P9-EMP-989

A WELL-PAID SLAVE

ALSO BY BRAD SNYDER

Beyond the Shadow of the Senators:
The Untold Story of the Homestead Grays and the Integration of Baseball

A WELL-PAID SLAVE

Curt Flood's Fight for Free Agency in Professional Sports

BRAD SNYDER

VIKING

VIKING
Published by the Penguin Group
Penguin Group (USA) Inc., 375 Hudson Street, New York, New York 10014, U.S.A.
Penguin Group (Canada), 90 Eglinton Avenue East, Suite 700, Toronto, Ontario, Canada M4P 2Y3
(a division of Pearson Penguin Canada Inc.)
Penguin Books Ltd, 80 Strand, London WC2R 0RL, England
Penguin Ireland, 25 St Stephen's Green, Dublin 2, Ireland (a division of Penguin Books Ltd)
Penguin Books Australia Ltd, 250 Camberwell Road, Camberwell, Victoria 3124, Australia
(a division of Pearson Australia Group Pty Ltd)
Penguin Books India Pvt Ltd, 11 Community Centre, Panchsheel Park, New Delhi – 110 017, India
Penguin Group (NZ), Cnr Airborne and Rosedale Roads, Albany, Auckland 1310, New Zealand
(a division of Pearson New Zealand Ltd)
Penguin Books (South Africa) (Pty) Ltd, 24 Sturdee Avenue, Rosebank, Johannesburg 2196,
South Africa

Penguin Books Ltd, Registered Offices: 80 Strand, London WC2R 0RL, England

First published in 2006 by Viking Penguin, a member of Penguin Group (USA) Inc.

10 9 8 7 6 5 4 3 2 1

Illustration credits: p. 1 *top,* p. 6 *top,* p. 7 *top,* p. 11 *top:* National Baseball Hall of Fame Library, Cooperstown, NY; p. 1 *bottom,* p. 2 *top and bottom,* p. 4 *bottom,* p. 11 *bottom,* p. 12 *top and bottom,* p. 13 *bottom: The Sporting News*/ZUMA; p. 3 *top:* Herb Scharfman/*Sports Illustrated;* p. 3 *bottom:* courtesy Marian Jorgensen; p. 4 *top,* p. 7 *bottom,* p. 9 *top,* p. 10 *bottom,* p. 13 *top,* p. 14 *top,* p. 15 *bottom,* p. 16 *top:* AP/Wide World Photos; p. 5 *top:* courtesy John Engels; p. 5 *middle:* courtesy Marge Brans; p. 5 *bottom:* courtesy Buddy Gilbert; p. 6 *bottom,* p. 8 *bottom,* p. 10 *top:* Corbis; p. 8 *top,* p. 15 *top:* Library of Congress; p. 9 *bottom:* courtesy Allan Zerman; p. 14 *bottom:* Fred Kaplan/*Sports Illustrated;* p. 16 *bottom:* William J. Clinton Presidential Library.

LIBRARY OF CONGRESS CATALOGING-IN-PUBLICATION DATA
Snyder, Brad.
A well-paid slave : Curt Flood's fight for free agency in professional sports / Brad Snyder.
p. cm.
Includes bibliographical references.
ISBN: 0-670-03794-X
1. Flood, Curt, 1938– 2. Baseball players—United States—Biography. 3. African American baseball players—Biography. 4. Free agents (Sports)—United States. I. Title.
GV865.F45S69 2006
796.357092—dc22
[B] 2006046139

Printed in the United States of America
Set in Adobe Caslon
Designed by Daniel Lagin

To John Thompson and Ray Gavins

A WELL-PAID SLAVE

CHAPTER ONE

The phone in Curt Flood's 19th-floor apartment rang at 4 a.m. on October 8, 1969. A sportswriter broke the news to him. A few hours later, another phone call made it official. The second conversation lasted no more than two minutes. The voice on the other end of the phone was so emotionless that it sounded almost like a prerecorded message.

"Hello, Curt?"

"Yes."

"Jim Toomey, Curt. Curt, you've been traded to Philadelphia. You, McCarver, Hoerner, and Byron Browne. For Richie Allen, Cookie Rojas, and Jerry Johnson. Good luck, Curt."

"Thanks. Thanks a lot."

Flood was polite but thought he deserved better. After 12 seasons of playing center field for the St. Louis Cardinals, he did not find out about the trade from the team's owner or general manager. He heard about it from a sportswriter and then from Toomey, a man Flood later described as a "middle-echelon coffee drinker from the front office." This was no way to treat Flood—the team's co-captain, a three-time All-Star, a seven-time Gold Glove winner, and a major cog in the Cardinals' World Series teams of 1964, 1967, and 1968.

It struck Flood as unfair that, like every professional baseball player at that time, he had no right to sign with another team or to test his value on the open market. In 1969, free agency was a foreign concept. The Cardinals could ship him off to Philadelphia because players belonged to their teams for life.

For 90 years, baseball players had been bought, sold, and traded like property. In 1879, the eight National League teams agreed to allow each team to "reserve" five players. This agreement forbade other National League teams from signing the reserved players and therefore prevented those players from changing teams based on their own free will. By the time the National League made peace with the upstart American League in 1903, reserving players was standard practice. Under the major league rules in 1969, each team reserved 40 players (25 on the major league roster plus 15 minor leaguers), all of whom were unable to sign with other teams.

The owners foisted the reserve system on the players by including in the standard player contract a provision referred to as the reserve clause. Paragraph 10(a) of the Uniform Player Contract said, "[T]he Club shall have the right . . . to renew this contract for a period of one year." Under this clause, a team could automatically renew a player's contract for another season at as little as 80 percent of the previous season's salary. Read literally, the Uniform Player Contract was a one-year agreement plus a one-year option on a player's services. But the players knew that they were not free to negotiate with other teams and their salaries could automatically be reduced by 20 percent for the following year. Before each season, therefore, they had no choice but to accept their teams' final salary offers and to sign new contracts containing the same one-year option provision. A contract for one year became, in effect, a contract for life.

Flood's trade from St. Louis to Philadelphia reawakened latent feelings of unfairness about the reserve system. His eventual decision to act on those feelings led to the first in a series of fights for free agency that altered the landscape of professional sports. Like his hero, Jackie Robinson, Flood had the courage to take on the baseball establishment. In 1947, Robinson started a racial revolution in sports by joining the Brooklyn Dodgers as the 20th century's first African-American major leaguer. Nearly 25 years later, Flood started an economic revolution by refusing to join the Philadelphia Phillies. The 31-year-old Flood sacrificed his own career to change the system and to benefit future generations of professional athletes. Today's athletes have some control over where they play in part because in 1969 Flood refused to continue being treated like hired help. But while Robinson's jersey has been retired in every major league ballpark, few current players today know the name Curt Flood, and even fewer know about the sacrifices he made for them.

The morning of Toomey's phone call, Flood woke up his two roommates—his oldest brother, Herman, and his friend and business manager, Marian Jorgensen—and swore to them that he was not going to Philadelphia. Like most proud ballplayers traded at the height of their careers, he threatened to retire.

Flood, however, was not like most ballplayers. He would joke around with his teammates one minute and stick his head in a book the next. He spoke in a soft, soothing voice and sounded like a college professor. He liked to draw, played classical piano by ear, and taught his best friend and road roommate, pitcher Bob Gibson, how to play the ukulele. Both Gibson and former Cardinals first baseman Bill White, Flood's closest friends in baseball, had attended college. Flood, however, had missed out on the college experience and engaged in constant self-education. "When Bob and I were reading the *Sporting News*, Curt was reading novels," White said. "We were listening to rock and blues, Curt was listening to classical music. We tried to play the harmonica, Curt had mastered the guitar."

Flood's quiet, artistic side obscured his lifelong battle against injustice. He had survived a childhood in a West Oakland ghetto, two minor league seasons in the Jim Crow South, and the racist attitudes of major league management. He persevered because of the courage Jackie Robinson had shown in 1947 and throughout his 10-year career with the Dodgers. After his playing days, Robinson inspired Flood to get involved in the civil rights movement. In 1961, Flood spoke out against segregated spring training camps in Florida. The next year, he spoke with Robinson at an NAACP rally in Mississippi. Flood integrated a white Bay Area neighborhood after the 1964 season with a court order and armed police protection. In 1969, he served as the president of Aunts and Uncles, a St. Louis organization that provided shoes and clothing to underprivileged children.

One of Flood's favorite authors was James Baldwin, the bard of the black freedom struggle. In November 1962, Baldwin shocked readers of *The New Yorker* with his essay about race in America, *The Fire Next Time*. He wrote not about Martin Luther King's nonviolent protest marches, but about Elijah Muhammad and the Nation of Islam, not about southern segregation, but of northern racial discontent. He awakened people to the changing face of the civil rights movement. Baldwin's prescient essay challenged "the relatively conscious whites and the relatively conscious blacks . . . to end the racial nightmare . . . and change the history of the world." He concluded by quoting an old slave song: "God gave Noah the rainbow sign, No more water, the fire next time!"

Inspired by the civil rights movement, Flood, too, was thinking about the future and was not making idle threats. The reserve clause gave him two choices—play for Philadelphia or retire. Flood knew one thing: He was not going to Philadelphia.

A few hours after his phone call from Toomey, Flood called Cardinals general manager Bing Devine. Devine was in the middle of a press conference, so Flood left a message for Devine to call him.

At 9:30 a.m., Devine explained to the media why he had traded his two co-captains, Flood and McCarver. Flood was a $90,000-a-year singles hitter showing signs of decline. In 1969, his batting average had fallen 15 points to .285, and his throwing arm, never strong, had not fully recovered from an injury two years earlier. McCarver had a sore arm and could be replaced by rookie catcher Ted Simmons or Joe Torre, an All-Star and former catcher acquired the previous season. The press conference lasted an hour and a half. As soon as it was over, Devine called Flood.

Devine had wanted all the players notified of the trade before the press conference, but it was odd that he had not called Flood himself. Toomey was one of the least respected members of the Cardinals organization. Perhaps Devine could have softened the blow. Vaughan Palmore "Bing" Devine was as respected by the Cardinals players as Toomey was disrespected. Best known for his shrewd trades, Devine had dealt pitchers for many of the cornerstones of the Cardinals' World Series teams of the 1960s: Sam Jones for Bill White; Vinegar Bend Mizell for second baseman Julian Javier; Don Cardwell (and shortstop Julio Gotay) for shortstop Dick Groat; Ernie Broglio for future Hall of Fame outfielder Lou Brock; and Willard Schmidt, Marty Kutyna, and Ted Wieand for a small but highly touted minor leaguer named Curtis Flood.

Devine had a soft spot in his heart for Flood, who was his first acquisition as general manager. On the last night of the 1957 winter meetings in Colorado Springs, Devine and Cardinals manager Fred Hutchinson skipped the annual minor league dinner and talked late into the night with their Cincinnati Reds (or Redlegs, as they were officially known from 1953 to 1958) counterparts, Gabe Paul and Birdie Tebbetts. Hutchinson and Tebbetts had been battery mates and roommates with the 1940s-era Detroit Tigers. Hutchinson knew that Tebbetts and the Reds needed pitching and that Flood might be able to fill the Cardinals' void in center field. The Cardinals' manager had seen Flood play in a B game in spring training two years earlier and was impressed that a kid right out of high school could play with such confidence. Devine and Hutchinson recessed for 30 minutes and at 3 a.m. made the deal.

At the time, the Reds were forcing Flood to play winter ball in Venezuela. They wanted him to learn second base, his third position in three years. He had played center field and third base during two minor league seasons in the Jim Crow South. In Venezuela, his body was racked for a month by dysentery and sore from taking hundreds of ground balls off his chest. He was sitting on a stool in the Pastora Milkers clubhouse in Maracaibo when a long telegram arrived from Gabe Paul announcing that he had been traded. For 30 minutes, Flood stared at the telegram in shock. He vowed that he would not allow himself to suffer the indignity of being traded ever again.

Twelve years later, during a lengthy phone conversation with Devine, Flood made good on his promise. He told Devine that he was not going to report to Philadelphia. At age 31, he was going to retire. He was physically and mentally exhausted. He had spent the first 14 years of his adult life playing baseball. There had to be more to life than playing center field. Besides, he wanted to focus on his St. Louis–based photography and portrait-painting business.

Flood had also threatened to retire before the 1969 season when Toomey had insulted him by offering a $5,000 raise from $72,500 to $77,500. In 1968, Flood was one of six major leaguers to bat .300 or better and helped lead the Cardinals to their second consecutive World Series appearance. A *Sports Illustrated* cover that season proclaimed him "Baseball's Best Centerfielder." For years, he had been making leaping catches over outfield walls in ways no one had ever seen before. From 1965 to 1967, he set a National League record by handling 555 chances in 226 consecutive games without an error. The press predicted that he would be baseball's first $100,000-a-year singles hitter, ahead of the Cincinnati Reds' Pete Rose. In those days, $100,000 was the salary barrier that separated All-Stars from superstars. Flood believed that this was his last best chance to achieve his salary goal. "If you don't pay me $100,000 to play baseball," he told Devine before the 1969 season, "then I am going to retire." He put it even more strongly in the *St. Louis Globe-Democrat*: "At this moment, I wouldn't consider taking even $99,999."

During his salary negotiations with Flood in March 1969, Devine knew that he could not find a comparable center fielder a month before the season. But he also recognized Flood's retirement talk as a common negotiating ploy. In his gentlemanly way, Devine explained to Flood that he was only 31 and had plenty of time to reach six figures. Devine made a final offer of $90,000. Flood accepted, but his retirement threat had been real. "I'm making $90,000 now," he told a reporter in March 1969. "If I have a good year I can hit $100,000. Three more years at that price and I'll be set financially for life. I won't have to work for money. I'll be able to do what I want, go where I want, say what I want. I want to get as far away from baseball as I can. I am just tired of the struggle, the pressures, the problems of making it, the problems of staying on top, the fighting with umpires, the struggling for the base hits, the fears, the insecurities."

To escape the pressures of the playing field, Flood often resorted to drinking and womanizing. He enjoyed the party scene, both in St. Louis and on the road. He always seemed to have a vodka martini in his hand and a beautiful woman on his arm. The popular drug of choice among Flood and his fellow ballplayers, alcohol had aged Flood beyond his years and had begun to erode his playing skills.

The first sign of Flood's physical decline came at the worst possible time—the seventh and deciding game of the 1968 World Series. With no score in the seventh inning, two men on base, and his good buddy Gibson on the mound, Flood misjudged a line drive hit by Detroit's Jim Northrup. The ball sailed over Flood's head for a triple, scoring two runs and costing the Cardinals the game and the Series. Bitterly sipping champagne in the clubhouse after the game, Flood accepted full responsibility for his team's defeat.

In light of his World Series gaffe and subsequent contract demands,

Flood's trade from the Cardinals was inevitable. During spring training in 1969, Cardinals and Anheuser-Busch president August "Gussie" Busch lectured Flood and his teammates about their ungrateful attitudes. Flood, who had been Busch's favorite player, went from being Busch's pet to a pariah. In May 1969, the team fined Flood $250 for missing a team luncheon (he had suffered a 10-inch spike wound during the previous game and, because of the medication, had overslept). His bat orders stopped arriving on time. He discovered that someone had begun to take his customary parking space beneath Busch Stadium.

"Something is happening," Flood confided to pitcher Jim "Mudcat" Grant, who lived with Flood after coming to the Cardinals in June 1969 from Montreal. "They're either going to trade me or something."

"They're not going to trade you," Grant said.

"Yes," Flood said, "they are."

In May 1969, the newspapers reported a possible trade of Flood, McCarver, and Javier to the Reds for second baseman Tommy Helms and 21-year-old star catcher Johnny Bench. In September, Flood made anonymous comments in the *St. Louis Globe-Democrat* criticizing management for giving up on the season by inserting rookies in key spots in the batting order. Devine responded that griping veterans could expect sweeping changes next season. Flood told McCarver during the last week of the season that he would retire rather than report to another team. "If they trade me," Flood said, "I'm packing it in."

During his October 8 phone conversation with Devine, Flood cited the same mental and physical exhaustion as when he had threatened to retire before the 1969 season. Then he said something that threw Devine for a loop.

Flood said he wished Devine had "shot me down" last spring.

"When you say, 'shot me down,'" Devine asked, "what do you mean?"

If Devine had come back with anything less than $90,000 during their contract negotiations in early March, Flood explained, he would have retired before the 1969 season.

Devine spent much of the conversation trying to talk Flood out of an "emotional reaction." The Cardinals general manager believed that Flood still had a few more good seasons left in him, that he obviously liked playing center field because he had been doing it so well and for so long, and that once Flood had a few days or weeks to reconsider, he would report to the Phillies. Devine wanted Phillies general manager John Quinn to call Flood as soon as possible. The sooner Quinn talked to Flood, Devine believed, the less likely Flood would follow through with his plan to retire. Devine told Flood that Quinn would be calling him immediately.

"Well, there's not much use," Flood replied. He had nothing to say to Quinn. There was no way he was going to report to the Phillies. He then offhandedly mentioned that Quinn had better call him soon because he was scheduled to leave for a previously planned vacation to Denmark. Devine told Flood to expect Quinn's call.

Flood sat in a chair by the phone for the rest of the day. The phone rang constantly, but he refused to answer it. Quinn called from Philadelphia, but one of Flood's roommates told Quinn that Flood was unavailable.

Flood publicly announced his plan to retire and responded to numerous media inquiries by issuing a press release. He said in the statement that the trade "comes as a surprise and a personal disappointment. . . . When you spend 12 years with one club, you develop strong ties with your teammates and the fans who have supported your efforts over a period of years. . . . Everyone in St. Louis—from Cardinals management to the various sportscasters and writers to the fans themselves—has made my baseball career a wonderful experience."

The remainder of Flood's statement explained his decision and echoed his conversation with Devine:

"For the past year or two it has been increasingly difficult to stay in top physical shape; as you know I'll soon be 32 years of age. In addition, with my playing days nearing an end due to physical considerations alone, I've had to think of my own and my children's future. Consequently, I've felt that I should give more time to the Curt Flood Photo Studio franchise business, as well as a large backlog of oil portrait commissions.

"I then told Mr. Devine that the trade to Philadelphia has caused me to make a personal decision that I have been putting off for some time. If I were younger I certainly would enjoy playing for Philadelphia. But under the circumstances, I have decided to retire from organized baseball, effective today, and remain in St. Louis where I can devote full time to my business interests."

Devine, Quinn, the media, and even his fellow players did not believe that Flood was going through with his retirement. He had several major league seasons and big paydays in front of him. His interest in his photography and portrait business could wait. He'll play, former Cardinals general manager Frank Lane said, "unless he's better than Rembrandt."

Flood was a decent sketch artist, but his portrait painting career was illusory. In March 1967, he had presented Gussie Busch with a portrait of the beer baron in his sailing outfit. Busch was so enamored of the painting that he hung it in his 84-foot yacht, *Miss Budweiser*, and commissioned Flood to paint Busch's children. Soon, Flood began accepting commissions to paint teammates, opposing players, and their families. He presented the governors of Illinois and Missouri with portraits, and the archbishop of St. Louis with a portrait of Pope Paul VI. He produced a portrait of a girl who had died of leukemia and donated his commission to the Leukemia Guild of Missouri. He usually gave portraits to teammates and friends as presents, then charged them if they wanted additional paintings of their children. During a two-year period, he had made an extra $15,000 on commissions. His teammates began referring to him as "Rembrandt."

Flood received the most publicity for a portrait of Martin Luther King Jr. After King's assassination in April 1968, Flood unveiled a pensive image of the slain civil rights leader. He discussed the painting on the *Today* show and donated the original to King's widow, Coretta, who liked the portrait so much that she hung it above her desk. "Your painting," Mrs. King wrote Flood in 1968, "comes closest to depicting the dignity and reverence—and especially the love—which characterized his life." In January 2002, she donated Flood's portrait of her husband to President George W. Bush. The portrait, which hangs in the East Wing of the White House, is signed by someone other than Flood.

Flood did not paint the King portrait or any of the others. Yes, he had been drawing since he was a child in West Oakland, and as a teenager he had earned extra money lettering signs for a local furniture store. During the fall of 1959, he had spent the first of two offseasons at

Oakland's College of Arts and Crafts. His sketches of teammate Dick Groat and manager Johnny Keane had appeared in the *St. Louis Post-Dispatch* and the *Sporting News*. But, as adept as he was with a pencil and a sketch pad, he could not paint oil portraits. Instead, he sent photographs of his subjects to a Burbank-based portrait artist who enlarged the photographs and painted over them. Flood simply signed his name to the finished products. Flood's business partner, Bill Jones, watched him unpack the paintings from crates. The commissions kept rolling in. Flood had started something that he could no longer control.

Flood's reaction to the trade after the 1969 season took him on a similar course. It eclipsed his baseball career and the publicity from his portraits and soon took over his life.

The day after the trade, Flood shut out baseball people and the media and brooded about what had transpired over the last 24 hours. That day an index card arrived in the mail.

"Notice to player number 614," the preprinted form said. The part of the form about being "optioned" or "released" had been crossed out. The remaining part indicated that Flood's contract had been assigned to the Philadelphia club of the National League. It was signed by Vaughan P. Devine. Accompanying the index card was a one-sentence letter from Devine ending with "Best of luck." "If I had been a foot-shuffling porter," Flood later wrote, "they might have at least given me a pocket watch."

Flood was so depressed during the first two days after the trade that he considered canceling his trip to Denmark. His friend and business manager, Marian Jorgensen, talked him out of it.

Few people understood Flood's relationship with Marian, a white woman nearly 30 years his senior. They often asked if "that white lady" still lived with him. Their questions implied some weird sexual relationship where none existed. Marian was more of a mother hen than a muse. Mean and sometimes Machiavellian, she kept Flood's business affairs in order and outsiders away. She had grown up in a prominent Bay Area family and lived off her inheritance. Flood met Marian and her husband, Johnny, through his junior high school art teacher, Jim Chambers, at the end of the 1962 season. The Jorgensens were progressive and freethinking in an era when most white people their ages could not comprehend the social and political upheaval of the 1960s. The Bay Area couple did not think in terms of skin color. Flood described them as "humanists."

The Jorgensens became Flood's intellectual mentors, his confidants, and his family. They opened their Oakland home to Flood, his parents, his siblings, and his teammates. They helped him as he continued his quest for education and self-improvement. Their library was his library. They even created a downstairs apartment for him.

The owner of an Oakland engraving and die company, Johnny taught Curt the trade. By virtue of his artistic talent, Curt was a quick study. He engraved the Lord's Prayer on a die so small that it could be stamped on the head of a pin. The meticulous work soothed his nerves. Johnny made Curt a partner and viewed him as his eventual successor at the shop. Curt's desire to work as a commercial artist after his playing days seemed to be coming true.

On December 15, 1966, however, Johnny was stabbed to death at the engraving shop. Oakland police detectives, skeptical about a friendship between a younger black man and an older white woman, brought both Curt and Marian in for extensive questioning even though Curt had been in Los Angeles at the time of the murder. Ultimately, the detectives believed that a mentally disturbed teenager had committed the crime, but he was never charged.

In 1967, Curt begged Marian to move to St. Louis. After two go-rounds, his marriage to Beverly, a model whose family owned a St. Louis nightclub, was over. Their five children lived with their mother outside of Los Angeles. His photography business needed supervision. His social life was out of control. He needed Marian to help him pull his life together. She responded to his cry for help.

Carl Flood also came to St. Louis to live with his brother. Marian had taken a particular interest in Carl. One year older than Curt, Carl had been serving 20 years in federal prison at Leavenworth and McNeil Island for robbing a West Oakland Bank of America. An artist and poet, Carl had won prison chess championships and taught himself several languages. Marian had successfully campaigned for Carl's early parole after he had saved the life of a prison guard who had been beaten up by other prisoners.

Trouble soon found Carl in St. Louis. Although he was supposed to be earning $100 a week selling Curt's portrait commissions, Carl had begun pocketing the prepaid commissions without providing any portraits in return. The money fed Carl's $300-a-day heroin habit, which Marian was trying to help him kick.

One mid-March morning in 1969, Carl and a convicted murderer held up a downtown St. Louis jewelry store. They took the store owners hostage when the police arrived, and tried to escape in a police cruiser. The police shot out the cruiser's tires. Carl was charged with two counts of armed robbery and attempted theft of the cruiser. He was sentenced to 20 years in a Missouri state prison. Carl's arrest only added to Curt's frustrations during the 1969 season.

Marian spent most of the 1969 season keeping tabs on Curt's photography and portrait business and his personal affairs. As his business manager, secretary, and social conscience, she could drink, swear, and trade barbs with Curt like one of his Cardinals teammates. Some people thought that Marian manipulated Curt, that she restricted access to him, and that she was the driving force behind his eventual response to the trade.

Two days after the trade, on the morning of October 10, Marian drove Curt to the St. Louis airport for the first leg of his flight to Copenhagen. As they sat in the airport bar, Curt bemoaned the unfairness of the reserve clause. Even before his trade, he had criticized the reserve clause in the press. Marian suggested that Curt challenge the system by suing Major League Baseball.

Curt pondered Marian's idea during his three-week trip to Copenhagen. Johnny's parents had come from Denmark, and he and Marian had raved about Copenhagen. After the Cardinals' postseason tour of Japan in 1968, Flood and some of his friends from St. Louis had toured Paris, Stockholm, and Copenhagen. "I went to Europe to relax, to get away from the pressures, to see museums and art galleries, to escape the things that are wrong here," he told a reporter in March 1969. Flood fell in love with Denmark and planned on settling there after his playing career. He invested in a Copenhagen cocktail lounge called Club 6. He intended to reopen it after the 1969 season under the name Club 21, his uniform number with the Cardinals.

Copenhagen was Flood's sanctuary. He could walk the streets unrecognized and unself-conscious about being black. Artistic, impeccably dressed, and handsome, he rarely lacked female companionship. In October 1969, he met a tall black Danish woman named Claire. They talked about her running the cocktail lounge in Copenhagen. Although she was married, Claire agreed to return to St. Louis with Flood to check out the American restaurant and bar scene.

Even in Copenhagen, however, Flood could not escape Major League Baseball. John Quinn called on his first night overseas. Flood reiterated his retirement plans to Quinn but promised not to make a final decision until he met with Quinn in person.

On November 7, after returning with Claire to St. Louis, Curt met with Quinn for 45 minutes to an hour at St. Louis's Chase Hotel. Quinn, who had stopped in St. Louis after a baseball meeting in Arizona, spent most of his time with Flood selling his team and his city. It was a tough sell.

The Phillies were one of baseball's worst organizations. They had lost in their only World Series appearances, in 1915 and 1950. In 1964, they had blown the National League pennant in a late-season collapse for the ages. They treated their players like second-class citizens, sending them across the country on late-night commercial propeller flights in an era when most teams chartered jet planes.

Flood described Philadelphia as America's "northernmost southern city." In 1947, Phillies general manager Herb Pennock reportedly urged Dodgers general manager Branch Rickey not to bring "the nigger here with the rest of your team." Phillies owner Bob Carpenter threatened to pull his team from the field if Jackie Robinson played at Philadelphia's Shibe Park. Rickey responded by inviting the Phillies to forfeit those games to the Dodgers. The Phillies played against Robinson and gave him a brutal reception. Philadelphia manager Ben Chapman, a Tennessee native who lived in Alabama during the offseason, led his players in yelling racial epithets across the field at Robinson, knowing that the black pioneer was not allowed to say anything back. The Ben Franklin Hotel in Philadelphia refused to allow Robinson to stay there, so the Dodgers moved to the Warwick. Ten years later, the Phillies became the last National League team to integrate. More recent charges of racism dogged the franchise, fans, and local media who vilified black slugger Dick (Richie) Allen. Allen tried to force a trade with unexcused absences and other rebellious behavior, leading the Phillies to send him to the Cardinals for Flood and McCarver. Allen's ordeal was fresh in Flood's mind.

Quinn explained to Flood that the Phillies were turning things around and building a new ballpark. He told Flood about the city's art museums and numerous galleries. He said that playing four or five more seasons would increase Flood's name recognition as an artist. He related his own family's experiences moving from Milwaukee, where he had been the Braves' general manager, to Philadelphia.

Flood insisted that his decision had nothing to do with Philadelphia. "It may be time for me to make my break from baseball," he told Quinn. Quinn said he would not be in a St. Louis hotel room if Flood were 37 or 38 years old. Philadelphia's scouts did not believe that Flood's skills had faded. Quinn said Flood had promised to "keep an open mind." Flood, however, said he had told Quinn: "I don't think there was anything he could say to make me change my mind." They never discussed salary but agreed to stay in contact.

Most people believed that after the November 7 meeting Flood was coming to Philadelphia. "Curt Nearly a Phil," the next day's *Philadelphia Daily News* headline declared. Quinn said that if he had $1,000 at stake, he would place it on Flood wearing a Phillies uniform in 1970. Two of Flood's former teammates, McCarver, who had signed with the Phillies, and Bill White, who had retired and worked as a Philadelphia sportscaster, believed that Flood would sign. So did Dick Allen, who said "the money" was the overriding factor.

Flood liked Quinn based on their initial meeting but publicly insisted that his plan to retire had not changed. He told reporters to talk to him again in March. His thinking, however, had changed—he was contemplating the idea of suing Major League Baseball over the reserve clause.

Soon after he had returned from Copenhagen and before meeting with Quinn, Flood visited Allan H. Zerman. A 32-year-old St. Louis attorney, Zerman had helped Flood acquire his first photography studio and incorporate the business as Curt Flood & Associates, Inc. Zerman also had represented Carl after the jewelry store robbery, negotiating a plea bargain with the state of Missouri and appearing in federal court about the parole violation. Zerman liked Flood's sense of humor and, as his lawyer, had earned Flood's confidence and trust. Flood had been impressed that Zerman was the only person to turn down Flood's free tickets to the 1964 World Series.

Zerman had never seen Flood as upset as he was that afternoon in Zerman's law office. Zerman listened as Flood vented about how the trade had turned his life in St. Louis upside down. It was clear to Zerman that Flood was not going to Philadelphia. Retirement seemed a certainty.

"There is one other alternative," Zerman said.

Flood was startled when Zerman brought up the idea of a lawsuit. Zerman had not read the two Supreme Court cases granting Major League Baseball a legal monopoly, but he knew that they were old and most likely outdated. He correctly believed that to challenge the reserve clause, Flood would first have to challenge baseball's exemption from the antitrust laws. Zerman's gut told him that the reserve clause was an injustice that a more liberal, modern Supreme Court would not tolerate. The more Zerman looked into it, the more he believed that Flood might have a viable legal claim.

Two of the people Flood trusted most, Zerman and Marian Jorgensen, suggested that he sue. Flood knew his next move. He called Marvin Miller.

CHAPTER TWO

Marvin Miller was not expecting Curt Flood's phone call. The executive director of the Major League Baseball Players Association, Miller was aware of the trade, Flood's announcement of his plan to retire, and even his vacation to Denmark. But Miller thought that Flood would either retire or report to the Phillies, and that would be the end of it. Instead, Flood called Miller about a lawsuit.

Miller did not know Flood well. Flood had supported the association's directive to the players to refuse to sign contracts during a pension dispute before the 1969 season. He had occasionally stopped by the association's New York offices when the Cardinals were playing the Mets. During Miller's annual spring training visits with Cardinals teams of the mid- to late 1960s, Flood had not stood out among the team's strong and intelligent personalities. Miller associated Flood with the center fielder's misplay of Northrup's line drive in Game 7 of the 1968 World Series.

Despite their lack of familiarity, Miller could tell from Flood's tone of voice that he meant business. Flood said there was no way he was going to report to Philadelphia, not after 12 seasons in St. Louis and not with his business interests there. Flood explained that he and his St. Louis attorney had discussed a legal challenge to the reserve clause. In response, Miller launched into a brief discussion of the two Supreme Court decisions in Flood's way. Miller mentioned that there was a slight chance that the Court might reverse those decisions, but he "wouldn't bet any money on it." Flood asked Miller if they could talk in person.

Flood had business soon in New York. Miller agreed that they should meet.

Many people meeting him for the first time underestimated Marvin Julian Miller. At 5 feet 8 and 150 pounds and with a right shoulder damaged at birth, he looked slight and vulnerable. He spoke in slow, measured sentences and never raised his voice. But beneath his polite and charming demeanor lay a no-holds-barred fighter and relentless negotiator. He believed that he could accomplish anything. Despite his bum shoulder, he willed himself into becoming a fine tennis and handball player. His wife, Terry, often teased him by calling him "J.C." or "Don Quixote." "He likes the impossible dream," she said. "He's eager for the impossible fight."

The son of a ladies' garment salesman and a schoolteacher, Miller grew up in the Flatbush section of Brooklyn not far from Ebbets Field. He lived and died with the Brooklyn Dodgers of the 1930s. When a San Francisco Giants public relations man once sought to confirm the owners' misguided notion that Miller did not like baseball by challenging him to name some Dodgers from that era, Miller rattled off the entire starting nine, the starting pitchers, and the backup catchers. His steel-trap mind was not limited to baseball. He finished high school at age 15 and spent the next three semesters working and taking night courses at Brooklyn College. He then began taking prelaw courses at St. John's at age 17, entered Miami University in Ohio a year later, and after two years transferred to New York University, where he graduated in 1938 with a degree in economics.

Miller spent the first 12 years of his adult life in a succession of short-term civil service jobs. He worked as a Treasury Department clerk in Washington in 1939, a welfare investigator in New York City from 1940 to 1942, a staff economist at the War Production Board in Washington from 1942 to 1943, an economist and dispute-resolution specialist for the National War Labor Board in Philadelphia from 1943 until the end of World War II, and a trainer of mediators for the Department of Labor's Conciliation Service back in Washington after the war.

By the late 1940s, the 32-year-old Miller was professionally rudderless. After briefly working for the Machinists Union and the United Auto Workers, he found a professional home in 1950 as a staff economist at the Pittsburgh headquarters of the Steelworkers Union. During the next 16 years, he climbed his way into the Steelworkers Union's inner circle.

In December 1965, the Players Association sought its first full-time executive director. For years, the owners had outsmarted the players' part-time legal advisers, who failed to protect the players' interests. Miller came to the players' attention through veteran pitcher Robin Roberts. One of several players entrusted with finding an executive director, Roberts asked University of Pennsylvania labor relations expert George Taylor to recommend "a strong man of established character." Taylor, having worked with him on the National War Labor Board and the Kaiser Steel Long-Range Sharing Plan Committee, suggested Miller. Roberts and fellow players Jim Bunning and Harvey Kuenn interviewed Miller and recommended him for the job. But the 20 elected player representatives, led by Pittsburgh Pirates pitcher Bob Friend, rejected the recommendation and offered the job to Milwaukee municipal judge Robert Cannon. Cannon had been the players' part-time legal adviser since 1959 and had collected his union fees from the owners. When he was offered the executive director position, Cannon balked at moving to New York City to run the union headquarters, tried to force the players to compromise by accepting Chicago, and asked them to match his judicial pension. What he really wanted was for the owners to name him the game's commissioner. The player representatives rejected Cannon's demands and offered the position to Miller. Miller reluctantly accepted, but a majority of the players still had to vote him into office.

The owners portrayed the Jewish Miller as a left-leaning labor goon. He wore what one writer described as a "pencil-thin" mustache (Roberts begged him to shave it off) and "shimmering blue" suits (Miller denied ever owning one) that made him look like a gangster. Despite the management-led smear campaign during Miller's visits to spring training camps in 1966, the players voted, 489–136, to hire him. The player representatives informed Miller that the owners had agreed to put up $150,000 to fund the association. After Miller's election, however, the owners reneged on their offer. The commissioner's lawyer, Paul Porter, informed the association that the payments were illegal under the Taft-Hartley Act, which Miller knew; but that had not stopped the owners from paying the legal fees of their man, Judge Cannon. The players agreed to fund the association and Miller's salary through $344 in annual union dues.

The 49-year-old Miller opened the Players Association's New York office at 375 Park Avenue with $5,400 in the organization's bank account and a beat-up file cabinet. He built his labor relations revolution in baseball brick by brick. He started a licensing arm that brought royalty checks to the players and financial solvency to the association. He tackled issues including the pension plan, the minimum major league salary (which was $6,000 in 1966), the scheduling of games, the structure and payment for the playoffs, and the grievance procedure. He negotiated the first comprehensive labor agreement in professional sports, a two-year pact between the players and the owners known as the 1968 Basic Agreement, and during their 1969 pension dispute he showed the players what they could accomplish by sticking together.

Miller educated the players. The owners had brainwashed them into believing that the game could not survive without the reserve clause and that it was for the players' own good. Miller explained that the reserve clause helped the owners artificially limit salaries and hold on to their players forever. The promanagement sporting press, however, insisted that Miller was the one doing the brainwashing. They portrayed him as the players' Svengali.

Miller was not ready for Flood's phone call or his proposed lawsuit in November 1969. The owners were too obstinate and the players were not yet unified enough to fight over the reserve clause. Nor was Flood the ideal plaintiff. At $90,000, his salary was one of the 10 to 15 highest in the game. He had earned substantial bonuses for playing in three World Series. He had been well compensated during 12 seasons with the Cardinals. He was not some middle-aged minor leaguer trapped in some team's farm system with no chance of making it to the major leagues. Miller's biggest concern was that Flood had no idea what he was getting himself into. Miller's mission was clear: to make Flood aware that the lawsuit's risks greatly outweighed any potential rewards.

On the morning of November 25, Flood and Zerman met Miller and his general counsel, Dick Moss, for breakfast at New York's Summit Hotel. Flood began by asking Miller about the slight chance that Miller had mentioned on the phone of overturning baseball's exemption from the antitrust laws.

Baseball's legal monopoly, Miller explained, was created out of whole cloth by the Supreme Court of the United States. In 1890, Congress had passed the Sherman Antitrust Act, which deemed "[e]very contract, combination . . . or conspiracy" illegal that restrained "trade or commerce among the several states." The goal was to ban monopolistic practices that prevented competition. The Sherman Act did not list exceptions for baseball or any other sport. The U.S. Constitution, however, allows Congress to regulate only commerce "among the several states." Therefore, federal antitrust law applies only to acts of interstate commerce (as opposed to in*tra*state commerce occurring within a single state).

The Supreme Court got into the act of deregulating baseball in a case brought by an obscure team known as the Baltimore Terrapins. The Terrapins played in the eight-team Federal League, a rival or third major league that competed with the National and American leagues for players in 1914 and 1915. After the 1915 season, the Federal League folded when most of its clubs joined the so-called Peace Agreement with major league ball. Under this deal, five Federal League owners received either cash settlements or ownership shares in major league franchises (the owner of the Chicago Federals, for example, invested in the Cubs and moved them into his ballpark, known today as Wrigley Field). Excluded from the settlement talks, the owners of the Terrapins balked at a belated cash payoff and demanded a major league team in Baltimore. They sued under the Sherman Act, arguing that the established leagues employed the reserve clause and other monopolistic practices to destroy the Federal League. A District of Columbia jury awarded the owners of the Terrapins $80,000, which was tripled under the antitrust laws to $240,000. A federal appeals court reversed the jury's verdict.

In a 1922 decision, *Federal Baseball Club of Baltimore, Inc. v. National League of Professional Baseball Clubs*, the Supreme Court unanimously agreed with the appeals court, ruling that the owners of the Terrapins were not entitled to damages under the Sherman Act, because professional baseball was not interstate commerce. *Federal Baseball* is often mischaracterized as a decision that baseball is a sport, not a business. The Court made no such distinction. "The business is giving exhibitions of base ball," the Court wrote, "which are purely state affairs." The Court said that the transportation of players from city to city was incidental to the "business" of professional baseball because the game itself, when played, was wholly intrastate. It borrowed the lower court's analogy of lawyers or lecturers traveling to distant cities as proof that travel alone did not make baseball games interstate commerce. *Federal Baseball* established Major League Baseball's legal monopoly, which today is referred to as baseball's antitrust exemption.

The author of this much-maligned opinion was not some jurisprudential hack, but one of the greatest jurists in the history of American law, Justice Oliver Wendell Holmes. With his thick white hair and white mustache, the 81-year-old Holmes looked like a god. Right or wrong, an opinion from Holmes was like Moses delivering the Ten Commandments. It might as well have been carved in stone. It did not help that Holmes "loathe[d] and despise[d]" the Sherman Act, which he referred to as a "foolish law," or that he knew almost nothing about baseball. A bookish, unathletic child who had grown up in Boston before the Civil War, he had probably never seen a baseball game. In Holmes's defense, radio broadcasts of baseball games in 1922 were in their infancy, the farm system concept was not popularized until the 1930s, and the first television broadcast of a major league game was not until 1939. In 1922, it was not obvious that baseball's effect on interstate commerce was more than "incidental."

The power of Justice Holmes was illustrated 31 years later in the second major Supreme Court case involving baseball's monopoly status. In *Toolson v. New York Yankees*, a 29-year-old pitcher named George Earl Toolson wanted out of the Yankees' minor league system. Toolson had signed with the Red Sox out of Willamette University, served in World War II, and ruptured a disk in his back in 1948 pitching for the Triple-A Louisville Colonels. After thc 1948 season, he was traded to the Yankees' organization. He struggled in 1949 after being sent from Triple-A Newark to the Oakland Oaks of the Triple-A Pacific Coast League. The following year, the Yankees demoted him to Class A Binghamton. Toolson refused to report to Binghamton and on May 25, 1950, was placed on the ineligible list. He returned home to California and worked as a film printer for a Hollywood studio. Blacklisted from the game, he challenged the reserve clause in federal court.

After two lower courts rejected Toolson's lawsuit by relying on *Federal Baseball*, the Supreme Court agreed to hear Toolson's case and combined it with two other unsuccessful baseball lawsuits. Toolson and his co-plaintiffs argued before the Court that radio and television broadcasts, train and air travel, and the expansion of the minor leagues had left no question that baseball was interstate commerce.

The Supreme Court, however, is extremely reluctant to reverse its own decisions. It is a principle known as *stare decisis*, which means "let the decision stand." Supreme Court decisions, or precedents, are interpretations of American law that are relied on year after year by judges, lawyers, businessmen, and scholars. This is particularly true when the Court interprets the meaning of federal legislation such as the Sherman Act. The general immutability of these decisions is based on *stare decisis*.

The Court in 1953 included some of the best and brightest justices. Chief Justice Earl Warren, an Eisenhower nominee, had recently joined such legal luminaries as Hugo Black, William Douglas, Felix Frankfurter, and Robert Jackson. A year later, the Court unanimously declared in *Brown v. Board of Education* that racially "separate but equal" public schools were "inherently unequal" and therefore unconstitutional. *Brown* reversed the Court's 1896 *Plessy v. Ferguson* decision, proving that *stare decisis* was not insurmountable. When it came to *Toolson*, however, Warren, Black, Douglas, Frankfurter, and Jackson were among the seven justices who voted in Major League Baseball's favor.

The Court's unsigned, one-paragraph opinion in *Toolson* refused to reexamine the "underlying issues" about whether Major League Baseball in 1953 had risen to the level of interstate commerce. It claimed to be a reaffirmation of Holmes's opinion in *Federal Baseball*. Yet, in a single paragraph, it completely changed *Federal Baseball*'s meaning. The Court in *Toolson* offered three additional reasons for baseball's legal monopoly:

1. Congress had done nothing to correct *Federal Baseball* despite hearings in 1951 about baseball's monopoly status;
2. Baseball had developed for the last 30 years under *Federal Baseball* and had relied on the assumption that it was a legal monopoly; and
3. Any future action on baseball's antitrust exemption should be taken by Congress.

One commentator described *Toolson* as the first step in "the greatest bait-and-switch scheme in the history of the Supreme Court." The key to the "scheme" consisted of the second half of the opinion's final sentence, a last-minute addition to the unsigned opinion. "Without reexamining the underlying issues, the judgments below are affirmed on the authority of *Federal Baseball* . . . ," *Toolson* concluded, "so far as that decision determines that Congress had no intention of including the business of baseball within the scope of the federal antitrust laws." But Holmes never said anything in *Federal Baseball* about what Congress had intended in 1890, only that professional baseball as it operated in 1922 was not interstate commerce. The second half of this final sentence was recently discovered to be the handiwork of the Court's new chief justice, Earl Warren. Warren was extremely uncomfortable with the opinion, which had been written by Hugo Black, the former U.S. senator among the justices. Warren asked Black to add the "so far as" clause "to make it clear that Congress has the right to regulate baseball if and when it desires to do so." Neither Black nor the other six justices in the majority objected to Warren's addition, which helped transform Holmes's opinion into an express "exemption" for baseball.

But, as Justice Harold Burton wrote in his eight-page dissent, Congress passed the Sherman Act without saying a word about baseball. The Court was the institution that claimed baseball did not have a sufficient impact on interstate commerce. Justice Holmes's decision also was based on an antiquated conception of interstate commerce, which the Court expanded dramatically in upholding the constitutionality of President Roosevelt's New Deal programs. Baseball in 1953 was obviously interstate commerce, given its radio and television revenue and extensive network of minor league teams. If the Court's prior decision was not wrong in 1922, it was definitely wrong now. Only Stanley Reed joined Burton's dissent.

Toolson also made it possible for baseball to enforce the reserve clause. Before and even after *Federal Baseball*, lower courts had been reluctant to enforce the reserve clause because the contracts were so one-sided against the players. *Toolson*, by redefining *Federal Baseball*, further insulated the reserve clause from legal challenge.

As Miller explained, Flood's chances of defeating *Federal Baseball*, *Toolson*, Oliver Wendell Holmes, and *stare decisis*—just to get to the issue of whether the reserve clause was illegal—were basically slim to none.

Miller was not a lawyer, but as an economist he was well versed in antitrust law. He also relied on the opinion of his general counsel, Dick

Moss, who had examined all the relevant cases since *Toolson*. A former assistant state attorney general for Pennsylvania, arbitration lawyer from the Steelworkers' legal department, and diehard Pirates fan, Moss had applied for Judge Cannon's position as part-time legal counsel in 1959. A brash 35-year-old Harvard Law School graduate, Moss was fire to Miller's ice. He played the role of attack dog, while Miller often stayed above the fray.

With Moss sitting beside him, Miller explained that since *Toolson* several Supreme Court decisions had cast doubt on the logic of *Federal Baseball*. The Court had abandoned *Federal Baseball*'s limited definition of interstate commerce in refusing to extend antitrust exemptions to theatrical performances, professional boxing, and professional football. The Court's 1957 decision in *Radovich v. NFL* acknowledged that *Federal Baseball* "was at best of dubious validity." Nor was there any reason why baseball deserved an exemption but football did not. "If this ruling is unrealistic, inconsistent, or illogical," a six-justice majority said in *Radovich*, "it is sufficient to answer, aside from the distinctions between the businesses, that were we considering the question of baseball for the first time upon a clean slate we would have no doubts."

But even if the Supreme Court agreed to hear the case and miraculously decided to reverse Justice Holmes, abandon *stare decisis*, and wipe out its two hallowed baseball precedents, Miller predicted, Flood would still lose. "It's a million-to-one shot, but even if that million-to-one shot comes home, you're not going to get any damages," Miller said. No trial court in America was going to award damages retroactively to a ballplayer making $90,000 a year under player contracts and trades that had been deemed legal by the Supreme Court for nearly 50 years. A win at the Supreme Court still meant a loss for Flood.

"But it would benefit all of the other players and all the players to come, wouldn't it?" Flood asked.

Miller said it would.

"That's good enough for me," Flood replied.

Miller knew he had found a man of uncommon principle, but the union's executive director was not done playing devil's advocate. He explained that a lawsuit would take at least two to three years to wind its way through the federal court system to the Supreme Court. By the time the Court reached a decision, Flood would be 34. He would lose three seasons and nearly $300,000 in salary. His playing career would be over.

Flood responded that he had no intention of playing for the Phillies and that he was serious about sacrificing his playing career to sue baseball.

The owners, Miller continued, were a mean and vindictive bunch. Flood's lawsuit would end any aspirations he had to be the first black major league manager.

Flood said he had no interest in managing.

What about working as a major league coach or scout? Miller said Flood would be blacklisted. He could forget about any future career opportunities in the game.

"You're not telling me anything new," Flood said.

Flood's lawsuit would be targeting not only Major League Baseball, Miller said, but also his former employer, Anheuser-Busch. Gussie Busch was the most powerful businessman in St. Louis. He had set up Flood's former teammate Roger Maris with a Budweiser distributorship in Florida. The head of the King of Beers could just as easily destroy Flood's photography and portrait business and reputation in St. Louis.

Flood had not thought of that, but was not deterred. He was not likely to be receiving any Christmas cards from Busch this year anyway.

Miller then pressed Flood about his financial condition. Miller's inquiries led him to tell Flood about another reserve clause lawsuit, involving New York Giants outfielder Danny Gardella.

A stocky, muscular man who liked to walk up a flight of stairs on his hands, burst into opera songs, and quote Shakespeare, the 5-foot-7-inch Gardella once left a suicide note on the bed of his Cincinnati hotel room blaming his road roommate, Nap Reyes, for his death. Reyes ran to the open window and saw a smiling Gardella hanging from a ledge 22 floors off the ground.

In 1946, Gardella risked his baseball life. He rejected a raise from $4,500 to $5,000 after batting .272 with 18 home runs the previous season. The Giants thought that wartime pitching had inflated Gardella's offensive numbers, and by all accounts, he could not field worth a lick. Gardella showed up at the Giants' spring training camp without a signed contract. He argued with the team's traveling secretary after barging into the main hotel dining room in a sleeveless sweater. The team kicked him out of the hotel and planned to auction him off to a minor league team. Gardella made his own deal, signing a $10,000 contract to play for Veracruz in the Mexican League. Baseball commissioner Happy Chandler placed a five-year ban on Gardella and 14 other players who had signed Mexican League contracts.

Gardella returned from Mexico after a year. He tried to play for the semipro Gulf Oilers in a 1947 game on Staten Island against the Negro American League's Cleveland Buckeyes and the legendary pitcher Satchel Paige. Alerted to Gardella's presence, Chandler sent a telegram that was read over the stadium loudspeaker: The black players would be banned from the majors for playing against Gardella or any other players who had jumped to the Mexican League. With major league teams beginning to open their doors to blacks that season, Paige and the Buckeyes obeyed Chandler's edict.

In 1948, a trial judge threw out Gardella's lawsuit against the reserve clause based on *Federal Baseball.* On appeal, however, Gardella landed two of the best federal judges in history, Learned Hand and Jerome Frank. The intellectual heir to Justice Holmes and perhaps the greatest American jurist never to serve on the Supreme Court, Hand wrote a careful opinion returning Gardella's case for a trial to determine whether baseball had developed into interstate commerce. Frank, a liberal New Dealer and "legal realist" who believed that economic, psychological, and sociological factors influenced judicial decisions, joined Hand's opinion and wrote a separate opinion that declared *Federal Baseball* an "impotent zombi," baseball interstate commerce, and the reserve clause both illegal and immoral.

As Gardella's case seemed headed for trial, the baseball world abandoned him. Branch Rickey charged that anyone who opposed the reserve clause had "avowed communist tendencies," even though Rickey's beloved reserve clause was antithetical to a capitalist, free-market system. The players believed the owners' rhetoric that the game could not survive without the reserve clause. Bob Feller, Stan Musial, fellow Mexican Leaguer Mickey Owen, and even banned Black Sox pitcher Eddie Cicotte all spoke in favor of it.

But Gardella's biggest handicap proved to be his attorney, Frederic Johnson. After Johnson conducted a pretrial deposition of Chandler in open court in 1949, Johnson persuaded Gardella to accept reinstatement and a $60,000 settlement. Johnson, who owed other lawyers money and did not see how he could prove Gardella's damages at trial, received half of Gardella's settlement. A few years later, Johnson represented one of the *Toolson* co-plaintiffs before the Supreme Court.

At the time of the settlement, Gardella was working as a hospital orderly for $36 a week. In 1949, he had played for an independent Provincial League team in Drummondville, Quebec, for more money than he had made with the Giants. In April 1950, he returned to the major leagues for one at-bat with the St. Louis Cardinals and flied out to right. On April 25, the Cardinals sold him to Houston in the Double-A Texas League. Gardella struggled with Houston, quit the game, and threatened to sue again (though he never did). Gardella's biggest regret was not seeing his lawsuit through to the end. Although he bought a house with his share, the settlement made him "feel like a Judas who had received his 30 pieces of silver."

Miller said it would not be acceptable if Flood began a legal attack on the reserve clause that affected all his fellow players and then succumbed like Gardella to a large settlement offer.

Flood said he could not be bought. He promised to fight the reserve clause to the finish. He did not reveal to Miller that his photography business was floundering and he was not keeping up with alimony or child support payments to Beverly.

Miller continued to grill Flood. Breakfast turned into lunch. Coffee sustained them.

During the course of his interrogation, Miller asked Flood if there was anything in his private life that Curt did not want to see on the front page of the newspaper. Miller had heard rumors about Flood's heavy drinking but was not going to bring them up unless Flood pressed him for specifics. If there was something, Miller warned Flood, the owners would make sure that it came to light.

Flood volunteered Carl's armed robbery conviction and drug addiction, but newspapers had already covered Carl's most recent brush with the law. Curt kept his drinking, womanizing, and financial problems to himself. Nor did he reveal the secret behind his portrait-painting business.

"Nothing you've said so far scares me," Flood said.

Miller tactfully broached the question of Flood's counsel. More than just Flood's interests were at stake here. His lawsuit would affect current players, future players, and the Players Association's current and future negotiations with the owners. Flood, therefore, needed the best possible legal representation. Zerman possessed neither the experience with antitrust law nor the stature to be able to litigate a case to the Supreme Court. Sitting at Flood's side, Zerman agreed with Miller's assessment. He was impressed by Miller's candor with Flood about the risks involved in the lawsuit.

Flood expressed concern to Miller that a top law firm's fees for a case like this could amount to hundreds of thousands of dollars. He asked Miller for the union's help. Flood's awareness of the legal costs impressed Miller.

At some point during their conversation, Flood volunteered a motivating force behind his lawsuit. He told the story about sitting on a stool in the clubhouse in Maracaibo, Venezuela, feeling the shock of being traded after two seasons in the Reds' minor league system and vowing that he would never let himself be traded again. Both Miller and Flood would repeat the Venezuela story many times. Many players, however, are traded early in their careers. They do not react by threatening to sue Major League Baseball.

After four hours of interrogation, Miller said he would not begin to seek the Players Association's help until Flood went home for two weeks and thought about what they had discussed.

Flood did not immediately return to St. Louis. That night he ate dinner at a Greenwich Village restaurant with Phillies general manager John Quinn. They talked for four hours over dinner and drinks. The more time Flood spent with Quinn, the more he liked him.

Flood broached the subject of a salary for 1970, following Miller's advice to explore all his options. Quinn offered him $90,000 plus $8,000 for spring training expenses. Spring training expenses usually amounted to a few hundred dollars. Quinn's offer was nearly the $100,000 contract that he had sought from the Cardinals before the 1969 season. Money, however, was not the issue. The issue was whether Flood wanted to play baseball in 1970 and whether he was willing to submit to a system that ignored his desire to stay in St. Louis or play for another team of his choice.

An incident later that evening persuaded Quinn that Flood would play for the Phillies. A woman at the next table interrupted Flood's conversation with Quinn and said to Flood: "I know you from somewhere. Don't tell me. Lou Brock!"

Flood wanted to spare himself further embarrassment and to send the woman on her way as quickly as possible. "No, I'm Curt Flood," he told the woman, "and this is John Quinn, the general manager of the Phillies. I'm with them now."

With the words "I'm with them now," Quinn believed that he had his man. He told several members of the Philadelphia media to expect a public announcement about Flood's signing.

To Flood, however, the words meant nothing. He never told Quinn about the meeting earlier that day with Miller and Moss or his problems with the reserve clause. At the end of four hours of dinner and drinks, Flood agreed to call Quinn in December.

On November 25, the day after dining with Quinn, Flood headed to a meeting in Philadelphia. Shortly after the trade, a Philadelphia-based executive for Gault Galleries, a national chain of art galleries, contacted Flood. Flood agreed to meet with the executive to explore possible business opportunities. He arrived at noon for a two-hour lunch at Penn Towers where they discussed the art franchise business. He visited the Gault warehouse, a suburban gallery, and then Gault's downtown offices. He even took home one of the gallery's paintings, a nude woman looking into her purse, painted by Paul Butterfield of the Paul Butterfield Blues Band.

During those seven hours, the two men could not agree on a business deal. Flood wanted part ownership in Gault and a possible tie-in with his own franchise business. Gault wanted him to work in public relations in conjunction with the opening of new galleries in the Philadelphia area. The Gault executive called Quinn and offered to serve as an intermediary in persuading Flood to come to Philadelphia. Quinn dismissed the offer, perhaps thinking that based on the "I'm with them now" comment, Flood was already on his way.

Flood returned to St. Louis and spent a week sitting around his apartment thinking about what Miller had told him. He and Zerman huddled at a St. Louis restaurant one night making a list of the pros and cons about suing baseball. They looked at each other after making the list. Flood decided to sue.

Flood called Miller in early December with his decision and his desire to enlist the union's help with legal fees. Miller suggested they meet once more in person. Miller and Moss had begun talking to some of the player representatives; Moss had also begun researching the law and plotting strategy. Miller wanted to give Flood an idea of their next move. He also wanted one last chance to look Flood over before they embarked on a lawsuit that would affect both of their futures.

One night in early December, Flood and a female companion arrived at Miller's Greenwich Village apartment for cocktails. Then they joined Miller and his wife, Terry, for a relaxing dinner at Nat Simon's Penguin, a steakhouse that billed itself as "the second most charming restaurant in the world." The conversation over dinner and drinks was light. They talked about the case, but not with the intensity that had marked breakfast at the Summit Hotel.

Miller believed that in Flood he had found a principled man. He was still curious about why Flood was throwing away his career for a lawsuit he had little chance of winning and no chance of benefiting from, but Miller knew he might never know the answer to this question. It did not seem to be a coincidence that the potential plaintiff was black. Four hours of interrogation and their most recent dinner had not revealed the depths of Flood's racial convictions. Miller supported Flood yet still wondered where this young man was getting his resolve.

CHAPTER THREE

To find a deeper reason why I took this on, you'd have to go back to my mother. Despite all of what had happened to her, she taught me to believe that America would live up to its promise, it would live up to the dignity it was supposed to give you. If you worked hard, you could achieve that dream, that American dream.

—Curt Flood's journal

Curt Flood's inner strength came from his mother, Laura. She never feared anyone or anything—except for the Louisiana lynch mob that once tried to take her life.

Laura's first husband, a Houston man named Ivory Ricks, worked as a supervisor at a lumber mill in De Ridder, a small southwestern Louisiana mill town north of Lake Charles. A black supervisor did not sit well with the white workers in De Ridder in 1915, or their wives.

One of the white wives, who ran the lumber mill's company store, frequently took out her husband's frustrations at reporting to a black man on Laura. But one afternoon in the store, the woman pushed Laura too far.

"Laura," the woman said, "I have been observing you, and you look like a clean nigger. I am going to let you wash my clothes."

"I don't know what you're talking about," Laura replied. "I wash my own clothes, but I wouldn't touch yours."

The woman slapped Laura. Laura beat her to a pulp. A black man might supervise white men in Louisiana in 1915, but no black person could lay a hand on a white woman and live to tell about it. The word was out: Laura Ricks was going to be lynched.

With the mill workers loyal to Ivory Ricks holding off the mob by guarding his family's home, Laura and Ivory packed up the family's belongings, received an armed escort to the train station, and escaped unharmed to Houston. They soon moved to Oakland, California. By 1920, Laura had divorced Ricks. He won custody of their two children, but she took them anyway.

Laura and her children occasionally took the train from Oakland to De Quincy, Louisiana, a town 30 miles south of De Ridder where her parents lived. Laura would disembark in Houston, while her children continued to De Quincy to see their grandparents. Her children thought that she stayed in Houston because she liked the big-city nightlife. They were unaware of Laura's lingering fear of returning home to Louisiana and being lynched.

During one of those nights in Houston, a young piano player spotted Laura at a blues club. With her caramel complexion, bobbed hair, and long pants, Laura stood out among other African-American women during the mid-1920s. She told the man eight years her junior that she was from Oakland, but she refused to give him her address or phone number.

Herman Flood left his native Texas and his job as a cook at a local drugstore and followed Laura to Oakland. He found a job there as a waiter on the ferry, figuring that one afternoon she would have to ride the ferry from Oakland to San Francisco (the San Francisco–Oakland Bay Bridge was not built until 1936). Though it took nearly a year, they finally met again on the ferry, and in 1928 they were married.

Herman and Laura Flood moved back to Houston in 1931 before their oldest son, Herman Jr., was born. Herman Sr. worked two jobs in Houston, as a hospital orderly and a janitor at a church, but he never saw a dime of his paychecks. He always handed them over to Laura, who had opened her own beauty salon. She ran the house. She also decided when they were going to move. They moved frequently. Anytime Laura disliked her home, her neighborhood, or one of her neighbors, she quickly packed up all her family's belongings. Rickie, Laura's daughter from her first marriage, would come home from school and find an address on the door with a three-word note: "We have moved."

Herman and Laura had four children of their own. Herman Jr. was born in 1931, followed by Barbara two years later and Carl a year after her. Then came the baby.

Curtis Charles Flood was born in Houston on January 18, 1938, in the black section of Jefferson Davis Hospital. It did not take him long to take to baseball. One afternoon on Elgin Street, Laura told Herman Jr. to take the baby for a walk. After they had been gone for some time, Rickie went looking for her younger brothers. She was astonished at what she saw on the local playground: Curt was up at bat. Although only 18 or 19 months old, he insisted on swinging a small wooden bat that was almost as big as he was.

The South had no impact on Curt's childhood. Just as Jackie Robinson's family had moved from Cairo, Georgia, to Pasadena, California, when Robinson was a toddler, Curt was two years old when his family left Houston for good for Oakland.

The Floods, like so many other black families, settled in West Oakland. They lived in a two-story white wooden house at 2839 Helen Street. Rickie and her husband, Alvin Riley, lived on the first floor. Herman and Laura slept in one of the two upstairs rooms. In the children's room, Herman Jr. and Curt shared one bunk bed, and Barbara and Carl shared the other.

Jobs were so plentiful in Oakland during World War II that the *San Francisco Chronicle* referred to it as a "Second Gold Rush." Herman initially found a job as a dockworker and later at a military installation in Vallejo. After the war, he worked 60-hour shifts as a janitor at Fairmont Hospital. On weekends, he played Texas-style blues guitar in Oakland's clubs.

At home, Laura worked as a seamstress and served as the family disciplinarian. She also opened a café in the back of a local tavern called the 1430 Club. She served Creole food from her native Louisiana and always left an open seat at the far end of the café's lunch counter. People too poor to afford a meal knew that they could sit in that empty seat, satisfy their hunger, and still preserve their dignity.

Herman taught his children to love art and music. Herman Jr. played the trumpet. Young Curt learned to play the piano by ear. Both Curt and Carl loved to draw. The Floods may have been poor, but Herman and Laura always had enough money for bowls of fresh fruit to fill their children's empty stomachs and for pencils and sketch pads to feed their dreams and imaginations. Curt credited his parents with teaching him "righteousness and fairness."

West Oakland was a working-class black community that produced Congressman Ron Dellums, the Pointer Sisters, basketball players Bill Russell and Paul Silas, and scores of baseball players, including Frank Robinson, Vada Pinson, and Curt Flood. The Floods and many other West Oakland parents moved there from the South in search of jobs and to give their children better lives.

The line between trouble and triumph in West Oakland was a thin one. Curt and Carl initially stayed out of trouble by playing baseball at Poplar Park, only a few blocks from their home. Carl pitched, and Curt caught. Together they played on Police Athletic League teams and rode to the games in the back of a paddy wagon. Carl, however, began to get into real trouble, and Curt started to follow him.

Curt wanted so badly to join his older brother, who had been locked up in juvenile detention, that he stole a truck from the local sawdust mill. Even though his feet could not reach the pedals, he started the truck and drove it for two blocks before plowing it into a parked car. Curt had never seen his father so angry or his mother so disappointed as when they had to bail their two youngest children out of jail on the same day. While trouble would always find Carl, Curt vowed never to get into trouble again.

Curt's ticket out was a man named George Powles (pronounced *Poles*). A failed outfielder with the Pacific Coast League's San Francisco Seals, Powles took a temporary position in 1931 with the Oakland Recreation Department. He enrolled at San Francisco State and received his teaching certificate in 1936, but was unable to find a teaching job. He worked at a brewery, an oil refinery, and a creamery to support his family. In his spare time, he coached baseball.

Powles worked one summer as the playground director at Poplar Park and took an instant liking to nine-year-old Curt. Powles arranged for Curt and Carl to play on his Junior's Sweet Shop midget league team. The two brothers were headed in different directions. Carl indulged in petty crime; Curt gravitated to art and athletics, mostly playing baseball for Powles. Competing against boys two to three years older than he was, Curt played catcher until he came home one afternoon with a badly bruised wrist. He had been hit by the bat while catching. Laura

Flood had a fit. She liked Powles, knew that he kept her children off the streets, and did not mind Curt playing with older boys. But she insisted that Powles move her baby boy out from behind home plate. He agreed. They never had any problems after that day.

It was hard not to like Powles. He, his wife, Winifred, and their two children lived on 60th Street, two blocks from two baseball fields at North Oakland's Bushrod Park. He provided the boys at Bushrod with bats and balls so they could play baseball from sunrise to sundown. A stocky, curly-haired man with an open face, large jowls, and prominent eyebrows, he often pitched for both teams during the course of their nine-inning sandlot games.

Powles turned his family's home into a clubhouse. Winifred served cookies, cakes, pies, and ice cream. She talked with the boys about their girlfriends. George talked baseball, endlessly plotting strategy on a green chalkboard that folded up like a briefcase. He taught them card games such as bridge, and he taught them about life. Curt vividly recalled George chastising him on one occasion: "Don't give somebody a dead fish to shake." It was a lesson that Curt never forgot. For many black children from working-class families, it was their first time inside a white person's home. Powles made them feel at ease.

Powles worked with black children for much of his life. In 1943, he finally landed a teaching job, at predominantly black Herbert Hoover Junior High School. After serving in the Battle of the Bulge, he returned to Hoover before transferring in 1947 to predominantly black McClymonds High School. Most whites hated teaching at McClymonds. Powles, however, was not like most teachers. As the basketball coach, he rescued a tall, gangly, and uncoordinated sophomore whose mother had died when he was 12 and who spent his evenings cooking dinner for his father. Powles made him the 16th man on the junior varsity basketball team (where he shared a uniform with the 15th man). "By that one gesture," Bill Russell wrote, "I believe that man saved me from becoming a juvenile delinquent."

In 1947, the same year Powles transferred to McClymonds, Jackie Robinson broke baseball's color barrier. For aspiring young ballplayers like Flood, Robinson symbolized hope. For southern black families in West Oakland, Robinson symbolized success. The Georgia-born Robinson had grown up in California, starred in football, basketball, baseball, and track at UCLA, and served as an army lieutenant. He had been acquitted during a 1944 court-martial for refusing to move to the back of a bus at Camp Hood, Texas. His signing with the Brooklyn Dodgers made Robinson a hero nationally and in the Flood household. "There was a feeling of enormous pride in someone of my color finally doing something that had the nation's ear," Curt said. "Everyone was talking about Jackie Robinson, the first black athlete to play Major League Baseball, and, daily, my father would get the newspapers to see what Jackie was doing. It was a great deal of pride."

Powles helped the next generation of black athletes to take advantage of Robinson's success. He sent 17 players, most of whom were black, from McClymonds and his Captain Bill Erwin Post 337 American Legion teams to the major leagues. The best was a fatherless, painfully shy eighth-grader on Powles's 1950 Bill Erwin team also named Robinson. Frank Robinson was so terrified about being away from home for the first time during the 1950 American Legion playoffs in Arizona and Nebraska that doctors initially diagnosed his nervous stomach as acute appendicitis. He completely clammed up around adults, except for Powles, who brought Robinson out of his shell by talking baseball. "He was terrific on the fundamentals, but he always went a step beyond them," Robinson said. "Powles taught us how to *think* baseball." Robinson played on the second of Powles's back-to-back American Legion national championship teams. During Robinson's senior year at McClymonds, the star third baseman lost the team batting title to Flood, a scrawny sophomore center fielder. Flood hit .429 to Robinson's .424.

Neither Flood nor Robinson played at McClymonds with Powles's other future star, Vada Pinson. Two years behind Flood, Pinson was more interested in music at that time than baseball. Powles told Pinson, a first baseman/pitcher in high school, to choose between "the trumpet or the bat." Pinson picked baseball and went on to become a fleet major league outfielder for 18 seasons, finishing his career with 2,757 hits.

Curt did not need the same type of prodding from Powles. He brimmed with self-confidence and charmed adults with his artistic ability and extroverted personality. In 1949 and 1950, he served as the Bill Erwin American Legion team's mascot, bat boy, and chief crowd pleaser. He traveled with the team throughout California, warming up pitchers, catching batting practice, and wowing players and spectators with his spectacular catches in the outfield. He was 11 years old in 1949 and weighed 105 pounds. "We'd put on a little show with him, because the customers couldn't help noticing the little guy and how clever he was," Powles told *Sports Illustrated* in 1968. By the time Flood reached McClymonds a few years later, the other players recognized that he and Powles shared a special bond. "George was the coach, and Curt was his pet," recalled Jesse Gonder, a catcher for eight major league seasons. "Curt was more mature than any of us at his age."

Curt made extra money on Saturdays and during school vacations lettering signs, moving furniture, and setting up window displays for a downtown Oakland furniture store called E. Bercovich and Sons. A woman walked into the store one afternoon and asked Sam Bercovich, "Where is your Negro salesman who helped me pick out a piece of furniture?"

"We don't have a Negro salesman," Bercovich replied.

Bercovich realized that the woman was referring to Curt, who knew nothing about furniture but everything about dealing with people. When Curt was 15 or 16 years old, he drew a pen-and-ink portrait of Bercovich. Beneath the portrait, Curt wrote: "To Sam, Your Friend Always, Curt." It still hangs in Bercovich's Bay Area home.

If Flood had two baseball benefactors, the first was Powles, and the second was Bercovich, whose family's furniture store sponsored decades of Oakland's youth baseball teams. The biggest problem Powles and Bercovich faced was how to keep Curt on their Bill Erwin team. The Oakland high schools were divided among nearly a dozen American Legion teams. Powles's McClymonds students had to play for the Colonel Young Post, whereas his Bill Erwin team could draw players only from Oakland Tech and St. Elizabeth's. Powles initially pulled the same trick with Curt that he had used with Frank Robinson: Curt joined the Bill Erwin team at age 14 before he entered the 10th grade at McClymonds. Even at 14, Curt led Bill Erwin in hitting.

Powles and Bercovich hatched a plan. They persuaded Curt to transfer schools by moving in with his older sister, Barbara. Bercovich bought Curt a new $8 bicycle so that he could get from Barbara's house to his new school, baseball games, and the furniture store. The mother of twin boys, Barbara was separated from her husband, John Henry Johnson, a Hall of Fame running back with the San Francisco 49ers and Pittsburgh Steelers, among other teams. Barbara and Curt became extremely close after Curt and Carl had begun to go in different directions. Curt moved into her North Oakland home ostensibly to look after her young children while she worked at night, but mostly so that he could play for the Bill Erwin team by attending Oakland Technical High School.

The same year Curt enrolled at Oakland Tech, the Supreme Court declared segregated schools unconstitutional in *Brown v. Board of Education*. In Oakland, southern-style segregation did not exist. Oakland was a multiethnic, multiracial city of blacks and whites, Italians and Portuguese, Mexicans and Japanese. "I recall little discussion and no excitement in 1954, when the Supreme Court supposedly outlawed the segregation of schools," Curt said. McClymonds was almost all black. Oakland Tech was 75 percent white. Curt's transition, however, was a seamless one. He thrived in Tech's art classes, designed sets for school plays, and painted banners for school assemblies. He joined the Art Club. He "fooled around, like most kids" but described himself as "an above-average student."

Flood's dream of leading Powles's Bill Erwin teams to glory came true. The 1955 team captured the American Legion state championship. As members of one of the state's few integrated teams, the players were as close as brothers. They won the state championship despite enduring racial slights along the way, such as being excluded from the team cafeteria at the state playoffs in Fresno and hearing racist catcalls directed at Flood during the regional playoffs in Lodi. In 27 Legion games that season, Flood hit .620 with 12 doubles, 5 triples, and 9 home runs. Despite his small size, he possessed strong hands and wrists and surprised other boys with his power. He confirmed his major league potential each winter as a member of the Bercovich-sponsored, Powles-coached semipro team in the Alameda Winter League. Major and minor leaguers from the Bay Area would stay in shape during the offseason by playing in that league. At age 15, Flood led his winter league team in hitting.

Because of his small size, scouts did not consider Flood a first-rate prospect. He was only 5 feet 7 and 140 pounds in high school, and eventually topped out at 5 feet 9 and 165. He had been prepared for the disappointment. A few years earlier, Powles had sat him down for a talk. He explained to Curt that a professional baseball career was possible, but that most scouts would write him off as too small.

One scout willing to overlook Flood's size was the Cincinnati Reds'

West Coast scout, Bobby Mattick. Mattick liked Flood's instincts at the plate and in center field. He found Flood easier to talk to than Robinson and Pinson. For Mattick, one thing stood out about Flood: "He had immense pride as a kid."

An infielder with the Cubs and Reds from 1938 to 1942 and the son of a former major leaguer and minor league team owner, Mattick spent much of his eight-decade career in the game as a scout in Oakland. Hot after Robinson and the city's other young black players, Mattick became a fixture at Powles's home with his dry wit and big, smelly cigars. Recognizing that Powles could make or break him in the Bay Area, Mattick persuaded Reds general manager Gabe Paul to put Powles on the team payroll as a bird-dog scout. Powles was Mattick's liaison to the city's top baseball prospects. Beginning with Robinson, the best black players from West Oakland signed away their baseball lives to Mattick and the Reds for a few thousand dollars apiece. Big bonuses went almost exclusively to white prospects. There was no other way into the system. "Everybody signed with him," outfielder Joe Gaines recalled. "If there were 30 guys in the area that signed, 25 of them signed with Cincinnati."

After Curt graduated from Oakland Tech at the end of January 1956, he signed for no bonus, a $4,000 salary, and an invitation to the Reds' spring training. "We were prepared to pay Curtis a bonus," Mattick claimed at the time, "but the boy decided against it." Under the bonus rule, anything greater than $4,000 would have made Curt a "bonus baby" and forced the Reds to keep him on their major league roster for two seasons. The *Cincinnati Enquirer* erroneously reported "that all 16 major league clubs sought to sign Flood after his graduation from high school last week." The *Oakland Tribune* claimed that "no less than 11 clubs" were willing to bid on Flood's services and that one team was prepared to offer him "around $25,000." In truth, Mattick was the only scout who had made him an offer.

At 18, Curt could not have cared less about the reserve system. Or that he would be competing with all his friends from West Oakland for a spot on the Reds' roster. He wanted to be a major league baseball player like his hero, Jackie Robinson, and to play for the Reds with his former high school teammate, Frank Robinson. In part because his class graduated in January, Curt received a plum invitation to spring training to show the Reds what he could do.

On the standard team questionnaire, Flood informed the Reds that he liked Dean Martin and Jerry Lewis movies and that San Francisco native Joe DiMaggio was the greatest player he had ever seen. Next to a question about women, Flood wrote "Eeeech."

The only one not enjoying Curt's success was his older brother Carl. Carl was more than 6 feet tall and, despite a lengthy criminal record (the armed robbery conviction came five years later), still possessed loads of pitching talent. As a 19-year-old semipro pitcher, he threw three consecutive one-hitters. "The three hits wasn't really hits," childhood friend Thomas Johnson recalled. "[It was] a couple of misplayed balls, and they gave them hits." Those misplays drove Carl crazy. His talent was enough to warrant a $2,000 minor league contract. "He turned it down," Herman Jr. recalled, "because little brother was making more than he was." Not that it mattered. Herman Jr., the soft-spoken but wise oldest brother, knew that Carl lacked Curt's discipline. Carl's pride held him back; Curt's propelled him forward.

By signing Curt for $4,000 and sending him to Florida in March 1956 for spring training, the Reds thrust him into the South's cauldron of racial discord. Nearly two months before Curt's graduation from Oakland Tech, on December 1, 1955, a tailor's assistant at a Montgomery, Alabama, department store refused to give up her bus seat to a white passenger. Rosa Parks was the second woman arrested for this act of racial defiance on a Montgomery bus in nine months. Parks's arrest led to the creation of the Montgomery Improvement Association (MIA) and to a massive boycott of the city's bus system. The reluctant leader of the MIA and the boycott was a 26-year-old pastor at Dexter Avenue Baptist Church, Martin Luther King Jr.

The Supreme Court's decision in *Brown v. Board of Education* and the courage of civil rights heroes such as Rosa Parks triggered a southern campaign of white violence, intimidation, and murder. In a decision known as *Brown II*, the Court declared in May 1955 that integration of the public schools should occur with "all deliberate speed." This "all deliberate speed" language encouraged white resistance to integration in the halls of Congress, in state legislatures, and on the streets.

In late August 1955, a 14-year-old Chicago boy went to Money, Mississippi, to visit his relatives. Unfamiliar with the South's unwritten rules, Emmett Till supposedly whistled at the wife of a white store owner. He was kidnapped from his great-uncle's home. Three days later, Till's body was found in the Tallahatchie River with a cotton gin fan tied around his neck. He had been shot in the head and bludgeoned to death. Till's mother left his casket open so that thousands could view his mangled corpse.

Curt Flood was as naive about and ignorant of the customs of the South as Emmett Till. The only things Curt had to protect himself from this storm of racial hatred were the inner strength his mother had exhibited in Louisiana, the courage Rosa Parks had shown that afternoon in Montgomery, and the self-confidence he had carried with him as a youngster growing up in Oakland.

CHAPTER FOUR

I am pleased that God made my skin black but I wish He had made it thicker.

—Curt Flood, *The Way It Is*

In late February 1956, Flood arrived in Tampa, Florida, after the first airplane flight of his life. Barely a month past his 18th birthday, Flood was waiting for his luggage in the Tampa airport's baggage claim area when he saw two water fountains, one labeled "White" and the other labeled "Colored." "For a wild instant," Flood said, "I wondered whether the signs meant club soda and Coke."

Upon arriving at the Cincinnati Reds' spring training headquarters at the Floridian Hotel, Flood could not wait to settle into his room and check out the town. He entered the lobby and asked for his room key. Before he could set down his bags, a black porter whisked him into a cab headed across town to a black boardinghouse named Ma Felder's after the black woman who ran it. All the Reds' black players, including Frank Robinson, were there.

Ashamed and in complete cultural shock, Flood did not dare tell the other black players that he had gone to the white hotel even though many of them had once made the same mistake. Chuck Harmon, one of the first two black players in Reds' history, tried to calm Flood down and give him a crash course on segregation. Putting up with separate spring training facilities was not about being an Uncle Tom, Harmon told Flood, it was about getting to the major leagues.

Flood had no chance of making the Reds straight out of high school. In his first few games, he impressed Cincinnati manager Birdie Tebbetts with his fielding and his poise, but flailed at the plate chasing outside curveballs. He wound up playing mostly in B games. His lone highlight that spring was getting into a March 31 game as a pinch runner against Jackie Robinson and the Brooklyn Dodgers. Trying to prevent Randy Jackson from taking his third-base job, Robinson stole bases and jawed with umpires that day as if it were the 1955 World Series. Robinson always played with a chip on his shoulder. Later that season, he spoke out about the segregated spring training and minor league facilities. He said that "after ten years of traveling in the South, I don't think the advances made there have been fast enough. . . . It is my belief therefore that pressures can be brought to bear by heads of Organized Baseball that would help remedy a lot of the prejudices that surround the game as it's played below the Mason and Dixon Line."

Immediately after playing against Robinson on March 31, Flood was sent to train with the Reds' Class B Carolina League affiliate in High Point, North Carolina. He joined the team at the Reds' minor league spring training facility in Douglas, Georgia.

Ma Felder's was a day at the beach compared with Douglas, Georgia, where more than 400 Reds minor leaguers trained at an old army base. If ever the farm system structure that had been popularized by Branch Rickey made players feel like cattle, this was it. The players lived in barracks, were awakened at 7 a.m., and wore numbered placards on their backs. Flood's number was 330. He and the other black players lived in separate barracks and ate in separate mess halls from their white teammates. At night, they could watch movies from the balcony of a local theater but preferred bars in black neighborhoods where no Reds officials dared go. The conditions affected Flood's play on the field. The *High Point Enterprise* reported that he "looked miserable at the start."

Life only got worse for Flood in High Point–Thomasville, the adjacent North Carolina furniture towns with a combined population of 60,000 and home to Flood's first minor league team. "I was ready for High Point–Thomasville," he said, "but the two peckerwood communities were not ready for me."

"Massive resistance," the campaign of white violence and intimidation in response to the Supreme Court's desegregation decisions, was in full swing. Whites rioted and burned crosses in February as a young black woman named Autherine Lucy unsuccessfully tried to attend the University of Alabama. In March, 100 southern congressmen and senators declared in a document known as the "Southern Manifesto" that the Supreme Court had abused its judicial power. Dr. King's Montgomery bus boycott lasted 382 days and would have lasted longer had the Supreme Court not declared in November 1956 that Montgomery's segregated bus service was unconstitutional. Whites were angrier than ever before about blacks ruining their southern way of life, and that way of life included minor league baseball.

Just because Jackie Robinson had integrated the major leagues in 1947 did not mean that small southern towns were going to accept black players on their minor league teams. The Carolina League's first black player, Percy Miller, lasted just two unhappy weeks with Danville, Virginia, in August 1951. Two years later, Flood's future Cardinals teammate Bill White, who also played for Danville, was the first black player to survive a full Carolina League season. A black player did not join a North Carolina–based Carolina League team until 1955, just a year before Flood's arrival. Racism plagued the southern minor leagues well into the 1960s and by 1956 had reached a fever pitch in the Carolina League, which Flood called the "peckerwood league."

Games at High Point–Thomasville's Finch Field generally drew between 500 and 1,000 people, and Flood could hear every heckler in the 3,500-seat ballpark. He internalized all the insults he heard in the stands. "One of my first and most enduring memories is of a large, loud cracker who installed himself and his four little boys in a front-row box and started yelling 'black bastard' at me," he said.

During the first few weeks of the season, Flood could not wait to get home to his room at a black boardinghouse, where every night he would break down and cry. "It's hell down here," he wrote home. "I didn't know that people could act like this. The home fans are swell to me, but on the road they are on me all the time. . . . I don't know how long I can take it."

He called his sister, Barbara, and told her that he wanted to come home. "I felt too young for the ordeal," he said. "I wanted to be home. I wanted to talk to someone. I wanted to be free of these animals whose fifty-cent bleacher ticket was a license to curse my color and deny my humanity. I wanted to be free of the imbeciles on my ball team." Barbara frantically phoned Reds scout Bobby Mattick. "His sister called me and said he wanted to come home," Mattick recalled. "I said, 'You call him back and tell him not to come home. Tell him to tough it out.'"

Flood understood the stakes. "What had started as a chance to test my baseball ability in a professional setting had become an obligation to measure myself as a man," he said. "As such, it was a matter of life and death. These brutes were trying to destroy me. If they could make me collapse and quit, it would verify their preconceptions. And it would wreck my life."

With the Hi-Toms (the name of the High Point–Thomasville team), Flood wore a stealth shield on his back, number 42, the number worn by Jackie Robinson. The number honored his hero, reminded him of what Robinson had gone through, and pushed him to go forward. It was like wearing Superman's cape.

Robinson had experienced the South, but not for a whole season. At the start of spring training in 1946, he had to leave Sanford, Florida, in the middle of the night because of threats on his life if he continued to stay there. Two other Florida cities, Jacksonville and DeLand, canceled spring training games in 1946 rather than allow him to play there with the Triple-A Montreal Royals. Later that season he played in two southern border cities, Baltimore and Louisville. The Dodgers tried to insulate him from future spring incidents by training in Havana in 1947 and later purchasing their own spring facilities and housing in Vero Beach, Florida. Robinson and his family, however, still experienced the Jim Crow South outside the walls of the Vero Beach training complex, at spring training games in other Florida towns and during a few exhibition games each spring on the Dodgers' annual trek north to Brooklyn.

Flood and other black players of his generation survived entire minor league seasons in the South. "We were Jackie's disciples," said Ed Charles, a member of the 1969 World Champion New York Mets who spent one of his eight minor league seasons in the South with Flood. "We were an extension of Jackie. We were the early trailblazers, on the heels of his trailblazing. He was up North. He assigned us to break the barriers in the South. . . . We had to complete the job that he had started, and that means we had to comport ourselves the way that he did. . . . We were on a tightrope all the time."

Fans in other Carolina League towns tested Flood's resolve. Greensboro was bad. Smaller, southeastern North Carolina towns such as Wilson, Kinston, and Fayetteville were worse. In Wilson, during one of the league's two midseason all-star games, a *High Point Enterprise* columnist noticed the "considerable amount of cat-calls directed at the all-Negro outfield." In Fayetteville, a military town, one fan called out upon seeing Flood: "There's a goddamned nigger son-of-a-bitch playing ball with them white boys! I'm leaving." In Durham, Flood hit a ball into the left-center-field gap, and his cap flew off as he rounded first base. A man sitting in a wheelchair halfway up the stands behind the Hi-Toms' dugout yelled: "Run, nigger, run."

The words "Run, nigger, run" stuck with Flood's lone black teammate, pitcher John Ivory Smith, for the rest of his life. A native of Cocoa Beach, Florida, Smith pitched for the Hi-Toms until he was transferred to another team in early May. A month later, Bo Bossard, a black infielder from Columbia, South Carolina, joined the team. These native-born southerners knew what to expect; for Flood, however, southern segregation was foreign territory.

The worst part of life in the Carolina League for Flood was the travel. White teammates saw Flood's shoulders drop as they got off the bus to eat while he was forced to stay on the bus and wait for them to bring him food. Sometimes he was told to go to the back of the restaurant. He once ate a hamburger in the yard of a diner among barking dogs while his teammates sat inside. His teammates went to the bathroom at rest stops; Flood had to ask the bus driver to pull over to the side of the road. At home and on the road, the bus dropped him off in the black section of town. The routine alienated him from his white teammates. His manager, 42-year-old former Reds utility player Bert Haas, did nothing to bridge the gap.

Like the Carolina League's dozen other black players, Flood learned an important early lesson: how to duck. As the league's best hitter, Flood saw more than his share of beanballs and knockdown pitches. Johnny Pesky, the former Red Sox infielder who managed the Durham Bulls that season, praised Flood's "attitude" and "courage." "They keep throwing at Flood to keep him loose up there at the plate and he continues to dig in," Pesky said.

One night, as Flood lit up Kinston's pitching, Kinston manager Jack Paepke decided he had seen enough. He inserted himself as the team's pitcher. Kinston outfielder Carl Long cringed when he heard what his manager was planning in the dugout. "The manager said, 'I'm going to hit that son-of-a-bitch upside the head,'" Long recalled. "And he hit him upside the head. Curt went to first, stole second, and stole third. After the ball game, he said he was going to steal home if he could. The next at-bat he hit a home run."

Black ballplayers and entertainers of that era were prime targets for white violence. On April 10, 1956, singer Nat King Cole was knocked to the floor as he performed before an all-white audience in Birmingham, Alabama. Six men were arrested before they could do him serious physical harm, but a plot was uncovered that involved more than 100 people and aimed to kill the singer. In a Carolina League game that year in Greensboro, Danville outfielder Leon "Daddy Wags" Wagner mysteriously dropped an easy fly ball. His manager began to yell at him between innings until Wagner explained the situation. "[A] guy was hiding out behind the left-field stands," Wagner said. "He pointed a shotgun at me and yelled, 'Nigger, I'm going to fill you with shot if you catch one ball out here.'" Police caught the man, and Wagner, though not the deftest fielder, at least tried to catch fly balls again.

Flood and the Carolina League's other minority players thrived despite the torrent of racial abuse. The league's best players were black or Hispanic, including future major leaguers Wagner (51 home runs, 166 RBIs), Hall of Fame first baseman Willie McCovey (.310), infielders Tony Taylor and Jose Pagan, and pitcher Orlando Pena. Flood outshone them all. He led the league with a .340 batting average, set a league record with 133 runs, tied for the league lead with 190 hits, finished second to Wagner with 128 RBIs, walked 102 times, stole 19 bases, and hit a team-record 29 home runs. He dazzled teammates with his running catches in the outfield and led the league with 388 putouts. Pesky proclaimed Flood the league's best prospect. The Carolina League named him its player of the year. "I lit up that league—I carried my ballclub, and if that sounds like bragging, I don't care," Flood said. "I played like I was on fire to prove to myself that you can always overcome anything from the outside."

Despite accolades from the league and quiet admiration from teammates and opponents, Flood was miserable all season. He did not care whether his team won or lost. There were times when he despised his team's pitcher so much that he contemplated making an error on purpose. He never did. "Pride was my resource," he said. "I solved my problem by playing my guts out." But for the first time in his life, baseball was not fun. It was a job, and a miserable one at that.

After the season's final game, Flood was excluded from the team party at an all-white establishment until owner Tom Finch, a Thomasville furniture dealer and friend of Sam Bercovich's, intervened. Nothing could change Flood's mind about High Point–Thomasville. By the end of the season, his weight hovered around 135 pounds. His face looked gaunt. He was exhausted. But he knew he had played his way out of the peckerwood league. "I believe that I would have quit baseball rather than return there," he said.

The Reds rewarded Flood for his fine season by calling him up to the major leagues. He had never been to a regular-season major league game before playing in one. On the plane flight to join the team in St. Louis, the airline lost his bag containing his baseball spikes and other equipment. He could not even get out of the Carolina League with his shoes. In St. Louis, he borrowed spikes from one of his new Reds teammates and traded his Hi-Toms uniform number 42 for a Reds uniform bearing number 27. The following spring, and for most of his major league career, he wore number 21—half of Jackie Robinson's number.

A week after joining the team, Flood found himself at Brooklyn's Ebbets Field on the same diamond as his hero. The Reds, Dodgers, and Braves were locked in a pennant race, with the Reds just two games behind the first-place Dodgers. On September 16, the Reds trailed the Dodgers 3–2 with two outs in the top of the ninth inning. When third baseman Ray Jablonski and catcher Ed Bailey both singled to keep the Reds' hopes alive, Cincinnati manager Birdie Tebbetts sent Flood to pinch-run for Bailey at first base. At that moment, Flood represented only one thing to Jackie Robinson—the winning run. Flood never made it past first. Robinson scooped up pinch hitter Stan Palys's ground ball at third base and threw to first for the final out. It was the only time the two men shared the same major league field. After the season, the Dodgers sold Robinson to their crosstown rivals, the New York Giants. Robinson had already decided to retire and accept an executive position with Chock full o' Nuts. He later explained that he wanted nothing more to do with the game or the racist people who ran it.

The Reds, who regarded Flood as the nation's best minor league prospect, were so eager to get him into their lineup that they sought to turn the graceful center fielder into a third baseman. The experiment began in pregame warm-ups during Flood's September call-up to the major leagues, continued during an aborted winter league season in the Dominican Republic and at spring training in 1957, and ended with the Savannah Redlegs of the Class A South Atlantic ("Sally") League.

After High Point–Thomasville, the last thing Flood needed was a year in the Sally League. With teams in Georgia, Florida, Tennessee, and North and South Carolina, the league was Flood's introduction to the Deep South. Hank Aaron had integrated the Sally League in 1953 along with several other players. Despite growing up in Mobile, Alabama, Aaron said he "wasn't prepared at all for what would happen that year." If anything, racial tensions had increased by the time that Flood played there four years later.

Before the 1957 season, the Georgia Senate passed a bill, 31–0, banning interracial athletics in an attempt to keep integrated teams out of the state's four Sally League towns. The bill would have ended many major league teams' affiliation with Georgia, but it died in the House of Representatives. Senator Leon Butts, the author of the legislation and a native of Lumpkin, Georgia, near Columbus, fumed: "I think it's a shame the major league ballclubs and the NAACP have gotten control of the Georgia House."

That same year, U.S. senator Strom Thurmond of South Carolina broke the record for the longest filibuster in Senate history by holding the floor for 24 hours, 18 minutes. He was defeated in his efforts to prevent the passage of the Civil Rights Act of 1957, the first civil rights legislation since Reconstruction. On September 4, Arkansas governor Orval Faubus enlisted the National Guard to prevent nine black students from integrating Little Rock's all-white Central High School. Faubus flouted federal court orders and forced President Eisenhower to bring in the U.S. military to oversee the integration of the school. The *Savannah Morning News* ran front-page stories about the "Little Rock Crisis" every day.

Flood knew what to expect after a season in the Carolina League, but life in Savannah was still hard. "The Georgia city had lately been in a high state of tension about school desegregation and other civil rights," he said. "When I saw how uptight the black community was, and how hostile the whites were, I realized that Cincinnati had arranged another full dose for me."

One day, in between games of a doubleheader, Flood peeled off his only uniform and threw it into a pile with those of his white teammates. The team trainer yelled as if Flood had lit him on fire. The trainer extricated Flood's uniform and jockstrap from the pile with a long stick with a nail on it and sent his clothes to the black laundry 20 minutes away. Flood cried as he sat naked waiting for his uniform to arrive while his white teammates took the field. He could not even wait in the same section of the clubhouse as his white teammates. He dressed in a cordoned-off section made out of corrugated tin next to the dugout. According to Flood, local law prevented him from dressing with his white teammates.

He could not find a place to live until the dean of men at the local black college, Savannah State, offered him a room. The college cafeteria was usually closed after games, so Flood sometimes cooked a piece of meat in his room. Sometimes he went hungry rather than eat the greasy food at the only late-night place that would serve him, the all-black lunchroom at the local bus station.

Savannah center fielder Buddy Gilbert thought that Flood was the loneliest man in the world. On road trips, Gilbert frequently brought food out to Flood and the other black players on the team bus. "Poor Gilbert's small kindnesses only accentuated the cruelty of prejudice," Flood said. Flood seethed as he waited for his food on the bus. "He took a lot," Gilbert recalled. "How he ever held it in was beyond my comprehension. There were times it really bothered him, more than the other guys. He would just get really quiet."

Playing third base made Flood an easy target for abuse. He committed 41 errors that season, and each error was an excuse for the fans, either home or away, to call him another name. In August, he injured the inside of his right arm sliding into the canvas bag at second base. An ugly mass of flesh formed on the joint and made throwing extremely painful. He played on, though he shifted to right field for the last two weeks of the season. For Flood, it was all about surviving physically and mentally and advancing to the major leagues. He could not do that on the bench.

Flood's Sally League season was solid but not spectacular. His .299 average was the fourth highest in the league. He finished among the Sally League leaders in most offensive categories. He made two Sally League all-star teams at third base despite his 41 errors.

The Reds thought enough of Flood's Sally League campaign to call him up again at the end of the season. His first major league hit was a home run, a two-run shot down the left-field line off Chicago Cubs pitcher Moe Drabowsky. The home run was a happy ending to two brutal seasons in the southern minor leagues. The name-calling, segregated facilities, and second-class citizenship had transformed Flood from an extroverted kid who charmed adults into a quiet, introverted man who had survived two trying years in the South because of his tremendous pride and inner competitive fire.

Flood discovered the effects of the reserve clause that winter in Venezuela. He was sent there to learn to play second base because of the outstanding 1957 season of Reds third baseman Don Hoak. Then came the first trade. In exchange for Flood and outfielder Joe Taylor, the Reds acquired three Cardinals pitchers whom sportswriter Jim Murray later described as "a flock of nobodies even the slot man on the *Sporting News* had to look up."

The Reds traded Flood to the Cardinals for the same reason they had tried to turn him into an infielder—Cincinnati was not ready for an all-black outfield. The Reds already had 1956 Rookie of the Year Frank Robinson in left field and preferred another West Oakland player, Vada Pinson, in center. Pinson was not the defensive outfielder that Flood was, but Pinson was bigger, stronger, and faster. After tearing up Class C Visalia in 1957, Pinson played so spectacularly in spring training in 1958 that he started in right field for the Reds on Opening Day before a slump sent him back to the minor leagues. The following year, Pinson emerged as the Reds' star center fielder.

Bobby Mattick, the scout who had signed all three players, rejected the all-black-outfield theory as the reason behind the Flood trade.

Mattick pointed out that another of his black Bay Area signees, Tommy Harper, started in the Reds outfield with Robinson and Pinson from 1963 to 1965. But that was years later. Mattick attributed the trade to Reds manager Birdie Tebbetts, who had told Mattick that Flood was too small. Tebbetts denied that race had anything to do with it, saying he had traded Flood because of a hitch in his swing. Flood did have a hitch (that he later corrected), but so did many other great players, including Frank Robinson.

An equally plausible explanation for Flood's trade to the Cardinals was the unspoken quota system employed by most major league teams of the late 1950s and early 1960s. "There was a quota on a lot of ball clubs," Frank Robinson said. "If you saw a few [blacks] at spring training at a major league camp and there was more than four, you said, 'Uh-uh, someone's got to go.'" The Reds opened the 1958 season with four black position players: Robinson, Pinson, George Crowe, and Bob Thurman. Flood would have made five, but he had already been sent to St. Louis.

At that time, St. Louis was the southernmost city in the major leagues, both geographically and politically. St. Louis was the city where the slave Dred Scott had sued for his freedom and lost, resulting in the infamous 1857 Supreme Court decision that some believe ignited the Civil War. In 1947, several southern members of the St. Louis Cardinals had threatened to boycott their team's games against Jackie Robinson and the Dodgers. After the boycott talk was crushed, Cardinals outfielder Enos "Country" Slaughter and catcher Joe Garagiola spiked Robinson at first base; Robinson also exchanged heated words with Garagiola, a St. Louis native, at home plate. A few years later, the Cardinals tormented Robinson and Dodgers pitcher Joe Black. The Chase Hotel in St. Louis had refused to allow black players to stay there until Robinson broke that barrier in 1954 by agreeing not to use the pool or dining room or hang out in the lobby. St. Louis was as segregated in 1958 as any southern city. Flood's first apartment there in a black hotel was so run-down that he found his own lodging in what turned out to be a whorehouse.

Cardinals president Gussie Busch and new general manager Bing Devine were bent on changing the team's racist image. They were succeeding until Busch replaced manager Fred Hutchinson—who had instigated the trade for Flood and started him in center field in 1958—

with Solly Hemus, who was named player-manager. A diminutive former Cardinals infielder known as "Mighty Mouse," Hemus wrote Busch an ingratiating letter in 1956 after the Cardinals had traded him to the Phillies. Hemus gushed about how much he had loved wearing a Cardinals uniform and how he wanted to return to the organization one day. Three seasons later, Busch granted the 35-year-old Hemus's wish.

During Hemus's managerial tenure from 1959 to 1961, Flood spent two and a half seasons as a pinch runner, late-inning defensive replacement, and second-fiddle center fielder. Hemus insisted on experimenting with anyone and everyone, including slick-fielding first baseman Bill White, in center. White nearly killed himself out there. Hemus also refused to put Bob Gibson into the regular starting rotation and often shuttled him back and forth between the Cardinals and the minor leagues. Hemus believed that the Creighton-educated Gibson lacked the brains to learn to control his fastball and master National League hitters. Flood and Gibson believed that Hemus, the son of an Austrian immigrant, was not simply making player evaluations. "Hemus acted as if I smelled bad," Flood said. "He avoided my presence and when he could not do that he avoided my eye."

Hemus's lack of confidence in him drove Flood to distraction. During the Hemus years, Flood rarely slept more than a few hours each night. He often stayed awake replaying the previous night's game in his head, which sportswriter Al Stump called Flood's "Midnight League." He had already been smoking a pack of cigarettes a day since he was 15. Now insomnia and indigestion were Flood's closest friends. Nearly every day there was a new center fielder auditioning for his job. A St. Louis sportswriter speculated in July 1961 that Flood might be left unprotected during the 1962 expansion draft.

Hemus revealed his true colors after inserting himself into the second game of a May 3, 1959, doubleheader against the Pirates' black rookie pitcher Bennie Daniels. During a second-inning at-bat, Daniels nicked Hemus in the leg. Hemus motioned toward the mound and yelled at Daniels, "You black bastard!" After Hemus doubled in the third inning, Daniels whizzed a fastball near Hemus's chin. Just as Daniels threw his next pitch, Hemus released his bat toward the mound. Both benches emptied. Fists flew. Hemus held a closed-door team meeting immediately after the game and revealed to his players what he had called Daniels. Flood, White, and George Crowe, acquired in the offseason from the Reds, sat there in stunned silence. They now understood where they stood with their manager. "Until then, we had detested Hemus for not using his best lineup," Flood said. "Now we hated him for himself."

Hemus was fired on July 6, 1961, and replaced with Johnny Keane. After briefly studying for the priesthood, Keane had played in the Cardinals' minor league system until a vicious beaning by pitcher Sig Jakucki in 1935 fractured Keane's skull and put him in a coma for a week and in the hospital for six more. Keane played one more year, then managed for 17 seasons in the Cardinals' minor league system before becoming one of Hemus's coaches. Keane had been passed over five times for the Cardinals' managerial post.

As the new Cardinals manager, Keane immediately inserted Gibson into the starting rotation. The 5-foot-9, 165-pound Flood finally heeded his coaches' advice, stopped trying to hit home runs, and turned himself into a singles hitter. A month later, Keane made Flood the starting center fielder. Flood finished the 1961 season with a .322 batting average and held the center field job for the next eight seasons. The former seminary student sensed the anxiety that lay behind Flood's calm clubhouse demeanor. He could read on Flood's face when things were bothering him, and he tried to put Flood's active mind at ease. Keane recognized that Flood, Gibson, and White were not just great natural athletes; they were also smart, educated, and proud men and budding team leaders. He respected them in a way that Hemus, according to Flood and Gibson, never did.

Flood, Gibson, and White led the Cardinals into the 1960s. They represented the next generation of outspoken black athletes. They also became the best of friends. Flood first met Bob Gibson during a September 1957 game in the Sally League. The starting pitcher for Columbus against Flood's Savannah team, Gibson did not get out of the first inning, walking five straight hitters with two outs—beginning with Flood. The segregation and discrimination in the Sally League infuriated Gibson. One of seven children whose father had died three months before he was born and whose mother worked in a laundry and cleaned houses and hospitals in her spare time, Gibson grew up a sickly child in an Omaha, Nebraska, ghetto. A rat once bit Gibson's ear. Pneumonia nearly killed him. His older brother, Josh (not the Hall of Fame catcher), promised to buy Gibson a baseball glove if he recovered. Raised by his older brother, Gibson starred in baseball and basketball playing with and against whites. He attended Creighton University on a basketball scholarship and played for several years with the Harlem Globetrotters, initially dividing his year between the Cardinals and the Globetrotters until Devine agreed to cover his basketball salary.

Gibson and Flood were reunited at the Cardinals' 1958 rookie instructional camp. Gibson arrived in St. Petersburg in 1958 and made the same mistake that Flood had made with the Reds in 1956—Gibson showed up at the white players' hotel. He was immediately sent to a black boardinghouse, where Flood happened to be one of his three housemates. They roomed together when Flood briefly began the 1958 season at Triple-A Omaha and were road roommates for nearly ten years with the Cardinals. Flood grew closer to Gibson than he was to his own brothers.

Flood and Gibson may have led the Cardinals on and off the field in the 1960s, but in early 1961 they could not crack Hemus's starting lineup. Rather, the mantle of leadership initially fell on the third member of their trio, Bill White. Born in Lakewood, Florida, and raised in the integrated steel town of Warren, Ohio, William De Kova White was the only child of a military secretary and never knew his steelworker father. White finished second in his high school class, attended Hiram College on an academic scholarship, and planned on becoming a physician. But the premed student could not bear asking his mother for any more spending money and instead accepted the New York Giants' $2,500 bonus to play baseball. As the first black player to survive a season in the Carolina League, White yelled at his tormentors and gave them the finger. White, like Flood, later developed an outward calm that masked his deep sensitivity and competitive inner fire.

One weekend before spring training in 1961, Flood and White drove to Miami and were introduced to a young man named Cassius Clay. The Louisville Lip charmed them. The light-heavyweight Olympic gold medalist in 1960, Clay had moved up to the heavyweight division and turned professional. During a two-week period in Miami Beach, he won his fourth and fifth professional bouts against Jim Robinson and Donnie Fleeman. He also sparred with former heavyweight champion Ingemar Johansson. "I'll go dancin' with Johansson," Clay said.

In between fighting palookas and dancin' with Johansson, Clay invited Flood and White to a Nation of Islam meeting. They were searched for weapons and forced to leave their wallets and watches at the door. A speaker stood up and started talking about white devils. The ballplayers, as well as Clay, got up and left. "Sounds as if black power would be white power backwards," Gibson said later. "That wouldn't be much improvement."

In 1961, White spoke up about one of the most important baseball issues of the day: segregated spring training facilities. White arrived in St. Petersburg, Florida, an All-Star first baseman only to be treated like a second-class citizen. His white Cardinals teammates either rented private beachfront condos for their families or sunned themselves by the pool at St. Petersburg's Vinoy Park Hotel. White and his fellow black players stayed in boardinghouses in the black section of St. Petersburg and were afraid to bring their families to Florida. As a result, any team unity fostered in spring training was destroyed once the Cardinals left the field.

That year, an incident in spring training finally made White speak up. He saw a list of Cardinals players invited to a March 9 "Salute to Baseball" breakfast for the Cardinals and Yankees at the local yacht club, sponsored by the St. Petersburg Chamber of Commerce. No black players were on the list. To make matters worse, the list included Doug Clemens, a white Cardinals outfielder who had appeared in exactly one major league game and had never even come to bat. White was so incensed that he mentioned the situation to Associated Press reporter Joe Reichler. At 5:20 p.m. on March 8, Reichler put White's comments on the national wire.

"When will we be made to feel like humans?" White asked Reichler. "They invited all but the colored players. Even the kids who never have come to bat once in the big leagues received invitations—that is, if they were white. . . . How much longer must we accept this without saying a word? This thing keeps gnawing away my heart. I think about this every minute of the day."

Cardinals public relations director Jim Toomey feebly replied that it was his fault. He had invited only the Cardinals players staying at the team hotel because it was close to the yacht club and the breakfast was at 8:15 a.m. Toomey said he had excluded white veterans such as Stan Musial staying in private condos with their families as well as the black players. Toomey's response ignored the bigger issue that the team's black players were not isolated from their white teammates by choice.

Flood had spoken out about the spring training situation a month before White helped make it a national issue. "The rookie who is trying to win my job can bring his wife to camp and live in the most lavish surroundings," Flood told a *Pittsburgh Courier* reporter the week of February 4. "Me, I'm forced to leave my wife at home because we can't find a decent place to stay. It just doesn't make sense."

At spring training, Flood broached the issue with Cardinals owner Gussie Busch. It was unfortunate, Flood told Busch, that he and the team's other black players had to stay in the black section of town.

"Do you mean to tell me," a surprised Busch said, "that you're not staying here at the hotel with the rest of the fellas?"

"Mr. Busch," Flood replied, "don't you know that we're staying about five miles outside of town in the Negro section?"

Busch said he did not know, and from that point on the Cardinals organization began to take White's and Flood's complaints seriously. Devine called Flood in the spring of 1961 and asked him if he was satisfied with the team's spring training accommodations. Flood did not mince words in voicing his displeasure, a bold move considering that his position with the Hemus-led Cardinals in the spring of 1961 was tenuous at best.

White and Flood were not the only ones blasting segregated spring training accommodations. Wendell Smith, who had led the *Pittsburgh Courier*'s campaign urging Major League Baseball to integrate and had served as Jackie Robinson's roommate and confidant in 1946 and 1947, wrote a front-page article in the January 23, 1961, edition of the *Chicago American* about the problems of black players at spring training. Smith tried to shame the black players into standing up for their rights to desegregated housing, calling them "Fat Cats" and "Uncle Toms" who refused to jeopardize their standing with major league clubs.

A week after Smith's initial article, the chairman of the St. Petersburg chapter of the NAACP, Dr. Ralph Wimbish, told the *St. Petersburg*

Times that he would no longer help the Cardinals and Yankees find housing for their black players. So did Dr. Robert Swain, a black dentist who owned a six-unit apartment building in St. Petersburg where some black players stayed. Wimbish asked the two major league teams to pressure their spring training hotels to integrate. He named White, Flood, and George Crowe of the Cardinals and Elston Howard and Hector Lopez of the Yankees as spokesmen. He also mentioned Flood's decision not to bring his wife to spring training.

Wimbish's home and swimming pool at 3217 15th Avenue South was the black players' unofficial clubhouse. The players ate, sat around the pool, watched television, and talked. Wimbish's wife, Bette, made a gumbo that Flood enjoyed. "After dinner, we'd sit around and talk about everything, including segregation," Bette Wimbish told the *St. Petersburg Times*. "Some players were conservative and didn't want to rock the boat. But others, like Curt Flood and Bill White, resented the way they were treated."

After White's comments hit the national wire on March 8, the talk at Wimbish's home centered on the chamber of commerce breakfast. White received a belated invitation, but he did not want to wake up early to eat breakfast with bigots. Flood and Bette Wimbish argued that White should go. "Curt thought it was important to break down the barriers, make inroads so that the black ballplayers could be recognized," Bette told her son, Ralph Jr., a *New York Post* sports editor, "but Bill held firm and said no. He wouldn't go." At 8:15 a.m. on March 9, 48 Cardinals and Yankees players attended the breakfast. Only one was black. At the behest of his team, Yankees catcher Elston Howard went in order to "help to break down some of the segregation mess." White, Flood, and the other black Cardinals players stayed home.

White's comments to Reichler, Smith's reporting, and Wimbish's activism planted seeds of change. "It was our own little civil rights movement," White said. The national civil rights movement had taken off on February 1, 1960, when four black North Carolina A&T students demanded service at a Woolworth's lunch counter in Greensboro, North Carolina, and refused to leave until they were served. The sit-ins swept the South. Integrated groups of "Freedom Riders" boarded interstate buses beginning in May 1961 to test the desegregation of southern airports, bus terminals, and lunch counters. The Freedom Riders suffered brutal beatings and arrests, attracting national media attention to the unfairness and cruelty of southern segregation.

On July 31, White and Detroit Tigers outfielder Bill Bruton addressed the Players Association's representatives in Boston at the second of two All-Star Games scheduled that year. The association backed a resolution sent to the owners asking them to ensure that black players at spring training would be treated like "first class citizens." When the owners of the spring training hotels for the Yankees and Cardinals refused to integrate their facilities, the Yankees, a team not known for its progressive racial policies, left St. Petersburg and found integrated housing across the state in Fort Lauderdale. The White Sox, Orioles, Braves, and expansion Mets also moved into integrated facilities in 1962.

The Cardinals reacted like a corporation with a crisis on its hands. Busch and his public relations man, Al Fleishman, knew that segregated spring training facilities were bad for beer sales. Rumors surfaced of a black boycott of Anheuser-Busch's beers. Devine knew that the segregated facilities were bad for his team. The Cardinals vowed not to return to the all-white Vinoy Park Hotel. During spring training in 1961, Busch asked city officials to help the team find desegregated housing.

A businessman purchased two adjacent motels, the Skyline Motel and the Outrigger Motel, on the southern tip of St. Petersburg and housed the Cardinals there in 1962. Twenty-nine of the 32 players stayed at the 49-unit Skyline Motel. (Three players with families from St. Petersburg lived elsewhere.) Captain Ken Boyer and future Hall of Famer Stan Musial sacrificed their private beachfront condos that season and moved into the motel with their families. The motel's food, based on its Polynesian theme, was awful. Cardinals players and their families responded by barbecuing their own food. White and Gibson cooked, pitching coach Howie Pollet made the salad, and Boyer and pitcher Larry Jackson purchased the meat and worked the grill. Players, front-office personnel, and sportswriters stayed there, 137 people in all, including 32 wives and 25 children. It was like Camp Cardinal. Each week the team held a fried chicken picnic dinner. The team showed nightly movies, held costume parties for the kids, organized fishing trips, toured Busch Gardens, and cruised on Gussie Busch's yacht. This was the beginning of the social integration of the Cardinals. Flood, Gibson, and White spent the next few years completing the job.

The civil rights movement grabbed Flood in 1962 and would not let go. His hero, Jackie Robinson, showed him the way. Since retiring after the 1956 season, Robinson had thrust himself into politics and the freedom struggle. In February 1962, he invited the 24-year-old Flood to join him, heavyweight champion Floyd Patterson, former light-heavyweight champion Archie Moore, and entertainer Harry Belafonte's former wife, Margurite, at the NAACP's Southeast Regional Conference in Jackson, Mississippi. Before 3,800 people at the Masonic Temple in Jackson, Flood and the other athletes spoke out on behalf of racial justice. Robinson, recently elected to the Baseball Hall of Fame, was the master of ceremonies. Grayer and about 50 pounds heavier than in his playing days, Robinson told the audience that these athletes were there "to let you know we are with you 100 percent." He swelled with pride over the comments by his fellow celebrities. "Our admiration for Patterson, Moore, Flood, and Marguerite [sic] Belafonte is unlimited," Robinson wrote in his column for two of the nation's largest black weekly newspapers. "They represent the kind of thinking and dedication which is helping to lick one of the toughest problems of our time."

In Mississippi, Flood and the other celebrities stayed in the homes of black families. Their host families escorted them to the rally with pride. The rally, in turn, inspired local black Tougaloo College students such as Anne Moody. "People felt relaxed and proud," she later wrote. "They appreciated knowing and meeting people of their own race who had done something worth talking about." Moody went on to risk her life in Mississippi voter-registration drives and lunch-counter sit-ins. Medgar Evers, the NAACP's first field secretary in Mississippi, was the group's official host. A year later, Evers pulled into his driveway, got out of his car, and was shot in the back and killed.

The athletes attracted the attention of the Mississippi State Sovereignty Commission, an anti–civil rights police force established by the state after the *Brown* decision to "do and perform any and all acts deemed necessary and proper to protect the sovereignty of the state of Mississippi, and her sister states," including spying on and intimidating civil rights workers. The Sovereignty Commission investigator at the February 25 rally reported that "Patterson and the other world-known Negroes" drew "one of the largest crowds I have ever observed for a meeting of this type." Cars jammed Lynch Street next to the Masonic

Temple and were so numerous that it was impossible for the investigator to record the license-plate numbers. By virtue of his participation, Flood earned himself a secret Sovereignty Commission file.

Flood told the Mississippi audience that the rally helped him realize his responsibility to the struggle for racial equality. He went to Mississippi not to gain notoriety among white authorities or for the thank-you note from NAACP executive secretary Roy Wilkins. Flood went because his hero had asked him to go. He went because he wanted to show his solidarity with southern blacks fighting for their freedom. He went because he felt the civil rights movement in his soul.

Flood was one of the first active major leaguers to join the civil rights struggle. Baseball is the most individualistic team sport, and baseball players are, by their very nature, self-interested loners. Black major leaguers were still fighting for their own rights in baseball in the early 1960s; few of them stood up for the rights of others. Some, like Frank Robinson and Willie Mays, refused to get involved. Flood and White felt differently. In 1963, White said that Flood "went to Jackson, Mississippi, to show by his presence that we in the big leagues were solidly with those unfortunate people down there."

Flood's participation in the rally was brave considering that Mississippi and Alabama were engulfed in racial intimidation, violence, and murder. President Kennedy was forced to mobilize federal troops in late September and early October 1962 so that James Meredith, a black air force veteran, could enroll at the University of Mississippi. Thousands of schoolchildren marched in the streets of Birmingham in April 1963 as Public Safety Commissioner Eugene "Bull" Connor turned police dogs and high-powered fire hoses on them. Medgar Evers was murdered in June. On August 28, Martin Luther King delivered his famous "I Have a Dream" speech at the March on Washington. Less than three weeks later, a bomb at Birmingham's 16th Street Baptist Church killed four black girls in the church restroom.

From April to September, Flood could not do much to stay involved because he went wherever the Cardinals' schedule took him. On the day of King's "I Have a Dream" speech, for example, Flood and the Cardinals were playing the Giants in San Francisco. It tore Flood up that he was not more involved in civil rights marches and demonstrations. "I should be there instead of here," he said. During the offseason, Flood traveled to places such as St. Augustine, Florida; Baton Rouge, Louisiana; and Jackson, Mississippi, because he wanted to see what was going on. Bill Patterson, the director of Oakland's De Fremery Recreation Center, once ran into Flood in Jackson. "What are you doing down here?" Patterson asked Flood. "You could get yourself killed."

Flood's moment of truth came after the Cardinals won the 1964 World Series. The Series victory over the Yankees capped off a spectacular season for Flood. He was named to his first National League All-Star team and won his second straight Gold Glove. He batted .311 and tied for the league lead with 211 hits, the second consecutive season he had finished with 200 or more. Branch Rickey, a senior consultant with the Cardinals, wrote in a scouting report that Flood had the "best hitting form of any man on the Cardinal club." Flood was 26 and an established star.

After the season, Flood remarried his first wife, Beverly, who had divorced him the previous winter. Curt and Beverly were first married in 1959 when he was only 21 and she was 20. Curt adopted her two children from a previous marriage, and the couple then had two children of their own, Curtis Jr. and Shelly. But Curt's infidelity on the road and during spring training, Beverly's frequent shopping sprees, and their different personalities strained their marriage. The young couple also had trouble finding a suitable home in segregated St. Louis. They lived there during the offseason because Beverly had grown up in St. Louis and her family owned a nightclub there. In 1962, Curt and Beverly tried to save their troubled marriage by moving from St. Louis to an integrated neighborhood in Pomona, California, outside Los Angeles. Cardinals broadcaster Harry Caray warned Curt not to move to California because it was a community-property state, entitling Beverly to half of everything Curt had earned during the marriage.

In October 1963, Beverly filed for divorce, alleging that Curt had made her feel "inadequate and inferior" and had struck her on one occasion. She charged that he preferred to spend more time with his sketch pads in the garage than he did with her. On February 27, 1964, a California judge granted the divorce and ordered him to pay her $100 a week in child support and $75 a week in alimony and to make Beverly the beneficiary on his $50,000 life insurance policy. She also received sole title to their home in Pomona.

By the time Curt and Beverly were married for the second time, they were expecting their fifth child, Scott. They decided to rent (with an option to buy) a home in Alamo, a white Oakland suburb just south of Walnut Creek. They returned to the Bay Area to be closer to Curt's family and so that Curt could work for Johnny Jorgensen's engraving company. Both Johnny and Marian had encouraged Curt to try to reconcile with Beverly. The house in Alamo was the key to a fresh start. On the morning of October 24, Curt and Beverly paid the $655 security deposit (two months' rent plus a $75 cleaning fee) and signed the $290-a-month lease to rent a three-bedroom, $35,000 ranch-style home with a pool at 170 La Serena Avenue. The next few days were anything but serene.

The real estate agent, Phyllis Schofield, did not tell George Finn, the owner's boyfriend who had power of attorney over the home, that the Floods were black. Finn found out shortly after the Floods had signed the lease; he demanded that Schofield meet him at the house to return the keys. When she arrived, Finn and another man blocked the driveway with their car. They opened up the trunk, pulled out two shotguns, and cocked them to let her know that they were loaded.

"No niggers are going to move in here," Finn warned Schofield as he took back the keys. "We will shoot them first."

The law did not concern George Finn. He and his identical twin brother, Charles, had been in and out of prison for most of their lives. In the early 1950s, they attracted national media attention as the "Flying Finn Twins" by purchasing a surplus government airplane, losing it to the government in a legal dispute, and stealing the plane back. In 1954, they were sentenced to a year in federal prison for making a citizen's arrest of the U.S. attorney from Los Angeles in connection with the airplane dispute. They claimed that the U.S. attorney had illegally kept the plane from them, but they were convicted of assaulting and impeding a federal officer. In prison, they went on hunger strikes and were paroled after 114 days. In 1969, they were blamed for the disappearance of a $100,000 government helicopter. Three years later, they sued the government over the ownership of Lake Tahoe. George Finn was part crackpot, part militiaman; there was no telling what he would do to Flood and his family.

Immediately after receiving Finn's initial phone call to return the keys, Schofield sent her husband to intercept Curt, Beverly, and Curt's half sister, Rickie Riley, before they reached their future Alamo home. They reconvened at the Schofield home, where Schofield and her husband explained to the Floods what had happened and begged them to consider another house she had showed them. The Floods explained that they did not like that house as much as this one. Beverly was intent on living in the Alamo house, and Curt was intent on standing up for what was right. It did not matter that his four children were cooped up in an Oakland motel or that his wife was six months pregnant. There was a principle at stake: He should be able to live where he pleased.

Curt turned to his friends, Johnny and Marian Jorgensen, who immediately took up the fight. Marian turned her Oakland home into mission control and found the Floods a lawyer, a former congressman from Martinez, California, named Robert Condon. On October 26, Condon filed a lawsuit in Contra Costa Superior Court against Finn and the owner of the home, Constance Oliver. The lawsuit sought access to the house as well as $10,000 in punitive damages. Condon also filed a complaint with the California Fair Employment Practices Commission. Contra Costa Superior Court judge Richard E. Arnason issued Flood a temporary restraining order—after Flood put up a $1,000 bond—forbidding Finn and Oliver to rent or sell the property for the next year. The court order permitted Flood to move into the house the following day.

Backed by the court order, 11 sheriff's deputies, several highway patrolmen, and two representatives from the state Fair Employment Practices Commission, Curt and Beverly attempted to move into their new home at 1:30 p.m. on October 27. Approximately a dozen supportive local women and their children, along with 30 members of the media, watched. No one knew what to expect. Condon had brought along a locksmith after correctly assuming that the locks had been changed. The locksmith drilled a hole in the back door and fitted it with new locks. Not knowing who or what might be inside, the sheriff's deputies searched every room and every kitchen cupboard before allowing the Floods to enter. As Curt and Beverly waited outside, Curt spoke with the neighbors and joshed with their children. Once it was declared safe, he gave the 30 newsmen a tour of the home. After the tour, he addressed the assembled media on his back porch with an eloquence, calm, and self-assuredness that belied the commotion of the day.

"Yes, we thought of chucking the whole thing to avoid trouble," he said. "But there's a great deal of pride involved.

"It doesn't make any difference whether I'm a professional athlete or a Negro or whatever—I'm a human being.

"If I have enough money to rent the house, I think I ought to have it.

"There was a challenge to be met, and I think we met it well."

Flood was eventually forced to drop his lawsuit after Finn and Oliver could not be found to be served with papers and did not show up for court; the battle, however, had been won.

"You don't do these things if you scare easily," Flood told the *Baltimore Afro-American*, "and this time I knew I was legally and morally right."

The housing ordeal made the front pages of the *San Francisco Chronicle* and *Examiner* as well as several other Bay Area newspapers. The *Washington Post* wrote an editorial arguing that Flood's housing dispute was the perfect example why Californians should vote against the referendum seeking to repeal the state's fair housing law.

Six women brought over a small tree for the Floods' backyard and cooked dinners for their first two nights in the house, bringing tears to Beverly's eyes. Several days later, two neighbors took her to the local grocery store. The men invited Flood to play golf and bridge.

Breaking barriers, however, came with a cost. The Floods' children endured racial taunts and got into fights. Debbie, their oldest daughter, was excluded from the local Brownie troop. Racists phoned the house and threatened the family. The police received a false report that someone had broken into the Floods' home and stolen the furniture. Both Finn and the owner refused to cash Flood's rent checks, much less sell him the house.

"I have no regrets," Flood told the *Los Angeles Times* in January 1965. "We've enjoyed living here and have met some wonderful people. The experience has been well worth all the difficulties we had at the start."

A few of Flood's Oakland baseball buddies slept outside the house in a parked car that first night to make sure that nothing happened to him or his family. They were not the only ones watching. J. Edgar Hoover was watching, too. On October 30, the FBI director ordered the special agent in charge of the San Francisco office "immediately [to] obtain facts pertinent to this alleged occurrence through established police and/or other sources." The San Francisco office had received its initial report on Flood's housing dispute three days earlier. On November 4, Hoover received a three-page memorandum and numerous news clippings as well as several updates about Flood's housing lawsuit. Hoover wanted the information in part because of Flood's "recent notoriety as a player in this year's World Series."

The FBI director was no friend of the civil rights movement. He appeared to be more concerned about Communist infiltration of the movement (which he was convinced of) than he was with protecting civil rights workers from white violence. In October 1963, Hoover persuaded Attorney General Robert Kennedy to approve wiretaps on Martin Luther King's home and office because King continued to consult with advisers with alleged ties to the Communist Party. In April 1964, Hoover bugged King's hotel rooms and later attempted to blackmail the civil rights leader about his extramarital affairs. Hoover's interest in Flood was about as beneficial as a file with the Mississippi State Sovereignty Commission.

Flood's interest in the civil rights movement continued during the assassinations and antiwar protests of the late 1960s. Not even the most self-absorbed major leaguer could ignore what was going on around him. Martin Luther King's April 4, 1968, assassination delayed Opening Day. Two months later, Senator Robert Kennedy's funeral caused the league to postpone games in New York and Washington. The New York Mets players forced the Giants to postpone that night's game in San Francisco. Several players protested their teams' decisions to play that Sunday on the national day of mourning for Senator Kennedy. Milt Pappas of the Reds; Dave Giusti, Rusty Staub, and Bob Aspromonte of the Astros; and Maury Wills of the Pirates refused to play. All the players were fined. A few days later, Pappas was traded; Giusti, Staub, and Aspromonte were traded after the season; Wills was left unprotected in the expansion draft.

Flood conveyed his feelings about King's assassination through his portrait of Dr. King. "When something happens like that your feeling is what can you do and generally you can't do anything," he said. "But I feel we owe this family a great deal, and I feel this is my small step in the right direction." A St. Louis calendar company had asked him to paint the portrait. Flood hesitated because he did not want to tarnish the memory of a man he had met a few times and had admired so deeply. What started out as a small commercial project became a standard part of his biography. The company reproduced over a million copies of the portrait. That fall, Coretta Scott King received the original work during an Atlanta benefit concert honoring Dr. King. The audience received 8-by-10 color reproductions. Flood was not there for the presentation; he was playing in a postseason tour of Japan with his Cardinals teammates. But he took full credit for the portrait, which he described as "the best work I've ever done."

The person who most likely painted the portrait of Dr. King was a California artist named Lawrence Williams. Williams owned a Burbank studio called Portrait Arts, Inc. In early 1967, Williams had entered into a similar arrangement with NFL wide receiver Tommy McDonald. McDonald was winding down his football career with the Atlanta Falcons after 10 seasons with the Eagles, Cowboys, and Rams. Like Flood, McDonald also placed his name on the portraits, but McDonald later claimed that he had done it so potential clients could contact him. In a 1967 *Los Angeles Times* article, McDonald made it clear that he did not paint the portraits; he was only selling them. Flood made no such distinction. He took full credit for the Gussie Busch portrait and every portrait thereafter. After the Martin Luther King painting earned national acclaim, it became difficult for him to reveal the truth.

Regardless of who painted the King portrait, Flood's feelings for Dr. King and the impact of the civil rights movement on his decision to sue baseball were genuine. As Flood related in Ken Burns's nine-part *Baseball* documentary in 1994:

> I guess you really have to understand who that person, who that Curt Flood was. I'm a child of the Sixties, a man of the Sixties. During that period of time, this country was coming apart at the seams. We were in Southeast Asia. Men, good men, were dying for America and for the Constitution. In the Southern part of the United States, we were marching for civil rights, and Dr. King had

> been assassinated, and we lost the Kennedys. And to think that merely because I was a professional baseball player I could ignore what was going on outside the walls of Busch Stadium is truly hypocrisy. And now I find that all of those rights that these great Americans were dying for, I didn't have in my own profession.

Flood sought to take what his hero, Jackie Robinson, had accomplished one step further. Unlike Robinson, Flood came of age during the civil rights movement and realized that a seat at a lunch counter, a house in a white neighborhood, or a spot on a major league roster was not enough. Flood recognized that racial equality could not be achieved without the freedom to sell one's talent to the highest bidder.

Five years after his housing dispute, Flood once again sought protection from the courts for what he believed was legally and morally right. This time he was not taking on a couple of gun-wielding racists; he was planning to sue Major League Baseball. To obtain the union's financial backing, Flood knew that he needed not only Marvin Miller's support but also the support of the players.

CHAPTER FIVE

On December 12, 1969, Flood boarded a flight from St. Louis to Miami en route to San Juan, Puerto Rico. The next day at the Players Association's executive board meeting, Flood's job was to explain to 25 player representatives why he wanted to sue baseball over the reserve clause and why he needed the union to pay for his legal fees. Marvin Miller promised to support Flood at the meeting, but it was up to Flood to persuade the players of his sincerity.

Flood tested his persuasive skills on both legs of the flight. As he boarded the first-class section of the plane in St. Louis, he saw the Cardinals' player representative, Dal Maxvill. A Washington University engineering graduate, the 5-foot-11-inch, 157-pound Maxvill was a good-field, no-hit shortstop. In May 1964, he quit the game after being sent back to the minors in Jacksonville and accepted a $10,000 engineering job with the Bussmann Fuse Company. After a week, he changed his mind. That October he started all seven World Series games in place of injured second baseman Julian Javier and wound up catching the final out. Two years later, he took over as the Cardinals' starting shortstop and became an integral member of the Cardinals teams of the mid- to late 1960s.

Maxvill had no idea why Flood was on his flight. Flood took a seat next to his former teammate in first class, revealed his plan to speak to the player representatives in Puerto Rico, and explained his decision to challenge the reserve clause in court. Maxvill's primary concern was Flood's personal well-being. He had watched Flood work for years to get to the top of baseball's salary scale. In those days, the only way to make close to $100,000 was through winning, consistent excellence, and longevity. A player's salary could be reduced by a maximum of 20 percent each season. Having made $90,000 in 1969, Flood was due several big paydays. Maxvill hated to see him throw them away.

"How can this work out for you?" Maxvill asked.

"It's just something I feel like I need to do," Flood replied.

"Everybody gets traded," Maxvill said.

"You haven't," Flood replied.

"It's early," Maxvill said. "I'm a few years younger than you." Maxvill was indeed traded to the A's during the 1972 season. "Everybody got traded then," Maxvill later remarked. "Even Willie Mays got traded."

"Why are you doing this to yourself?" Maxvill finally asked. "Do you know that you're going to be out there like the Lone Ranger?" Nothing Flood said satisfied his friend and former teammate. Maxvill did not realize at the time the full impact of Flood's lawsuit. They talked all the way to Miami.

While waiting in the Miami airport to change planes, they encountered another cornerstone of those great Cardinals teams (and Maxvill's former road roommate), catcher Tim McCarver. Of all the white players on the Cardinals, McCarver had been Gibson's and Flood's guinea pig. The son of a Memphis police detective, McCarver had signed with the Cardinals right out of high school as a $75,000 bonus-baby catcher. He was cocky and intelligent, but also filled with a lifetime of southern prejudices. It was Gibson's and Flood's job to disabuse him of them.

McCarver once walked onto the team bus after a 1960 spring training game eating an ice-cream cone (McCarver says it was an orange drink). Gibson nudged Flood and then asked McCarver in a voice loud enough so that the rest of the team could hear: "Hey, Tim, can I have a bite of that ice-cream cone?" The young catcher did not know what to do or say. He had never shared an ice-cream cone (or an orange drink) with a black person. "I'll save you some," McCarver mumbled in response. Gibson and Flood burst out laughing. McCarver knew they had gotten him. Another time, McCarver informed Gibson that there was a "colored guy" waiting for him outside the locker room. "Which color is he?" Gibson asked his catcher.

Sometimes the lessons were more serious. At spring training, McCarver saw a black kid stealing some baseballs from the outfield and yelled:

"Hey, stop that, you little nigger!" Flood just stared at McCarver, who insisted that he had said "you little cannibal." Gibson read McCarver the riot act. McCarver apologized. But what Gibson wanted McCarver to do was to think about why he had said it. Flood and Gibson saw McCarver's racial attitudes change completely over time. "Tim McCarver was a rugged white kid from Tennessee and we were black, black cats," Flood wrote. "The gulf was wide and deep. It did not belong there, yet there it was. We bridged it."

Gibson and Flood targeted McCarver not because they thought he was an irredeemable southern racist. They recognized him as a potential team leader and good friend. They were right on both counts. Although Gibson reigned as the team's unquestioned leader, Flood and McCarver were named co-captains in 1966 in a move that a St. Louis toastmaster described as pleasing "everybody but the Ku Klux Klan." Four years later, they were traded together to Philadelphia. Their reactions to the trade were starkly different. McCarver quickly signed; Flood wanted to sue.

In the airport and on the short flight from Miami to Puerto Rico, Flood once again explained his plan to sue baseball. McCarver, who had flown in from Memphis, sat there in "complete shock." He'd had no inkling that such a lawsuit was in the works. Nor did he have any idea why Flood would do such a thing.

"Curt, do you really want to do this?" McCarver asked. "Do you know what you're doing?"

Like Maxvill, McCarver soon realized that Flood was deadly serious. McCarver peppered Flood with many of the same questions that would be asked the next day. He asked about the more than $90,000 in salary that Flood would be leaving on the table. He asked whether Flood knew that he would be blacklisted from the game forever. He asked how Flood could survive financially. Even though he had known Flood for a long time and knew how determined Flood could be, McCarver still believed that the other players and Miller would talk him out of suing.

Flood knew that Maxvill and McCarver would support him during the union meeting in Puerto Rico and throughout his lawsuit, not because they understood his decision but because they admired him as a teammate and a friend.

Flood had another person in his corner in Puerto Rico: his on-again, off-again girlfriend, actress Judy Pace. Pace flew in from an appearance on *The Dating Game* in Copenhagen to give Flood moral support. The daughter of a Los Angeles airplane mechanic and a dress shop owner, she had broken racial barriers in 1968 as television's first black villainess on the show *Peyton Place*. Among a small cadre of black actors appearing regularly in movies and on television at that time, Pace starred in the television show *The Young Lawyers* and played Gale Sayers's wife in the ABC television movie *Brian's Song*.

Flood first noticed Pace when she appeared as a bachelorette on a 1965 edition of *The Dating Game*. On the show, Pace sat behind a partition and asked questions of her three celebrity suitors. She chose Willie Mays, not because she had figured out who he was but because in her mind his high, squeaky voice meant that he must be someone important. "That's awful. That's a beautiful woman," Flood told his friends while watching the show on television. "I deserve her more than Willie does."

For nearly a year, Flood clamored to meet Pace. He tracked her down through Sy Marsh, her agent at William Morris. "[Curt] thought I was the prettiest little chocolate thing he had ever seen in his life," Pace said. She had no idea who he was. Flood called her everywhere he went. He sent her baseball cards, news clippings, and flowers. Her father was impressed and encouraged Pace to go out with Flood. She finally agreed to meet him but only in a crowded place and with a chaperone. Flood's father, Herman Sr., having divorced his mother, Laura, and moved to Los Angeles, accompanied them on their first date. They went to Dodger Stadium for one of the first two games of the 1966 Dodgers-Orioles World Series. After the game, Flood ate with Pace's parents at their home. He then flew back to St. Louis, but the phone calls continued. A week later, he called Pace after moving into the Shoreham Towers in West Hollywood. "Now you can see me all the time," he said. The following year, she was his guest, sans chaperone, at the 1967 World Series between the Cardinals and the Red Sox. After one of the games in Boston, they dined with Bob Gibson and his wife. Over the years, Flood visited Pace on the sets of the movie *Three in the Attic*, the television show *The Young Lawyers*, and Ossie Davis's film *Cotton Comes to Harlem*.

Flood and Pace shared a bond as successful black entertainers. They both knew what it meant to have to be three times better than their white counterparts and shared the fatigue of striving for perfection all the time. They were both living the American dream but knew how hard living that dream could be. Pace admired Flood's decision to sue baseball and flew to Puerto Rico to support him.

Before the meeting, Flood conferred with Marvin Miller.

"Why is it nobody's ever done this before?" Flood asked Miller.

Miller reminded him of Gardella's and Toolson's lawsuits, how Gardella had been paid off and Toolson had lost. Any player willing to sue Major League Baseball, Miller said, must have either no choice or nothing to lose. Flood was risking everything so that his fellow ballplayers might have more bargaining power and more control over their careers.

Before Flood spoke that morning, he waited outside the meeting room as the players addressed several related items on their agenda. For nearly two months, the players and owners had been trying unsuccessfully to negotiate a new labor agreement. The players proposed several modifications to the reserve clause. The owners rejected all of them. Instead, the owners offered to raise the minimum salary by $500 per year (to $10,500 in 1970), daily meal money at spring training by 50 cents (to $12.50 in 1970), and in-season meal money by 50 cents (to $15.50 in 1970). They also agreed to allow lawyers or agents to participate in salary negotiations but refused to include it in writing. The player representatives voted unanimously to reject the owners' counteroffer because of their refusal to compromise on the critical issue in the labor agreement, the reserve clause.

The players also reviewed the lack of progress of the joint study committee. As part of the 1968 Basic Agreement, the players and owners had agreed to form a committee to discuss "possible alternatives to the reserve clause as now constituted." The committee had been meeting for the last two years. Each time the players proposed an alternative to the reserve clause, the owners rejected it. "If you want to change one comma," Miller said, describing the owners' position, "Yankee Stadium will fall."

Flood's timing was perfect. The player representatives were primed to listen to a challenge to the reserve clause. Miller spoke first. Most of the player representatives knew only that Flood had been traded to the Phillies and had announced his intention to retire. Miller explained that Flood planned to challenge the legality of the reserve clause in court. He told the player reps that he had met with Flood on several occasions and had given Flood the "third degree" about the risks. Flood was determined to sue with or without the Players Association's support. Thus, Miller explained, it would benefit the association to provide Flood with the best possible legal counsel and to have input on his legal strategy. Miller proposed that in exchange for the right to select Flood's counsel, the Players Association would agree to pay Flood's legal fees and related travel expenses.

The players were skeptical of Flood's retirement announcement. They knew that their only leverage in salary negotiations was to threaten to quit. They also knew that Flood was not the first player to make such a threat after being traded. Earlier that year, Montreal Expos first baseman–outfielder Donn Clendenon had balked at being traded to the Houston Astros for outfielder–first baseman Rusty Staub. On February 28, 1969, Clendenon announced his retirement and said he planned to take a $40,000-a-year public relations job with the Atlanta-based Scripto pen company. The Expos coaxed Clendenon out of retirement with a two-year contract and a $14,000 raise on his $35,000 annual salary. Staub, for his part, refused to return to Houston, which filed suit against Montreal before receiving additional players and monetary compensation.

A few weeks after Clendenon's change of heart, retirement talk surfaced from the shaggy-haired, mod-dressing Boston Red Sox outfielder Ken "Hawk" Harrelson. Two years earlier, Harrelson had joined the Red Sox during their "Impossible Dream" season after being released by the Kansas City A's at midseason because of a dispute with A's owner Charlie Finley. In April 1969, the Red Sox traded Harrelson to the Cleveland Indians. The 27-year-old Harrelson, wearing dark glasses, a maize sweater, multicolored pants, and high-heeled white boots, immediately announced his retirement, citing his Boston-area business interests. Cleveland changed his mind with a new contract that reportedly paid him $75,000 plus $25,000 for promotional work.

Finally, on June 3, 1969, Montreal Expos shortstop Maury Wills shocked his team a few hours before game time by announcing his retirement. This was not about money; Wills was making the highest salary of his career, $80,000. The former Dodgers star and team captain, whom the Expos had acquired from the Pirates in the previous winter's expansion draft, wanted to return to the West Coast. He planned on franchising a dry-cleaning business. Eight days later, the Expos traded Wills back to the Dodgers. The 36-year-old Wills unretired and played through the 1972 season.

As a result of the Clendenon and Harrelson incidents, the owners passed a *caveat emptor* ("let the buyer beware") rule. All trades were final regardless of who retired or threatened to retire. The rule was passed in early December, a few weeks after the Flood trade, and therefore did not apply to him.

After Miller spoke, Flood took the podium and punctured the players' skepticism about his lawsuit with his brutal honesty. He was not threatening to retire as a negotiating tactic. He was going to sue baseball, with or without their help. He explained that he was not doing it for the money. He was doing it because the reserve clause as it currently existed was inhumane and unjust. This was a question not only about how the business of baseball should be conducted, but also of human dignity. We are all "under the same yoke," he said. "I can't be bought off. Someone has to do it. . . . I feel I'm qualified and capable of doing it."

Flood knew most of the players in the room. Player representatives were usually smart, veteran players who were not afraid of management retaliation. For 20 minutes, he spoke from his heart before a group that included four future Hall of Famers (Jim Bunning, Roberto Clemente, Reggie Jackson, and Brooks Robinson), a future U.S. congressman and senator (Bunning), two future major league managers (Phil Regan and Joe Torre), and three future general managers (Tom Haller, Dal Maxvill, and Woody Woodward).

After Flood finished, the player representatives asked Miller for his views. Miller reminded the group that Flood was a member of the association with a problem that affected all of them. It was "of tremendous importance," Miller said, that the association help Flood as much as possible. More important, it was incumbent on the association to make sure that Flood had the best possible legal counsel so that he would not make "bad law." The players were the ones who would have to live with it.

The player representatives questioned Flood for more than an hour. With Miller serving as moderator, Flood and his fellow players acted like a group of business executives in a board meeting but with the candor and casual dress of ballplayers in a pregame strategy session. "A lot of people think baseball players are clods," Maxvill said a month after the meeting. "But I never was prouder than when I listened to the questions the player reps put to Flood at that meeting."

Tom Haller of the Dodgers asked an early but pivotal question: During this period of black militancy, was Flood doing this as part of a movement? Was he doing this because he was black?

The room fell silent. Haller's question had taken Miller by surprise. But the question was on the minds of many of the players in the room, all of whom, except Jackson and Clemente, were white.

The black power and antiwar movements of the late 1960s inspired several high-profile black athletes to take political stands. In 1966, Jim Brown retired from pro football at age 30 to pursue an acting career and tackle racial issues. A year before his retirement, the running back had helped to organize the Negro Industrial and Economic Union to benefit black businesses. The same year as Brown's retirement, Muhammad Ali spoke out against the Vietnam War ("I ain't got no quarrel with them Vietcong," he said). The following year, Ali refused induction into the military and was stripped of his heavyweight title. A jury disagreed with his contention that as a member of the Nation of Islam he was a conscientious objector. In December 1969, Ali's draft-evasion conviction was still being appealed. At the 1968 Olympics in Mexico City, sprinters Tommie Smith and John Carlos bowed their heads and raised their black-gloved fists on the medal stand in support of black power and unity. UCLA basketball star Lew Alcindor (known today as Kareem Abdul-Jabbar) and other African-American athletes boycotted the Olympics altogether. Tennis star Arthur Ashe sought to raise awareness about South Africa's racist system of apartheid by attempting to compete in the 1970 South African Open. After denying Ashe a visa to play in its tournament, South Africa was banned from the 1970 Davis Cup.

Haller did not want to be associated with black militancy. "I didn't want it to be just a black thing," Haller recalled. "I wanted it to be a baseball thing." Other players agreed. "I wanted to make sure that he didn't have a personal ax to grind," the Expos' Ron Brand recalled. Flood later described Haller's query as a "fascinating question, well-meant." The players' financial support for Flood's lawsuit hinged on his response.

Flood explained that as a black man he had experienced many hardships in baseball, hardships that may have made him more sensitive to injustice than the average white player. Yet, he was not suing baseball as a black man; he was suing as a major league ballplayer. The reserve clause, he said, was an injustice that affected players of all races, and it was time that someone did something about it. He believed he was the right man to do it.

Flood knew that his answer may have satisfied his fellow players, but it again raised the question about his true motivations. The players in Puerto Rico knew nothing about Flood's past racial battles. Not even McCarver, one of Flood's friends and teammates, knew the full extent of his housing dispute. Flood did not tell any of the players about the racism he had experienced in and out of baseball or his passion for the civil rights movement. His answer to Haller's question was technically right—the reserve clause did affect players of all races—but the answer avoided the lifetime of motivations behind his lawsuit.

After he answered Haller's black-militancy question, the players indicated by their questions that they supported Flood.

Jim Bunning of the Phillies asked, if he had not been traded, what Flood would have done.

The trade brought things to a head; he was tired of being treated like chattel.

Reggie Jackson of the A's asked why Flood wanted to challenge the trading of players from one team to another.

To make things between the players and owners more fair.

Haller asked what Flood would do if the Phillies gave him his release.

Miller said that would be okay if other teams bid on his services.

McCarver asked what would happen if Flood won in court.

Miller said a court would determine whether the reserve clause was legal, but a solution would still need to be negotiated between the owners and the Players Association.

Moe Drabowsky of the Royals asked if Flood would play again after the lawsuit.

Yes, if he wasn't too old.

Bob Locker of the Seattle Pilots asked if there were any dangers if Flood won.

Miller said there was no danger, as long as everyone realized that the objective was to modify the reserve clause and not abolish it. Miller recognized the owners' right to recoup their investments in players developed in their minor league systems. He also knew that making all the players free agents at the end of every season would flood the market and cause too much uncertainty. Miller's goal, therefore, was to modify the reserve clause to allow players to test the market after a certain number of years.

Several players, including Bunning and Milt Pappas of the Braves, asked what would happen if other players wanted to join the lawsuit.

Roberto Clemente reminded them that no other players had stepped forward. Reggie Jackson said that no other players could afford it. Other players, Miller said, would either have to wait for the outcome of Flood's case or file their own self-sponsored lawsuits. Flood's would be the test case.

Steve Hamilton of the Yankees asked Flood how far he would go with his lawsuit.

As far as necessary.

Bunning asked Flood what would happen if the owners offered him a $1 million settlement but refused to modify the reserve clause.

It was a classic Bunning question. He was not concerned whether the union should support Flood, but what might happen a year or two into Flood's lawsuit. Bunning, like Miller, was testing Flood's resolve. Bunning's support meant more than that of any other player in the room. He had served on the player committee that hired Miller. He had made it his mission to improve the major league pension. Traded from the Pirates to the Dodgers in 1969, Bunning was released by the Dodgers after the season and re-signed with the Phillies. He was attending the meeting as the union's pension representative and reigned as the group's intellectual leader.

The settlement, Flood replied, must be satisfactory to all the players. The answer seemed to satisfy Bunning. Flood had gained an important ally.

Drabowsky asked Flood what he had told Philadelphia.

Flood said he had told them nothing but planned to hold a press conference December 22 and to send letters to Miller and the commissioner stating that, as a free man in a free society, he should have the right to negotiate with the team of his choice.

Roberto Clemente knew exactly what Flood meant. No one in that room had earned more respect as a player than Clemente. His speed, swing, and incredible throwing arm made him baseball's first Latin American superstar. His social conscience eventually made him a legend. After collecting his 3,000th hit at the end of the 1972 season, he died in a New Year's Eve plane crash while on a relief mission to Nicaraguan earthquake victims.

Miller understood the importance of minority voices such as Clemente's and Reggie Jackson's among the player reps. When Bunning was traded from the Phillies to the Pirates after the 1967 season, his new teammates immediately wanted to make him the player rep. With Miller's support, Bunning urged the Pirates to ask Clemente instead. They agreed.

Clemente took up Flood's cause that day at the Sheraton Hotel in Puerto Rico. He related how the reserve clause had led to his playing his entire 18-year career in Pittsburgh. In February 1954, the 19-year-old Clemente turned down a $35,000 offer from the Milwaukee Braves in favor of a $10,000 bonus (and $5,000 salary) from the Brooklyn Dodgers because he wanted to play in New York. After the 1954 season, the last-place Pittsburgh Pirates drafted Clemente, a bonus player who was supposed to remain on the Dodgers' active roster, from Brooklyn's Triple-A club in Montreal for $4,000. Clemente later offered to refund the Pirates' $4,000 in exchange for his freedom. Pirates general manager Joe Brown refused. "He had me," Clemente told his fellow players, estimating that during his career the Pirates had "made $300,000 on me."

The tenor of the meeting soon changed from whether the players would back Flood, to how.

Max Alvis of the Indians asked how quickly this could get into court.

Dick Moss, who had been taking detailed notes of the proceedings, said no earlier than the spring.

Jackson asked Flood if things would have been different if St. Louis had consulted with him about the trade.

Basically, yes.

Drabowsky said that the timing could not be better and that taking the reserve clause to court was preferable to a strike. His comment reflected the players' anger over the owners' refusal to modify the reserve clause during the joint study committee meetings or negotiations about the 1970 Basic Agreement. As the minutes of the meeting indicated, the owners had left the players with only two choices about the reserve clause: "(1) to take concerted action on the issue by withholding their services, or (2) to test the matter in the courts. As between the two, it was felt that the latter was a far less disruptive course of action, and therefore was preferable." The players were not unified enough in December 1969 to strike over the reserve clause; they chose to let Flood do their striking for them.

Joe Torre of the Cardinals was the first player at the meeting to say that the association must back Flood. Torre knew all about being traded. Atlanta Braves vice president Paul Richards, a frequent union and Miller critic, had blasted Torre for his participation in the 1969 pension dispute. He wanted to cut Torre's salary $5,000 and take away his complimentary Cadillac. Torre refused to sign his contract. "I don't care if he holds out until Thanksgiving," Richards said. Before the 1969 season, Richards traded Torre to the Cardinals for popular first baseman Orlando Cepeda.

During his one season as Flood's teammate in 1969, Torre bonded with both Gibson and Flood. "Knowing how entrenched Curt was in St. Louis, it didn't surprise me," Torre said of Flood's decision to sue. An alternate player rep with the Cardinals and a mainstay on the union's negotiating team, Torre saw the necessity of Flood's lawsuit and never doubted Flood's sincerity. "I knew Curt didn't do something just for the sake of doing something. He did something because he felt very strongly about it," Torre recalled. "He was a sensitive, personal, passionate person. And he just sort of felt violated. He was making a stand. He was certainly forewarned by Marvin Miller and Dick Moss that you may not play baseball again, and he understood that. He just didn't think someone should tell him that he has to go play somewhere."

Bunning said the representatives needed unanimity.

Alvis said that unanimity among the player representatives did not necessarily mean that all the rank-and-file players would support Flood's lawsuit.

As their questions turned into commentary, the players excused Flood from the room and discussed with Miller how to explain their prospective decision to their fellow players, when to make the lawsuit public, and what effect the lawsuit would have on their labor negotiations with the owners. Miller said that it was up to him and the player representatives to educate their fellow players, but it was up to Flood when to make the lawsuit public. His lawyers would decide when to file. The labor negotiations could continue as planned.

A question then arose that had not been asked of Flood. If he won a large damage award, would he pay the association back for legal fees and expenses? And would he agree to such an arrangement in writing? Miller explained that the chances of Flood receiving any monetary award were almost none, but that he had not broached the subject with Flood. Miller left the room, found Flood in the hotel, and explained the players' request. Flood readily agreed to sign a written pledge to pay the association back if he was awarded damages that exceeded his legal fees. This may have seemed like a petty request by the players considering that Flood was the one risking everything, but the association's entire operating budget for 1970 was $195,000, and Flood's legal fees could run $200,000 to $300,000. When Miller returned to the room, he assured the players that Flood would sign such a document.

Miller then asked if there was anyone in the room who felt that the association should not assist Flood. No one said anything. Ron Brand made a motion to take all necessary action to support Flood. McCarver quickly seconded it. The player representatives voted 25–0 to pay Flood's legal fees—with all legal bills still subject to the association's approval—in exchange for the right to select his lawyer.

Flood was ecstatic about the unanimous show of support—all of which still remained a secret. He and the players posed one more question to Miller: Whom should they hire as Flood's lawyer? Miller assured them that he had an extremely prominent attorney in mind. He did not tell them that his choice was a former Supreme Court justice.

CHAPTER SIX

The nameplate on the door of his office read "Mr. Justice Goldberg." It had been more than four years since he had resigned from the Supreme Court. His partners at the New York law firm Paul, Weiss, Goldberg, Rifkind, Wharton & Garrison included former U.S. attorney general Ramsey Clark; President Kennedy's chief speechwriter, Theodore Sorensen; and a former federal judge, lead partner Simon Rifkind. Yet Arthur Goldberg preferred that they refer to him as "Mr. Justice."

Marvin Miller called him Arthur. Before Goldberg was the U.S. ambassador to the United Nations, a Supreme Court justice, or the secretary of labor, Miller knew him as the brains behind the Steelworkers Union. From 1948 to 1961, Goldberg served as general counsel for the Steelworkers and the Congress of Industrial Organizations (CIO). Many people believed that he was more powerful than the Steelworkers Union's president. He argued Supreme Court cases, brokered the merger between the American Federation of Labor (AFL) and the CIO, negotiated with steel industry executives, and drafted legislation for members of Congress. He also worked closely with Miller.

As Miller rose from an obscure staff economist to chief economist and assistant to the Steelworkers' president, Goldberg raised Miller's public profile. He selected Miller (over Miller's immediate boss) as a member of the Human Relations Committee, which was designed to prevent another massive steel strike by addressing issues with management before labor contracts expired. When Goldberg left to become

Kennedy's labor secretary, Miller replaced him on the nine-member Kaiser Steel Long-Range Sharing Plan Committee. The Kaiser committee revolutionized labor negotiations by employing three public representatives, three management representatives, and three labor representatives to resolve issues between the Steelworkers and California-based Kaiser Steel. One of the public representatives and the chairman of the Kaiser committee was University of Pennsylvania professor George Taylor, who later recommended to pitcher Robin Roberts that the Players Association hire Miller.

Miller called Goldberg on December 3, ten days before Flood addressed the union meeting, and briefly explained Flood's proposed lawsuit. Goldberg suggested that they meet for breakfast.

On the way to breakfast two days later, Miller noticed a story on the front page of the *New York Times*. There was Goldberg, pictured standing next to smiling former New York governor W. Averell Harriman, below the headline "21 Leaders Urge Race by Goldberg." For several months, state Democratic leaders had been goading Goldberg to run either for the late Robert Kennedy's U.S. Senate seat or for governor of New York. Polls indicated that Goldberg—a liberal Democrat in a heavily Democratic state, a Jew in a very Jewish city, a former Supreme Court justice, and holder of two cabinet positions (labor secretary and UN ambassador)—would win either office. In the 1966 gubernatorial race, Republican governor Nelson Rockefeller had captured only 44.6 percent of the vote. An October 1 poll showed Goldberg leading Rockefeller by 25 percentage points.

Before they began discussing the Flood case, Miller asked if Goldberg was planning on running for office. Miller needed not only big-name legal counsel but also someone committed to litigating Flood's case for two to three years through the federal courts. Miller did not need a lawyer who would run away in the middle of the fight if he won an election.

When he won the election, Goldberg quickly corrected him, not *if*.

Goldberg was only joking. He often said that after serving on the Court, "I took myself out of the political arena." Declining to go into politics was his way of still acting as if he were a Supreme Court justice. "I personally do not think it is a good thing for a man who has served on the nation's highest Court and who has dealt with political issues, even though he has resigned, to re-enter the political arena," he said when he resigned as UN ambassador in 1968. "I do not intend to do so."

With this in mind, Goldberg assured Miller that he had no intention of running for governor, the U.S. Senate, or any other elected office. He did not want to be governor, he had never run for office in his life, and he was not about to embark on a career in electoral politics at age 61. Five days later, Goldberg confirmed what he had told Miller by announcing that he had no intention of running for any office in 1970. "This decision is final and not subject to change," Goldberg said.

With Dick Moss at his side, Miller went through the background of the case. He discussed the players' unsuccessful negotiations with the owners to modify the reserve clause; the two Supreme Court precedents, *Federal Baseball* and *Toolson*, which exempted baseball from the antitrust laws; and the 31-year-old ballplayer willing to sacrifice his career to challenge it all in court. He explained that Flood had retained local counsel in St. Louis, but that Miller wanted a lawyer with a national reputation to take the case all the way to the Supreme Court.

Miller could think of no one better suited for that task than Goldberg. He had seen Goldberg argue for two hours straight before a federal appeals court with only a scrap of notes in his hands. Although Goldberg was unsuccessful in overturning a lower court's order forbidding the Steelworkers Union from going on strike, one of the three appellate judges congratulated him from the bench on his outstanding argument. In the span of three weeks in late 1959, he challenged the constitutionality of that injunction all the way to the Supreme Court. His first Supreme Court argument, representing the Steelworkers Union as a third party when President Truman seized the steel mills in 1952, had been so good that, according to Judge Abner Mikva, a Supreme Court law clerk that term, "[i]t was the overwhelming consensus of the law clerks that he was the best oral advocate not only of the day but of the entire year." In 1957 he argued and won a Supreme Court case in the Textile Workers Union's favor, and three years later he litigated a steelworkers' case to the Court before allowing one of his colleagues to argue it.

No one knew more about labor-management relations than Goldberg. He educated a callow Massachusetts senator named John Kennedy on the subject and drafted labor-reform legislation for him. Goldberg could see that Kennedy was going places. Goldberg endorsed Kennedy for president in 1960 and rallied support for him among the labor unions. Kennedy rewarded Goldberg by naming him secretary of labor. After accepting the cabinet position, Goldberg severed his ties to the labor movement and even gave up the $25,000-a-year Steelworkers Union pension that would have kicked in after he turned 60. One of the most visible members of the Kennedy cabinet, Goldberg traveled the world making speeches, mediated massive labor disputes, and earned the president's trust. When Kennedy nominated Goldberg to be a Supreme Court justice in 1962, the president wrote Mrs. Goldberg: "I gave away my right arm."

Arthur Joseph Goldberg had dreamed of becoming a Supreme Court justice since he finished with the highest grade point average in the history of Northwestern's law school. The youngest of eleven children (including two who died before his parents emigrated from Russia), Goldberg grew up in a working-class neighborhood on the west side of Chicago. He was the only one in his family to attend school beyond the eighth grade. His father had left a Russian town near Kiev and traveled through Siberia, Manchuria, California, and Texas before settling in Chicago, where he peddled produce on a cart drawn by a one-eyed horse. He died at age 51, when Arthur was eight. Goldberg later worked his way through Crane Junior College (while taking night classes at DePaul University), Northwestern University, and Northwestern's law school. He then sued the Illinois Bar Association over its age minimum and won admittance before the age of 21.

Goldberg assumed the Court's "Jewish seat," which had belonged to Benjamin Cardozo and Felix Frankfurter. Frankfurter had stepped down on August 28, 1962, shortly after suffering a stroke. His replacement could not have been more philosophically different. Frankfurter believed in judicial restraint—strictly adhering to the Court's past decisions and deciding cases on the narrowest possible grounds. Goldberg was a judicial activist—he saw the Court as the protector of the rights of individuals and minorities.

Goldberg's appointment reinvigorated the Warren Court's rights revolution, which had begun eight years earlier with the school-desegregation cases. Goldberg and fellow liberals Earl Warren, William Brennan, and

William Douglas could often wangle a fifth vote from an increasingly conservative Hugo Black or moderate Tom Clark. They protected the powerless: instructing state legislatures to draw fairer voting districts, enforcing the separation between church and state, establishing new constitutional protections for the freedom of the press, safeguarding the rights of the accused, and overturning convictions of civil rights demonstrators.

Goldberg was in many ways perfectly suited to be a Supreme Court justice. Although not a gifted writer, he loved to generate ideas and relied on his law clerks to refine them into cogent judicial opinions. He circulated a confidential memorandum in 1963 urging his colleagues to declare the death penalty unconstitutional. Even though none of the six capital cases that term raised the issue, Goldberg made his views public in a three-page dissent. It was an idea that was a decade ahead of its time (the Court outlawed capital punishment in 1972 but changed its mind four years later). The law clerk who helped Goldberg plant those seeds of change was future Harvard law professor Alan Dershowitz. In *Griswold v. Connecticut* in 1965, Goldberg helped overturn a Connecticut ban on contraceptives. In a separate opinion, he wrote that the seldom-cited Ninth Amendment, which says the people retain any rights not enumerated in the Constitution, created a right to privacy.

Goldberg's ability to mediate disputes was a valuable skill for someone who must persuade four other justices to join his opinions. He wrote several important decisions, including *Escobedo v. Illinois*, which overturned a murder conviction because the confession was obtained after the defendant's request for a lawyer had been denied. *Escobedo* established a right to counsel at the interrogation phase of a criminal case, which led to the famous Miranda warnings.

Goldberg reveled in the law's doctrinal intricacies. For Goldberg, the law was a religion consisting of a search for Talmudic truths; the justices were the rabbinical scholars. The rituals and formality of the Court appealed to a man who wore a three-piece suit to work every day. "He was happy on the Court; indeed, he was in his element," wrote Stephen Breyer, a former Goldberg law clerk who later became a Supreme Court justice. Dorothy Goldberg wrote that her husband's "three years on the Court were like three days."

But as much as he loved the law, he had trouble adjusting to the slow pace of life as a Supreme Court justice. "The [labor] secretary's phone rang all the time," he said. "The justice's phone never rings." Goldberg and his wife adapted to their more insular lifestyle by socializing with the other justices and their wives. The Goldbergs became close to the Blacks, the Warrens, and the Brennans.

In July 1965, Goldberg made the biggest mistake of his life. He listened to the pleas of President Lyndon Johnson. Johnson yearned to put his friend and closest adviser, Washington lawyer Abe Fortas, on the Court. The president also needed a new ambassador to the United Nations after Adlai Stevenson's death. John Kenneth Galbraith, a Harvard economist and former ambassador to India who wanted no part of the UN job, fed Johnson rumors that Goldberg was "bored" on the Court. A week earlier, Goldberg had given a speech at Harvard Law School and confided to Galbraith about his difficult adjustment to the slower pace of life as a justice (Goldberg later denied to journalists, historians, and even Johnson himself that he was ever bored on the Court or had any desire to leave).

Johnson seized on Galbraith's information to cajole Goldberg into one of the quickest exits in the Court's history. Three days after Stevenson's death, Johnson called Goldberg to the White House. While Goldberg waited outside the Oval Office, Johnson aide Jack Valenti offered him the post of secretary of health, education, and welfare. Earlier that year, Johnson had offered Goldberg the job of attorney general. "I'm not an applicant for any post—including the U.N. one," Goldberg told Valenti. In the Oval Office, Johnson reviewed a list of more than 20 potential candidates for the UN post with Goldberg, but both men knew why Goldberg was really there. Johnson wanted Goldberg. Two days later, Goldberg flew with Johnson to Stevenson's funeral in Bloomington, Illinois, aboard Air Force One. During the plane ride home, Johnson pushed all the right buttons. He appealed to Goldberg's patriotism. The nation was at war in Vietnam; his country needed him. A former member of the Office of Strategic Services (OSS) during World War II, Goldberg was proud of his wartime service and even prouder of being an American. As the son of Russian-Jewish immigrants and the embodiment of the American dream, he felt that he owed his country. Johnson appealed to Goldberg's ego. Only someone with Goldberg's negotiating skills could end the Vietnam War. Johnson said he was serious about peace; Goldberg could get the credit for making it happen. Finally, Johnson appealed to Goldberg's ambition. If Goldberg could end the Vietnam War, he might be named secretary of state or even replace Hubert Humphrey as Johnson's next vice president. And if Goldberg were vice president, he might even become the first Jewish president of the United States. That night, after they had returned to Washington, the president called George Washington University Hospital, where Goldberg was visiting his ailing mother-in-law, and officially offered him the job. For the rest of his life, Goldberg would answer questions about why he had left the Supreme Court after just three years. He gave up his dream job for God, country, and a political pipe dream.

Goldberg's three years at the UN aged him 30 years. Referring to the UN's 117 member countries, Goldberg said he felt like "a lawyer with 116 clients." The real problem was the 117th client at home. On the Vietnam War, he was a dove in a presidential administration dominated by hawks. Syndicated columnist Joseph Alsop speculated that Goldberg would temper his views in order to preserve his vice-presidential chances. Alsop could not have been more wrong. In cabinet meetings and confidential memos, Goldberg made a persistent and persuasive case to halt the bombing in Vietnam and negotiate a settlement. Johnson, however, had no intention of pulling out of Vietnam without a victory and continued to escalate the war. Goldberg believed that Johnson froze him out of strategy sessions and kept key memos from him. The more correct Goldberg's assessment about Vietnam proved to be, the more Johnson hated him for it. As early as December 1967, Goldberg considered resigning. The last straw was Johnson's decision to leave Goldberg out of the Vietnam peace talks.

On March 31, 1968, Johnson publicly announced that he would not seek reelection and privately told members of his cabinet that he would understand if they decided to resign. On April 23, Goldberg submitted his letter of resignation before the entire cabinet. Two days later, Johnson accepted it. It was not a warm good-bye on the part of either man. "I don't want the impression to be created that I am hanging around for a Supreme Court appointment," Goldberg told the president and his cabinet. "This is not good for the country, the President, nor is it personally dignified for me."

Although Goldberg denied that he had made a deal with Johnson to return to the Court, some Goldberg intimates believe that Johnson promised to reappoint him as chief justice. Ten days before Johnson announced that he would not seek reelection, Chief Justice Earl Warren had summoned his close friend Goldberg to his chambers. Warren had not even told his wife yet, but he was planning to step down from the Court. He wanted Goldberg to replace him. Goldberg was moved nearly to tears and urged Warren not to resign. Warren, however, had detested Richard Nixon since their days in California Republican politics and did not want Nixon appointing the next chief. Goldberg's wife told him that even if "nothing later may measure up to the Supreme Court experience you have had, you still have a treasure in this to remember—that the Chief should have come to you and said I know no other man who should be the Chief Justice of the United States."

Goldberg knew that there was no way—particularly after his latest get-out-of-Vietnam memo to the president, Secretary of Defense Clark Clifford, and Secretary of State Dean Rusk—that Johnson was going to name him chief justice. Syndicated columnist Drew Pearson lobbied Johnson to nominate Goldberg. Johnson told Pearson that the country was not ready for two Jewish justices (Abe Fortas had filled Goldberg's "Jewish seat"). Goldberg, who reminded his wife that two Jewish justices, Louis Brandeis and Benjamin Cardozo, had served on the Court together during the 1930s, was so incensed that he wanted to confront the president: "I'll ask him where the Constitution says the country has a god-given right to have seven Protestants on the bench but only one Catholic [William Brennan] and one Jew?"

After Warren announced his retirement in June 1968, Johnson tried to replace him with Fortas. Fortas's nomination as chief justice failed because of Johnson's lame-duck status, anti–Warren Court sentiment, and a financial scandal that eventually forced Fortas to resign from the Court. Fortas had lied about agreeing to a $20,000-a-year lifetime salary to serve on a foundation started by financier Louis Wolfson, who was convicted of securities fraud (Goldberg had turned down a similar offer from Wolfson after leaving the Court for the UN). After Fortas resigned, Johnson asked Goldberg about nominating him as a recess appointment (when Congress was out of session). But Johnson changed his mind after his staff discovered the president had spoken out against recess appointments. He later recommended that his successor, Richard Nixon, nominate Goldberg instead. There was no chance of that happening; thus Goldberg was forced to return to private practice, making him available to Flood.

For Miller, having a former Supreme Court justice take on Flood's case accomplished several goals. It let the owners know that the players meant business. It attracted media attention. And it gave Flood a better chance to persuade the Court to hear his case.

For Goldberg, the Flood case was a chance at redemption. He could match wits with the nine men on the Court, remind the country that he was one of its brightest legal minds, and justify why he still carried himself like a Supreme Court justice.

Since leaving the UN and joining Paul, Weiss, Goldberg had championed several left-wing causes. In July 1969, he won a federal appeal of Yale chaplain William Sloane Coffin Jr.'s conviction for conspiring to aid draft resisters. He took on a massive land rights case involving Alaskan Indians. And he co-chaired a committee to investigate the numerous police clashes with the Black Panthers.

Goldberg grasped the moral implications of Flood's lawsuit. As a Chicago lawyer in December 1946 and January 1947, Goldberg had litigated a similar dispute involving professional basketball's first giant, George Mikan. A bespectacled 6-foot-9 All-American at DePaul, Mikan signed a professional contract with the National Basketball League's Chicago American Gears. On December 11, 1946, Mikan quit the team after its first home game because of a contract dispute. Mikan, who was pursuing his law degree at DePaul, claimed that the American Gears had reneged on an oral agreement to pay him an additional $25,000. His five-year contract paid him $7,000 a year. The team also agreed to pay him a $50 weekly salary to work in its legal department, $5 for each basket, $2 for each free throw, and an insurance policy equal to his salary. Publicly, the American Gears boasted that Mikan's contract was worth $60,000. Privately, the owner of the team asked him to take a pay cut. Mikan was also upset about the way the team was being run: Mikan's brother, Joe, was one of four players cut at the train station just before the team left for an eastern road trip, and the head coach did not show up for the team's first home game.

The day after Mikan quit the team, Goldberg filed a declaratory judgment action seeking to void Mikan's contract and declare the star center a free agent. He argued that the contract was invalid because it was unilateral or one-sided—the American Gears could release Mikan at any time, but the player was not allowed to quit and join another team. The American Gears also were under no obligation to pay Mikan if they went out of business, and could assign his contract to another team. As proof of the contract's invalidity, Goldberg's brief cited two pre–*Federal Baseball* cases in which the owners were unable to enforce the reserve clause and prevent stars Napoleon Lajoie and Hal Chase from jumping to rival leagues. The Cook County judge never ruled on the issues. After six weeks of legal wrangling, Mikan and the American Gears settled their differences on January 28; three nights later, he returned to the team.

Thanks to the Mikan case, Goldberg arrived at breakfast with Miller and Moss armed with a firm understanding of the reserve clause. A former Wrigley Field stadium vendor, he had sold coffee at Prohibition-era Chicago Cubs games. His allegiance to the Cubs notwithstanding, Goldberg saw the need to challenge the lifetime ownership of players. As a labor lawyer and a leader of the Warren Court's rights revolution, he was outraged.

Goldberg regarded this as "an important case in principle" and offered to take the case without collecting his hourly fee. He asked only that the Players Association pay his expenses and the hourly fees and expenses of the other partners and associates on the case. "Arthur Goldberg for expenses!" Miller wrote. "That was like Sandy Koufax pitching for pass-the-hat."

Goldberg's giveaways infuriated his Paul, Weiss partners. He frequently brought in high-profile clients and, without consulting his partners, grandly announced that he would not collect his hourly fee. Goldberg did not work for the American Civil Liberties Union or the government; he worked for a large New York law firm. He insisted on riding in a chauffeured limousine to and from work. He retreated to a 28th-floor Park Avenue corner office and collected a mid-six-figure salary. His salary derived from the billable hours of his fellow partners and associates whether or not he charged for his own time.

A few days after Flood had addressed the Players Association in Puerto Rico, he flew to New York with Allan Zerman to meet Goldberg. Flood was nervous about making a good first impression on a former Supreme Court justice. What should he call him? Your Honor? Mr. Ambassador? Mr. Justice? Mr. Goldberg? He was so nervous that he was afraid he was going to bungle Goldberg's last name.

Flood was in awe of Goldberg even though there was nothing physically imposing about him. The former justice was 5 feet 9 and 150 pounds, with a double chin, wavy white hair, and thick black plastic glasses. Nor was his gray and white corner office very intimidating. The blond wood and modern furniture—a couch, a glass table, and a few armchairs—were more befitting a Hollywood studio executive than a former justice. Goldberg nonetheless made a good first impression on Flood. "When he talks about legal ideas and his business," Flood said, "he becomes 6 feet 8. His office on Park Avenue looks like Busch Stadium."

Goldberg put Flood at ease by asking factual questions about the case. Goldberg alluded to his experience with the issues. He raised many of the same concerns as Miller and the player representatives. He reiterated the difficulties of persuading the Court to hear a case about an issue it had decided two previous times. He wanted Flood to know that they faced long odds and that Flood had little to gain even if they succeeded.

"I won't be treated as if I were an IBM card," Flood said.

"All right," Goldberg replied. "Let's go."

Flood could not believe that "the most famous lawyer in the world" had just agreed to represent him.

The next decision was how to fire the first shot. It was the third week of December and Flood's intentions to sue baseball had not been made public. One reason was the location of the players' 1969 winter meetings. Incensed at the owners' refusal to meet with them at the 1967 winter meetings in Mexico City or the 1968 winter meetings in San Francisco, the players decided in 1969 to hold their meetings in Puerto Rico a week after the owners' meetings in Florida. Another reason was that most of the sporting press was in the owners' pocket. Sportswriters attended the owners' meeting in Florida, but they neglected to go to Puerto Rico. Nor did they follow up with the players upon their return. In an era before cellular phones, cable television, and the Internet, the news cycle was slower; it was easier to keep something like Flood's lawsuit under wraps. The Phillies and the Cardinals, along with the rest of the baseball establishment, remained in the dark.

Miller clued in one of his social friends, *New York Times* baseball writer Leonard Koppett. One night in mid-December when they went out to dinner with their wives, Miller revealed Flood's proposed lawsuit and the Players Association's decision to hire Goldberg. Miller asked Koppett's thoughts. Koppett predicted that Flood would lose at trial and on appeal, but he would get a fair shot with the Supreme Court. Koppett agreed at dinner to hold off on writing the story, but there was no doubt he was going to break it.

Flood's first shot came in the form of a letter to the commissioner, which has since found its way into a book about the best letters of the 20th century and into the Baseball Hall of Fame. Miller and Moss wrote the letter, Goldberg edited it, and Flood approved it. All of their voices can be heard.

For Miller and Moss, the letter staked out the union's position that the reserve clause was unjust. Seven months into his job as the union's executive director, Miller had predicted in a February 12, 1967, *New York Times* interview:

> The idea that a baseball player is a piece of property that can be owned, traded, sold or released, and that his only recourse is to take it or quit, has been accepted for too long. Sooner or later the players will want to get into this question of whether they are someone's property, or whether they are not. When that happens, there will have to be some fundamental changes in the thinking of baseball club owners.

Less than three years later, Flood proved Miller right. Many of Flood's fellow players, however, still believed the owners' line that baseball could not survive without the reserve clause. Anything less than complete control over player mobility, the owners claimed, would destroy the game. Flood's letter marked the first step in changing people's minds.

For Goldberg, the letter set up Flood's legal claim that Major League Baseball used the reserve clause to operate as an illegal monopoly. It put the owners on notice of Flood's grievances and offered them the opportunity to rectify the situation. The failure to meet those demands would give Flood no other recourse but to quit the game and take the owners to court.

For Flood, the letter declared his freedom. He had told the player representatives in Puerto Rico that he planned to write the commissioner a letter announcing that he was a "free man in a free society" and he "should have the right to decide" where to make his living. Miller and Moss wanted to begin the letter with the words: "I'm free, black, and 31"—inspired by *To Be Young, Gifted, and Black*, a popular off-Broadway play in 1969 about the life of the late playwright Lorraine Hansberry (*A Raisin in the Sun*). Flood was certainly young, gifted, and black. Goldberg, however, nixed the opening as too flippant for such a serious document.

After Miller, Moss, Goldberg, and Flood agreed on the document's tone and the language, the two-paragraph letter was typed onto stationery from Flood's photography studio business, Curt Flood & Associates, Inc., and signed by Flood in New York. Fear swept through Flood before they mailed the letter. He feared bucking the establishment. He feared he was destroying his life, because he had no idea how this was going to turn out. But relief soon replaced fear as Flood realized that someone was finally doing something about the unfairness of the reserve clause.

The letter, copies of which were sent to Miller and Phillies general manager John Quinn, was mailed on December 24, 1969, and addressed to only one person: the commissioner of baseball, Bowie Kuhn.

> Dear Mr. Kuhn:
>
> After twelve years in the Major Leagues, I do not feel that I am a piece of property to be bought and sold irrespective of my wishes. I believe that any system which produces that result violates my basic rights as a citizen and is inconsistent with the laws of the United States and of the several States.
>
> It is my desire to play in 1970, and I am capable of playing. I have received a contract offer from the Philadelphia Club, but I believe I have the right to consider offers from other clubs before making any decisions. I, therefore, request that you make known

to all the Major League Clubs my feelings in this matter, and advise them of my availability for the 1970 season.

Sincerely yours,
Curt Flood

Flood's letter miffed Kuhn. The commissioner had met with the player representatives in Puerto Rico on December 14, the day after they had voted to support Flood's lawsuit. He addressed a number of the players' concerns: fan voting for the All-Star Game, earflaps on helmets, the length of the season, artificial turf, and signing autographs before games. Neither Flood's proposed lawsuit nor the reserve system ever came up.

Kuhn attributed the players' silence to Miller. He claimed that the union chief had placed a gag order on any discussion of Flood or the reserve clause. The owners began repeating a single theme: Miller was the man behind this lawsuit, not Flood.

Indeed, Kuhn's legal advisers chuckled when they read Flood's letter. Language such as "irrespective of my wishes" and "inconsistent with the laws of the United States and of the several States" was a dead giveaway. This was Miller's and Moss's handiwork, not Flood's.

Phillies general manager John Quinn felt more embarrassment than amusement. After spending time with Flood in St. Louis and New York, he had been convinced that Flood was going to sign. He had even confided to a black Philadelphia weekly newspaper that he planned to announce Flood's signing at the team's January 7 Newsy Notes Club meeting. On December 4, Flood had sent Quinn a dictated letter apologizing for not returning Quinn's phone call. "I feel that I must resolve a number of personal problems before I make a final decision," Flood said. He was out of town and promised to call Quinn the week of December 22. Instead, Quinn simply received Flood's December 24 letter along with the commissioner. Quinn's secretary read it to him over the phone while he vacationed in Arizona. Like the commissioner, Quinn blamed Miller for Flood's supposed change of heart.

The letter's biggest stroke of genius was its first three words: "Dear Mr. Kuhn." Miller knew that by addressing the letter to Kuhn, rather than to Quinn of the Phillies or Devine of the Cardinals, Miller was placing Kuhn squarely on the owners' side of the ball. Miller wanted to smash the myth that the commissioner was impartial. If the owners' principal theme was that Flood's lawsuit was conceived and driven by Miller and the Players Association, then Miller's theme was that Kuhn was employed by and a water carrier for the owners. A former lawyer for the National League, Kuhn had worked for much of his adult life protecting the owners' cartel.

Bowie Kent Kuhn grew up a die-hard Washington Senators fan. His first memories of baseball coincided with the Senators' last World Series appearance in 1933. Six years later, he worked inside the Griffith Stadium scoreboard for $1 a day. He started as an assistant to the scoreboard operator and rose to head of the scoreboard. His first Social Security card, which he kept in his wallet as commissioner, listed Senators owner Clark Griffith as his employer. His immediate boss was Griffith's nephew, Calvin. Kuhn picked up his love for the Senators through his mother. His father, the head of the Washington, D.C., office of the Petroleum Heat and Power Company, did not have time for baseball.

Born into a devout Catholic family, Kuhn was the youngest of three children and, at 6 feet 5, the tallest. At Theodore Roosevelt High School, the basketball coach spotted Kuhn in the hallway and asked: "Son, you're the tallest boy in the school. How come you're not out for the basketball team?"

"Because I'm a lousy player," Kuhn replied.

"You let me be the judge of that," Red Auerbach said.

After a week, Auerbach informed Kuhn: "Son, you were right, and I was wrong. You won't have to come back tomorrow."

Auerbach left Roosevelt High shortly thereafter and went on to coach the Boston Celtics; Kuhn returned to the team but never amounted to anything as an athlete.

Kuhn's athletic shortcomings did not diminish his love for baseball. After two years of stateside military service beginning in June 1944, he graduated from Princeton and the University of Virginia law school. In September 1950, he joined the New York law firm of Willkie Owen Farr Gallagher & Walton (later known as Willkie Farr) because one of its name partners was one of his political heroes, former Republican presidential candidate Wendell Willkie, and because the firm represented the National League.

Shortly after joining the firm in November 1950, Kuhn knocked on the door of senior partner Louis Carroll. Carroll had represented the National League since the 1930s and was known in baseball circles as "The Wise Man." Any thorny legal issue in baseball prompted someone to ask: "What does The Wise Man say?" Kuhn let Carroll know that he wanted to work on baseball issues.

The midcentury challenges to baseball's antitrust exemption provided Kuhn with the opportunity. The Second Circuit's decision in *Gardella v. Chandler* in 1949 suggested that the exemption was on shaky ground. Yankees farmhand George Toolson filed suit in the summer of 1950, as did two other plaintiffs. Carroll pulled his eager young associate into the litigation. For the next three years baseball fought those cases, until the Supreme Court reaffirmed *Federal Baseball* in *Toolson*. Along the way, Kuhn met baseball commissioner Ford Frick, American League president Will Harridge, and National League president Warren Giles, and became Carroll's right-hand man on baseball matters.

Kuhn earned his stripes with the baseball establishment 14 years later in an important but often overlooked antitrust victory in Milwaukee. After the 1964 season, the owners of the Milwaukee Braves decided to move the team to Atlanta. In an effort to keep their team, the people of Wisconsin sued Major League Baseball in state court. They hired Louis Oberdorfer—a future federal judge, former head of the Kennedy Justice Department's tax division, and one of Washington's best lawyers—as a special consultant. They did not try to attack *Federal Baseball* and *Toolson* or to apply federal antitrust law. Instead, they argued that moving the Braves to Atlanta violated Wisconsin's antitrust laws. A state trial judge agreed, issuing an injunction that prevented the Braves from playing anywhere but Milwaukee until baseball granted the city an expansion team.

Kuhn took the lead in arguing baseball's case before the Wisconsin Supreme Court. Baseball was caught in a clever trap: It was either interstate commerce subject to federal antitrust law or intrastate commerce subject to Wisconsin's antitrust law. Put another way, either *Federal Baseball* was wrong (and baseball lost its exemption) or the Wisconsin trial judge was right (and the Braves stayed in Milwaukee). The future of the game's legal monopoly was at stake.

Kuhn and his colleagues conceded that baseball was interstate commerce. They said that *Toolson* rested on *stare decisis*—the exemption should stand because it had been around a long time and baseball had relied on it. Then they argued that the enforcement of each state's antitrust law would throw baseball into organizational chaos. They compared Major League Baseball to a railroad. If each state enforced different regulations on the length of rail cars, then cross-country train travel would be impossible. If each state enforced different regulations on baseball, then major league teams would have to go back to barnstorming. Federal law, therefore, preempted state law in this instance. Agreeing on the result but not on the rationale, the Wisconsin Supreme Court voted 4–3 to reverse the trial court's order. The Braves moved to Atlanta. Baseball narrowly escaped with its antitrust exemption intact. Kuhn was the hero. "Bowie Kuhn is a very good lawyer," his Willkie Farr colleague Lou Hoynes said, "and this was no hanging curveball."

Miller did not hold Kuhn's legal acumen in the same high regard. Miller's first impression of Kuhn came after a July 1966 meeting in Chicago where baseball officials had signed a new television contract. A lawyer for the National League, Kuhn informed Miller that then-commissioner William Eckert was about to hold a press conference announcing the deal as well as the amount the owners planned on contributing to the players' pension fund. Miller pulled Eckert aside and informed him that any announcement about the pension fund would be a gross violation of federal labor law. The amount of the owners' pension contribution must be negotiated with the union. Eckert heeded some of Miller's advice, announcing only the new television contract, but not the part about finding a lawyer who knew something about labor law.

Five months later, with Lou Carroll beginning a battle with cancer and relinquishing his National League counsel duties, Kuhn joined the owners' three-man Players Relations Committee (PRC), which negotiated labor and pension agreements with the players. Kuhn found himself on the opposite side of the negotiating table from Miller. He came to view Miller as "pedantic, fussy over details and unwilling to deal straightforwardly with issues. . . . The result was a never-ending game of cat and mouse in which Miller conducted union affairs with such endless slyness that he soured the relations between clubs and players." It was the beginning of a hate-hate relationship. For the next three years, the two men butted heads at the negotiating table. Then, in early February 1969, Kuhn became commissioner and declared himself impartial.

Kuhn's Willkie Farr partners saw the commissionership as his perfect exit strategy from the firm. He had no clients of his own. And Lou Carroll's heir apparent as National League counsel was not Kuhn, but Lou Hoynes. Many people considered Hoynes the genius behind the strategy in Milwaukee. After Hoynes became National League counsel, he worked so closely with Kuhn that people referred to Hoynes as "the shadow commissioner" or "Bowie Kuhn's brains."

Kuhn was a compromise choice for commissioner. The only thing the owners could agree on at the 1968 winter meetings in San Francisco was firing retired air force lieutenant general William Eckert. A few weeks later at a meeting at the O'Hare Inn outside Chicago, they stayed up all night and voted 19 times without coming up with Eckert's successor. None of the four candidates—Yankees president Mike Burke, Yankees general manager Lee MacPhail, Montreal Expos president John McHale, and San Francisco Giants vice president (and future National League president) Chub Feeney—garnered the necessary approval of three-quarters of the owners in each league. One of the game's most powerful figures, Dodgers owner Walter O'Malley, decided to bless Kuhn's candidacy. Less than two months later in Miami, the owners unanimously elected Kuhn to a one-year trial run as commissioner *pro tem*.

Kuhn believed that he was the second coming of Judge Landis. A white-haired, steely-eyed federal judge, Kenesaw Mountain Landis earned national acclaim in 1907 for fining John D. Rockefeller's Standard Oil Company $29 million for antitrust violations. Like many of Landis's judicial decisions, the fine was reversed on appeal. In 1915, Landis curried favor with the major league owners by refusing to rule on an antitrust lawsuit filed by the Federal League in his courtroom. Landis's delay tactics helped the major league owners run the Federal League out of business. After the 1919 Black Sox scandal destroyed baseball's credibility, the owners tapped Landis as their first commissioner and gave him unlimited authority to clean up the game.

Until he died 24 years later, Landis ruled the game like a benevolent dictator. He banned nearly two dozen players for life for gambling and other illegal activities. He was a leading force in keeping blacks out of

Major League Baseball during his lifetime. Dodgers general manager Branch Rickey signed Jackie Robinson less than a year after Landis's death in November 1944.

As insensitive as Landis was about race, he was sensitive to the injustice of the reserve clause. He declared outfielder Fred Bennett a free agent in 1930 after the St. Louis Browns kept shuttling him back and forth between their minor league teams. Browns owner Phil Ball was so incensed that he challenged Landis's authority in federal court; Landis won. Landis also freed Tommy Henrich, who wrote the commissioner after the 1936 season about being stuck in the Indians farm system. Henrich signed for a $20,000 bonus and $5,000 contract with the Yankees. The commissioner crusaded against the farm system, freeing 91 of the St. Louis Cardinals' minor leaguers in 1938, and 87 of the Detroit Tigers' minor leaguers and 5 of the Tigers' major leaguers two years later. One of those Tiger minor leaguers was Danny Gardella. When it came to reserve clause abuses, the players had a friend in Judge Landis.

Kuhn deluded himself into believing that he possessed Landis's power and impartiality rather than a lifetime record as a management lawyer. He was the youngest commissioner in the history of the game at age 42, but with his baritone voice, 6-foot-5-inch and 230-pound frame, receding brown hair, blue eyes, graying sideburns, light plastic eyeglasses, and conservative three-piece suits, he looked and acted the part. His defining characteristic was his pomposity. He delivered his decisions as if he had brought them down from a mountaintop. Syndicated columnist Red Smith, a Wisconsin native who blamed Kuhn for the Braves' move to Atlanta and blanched at Kuhn's self-important manner, referred to the commissioner as "the game's upright scoutmaster." Smith, more than any other sportswriter, helped portray Kuhn as "the ultimate stuffed shirt."

Like Landis, Kuhn saw himself as the protector of the game's integrity. The Major League Agreement gave the commissioner the power to investigate and punish "any act, transaction or practice charged, alleged or suspected to be not in the best interests of the national game of baseball." Although Kuhn rarely invoked the "best interests" clause, he took action when anything offended his sensibilities. Flood's lawsuit plainly fell under that category.

Kuhn acted firmly and decisively in his first few months as commissioner. He won praise in late February 1969 from the press and even from Miller for persuading the owners to settle the pension dispute that threatened to keep the players out of spring training. He talked Donn Clendenon out of retirement by returning him to Montreal and ordering the Expos to compensate the Astros with additional players and cash. He also ended post-trade retirement talk from Ken Harrelson, persuading him to report to Cleveland after the Indians guaranteed him a new contract worth $100,000. "Baseball," Kuhn said, "needs Ken Harrelson." In late May, the owners gave Kuhn a vote of confidence by removing his temporary tag.

Kuhn assumed that, as he had done with Clendenon and Harrelson, he could make Flood's threatened lawsuit go away. Kuhn figured that after a few meetings with Flood or his counsel, Kuhn could persuade Flood to report to spring training with the Phillies. Kuhn, however, refused to make Flood a free agent. He was no more willing as commissioner to reduce the owners' power to enforce the reserve clause than he had been as a member of the PRC from 1966 to 1968. Baseball's antitrust exemption, which he had worked most of his legal life to preserve, was not going down without a massive fight.

Kuhn called Flood at home on the evening of December 30 and in a monotone voice read Flood the following response to his December 24 letter:

> Dear Curt:
>
> This will acknowledge your letter of December 24, 1969, which I found on returning to my office yesterday.
>
> I certainly agree with you that you, as a human being, are not a piece of property to be bought and sold. This is fundamental in our society and I think obvious. However, I cannot see its applicability to the situation at hand.
>
> You have entered into a current playing contract with the St. Louis club which has the same assignment provision as those in your annual Major League contracts since 1956. Your present contract has been assigned in accordance with its provisions by the St. Louis club to the Philadelphia club. The provisions of the playing contract have been negotiated over the years between

the clubs and the players, most recently when the present Basic Agreement was negotiated two years ago between the clubs and the Players Association.

If you have any specific objection to the propriety of the assignment, I would appreciate your specifying the objection. Under the circumstances, and pending any further information from you, I do not see what action I can take and cannot comply with the request contained in the second paragraph of your letter.

I am pleased to see your statement that you desire to play baseball in 1970. I take it this puts to rest any thought, as reported earlier in the press, that you were considering retirement.

Sincerely yours,
Bowie K. Kuhn

After Kuhn finished reading Flood the contents of the letter, Flood thanked the commissioner for his quick reply. Flood remarked that he would decide his next step in a day or two. The commissioner sent copies of the letter to Flood, Miller, Bing Devine, and John Quinn. He then released both letters to the press.

Miller, however, had already beaten his adversary to the punch. On December 29, he sent a short memo to all the players informing them of Flood's meeting with the player representatives and the union's decision to pay for his legal counsel. The next day, the *New York Times* and *New York Post* ran stories revealing Flood's plan to test the reserve clause in court with Goldberg as his lawyer and the Players Association's financial backing. The national wires picked up the stories. Kuhn's letter hit the paper the following day. Red Smith translated the commissioner's response to mean: "Run along, sonny, you bother me."

Flood knew that Kuhn and the owners had not yet realized the depth of his resolve. "I think the owners are underestimating me," Flood said January 2 before leaving for New York. "They think I'm just trying to get more money for next season. They'll probably begin taking it serious around March."

CHAPTER SEVEN

Four days after his decision to sue was made public, Flood went on national television and attacked the reserve clause in the starkest moral terms. He shocked and offended the American people during an interview with the man people loved to imitate but claimed to hate, Howard Cosell.

A lawyer by trade, Jew by birth, and friend of outspoken black athletes by choice, Cosell ruled 1970s sports television. He spoke in a slow, nasal Brooklyn accent and offered an opinion about everything. Before *Monday Night Football* turned him into a legend, Cosell championed Muhammad Ali's right to refuse to serve in the Vietnam War; he landed the first interview with Tommie Smith after his black-gloved salute at the 1968 Olympics in Mexico City; and he regarded Jim Brown, Bill Russell, and Jackie Robinson as close friends.

Cosell, who saw Flood as continuing the fight for social change begun by Robinson and Ali, supported Flood at every turn. Their friendship began on the morning of January 3 when Flood arrived at ABC's New York studios to tape his interview for a *Wide World of Sports* episode that aired later that day.

Dressed in a royal blue suit and accompanied by Marvin Miller, Flood explained his reason for wanting to sue baseball: "I don't think there is anything more damaging to a person's ego as a human being than to be traded or bought and sold like a piece of property."

Never at a loss for words, Cosell followed up with the question on the mind of every thinking sports fan in America:

"It's been written, Curt, that you're a man who makes $90,000 a year, which isn't exactly slave wages. What's your retort to that?"

The camera zeroed in on Flood. He cocked his head toward Cosell and responded as if he were in Cosell's living room rather than being beamed into America's.

"A well-paid slave," Flood said, "is nonetheless a slave."

During the past four days, Flood had compared the reserve clause to being treated like cattle or property. This was the first time he had invoked slavery.

Cosell asked Miller if it was possible to generate public support for a ballplayer making $90,000. "If people think slavery is all right as long as the money's OK, then maybe we won't," Miller said.

Several months later, other athletes quit their respective sports and expressed similar feelings of powerlessness. Stripped of his heavyweight title for refusing to fight in Vietnam, Muhammad Ali explained in May 1970 why he was "through" fighting in the ring as well. "We're just like two slaves in that ring," he said. "The masters get two of us big black slaves and let us fight it out while they bet, 'My slave can whup your slave.' That's what I see when I see two black people fighting." That same month, two 20-something white linebackers suddenly retired from the NFL. Chip Oliver left the Oakland Raiders to live in a Bay Area commune. "Pro football is a silly game," he said. "It dehumanizes people. They've taken the players and made them into slabs of beef that can charge around and hit each other." A few days later, Dave Meggyesy quit the St. Louis Cardinals. He moved to Berkeley, described his football experiences in his groundbreaking book, *Out of Their League*, and later worked for the NFL Players Association. "What is wrong with professional football is not that the players are not getting a decent wage," Meggyesy wrote in October 1970, "but the dehumanizing conditions they are required to work under."

Flood was striving for the same thing as Ali, Oliver, and Meggyesy: human dignity. He wanted to feel like a person and not like an object. As a black man, he expressed those feelings in terms of slavery.

Comparing baseball's system of player ownership to slavery was not an original idea. Almost as soon as the owners had begun the practice of reserving five players per team in 1879, the players decried it as a form of slavery. The leading critic among the players was future Hall of Famer John Montgomery Ward. A white Columbia-educated lawyer and founder of the rival Players League in 1890, Ward wrote an article in August 1887 titled "Is the Base-Ball Player a Chattel?" "Like a fugitive-slave law," Ward wrote less than 25 years removed from the Civil War, "the reserve-rule denies him a harbor or a livelihood, and carries him back, bound and shackled, to the club from which he attempted to escape."

In 1914, a New York judge rejected an attempt to enforce the reserve clause and prevent Chicago White Sox first baseman Hal Chase from jumping to Buffalo's Federal League team. The judge described the reserve clause as a "system of servitude" based on "the purchase, sale, barter and exchange of the services of the baseball players—skilled laborers—without their consent. . . . The *quasi* peonage of baseball players under the operations of this plan and agreement is contrary to the spirit of American institutions, and is contrary to the spirit of the Constitution of the United States."

In his opinion in the 1949 *Gardella* case, Judge Jerome Frank wrote that the reserve clause "results in something resembling peonage of the baseball player" and "possesses characteristics shockingly repugnant to moral principles that, at least since the War Between the States, have been basic in America, as shown by the Thirteenth Amendment to the Constitution, condemning 'involuntary servitude.'" Frank foreshadowed Flood's "well-paid slave" comment by writing that "if the players be regarded as quasi-peons, it is of no moment that they are well paid; only the totalitarian-minded will believe that high pay excuses virtual slavery."

During the 1960s, other people compared the reserve clause and the plight of black athletes to slavery. No one, however, had done so in the context of suing America's national pastime. The reaction to Flood's comments reflected a backlash against the idealism of the 1960s. The public's distaste for the perceived excesses of the civil rights and antiwar movements seemed to come to a head over a rich black athlete portraying himself as a slave. Flood's "well-paid slave" remark turned America against him. The media seized on it. The public vilified him for it.

Before returning to St. Louis after three days in New York, Flood and his St. Louis lawyer, Allan Zerman, met their new legal team. Goldberg had enlisted one of Paul, Weiss's top litigation partners in Jay Topkis. The firm's most senior antitrust lawyer, Topkis was also regarded as one of its best brief writers. They were joined by two recent Yale law graduates, Max Gitter and Bill Iverson.

The major decisions facing Flood's legal team included where and when to file a lawsuit and what type of lawsuit to file. They settled on federal district court in Manhattan, the home of the commissioner's office. They gave themselves less than two weeks to do it. And they decided to file both a request for a preliminary injunction and a complaint.

The purpose of a preliminary injunction was twofold: First, it asked the court to prevent Major League Baseball from enforcing Flood's trade to the Phillies. This would allow Flood either to play for the Cardinals or to become a free agent. Either way, Flood could play baseball in 1970. Second, and more important, the injunction placed Flood's case on the fast track for trial. A judge would hear from both sides before deciding whether to grant or deny the injunction. Although the chances of the court granting Flood an injunction were low because he was required to show an extremely high likelihood of winning his case, the injunction hearing moved up Flood's case on the trial judge's docket.

Flood's complaint declared war on the reserve clause. It named commissioner Bowie Kuhn, league presidents Chub Feeney and Joe Cronin, and the 24 major league teams as defendants. The lawsuit claimed that the reserve clause violated two federal antitrust laws; the state antitrust laws of New York, California, and several other states; and the common law. It also included separate antitrust claims against Anheuser-Busch for allegedly selling only its beer at St. Louis Cardinals games and against CBS because its ownership of the New York Yankees allegedly interfered with the selling of baseball's television rights. Finally, it claimed that the reserve clause violated federal statutes against "peonage and involuntary servitude" as well as the 13th Amendment's prohibition against slavery.

At least one member of Flood's legal team believed that by invoking peonage, involuntary servitude, and the 13th Amendment, they were fanning the racial flames that threatened to engulf Flood's case. The goal of Flood's lawsuit was to persuade the Supreme Court of the United States that baseball did not warrant an exemption from the antitrust laws and that the reserve clause violated those laws. The goal was not to prove that Curt Flood was a $90,000 slave. Goldberg, however, insisted on the 13th Amendment and peonage claims. The 13th Amendment claim added a constitutional dimension to the case and did not depend on baseball's status under the antitrust laws. By invoking slavery, peonage, and involuntary servitude, the complaint highlighted the injustice and immorality of the current system.

Flood's complaint sought $1 million in damages. If Flood won at trial and proved all his damages, federal antitrust law would automatically triple his damages award to $3 million. The money, however, was an afterthought. Zerman and Max Gitter estimated the $1 million figure based on Flood's possible future earnings. Flood neither knew nor cared about the amount of damages. Miller told him repeatedly that he would never see any money. Flood knew that he would never recover his 1970 salary of at least $90,000. "Sometimes money's not that important," Flood told the *St. Louis Globe-Democrat* on January 6. "I know it sounds corny, but that's the way I feel."

Zerman and Flood returned to New York City in mid-January to sign the complaint and an affidavit accompanying the injunction request, respectively. On January 16, civil action number 70 Civ. 202, *Curtis C. Flood v. Bowie K. Kuhn, et al.*, was filed in the clerk's office of the United States District Court for the Southern District of New York. The 17-page complaint also contained five exhibits: the Uniform Player Contract signed by Flood and the Cardinals, the notice of transfer of Flood's contract to the Phillies and accompanying letter from Bing Devine, and the letters exchanged between Flood and Kuhn. The 35-page injunction request was accompanied by affidavits signed by Flood and Miller asking the court to nullify Flood's trade to the Phillies.

The motions judge on duty that day, Judge Dudley B. Bonsal, ordered the team owners to appear in his courtroom on January 20 to respond to Flood's request for a preliminary injunction. The owners received a copy of Flood's complaint and Judge Bonsal's order later that afternoon while seated across the negotiating table from Miller and several players. Lou Carroll, who had resumed his role as National League counsel, exploded. He leaped up from the table and accused Miller of undermining their efforts to negotiate a new labor agreement and of violating the old one. Miller calmly replied that if the owners were prepared to modify the reserve clause, then Flood would drop his lawsuit.

"I just wanted to raise the question," Carroll responded.

Miller realized that Carroll's anger had been more calculated than real. Carroll was merely testing out legal arguments at the negotiating table.

While Miller sparred with Lou Carroll, Flood sat in a large paisley armchair in the lobby of the Warwick Hotel and answered reporters' questions. He waved at passersby as photographers snapped pictures of him. Dressed in a dark double-breasted herringbone suit and a white shirt with cuffs, he wore a World Series ring and a gold watch given to him by a female fan on one hand and a gold pinky ring on the other. He looked like visiting royalty sitting on a throne.

Flood was the talk of the sports world. "Baseball Is Sued Under Trust Law" declared the front page of the next day's *New York Times*. Leonard Koppett wrote the story. Inside the paper, George Vecsey wrote a profile of Flood accompanied by a photo of Flood with the portrait of Dr. King. Nearly every newspaper in the country ran at least one story about Flood's lawsuit.

The day after Flood filed his lawsuit, the owners issued a two-page press release claiming that Flood's lawsuit was trying to destroy baseball. The statement was released under the names of American League president Joe Cronin and National League president Chub Feeney. Cronin was interviewed by telephone on Howard Cosell's January 3 show and told the television audience that "the reserve clause is part of baseball. It has stood the test of time." He knew from experience how it worked. As the player-manager of the Washington Senators in 1934, Cronin had been sold by his uncle-in-law, Senators owner Clark Griffith, to the Boston Red Sox for $225,000. Cronin's and Feeney's statement predicted "chaotic results" if Flood's lawsuit was successful. "Without the reserve clause," the statement said, "the wealthier clubs could sign an unbeatable team of all-stars, totally destroying league competition." The poorer, weaker teams would fold. The scouting and minor league system would no longer be profitable. Trades would be "impossible" if player consent were required. "Professional baseball," the statement concluded, "would simply cease to exist."

The opening of Cronin's and Feeney's statement emphasized the "well-paid" part of Flood's "well-paid slave" remark, characterizing him as a "highly paid star" who had "contributed much to and obtained much from baseball." The reserve clause, the statement said, "permitted players such as Curt Flood to reap rich personal rewards." Reiterating Lou Carroll's comments at the negotiating session, Cronin and Feeney also accused the Players Association of violating the labor agreement by not using its best efforts to enforce the Uniform Player Contract. Two days later, Miller charged Cronin and Feeney with issuing a "phony" statement. During labor negotiations in 1968, the players had asserted that the reserve clause was illegal and therefore the players could not use their best efforts to honor an illegal provision.

Cronin's and Feeney's comments polarized the public debate. The back page of the *New York Daily News* proclaimed: "Curt Win Kills Baseball." In the *New York Times*, Leonard Koppett accused both sides of overstatement: the owners for claiming that the only alternative to the reserve clause was "chaos"; the players for framing the debate in terms of "freedom" and "slavery."

Kuhn remained conspicuously above the fray. The commissioner sent Cronin and Feeney to do his dirty work for him. It was Kuhn who had asked Cronin to participate on Cosell's January 3 program, declining to appear himself because he "occupie[d] a judicial position." Kuhn still believed that he could swoop down like his hero, Judge Landis, and resolve at least part, if not all, of this mess.

In January, Kuhn and his lawyer, Paul Porter, met with Goldberg, Topkis, and Moss for the first of several times to try to resolve Flood's lawsuit. Goldberg spoke on Flood's behalf. Kuhn spoke for the owners. Goldberg insisted that Flood should have the right to negotiate with any team. Kuhn said Flood's contract did not permit it. Goldberg countered that the contract was illegal. "I could not communicate with Goldberg, whose starchy, formalistic assertions left little room for even polite conversation," Kuhn later wrote. "I almost wished everybody would go away and let me talk to Miller. Mr. Justice Goldberg sailed off, leaving me to wonder if he had not somehow managed to top even my well-honed reputation for pomposity."

Mr. Justice Goldberg was not about to let some midlevel former Wall Street partner back his client into a legal corner. At one meeting, Kuhn told Goldberg that Flood could continue to play while suing baseball. Goldberg replied that if Flood played, he would not have suffered any harm and his lawsuit would be moot.

"You mean, Mr. Justice, that you are advising Flood to not play?" Kuhn asked.

"If you want to do any quoting," Goldberg quickly replied, "you had better be accurate in what you quote. The decision about whether

Mr. Flood will play will be made by Mr. Flood. I have given him legal advice as to the impact of his decision. The decision is his."

On January 8, Phillies general manager John Quinn sent Flood a contract for $90,000. Flood announced that he would not sign it. Quinn still believed that Flood would play baseball in 1970, just not for Philadelphia.

"Is it true that negotiations are out—that the suit will proceed regardless?" Kuhn asked Goldberg.

"You have a terrible habit of misquoting," Goldberg said. "It is my understanding that if appropriate modifications can be made through negotiation, they would satisfy Curt Flood. Therefore, if you want to carry out your legal right to negotiate, please do so."

In one of his few public comments about the case, Kuhn declared at the Phillies' January 7 Newsy Notes Club meeting (at which the Phillies had intended to announce that they had signed Flood) that Flood's lawsuit was a tactical mistake. Kuhn said if he were advising the Players Association, he would not file a lawsuit that could jeopardize ongoing negotiations about the reserve clause as part of the new labor agreement.

A labor negotiation session a few weeks earlier in New York City had revealed the ridiculousness of this logic. Miller and Moss met with the owners' lead negotiator, John Gaherin; Cronin; Feeney; American League counsel Sandy Hadden; and Lou Carroll, the National League counsel. Four players also were seated around the negotiating table: Joe Torre of the Cardinals, Steve Blass of the Pirates, Ed Kranepool of the Mets, and Jim Bouton of the Astros. A few months before his book *Ball Four* turned the baseball establishment on its ear, Bouton made waves during the late-December negotiation session.

Bouton asked Lou Carroll if the players could be declared free agents at Social Security retirement age.

"What age do you mean?" Carroll asked.

"Age 65," Bouton said.

"No," Carroll replied, "because then you would get your foot in the door." There was some subsequent debate about whether Carroll was joking. Miller said he was not, because Gaherin reiterated Carroll's concern that the players would use that concession to "disturb the entire system." The only way the players were going to get the owners to modify the reserve clause was for someone to take them to court.

Neither Flood nor Kuhn showed up for the first hearing in the case. On January 20, Judge Bonsal granted the owners a two-week delay to respond to Flood's request for an injunction. The lawyer for the Phillies told Judge Bonsal that they would allow Flood to report to spring training without prejudicing his lawsuit. "That's exactly what he doesn't want to do," Topkis replied. "He lives in St. Louis, has a business there and doesn't want to be treated like cattle."

That same night, Flood and Cosell appeared together on *The Dick Cavett Show*. Zerman, who declined to appear on the program, watched in the wings as Flood told another national television audience that the Phillies had offered him "at least $100,000" to play for them in 1970. And there was no way that he was going to take it.

Judge Bonsal's two-week delay gave additional time for the media, players, and fans to take sides about Flood's lawsuit. The owners' "baseball will cease to exist" rhetoric carried the day over Flood's "well-paid slave" comment by a wide margin—especially among the country's baseball writers.

During the 1960s and early 1970s, members of the press were firmly on the side of management. They rode on team buses and planes, reveled in the hometown team's victories, and bonded with owners and general managers. They distrusted Marvin Miller and the Players Association. They could not get over the fact that Flood made $90,000 in 1969. And they often wrote columns about Flood that lacked any racial sensitivity or understanding.

Flood's most incisive and persistent critic was *New York Daily News* columnist Dick Young. Young had dubbed the owners "the Lords of Baseball," but he had been decidedly promanagement ever since. He took shots at Miller and the Players Association, portrayed Flood as Miller's puppet, and denigrated Flood's slavery comparison. "Curt Flood isn't helping his case with that tired slavery line," Young wrote. "Any guy who has to cut short his six-months vacation in Scandanavia [*sic*] to fly here and file his suit doesn't paint a bad picture for the Plantation Owners' Association."

UPI's Milton Richman rejected any comparison between Flood and cattle. "That's where I stop feeling for Flood," Richman wrote. "I know we're in the middle of paralyzing inflation but $90,000 for one head of cattle still staggers the imagination. . . . I don't believe his rights as a human being have been abrogated or annulled in any way by baseball, particularly when I think about the various businesses he has been able to operate both in this country and in Denmark because of the money he earned in the game." Bill Conlin of the *Philadelphia Daily News* cracked: "Flood may become the first petitioning slave in the history of the Republic with a Swiss bank account."

The leader of the St. Louis press corps, *Post-Dispatch* columnist Bob Broeg, epitomized the conservative breed of baseball writers. Broeg bled Cardinal red. He had begun his career working in the team's public relations department in 1939 with future general manager Bing Devine. Before the seventh game of the 1967 World Series in Boston, he had dashed off the team bus in order to buy famished Cardinals starter Bob Gibson two ham-and-egg sandwiches. And he adored Cardinals owner Gussie Busch. Broeg had bristled in 1969 when Flood demanded $100,000, and "not $99,999." He viewed Flood's salary demands as betrayal of a team owner who had been so good to his players.

Broeg contended that Flood's lawsuit was "not a matter of principle, but of principal." He pointed to the $3 million in damages sought by Flood's lawsuit as proof, ignoring the reality that Flood had turned down a six-figure salary with the Phillies and never expected a dime from his lawsuit. All Flood wanted to do was to stay in St. Louis and play for the Cardinals. Broeg brushed aside Flood's hometown allegiance; the St. Louis sports columnist could not get past Flood's big salary. "If the legality of the baseball reserve clause were being contested by a player less affluent than Curt Flood," Broeg wrote, "the sympathy would be considerably greater." He urged his readers not to "gag on" the idea that Flood and his fellow ballplayers were "the poor victims of 'peonage and servitude.'"

St. Louis Globe-Democrat sports editor Bob Burnes infuriated Flood even more than Broeg. Burnes made no secret in his columns that he supported management's right to the reserve clause, but he also believed that Flood's lawsuit was "an absolutely necessary step." On his radio show and in print, Burnes made it seem as if he knew Flood "inside and out." In reality, however, Burnes had never even spoken to Flood. Flood had one of his friends call Burnes's radio show and ask him why Burnes had never interviewed Flood during his 12 seasons with the Cardinals.

Burnes said Flood had never been available for an interview, yet continued to write and talk as if he knew him.

A few sportswriters embraced Flood's slavery argument. Red Smith wrote more supportive columns about Flood than anyone else in the business. As a columnist for the *New York Herald Tribune*, Smith captivated readers with his wit and prose. He was a favorite of Ernest Hemingway's. In his 1950 novel, *Across the River and into the Trees*, Hemingway wrote of one of his characters: "He was reading Red Smith, and he liked it very much." Smith despised the reserve clause, blasting it as early as 1938 and referring to it in a 1957 column as "the Slave Trade." In those days, however, Smith had not been as enlightened about racial issues. He remained silent while other white columnists advocated the integration of baseball. He later insisted on referring to Muhammad Ali as Cassius Clay in columns that Robert Lipsyte of the *New York Times* described as "borderline racist." But in November 1968, after the death of his first wife, Smith married a younger woman with counterculture teenage children. Smith's young family helped transform him into a racial and social progressive.

The 64-year-old Smith combined his new philosophical outlook and long-standing antipathy for the reserve clause in writing about Flood. In 1970, his syndicated columns ran in many of the country's largest newspapers. He introduced readers to Judge Frank's opinion in *Gardella*, blasted his favorite punching bag, Bowie Kuhn, and articulated Flood's point of view with unmatched eloquence. "Curtis Charles Flood is a man of character and self-respect," Smith wrote. "Being black, he is more sensitive than most white players about the institution of slavery as it exists in professional baseball." Smith later advised the trial judge not to be fooled by the defense that "because Flood earned $90,000 a year playing center field for the St. Louis Cardinals, he could not be a slave. . . . you can't change muskrat to mink just by changing the prices."

Los Angeles Times syndicated sports columnist Jim Murray agreed with Smith, describing the reserve clause as "just a fancy name for slavery. The only thing it doesn't let the owners do is flog their help." Although he often wrote with his tongue firmly in his cheek, Murray sided with Flood. "It is pretty late in history for the slave mart anyway," Murray wrote. "If a Curt Flood wants to remain in St. Louis, baseball (and society) should let him."

Smith and Murray represented exceptions to the rule. There were a few others: Koppett and Lipsyte of the *New York Times*, Milton Gross of the *New York Post*, Gene Ward of the *New York Daily News*, and former NFL star-turned-broadcaster Kyle Rote and, of course, Cosell on television. But the bulk of the white media blasted Flood's "well-paid slave" comment and backed the owners' contention that baseball needed the reserve system to survive. In an editorial titled "A Threat to Baseball," the *Houston Chronicle* concluded: "We think Flood and the players association are making a mistake which can backfire against the players themselves and can seriously cripple baseball."

Flood's most consistent supporter was the black press. Sportswriters at weekly black newspapers had led the fight to integrate Major League Baseball and played a critical role in Branch Rickey's selection of Jackie Robinson as the 20th century's first African-American player. They had also fought for the integration of spring training camps and major league hotel accommodations and had railed against the reserve clause.

Flood graced the February 15 cover of *Jet* magazine, which declared him "The Man Who Fights Power Structure of Baseball." *Jet*'s sister publication, *Ebony*, said it had been looking since 1964 for an "Abe Lincoln of Baseball" to challenge the owners' stranglehold on the players' services and had finally found one in Flood. "It will be a bit of poetic justice should it turn out that a black man finally brings freedom and democracy to baseball," *Ebony* wrote in a March 1970 editorial. The *Pittsburgh Courier*, one of the nation's most prominent black newspapers, frequently chimed in with praise. "Even if you don't agree with Curt Flood in his fight against organized baseball concerning the reserve clause, his fortitude in fighting for what he believes to be right has to be admired," *Courier* columnist Bill Nunn Jr. wrote. "Flood thus joins a growing list of black athletes who have placed principal [*sic*] above personal gain." Nunn Jr. compared Flood's selflessness to that of Robinson, Ali, Jim Brown, Arthur Ashe, and Bill Russell.

One of Flood's most ardent supporters was *Baltimore Afro-American* columnist Sam Lacy. Along with the *Pittsburgh Courier*'s Wendell Smith, Lacy had led the fight to integrate Major League Baseball and served as one of Jackie Robinson's traveling companions and confidants. Lacy was the social conscience of the black press. From his January 6 column "Cheers for Flood and His Compatriots" until the end of

Flood's lawsuit, Lacy stood in Flood's corner. "Flood's decision last week to challenge organized baseball's reserve clause wins admiration here," Lacy wrote on January 6. "It is high time that someone should be made to say how far baseball can go in its one-way travels."

The most prominent black writer to come to Flood's aid was Bayard Rustin. A longtime adviser to Martin Luther King and leading organizer of the March on Washington in 1963, Rustin was relegated to the fringes of the civil rights movement because of his homosexuality, Communist ties, and steadfast belief in nonviolent social protest. He was a pacifist in a violent age, but he knew courage and possibility when he saw it. He went to Montgomery to help King with his bus boycott, and he stood up for Flood in print. "Flood stands in the tradition of such black athletes as Jackie Robinson and Muhammad Ali who, in addition to achieving great status within their professions, took courageous stands on issues of human rights," Rustin wrote February 17 in the *Philadelphia Tribune*. "For these reasons, Curt Flood deserves our support and our respect."

Dr. Harry Edwards, a black sociologist and a former member of the San Jose State basketball and track teams, had encouraged black athletes to boycott the 1968 Olympics in Mexico City to call attention to the continued struggle for racial equality in America. Edwards recognized Flood's lawsuit, like Tommie Smith's and John Carlos's black-gloved salute at the Olympics, as helping both black and white athletes regain their dignity. "Flood is fighting this master-slave relationship that exists between baseball owners and baseball players . . . ," Edwards wrote in his 1970 book, *The Revolt of the Black Athlete*. "[I]f Flood is successful, he will have pulled off the greatest victory for justice in pro athletics since another black man turned a similar trick in the late 40s when Jackie Robinson entered professional baseball."

Despite the support for Flood in the black press, the alphabet soup of civil rights organizations—the NAACP, SNCC, SCLC, CORE, the Urban League, and the Black Panthers—failed to make the connection between Flood's lawsuit and the freedom struggle. Many of them threw their support behind Ali and his refusal to fight in the Vietnam War. Supporting Ali was understandable given that Vietnam affected the lives of thousands of black soldiers. Ali paid a heavy price. He was stripped of his heavyweight title and did not fight again competitively for 43 months. He was also convicted of evading the draft and risked going to prison. Ali's stand reflected America's growing frustration over the war and launched his career as a legendary international figure. But, as heroic as Ali was, he acted out of self-interest in not wanting to fight in an unjust war. Ali never spoke out for the rights of his fellow boxers.

Flood, by contrast, fought against the system not to enrich himself, but to benefit future generations of ballplayers. Maybe civil rights organizations were overwhelmed by the turmoil of the late 1960s and early 1970s and therefore too busy to stand up for Flood's cause. Maybe they lacked sympathy for a small group of athletes perceived to be spoiled and overpaid, rather than subjugated and oppressed. The reserve clause was not strictly a racial issue. Flood, however, stood up for employee rights that Martin Luther King had fought for at the end of his life. King was murdered after marching with Memphis sanitation workers. King realized that the freedom struggle had grown beyond seats on buses or at lunch counters; it was about economic justice. Flood carried on King's fight for economic freedom, a fight that affected future generations of black athletes. The civil rights organizations, however, failed to see the larger implications of Flood's lawsuit.

Many fans believed what they read in the press about Flood ruining baseball. They wrote angry letters to the promanagement *Sporting News* and to daily newspapers. Most Cardinals fans shared Bob Broeg's outrage and refused to cut Flood any slack for wanting to stay in St. Louis. Soon after Flood's lawsuit became public, Ron Jacober of Channel 5 in St. Louis interviewed Flood on the street outside Flood's Central West End apartment at the Executive House. After Flood referred to himself on the air as a slave, the station received dozens of angry phone calls. Of the hundreds of letters that Flood received at home, he said, 90 percent of them were favorable. But the hate mail seemed to stick out in his mind. "Once you were compared with Willie Mays," one fan wrote. "Now you will be compared with Benedict Arnold."

Flood said at the end of January that the pressure "is making it a little difficult to sleep at night. I'll toss and turn and try to evaluate what I've done. In my mind I'm doing the right thing." He acknowledged having second thoughts. He wanted to play but vowed never to sign another contract with the reserve clause. There was no chance that he was turning back. "I'm not trying to create chaos or end baseball," he told

Jack Herman of the *St. Louis Globe-Democrat*. "I just want to stand up like a human being. I want something we can live with."

The media reaction and the hate mail from the fans did not hurt Flood nearly as much as the criticism from his fellow players. "If I had 600 players behind me," he said later, "there would be no reserve clause."

Boston Red Sox outfielder Carl Yastrzemski led the parade of players who spoke out against Flood's lawsuit. One of the game's highest-paid players, Yastrzemski was fiercely loyal to Red Sox owner Tom Yawkey, who paid him $130,000 a year. Yastrzemski charged that all the players, not just the player representatives, should have voted whether to pay Flood's legal fees. "That backing should never have been given to Flood," Yastrzemski said. "Personally I am against what Curt Flood is trying to do because it would ruin the game." On January 15, Yastrzemski wrote Marvin Miller a two-page letter urging that all major league players be polled about Flood's lawsuit.

Rather than try to stifle dissent within the union, Miller used it as an opportunity to educate the players. On January 22, he sent Yastrzemski's letter to all the Players Association's members accompanied by his own seven-page reply. In his reply, Miller explained that all the players had been questioned about their views on the reserve clause before the current labor negotiations. He also said that the union had only two choices regarding Flood's lawsuit: whether to support him or not. Either way, Flood was going to file a lawsuit that affected the entire union. It was in the union's interest to facilitate the best possible outcome. In exchange for the union's financial backing, Flood agreed to allow the union to select his counsel and to drop his lawsuit if the union negotiated reserve clause modifications.

Miller wrote that before the 1969 season Yastrzemski had tried to undermine the union's pension negotiations, and that Yastrzemski's friend, American League president and former Red Sox general manager Joe Cronin, had tried to force a playerwide vote on an inferior pension proposal in an effort to divide the union. Mets player representative Ed Kranepool was less tactful in calling Yastrzemski Cronin's "yo-yo." Kranepool and other players correctly observed that Yastrzemski was trying to prevent the union from operating as a representative democracy. "If Yastrzemski doesn't like an association supported by 700 players," Kranepool said, "perhaps he should start his own."

Yastrzemski, however, was not alone among superstar players in opposing the union's decision to back Flood. Many of the game's top-salaried players had been brainwashed by their owners that Flood's lawsuit would ruin the game. Harmon Killebrew, who was in line to become the Minnesota Twins' first $100,000 ballplayer, also called for a player-wide poll. "As far as I'm concerned, the reserve clause is something all of us knew about when we came into baseball . . . ," he said. "Without control, there would be no baseball." Washington Senators slugger Frank Howard agreed with Killebrew: "I can't speak for Curt Flood, but if he believes in what he's doing, God bless him. I don't agree with him. The reserve clause is the foundation of the game. It protects the clubs' investment in a player." A few months later, Howard signed with the Senators for a team-high $125,000.

Part of the negative reaction among baseball's star players stemmed not from self-interest but from ignorance. Howard said he did not agree with Flood's lawsuit, yet in the next breath volunteered that the reserve clause should be modified. Years later, Howard admitted he had no understanding of the reserve clause or the issues behind Flood's lawsuit. Yastrzemski also confessed that his loyalty to Tom Yawkey clouded his judgment about the reserve clause. "We played for a great owner," Yastrzemski said. "The players on the Red Sox didn't understand the conditions on the other teams."

Many retired superstars from the 1950s and early 1960s opposed Flood's lawsuit. Ted Williams described Flood as "ill-advised" and "wrong." Joe DiMaggio, who had endured the wrath of the media and the fans for holding out several times during his career, said the reserve clause did not hurt the players. Only the highest-paid players, he said, would benefit from a change. Ralph Kiner, who had helped form an earlier version of the Players Association in 1954, echoed the management line that any change to the reserve clause would cause the weaker teams to go out of business. Robin Roberts, who along with Jim Bunning had been instrumental in hiring Miller, said: "Curt's doing the wrong thing." Bob Feller, who had feuded with Jackie Robinson about the lack of minority hiring in baseball management during baseball's 1969 centennial celebration, took aim at Flood: "Flood is just a crusader. Baseball hasn't hurt him. He's selling his paintings for $1,000 each, so what does he care." Mets manager Gil Hodges could not look past Flood's salary: "It's hard for me to sympathize with any individual making $90,000 a year. That's a lot more than I make, and I can't understand why he's doing what he is. My own personal opinion is that the reserve clause is good the way it is. It's been good to me for over 20 years in baseball." Former players usually resist changes to the system because they tend to think that the game was better in their day and that modern players are spoiled and lazy.

But even Flood's contemporaries, many of whom could have benefited from a loosening of the reserve clause, reacted to his lawsuit with either skepticism or contempt. San Francisco Giants pitcher Gaylord Perry blasted the player representatives, even though one of them was his brother, Jim: "How these two-dozen player reps ever voted unanimously in support of something the majority of the players weren't even asked about is a mystery." Chicago Cubs third baseman Ron Santo said Flood's lawsuit reminded him of another "Ken Harrelson deal." Even Harrelson, who had landed a $75,000 salary and $25,000 for promotional work in 1969 by threatening to retire after being traded to the Indians, said Flood was "making a mistake. . . . This is biting the hand that feeds you."

Black superstars also refused to come to Flood's aid. Many of them felt the same loyalty to their owners as the white superstars and bought into the current system. A climate of fear also prevented minority ballplayers from speaking out. They had fought hard for their places in the game. Many of them, like Flood, had come up through the southern minor leagues. Some had even spent time in the Negro leagues. They did not want their professional success ripped away from them because of newspaper comments supporting baseball's number one persona non grata.

Hank Aaron sided with the Yastrzemski-Killebrew position that players were "left out in the cold" and "should have been consulted." Soon after those comments, he signed a two-year, $250,000 contract. Aaron had not yet endured the torrent of racist hate mail and abuse as he chased Babe Ruth's career home run record in 1974. After that record-breaking season, he was traded to the Milwaukee Brewers. He later went to work in the Atlanta Braves' front office.

Willie Mays refused to take a position. "If Curt is doing something he thinks is right, I think he should do it," Mays said. "I haven't really studied it too much. I don't know all the arguments that are going on and I'm not going to get involved." Two years earlier, Jackie Robinson had blasted Mays for not speaking out about racial issues and called him a "do-nothing Negro." With his salary approaching $150,000, Mays was the highest-paid player in baseball. Two years later, he was traded to the Mets.

Ernie Banks waffled: "I can understand his side. . . . I certainly want to see him back." The *Chicago Tribune*, however, reported: "Willie Mays, Ernie Banks, and Henry Aaron have indicated—ever so lightly—that they are not in complete sympathy with an attempt to destroy the reserve clause."

Cubs outfielder Billy Williams also straddled the fence. "If he wins the case, he made the right decision. If he doesn't, it was wrong," Williams said. "I hope they don't think our association is going to pay his salary if he doesn't play, tho[ugh]."

Frank Robinson, Jackie Robinson believed, was too fixated on becoming baseball's first black manager to speak out on racial and social issues. "To me, your personal desire hurts the cause of your people," Jackie wrote Frank in May 1970, "but if that's your bag, so be it." Frank, like most black players, remained silent about his former high school teammate's lawsuit.

It is not surprising that these five black future Hall of Famers failed to support Flood. At the time of Flood's lawsuit, none of them spoke out on racial or social issues. All of them, except Frank Robinson, had grown up in the South. Aaron, Banks, and Mays had played in the Negro leagues. Williams and Frank Robinson had started in the minors straight out of high school. They succeeded by obeying the system. They were not boat rockers. They feared retribution from the owners and did not want to jeopardize their salaries, their playing careers, and their futures in the game.

Athletes in other sports, however, spoke out in favor of Flood's lawsuit. National Basketball Association (NBA) contracts included the same renewal provision as in baseball, but basketball players could jump to the rival American Basketball Association. Oscar Robertson, a black superstar guard, had spoken out about the reserve clause as early as 1966 and had negotiated a contract with the NBA's Cincinnati Royals allowing him to veto any trade. In late January 1970, he rejected a trade to the

Baltimore Bullets before accepting a trade to the Milwaukee Bucks a few months later. The president of the NBA Players Association, Robertson understood the ramifications of Flood's fight against the reserve clause. "We hope he makes it illegal," he said. "I'm certainly behind him." Chicago Bulls forward Chet Walker agreed: "It's going to affect all sports. I'm definitely behind him. . . . That's a lot of hogwash about it destroying baseball." Hockey players, who were also subject to a reserve system, expressed similar support for Flood's lawsuit through NHL Players Association president Red Berenson of the St. Louis Blues.

Flood soon found out who his real friends were in baseball. Privately, his best friend, Bob Gibson, told him: "You're crazy." Gibson let Flood know that he supported him but planned on standing "a few hundred paces" behind him to avoid any fallout. Publicly, Gibson could not remain silent as others took potshots at his old roommate and the lawsuit. "Guys who come out against it see themselves as having futures in baseball management," Gibson said. "How many black guys you know are going to make it in baseball management?" Gibson admired the selflessness of Flood's actions: "If he succeeds it won't benefit him nearly as much as it will most of the other players."

Vada Pinson publicly supported his childhood friend and former teammate. Flood and Pinson were reunited on the 1969 Cardinals. It rekindled their friendship, which had begun in West Oakland. Professionally, it was an unhappy season for both men. Flood slumped and was traded to Philadelphia. Pinson played most of the season on a broken leg and was traded after the season to Cleveland. Pinson was so incensed about the trade that he considered joining Flood's lawsuit. "Something had to be done and Curt is doing it," Pinson said. "Curt's doing it for all of us. But it's too bad all the players don't dig what he's doing." Pinson knew that Flood was not backing down. "Flood is going to go through with it all the way in my opinion," he said. "He's convinced the reserve clause is a bad one and he'll fight it to the end, regardless of what happens to him. That's just the way it is."

Pitcher Jim "Mudcat" Grant grew close to Flood after being traded to the Cardinals midway through the 1969 season. Flood invited Grant to live at his apartment and refused to accept any rent money. Grant learned a lot about Flood's values. "You have to understand Curt,"

Grant said. "He was raised by a couple who were highly principled. His upbringing has affected his whole life. Money always has been secondary to him."

Dick Allen, the player the Phillies traded for Flood, publicly supported him. Allen, who eventually agreed to a $90,000 contract with the Cardinals, admired Flood's guts for turning down the same salary. "Curt Flood, my hat's off to him. I think he's all man, that 160 pounds," Allen said. "Would you have done it at that price? Would you walk away from $90,000? Maybe my kids will benefit from what he's doing, maybe yours will." Allen's Cardinals teammate Lou Brock also backed Flood. "If you want to know where I stand," Brock told *Jet*, "I am prepared to go as far as backing the suit financially."

One former player and labor pioneer applauded Flood—Sandy Koufax. Before the 1966 season, Koufax and fellow Dodgers ace Don Drysdale had hired an agent (a taboo at the time), demanded a combined salary of $1 million over three years, and staged a preseason double holdout. After much public criticism, they had secured one-year deals for $125,000 and $110,000, respectively. Koufax, who retired after that season because of chronic arm problems and became a television announcer, admired Flood's fortitude. "I have to give Curt the greatest amount of credit for believing in what he's doing," Koufax said. "At the salary he's making that's the kind of money which he's never going to get back."

Union representatives expressed cautious support for Flood in anticipation of the backlash from their fellow players. Joe Torre told the press the same things he had told the player representatives in Puerto Rico. "We just feel it is our duty to back him," Torre said. "Being that the reserve clause is one of the points on the table right now, it is only right for us to back what we believe."

"We're not interested in helping Curt Flood make more money," New York Yankees player representative Steve Hamilton said. "We're interested in modifying the reserve clause."

"I think he's right," Brooks Robinson, the Baltimore Orioles' player representative, said a few weeks later. "The way I feel—and a lot of other guys feel the same way, too—the reserve clause could be loosened."

Cardinals player representative Dal Maxvill also explained to the press the union's decision to support Flood.

Several fringe players understood Flood's freedom fight. Gene

Michael, who had spent seven years behind shortstop Dick Groat and others in the Pirates organization, said: "Maybe I would have had a little more time in the majors if I could have sold my services to another club." Orioles pitcher Pete Richert, stuck behind three 20-game winners, declared, "[a]s far as I'm concerned, I think Curt Flood deserves a lot of praise. He has guts. I don't know if I would give up a good salary for a principle. I'm behind him."

Other fringe players, however, failed to understand how Flood's lawsuit affected them. They could not relate to a star player walking away from his big salary. "I'd play in Alaska for $90,000 a year," Atlanta Braves reserve infielder Bob Aspromonte said. Braves pitcher Pat Jarvis agreed: "I can't understand how Curt Flood can make $90,000 and turn it down. That's a lot of money—even if you do play in Philadelphia." Jarvis said Flood was "the wrong guy" and "a player making about $15,000 a year" would have made a better test case. No one else, however, was willing to put his career on the line.

The player reps tried to educate their fellow players and even their managers. Montreal Expos player rep Ron Brand discussed Flood's lawsuit with his manager, Gene Mauch. "I remember Gene Mauch, who I loved, was so angry at Curt Flood, because baseball was sacred to him," Brand recalled. "I tried to explain it to him: 'He's going to give up his career to do this. He's just looking for a rule to be changed.' [Mauch] didn't have much of an open mind about it."

Management was not shy about bashing Flood. Braves vice president Paul Richards welcomed Flood's lawsuit. He compared players getting rid of the reserve clause to "the Pope burning down the Vatican." "If they wipe it out, you'll see a march on Washington by baseball players trying to get legislation to get it back," he said. Richards explained that star players would be worse off because under the current system salaries could be reduced by no more than 20 percent per season. Dodgers owner Walter O'Malley said the elimination of the reserve clause would favor his franchise because players would clamor to play in Los Angeles. "Realistically," O'Malley said, "there would be such imbalance that the game couldn't exist."

The angriest cries came from Cardinals owner Gussie Busch. Flood's lawsuit was the least of his problems heading into the 1970 season. His team could not come to terms with Dick Allen or pitcher Steve

Carlton. With both players still unsigned in March, the Cardinals exercised their right under the reserve clause to renew their contracts automatically and demanded that the players report to spring training. Allen, whose demands ranged from $125,000 to $150,000, signed on March 12 for $90,000. Carlton, who had rejected a raise from $24,000 to $30,000, refused to budge after lowering his demands from $50,000 to $40,000. He reported to camp without a contract and on March 16 signed a two-year deal for $80,000. Carlton's holdout sent Busch over the edge:

"Instead of a sport, baseball has become a headache. I can't understand the Curt Flood case and I can't understand the Allen case.

"Baseball is in a helluva turmoil. I think one of us has to take a stand for the good of the game. I hate to be a sucker, but I'm perfectly willing to do it.

"I can't understand what's happening to our country. My hope is some other owners will have the guts to do what I'm doing—help the people reverse this thing and get them to some degree of normalcy."

Busch ordered general manager Bing Devine to trade Carlton after the 1971 season, the first of several trades that set the Cardinals back for more than a decade.

Busch's tirade may have encouraged Cardinals assistant general manager Jim Toomey to kick Flood on his way out of the organization. "We're much better off in center field this year than we were last year," Toomey boasted before the season. Indeed, the new Cardinals center fielder, Jose Cardenal (.293, 10 home runs, 74 RBIs), played well in 1970. Toomey may have been currying favor with management, but he did not win any friends in the clubhouse by ripping Flood. "How good was he?" Toomey asked. "If he was *that* good, do you think we'd have gotten rid of him?"

The most hurtful charge leveled at Flood was that he was Miller's puppet. Both reporters and management portrayed Miller as a Svengali who had seduced Flood into suing baseball. "I can only believe that Curt Flood's taking baseball to court is an idea prompted by Marvin Miller," Phillies general manager John Quinn said. "I'm certain that Miller psyched Flood," former Cardinals general manager Frank Lane said. "He has psyched everyone else." The deepest cut of all came from the man who had made Flood's major league career possible, his old American Legion coach, George Powles. "I think Curt is being used," Powles said. "I believe Marvin Miller, the players' union representative, put the whole idea in Flood's head." Such comments were meant to distance Flood from a lawsuit that these men believed could ruin baseball and ruin Flood's career. But they implied that Flood was not smart enough to come up with the idea. They denied his vision, intelligence, and creativity. They suggested that a black man with only a high school education could not have done this. They underestimated him.

CHAPTER EIGHT

The February 3 preliminary injunction hearing was Flood's last chance of playing baseball in 1970. Only an injunction could block his trade to Philadelphia, thus keeping him in a Cardinals uniform or making him a free agent. Otherwise he remained the property of the Phillies and planned on sitting out the season.

For Flood's legal team, the hearing was a formality. None of his lawyers expected to win. Requesting an injunction was simply a way to get Flood's case before a federal trial judge as quickly as possible. The question was which judge. Judge Bonsal was only the motions judge. Another judge would be randomly assigned to the injunction hearing and probably preside over the trial. Jay Topkis hoped for anyone but the judge who was assigned to the injunction hearing—Irving Ben Cooper.

In 1962, former U.S. attorney general Herbert Brownell, several past and future presidents of the American Bar Association (ABA), and numerous lawyers testified against Cooper's nomination to the federal bench. The ABA found Cooper "not qualified." The president of the Association of the Bar of the City of New York testified that Cooper had been "emotionally unstable for a number of years." As a state criminal court judge, Cooper was famous for his temper tantrums on and off the bench. He berated and humiliated lawyers so frequently that they called it being "Cooperized." In April 1955, he accused a New York City bus driver of trying to run him over as he rode his bicycle on Riverside Drive, twice called the bus driver "a son of a bitch," and engaged him in a shoving match on the sidewalk. A few days later, Cooper ordered the driver to appear in his courtroom and then refused to accept "an apology from any scum like that." In January 1960, when Cooper resigned as the chief justice of the court of special sessions, he cited "personal wear and tear" and "constant anxiety, irritation and strain."

The son of a British tailor, Cooper came to the United States at age nine. He grew up in New York City and Missouri and worked his way through the University of Missouri and law school at Washington University in St. Louis. He made his name in New York City as a government lawyer investigating ambulance-chasing lawyers, dirty doctors, and Jimmy Walker's corrupt mayoral administration. Mayor Fiorello H. La Guardia appointed Cooper a city magistrate in 1938 and a year later made him an associate justice on the court of special sessions, the city's criminal court. Cooper later became chief justice of the special sessions court and, according to one Legal Aid lawyer, behaved "like a baby in a high chair." He called her "a crummy little lawyer from the crummy little Legal Aid Society." Cooper sometimes held special evening sessions so that he could show off for dignitaries while sentencing juvenile defendants, once telling a group of defendants, "You are all punks." The lawyers at the criminal court referred to him as "Bellevue Ben." One of his former judicial colleagues testified that he had "a persecution complex."

President Kennedy, looking for a Democrat with bipartisan support, nominated the 60-year-old Cooper to be a federal trial judge at the behest of Representative Emanuel Celler (D-NY). Cooper was the most controversial of Kennedy's first 102 judicial nominees and the first to be challenged by the Senate. Kennedy sought to ensure Cooper's eventual confirmation by putting him on the bench as a recess appointment. Cooper managed to behave himself during his trial run on the federal bench, and both Republican senators from New York eventually supported his nomination. Six months, numerous appearances before the Senate Judiciary Committee, and 399 hearing transcript pages later, Cooper was confirmed. The only way to get rid of Cooper, a life-tenured federal judge, was impeachment.

Cooper spent the remainder of his judicial career trying to prove that he deserved his position. He struggled to keep his Dr. Jekyll/Mr. Hyde personality in check. He terrorized his law clerks and litigants. In 1969, Alan Dershowitz appeared in Cooper's courtroom and incurred his wrath. Cooper called Dershowitz into his chambers and for no apparent reason "screamed at me the way no judge has ever done." Cooper usually kept his temper in check during high-profile cases. The *Flood* case was the biggest to date of Cooper's career and thus the ultimate opportunity for Cooper to prove himself.

Cooper was the worst combination for Flood—a baseball fan and a publicity hound. Although he would not be able to damage Flood's lawsuit at the preliminary injunction stage, Cooper could prevent Flood's lawyers from developing a good factual record as the case made its way to the Supreme Court. Topkis and his Paul, Weiss colleagues did have one thing going for them: The firm's lead partner, former federal judge Simon Rifkind, had chosen to testify before the Senate Judiciary Committee in favor of Cooper's nomination. Rifkind's partners had disagreed with his decision at the time but benefited from it when Cooper drew Flood's case. Cooper reportedly kept a list in his desk of the lawyers who had testified against him at his confirmation hearings.

The owners' lawyers expressed their own disappointment in landing Cooper. "We got the madman," one of them said. But they, too, had a trump card. Compared with Flood's trial team of seven lawyers (five at Paul, Weiss, plus Moss and Zerman), Kuhn and the owners had hired a litigation army. Two law firms, Arnold & Porter in Washington and Donovan, Leisure in New York, represented Kuhn. Paul Porter led a team of six lawyers for the commissioner. Baker & Hostetler, led by Sandy Hadden, represented the American League teams and added three lawyers to the owners' brief. Willkie Farr, including Lou Carroll and Lou Hoynes, represented the National League teams and added six lawyers. Each team also had its own general counsel keeping tabs on the litigation.

The owners' ace in the hole was their lead lawyer, Willkie Farr's Mark F. Hughes. Hughes knew baseball and antitrust law, having represented the New York Giants in the *Gardella* case. More important, he also knew Judge Cooper. Hughes was former president of the New York County Lawyers Association (NYCLA). NYCLA was divided over Cooper's nomination and, unlike the ABA and the New York City bar association, refused to send anyone to the Senate Judiciary Committee to testify against him. During his own testimony, Cooper pointed out NYCLA's absence to the committee. The vice chairman and then chairman of NYCLA's judiciary committee during Cooper's nomination fight was Mark Hughes.

On the morning of February 3, lawyers from both sides as well as the press gathered in Cooper's courtroom, room 1505 in the federal courthouse at Foley Square, for Flood's preliminary injunction hearing. Neither Flood nor Kuhn was there. Flood's lawyers sought a preliminary injunction that would make Flood a free agent during his lawsuit, thus allowing any major league team to sign him. They had a high bar to clear—they had to show that Flood would be "irreparably harmed" by not being a free agent and that he had a high degree of likelihood of winning his case at trial. That was a tough argument with two Supreme Court precedents in his way.

In requesting an injunction, Arthur Goldberg made three key points: (1) Judge Cooper was not bound by *Federal Baseball* and *Toolson* because subsequent factors, such as radio and television revenues, plainly made baseball interstate commerce; (2) the reserve clause was illegal; and (3) the trade prevented Flood from playing for the team of his choice and was a form of slavery. "The fact that he is a high priced player is completely irrelevant," Goldberg said. "In the times of the Romans there were very high priced slaves who were counselors to emperors and to generals who had access to kings' treasury. Price has nothing to do with it. The basic concept is the morality of the situation and the legality of the situation."

Goldberg concluded by making a "counteroffer" to declaring Flood a free agent: Cooper could allow Flood to continue to play for the Cardinals under his old contract or with no contract at all until the case was resolved. Players were due to report to spring training in 22 days.

Cooper took every opportunity to ham it up for the press. After Goldberg's 40-minute argument, Cooper said: "The Court announces a seventh-inning stretch."

When the hearing resumed, Hughes countered that Flood had shown no chance of winning at trial and no irreparable injury. An injunction, Hughes said, would disturb rather than preserve the status quo. He also said that Goldberg was basically asking the court to ignore a binding Supreme Court decision in *Toolson*.

Hughes attacked Goldberg's slavery argument by drawing attention to Flood's salary: "It is very difficult to come to any conclusion that he is a slave. He is certainly making more money than most professional people. He is making more money than most well-paid executives. He is making more money than any judge I know or any writer or any poet or any other occupation you choose to name. It is his choice, your Honor, either to stay within the framework, the reasonable framework of the reserve system, or not to play."

Hughes also exposed weaknesses in Flood's contention that his "business may fail if I am forced to leave St. Louis." Flood had opened two photographic studios and a portrait studio in St. Louis. Hughes said that Flood's request to negotiate with other teams conflicted with his argument that he needed to stay in St. Louis to support his "fledgling business." Hughes also read a January 18 *St. Louis Post-Dispatch* advertisement for Curt Flood Studios, Inc., listing its headquarters as Lincolnwood, Illinois, a Chicago suburb. Hughes and the owners never pursued Flood's photography or portrait business any further. If they had, they might have uncovered the secret behind Flood's portraits.

Hughes concluded his argument by taking the sky-is-falling approach. He claimed that "if this system as it now exists and has worked through the years is destroyed, your ball players coming up won't have any leagues to play in."

Porter briefly added that the commissioner took no position in the dispute, but that the way to modify the reserve clause was through labor negotiation.

In rebuttal, Goldberg argued that the status quo was keeping Flood in St. Louis.

Judge Cooper declined to decide on the spot whether to grant the injunction. Instead, he gave both sides 20 days to file any additional briefs. Cooper, however, could not resist showing the press that he was a great baseball fan. "You have thrown the ball to me," he said. "I hope I don't muff it."

He concluded the hearing by comparing his job to that of an umpire: "You do not ask that he shall never make a mistake or always agree with you or always support the home team. You want an umpire who calls them as he sees them. That, I promise you, I shall do."

Flood was not amused by Judge Cooper's comments. Nothing amused Flood these days. There had been an unreality to the first few months of his decision to quit the game and sue baseball. Aside from the added media and fan attention, November, December, and January had seemed like any other offseason. But by February's preliminary injunction hearing, the reality had begun to sink in that for the first time in 13 years he was not going to spring training with the St. Louis Cardinals. As part of his ongoing effort to undermine public support for Flood, Dick Young reported that the Phillies had increased their offer to $105,000 and that Flood was "having second thoughts about his slave-status." Flood's only thoughts were of not playing baseball in 1970 and of despair.

Flood's world came crashing down. He had put his portrait sales on hold. His photography business was on the rocks. So was his relationship with Claire, the woman he had met in Denmark. His chances of opening a bar in Copenhagen crumbled along with it. Flood went from not being able to sleep at night to not being able to keep food down. The tension also took its toll on his good friend Marian Jorgensen, whose nose began to bleed so badly that she had to be hospitalized. Flood cried over how his lawsuit had affected both of their lives.

Needing money and a new challenge, Flood embarked on a career as an author. He collaborated on an article for *Sport* magazine's March 1970 issue titled "Why I Am Challenging Baseball." He also began working on a book, thanks to a phone call from an old Sally League adversary, Dave Oliphant. Oliphant had pitched against Flood as a member of the Macon Dodgers. Originally signed by the Yankees for $3,000, Oliphant, a Jew, experienced so much anti-Semitism from his minor league manager that his father purchased his contract for $2,000. The Yankees gave Oliphant's family $1,000 back after he hooked on with the pitching-rich Dodgers. Oliphant never made the major leagues, but the unfairness of the reserve clause stuck with him as a Connecticut businessman. The president of a small publishing company and a consultant for Simon & Schuster, Oliphant set Flood up with Herbert Alexander, an editor at Simon & Schuster's Trident Press.

Alexander found Flood a collaborator in Richard Carter. The author of several nonfiction books about science and medicine, Carter also wrote books about handicapping horses under the pseudonym Tom Ainslie. To disassociate them from gambling, Carter wrote under his given name with Flood. In late February, Carter arrived in St. Louis and stayed at the Holiday Inn on the publisher's dime. After a few weeks, Alexander became alarmed because he could not reach Carter. Flood's collaborator had neglected the book and immersed himself in the ballplayer's lifestyle of drinking and partying, spending his nights at Flood's favorite hangout, the Playboy Club in St. Louis. In mid-March, Alexander ordered Oliphant to pay Carter and Flood a surprise visit. "I read them the riot act," Oliphant recalled.

"The book's gone," he told Flood. "You will have to return the money."

He was even harsher with Carter, accusing him of acting like a drunk.

That same afternoon, Flood pulled two baseball gloves out of the trunk of his car. He and Oliphant played catch in the parking lot of Flood's apartment building, the Executive House. Flood's mood lightened. Later that afternoon, he and Oliphant put on an impromptu Ping-Pong exhibition at a nearby recreation center. For three hours, Flood was like a different person—upbeat and sober. Without baseball, drinking had come to dominate Flood's life. He no longer had an incentive to remain sober each day. "Curt was addicted to alcohol," Oliphant said. "There's nothing new that I can tell you about that. It was his demon."

Flood and Carter promised to change their ways and get to work on the book. After Oliphant returned home to Connecticut, they finished most of the book in about 30 days. "I really thought Curt was getting it turned around," Oliphant said. The drinking, however, resumed. And the bad news kept coming.

Judge Cooper's inevitable decision came down March 4, denying Flood's request for a preliminary injunction. Cooper issued a scholarly 55-page decision replete with 71 footnotes. He wrote about every facet of the case and, despite only denying the request for an injunction, indicated how he was likely to decide a possible trial. Cooper's order made no secret of his love of the game:

> Baseball's status in the life of the nation is so pervasive that it would not strain credulity to say the Court can take judicial notice that baseball is everybody's business. To put it mildly and with restraint, it would be unfortunate indeed if a fine sport and profession, which brings surcease from daily travail and an escape from the ordinary to most inhabitants of this land, were to suffer in the least because of undue concentration by any one or any group on

commercial or profit considerations. The game is on higher ground; it behooves every one to keep it there.

Cooper was not likely to find that baseball no longer deserved its antitrust exemption. Nor did anyone expect him to make such a ruling. Only the Supreme Court could reverse its own precedents. Cooper's overriding concern seemed to be the legality of the reserve clause. In concluding his opinion, he acknowledged that "[f]or years professional ballplayers have chafed under the restrictions of baseball's reserve system. . . . Many of their grievances appear justified." Cooper said that the only way to resolve them was through a "full trial." Nine days after the March 4 order, the chief judge of the district court permanently assigned the case to Cooper.

The day of Cooper's decision, Flood released a statement announcing what he had known all along—he would not be playing baseball in 1970. Flood called Zerman, who lay in bed with the flu and a 102-degree temperature, and Zerman drafted and released a two-paragraph statement. "The failure to obtain a restraining order means I've lost my one chance to play ball this year," Flood's statement said. "I can only hope that after a full hearing on the merits that my position will have been vindicated and that my career will not have been ended by the time lost pursuing what I believe to be right."

Flood told Jorgensen to put off numerous interview requests. The last thing he wanted to do was talk to the press. He told Carter that he did not want to lie to reporters that his photography business was booming (it wasn't), that he was painting portraits (he certainly wasn't), or that he could live without baseball (he couldn't). Four days earlier, the St. Louis Cardinals' position players had reported to spring training. Flood's body—except for that brief afternoon playing catch with Oliphant—was going through baseball withdrawal. "I'm a baseball player and I'm supposed to play out my string," Flood told Carter that day. "I'm supposed to be in Florida now, romping around and hitting the ball and cussing with Gibson and banging the chicks."

Flood confronted the reality that his baseball career was over. He decided to make his conclusions public by instructing Jorgensen to arrange a press conference on the afternoon of March 5 at Zerman's Clayton,

Missouri, law office. That morning Flood took Claire to the airport for her noon flight back to Denmark. It was a permanent farewell. Flood drowned his sorrows at the airport bar and hid his pain behind a pair of big, dark sunglasses. At the press conference, he wore a double-breasted black sport jacket, light purple shirt, and plaid trousers. Before the assembled reporters, he removed his sunglasses and then exposed his soul. "It's my life, and I'm on pins and needles," he said.

Flood shared his belief that Cooper's order meant the end of his baseball career. "Let's face it, I'm 32 now and if the case does drag on for two years, I'd be 34. It would be difficult to come back. And besides, I don't think I'll get the opportunity to play again. As big as it is, baseball is a closely knit unit. I doubt that even one of the 24 men controlling the game would touch me with a 10-foot pole. You can't buck the Establishment."

Flood said the Phillies had offered him a salary "very close" to $100,000 but he had turned it down. "I'm not a millionaire but I'm not that bad off, either," he said. "Sure, it's tough to turn your back on $90,000 or $100,000 a year, but the reserve clause is not democratic and I intend to continue my fight." He denied rumors that he was being compensated by the Players Association. He mentioned his new book contract with Simon & Schuster as proof that he would not starve. He tried to place Judge Cooper's decision the previous day in perspective. "It's just the first step in a long battle," he said. "I do not intend to give up. People literally died for a cause such as mine, and I feel as strong as ever about my rights."

Flood felt better after getting all that off his chest. His appetite returned. He found peace of mind with the idea of not playing baseball and turned his attention to the action in the courtroom.

The day after Judge Cooper's decision, Mr. Justice Goldberg delivered an unexpected blow to Flood's lawsuit. Goldberg gave a speech at Columbia University designed to revive his candidacy for governor. He had been meeting with New York politicians since February about a possible gubernatorial run while continuing to deny publicly any interest in electoral politics. Several former aides were trying to talk him into the race. Before Goldberg's speech at Columbia, the *New York Times* ran a front-page story saying he was using it to test the political waters.

New York politics at that time was dominated by four parties: Conservative, Republican, Democratic, and Liberal. Liberals blasted Goldberg for his role in promulgating Johnson's Vietnam War policy as UN ambassador. Despite Goldberg's behind-the-scenes efforts to end the conflict, *New York Post* columnist Pete Hamill wrote that Goldberg should be tried as a war criminal. But the polls still showed that Goldberg held a sizable lead over incumbent Nelson Rockefeller. Goldberg went to Columbia, the heart of the antiwar student movement, to test out his message before 400 students and 17 radio and television stations. "I don't want to contribute to the polarization of liberal forces in this country," he told a student who asked about his possible candidacy. Goldberg talked about the Black Panthers and criticized the contempt convictions of the "Chicago Seven" by Judge Julius Hoffman. He attacked Governor Rockefeller but again denied any interest in being a candidate. "How can you revive a non-candidacy?" he asked.

In an interview at his office the day after his Columbia speech, Goldberg pointed to another reason why he was not running. "Meanwhile, goddamnit, I have to take care of Curt Flood!" he told the *Village Voice*. "We'll be asking for an immediate trial—he *ought* to proceed at once. So *that's* where I'll be *next* week in New York!" At least one newspaper columnist suggested that the *Flood* case would propel Goldberg toward the 1972 Democratic presidential nomination. But Goldberg took on the *Flood* case—just as he had appealed William Sloane Coffin's draft conspiracy conviction, fought for the Alaskan Indians, and co-chaired the Black Panther commission—because of his profound belief in social justice, not for political gain.

On March 19, Goldberg made it official: He was running for governor. He had allowed the New York politicians to seduce him into believing that he would be handed the Democratic gubernatorial nomination and easily defeat Rockefeller in November. His ego and ambition once again clouded sound personal judgment. He had also broken his promise to his friend Marvin Miller about not running for office.

Miller called Goldberg on March 19 and 20 from Sarasota, Florida. Miller was on his annual tour of spring training camps updating players about the labor negotiations, Flood's lawsuit, and other union matters. He did not have the heart to criticize Goldberg for sacrificing his commitment to Flood's case. Nor would it have done any good. He wanted to discuss the legal team's next move.

Goldberg still planned on taking an active role in Flood's lawsuit but turned over the day-to-day management of the case to his partner, Jay Topkis. Topkis had played a major role in Goldberg's other important cases. When Coffin hired Goldberg to appeal his draft conspiracy conviction, Goldberg told him: "Topkis will do all the work. He's as good as I am."

At this stage in their legal careers, Topkis was better. He was an antitrust expert, one of the firm's best brief writers, and quick on his feet. Feared by associates and respected by opposing counsel, he was one of the few partners who called Goldberg "Arthur." Goldberg's decision to run for governor delighted Topkis. It meant that he would get to try the bulk of Flood's case without Goldberg looking over his shoulder.

For Topkis, Flood's case was personal. As a Yale law student in 1949, he wrote an essay for Professor Fred Rodell's expository legal writing class about the *Gardella* case. Rodell sent Topkis's essay to Red Smith, who liked it so much that he ran part of it as one of his columns in the *New York Herald Tribune*. For Topkis, who had grown up in New York City reading Smith in the *Herald Tribune*, it was a dream come true. Rodell also recommended Topkis for a postgraduate clerkship with the most outspoken voice in *Gardella*, Judge Jerome Frank. While clerking for Frank, Topkis arranged a lunch with Smith and the judge. Topkis also turned his essay into an article for the *Yale Law Journal*, titled "Monopoly in Professional Sports," which called for an end to baseball's antitrust exemption. Flood's case gave Topkis the chance to vindicate his judge's *Gardella* opinion, his literary idol's columns, and his own belief that Justice Holmes had gotten it wrong in *Federal Baseball*.

Before handing over the reins to Topkis, Goldberg won a critical victory. At a March 24 closed hearing in his chambers, Cooper announced to lawyers from both sides that he was inclined to grant an early trial. Goldberg said all the right things to make it happen, reminding Cooper what was at stake. "It is of great importance to the industry and of great importance to this man," Goldberg said. "The season is starting April 6th. He is not playing ball." Goldberg agreed not to file written responses to any of the owners' motions and not to slow the process by disputing any of the case's essential facts. "We are ready to go to trial," Goldberg said. "We will take one day. I might as well tell you that. Or perhaps part of a day. We do not intend to encumber this record with non-essential matters."

The owners' lawyers, led by Lou Carroll and Paul Porter, said anything to avoid any trial at all, much less an early one. Carroll said the Phillies wanted to speak with Flood about joining their team.

"Mr. Flood will not play for Philadelphia, whether I advised him or not," Goldberg replied. He gave the Phillies permission to contact Flood. "But I can tell you what his answer will be: His answer will be no."

Paul Porter added: "Because speaking for the Commissioner, and I think everybody in baseball, they would like to have this boy back in baseball where he belongs."

Goldberg corrected Porter's insulting characterization of the 32-year-old Flood: "Flood is a mature man. He knows his mind. He made it up before he came to see me. I interrogated him at length as to the consequences and difficulties about litigation, possible duration, all of these I went through. He is not uninformed. I saw to it that he was informed in this issue. He knows precisely what he is doing and the evidence of that will be apparent when this proposal is renewed. He submitted another offer, which was to play in St. Louis without prejudice."

Carroll reminded Cooper that preparing for a trial was not as simple for the owners as it was for Flood. After a brief off-the-record discussion, the lawyers agreed to reconvene at Cooper's chambers on March 31 to discuss potential trial dates.

Cooper's decision to have an early trial was astounding. He agreed that there was no dispute about the facts of Flood's case and therefore skipped almost all of the pretrial fact-finding process known as discovery. In a modern civil action, discovery could take weeks, months, or even years. Cooper, however, saw no need for the production of a massive collection of documents. Nor did he allow the pretrial interrogation of potential witnesses known as depositions. One reason may have been that document productions and depositions take place largely outside the purview of the judge. Cooper was determined to remain at center stage.

A week later in Cooper's chambers, the owners argued that Cooper had no choice but to dismiss the case because of baseball's antitrust immunity per *Toolson*. Mark Hughes pressed Cooper to rule on the motion to dismiss Flood's lawsuit. Cooper refused to decide the motion, because that way he could ensure that the case would go to trial. If he granted the motion, the case would be dismissed. If he denied the motion, he probably would have been reversed on appeal because of *Federal Baseball* and *Toolson*.

The question returned not to if there would be a trial, but when. The owners wanted to push it back to September. But, realizing that Cooper would not go along with that, they argued for no sooner than early June. They predicted that the defendants' case could take two weeks. Paul Porter wondered, if Flood was not willing to play this season, "what the rush is on this." Lou Carroll put it even more harshly: "Mr. Flood has waited fourteen years to assert a principle, which, if accepted, would destroy a structure that has existed for over a hundred years."

Goldberg wanted to begin the trial immediately. "The rush is a simple rush," he said. "The rights of an individual are at stake. With due respect, the rights of that individual are as important to me as the rights of twenty-four club owners. . . . Our posture is simple: It is an illegal transfer. He will not submit to illegality. He has a right to take that posture. He may have to pay a heavy price for it. I think he is being made to pay a heavy price by protracted litigation."

As he so often did in these pretrial conferences, Goldberg injected his personal experiences on the Supreme Court and as a candidate for governor into the discussion. In doing so, he reiterated his commitment to litigating Flood's case: "I was told by my political managers that I ought to be in Grossinger's, shaking hands with adversaries. I am not there. I represent a client, and that takes priority over everything, and I have an engagement with a Judge. They will have to get along without me, whatever the consequences are. Now, we want an early trial, and by an early trial we mean an early trial."

The next day at Grossinger's, a Catskills resort, Goldberg won the State Democratic Committee's designation for governor—but not without incident. Representative Shirley Chisholm (D-NY) organized a walkout of some delegates and attacked Goldberg as a candidate of the party bosses. After he won, Goldberg renounced the party's endorsement to fend off Chisholm's charges of backroom party politics and instead chose to get on the ballot by obtaining the requisite number of signatures. The crowd booed and hissed at him as he made the announcement.

Goldberg had fared far better the previous day in front of Judge Cooper. Cooper set Flood's trial for May 18. At Hughes's request, Cooper later pushed the start of the trial back a day.

Cooper's decision ignored a fundamental rule—only the Supreme Court could reverse its own decisions. He was bound by *Federal Baseball* and *Toolson*, which compelled him to dismiss Flood's lawsuit because of baseball's antitrust exemption. If this were a case about widgets, any federal judge in America would have granted the owners' motion to dismiss. But it was not about widgets; it was about baseball. And this was not just any federal judge; it was Irving Ben Cooper.

At best, Cooper ignored two controlling Supreme Court precedents because he wanted to give the court of appeals and the Supreme Court a complete factual record about the reserve clause's legality. At worst, he wanted to preside over a case about baseball and to show the world that he was a competent federal judge. During pretrial hearings, Cooper sought to dispell such notions. "I think it would be dead wrong if this judge or any judge sought in this trial the publicity angle," he said on March 31.

Bowie Kuhn was working behind the scenes to avoid a trial. As the commissioner and protector of the integrity of the game, he saw Flood's lawsuit casting a pall over the 1970 season. Kuhn had already struck out once that spring in an attempt to protect the game's integrity. Detroit Tigers pitcher Denny McLain, winner of the American League's last two Cy Young Awards, had lost $5,700 investing in a Flint, Michigan, bookmaking operation. After two meetings with McLain, Kuhn suspended the ace pitcher until July 1. He contended that McLain had been duped into the investment and had not shared in the profits. The light sentence showed how beholden Kuhn was to the owners (in this case the owner of the Detroit Tigers). Kuhn seemed to take challenges to the reserve clause more seriously than he did gambling. Pete Axthelm of *Newsweek* called McLain's suspension a "farce." "The 'Alice in Wonderland' quality of the ruling," Axthelm wrote, "only becomes stranger when contrasted with the case of Flood, who must sacrifice his $90,000 salary entirely in order to test the legality of a clause in his contract."

Kuhn wanted Flood back in uniform. He thought he could work the same magic he had worked with the retirement threats of Donn Clendenon and Ken Harrelson. The key was getting Flood to meet with him.

The commissioner sent his special assistant, Monte Irvin, as an emissary. An infielder with the Newark Eagles in the Negro National League and an outfielder with the New York Giants, Irvin was a northern-bred, college-educated World War II veteran. His background and ability had placed him high on Branch Rickey's list of candidates to integrate the game. Unlike Jackie Robinson, however, Irvin was a company man, not a boat rocker. After their playing careers, Irvin and Robinson clashed at a banquet honoring Montclair, New Jersey, high school baseball star Earl Williams. "I don't owe baseball anything," Robinson told the audience, "and baseball doesn't owe me anything." Irvin took the microphone and tried to smooth things over. "Jackie was great for baseball," Irvin said, "and baseball was great for Jackie." The incident cooled relations between the two men. Irvin's service in the commissioner's office aided his 1973 induction into the Baseball Hall of Fame.

It was Irvin's job to get Flood to meet with Kuhn. Irvin called Flood's St. Louis apartment several times in mid- to late March. The first time he told Marian that Kuhn wanted to arrange a private meeting with Flood. Two days later, Irvin called again and spoke directly with Flood. The commissioner offered to fly Flood out to Los Angeles, where the Dodgers were holding a March 28 benefit game for the King Center, a memorial to Martin Luther King in Atlanta, for a private meeting. The commissioner wanted to talk with Flood and to listen to his concerns. Irvin promised that there would be no publicity.

"Damnit, Monte, the last guy who saw the Commissioner for an informal chat wound up getting a boot in the ass," Flood said, alluding to McLain.

"He'd have been in more trouble if he hadn't come in," Irvin replied, which Flood interpreted as a "threat."

Flood declined Irvin's offer.

"Listen, Curt, at least you can meet with the commissioner of baseball," Irvin said.

"I don't have anything to say to him," Flood replied.

"I think you're making a mistake, Curt," Irvin said. "A lot of good can come from this. . . . Maybe after your career you can get a job in the commissioner's office."

Flood wasn't buying it.

Irvin was "disgusted." He thought he had established a rapport with Flood after meeting him through Bill White. Irvin acknowledged that arranging a meeting between Flood and Kuhn would have been "a feather in my cap." But most important, Irvin could not understand why Flood did not have enough respect for the commissioner to at least meet with him. "I thought he made a terrible mistake in not meeting with him. I lost my respect for him," Irvin recalled. "I didn't understand how he could be so stupid."

Still, Irvin would not give up. He called Flood's apartment again and spoke with Marian. Irvin, like most people, assumed that Flood "was in love with that secretary." He told her this was Flood's last chance to meet the commissioner in Los Angeles. She questioned Kuhn's motives.

"The commissioner has worked out a deal," Irvin said. "Curt can play for any National League club of his choice without jeopardizing the litigation."

"Oh, come on, Monte!" Marian replied. "You know the commissioner can't change the rules of the Federal judiciary. If Curt plays ball, his case becomes moot. Now tell me what the Commissioner really wants."

"He's a very compassionate man," Irvin said. "He just wants everybody to be happy."

League lawyers had indeed agreed to arrange a trade for Flood to the team of his choice. Flood rejected the offer because it would have meant the end of his lawsuit. As Goldberg had explained to him, even a pretrial agreement between opposing parties not to prejudice ongoing litigation could not prevent a federal judge from declaring the lawsuit moot. The dispute must be real, not hypothetical; one side must have been harmed. To challenge his trade to the Phillies in court, Flood had to show harm by sitting out the season.

The March 28 Martin Luther King benefit game came and went, but Kuhn's efforts continued. On April 2, the commissioner sent Flood the following telegram:

> AM DISAPPOINTED YOU DECLINED MY INVITATION FOR A PERSONAL CONFERENCE IN LOS ANGELES ON FRIDAY. I DESIRED AN OPPORTUNITY TO DISCUSS

WITH YOU PERSONALLY YOUR BASEBALL CAREER WITHOUT PREJUDICE TO THE BASIC ISSUES INVOLVED IN THE PENDING LITIGATION. MY COUNSEL HAS ASCERTAINED FROM YOUR COUNSEL THAT THE LATTER HAD NO OBJECTIONS TO SUCH A CONFERENCE WITH THE EXPLICIT CONDITION THAT HE WAS NOT RECOMMENDING THAT YOU ASSENT OR DECLINE. THIS IS TO ADVISE YOU THAT IF YOU RECONSIDER I WILL CONTINUE TO BE AVAILABLE.

BOWIE KUHN

Kuhn's insistence on meeting with Flood helped the commissioner perpetuate the myth that he was an impartial judge rather than the owners' man. It also reinforced the idea that Flood was Miller's puppet. If Kuhn could just get Flood away from Miller and Goldberg, then Kuhn could talk some sense into Flood. As the commissioner and a fan, Kuhn also wanted one of the game's better players on the field. That's why he had talked Clendenon and Harrelson out of retirement. Kuhn did not realize that Flood was nothing like Clendenon or Harrelson. "I can't be bought," Flood told players and reporters many times. The owners soon discovered that Flood meant it.

Kuhn had more success resolving the dispute between the Cardinals and the Phillies. For months, the two teams had been unable to agree on additional compensation as part of the Flood-McCarver-Allen trade. Kuhn spoke with Cardinals executives Bing Devine and Dick Meyer and Phillies general manager John Quinn. Even owners Gussie Busch and Bob Carpenter got involved. The Phillies expressed interest in Cardinals third baseman Mike Shannon. Shannon, however, had contracted a career-ending kidney disease. Instead, the Cardinals sent the Phillies a list of players to choose from—not a single major leaguer was on the list. The Phillies spent all spring training scouting the Cardinals' minor leaguers. On April 8, the Phillies selected outfielder Guillermo "Willie" Montanez. They had until August 31 to select another Cardinals minor leaguer who was not on St. Louis's 40-man roster in April or who did not join the Cardinals' active roster later that season. The Flood trade was almost complete.

The Phillies selected Montanez only after going through another month of formalities of trying to get Flood into a Philadelphia uniform. Flood had never gone through with his retirement plans by filing the proper paperwork with the commissioner's office, so the Phillies were required either to renew his contract or make him a free agent. On March 4, the Phillies sent Flood a notice automatically renewing his contract at $90,000 under paragraph 10(a) of the Uniform Player Contract. After Flood failed to report to spring training with the Phillies by March 15, Quinn requested Kuhn's permission to place Flood on the restricted list. This prevented Flood from counting against the Phillies' roster and reassured the Cardinals that Flood would not be playing for another team. Part of the reason Kuhn had contacted Flood through Irvin and by telegram was to avoid putting him on the restricted list. On April 7, the day before they selected Montanez, Kuhn granted the Phillies' request and placed Flood on the restricted list.

The restricted list placed Flood in close company with some of the game's most notorious characters. Under the Major League Rules, "[a] player on the Restricted List shall not be eligible to play for any Major League or National Association Club until he is reinstated." Although Flood or the Phillies could request his immediate reinstatement if he decided to report to Philadelphia, he was technically banned from the major and minor leagues. The restricted list is a close cousin to the ineligible list—home to Shoeless Joe Jackson and the 1919 Black Sox as well as other players banned from the game for gambling and other misconduct. Danny Gardella (for jumping to the Mexican League) and George Toolson (for refusing to report to Binghamton) also found themselves on the ineligible list. Flood was now associated with players who had sullied the game's image or bucked the system.

For refusing to report to Philadelphia, Flood had been blacklisted from professional baseball. As the major league season started without him on April 6, he sat at home drinking vodka martinis, working with Carter on his book, and waiting for his trial.

On April 23, Cooper issued a 19-page opinion formally refusing to rule on the owners' motion to dismiss Flood's federal, state, and common law antitrust claims, as well as his claims of slavery and involuntary servitude. Cooper dismissed the claims against Anheuser-Busch and CBS. He had no other choice because Goldberg had decided not to contest the companies' opposition motions. Flood's legal team sacrificed those claims, which were weak and tangential to Flood's case against the reserve clause, so the rest of the lawsuit could proceed to trial.

In hindsight, if Cooper had relied on *Toolson* and dismissed the entire case, Flood could have immediately appealed Cooper's decision to the court of appeals and then to the Supreme Court. A dismissal would have sped up the appeals process and increased Flood's chances of returning to the major leagues. Flood's lawyers, however, wanted to develop the facts at trial about the evils of the reserve clause. Cooper gave them their opportunity.

CHAPTER NINE

On May 19, Curt Flood walked into room 1505 of the federal courthouse at Foley Square in lower Manhattan. For the next three weeks, he made baseball history, not in the National League ballparks he had once played in, but in a small courtroom with high ceilings, polished wooden tables and benches, and green leather chairs. He received what Danny Gardella, George Toolson, or any other disgruntled professional baseball player since *Federal Baseball* had failed to obtain—a full trial about the legality of the reserve clause.

Flood and his trial team—Goldberg, Topkis, Zerman, Miller, and Moss—sat at a long rectangular table directly in front of the court reporter and the judge's bench. To their left the nine lawyers for the commissioner and the owners—Mark Hughes, Lou Carroll, Lou Hoynes, Sandy Hadden, Victor Kramer, George Leisure, and three young associates—sat at a similar table close to the jury box. Kuhn sat in the first row of wooden benches behind his counsel's table with league presidents Cronin and Feeney on each side of him.

From a door to his chambers on the right side of the courtroom, Judge Cooper walked to his bench in his black judicial robe. Short, squinty-eyed, and bald with white hair on the sides of his head and a white mustache, Cooper spoke with a British accent from his youth and presided over the court on a high bench. The court clerk and the stenographers sat in a well below him. The witnesses testified in a box below him to his right. This was a bench trial, so there was no jury.

Members of the press sat in the jury box, two rows of six green leather chairs that lined the front left of the courtroom and were enclosed by a semicircular railing. Other journalists sat on the crowded rows of wooden benches, which were separated by an aisle and stretched from behind the counsel tables to the back of the courtroom. They scrambled for seats with lawyers, court watchers, and the public. Sports columnists came in for the first day of the trial from Baltimore and Philadelphia. The New York media was out in full force. *New York Times* sportswriter Leonard Koppett, syndicated columnist Red Smith, and ABC's Howard Cosell were regulars.

Cosell sat in the back right of the jury box where the railing opened behind Douglas Robinson, a young Arnold & Porter associate seated at the far end of the defense table. "Howard Cosell's big beak would be hanging over my shoulder," Robinson recalled. "He would often tap me on the shoulder and ask me questions." Cosell smoked his trademark cigars in the hallway during courtroom breaks. "A great day for the scribes," Cosell kept repeating that first day. "A great day for the scribes."

During those three weeks, Flood and the owners tried two cases in Cooper's courtroom: one in the court of law and the other in the court of public opinion. The legal outcome of the trial seemed preordained in baseball's favor given the Supreme Court's two decisions exempting the game from the antitrust laws. A trial, however, gave Flood's lawyers an opportunity to change public opinion about the reserve clause and to develop testimony in the hopes of persuading the Supreme Court to consider reversing itself.

As Judge Cooper entered the courtroom, the court clerk, Joseph Cannata, asked both sides if they were ready.

"We are not ready, your Honor," Mark Hughes announced on behalf of the owners, "but we have been directed to be here at this time and proceed with the trial, so we are here."

Flood's trial was like a Broadway show without any dress rehearsals. Both sides had only six weeks to prepare. They had no idea who some of their witnesses were going to be or what the other side's witnesses were going to say, because there had been no pretrial depositions or even answers to written questions in the form of interrogatories. They exchanged a few financial documents. They also agreed to estimate Flood's damages at $1 million. But damages were irrelevant. This was a trial about the legality of the reserve clause.

No one was more ill-prepared for trial than Flood's lead counsel, Arthur Goldberg. The Democratic gubernatorial nomination that he had expected to be handed to him was turning out to be a dogfight. Howard Samuels, a wealthy Long Island businessman and former undersecretary of commerce, exposed Goldberg as a weak candidate. Goldberg was running for governor of New York out of the same exalted sense of duty and ego that prompted him to give up his Supreme Court seat rather than out of any passion for the job. He had never campaigned for a governmental position in his life. Shaking hands and kissing babies was not his style. He loathed calling people up and asking them for money. He gave long-winded speeches and convoluted answers to simple questions. He was aloof. Stories that began with "Then I told President Kennedy . . ." and "Like Justice Holmes, I . . ." alienated reporters. He insisted that they read the British version of his Who's Who biography because it was more complete than the American version. "I spent a month with Arthur Goldberg yesterday morning," one reporter joked. Every time Goldberg left his apartment at the Pierre Hotel, he lost votes.

Goldberg spent the month before Flood's trial campaigning. Topkis, Bill Iverson, and Max Gitter scheduled appointments to speak with Goldberg about the case by leaving phone messages with his secretary. On May 6 and May 7, Topkis and Gitter received half-hour time slots from 10:30 to 11 a.m. Goldberg's schedule was otherwise booked solid with campaign events from morning until night. The day before the trial, Goldberg left his apartment at the Pierre Hotel at 9:45 a.m. and returned home at 8:45 p.m. His secretary penciled in a 15-minute meeting with Gitter from 2 to 2:15 p.m. about the *Flood* case. That was the only indication that Goldberg had prepared for the first day of trial.

The morning of Flood's trial, Goldberg ate breakfast with I. W. Abel, the president of the Steelworkers Union. As the general counsel of the Steelworkers for nearly 20 years, Goldberg had displayed unparalleled ability as a lawyer and courtroom advocate. The breakfast with Abel failed to rekindle any of Goldberg's old legal magic.

Flood's trial began at 10 a.m. with the lawyers introducing themselves to Judge Cooper. After these introductions, Goldberg said, "I would like to call as—"

Before Goldberg could even get the name of the first witness out of his mouth, Hughes jumped up and said: "Mr. Justice Goldberg, may I interrupt for a moment." Hughes once again asked Cooper to dismiss Flood's lawsuit. Cooper refused. Hughes also asked if Cooper planned on ruling on the owners' prior motion to dismiss. Cooper said he did not. The trial was on. Since there was no jury, lawyers on both sides agreed to waive their opening statements.

"Very well," Cooper said. "Call your first witness."

"Mr. Curtis C. Flood, your Honor," Goldberg replied.

The month before trial had been extremely difficult for Flood. The press would not leave him alone. Per Goldberg's instructions, he tried to keep a low profile in the days leading up to the trial. "I've really got nothing to say," Flood told United Press International (UPI). "That's all. I haven't been doing anything."

He continued to go through baseball withdrawal. His mind was still on the Cardinals. The day before his trial, they played in Houston. Gibson, off to a slow start, lost to the Astros, 6–0. A month of the major league season had come and gone without Flood. For the first time since he was a small boy, he was not playing baseball.

When Flood flew with Zerman to New York for his reserve clause trial, he left a pile of legal troubles back in St. Louis. On April 29, a North Carolina–based printing company filed a federal lawsuit against Curt Flood Associates, Inc., demanding $67,695 for photo-finishing services. The company also sued Flood and his partners personally for an additional $150,000 for allegedly concealing corporate assets. He did not know if his photography business would be there when he got back.

The day before Flood's trial, his lawyers handed him a script of his direct examination. They tried to prepare him as best they could that day. But Goldberg was not around to run through the questions with Flood or to put his mind at ease.

As Flood approached the witness chair on the morning of May 19, he was a nervous wreck. His eyes looked tired; his face looked fuller. It was as if the last six months had aged him six years. Dressed in a navy blue pin-striped double-breasted suit, a white shirt, and a dark tie with a white stripe at the top, he wore a pinky ring on one hand and a World Series ring on the other. He swore to tell the whole truth and nothing but the truth.

Before Flood gave even a word of testimony, Judge Cooper warned him to keep his voice up because of the high ceilings and bad acoustics in the room. By legal standards, it was not a large courtroom, but to Flood it seemed huge. The benches behind the counsel tables seated about 80 people.

Goldberg made it through only two questions about Flood's name and hometown before Hughes jumped up and objected. Hughes stated for the record that the court lacked jurisdiction over the case because of baseball's antitrust exemption.

The objection only added to Flood's discomfort. He was so nervous and uptight that he could not remember when he graduated from high school. First, he said 1968. He quickly corrected himself with 1958. Finally, Goldberg was forced to correct the record again by informing Flood that it was 1956.

Goldberg tried to take Flood through the start of his professional career—signing with the Reds out of high school for $4,000 without even reading the contract, playing in the segregated South in High Point and Savannah, and learning in Venezuela that he had been traded from the Reds to the Cardinals. It was difficult, however, for Goldberg to evoke sympathy about the way the reserve system had treated Flood because of Goldberg's lack of knowledge about Flood's career and Flood's nervousness and inexperience as a witness.

Flood's voice could barely be heard by the audience. He sat hunched over, nervously rubbed his hands together, and looked down as he spoke. Goldberg gently reminded Flood to speak louder and to talk with his head up instead of down. The young man who had spoken so eloquently at the Mississippi NAACP rally in 1962, to the media assembled outside his rented home in Alamo, California, in 1964, and after his misplay in Game 7 of the 1968 World Series was nowhere to be found. In Judge Cooper's courtroom, he was so afraid of saying the wrong thing that he could not find the words to say much at all.

Flood remembered that he had batted .261 in 1958 but could not remember his batting averages from the next three seasons. Goldberg believed that Topkis had Flood's averages on a piece of paper. Topkis looked for help from his two young associates in charge of the exhibits.

Bill Iverson happened to have Flood's Topps baseball card in his wallet. The 2½-by-3½-inch card pictured Flood in his Cardinals uniform on the front and listed his season-by-season statistics on the back.

Iverson kept Flood's card in his wallet "because he was one of my current heroes."

Iverson handed the card to Topkis. Topkis handed it to Goldberg at the lectern. Goldberg passed it up to Flood.

"What are you looking at?" Goldberg asked Flood so that he could identify it for the court.

"A baseball card," Flood replied.

Flood used his baseball card to refresh his recollection about his batting averages. The press loved it. It was great theater and completely improvised.

Cooper was not amused. He soon put Flood in his place. Goldberg asked Flood about his salary negotiations with Bing Devine before the 1959 season. Goldberg was trying to show the unequal bargaining relationship between player and general manager under the reserve clause.

Flood understood Goldberg's point, but he could not remember the facts to be able to answer the question. Flood instead answered with an argument about the inequities of the salary negotiations. Hughes objected. Sustained. Cooper launched into a lecture about the rules of evidence. He told Flood to stop arguing and to answer the question with his best recollection of the facts.

Flood could not regain his train of thought. He tried to answer the question with conditional statements and hypothetical dialogue. Cooper again interrupted him. He told Flood that "I state" was okay, but "I would state" was not. Flood was so unnerved that he could not understand Cooper's distinction.

Cooper could not keep the bully who had tormented Legal Aid lawyers and juvenile defendants completely under wraps. He showed Flood no respect and took advantage of an obviously nervous witness.

"Now, Mr. Flood, I presume you are not finding this as easy as getting up at bat, is that right?" Cooper asked.

"No sir, it is not," Flood replied.

"I want you to remember other people have problems and now you are seeing it is not an easy thing to testify," Cooper said. Cooper forced Flood to concede that he could not remember what took place during his 1959 salary negotiations with Bing Devine.

For a cooperative witness, direct examination is not supposed to be this difficult. The witness's lawyer asks the questions. The lawyer either has written out all the questions and even the answers in advance or has asked the witness all the questions in advance and knows how the witness is supposed to answer. A direct exam usually consists of who, what, when, why, and how questions. The lawyer is not allowed to lead the witness by planting the facts of the answer in the question. Instead, the lawyer is trying to get the witness to tell the story by asking the witness simple questions like "What happened next?" The lack of preparation by Goldberg and Flood added to Flood's difficulties. The fault rested with Goldberg. Cooper's snide comments exacerbated the situation. "I guess that they were looking for a Sidney Poitier playing me," Flood said, alluding to Hollywood's leading black actor at the time. "I was me playing me."

The rest of Flood's direct examination testimony was uneventful but certainly not smooth. Flood used the baseball card to review the rest of his batting averages: .296 in 1962, .302 in 1963, .311 in 1964, .310 in 1965, .267 in 1966, .335 in 1967, .301 in 1968, and .285 in 1969. He could not remember the salaries he had made after his first season. Goldberg asked his opposing counsel for the salary information. All player salaries had been kept secret. Goldberg read Flood's into the record:

1956	$4,000
1957	$4,000
1958	$5,000
1959	$12,000
1960	$12,500
1961	$13,500
1962	$16,000
1963	$17,500
1964	$23,000
1965	$35,000
1966	$45,000
1967	$50,000
1968	$72,000
1969	$90,000

His salary—which excluded World Series bonuses in 1964, 1967, and 1968—averaged $28,500 per season. That was nearly six times what the average American made during the 1960s. But Flood had spent most of that money, and his income stream, given his decision to sit out the season, had dried up. For all the talk about Flood being a rich, ungrateful ballplayer, he was not a wealthy man.

Goldberg walked Flood through some things that had happened to him during his career—receiving $500 for being named co-captain in 1965 and getting fined $250 for missing a team banquet in 1969. Flood discussed his trade from the Cardinals to the Phillies, his meetings with John Quinn and Miller and Moss, and his decision to sue.

"Why did you bring this lawsuit?" Goldberg asked.

"I didn't think that after twelve years I should be traded and treated like a piece of property," Flood said in one of his testimony's few bright spots. Flood also said that he would agree to play for another team "[i]f I had the choice of playing for whom I chose, whoever offered me the best deal." He also testified that he "could play another five years easily."

Flood concluded his direct testimony shortly before 1 p.m. after two and a half hours on the witness stand. The trial broke for lunch. After lunch but before the trial resumed, Flood and Goldberg chatted on a park bench outside the courthouse. Their little chat—more time than Goldberg probably had spent with Flood in the last month—seemed to help Flood relax.

Cross-examination was no picnic. The goal of cross-examination is not to engage the witness in a debate, nor is it always to achieve a revelatory or gotcha-type moment. The purpose is to read statements to the witness and get him to agree with them. The best answer from a witness on cross-examination is "Yes." Through a series of "yes" answers, the cross-examiner tries to point out inconsistencies in the witness's testimony, damage the witness's credibility, and destroy the witness's position.

Mark Hughes began by pointing out a few minor inconsistencies in Flood's testimony based on his prior statements in the press. He also received some help from Cooper. Flood, who sat hunched over and talked at the floor, incurred another of Cooper's lectures.

"The trial is a public trial," Cooper said. "People have a right to come into this courtroom. That is the American way. I presume a good number of them have come here purposely to see you. They want to hear you. They have a right to know what is going on, and I am going to ask you, and I hope it will be for the last time, to really almost shout, if you have to, because we want to hear what you have to say."

Hughes's main strategy on cross-examination was to persuade Judge Cooper that the real plaintiff in this case was the Players Association, not Flood. Hughes sought to divorce Flood from the litigation.

First, Hughes asked Flood who was paying his legal fees. Goldberg immediately jumped up and answered for his client. "[W]e, in conversation with Mr. Miller, not Mr. Flood, have made arrangements that we will look to the Players Association for compensation in this litigation," Goldberg said. "Thus far we have received none."

"I'm sorry to hear that," Victor Kramer piped up for the commissioner.

"That is mutually shared," Goldberg replied.

Despite this moment of levity, Hughes was determined to make Flood's participation in this trial irrelevant. He succeeded through a series of cross-examination questions about what would satisfy Flood regarding changes to the reserve clause. At first, Flood stuck to the union's party line: "I think some modification would do that for me."

In supporting Flood's lawsuit and during labor negotiations with the owners, the union had indicated that it only wanted to see the reserve clause modified, not destroyed. It recognized that the owners had a right to recoup their investments in player development but that the players deserved at some point in their major league careers to be free agents. The owners, however, had rejected any modifications. The union knew that the only way to bring the owners to the negotiating table was to get the reserve clause struck down in court.

Hughes kept after Flood. The owners' lawyers suspected that Flood, a vulnerable and ill-prepared witness, might not be able to differentiate between seemingly inconsistent aims: getting the reserve clause struck down in court and seeking modification at the negotiating table. Hughes took advantage of Flood's nervousness and lack of legal expertise.

"Well, which is it that you want?" Hughes asked. "Do you want a modification or do you want the whole system to be struck down and declared illegal?"

The correct answer was both—in order to modify the reserve clause at the negotiating table, the players had to get it struck down in court. Flood, however, picked one.

"I would like the whole system to be struck down and declared illegal," Flood replied.

Hughes had laid a trap. He claimed that Flood was advocating two inconsistent positions—modification and complete elimination—in the span of a few seconds. Hughes attempted to clarify Flood's views by reading a comment Flood had made during his Howard Cosell interview: "Any revision of the reserve clause, something both parties can live with, would be just fine with me."

Renouncing those earlier views, Flood took an absolutist position: "Well, I feel that we ought to start all over again, just wipe the thing out and do something different."

The owners' lawyers silently rejoiced. They knew that they had boxed Flood into an indefensible position. No one—not Marvin Miller or any former or current players—believed that as a practical matter the reserve clause should be eliminated. Hughes had succeeded in making Flood irrelevant. On appeal, the owners could successfully portray Flood as a figurehead whose views did not matter; what mattered were the views of Miller and the Players Association. This was an extension of the owners' theory that Flood was not smart enough to come up with the idea of suing baseball. Through Hughes's lawyer tricks, they had factual support for their theory.

Flood's cross-examination, however, was not a total detriment to his case. A few moments after scoring big points, Hughes asked: "Mr. Flood, what do you think would happen if every player were a free agent at the end of each playing season?"

Goldberg objected. He argued that Cooper had sustained Hughes's objection to a similar question of Goldberg's. Overruled. Cooper instructed Flood to answer the question.

"I think then every ballplayer would have a chance to really negotiate a contract just like in any other business," Flood said.

"Do you want that answer stricken, Justice Goldberg?" Cooper asked.

"No, I like that answer," Goldberg said.

"Engraved in gold," Topkis whispered.

After a few more questions from Hughes and a few from Kuhn's lawyer, Victor Kramer, the owners finished their cross-examination. Flood stepped down from the witness stand after nearly five hours of testimony.

Instead of trying to redirect Flood and exposing him to further cross-examination, Goldberg called his next witness, Marvin Miller. As smooth as Flood was nervous, Miller described how the owners had refused to negotiate about the reserve clause, that he had explained to Flood the risks of suing baseball, and that the Players Association had voted to pay Flood's legal bills.

Miller also detailed the association's fee arrangement with Goldberg. At first, Goldberg had waived his own hourly fees but asked the association to pay the fees and expenses of his colleagues. After Yastrzemski and several other players loyal to ownership objected to the arrangement, Goldberg told Miller that his firm would not collect any fees and expenses if further objections arose. That was not going to happen, not if Goldberg's Paul, Weiss partners had anything to say about it. Goldberg, however, was not going to allow the owners to "scare" him out of the case.

After Miller's brief testimony, Cooper granted the request of Flood's lawyers to delay the continuation of the trial one day until May 21. Flood was done testifying, but he was "on short notice" in case he needed to be recalled. The first day of the trial produced two conclusions: Flood was a nervous, unprepared witness, and Goldberg was not a good trial lawyer. Flood's hopes of generating a good trial record or favorable publicity seemed to be in trouble.

Several sports columnists were not impressed with Flood's testimony. "On the surface it would appear that the most damaging evidence to Flood's case was Flood himself," Larry Merchant wrote in the *New York Post*. Flood "trailed on several unofficial scorecards . . . ," according to Stan Hochman of the *Philadelphia Daily News*. "A player like Flood, in the $90,000 category, with business off-shoots, does not evoke much sympathy in the turbulent streets."

Flood's trial team did not want to be at the courthouse on May 20, because as many as 150,000 construction workers were planning to march on Foley Square to show their support for the Vietnam War and to protest against the antiwar protesters. It was a reactionary time. On

March 3, an angry white mob in Lamar, South Carolina, attacked three buses of black schoolchildren on their way to a desegregated school. On April 30, President Nixon announced that he was sending troops into Cambodia, which reinvigorated antiwar protests on college campuses. On May 4, National Guardsmen killed four white students at Kent State. Ten days later, police killed two black students at Jackson State. The construction workers' May 20 rally responded to the student protests and the antiwar stance of New York City mayor John Lindsay with American flags, hardhats, and signs that said "Lindsay for Mayor of Hanoi."

These same reactionary forces were arrayed against Flood and his lawsuit. The commissioner's lawyer, Victor Kramer, knew nothing about baseball. When he took over Paul Porter's trial duties in the case, he asked his young associate Douglas Robinson how many players were on a baseball team. But Kramer was an antitrust expert, a great trial lawyer, and an astute observer of public opinion. Every time Kramer hopped into a New York City cab, he asked the white ethnic cabdriver his thoughts about the *Flood* case. Every time, the cabdriver sympathized with the owners rather than with the black player making $90,000 a year. "Some of that was racial," Robinson said, "and some of it was more this feeling that why should anyone who's making $90,000 a year be complaining."

For Flood's legal team, the key to changing public opinion was to find powerful witnesses. No current players would dare testify. And most former players were equally reluctant. But one former player immediately jumped to the minds of Flood's legal team: Ned Garver. A former pitcher, Garver accounted for 20 of the last-place St. Louis Browns' 52 victories in 1951. The previous season, he had led the American League with 22 complete games but suffered 18 losses. He toiled for the Browns for nearly five seasons before being traded to the Detroit Tigers near the end of the 1952 season. He never made more than $30,000. "If ever there was a guy who had been victimized by the reserve clause, it was Ned Garver," Iverson said. In response to questions from a House subcommittee in 1951, Garver had written that baseball "could not exist" without the reserve clause, but he had suggested modifications to allow an underpaid player on a second-division club to get paid what he was worth or switch teams. Garver, however, rejected Iverson's invitation to testify on Flood's behalf.

Flood's witness list was shrouded in secrecy. The Associated Press reported shortly before trial that Satchel Paige, the great Negro league pitcher, might testify for Flood. Paige had made his major league debut in 1948 at age 42 with the Indians, had pitched for the St. Louis Browns until he was 47, and became the oldest pitcher in major league history by throwing three scoreless innings in 1965 for the Kansas City Athletics at age 59. The owners, in recent labor negotiations, had refused to make players free agents at age 65. The Athletics had granted Paige his unconditional release after the 1965 season, but technically they could have owned him for the rest of his life. Flood's lawyers, however, were looking for former players with more gravitas than Paige.

Goldberg, Topkis, Miller, Gitter, and Iverson all spent time tracking down obvious witnesses—great players on bad teams like Ned Garver who did not get paid very much. None of them wanted to testify. A huge Brooklyn Dodgers fan growing up in upstate New York, Iverson decided to start calling the people he most wanted to see in court—the mid-1950s Dodgers. Iverson called almost every Dodger except Roy Campanella, the catcher who had been paralyzed in an automobile accident. Iverson did not want to bother Campanella; nor was Campanella one to speak out on racial or social issues. Iverson talked to all the heroes of his youth: Sandy Amoros, Billy Cox, Carl Furillo, Junior Gilliam, and Duke Snider. "None of them wanted to testify," Iverson said, "but my reaction was, 'Hey, I'm getting paid for this.'" There were, however, a few notable exceptions. The media was alerted that when the trial resumed May 21, several former players would be testifying on Flood's behalf.

CHAPTER TEN

Flood's trial resumed at 10:15 a.m. on May 21. Goldberg announced that he had a few more questions for Marvin Miller, but first he would like to call a special witness.

Goldberg called Jack R. Robinson to the witness stand.

White-haired, diabetic, and going blind, Jackie Robinson looked like the oldest 51-year-old man on the planet. He had suffered a mild heart attack a few years earlier. Diabetes had destroyed the circulation in his legs. His doctor had given him only two to three years to live. Robinson walked in his distinctive pigeon-toed gait down the center aisle of Judge Cooper's crowded courtroom with the help of a cane. To Flood, however, Robinson may as well have been Superman. As he made his way down the aisle, Robinson stopped at the table for plaintiff's counsel. He shook Flood's hand and whispered words of encouragement into Flood's ear. Tears welled in Flood's eyes.

Flood knew that he was doing the right thing. It all seemed worth it now—giving up his baseball career, turning his back on more than $90,000, the hate mail at home, and the humiliation two days earlier on the witness stand. It all seemed worth it because his hero had come to testify on his behalf, to help Flood make professional athletes more free than they had been in Robinson's day.

A hush fell over the courtroom as Robinson approached the witness stand. Aside from his 1962 Hall of Fame induction and a stint as a color commentator for ABC television in 1965, Robinson had exiled himself from baseball. He railed against the game's refusal to hire black coaches and managers. He criticized Frank Robinson and Willie Mays for refusing to speak out on racial issues. He clashed with Bob Feller during the game's centennial celebration at the 1969 All-Star Game in Washington over the lack of minorities in baseball management. The racism in baseball that Robinson had experienced beginning in 1946 had taken on new forms, and he saw no one willing to confront them. "I don't know if anyone could get me back into baseball today, where I would have to deal with the kind of people that I feel are associated with baseball," Robinson said in 1966. "I think there is a narrow-minded, bigoted group of people who believe that the only way the Negro should get opportunities is if he is willing to go along with what they say—'Don't rock the boat.'"

Robinson admired boat rockers such as Flood and his former Cardinals teammate Bill White because "when there's an issue Curt Flood is ready; Bill White is ready. But there are not enough Curt Floods and Bill Whites." In the February 15 issue of *Jet*, Robinson had spoken out on Flood's behalf: "I think Curt is doing a service to all players in the leagues, especially for the younger players coming up who are not superstars. All he is asking for is the right to negotiate. It doesn't surprise me that he had the courage to do it. He's a very sensitive man concerned about the rights of everybody. We need men of integrity like Curt Flood and Bill Russell who are involved in the area of civil rights and who are not willing to sit back and let Mr. Charlie dictate their needs and wants for them or spread the message for them."

An ardent civil rights advocate, Robinson had raised money for the NAACP and the SCLC, participated in the March on Washington, and marched in Birmingham. He was an integrationist who clashed publicly with younger, more militant black activists including Malcolm X. A registered independent, he often supported Republican candidates because he believed blacks should be represented in both political parties. He had campaigned for Richard Nixon during the 1960 presidential election and again two years later when Nixon ran for governor of California. He had served as one of six deputy directors of Nelson Rockefeller's presidential campaign in 1964, worked on Rockefeller's reelection campaign for governor in 1966, and that same year was appointed the governor's special assistant for community affairs. Robinson had come to regret his earlier support of Nixon, who was not as progressive on civil rights issues as

Robinson had been led to believe. After Rockefeller lost the 1968 Republican presidential nomination to Nixon, Robinson endorsed Democratic nominee Hubert Humphrey. In politics, as in life, Jackie Robinson was his own man.

Robinson also was active in business, with mixed results. For seven years after his playing career ended, he had worked for Chock full o' Nuts as a vice president and director of personnel. Robinson's main function for the coffee shop chain was to serve as an intermediary to prevent its employees from unionizing. He had helped start a black-controlled bank, Freedom National Bank, and the Jackie Robinson Construction Corporation that built low- and middle-income housing. Nonetheless, he and his wife, Rachel, a psychiatric nurse, struggled to make ends meet.

After meeting with Marvin Miller, Robinson agreed to see Iverson at his office at Proteus Foods, Inc. Iverson thought the cramped office in a grimy building was not befitting a man of Robinson's stature. Although nominally a vice president, Robinson had no decision-making authority. His job was to encourage people to invest in fish and seafood fast-food restaurants in low-income neighborhoods. He was paid $10,000 a year plus some small stock options and a $500 bonus for each franchise he sold through personal contacts. In July, the company fired him a few months before it filed for bankruptcy. "It had seemed clear that he didn't have a whole lot to do. . . . It was kind of sad that this was what he was doing now," Iverson said. "And frankly, because of the system, he had to do it to make a living he needed to make."

Robinson showed no fear of alienating the Lords of Baseball. He had retired after the 1956 season when the Dodgers sent him to the Giants. He understood the injustice of the reserve clause but did not purport to be an expert on reserve clause issues. He had agreed to testify, he told Miller, because he "thought Flood was a courageous young man." Miller knew that Robinson's testimony came with some baggage. He reminded Robinson that he had told a 1958 Senate subcommittee, "I am highly in favor of the reserve clause." The owners, Miller said, would use Robinson's prior testimony to discredit him. Robinson was unfazed. "I was young and ignorant at the time," he told Miller. "That is what they told me, and that is what I said. But I know differently now, and I won't hesitate to say so."

Robinson spoke in a nasal, high-pitched voice. His white hair, self-confidence, and emotion gave him tremendous stage presence. The courtroom hung on his every word. Even lawyers sitting at the defense table listened in awe.

Robinson discussed his career with the Dodgers: his $600-a-month salary in 1946 with the Montreal Royals, the Dodgers' Triple-A farm club; his $5,000 salary his first year with the Dodgers in 1947; his 1949 Most Valuable Player Award; his .311 lifetime batting average; his six World Series appearances; and his 1962 induction into the Baseball Hall of Fame. Yet he was not certain that his lifetime batting average was .311 or that his highest single-season batting average of .342 came in 1949.

"You don't have one of those little cards?" Goldberg asked.

"No," Robinson replied as he fidgeted with a pair of glasses in his hands.

Judge Cooper tried to get the court reporter to strike the words "I think" about his .311 career average and .342 average in 1949. Robinson interrupted him.

"Well, sir, I hate to dispute you, but I don't know full well whether it was 1949," Robinson said.

"How about your total average?" Cooper asked.

"I am pretty sure it is around .311," Robinson said.

"Aren't you positive of it?" Cooper asked. "I would be if I had something like that in my favor."

With the press and public watching, Cooper fawned over Robinson, the hero of Brooklynites everywhere. Although the lawyers did not know it yet, the judge had more than good publicity in mind.

Robinson discussed his trade from the Dodgers to the Giants after the 1956 season. The Dodgers sold Robinson for $30,000 plus pitcher Dick Littlefield. Dodgers owner Walter O'Malley wanted Robinson out of the organization because Robinson adored O'Malley's nemesis, Branch Rickey, the team's former part owner and general manager. Trading Robinson to their National League rivals, the Giants, was the ultimate slap in the face. Robinson had already decided to retire and accept a $30,000 offer from Chock full o' Nuts "because, in my view, a black man had very little chance in organized baseball to go from the playing ranks to the front office to the managerial role regardless of whether he had any ability alone or not, and I had to protect my family as best as I possibly could." After the trade, Robinson nearly changed his mind when the Giants raised their initial salary offer of $35,000 to $50,000 or more (he had never made a salary of more than $42,500 with the Dodgers and had made only $33,000 in 1956 after accepting several salary cuts). Dodgers general manager Buzzie Bavasi was angry that Robinson had kept his retirement a secret in order to sell the story to *Look* magazine. According to Robinson, Bavasi's "statement that the only thing that I was doing when I was refusing to play was trying to get more money so angered me that nothing would have kept me in baseball at that particular time."

Robinson discussed the reserve clause with hurt, anger, and sensitivity. During his first two seasons with the Dodgers, he had been spiked, spit on, thrown at, and called every nasty racial epithet in the book, but had kept his promise to Rickey that he would not fight back. During the 1949 season, Robinson began to assert himself more. He had been fighting back on and off the field ever since.

Goldberg asked Robinson his opinion about the reserve clause. Robinson's response anchored the stories about Flood's trial in the next day's editions of the *New York Times*, the *Daily News*, and the *Post*: "[A]nything that is one-sided in this country is wrong, and I think the reserve clause is a one-sided thing in favor of the owners, and I think it certainly should at least be modified to give a player an opportunity to have some control over his destiny. Whenever you have one-sided systems, in my view, it leads to serious, serious problems, and I think that unless there is a change in the reserve clause that it is going to lead to a serious strike in terms of the ballplayers. . . . I sincerely believe that the reserve clause is so one-sided in favor of the owners that the players don't really have control over their own destinies."

Robinson said the reserve clause harmed younger players, especially those who since 1965 had been assigned to major league teams through a leaguewide draft of the best high school and college prospects. He added that "the reserve clause does not affect the $90,000 ballplayer as much as it affects that guy who sits upon the bench."

Robinson discussed the careers of three of his former Dodgers teammates—Don Zimmer, Eddie Miksis, and Don Hoak—who wasted many seasons on the Dodgers' bench when they could have been starters on other teams. Zimmer, Robinson said, would have been an extremely good shortstop, but for four years he was stuck behind All-Star Pee Wee Reese. Because of the reserve clause, Zimmer lost the prime of his career as the Dodgers organization's insurance policy in case Reese ever got hurt. Miksis backed up Robinson at second base and then Hoak backed up Robinson at third. Of Hoak, Robinson said the reserve clause "hurt his chances for a few years to become a better ballplayer, to become a person to make more money in the game."

Robinson ran afoul of Judge Cooper only one time on direct examination. Goldberg asked Robinson whether baseball as a sport would be affected if the reserve clause was modified. "I would like to say first—I don't know whether this is in the rules—I don't consider baseball a sport," Robinson said. "I think it is a big business, first of all." Hughes objected to the answer as "unresponsive." Cooper asked if Hughes moved to strike it. Hughes said yes, and Cooper struck the answer about baseball being big business because "that is the issue that I must resolve." The Supreme Court had never created a distinction between professional sports and other for-profit businesses; it had simply decided that the business of baseball was exempt from the antitrust laws. And Cooper, whether he was willing to admit it or not, was bound by those decisions.

On cross-examination, Hughes predictably asked Robinson if he had testified in 1958 before a Senate subcommittee. Robinson said he could not remember; he had testified before the Senate many times. Hughes then read one sentence on page 295 of Robinson's 1958 testimony in which Robinson had said: "I am highly in favor of the reserve clause." Robinson said he could not remember saying it. Nor did the rereading of the sentence refresh his recollection. Hughes kept badgering Robinson about his prior testimony. The most he could get Robinson to admit was that "I could have said that." Robinson was as stubborn on the witness stand as he had been on the ball field.

Goldberg finally objected that Robinson had been asked and answered the question. Goldberg suggested putting the entire testimony into the record. Hughes evaded the suggestion. Robinson indicated that he had made additional comments before the Senate, but Goldberg failed to follow up on this line of questioning on redirect.

Two witnesses and a lunch recess later, Goldberg realized that he should have read the entire paragraph into the record. Robinson's testimony on page 295, which Goldberg read aloud for the court after lunch, said:

> I think they should in some way be able to express themselves as to whether or not they do want to play for a certain ball club. I am highly in favor of the reserve clause. I do not want to get this out that I don't believe there should be some control. But on the other hand, I don't think the owners should have all of the control. I think that there should be something that a ballplayer himself could say that would have some effect upon his particular position with a ballclub.
>
> As it stands now, the players, in my opinion, don't really have the opportunity to express themselves in a way they should be able to.

Hughes, who had been guilty of taking Robinson's statement completely out of context, could only muster: "Could I have the book, please."

Goldberg's failure to catch the mistake at the time of Robinson's testimony was another result of his not doing enough trial preparation and thus not being as quick on his feet as a trial lawyer should be. Read in its entirety, Robinson's 1958 Senate testimony was consistent with his testimony at Flood's trial. Robinson had testified before the Senate that the reserve clause hurt bench players on stronger teams because those players could be starters on weaker teams. "So I believe that after five, six years, or so, that a player should have the right to express himself and perhaps go to some other club," Robinson had told the Senate.

Not even Goldberg could prevent Robinson from enrapturing the courtroom during cross-examination and on redirect. Hughes asked Robinson what the reserve clause meant to him. "It means to me that a player is tied to a ballclub for life," Robinson said. "That's all it means to me." On redirect, Goldberg asked Robinson about the type of reserve clause modification that he favored. Robinson said that a player should be able to ask for the chance to improve his condition with a new team "after a certain number of years."

Robinson concluded his testimony with a ringing endorsement of

Flood: "It takes a tremendous amount of courage for any individual—and that's why I admire Mr. Flood so much for what he is doing—to stand up against something that is appalling to him, and I think that they ought to give a player the chance to be able to be a man in situations like this, and I don't believe this is what has happened. Give the players the opportunity to be able to say to themselves, 'I have a certain value and I can place it on myself.'"

For Flood, Robinson's "soliloquy . . . sent chills up and down my spine." His hero had just stood up for him in open court for taking on the baseball establishment just as Robinson had done 23 years earlier. Flood had endured similar things in the southern minor leagues that Robinson had endured with the Dodgers. He had overcome racism in the Reds organization and with Solly Hemus to become an All-Star and Gold Glove center fielder. He had experienced the thrill of winning two World Series. He had ascended to the upper levels of baseball's salary scale. Now it was Flood's turn to take what Robinson had taught him over the years and to stand up and be counted. Robinson had just given Flood the encouragement he needed to fight on.

Flood was not the only one inspired by Robinson's testimony. As soon as he excused Robinson from the witness stand, Judge Cooper called for a short recess and brought lawyers from both sides into his chambers. He invited Kuhn, Feeney, and Cronin. He also invited Robinson. The defense thought that Cooper had a problem with Robinson's testimony. Instead, Cooper requested both sides' permission to ask Robinson for an autograph for his grandson. No one objected, and the starstruck Cooper received Robinson's signature. Robinson was not the last celebrity in the courtroom that day.

As soon as they returned from the impromptu autograph session, Cooper ordered people to be seated and called for the next witness.

"Mr. Greenberg will be our next witness," Goldberg said.

Hank Greenberg knew about discrimination. The 6-foot-4½-inch Detroit Tigers slugger battled anti-Semitism his entire career, particularly in 1938 when he chased Babe Ruth's single-season home run record and finished two shy of Ruth's mark with 58. Despite losing more than four seasons to military service in World War II, he finished his 13-year career with 331 home runs and 1,276 RBIs. Before anyone had ever heard of Sandy Koufax, Greenberg had been baseball's most legendary

Jewish player. In 1947, Greenberg's last season and Jackie Robinson's first, Robinson collided with the big Pittsburgh Pirates first baseman on a close play at first. During Robinson's next time on base, Greenberg asked Robinson if he was okay and told him to ignore Greenberg's stupid, racist teammates. "Stick in there," Greenberg said. "You're doing fine. Keep your chin up." He even invited Robinson to dinner. "Class tells," Robinson said at the time. "It sticks out all over Mr. Greenberg."

Greenberg also knew about the evils of the reserve clause. He had been in the Tigers organization since 1930 and came back in his first full season after World War II to lead the American League in home runs (44) and RBIs (127) in 1946. But the Tigers no longer wanted to pay Greenberg's $75,000 salary in 1947, so they put him on waivers. They refused to allow any of their American League rivals to claim him and then sold him for the $10,000 waiver price to the Pirates. Greenberg heard about the sale on the radio and then received a one-paragraph telegram making it official. The 36-year-old Greenberg informed Pirates owner John Galbreath that he was retiring. Galbreath talked Greenberg out of it by agreeing to the following conditions: (1) moving in the left-field fences at Forbes Field to 335 feet; (2) allowing Greenberg to fly instead of take trains and to have his own room on the road; and (3) raising Greenberg's salary from $75,000 to $100,000. Greenberg agreed to play for just one more season, provided the Pirates agreed to release him at the end of the year. "Mr. Galbreath," Greenberg said, "I'm never going to go through the shock of being traded or sold like a piece of merchandise like what just happened to me with Detroit."

True to his word, Greenberg retired after one season in Pittsburgh. Unlike Jackie Robinson, he was welcomed into management. Bill Veeck, the maverick owner of the Cleveland Indians, made Greenberg the team's vice president in 1948, farm director in 1949, general manager in 1950, and part owner and director in 1955. Greenberg sold his interest in the Indians in 1958 and the following year was part of Veeck's group that bought the Chicago White Sox. Greenberg worked as the team's general manager until 1961. Two years later, he left the White Sox and baseball. In 1956, he was inducted into the Baseball Hall of Fame. Greenberg lived a good life. He had married Caral Gimbel, whose family owned the Gimbel Brothers and Saks Fifth Avenue department stores. After they divorced, Greenberg remarried and moved to Southern

California. His son, Stephen, became the deputy commissioner of baseball under Fay Vincent.

Greenberg, knowing that it meant the end of his ties to Major League Baseball, had been reluctant to testify for Flood. "Greenberg said he agrees with our position on the reserve clause, but he had some qualms about testifying, and asked to think it over," Max Gitter and Topkis wrote in a May 7 memo to Goldberg. "Perhaps a phone call from you would resolve his doubts in our favor." Goldberg called Greenberg. Whatever Goldberg said to one of the other most prominent Jewish-American figures of the 20th century, it must have worked.

Healthy, tanned, and with dark, slicked-back hair, Greenberg was a physically imposing yet soft-spoken witness. As emotional as Robinson was on the witness stand, Greenberg, speaking in the thick Bronx accent of his boyhood, was calm, reserved, and almost aloof. He discussed his career with the Tigers, the telegram he received announcing his trade to the Pirates, and his part ownership of the Indians and the White Sox.

Greenberg testified that "the reserve clause as it is constituted now and has been is obsolete and antiquated. . . . It seems to me that the times have changed and that the owners and the players are going to have to get together and work more harmoniously and with a more cooperative spirit so that the game can go forward, and the first step or the last step is the reserve clause in the contract."

Judge Cooper asked Greenberg why the reserve clause was not in the best interests of baseball.

"[I]t's a unilateral contract, Judge," Greenberg replied. "The ballplayer has no choice other than accept the terms offered to him, because he can't play elsewhere." Greenberg had been rankled by the Tigers organization's callousness in selling him to the Pirates. After 17 years with Detroit, Greenberg felt that he deserved some consideration about where the Tigers were going to send him. Greenberg empathized with Flood: "I think that baseball must recognize that, that the player has built up some equity in playing with the club over a period of years, that he has a family, has friends, has business associations in the city, and they can't just arbitrarily say, 'You play in Philadelphia next season.'"

"That is the kind of testimony I want you to give," Cooper remarked. "I am not passing on the weight of it, but that is really the sort of thing I seek."

Greenberg, who believed that the reserve clause should be replaced by a contract for a term of years, helped both the owners and players on cross-examination. He conceded that both sides should sit down and negotiate reserve clause modifications—undercutting Flood's lawsuit and supporting the owners' argument that this issue should be resolved through labor negotiation. Greenberg, however, added that he was not a member of the Players Association and had met Marvin Miller for the first time that day. Greenberg also admitted that the owners had some equity interest in the players they developed and that it had taken him three minor league and two major league seasons to round into peak form. But, as a former owner, Greenberg said: "I would be perfectly willing to invest in baseball tomorrow if we had no reserve clause."

After Greenberg's testimony, Marvin Miller retook the witness stand to testify about the owners' refusal to negotiate about the reserve clause. American League counsel Sandy Hadden cross-examined Miller after lunch. Miller conceded that the owners had compromised on a number of other issues in the upcoming basic agreement, just not on the reserve clause.

Flood's legal team called one more star witness on this second day of Flood's trial: pitcher-turned-author Jim Brosnan. A major league relief pitcher for nine years, in 1954 and from 1956 to 1963, Brosnan spent his offseasons working for a Chicago advertising firm but really wanted to be a writer. He dared to read books in the clubhouse. His teammates called the bespectacled pitcher "Professor." After writing several magazine articles for Robert Creamer at *Sports Illustrated*, Brosnan kept a diary while splitting the 1959 season between the St. Louis Cardinals and Cincinnati Reds. The result was *The Long Season*, the first baseball book to capture the way ballplayers really talked. Although tame by modern standards, *The Long Season* pulled back the curtain on life inside the clubhouse. Brosnan cast a critical eye on his fellow players and coaches. One of his main targets was Flood's old nemesis, Cardinals manager Solly Hemus. Brosnan wrote that Hemus "tried too hard. He tends to overmanage and he gets panicky for no good reason at all." Hemus later said of Brosnan: "He's the first pitcher I ever heard of who won nine games and felt he had to write a book about it." Literary critics loved *The Long Season*, which became a bestseller. Brosnan followed it up with *Pennant Race*, a diary of the Reds' 1961 season.

Brosnan's literary success curtailed his baseball career. The Reds' new general manager, Bill DeWitt, objected to Brosnan's books and magazine articles. NBC offered Brosnan $4,000 to be miked for a baseball documentary. DeWitt demanded prior approval of the script. NBC said not even President Kennedy received prebroadcast approval. DeWitt prevented Brosnan from doing the documentary by invoking paragraph 3(c) of the Uniform Player Contract, which said:

> The Player further agrees that during the playing season he will not make public appearances, participate in radio or television programs or permit his picture to be taken or write or sponsor newspaper or magazine articles or sponsor commercial products without the written consent of the Club, which shall not be withheld except in the reasonable interests of the Club or professional baseball.

DeWitt withheld his consent. Brosnan wrote to commissioner Ford Frick, National League president Warren Giles, and Players Association part-time adviser Judge Robert Cannon for help. No one responded.

"You're being censored," a New York columnist told Brosnan. "That's unconstitutional."

"Obviously," Brosnan replied, "but so is the reserve clause."

DeWitt traded Brosnan in May 1963 to the Chicago White Sox. White Sox general manager Ed Short met Brosnan at the airport and said: "You can't write here, either." After Brosnan finished the 1963 season with a 3–9 record, 3.13 ERA, and 14 saves, Short tried to cut Brosnan's contract from $32,000 to $25,000 and refused to allow him to make up the difference by writing two magazine articles. Brosnan turned down the White Sox contract offer. Short responded by releasing him in February and boasting that "Brosnan can be had for a dollar." No teams called. After deciding against moving to Europe, Brosnan took out a tiny ad in the March 7, 1964, edition of the *Sporting News*. "Situation Sought. Bullpen operator, experience." After breaking down his statistics, Brosnan's ad concluded: "Free agent. Negotiable terms available. Respectfully request permission to pursue harmless avocation of professional writer." Only the unconventional Kansas City Athletics owner Charlie Finley responded to Brosnan's ad, but he wanted the pitcher to take a $5,000 pay cut. Brent Musburger, then writing for the *Chicago American*, told Brosnan that he was being blackballed. The American Civil Liberties Union (ACLU) accused the White Sox of censorship. Brosnan worked in 1964 and 1965 as a television and radio sports commentator and after that became a full-time freelance writer. He wrote magazine articles about baseball and had started to write a novel.

Bill Iverson called Brosnan May 1 at his home in Morton Grove, Illinois, and asked if Brosnan would come to New York to testify for Flood. Brosnan agreed. On the plane flight from Chicago to New York, Brosnan questioned his decision. "Why am I doing this?" Brosnan thought. "Our people asked me to do it. And we've got some weapons that we've never had before. The least I could do was put my ten words in, or two words."

Brosnan barely knew Flood, even though they had been teammates for half of the 1958 and 1959 seasons with the Cardinals and they both detested Solly Hemus, but Brosnan knew how cruel the game could be to players who dared to be different. He saw Flood's fight against the reserve clause as a noble one. "I didn't perceive this as a race thing," Brosnan recalled. "I perceived it as a player thing. I had been thinking about these things for a long time." Brosnan spent two delightful weeks in New York City hanging out with sports journalist Dick Schaap but had almost no contact with Flood at the trial except to shake hands with him and wish him luck.

On the day of his testimony, Brosnan ate lunch with Red Smith and Jackie Robinson. Smith and Robinson had not been friends during Robinson's playing days. Smith thought that Robinson was "fiercely racist" and "saw racism and prejudice under the bed." Inviting Robinson to lunch showed how progressive Smith had become. Smith also was a great admirer of Brosnan's books. The two men spent most of lunch discussing writing and art. Smith worked for the "Famous Writers School," a group of renowned writers who critiqued the work of people who paid to send them weekly submissions. Brosnan wanted to get his daughter, an aspiring artist, into the "Famous Artists School." Robinson, a political and social activist who knew little about writing or art, found it difficult to get a word in as Brosnan and Smith discussed their craft, and thus said almost nothing.

Brosnan was eager to testify by the time he approached the witness stand. He needed no more incentive than to see Bowie Kuhn taking notes on a yellow legal pad in the front row. At lunch, Smith informed Brosnan what Kuhn had been telling people: "What has [Brosnan] done in baseball that he can be involved in this?"

Brosnan responded with his wit. Six feet four, lanky, and wearing large black horn-rimmed glasses, he spoke with a slow midwestern accent. He enlivened every story with his writer's eye for detail, easygoing smile, and wry sense of humor. "He is a large, amiable, four-eyed, pipe-smoking martini man out of Xavier College in Cincinnati, whose literary leanings made his employers nervous," Red Smith wrote. Brosnan explained how he had bounced around the minor leagues and nearly quit the game after the 1953 season until the Chicago Cubs invited him to spring training. He spent half the year with the Cubs in 1954, was sent to Des Moines, and then was recalled to the Cubs a week later. The Chicago–Des Moines–Chicago moves wreaked havoc on Brosnan's family life.

"My wife threatened to divorce me," Brosnan testified about living in Des Moines. "She had just purchased two weeks of steaks, put them in the freezer in a house we had just rented, and she had done all this on her own because I was on a road trip to Denver. When I arrived in Denver there was a telegram saying, 'You are recalled. Get on a plane and report to St. Louis.' Then when I called her, she said, 'What do I do with the steaks and the rent?'"

Brosnan was not compensated for the lost rent or steaks. Topkis asked him what happened to the steaks.

"She gave them to the ballplayer that reported in my place."

The minor league pitcher who had replaced him, Paul Menking, lucked out.

Brosnan discussed his conflicts with Reds general manager Bill DeWitt and White Sox general manager Ed Short over his writing. Brosnan recalled that after he had refused to sign a contract with the White Sox in 1964, the package containing his notice of unconditional release came with 36 cents postage due. He then explained how he had been blackballed and had taken out an ad in the *Sporting News*.

As the audience laughed, Hughes objected. Judge Cooper admonished Brosnan. "This is your testimony under oath and while I like a certain amount of humor and humanity in the proceedings, there must come a time when we must make real progress with regard to the substantive matters before me," Cooper said. "So I am going to ask you to forfeit the indulgence that prompts you to add a little extra here and there."

On the reserve clause, Brosnan mentioned three former teammates that he thought could have been starters on other major league teams. He also advocated modifications to the reserve clause. Such modifications, Brosnan said, would not result in superstars jumping from team to team. "When a ballplayer develops his talents to the point where he is recognized as an outstanding player in a particular town with a particular club, his involvement with that club and with that town is of a unique nature, that is he does not want to leave that particular town for many reasons," Brosnan said. "In many case[s], he will have his family there, he will build a home there, he will have business contacts and businesses, probably, there. He is part of the community. His social life on and off the field, during the offseason, is bound up within the community in that particular town. For him to go to another town strictly on the basis of more money, for a star—we're talking about stars, he is making good money in the first place—would not be a good enough reason, in my mind, to leave a club with whom he has a solid position."

Brosnan stepped down from the witness stand after a brief cross-examination, and court adjourned for the day. Brosnan never even had the chance to say good-bye to Flood. As they left the courthouse, Goldberg grabbed Brosnan and pulled him into a cab. He was not happy with Brosnan's humorous testimony.

"Why was Irving Ben Cooper laughing?" Brosnan said as the cab drove him back to his hotel.

"There's a time to laugh and there's a time to be serious," Goldberg replied, "and this is a serious matter."

Goldberg's problem did not seem to be with Brosnan. Goldberg's involvement in the trial was at an end, and he had not really helped Flood's cause. Goldberg confided to the former pitcher after two days of trial: "We don't seem to be winning."

"When your chief lawyer says 'we're not winning,'" Brosnan recalled, "I already knew it was over."

CHAPTER ELEVEN

For Flood, the rest of the trial after Jackie Robinson's testimony was a "blur." He was at loose ends in New York City. He shared a suite with Allan Zerman at the Warwick Hotel. They hung out at the hotel bar, which was across the street from ABC News. Flood and Zerman drank with Howard Cosell and Don Meredith after the sportscasters had signed their first contract to do a weekly sports broadcast known as *Monday Night Football.* They also met the brains behind ABC Sports, producer Roone Arledge.

Flood also went out for drinks with the two young Paul, Weiss associates working on his case, Bill Iverson and Max Gitter. They were only a few years younger than Flood, but whereas Flood's baseball career was at an end, their legal careers were just beginning. For Iverson and Gitter, Flood's trial was a joyride. On lunch breaks, Flood and his trial team retreated to a Chinese restaurant near the Bowery. Cosell and Red Smith joined them a few times, as did a few of Flood's friends. One afternoon, Iverson and Gitter left the trial early to order the food. They became so enamored of the restaurant's dumplings that they placed six orders—72 dumplings in all. Flood and the rest of the group ate only a dumpling or two apiece and left the other 60 dumplings on the table. Iverson and Gitter finished them all.

One of Flood's lunch guests was the brother-in-law of Judy Pace, Oscar Brown Jr. An accomplished singer, songwriter, poet, and playwright, Brown was a theatrical revolutionary. He produced two Broadway musicals but spent his life challenging the establishment. In 1967, he put on a revue, *Opportunity Please Knock*, with the Blackstone Rangers street gang in his native Chicago. In December 1969, he cast former heavyweight champion Muhammad Ali—during his exile from the ring—in the starring role of a Broadway musical, *Buck White*. Wearing an Afro wig, Ali sang the chorus of the title song with his black fist raised in the air:

If you're expecting us to Uncle Tom
You might as well send and get your bomb
'Cause that's all over now, Mighty Whitey.
All over now.

Critics panned *Buck White*, which had only four Broadway performances. Ali, after mixed reviews, waited for the courts to reverse his draft-evasion conviction before returning to boxing. But Brown and his wife, Jean Pace, returned a month later with another musical revue, *Joy*, which was in its fifth month of a successful off-Broadway run during Flood's trial. Brown, like Flood, was his own man. They bonded in New York City. Brown even came to Flood's trial.

Flood did not lack for female companionship. His Warwick Hotel suite was a revolving door of beautiful women—a black schoolteacher, a beautiful blonde, and even a few prostitutes. The secretaries at Paul, Weiss swooned over him when he walked through the halls of the law firm. He looked and talked like a movie star. Women could not get enough of him, and he did not turn many of them away.

Women served as a welcome distraction from Flood's problems with his photography business. Feeling the pressure in the months leading up to his trial, he had neglected his business interests. While the trial proceeded in New York City, Marian Jorgensen stayed in St. Louis trying to keep the power company from turning off the electricity at Flood's photography studios. More creditors closed in on him. The demise of the business was imminent.

The rest of the trial bored Flood. The testimony during the remainder of his case—by economist Robert Nathan, NFL commissioner Pete Rozelle, NBA commissioner J. Walter Kennedy, NHL Players Association chief Alan Eagleson, and NHL president Clarence Campbell—was uneventful.

Cooper praised Rozelle's testimony. "Did you ever have any legal training?" Cooper asked.

"No, your Honor," Rozelle replied.

"This is the way," Cooper said. "Very good. You handled yourself very well. I compliment you."

Cooper's treatment of Rozelle gave Flood's lawyers a clue as to the way he would cater to the egos of the baseball dignitaries taking the stand for the owners.

After Robinson, Greenberg, and Brosnan testified, Goldberg returned to the campaign trail—a move that must have disappointed Cooper. Cooper wanted to prove that he was a competent judge under the brightest possible spotlight. That spotlight dimmed in Goldberg's absence. Goldberg had promised Cooper that Flood's trial would be his first priority. He had also promised that Flood's case would take only one day. He had broken both promises.

Flood's biggest disappointment with his ongoing trial was that no current players testified on his behalf. "So far as I know no one volunteered," Flood said on June 1. "I understand the situation. If a guy comes here and publicly says I'm right, he could be risking his future career in baseball." Miller and Moss explained the players' predicament to Flood and the press. "Some of Curt's friends indicated to him that they would like to testify but were fearful of jeopardizing their baseball careers," Moss said. "They said they hope Curt understands—and I think he does."

Not a single active player came to the trial to show his support by sitting in the gallery. The players were the ones paying for it; they could at the very least have come to the trial to see what they were getting for their money. The Cardinals played night games May 26 and 27 in New York against the Mets. Flood's best friend in baseball, Bob Gibson, started the series finale on the afternoon of Thursday, May 28. Flood asked Gibson for two tickets that day. Flood and Zerman skipped the trial to watch Gibson strike out 11 Mets at Shea Stadium during a 9–2 Cardinals win. "Curt Flood still likes baseball," Gibson told reporters, citing the ticket request as proof. The night before he pitched, Gibson had stopped by for several hours at Flood's Warwick Hotel suite. But Gibson made good on his promise to stay "a few hundred paces" behind

Flood to avoid any fallout. Gibson and a few of Flood's former Cardinals teammates could easily have come to lower Manhattan one of those mornings and quietly watched Flood's trial from the back of the courtroom. They never did. "I know we talked about it, and I know we were aware of it," Joe Torre recalled. "I can't give you a good reason why we weren't there."

Miller later admitted that one of his biggest tactical mistakes was not encouraging the players to be seen watching the trial and leaving the courthouse. "[I]f I had it to do over again I would say, 'For God's sake, this man is a colleague of yours!'" Miller wrote. "'What happens to him could have a dramatic impact on *your* life, so when your team comes to New York, if you've got a night game, come on down to Foley Square for a couple of hours during the day and show him some support.'" Miller blamed himself. But he had been on the job for only four years; he and the players were not as united as they would later be.

As soon as Flood's lawyers rested his case, the owners again asked Cooper to dismiss the lawsuit. Hughes argued that Flood had not proved any of his claims. Flood was "obviously not a slave" because, as Cooper had said in denying the preliminary injunction, Flood "was free to quit and refuse to play for Philadelphia." All of Flood's witnesses, except Flood himself, favored modification, not elimination, of the reserve clause. This did not amount to an antitrust violation. Hughes reminded the judge that *Toolson* exempted baseball from the federal antitrust laws. Hughes characterized Flood's lawsuit as merely a union negotiating tactic. Any changes in the reserve clause, he said, must be accomplished at the negotiating table. Baseball, Hughes argued, also was exempt from Flood's lawsuit under federal labor law. The players, according to this theory, could choose either to join forces as a union and negotiate collectively with the owners or to sue the owners under the antitrust laws, but not both. Relying on this "labor exemption," Hughes argued that the Players Association, or one of its members, could not bring an antitrust lawsuit about the reserve clause while engaging in labor negotiations about the same issue. Finally, Hughes cited the Wisconsin Supreme Court's decision in the Milwaukee Braves case as proof that baseball's federal antitrust exemption trumped Flood's state and common law antitrust claims.

Flood's biggest asset for the remainder of his trial was the leadership of Jay Topkis. In a stirring response, Topkis told Cooper that "we are fortunate to live in a time of change, great change," reminded him that the Supreme Court had struck down its long-standing decisions permitting racial segregation, and argued that it was time for *Toolson* to go the way of the Court's other decisions that restricted personal freedom. Topkis understood if Cooper was waiting for the Supreme Court to overrule *Toolson*. But the state antitrust laws applied to insurance companies; there was no reason they should not apply to baseball. Cooper, as a federal judge, was not bound by decisions of the Wisconsin Supreme Court. And as for Flood not being a slave, Topkis remarked: "The only difference that I can see between peonage and involuntary servitude on the one hand and Curt Flood's position on the other is that he was being paid $90,000 a year. That makes him a mighty high-paid slave. There is no doubt about that. But you remember Winston Churchill's great remark about the lady of easy virtue who was paid a great deal of money and the label that was still hung on her, the same thing is true here. As long as Curt Flood has pressed down upon him the restraint of baseball, he must feel himself a slave because, in fact, he is a slave. To use his skills, he must submit to slavery."

Topkis employed his ample rhetorical skills to remind Cooper about Flood's courage. "I would ask your Honor to consider what a remarkable sacrifice it is that this young man is making by coming into this court," Topkis said. "He is at the peak of his powers today as a baseball player, or he was two months ago, being compensated quite handsomely. But he is putting that all aside, saying, 'To me freedom is worth more.'"

After a brief recess, Cooper denied the owners' motion to dismiss. He forced the owners to put on their defense. The next morning at 10 a.m., the owners called their first witness—commissioner Bowie Kuhn.

Kuhn's problems as commissioner continued to mount. The city of Seattle was suing baseball because after a single season the expansion Pilots had left town to become the Milwaukee Brewers. Kuhn was fending off criticism for his lenient suspension of pitcher Denny McLain. Even his self-described "Washington mentor," lawyer Paul Porter, advised Kuhn on a limousine ride from New York to Washington to abandon his "high moral tone." Kuhn replied: "I think it's the commissioner's job to strike a high moral tone, come what may."

A high moral tone was all that Kuhn had left after the union and the owners agreed in principle to a new labor agreement, known as the 1970 Basic Agreement. The owners agreed to allow the players to take future grievances, except those involving "integrity issues," to an independent arbitrator. Kuhn acceded to the arrangement after a chance meeting with Miller on a midtown Manhattan street corner. Miller explained that the union intended to inundate the commissioner with grievances and that every decision Kuhn made would alienate either an owner or the union. In the long run, independent grievance arbitration turned out to be a powerful weapon for the players to resolve disputes with management and another way for them to attack the reserve clause besides the courts. In the short run, the decision to permit independent grievance arbitration eviscerated Kuhn's authority. "[T]he Lords of Baseball have sold out the commissioner," Dick Young wrote a few days before Flood's trial. "They have peddled away his power. They have conceded, at last, that he is their commissioner, not the players' commissioner."

With his only remaining role to protect the game's integrity, Kuhn embarked on a moral crusade against pitcher Jim Bouton and his new book, *Ball Four*, a behind-the-scenes account of Bouton's 1969 season as a knuckleballer for the Seattle Pilots and the Houston Astros. Bouton's irreverent look at the game portrayed his former New York Yankees teammates as Peeping Toms, described Mickey Mantle drinking too much and slamming bus windows in the faces of kids asking for his autograph, and revealed players popping amphetamine pills they called "greenies." Bouton's *Ball Four* made Brosnan's *The Long Season* look tame.

On June 1, Kuhn called Bouton into his 20th-floor, corner office on Fifth Avenue, which Bouton described as "decorated in Early Authority—paneled walls with pictures of presidents and a large desk between two American flags." Kuhn tried to persuade Bouton to sign a document that repudiated everything in his book and placed the blame on his editor, sportswriter Leonard Shecter. Bouton, accompanied by Miller and Moss, refused. Kuhn then spent the next three hours urging Bouton not to reveal what had happened at their meeting. The commissioner let Bouton off with a warning and turned his book into a bestseller.

A week before meeting with Bouton, Kuhn testified against Flood. The commissioner viewed Flood's lawsuit not as *Flood v. Kuhn*, but as

Miller v. Kuhn. This was Kuhn's chance to one-up his labor adversary in the commissioner's legal domain.

Kuhn's two days of testimony represented an argument against change. Kuhn testified that "baseball as we know it simply could not survive" without the reserve clause. "Baseball as we know it," Leonard Koppett wrote after the trial, was an elusive concept. It meant 16, 20, or 24 teams; 154 or 162 games; natural grass or artificial turf; a dead or lively ball; big or little gloves; 400 or 600 major leaguers; two or four umpires; day or night games; franchises in 11 Northeast cities or 16 franchise shifts in 17 years; massive farm systems or a free-agent draft; complete-game pitchers or starters followed by relievers. "The only aspect 'preserved' by the reserve system," Koppett wrote, "is the reserve system itself."

Without the reserve clause, Kuhn predicted, the rich teams would sign all the star players, the poor teams would go out of business, and the operation of a league would be impossible. Major League Baseball would devolve into an "exhibition business." He based his predictions on the "chaotic conditions [that] prevailed when there was no reserve clause" in professional baseball from 1871 to 1879, when players jumped to rival teams and leagues and fixed games. Kuhn's argument, however, lacked historical context. He was comparing baseball in Reconstruction-era America in the 1870s to modern-day baseball in the 1970s. The argument ignored the industrialization of America, the evolution of the game, the rise of the modern print and electronic media, and a century of progress.

Kuhn rejected all Miller's proposed reserve clause modifications by rigidly analyzing their effects on four criteria: (1) integrity of the game; (2) economics of the sport; (3) mechanical workability; and (4) equality of competition. Topkis countered on cross-examination that the reserve clause accomplished none of these goals except to limit player salaries. Player salaries constituted 59 percent of team expenses in 1879 compared with 22 percent in 1950 and 21.5 percent in 1970. It certainly did not help equalize competition. Four teams won 63 of the 100 pennants from 1920 to 1969.

Both Kuhn and National League president Chub Feeney testified that free agency would compromise the game's integrity by inducing players to cheat. Feeney raised the possibility of a potential free agent committing a key error during the pennant race and then joining the opposing team the following season. According to Feeney, "the public's confidence in the integrity of the game would be shattered." Feeney did not explain what incentive a free agent would have to perform below his best or what incentive another team would have to sign a player who did so. Kuhn made an equally implausible prediction that free agency would stifle trades and end offseason discussion of baseball known as the Hot Stove League.

On June 2, after Cardinals general manager Bing Devine's testimony, former Cardinals catcher Joe Garagiola brought 13 minutes of promanagement cheer. Garagiola's image had come a long way since his heated 1947 encounter with Jackie Robinson. During a routine double play at first base, Garagiola stepped on Robinson's heel. Robinson—who had been spiked by Cardinals outfielder Enos Slaughter a few weeks earlier—exchanged angry words with Garagiola before Robinson's next time at-bat. Garagiola, according to Robinson, "made a crack about my race." Umpire Beans Reardon stepped in between them. Dodgers coach Clyde Sukeforth, knowing that Rickey had ordered Robinson not to fight back, tried to push Robinson away. Nothing more came of the incident. Garagiola spent the rest of his life trying to make people forget that it had ever happened. The gregarious host of NBC's *Today* show, the game show *He Said, She Said*, and several radio programs, Garagiola endeared himself to a subsequent generation of baseball fans as one of the voices of television's *Game of the Week*.

Garagiola spelled his name for the court reporter. Even before his testimony began, he and Judge Cooper formed a mutual admiration society.

"Do you always have a smile like that?" Cooper asked.

"Yes, always."

"That is a blessing."

Garagiola returned the compliment: "I wish you were on a bubble gum card, Judge. I'd have you."

In his only substantive testimony, Garagiola said of the reserve clause: "To me this is the best system so far. Nobody's come up with anything better. I think if they might change the name but have the same thing, everybody would be happy."

Topkis declined to cross-examine Garagiola. It would have been like interrogating Santa Claus. Nothing could have been gained except alienating Judge Cooper.

The only nondefendant in baseball to testify against Flood, Garagiola made light of the system of player ownership years later. "Being traded is like celebrating your hundredth birthday," he said. "It might not be the happiest occasion in the world, but consider the alternatives." Garagiola lacked Flood's vision to do just that.

Another former player who testified against Flood was American League president Joe Cronin. As the Washington Senators' player-manager, Cronin was traded to the Boston Red Sox for $225,000 and shortstop Lyn Lary by his uncle-in-law, Senators owner Clark Griffith. After sending Cronin to the Red Sox, Griffith and the Senators never won another pennant. Cronin testified that Griffith—known during his pitching days as "the Old Fox"—was "one of the finest baseball talents (and one of the finest human beings) he had ever known."

"Didn't he attain some fame by jumping his reserve clause?" Topkis asked on cross-examination.

"That I don't remember," Cronin replied.

Topkis then read Griffith's testimony before a 1951 House subcommittee in which Griffith said he had "jumped his reserve clause and joined the American League at the time of its formation." Griffith had been instrumental in persuading other National League players to jump their contracts and join the league known as the junior circuit.

The defense's next four witnesses were baseball executives—Cincinnati Reds president Francis L. Dale, Montreal Expos president and CEO John McHale, California Angels president Robert Reynolds, and Kansas City Royals owner Ewing Kauffman. They testified that they would not have purchased their teams without baseball's antitrust exemption and without the reserve clause.

Of the four, Kauffman was the most impressive witness. In 1950, the Royals' owner founded a pharmaceutical company, Marion Laboratories, in his 500-square-foot basement with $5,000 and turned it into a three-acre laboratory worth millions. In 1968, he bought the Royals as an expansion team and started a baseball academy in an effort to find young men with the right athletic gifts to turn them into professional baseball players. On the stand, he toed the party line about baseball not being able to survive without the reserve clause. But when Topkis asked him how much he would pay Curt Flood on the open market, Kauffman said $125,000 a year and even more than that if Flood was willing to sign a long-term deal.

"How much for a five-year contract?" Topkis asked.

"I don't know," Kauffman replied. "You let me choose my players, we'll go pretty high."

It was an honest admission that revealed the main purpose of the reserve clause: to prevent deep-pocket owners such as Kauffman from paying players what they were worth.

As their last two witnesses, the owners called economist John Clark and their labor negotiator, John Gaherin. A veteran negotiator for the railroad and newspaper industries, Gaherin was the owners' most credible witness. He countered many of Marvin Miller's assertions that the owners had not negotiated about the reserve clause in good faith. He said that Miller and the Players Association had thrown out ideas about how to modify the reserve clause, but they had not made any formal proposals. He also said that the union's decision to fund Flood's lawsuit undermined their efforts to negotiate a new labor agreement. Gaherin came off as a professional negotiator rather than a baseball partisan.

Between rebuttals by Miller and Gaherin, Flood's legal team called its best witness last—former Cleveland Indians, St. Louis Browns, and Chicago White Sox owner Bill Veeck. Known as the P. T. Barnum of baseball because of his crazy promotions, Veeck was not so much a clown as a visionary. He originated exploding scoreboards, bat days, ball days, cap days, and names on the backs of uniforms. He would do almost anything to help his team at the box office and in the standings.

Veeck is most famous for sending a midget—3-foot-7-inch, 65-pound Eddie Gaedel—to bat with the Browns. Gaedel jumped out of a cake to pinch-hit for the leadoff batter, and stepped to the plate wearing the number 1/8 and holding a toy bat. "Eddie," Veeck had earlier told Gaedel, "I'm going to be up on the roof with a high-powered rifle watching every move you make. If you so much as look as if you're going to swing, I'm going to shoot you dead." Gaedel walked on four pitches. Detroit Tigers pitcher Bob Cain was laughing so hard that balls three and four sailed over Gaedel's head. Cain's catcher, Bob Swift, caught the pitches on his knees. The Browns immediately sent in a pinch runner. The following day, American League president Will Harridge banned

Gaedel from baseball. Veeck claimed Harridge's ruling "discriminate[d] against the little people." Veeck demanded that Harridge set a minimum height requirement and wanted to know whether diminutive Yankees shortstop Phil Rizzuto was "a short ballplayer or a tall midget." Veeck befriended Gaedel and hired him for several other baseball-related promotions until Gaedel's death in 1961. The last line of Veeck's Hall of Fame plaque reads: "A champion of the little guy."

As the owner of the minor league Milwaukee Brewers, Veeck installed movable outfield fences. A gadget lowered the fences when the Brewers batted and raised them for opposing teams. In Cleveland, he moved the fences in and out depending on the opposing team's power. Both leagues immediately outlawed Veeck's fence manipulation. "I have tried always not to break any rules," Veeck testified at Flood's trial, "but to test highly their elasticity."

Veeck purchased the Brewers in 1941 with $11 in his pocket and a $25,000 loan to cover the team's pressing debts and left the game in 1961 after selling his share of the Chicago White Sox for $1.1 million. The son of the president of the Chicago Cubs, Veeck had been thrown out of several boarding schools and dropped out of Kenyon College upon learning that his father was dying of leukemia. The younger Veeck worked for the Cubs from 1933 until 1941. He lost part of his right leg after injuring his foot as a World War II marine. Over the years, he had bought and sold a number of franchises: the Brewers, Indians, Browns, minor league Miami Marlins, and White Sox. He persuaded Hank Greenberg to join the Indians' front office in 1948. The two men later bought the White Sox and were best friends. Veeck likely influenced Greenberg to testify at Flood's trial.

In his quest for success, Veeck disregarded not only size but also age and race. Although disputed by some historians, he claimed that Judge Landis had scuttled his plan to purchase the Philadelphia Phillies after the 1942 season and stock the team with black players. He signed Larry Doby, the American League's first black player, in July 1947, only a few months after Jackie Robinson had broken in with the Dodgers. The following year, Veeck signed Negro league pitching legend Satchel Paige. Paige and Doby helped the 1948 Indians become the first team to draw more than 2 million fans and capture Cleveland's last World Series trophy. Paige also pitched for Veeck with the Browns and the Marlins.

Veeck was a man ahead of his time. In 1952, he suggested at an American League meeting that the owners increase the visiting team's share of the gate receipts and pool their television revenues. "After all," Veeck reasoned, "it takes two teams to put on a game." After Veeck received a second for his proposal, the owners voted against it, 7–1. The NFL adopted Veeck's television idea in 1961 at the urging of NFL commissioner Pete Rozelle, which helped football maintain competitive balance and overtake baseball as America's most popular professional sport.

For nearly 30 years, Veeck had been on record as opposing the reserve clause. While taking night law school classes at Northwestern in 1941, Veeck wrote Judge Landis a letter that described the reserve clause as "legally and morally indefensible." Veeck recalled Landis's tersely written response by heart: "Some very knowledgeable fellow once said that a little knowledge is a dangerous thing and you just proved him a wizard."

Veeck sold the White Sox in June 1961 after doctors at the Mayo Clinic had told him to slow down. He had been smoking four packs of cigarettes and drinking a case of beer a day. He had lost the rest of his right leg to subsequent operations. He had suffered a chronic case of walking pneumonia, and had been coughing so hard that he was blacking out.

For Veeck, however, there was no slowing down. Even though he retired to a farm on Maryland's Eastern Shore, he purchased Suffolk Downs racetrack outside Boston. He also wrote, with Ed Linn, two of the best baseball autobiographies ever published, *Veeck As in Wreck* and *The Hustler's Handbook*. An insomniac and voracious reader, Veeck read an average of five books a week.

Miller, Topkis, and Goldberg all spoke with Veeck about testifying. It did not take much persuading. During a three-hour dinner with Miller in Washington, Veeck readily agreed to testify. Topkis and Gitter visited with Veeck for several hours at Suffolk Downs. The two lawyers barely got a word in as Veeck regaled them with stories just as he had done with Miller. Topkis, who, like Miller, had read Veeck's books, knew what to expect. "I was prepared to love him and be charmed by him, and I was," Topkis recalled.

Veeck refused to allow his desire to return to baseball to prevent him from testifying against the owners. He had already revealed many of their foibles in his two books. He had testified against them in 1966 during the Milwaukee Braves relocation case. A prior speaking engagement, however, had prevented him from testifying May 19 or 20 for Flood. Veeck initially agreed in a phone conversation with Goldberg to testify on May 21, but Veeck could not make it that day either. He wanted to testify June 1—in the middle of the defense's case. The owners' lawyers balked at the idea of interrupting their defense. Flood's lawyers agreed to call him as a rebuttal witness.

Veeck arrived in New York City late on the night of June 9. The next morning, Topkis and Iverson met Veeck at 7:45 in his suite at the Waldorf-Astoria Hotel, where they ate salmon omelets and discussed his testimony. Iverson was concerned that during cross-examination the owners—by bringing up midgets and movable fences—would make Veeck look like a crackpot. Veeck told Iverson not to worry. He pulled out a large embossed book that American League owners had given him in 1961 after he had sold the White Sox. The book contained a list of his accomplishments and a citation that read as follows:

> Tribute to Bill Veeck
>
> It is a matter of deep regret to the American League that Bill Veeck has been forced by illness to divest himself of his interests in the Chicago White Sox and to resign from the presidency of that club. The American League expresses its appreciation to Bill Veeck for his many valuable contributions to baseball, the league and the Chicago club, and extends sincere wishes for his speedy recovery to good health and to the personal vibrancy which has so characterized his career in baseball.
>
> Resolution unanimously adopted by the members of the American League of Professional Baseball Clubs at its meeting in Chicago on Monday, June 26, 1961.

The owners thought that Veeck was dying. Doctors at the Mayo Clinic believed that lung cancer had spread to his brain. He turned out to have a chronic concussion exacerbated by the coughing fits that caused his blackouts. His health improved with rest. He spited his American League adversaries by living an additional 25 years and testifying against them at Flood's trial.

Before his testimony, Veeck waited in Cooper's courtroom to be called to the witness stand. He wore an open-neck, wide-collared shirt and no tie. He hated to wear ties on account of a skin condition. He ignored the No Smoking signs in the courtroom and lit a cigarette. Miller sat there bemused by Veeck's wearing an open-collared shirt and smoking in federal court. Goldberg, who had declined Topkis's and Iverson's repeated invitations to join them at breakfast, was horrified. "Bill," Goldberg said, "you can't smoke in the courtroom." Veeck pulled up his right pants leg and extinguished the cigarette in an ashtray carved into his wooden leg.

Fortunately for Veeck, Topkis conducted his direct examination. After reviewing Veeck's background, Topkis asked whether he had received any awards from the American League. "Well, I presume it was an award," Veeck said. "It was a very nice citation or call it what you will. I have a feeling that maybe it was kind of in memoriam." The crowd laughed. Topkis then read the entire resolution into the court record. The owners could not portray his witness as a kook.

Veeck set himself apart from Flood's other witnesses because of his quick wit and because, in Topkis's words, "he had thought about these issues more than anyone else." Veeck opposed the complete elimination of the reserve clause, but phasing in a different form of the reserve clause "wouldn't dislocate baseball horrendously and wouldn't cause any chaotic conditions." Veeck advocated seven-year contracts like the ones between movie stars and Hollywood studios, which called for automatic raises at designated option periods. He suggested a system similar to pro football's, in which the player played out his one-year option and joined a new team as long as the new team was willing to pay his former team mutually-agreed-upon financial compensation. He also endorsed signing players to a combined major league–minor league contract for a period of years.

Modifying the reserve clause, Veeck argued, would benefit management. The wealthiest teams, Veeck said, could not sign all the best players. He attributed the Yankees' dominance not to their wealth but to their scouts and added, "though it grieves me to say it, they had probably the best administrator in the game in a fellow by the name of George Weiss, with whom I did not see eye to eye on much of anything except that he is a very talented man." Veeck believed winning was "not a question of dollars" but "a question of the ability of the people operating and their willingness to work hard."

Veeck also recognized the principles at stake: "Everyone should once in their business career have the right to determine their future for themselves." He envisioned more equitable contractual negotiations and distribution of talent. Teams could not stockpile players if the players were free to negotiate with another organization where they could receive more playing time. He believed that teams recouped their investments in their players after five major league seasons.

Unlike most of the owners, Veeck understood why Flood felt like a slave and why the current system was bad for the game. "I think that it would certainly help the players and the game itself to no longer be one of the few places in which there is human bondage," Veeck said. "I think it would be to the benefit of the reputation of the game of baseball. . . . I still think it is a game that deserves to be perpetuated and to restore it to the position of honor it once held, and I think this would be a step in that direction. At least it would be fair."

Kuhn's lawyer, Victor Kramer, cross-examined Veeck. "I would say I found *Veeck As in Wreck* an extremely enjoyable book," Kramer announced. "I recommend it to everyone within the sound of my voice." Kramer then turned Veeck's literary genius against him. He adopted the same strategy that baseball's lawyers had used in the Milwaukee case: He read sentences from Veeck's books and asked Veeck whether he agreed or disagreed with them. A contrarian by nature, Veeck disagreed several times with statements from his own books.

Goldberg, in one of his few speaking roles since the beginning of the trial, stood up and objected to Kramer's marking selected pages from Veeck's books as exhibits. Goldberg wanted Veeck's entire books entered into the record. Goldberg had already been burned by the owners' selective quotation of Jackie Robinson's prior statements. Judge Cooper refused to admit the entirety of both books into evidence. Instead, they compromised on the admission of a complete chapter.

Despite a few early inconsistencies, Veeck was too quick for both Kramer and Judge Cooper on cross-examination. Cooper asked Veeck to stick to yes-or-no answers when asked yes-or-no questions on cross-examination. "I know that you are a colorful witness," Cooper said, "and it is good to have a colorful witness, but would you remember that it is important to address yourself to the particular question." "I'm sorry to have spoiled your morning," Veeck replied.

Kramer asked Veeck a hypothetical question about an unhappy star shortstop who wanted just compensation and therefore wanted to leave the team. "I find that question impossible to answer," Veeck said, "because I can't anticipate as an owner, when I was an owner, that I would have a shortstop who would be so unhappy with being with me." Kramer also asked Veeck why he seemed to be so fond of the American League owners. "I think it is that I don't have to associate with them as directly," Veeck replied. During a recess, however, he told a reporter that the owners have "intractable minds that respond only to necessity." After an hour and a half, Veeck stepped down from the witness stand. He walked out of the courthouse and smiled for waiting photographers.

Only baseball's outsiders—black, Jewish, pitcher-turned-author, and maverick—had the guts to support Flood. Robinson, Greenberg, Brosnan, and Veeck brought an enormous amount of publicity to Flood's case. The American people—69 percent of them according to a September poll—believed that the reserve clause was "necessary." But these four men reminded everyone why it needed to be modified.

John Gaherin briefly rebutted Miller's third and final appearance on the witness stand, and both the plaintiff and the defense rested. Lawyers from both sides asked Judge Cooper to decide the case in their favor; Cooper refused to rule. Instead, he ordered post-trial briefs due July 7 with replies due July 13. Cooper's decision was going to come in the form of a written opinion.

Just past 3:37 p.m. on June 11, Cooper concluded Flood's trial after 3 weeks, 15 trial days, 21 witnesses, 56 exhibits, and 2,078 pages of transcript. Cooper singled out each of the lead attorneys in the courtroom for praise. He reminded the audience that Hughes was the past president of the New York County Lawyers Association, a subtle reference to the only local bar organization that had refused to testify against him at his confirmation hearings. He praised Goldberg's "leadership" as "exemplary" and told Topkis "your hair-trigger alertness was remarkable and at times truly fascinating."

"As to the case itself," Cooper said, "it really is a cause in the truest classical sense. Interwoven with the rights of the litigants named in the caption of this matter is baseball itself. This is enough to compel us to proceed with utmost care. . . . It goes without saying that we are resolved to call them as we see them as they come across the plate."

Cooper wrapped up his remarks with a quotation from Judge Jerome Frank, the famed liberal jurist who in the *Gardella* case had equated the reserve clause with slavery. Cooper quoted another of Frank's opinions:

"The law doesn't require a judge to anesthetize his emotional reflections. 'Only death yields such complete dispassionateness, for dispassion signifies indifference. Much harm is done by the myth that merely by putting on a black robe and taking the oath of office as a judge a man ceases to be human and strips himself of all predilections and becomes a passionateless unthinking man.'

"That is the effect that this case has had on this judge," Cooper said.

For three weeks, Cooper had tried hard to prove to the world that he was an erudite jurist and not a raving madman. He had no intention, however, of following Frank's thinking in *Gardella*. Cooper's true feelings about the case came out in the ways he bullied Flood, browbeat Brosnan, and bristled at Veeck, yet ingratiated himself with celebrities including Robinson, Kuhn, Rozelle, and Garagiola. Cooper was a prisoner of the game's establishment. And the two Supreme Court precedents in baseball's favor did not give him much room to prove otherwise.

Flood was not present for Veeck's testimony or Cooper's closing remarks. Nor was he there June 8 for the cross-examination of the owners' economist, during NHL president Clarence Campbell's May 26 testimony, or for Topkis's stirring defense against the owners' motion to dismiss.

Flood most likely retreated to the Westchester County home of his literary collaborator, Richard Carter. For a month in early summer, he lived at Carter's home in Ossining, about 25 miles outside of New York City, ostensibly working on his book but mostly getting drunk. He admitted later that he spent most of that summer "bedding and boozing." The boozing was more evident. He began each day with a vodka martini. Members of Flood's legal team noticed his drinking during the trial. It got worse at Carter's home.

Carter's 12-year-old son, John, idolized Flood. One afternoon, John invited several friends over to play some backyard baseball. Not believing their good fortune that they had a major leaguer in their midst, they invited Flood to join them. Flood was so drunk that he was in no condition to do anything. He uncorked a wild throw and heaved the ball into the woods behind the Carter home. The boys never found the ball. Flood retreated inside the house.

Flood's life was a mess. He had thrown away his baseball career for a lawsuit that he had little chance of winning. Even though Marvin Miller had warned him that it would be like this, Flood was unprepared to deal with the harsh realities of his daily life without baseball.

St. Louis—despite Flood's protestations about being traded from the Cardinals—no longer felt like home. The lawsuits against Curt Flood & Associates and Flood personally represented the least of his problems. The IRS was on his tail. Curt Flood & Associates owed the government $6,888.42 in unpaid withholding taxes. The IRS auctioned off a camera and camera stand from one of Flood's two St. Louis photo studios. The telephones had been disconnected. Flood's attorney, Allan Zerman, no longer knew if the corporation was even in business. Neither did Flood. He took no part, nor did he want any part, in his business affairs.

In early August, Marian Jorgensen forced Flood to confront the reality that his portrait and photography businesses were finished. Flood lacked the business sense, the desire, and the money to keep them afloat. The failure to file annual corporate disclosure forms with the state of Missouri by the end of 1970 spelled the official end of Curt Flood & Associates, Inc.

The demise of Flood's business interests in St. Louis also led to the end of his close friendship with Marian Jorgensen. Flood decided to clear his head by returning to Denmark. So Marian packed up the St. Louis apartment and moved back to Oakland. Marian's family money began to run out. She went to work for Oakland's welfare department and later moved in with her son about an hour outside Oakland. She never remarried and became reclusive, eventually severing her ties with Carl, Flood's sister, Barbara, and Flood himself. Without Marian, Flood had no support system, no way of coping, other than vodka.

Denmark helped Flood escape from reality. He initially checked into the same Copenhagen hotel as the Rolling Stones, but the groupies who pounded on the door of the band's room and bombarded it with phone calls reminded Flood of his hectic life at home. He checked out and rented a room that overlooked a harbor in Vedbaek, a suburb 15 miles north of Copenhagen. He grew a goatee, bought a sketch pad and a beret, and sat in Copenhagen's Tivoli Gardens flirting with Danish women. He enjoyed the anonymity of a black expatriate artist much more than the constant celebrity of a major league ballplayer. "In Denmark, I can walk down the street and nobody recognizes me," Flood said. "I can have a beer and nobody recognizes me. I feel free here." He also was free from answering reporters' questions about his lawsuit against baseball.

On July 7, both sides filed massive post-trial briefs that set up their arguments for the inevitable appeal. The 88-page brief filed by Flood's legal team exposed inconsistencies in baseball's position. In *Federal Baseball* and *Toolson*, baseball's lawyers had encouraged the Supreme Court to exempt the game from the federal antitrust laws because the state antitrust laws still applied. Flood's lawyers recognized that no trial court was going to reverse two Supreme Court precedents but that it might rule in Flood's favor on state law grounds. If baseball was not interstate commerce, as *Federal Baseball* had claimed, then it was intrastate commerce subject to state law. State antitrust law, therefore, might provide the federal court of appeals or the Supreme Court with another way of ruling in Flood's favor.

The opening of the owners' 133-page brief drove a wedge between Flood and the Players Association by asking: "Who is the real plaintiff in this action?" The owners' lawyers pointed out that the union was paying for the litigation and that the goals of the union (modifying the reserve clause) and of Flood (eliminating the reserve clause) were at odds. On appeal, they sought to make Flood and his enormous personal sacrifices irrelevant. They wanted to remove the human face from the lawsuit and expose it as a mere labor negotiation tactic. They, too, were looking ahead for ways that the Supreme Court could rule in their favor.

On July 13, Flood and the owners' lawyers filed short replies to each other's briefs. A month later, on August 12, Cooper issued his decision. Cooper's 47-page typewritten opinion said what both Cooper and everyone else already knew before Flood's trial: He could not overrule the Supreme Court's decision in *Toolson* upholding baseball's antitrust exemption. He rejected Flood's state and common law claims as preempted by federal law. He found it unnecessary to rule on whether federal labor law also thwarted Flood's antitrust claims. Finally, he dismissed Flood's claims of involuntary servitude because Flood "has the right to retire and to embark upon a different enterprise outside organized baseball." After reading this section of Cooper's opinion, Red Smith wrote: "To the Four Freedoms of Franklin Roosevelt—freedom of speech, freedom of worship, freedom from want, and freedom from fear—Judge Cooper has added freedom to starve."

Cooper, however, refused to stop there. He could not let his moment in the spotlight slip away without expressing his personal views about the reserve clause:

> Prior to the trial we gained the impression that there was a view, held by many, that baseball's reserve system had occasioned rampant abuse and that it should be abolished. We were struck by the fact, however, that the testimony at trial failed to support that criticism; we find no general or widespread disregard of the extremely important position the player occupies.
>
> Clearly, the preponderance of the credible proof does not favor elimination of the reserve clause.

Cooper also predicted that the solution to this lawsuit lay at the bargaining table. He rejected Flood's argument that the owners had refused to negotiate in good faith and expressed optimism that "the reserve clause can be fashioned so as to find acceptance by player and club." Cooper concluded: "We are bound by the law as we find it and by our obligation to 'call it as we see it.'" He ordered judgment for the defendants.

Bowie Kuhn commended Judge Cooper's decision. "I am particularly pleased," Kuhn read from a prepared statement, "that the court has recognized the need for a reserve system and has recognized further that baseball has not disregarded the extremely important position the player occupies." The commissioner used Cooper's decision to urge the players to abandon Flood's lawsuit and settle their issues with the reserve clause at the bargaining table.

Miller was unfazed by Cooper's opinion or Kuhn's response. "Judge Cooper only held that it is up to the Supreme Court to overrule the

Supreme Court," he said. "I think everyone knew that it would be very difficult for a district court to overrule the Supreme Court." Miller chided Kuhn and his call for negotiations as disingenuous given that the union and the owners had agreed not to negotiate about the reserve clause while Flood's lawsuit was pending. The owners, moreover, had never wanted to negotiate about the reserve clause when there was no lawsuit. Miller welcomed sincere efforts by management to modify the reserve clause but doubted any real possibility of change.

Arthur Goldberg heard the news while hiking with a half dozen reporters in the Adirondacks. For this reluctant campaigner, the 10-mile hike was the highlight of the campaign trail. He ditched his conservative suit and vest for a backpack, a sweater, khaki pants, and a jacket. He spoke with environmentalists, slept overnight in a pup tent, and washed in a stream. He won over a few reporters, who discovered beneath Goldberg's aloof and somewhat pompous exterior a real human being.

As he had told Brosnan in the cab, Goldberg saw Cooper's decision coming. "This is the end of the first inning," Goldberg said from Long Lake, New York. "The second inning will be in the Circuit Court of Appeals." On August 24, Flood's lawyers filed a notice of appeal.

Phillies general manager John Quinn, informed of Judge Cooper's decision while in Hampton, Virginia, repeated his offer that if Flood "wants to come back and play for the Phillies we'd be happy to take him back." But Quinn knew that Flood would never play for Philadelphia. On August 31, the Cardinals sent the Phillies Bob Browning, an 18-year-old minor league pitcher on the disabled list with a broken collarbone, as final compensation in the Flood deal.

In Denmark, Flood read about Judge Cooper's decision in the *International Herald Tribune*. He, too, viewed it as a perfunctory step on the way to the Supreme Court. Flood told reporters that Denmark was his "permanent home." He had begun negotiations to buy a restaurant-bar but was having trouble obtaining a liquor license. His only American visitor was his onetime girlfriend, Judy Pace. American soldiers on leave from Germany kept him abreast of the baseball season. They told him about the success of Bob Gibson (who won the 1970 Cy Young Award), the failure of the Cardinals (who finished fourth in the NL East), and the World Series victory by the Orioles.

Flood's financial problems began to weigh on his conscience. The

IRS and other creditors hounded him. He owed his ex-wife, Beverly, back alimony and child support. He realized that it looked like he was running away from his debts. He viewed Copenhagen no longer as "a vacation resort but a jail."

A phone call from a *Washington Post* reporter offered him an escape.

CHAPTER TWELVE

Washington Post sportswriter Leonard Shapiro told the transatlantic operator to dial 891-711 in Vedbaek, Denmark.

Curt Flood picked up the phone.

Shapiro asked Flood what he thought about playing for the Washington Senators. The previous day, Senators owner Bob Short had upstaged the last day of the Orioles-Reds World Series by agreeing to send utility player Greg Goossen to the Philadelphia Phillies just for the right to negotiate with Flood.

"This is the first I've heard of it," Flood said. "Are you really calling from America? I have a lot of flaky friends in Denmark."

Flood expressed interest in playing for the Senators to Shapiro but doubted that he could do so without prejudicing his legal battle against the reserve clause. "If I signed a contract with that clause, I'd be making a big farce of my case," Flood said. "I'm seriously fighting it. How can I fight it on the one hand and accept it on the other? It would be ludicrous."

A few moments after Flood hung up the phone with Shapiro, Short called. Flood repeated that he wanted to play baseball but that he had no desire to jeopardize his lawsuit. He referred any other questions to his lawyers. But Short was not giving up that easily. He explained that sitting out an entire season was enough of a financial and professional sacrifice to sustain Flood's lawsuit. It was time for Flood to play ball. During a second phone conversation with Flood, Short knew he had him. Flood was talking about how much he loved the game and missed playing it. Short offered to fly to Denmark or have Flood fly to Short's home base in Minneapolis. Instead, Flood agreed to fly to New York City, on Short's dime, to discuss the possibility of playing for the Senators. Flood sent a telegram to Marvin Miller about his impending meeting with Short and headed for New York.

A Minneapolis-based hotel and trucking magnate, Robert Earl Short could talk anyone into anything. In February 1968, about two months after buying the Senators, he talked Ted Williams out of retirement and into managing. It happened to be the same year that Williams's deferred payments ended from the Boston Red Sox. More than eight years since his last game with the Red Sox, Williams had no desire to manage or to leave his life of fishing and leisure in the Florida Keys. Short engineered a return phone call from Williams by pretending to leave a message from American League president Joe Cronin but with Short's phone number. Williams could not resist Short's sales pitch. Few could.

Short possessed the persistence of a lawyer, the people skills of a politician, and the hucksterism of a businessman. A Georgetown law graduate, he was the youngest delegate to the 1940 Democratic convention at age 21. He ran Hubert Humphrey's 1964 vice-presidential campaign and later served as the treasurer of the Democratic National Committee. He bought the nearly bankrupt Minneapolis Lakers in 1957, moved them to Los Angeles three years later, and began building a basketball dynasty by talking Elgin Baylor out of returning to college for his senior season and Jerry West into signing by hiring West's college coach, Fred Schaus. Short sold the Lakers in 1965 to Jack Kent Cooke for an NBA-record $5.175 million because, as Dodgers owner Walter O'Malley advised Short, for that kind of money he could get into baseball.

Three years and $9.4 million later, Short purchased the Senators, leveraging himself to the hilt to buy the team after his partner backed out. He figured that the tax benefits from depreciating his ballplayers like machinery would offset profits from his trucking and hotel businesses. The profits, however, never materialized, and the losses from the Senators mounted. Short threatened to move the franchise to Dallas–Fort Worth unless things changed in Washington. He wanted a rent-free lease at RFK Stadium, all the profits from parking and concessions, and a radio and television contract that rivaled those of other major league cities.

Short believed that he could put people into the stands by identifying the Senators with "faces." Ted Williams was a face. So was troubled Detroit Tigers pitcher Denny McLain. A week before contacting Flood, Short had traded pitcher Joe Coleman, who went on to win 20 games for the Tigers in 1971, and the left side of the Senators' infield, shortstop Eddie Brinkman and third baseman Aurelio Rodriguez, in a seven-player deal for the former 31-game winner and failed bookmaker, McLain. Williams was furious about the McLain trade and particularly about the loss of Brinkman and Rodriguez. But McLain was a face.

In Flood, Short focused on a new face, a black face for a majority-black city thirsting for a black star. "I think Flood can be merchandised in this town," Short said. Flood piqued Short's interest at the owners' meeting July 29–30 in Montreal. Rumors surfaced before the meeting that the owners wanted to settle Flood's lawsuit. Short was the only owner supposedly in favor of a cash settlement. What Short wanted to do was to avoid paying his share of the owners' $1 million in projected legal fees. At the meeting, he proposed that someone other than the Phillies be given the opportunity to sign Flood. And if that was not possible, then the Phillies should pay the bulk of the legal fees. After the meeting, Phillies general manager John Quinn facetiously asked the Senators owner if he could sign Flood. Short said yes, he could. Quinn responded that they could not discuss a possible trade until after Judge Cooper's decision.

During the World Series, in Cincinnati, Short again approached Quinn about Flood. Short offered Quinn $100,000. Quinn, however, wanted ballplayers. Later that week, after consulting with Bowie Kuhn, they announced the deal at the official World Series hotel in downtown Baltimore. They agreed on Greg Goossen for the right to negotiate with Flood, and an additional player and the Senators' number one draft pick in the 1971 amateur draft if Flood signed. Quinn saw no chance of Flood's signing with Philadelphia and not much chance of his signing with Washington. "What the hell," Quinn said in Baltimore. "We've got nothing to lose." Like most people, Quinn underestimated the power of Short's sales pitch. "I'm going to sign Curt Flood," Short said. "You can make book on that."

On October 22, Flood arrived in New York City. Two days later, Flood, Goldberg, associate Max Gitter, Miller, and Moss met with Short at Goldberg's apartment at the Pierre Hotel. It was ten days before Election Day. Goldberg trailed badly against incumbent Nelson Rockefeller in the New York gubernatorial race. That summer, Goldberg had asked Miller for a photo opportunity in the New York Mets clubhouse, and Miller had reluctantly agreed. Miller, Goldberg, Goldberg's running mate, Basil Paterson, and writer Jimmy Breslin rode in a limousine to Shea Stadium for a Mets-Cubs game. Breslin talked Goldberg's ear off about drug treatment issues. All Goldberg wanted was to get his picture taken with Cubs legend Ernie Banks. Their starkly different agendas indicated how unenthusiastic Goldberg was about running for office. At one point during the game, Goldberg came close to apologizing to Miller for breaking his promise not to run. "It wasn't supposed to turn out like this," Goldberg said.

During the meeting with Short at Goldberg's apartment, Goldberg and Miller sought to protect Flood's lawsuit while reaching an agreement that would get Flood back into a major league uniform. Goldberg agreed with Short's analysis that Flood could play for the Senators in 1971 without prejudicing the lawsuit. By sitting out the entire 1970 season, Flood had incurred actual damages and created a real "case or controversy." The lawsuit would not be moot if Flood retook the field.

Miller insisted that Flood not sign a contract containing the reserve clause. The layman in Miller feared that the Supreme Court would use Flood's Senators contract as an excuse to declare the lawsuit moot. "In my mind's eye, my mind's ear, I could hear a Supreme Court justice asking Goldberg, 'How do you explain this, Counsel?'" Miller recalled. "It was very practical."

Goldberg handed Short a two-page memo containing six modifications to the Uniform Player Contract with the following goals:

- a no-cut clause
- a no-trade clause
- automatic free agency at the end of the contract
- an agreement by the owners that the contract did not prejudice Flood's lawsuit

Short agreed to all their demands on the spot. He offered Flood a two-year contract worth $100,000 per season.

As much as Flood loved the game, the real reason he decided to come back was the money. In addition to the back alimony and child support payments he owed to Beverly, the IRS was after him, he had two lawsuits pending against him and his corporation in St. Louis, and he had failed to start up his restaurant-bar and had no income while he was living in Copenhagen. He found it difficult to maintain the lifestyle of a ballplayer without a ballplayer's salary. Taking on the reserve clause was breaking him mentally and financially. Short, who had built up $6 million in organizational debt as the treasurer of the Democratic National Committee and piled up debt as the owner of the Senators, promised to help Flood get his own personal finances in order. Two $100,000 annual salaries would definitely help.

Three hours after the meeting, Short returned to the apartment with bad news about their deal: "Commissioner Kuhn will not permit it." No one had ever modified the Uniform Player Contract. The commissioner's office was not going to allow Flood to set a precedent by signing a contract without the reserve clause. The only thing that Sandy Hadden, Kuhn's counsel, agreed to was a statement that signing the Uniform Player Contract would not prejudice Flood's lawsuit.

Kuhn had already turned Short's quest for a face into a farce. Under Kuhn's watch, Short and Quinn had violated at least two major league rules. First, trading for the right to negotiate with another player broke the rule against tampering with a player on another team. Technically, Flood was still on the restricted list. And even if Kuhn removed him from the list, Flood was still the property of the Phillies. Short was not allowed to negotiate with a player who was owned by another team. Second, Short had offered to give Quinn the right to use the Senators' first-round draft pick if Flood signed. Although trading draft picks was a common practice in pro football, baseball forbade it. Kuhn was determined not to allow Flood to flout any more of baseball's laws—especially the reserve clause.

Miller balked at Short's news. "Then there's no deal," Miller declared. He advised Flood to break off negotiations until Short had written permission to make a deal. The negotiations, however, continued. "In effect, you might say that I was overruled," Miller said. "Everything went on as if it hadn't happened."

The commissioner's ruling, Short said, was irrelevant. "If you think about it," he said, "you'll see that you've got everything you've asked for." If Flood had a good year, Short argued, the Senators would want to re-sign him. If Flood hit .100, no team would want him even at a 20 percent cut of $80,000. Short said he had no intention of cutting or trading Flood. "Do you think I'm going through all this to trade him?" Short asked. "I'd have to be an idiot."

At one point during Goldberg's explanation of why he and Miller wanted the no-cut, no-trade language in writing, Short said: "Well, I understand, and these are all good points and we're going to do everything possible to make sure that the boy is comfortable." Miller looked at Flood for a reaction to being called a "boy." Flood just winked at him. He had been through too much to let such racial slights unnerve him.

Short's financial terms showed how much he wanted Flood in Washington. He orally agreed not to cut or trade Flood and to make him a free agent at the end of the season. "And if anybody says that I agreed to such an arrangement," Short said, "I'll deny it." He also agreed to begin paying Flood as of November 1 (as opposed to when the season started) and to pay Flood's entire salary if he stuck with the team past June 15. Finally, at Goldberg's suggestion, Short increased the amount of the one-year contract offer to $110,000. Only the amount of the salary was in writing. Flood said he would think it over.

Kuhn approved Short's $110,000 offer and the accompanying statement that neither Flood nor the owners believed that the contract prejudiced his lawsuit. He even met with Goldberg to discuss the issue. Any other oral agreements, Kuhn said, were not legally enforceable. But they did not have to be if Short kept his word. The Senators owner subverted the power of the reserve clause and the power of the commissioner by promising Flood his freedom.

A few days after making his pitch to Flood, Short met in Philadelphia with Quinn. They spent four and a half hours talking on the phone with Kuhn and haggling over players. "You're going to have to make a deal," Kuhn told Quinn. Short and Quinn eventually agreed on compensation for Flood: Goossen and two minor leaguers, first baseman–outfielder Gene Martin, and pitcher Jeff Terpko. The Phillies had the right to return Terpko, which they did later that season. Instead, they selected the Senators' first-round draft choice in 1971, pitcher Roger Quiroga, whom Short had signed for a $60,000 bonus. Flood, therefore, ended up costing Short $170,000.

After making his deal with Quinn, Short flew back to New York to have lunch with Flood. During lunch, Flood excused himself from the table and made one last phone call to Marvin Miller.

"You're not going to think I'm running out on the case?" Flood asked.

"Of course not," Miller said.

"I wouldn't do this if I weren't in a financial bind," Flood explained.

Flood returned to the table and told Short, "I'll do it."

Flood's signing with the Senators was a victory of sorts. Yes, he signed a contract containing the reserve clause, but all he had sought in his initial letter to Kuhn was the right to negotiate with the team of his choice on his terms. He accomplished that goal by signing with a team besides the Phillies and for more money.

But he had undoubtedly hurt his case. It did not matter that the owners had signed a document stating that Flood's contract with the Senators did not prejudice his lawsuit. The urgency of his situation was gone. He was no longer sitting out to protest the injustice of the reserve clause. With Flood in a Senators uniform, his lawsuit appeared more hypothetical than real.

Some of Flood's fellow players, at least the ones who claimed to be supporting him, felt he had let them down. At their winter meeting in Maui, the player representatives voiced frustration that he had jeopardized his lawsuit for a six-figure payday. Miller explained Flood's financial problems. He also reassured the player representatives that Flood's lawsuit was still going forward as scheduled and that Flood was keeping his promise about seeing his lawsuit through to the end. "The Players Association is still very much in Flood's corner," Miller told the press.

After returning to Denmark for a week to pack up all his possessions and to put his restaurant plans on hold, Flood flew back to America. He saw a few people who appeared to be waiting for him in New York as he passed through customs. He thought it was because he had lost his medical records about his vaccinations. Then he thought he might be on "a list of all the notorious characters entering the country." Instead, a Mets fan wished him a successful comeback.

On November 14, Flood's comeback began at the Senators' winter instructional league camp in St. Petersburg, Florida. His goal was to get back into baseball shape. "Baseball," he said, "is like sex. You don't forget overnight." It sounded good, but Flood had not hit a baseball or put on a uniform in more than a year. By the time the 1971 season started, it would be a year and a half since he had played in an official major league game. He had spent his layoff "bedding and boozing" and claimed to have stayed in shape "by chasing those Danish girls."

Flood pointed to Muhammad Ali, who had knocked out Jerry Quarry in three rounds on October 26 after a 43-month layoff, as proof that he could come back. But Ali was only 28. And, as he revealed in his 15-round loss to Joe Frazier the following March, a different Ali returned than the one the boxing world had seen before.

It would be a different Flood as well. He turned 33 on January 18. He told the press his goal was to reach 200 hits in 1971, but it had been seven years since his last 200-hit campaign and three years since his last .300 season. He felt the pressure of living up to his past glory with the Cardinals. "I feel like I'm under this huge microscope, and they're all watching to see what I can do," he said.

The Senators tried to make Flood as comfortable as possible in St. Petersburg. He was given two days to acclimate himself before having to take the field. When he did, he was greeted by an old Cardinals catcher turned Senators coach, Del Wilber. Another Senators coach, George Susce, ran Flood through the lightest of 45-minute workouts. After changing into uniform number 51 between rookie pitchers Mike Thompson and George Boseker, he started with a few push-ups, sit-ups, deep knee bends, and calisthenics. Susce then lobbed him about 50 pitches of batting practice. After some light running and throwing in the outfield, the workout was over. *Washington Post* sportswriter William Gildea, who watched that first workout, was amazed by its brevity and laxity. "There was nothing to it," Gildea recalled. "It suggested to me that he was not in shape." Despite its ease, the first workout left Flood breathing hard.

Day two at the Mets' Payson Field was more of the same—soft

tosses from Susce. "God, was I glad it was Susce out there and not Bob Gibson," Flood said. The workouts left him "stiff and sore."

Newspaper and television reporters swarmed around Flood's locker after each workout. They made it difficult for rookie pitcher Mike Thompson to get to his neighboring locker. The Senators brought in their public relations director, Burt Hawkins, to help Flood juggle the interview requests, but Flood displayed little patience with the media. He turned down interviews with three Florida television stations. He was kinder to the Washington press corps. He spoke with Gildea for a two-part series in the *Washington Post*. He opened up to the *Washington Star*'s Russ White over dinner at Bern's Steak House in Tampa. But, in a telephone interview with *Washington Daily News* reporter Charlie Rayman, he asked: "Are you writing all of this down?" When the answer was yes, Flood retorted, "Don't misquote me, or I'll sue you."

Flood spent his three or four days in St. Petersburg in familiar surroundings. He stayed in room 23 of the Sheraton Outrigger, the same hotel the Cardinals had moved into after integrating their spring training facilities. He also read the galley proofs of his book. He promised the D.C. sporting press that it would be "a rather angry book." "I'm concerned about principles," he said. "A lot of people don't understand how you can make a lot of money and complain."

Short formally introduced Flood to the Washington media during a November 24 press conference at RFK Stadium. Flood had visited the nation's capital only one other time "for a few hours" at the end of spring training in 1957 with the Reds. There had been snow on the ground that day. Before the Reds moved on to play in Baltimore, they had sent Flood down to Savannah for his second season of segregated southern minor league hell.

Flood returned to Washington a well-paid, yet controversial, star. He wore a conservative double-breasted suit and dark tie and spoke softly. Three Senators teammates, Bernie Allen, Tim Cullen, and popular slugger Frank Howard, sat in the audience. After the press conference, they posed for a photograph with their new teammate.

Senators manager Ted Williams, who was driving from New Hampshire to the Florida Keys, was conspicuously absent. Williams claimed to have been unaware of the press conference and spent the night in a South

Carolina motel. Despite all his positive public statements, Williams had warned Short and team vice president Joe Burke not to sign Flood. He was already furious with Short for trading away the left side of his infield for McLain. "Short's a star fucker," Williams bellowed to his friend, radio man Shelby Whitfield. "It's another McLain deal."

The press asked Flood repeated questions about his lawsuit. "I just want a chance to play again," he said. "I haven't changed my philosophy. Sometimes you have to do things that aren't tasteful." The reporters asked him if he had anything against Philadelphia. No. They asked if he would have brought the lawsuit if he had not been traded. Maybe. "A trade doesn't affect you until you're moved against your will," he said. "I have been told that my choice of words wasn't accurate when I said I was a 'slave.' But I think a slave is a slave if he is bought and sold outright. I believe a man should have the option to control his career at some point in his career." Flood knew that he would have to deal with questions about his lawsuit all season, but he didn't like it one bit. "I can't think of any question that I haven't been asked," he said.

A reporter unwittingly brought up another sore subject.

"How good a painter are you?" the reporter asked.

"I don't know how good I am, but my work sells," Flood replied. A few days earlier, he had claimed not to have found any free time to paint since his retirement.

With that, Flood returned to California to relax and to escape unwanted media attention. He lived for much of that winter in Los Angeles with Judy Pace, and he had no plans to return to Denmark. "Right now I feel like a vagabond," he said. "Everything I own has handles on it." His next move was to find an apartment in Washington. "Of course America is a nice place to live," he told the reporters in Washington. "It doesn't take Bob Short to convince me of that." But in America, the press would not leave him alone.

In January 1971, Flood returned to the public eye. He appeared January 18 at the annual dinner of the Washington chapter of the Baseball Writers' Association of America at Washington's Shoreham Hotel. The three men who were named as defendants in his lawsuit also attended: Kuhn, Cronin, and Feeney. Flood sat at the head table with Short, McLain, Jim Bouton, Jimmy Breslin, and the outspoken wife of the U.S. attorney general, Martha Mitchell. Ted Williams skipped the dinner, showing up Short by appearing the next night at the Waldorf-Astoria Hotel in New York City at a Save-the-Salmon dinner.

Even in absentia, Short, Williams, and Flood served as featured attractions at the New York baseball writers' 1,400-person dinner January 31 at Manhattan's Americana Hotel. The New York writers put on their annual comedy show and in their "chief masquerade" mocked Short's collection of faces on the Senators. Maury Allen of the *Post* played Flood, with Louis Effrat of the *Times* as Kuhn, Dick Young of the *Daily News* as McLain, and John Drebinger of the *Times* as Williams. Allen, as Flood, singing to the tune "There Is Nothing Like a Dame," lamented:

I got Denmark in the winter
I got Florida in the spring
I got lots of lovely lassies with whom
I always sing
I got hordes and hordes of lawyers
And a Goldberg you must know
What ain't I got?
Reserve clause dough!

The show ended with the writers predicting to the baseball officials in attendance: "We know this year will be a thriller, courtesy of Marvin Miller."

A few days before the New York chapter's dinner, Flood attended a much more serious theatrical event in Manhattan—the January 27 oral argument of his case before a three-judge panel at the United States Court of Appeals for the Second Circuit.

The Second Circuit appeal was even more of a formality for Flood than the trial. The last step before taking his case to the Supreme Court, the Second Circuit did not review the trial court's factual findings; it only determined whether Judge Cooper had followed the law.

Another recent Second Circuit decision about baseball foreclosed any possibility of its reversing Judge Cooper. Two former umpires, Al Salerno and Bill Valentine, claimed that AL president Joe Cronin had fired them for trying to unionize their fellow umps. Cronin contended that he had fired them for incompetence. Salerno and Valentine sued baseball in federal court in lower Manhattan. *Salerno v. American League of Professional Baseball Clubs* had been dismissed before trial on December 10, 1969, because of *Toolson* and the antitrust exemption.

Before the appeals court's decision, Salerno and Valentine passed up several opportunities to settle their case. Baseball offered to pay them $20,000 each, provide them annual salaries of $20,000, and, after brief minor league stints, reinstate them to the major leagues. Valentine wanted to accept the deal, but Salerno held out for $100,000. Neither ump was reinstated. They lost in a hearing before the National Labor Relations Board (NLRB) and on appeal to the Second Circuit.

The Second Circuit's decision in *Salerno* came down July 13, 1970—after Flood's trial but before Judge Cooper's decision. *Salerno* gave Cooper additional fodder for ruling against Flood because it represented controlling law in the circuit that baseball was immune from the antitrust laws. Trial and appellate judges in the Second Circuit were bound by the appeals court's decision in *Salerno* as well as by the Supreme Court's decision in *Toolson*. Flood, therefore, was destined to lose in the Second Circuit at least two ways.

Salerno, however, was not a total blow to Flood. Judge Henry Friendly, a very well-respected appeals court judge, wrote a short opinion for the three-judge panel that all but invited the Supreme Court to overrule *Federal Baseball* and *Toolson*. Friendly concluded:

> We freely acknowledge our belief that *Federal Baseball* was not one of Mr. Justice Holmes' happiest days, that the rationale of *Toolson* is extremely dubious and that, to use the Supreme Court's own adjectives, the distinction between baseball and other professional sports is "unrealistic," "inconsistent," and "illogical." . . . [W]e continue to believe that the Supreme Court should retain the exclusive privilege of overruling its own decisions, save perhaps when opinions already delivered have created a near certainty that only the occasion is needed for pronouncement of the doom. While we should not fall out of our chairs with surprise at the news that *Federal Baseball* and *Toolson* had been overruled, we are not at all certain the Court is ready to give them a happy despatch.

On January 11, about two weeks before the Second Circuit oral argument in Flood's case, the Supreme Court declined to hear the case now known as *Salerno v. Kuhn*. The Second Circuit's decision in *Salerno* remained the law of the circuit, but the tone of Judge Friendly's opinion gave Flood's legal team encouragement as it sought the attention of the Supreme Court. After *Salerno*, the Second Circuit served merely as the warm-up act to persuade the Supreme Court to hear Flood's case. As typically happens on appeal, both sides used their briefs to reprioritize and refine their legal arguments.

On November 2, 1970, Flood's legal team filed a 100-page appellate brief emphasizing his claims under state antitrust law. The owners "may not have it both ways," the brief said; baseball is either interstate commerce subject to federal law or intrastate commerce subject to state law. "If Curt Flood must bear the burden of *Federal Baseball Club* and *Toolson*, he should receive the benefit of those decisions as well," the brief said. Goldberg and other members of Flood's legal team believed that the state law argument gave the Supreme Court a way to wiggle out of its prior decisions and rule in Flood's favor. It also represented a fresh issue before the Second Circuit. *Salerno* did not address any state law claims. Flood's brief relegated his involuntary servitude and peonage claims to a mere footnote—an indication that his lawyers considered their slavery arguments to be weak and inconsequential.

The owners' lawyers responded in their 46-page brief that *Toolson* and *Salerno* controlled this case, that the decision to remove baseball's antitrust immunity was up to Congress, and that Congress had not acted. They used a large chunk of their brief to push their labor exemption argument—that federal labor law prevented Flood and the Players Association from challenging the reserve clause under the antitrust laws. The players either could aggregate as a union under federal labor law or sue the owners under federal antitrust law, but not both. Since the players had chosen to form a union, the brief argued, the only way to change the reserve clause was through labor negotiation, not an antitrust lawsuit. The owners' lawyers figured that if the Supreme Court decided to hear Flood's case and reconsider the game's antitrust exemption, then the labor exemption was the next best way to defeat Flood's lawsuit. They rebutted Flood's state law claims by relying on the logic of the

Milwaukee Braves case that inconsistent state court rulings would imperil the national pastime. They also informed the court that Flood had signed with the Senators, but that both sides had agreed November 13 that his signing did not prejudice his case.

In their eight-page reply brief, Flood's lawyers pointed out that the owners had "run from one forum to another, arguing before each that that particular forum [was] not the proper one to regulate baseball." In *Federal Baseball* and *Toolson*, they had argued that state law still applied. In the Milwaukee Braves case before the Wisconsin Supreme Court, they had argued that federal law controlled state law. After *Toolson*, they had argued it was up to Congress. Before Congress, they had said the legality of the reserve clause would be subject to the courts. In a dispute related to Salerno's and Valentine's attempt to unionize the American League umpires, they had said the NLRB lacked jurisdiction because the dispute did not affect interstate commerce, and baseball was international in scope. In Flood's case, they said his lawsuit should not go forward because the reserve clause was the mandatory subject of labor negotiations. Somewhere, in some forum, Flood's reply brief argued, the owners should be subjected to the law.

The Second Circuit lacked the authority to end the owners' shell game. It did, however, grant Flood's request for expedited review of his case. Despite Flood's presence at oral argument, the January 27 hearing did not receive much press coverage. The lawyers presented a preview of the possible lineup and arguments if the Supreme Court decided to hear the case. Arthur Goldberg argued for Flood. Lou Hoynes, representing the owners, and Paul Porter, the commissioner's counsel, took turns on the podium for baseball. Each side spoke for 45 minutes before three federal appellate judges: Sterry R. Waterman, Leonard P. Moore, and Wilfred Feinberg. Oral argument mostly served as an opportunity for the judges to ask the lawyers to amplify or explain aspects of their briefs or to expose weak points in their arguments.

The lawyers treated the hearing almost as cavalierly as the press. On the day of the argument, Hoynes juggled the needs of several other clients at Willkie Farr's offices in lower Manhattan and could not get out of the office. About a half hour before the argument, he hopped onto the subway near Wall Street for the two-stop subway ride to the courthouse. The train was delayed. Flood's case was the fifth and final argument of the day. Even so, Hoynes slipped into courtroom 1707 about 10 to 15 minutes after Goldberg had begun. As soon as Goldberg finished, Hoynes stood up and argued for the owners. After 90 minutes, the three judges reserved their decision on the case. A decision was expected in about a month but could take longer.

A week after the Second Circuit argument, Flood found himself back in the headlines because the February 1 issue of *Sports Illustrated* contained an excerpt of his soon-to-be-published book, *The Way It Is*. A cross between Eldridge Cleaver's *Soul on Ice* and Bouton's *Ball Four*, *The Way It Is* revealed the pain Flood had felt after being turned away from the Reds' spring training hotel and the shock of the name-calling and isolation he had experienced during his two minor league seasons in the segregated South. "The book in some parts is as sad as a suicide note," *Los Angeles Times* columnist Jim Murray wrote.

The Way It Is included a hilarious chapter about ballplayers' sexual habits. Flood declared that most major league players and coaches were "as randy as minks." Unlike Bouton in *Ball Four*, Flood told tales only on himself: throwing baseballs with his hotel phone number on them to attractive women at the ballpark, sneaking down to the lobby to check out groupies who had called up to his room, and discovering another player's little black book in a Chicago hotel room only to find that it contained all the same names and numbers as his own book. Flood and some of his Cardinals teammates bonded as they "swapped booze and chicks from one end of the country to the other." But he issued this tongue-in-cheek disclaimer: "In case any baseball wife boggles at this, let her rest assured that her own husband was never involved. We admired and respected his sobriety and his ministerial rectitude. He was an inspiration to us all. So were his closest friends on the club. None of them ever had any fun."

The Way It Is was about much more than sex. It was about the principles that lay behind Flood's fight against the reserve clause, the rise of the Players Association under Miller, Flood's unique bond with Johnny and Marian Jorgensen (he dedicated the book to them), his close friendship with and admiration for Bob Gibson, and the interracial brotherhood of the 1960s-era St. Louis Cardinals. *The Way It Is* endures as an important historical document. "As a star, a black man, and a forthright critic of the baseball establishment, Flood has much more to say than

Bouton did," syndicated columnist Red Smith wrote. "He is candid about his own pleasures off the field and he can discuss physical appetites without the leering prurience that made Bouton's disclosures distasteful."

The baseball establishment loathed Flood's book. Bowie Kuhn was rumored to be more upset about Flood's discussion of sex in baseball than he was about Bouton's. Kuhn, however, did not make the same mistake he had made with Bouton. Flood's lawsuit prevented Kuhn from calling him into his office. Kuhn got his revenge later that spring by leaving Flood off the All-Star ballot. The move turned out to be more prescient than spiteful.

Other than Jim Murray, Red Smith, and Robert Lipsyte of the *New York Times*, most of the sporting press teed off on *The Way It Is*. Flood took aim at too many sacred cows—especially in St. Louis. *The Way It Is* got Flood excommunicated from Cardinal Nation. He portrayed his second manager, Solly Hemus, as a racist—discussing Hemus's behavior during the Bennie Daniels incident, his disdainful treatment of Flood and Gibson, and his carping comments after Flood had made it big with the Cardinals. Flood also revealed the paternalism and condescension of Cardinals owner Gussie Busch. He blamed Busch's spring training diatribe against the players for ruining the team's morale during the 1969 season, even publishing the speech in its entirety as an appendix.

Harry "the Hat" Walker, the manager of the Houston Astros and a former Cardinals player and coach, called Flood's book "tripe" and claimed that several years earlier Busch had vetoed a proposed trade of Flood to the Pittsburgh Pirates. "Mr. Busch pets his players, takes care of them in so many ways. For example, I know he gave Flood's wife a good job modeling," Walker told the *Birmingham News*. "I know Mr. Busch has bailed Flood out of several money jams, too." Walker, despite his Alabama home and Mississippi roots, was extremely close to Flood's friend Bill White. Flood acknowledged Walker's help with his development as a hitter. Walker admired Flood's grit and determination as a ballplayer, just not his opinions about the game. "Philadelphia offered him $100,000 to play," Walker said. "It's his right not to take it, but I can't stomach his crying that baseball mistreated him."

Bob Broeg of the *St. Louis Post-Dispatch* stood up for Gussie Busch as well. Flood, Broeg wrote, "emerges as a cynic and as an unforgiving guy whose racial resentment runs deep." Broeg claimed that after Busch's 1969 speech to the players, Flood was quoted as saying: "He's the man." What else was Flood supposed to say? Broeg also reminded readers that Flood had demanded a $100,000 salary after the 1968 season and had bristled over the team's decision to try younger players at the end of the 1969 season. He quoted Flood as saying: "I want everything that's coming to me even if it's only a dime." No one had quoted Flood or any other players as saying that at the time. "Curt is indeed curt," Broeg concluded of *The Way It Is*. "I never knew he was so damned unhappy."

Flood further alienated Cardinals fans by ripping into the real patron saint of St. Louis: Stan "the Man" Musial. Flood described an incident in which he and a date had been refused late-night service at Musial's restaurant, Stan & Biggie's. Musial later said it "was a long time ago" and the kitchen closed at 12:30 a.m.—no exceptions. Flood said Musial would have made a decent major league manager because he would not think too much and would just let the players play. But he also portrayed Musial as a simpleminded company man and derided Musial's frequent use of the word "wunnerful." Musial was deeply hurt by Flood's comments.

Bob Burnes of the *St. Louis Globe-Democrat* rushed to Musial's defense. He called Musial "a great American" and suggested "it would appear someone does begrudge him his hard-earned success." Burnes lumped Flood's book in with those of Bouton and former St. Louis Cardinals linebacker Dave Meggyesy. "The one common denominator is that all three have walked away as losers," Burnes wrote. "They are admitting that they couldn't or wouldn't keep up with the rest and now find some vicarious satisfaction in abusing those who made a success of things."

Flood's new bosses were not pleased, either. Ted Williams disliked Flood's book because of "Curt's public disclosure of his exploits with women and his resentment of authority in general." Williams made no secret of his disagreement with Flood's lawsuit, which he had termed "ill-advised" and "wrong." "Baseball has been played for 100 years and for more than 50 the reserve clause has been in effect, and Curt Flood is the first player I've ever heard of who said he's being treated like a slave," Williams had said in January 1970.

Williams toned down his comments but stood by his opinion after

Flood joined the Senators. "Tell you this, I love baseball so much, I hate to see it torn apart by irresponsible writers," Williams said.

"Like Curt Flood?" Robert Lipsyte asked.

"No, he's entitled to say and do what he wants," Williams replied. "I think he's wrong, that's all."

Even one of Flood's biggest boosters, Bob Short, took offense at *The Way It Is*. Short forced Flood to delete a paragraph from the book's galleys quoting Short about their oral agreement. The lawsuit, *The Way It Is*, and a skeptical manager ensured that Flood's first spring training in two years would not be easy.

CHAPTER THIRTEEN

On February 22, Flood walked into the Senators' spring training camp in Pompano Beach, Florida, on edge. He had vowed to come in two weeks early to get into shape, but arrived only a day before the team's other position players. It was the first indication that he did not really want to be there. He quietly passed out 40 copies of *The Way It Is* to his new teammates and coaches. He did not hold any massive book signings or conduct any press conferences. He kept to himself on a team composed mostly of younger players, save for slugger Frank Howard and a few others.

Elliott Maddox made a distinctly different first impression the next day. A 23-year-old black outfielder, he had come over to the Senators from the Detroit Tigers as part of the Denny McLain trade. Street-smart from having grown up in East Orange, New Jersey, and book smart on his way to graduating from the University of Michigan, Maddox learned from the antiwar protests at Ann Arbor how to stand up for himself.

On Maddox's first day in Pompano Beach, he pasted a "Free Angela Davis" sticker above the nameplate on his locker. The Senators objected to the yellow-and-black bumper sticker about the black activist accused of murder. During the first day of practice, someone had written "Fuck you" on the sticker. Management asked him to take it down. He asked why. If the manager, Ted Williams, could have a picture of Richard Nixon in his office, why couldn't Maddox put up a lousy bumper sticker? Maddox responded by pasting the sticker inside his locker and adding a poster of Black Panther Party co-founder Huey P. Newton. In the poster,

Newton wore a beret and sat in a high-back wicker chair that looked like a throne. He held a rifle in one hand and a large spear in the other. Newton had attended Oakland Tech, the same high school as Curt Flood.

Flood walked by Maddox's locker and stopped when he saw the poster. "I like that," he said.

Maddox idolized Flood. He admired the way Flood had played center field for those great Cardinals teams, respected Flood for sitting out the previous season and for suing baseball, and made a concerted effort to win Flood's friendship.

For a brief time, Flood and Maddox roomed together in spring training. Flood holed himself up in their room at the Surf Rider Motel and drank vodka all night until he passed out. He refused to leave the room for breakfast or dinner. Either he ordered room service or Maddox brought him something to eat. If there was no food, Flood simply drank. Maddox tried to keep Flood from drinking by talking about baseball. A converted infielder, Maddox had begun to learn to play the outfield the previous season from Tigers great Al Kaline. Rooming with Flood served as Maddox's postgraduate outfield education.

One baseball subject was taboo—the St. Louis Cardinals. On his first day in camp, Flood said: "I have one goal this year—to kick [the] hell out of the Cardinals in the World Series." He later claimed to have been misquoted. Back in the room, the Cardinals were off-limits. Even though it had been nearly a year and a half, the trade made his old team too painful even to discuss. On the other side of the state in St. Petersburg, a reporter asked Flood's old friends Lou Brock and Bob Gibson about his comeback. Brock was optimistic: "He's out there because he has something to prove." Gibson knew better: "Curt came back because he needed the money. It's as simple as that." Neither of them could help Flood with his problems.

Maddox knew that he could not talk baseball with Flood all night long. Flood would not talk about his career with the Cardinals, nor would he discuss his year away from baseball. And when Maddox stopped talking baseball, Flood's drinking resumed. That spring, Flood spent most of his time off the field in his room either abusing alcohol or sleeping it off.

Flood found no relief on the playing fields of Pompano Beach. His manager, Ted Williams, was part of the problem. Flood tried to make a good first impression with Williams. "Ted is a nonconformist," Flood remarked during his instructional league stint. "He's unafraid of rocking the boat, of going upstream. Hell, I really like that in a man." Williams recalled seeing Flood at the Reds' spring training in 1957 as a young third-base prospect. Flood recalled eavesdropping by the batting cage in spring training as a young player with the Cardinals while hitting coach Harry Walker and Williams talked hitting.

On Flood's first day in camp, he impressed Williams by hustling over to him after calisthenics.

"I'm glad you're here," Williams said, "but more important, I'm glad you're back in baseball. This is where you should be."

Williams meant in baseball, not with the Senators. He opposed Flood's lawsuit and did not think Flood could be a useful player anymore. But now Curt Flood was Ted Williams's problem.

Williams indoctrinated Flood the way he did every new player—he talked hitting. He asked Flood where the good right-handers pitched to him. Flood pointed to the outside corner. "I thought so," Williams said. "That's what I would do if I was managing against you. You're a good opposite-field hitter, so I'd pitch to your strengths and defense against it. You're going to get your share of hits that way, but the other club has to depend on its defense to hold the damage to a minimum."

Hitting was Williams's obsession. His book, *The Science of Hitting*, landed in bookstores that May and remains the definitive work on the subject. In 1969, Williams had talked the Senators into becoming hitters. He raised the team's batting average 27 points that season from .224 to .251—tied for third best in the American League. He even made a hitter out of shortstop Eddie Brinkman, who raised his average 79 points from .187 to .266. In doing so, he also turned the Senators, who finished the season with an 86–76 record, into winners. For producing the first winning season in the expansion Senators' nine-year history (and the first above-.500 season by a Washington team since 1952), Williams was named the American League Manager of the Year.

But sustained managerial success eluded Williams. A staunch Republican and Nixon fan, Williams had gained weight and had begun to look and sound like John Wayne. He had trouble communicating with players from the counterculture generation. Several players, led by McLain, started an anti-Williams faction called "the Underminers Club."

Even though the group included at least two black players, race did not seem to be the issue. Williams had used his 1966 Hall of Fame induction speech to lobby for the induction of Negro league legends Satchel Paige and Josh Gibson "because they were not given a chance." Williams's color blindness may have stemmed from his Mexican mother and his childhood in working-class San Diego. For Ted, baseball ability was the great equalizer. Indeed, in 1971, half of the position players in his Opening Day lineup were black.

Williams's problems were more generational than racial. Maddox and some of the team's other young players could not relate to him. During the 1971 season, Maddox marched into Williams's office and asked why he had been benched in favor of Larry Biittner. Williams said he wanted to look at a younger player. Maddox pointed out that Biittner was two years older than he was. Williams told Maddox not to be such a smart-ass.

Publicly, Williams said all the right things about Flood and what he expected from him coming back from his year-and-a-half layoff. "As good a player as he is," Williams said, "it shouldn't make any difference at all." Williams pointed out that he had enjoyed one of his best seasons in 1946 after three years as a World War II pilot. He also hit .407 at the end of the 1953 season after nearly two years as a Korean War pilot. Flood, however, was not Ted Williams. He was a singles hitter who relied on his speed to leg out base hits.

Privately, Williams gave Flood almost no chance of coming back. Williams received reports from his friends in the National League that Flood's play had fallen off dramatically in 1969. Having read Flood's book, he also knew about Flood's "bedding and boozing" in Denmark.

Flood defended his physical conditioning during his layoff. "Sure, I lived the good life in Copenhagen during the time I was out of action," he said. "But I took care of myself. I like a drink once in a while. Yet I also know when to stop."

The medical experts begged to differ. "Flood has to have the oldest 33-year-old body I've ever examined," Senators team doctor George Resta said. Team trainer Bill Zeigler agreed. Flood had no strength in his arms and no muscle tone. A small man at 5 feet 9 and 165 pounds, he now looked even smaller. His washboard stomach and sinewy arms and legs had atrophied since his missed fly ball in the 1968 World Series.

Even his face looked different. His cheeks looked fuller, and the circles under his eyes were more pronounced. Broadcaster Harry Caray saw Flood in spring training and thought Flood had "aged ten years." He mentioned the bags under Flood's eyes to Williams. Williams said he had noticed the same thing.

Flood's first day in camp did nothing to change Williams's mind. During his first time in the batting cage, Flood flailed against a nonroster sinkerball pitcher, Jim Southworth. Southworth never made it to the major leagues, but that day he made Flood look foolish. Flood struggled to get any of Southworth's pitches out of the batting cage. A few dribbled into the infield. Williams made excuses for Flood, saying he should not have faced a sinkerballer like Southworth in his first few at-bats. But the next hitter, a switch-hitting outfielder named Richie Scheinblum, roped Southworth's offerings into the outfield.

Flood's struggles at the plate continued during the first few intrasquad games. He failed to get a ball out of the infield in the first two games and finished 0-for-7. Flood sat next to Williams to try to pick up batting tips. Williams held Flood out of the first few exhibition games against the Montreal Expos and then used him for four games as a designated hitter. He wanted Flood to get as many at-bats, particularly against American League pitching, as possible. Williams thought the biggest problem for Flood would be learning the American League pitchers. "They don't know me, either," Flood said. He finally got his first base hit of spring training in his 10th at-bat, a solid liner to left off Orioles pitcher Dave Leonhard, but Leonhard picked him off first base. "The toughest thing is the hitting," Flood said. "You can almost fake the fielding if you want to, but you can either hit or you can't."

Flood flopped in the field as well. He dropped an easy fly ball March 15 against the Kansas City Royals. His arm also proved to be suspect. As a runner tagged from third later in the game, Flood pumped once. His throw then bounced in to cutoff man Frank Howard. It revived speculation that Flood's arm was shot. Williams later criticized Flood for playing too deep in center field. Flood even took to borrowing his son Gary's Mickey Mantle glove to try to cure his fielding woes.

After the first few days of spring training, Flood quietly booked his own room in the team's spring training hotel. Maddox switched into a room with one of his former Tigers teammates, pitcher Norm McRae, just down the hall.

Maddox was constantly knocking on Flood's door. He wanted to keep Flood company, to learn about the game, and to keep Flood from drinking too much. Sometimes Flood told him to come back in an hour. If Maddox did not come back in exactly an hour (or sometimes even if he did), Flood would open the door only four inches. His bloodshot eyes glared at Maddox. Never mind, Flood would say. Sometimes he said he was tired or in bed. Sometimes Flood did not even bother to get up; he simply yelled through the door.

During the nights when Flood let him in, Maddox could see that his new friend was a troubled soul. Flood spent only a few minutes talking about his problems at the plate or in the field. Normally, if a ballplayer was not playing well, he would spend much of the night obsessing over his swing or his fielding techniques. Playing baseball, however, was not the first thing on Flood's mind.

After a while, Flood told Maddox that he wanted to be alone. "I've got things to think about," he said. Maddox replied that Flood's hitting and fielding would come around. "No," Flood said, "it's not about that."

Sportswriters who had known Flood for years could see that his heart was not in his comeback. "He is in baseball but not of it," *Los Angeles Times* columnist Jim Murray wrote. "Curt Flood, quite clearly, would rather make $10,000 a year painting oils than $110,000 catching baseballs." *Washington Daily News* columnist Jack Mann wrote that after the first week of spring training Flood did not try very hard to hide his unhappiness. "One gained an impression during spring training, from the sardonic words and themes Flood chose, that his displeasure was not so much with the game of baseball itself but the game of life in the society where it is played," Mann wrote. "He had discovered Denmark, but it was as if in Denmark he had discovered Curt Flood, one he had never allowed himself to be before."

Flood resented what had been written about him in the months leading up to his comeback. Bob Short referred to him as "tarnished goods"; *Sports Illustrated* called him a "stormy petrel." The press and public lumped him in with McLain, who had been suspended for investing in a gambling operation, as one of baseball's bad boys.

As Flood, McLain, and Williams posed for a national magazine cover, a photographer asked them not to smile.

"What's it gotta be serious for?" McLain asked.

"Don't you know, Denny?" Flood said. "We're supposed to be mad at the world."

Reporters who had covered Flood in the National League could not believe the change in his attitude. Once a great talker, Flood had turned reluctant and shy. A former *Sports Illustrated* writer, Mann had known Flood since his rookie season. Twelve years later with the Senators, Flood met Mann at the hotel bar near the swimming pool and drank a 7UP. He complained that he and his teammates were not allowed to drink at the team hotel bar. When Mann's wife, Judy, approached them, Flood quickly got up and left. He did not want to be seen with a bikini-clad white woman. "[I] better get the hell out of here," Flood said to Judy. "They'll think I'm with you, and I've got enough troubles."

Flood could not understand the media's fascination with him or his lawsuit. As he had done during his instructional league stint, he turned down several requests for television interviews. "As long as he isn't hurting anybody else," he asked Mann, "why can't a man do his own thing? Why do they care so much?"

Bernie Allen watched from the next locker as reporters swarmed around Flood. Allen could see the frustration mounting in Flood each day. "They all had Flood trapped," Allen said.

Flood's reticence boiled over into surliness during another round of questions about his lawsuit at the Dodgers' spring training camp in Vero Beach. "Look!" Flood said. "I just don't wanna talk about it! A guy can bury himself with his own words. This game is hard enough, and I've been gone for over a year. I'm having enough trouble. I'm very sensitive about it. It's tough enough to hit the curveball when you can concentrate."

Flood read books on the bus during spring training road trips. He kept his distance from most of his teammates. They liked and admired him, but also pitied him. They knew that he was not the player he had once been.

"I was expecting him to be the second coming of Lou Brock," catcher Dick Billings said. "He looked like kind of a regular player, a rookie who wasn't quite sure of himself."

"He was a speed guy, and he didn't have the speed anymore," outfielder Del Unser said.

"You hear about guys who have lost a step or two; he lost three," pitcher Dick Bosman said. "I'm not sure he hit four or five balls hard all spring."

He hid his drinking from everyone but Maddox and a few close friends. The day before the season started, the Senators played an exhibition game in Richmond against the Atlanta Braves. Flood went out with a former teammate, Braves first baseman Orlando Cepeda. For the first time, Cepeda realized that Flood had a drinking problem, but Cepeda did not believe it was his place to say anything. No one else seemed to notice. "Hell, in those days," Frank Howard said, "we all drank."

Flood tried to acclimate himself to Washington's social scene. A month before spring training, Howard had taken Flood out to dinner at several of the city's best restaurants. He had also introduced Flood to Fran O'Brien's. Whereas politicians dined at Duke Zeibert's, athletes drank beers and chased women at Fran O'Brien's. Started by a former Redskins lineman, the restaurant-bar served as the unofficial clubhouse of the Redskins and Senators. Beautiful women flocked there and usually drank for free. Fran O'Brien's operated on the ground floor of a five-year-old apartment building–hotel at 18th and L streets known as the Anthony House. During the season, Howard and pitcher Casey Cox lived at the Anthony House, as did Flood.

Flood was not a regular at Fran O'Brien's. He sometimes ate lunch or dinner there. He also made an appearance there on Shelby Whitfield's weekly one-hour radio show, but he preferred the privacy of his room. "He didn't spend a lot of time downstairs," Whitfield said. "He was upstairs screwing women most of the time. He was a good-looking guy. He could have any woman he wanted."

Whitfield, who also conducted a weekly radio show with Williams after Short had fired him as the team's color commentator, was privy to Williams's side of the Williams-Flood relationship. Williams disapproved of Flood's lifestyle—drinking vodka martinis at noon and sleeping with countless women. Williams also once spied Flood in the clubhouse smoking a pipe. Williams hated pipe smokers. He thought they were too laid-back and lacked the "piss and ginegar," as he liked to say, to be great ballplayers.

With some reservations, Williams penciled Flood into the number two spot of the Senators' Opening Day lineup. Flood's hitting had started to come around at the end of spring training. He batted only .210 (17-for-81) that spring, but Williams knew that spring training statistics often meant nothing, especially for veteran players. "I have a feeling that Flood's the type of player who will do it during the season," he said. Privately, he felt otherwise but knew that he could not keep Bob Short's $110,000 prize out of the lineup. At least not yet.

Opening Day marked the high point of Flood's comeback. After Master Sergeant Daniel L. Pitzer, a prisoner of war for four years in Vietnam, filled in for President Nixon and threw out the first ball, Bowie Kuhn and Joe Cronin watched with Bob Short from the presidential box as Flood helped the Senators defeat Vida Blue and the Oakland A's, 8–0. Flood walked twice, scored two runs, and laid down a perfect fourth-inning bunt in front of Oakland third baseman Sal Bando for a base hit. "He's the guy you really have to stop to stop the Washington ballclub," Blue said. "He gets on base, and he scores runs." Flood was nervous in his first game back and relieved that he had contributed, but he was realistic about his situation. "I'm just the same poor little colored boy," he said. "Nothing's changed."

Flood cautioned that he "was not out of the woods yet." The next game, he singled in the first inning off Orioles pitcher Dave McNally, and reached on an error in the seventh and was caught stealing. The Senators lost to the World Champion Orioles, 3–2.

Before the game, Flood found out about another loss. The United States Court of Appeals for the Second Circuit had denied his appeal; the three-judge panel had affirmed Judge Cooper's decision.

Judge Sterry R. Waterman, who had presided over the oral argument in Flood's case and had participated in the *Salerno* appeal, wrote a measured majority opinion. A Vermonter who never graduated from law school, Waterman rejected Flood's federal antitrust claims based on *Federal Baseball* and *Toolson*. He denied Flood's state antitrust claims because baseball was interstate commerce and therefore federal law preempted state law. "We readily acknowledge that plaintiff is caught in a most frustrating predicament," Waterman wrote. Baseball was not subject to federal law because the game was not interstate commerce according to the Supreme Court in 1922; however, baseball was not subject to state law because the game was "so uniquely interstate commerce" according to the Second Circuit in 1971. "[W]e do not consider our decision to be internally inconsistent. . . ," he wrote. "Any apparent inconsistency results not from faulty logic, but from the vagaries of fate and this court's subordinate role to the Supreme Court." In other words, it would be up to the Supreme Court to clean up the mess it had made. Waterman's opinion was thorough yet concise, scholarly yet commonsensical, and above all fair. It was the way Flood and his lawyers had expected to lose.

One of the other two judges, Leonard P. Moore, felt more strongly about preserving baseball's legal monopoly. The former U.S. attorney in Brooklyn and a loyal Republican, Moore had won a fierce political battle to replace a judicial legend on the court of appeals, Jerome Frank. Frank—who in *Gardella* had declared *Federal Baseball* an "impotent zombi" and had written that "it is of no moment that [ballplayers] are well paid; only the totalitarian-minded will believe that high pay excuses virtual slavery"—died on January 13, 1957. He did not live to see if his prediction about the Supreme Court overruling *Federal Baseball* ever came true. "In my opinion," Moore wrote in his concurring opinion about the *Flood* case, "there is no likelihood that such an event will occur."

Moore tipped his hand with his opinion's opening sentence. "Baseball for almost a century has been our country's 'national' sport," he wrote. The remainder of his first paragraph referred to A. G. Spalding and Abner Doubleday; baseball greats "Christy Mathewson, Walter Johnson, the remarkable Ty Cobb, Babe Ruth of home-run fame, Lou Gehrig, and more recently Ted Williams and Willie Mays"; and the Chicago Cubs' poetically famous double-play combination, "Tinker-to-Evers-to-Chance." This was not a judicial opinion; it was a glorified history of baseball.

After discussing the relevant precedents, Moore extolled the virtues of Justice Holmes's opinion in *Federal Baseball*:

> The Supreme Court in 1922 undoubtedly felt that it should adopt a "hands off" policy as to this one particular sport which had attained by then such a national standing that only Congress should have the power to tamper with it. And properly so. Baseball's welfare and future should not be for politically insulated interpreters of technical antitrust statutes but rather should be for the voters through their elected representatives. If baseball is to be damaged by statutory regulation, let the congressman face his constituents the next November and also face the consequences of his baseball voting record.

Moore concluded that he had no "reservations or doubts as to the soundness of *Federal Baseball* and *Toolson*" and wrote that he "would limit the participation of the courts in the conduct of baseball's affairs to the throwing out by the Chief Justice (in the absence of the President) of the first ball of the baseball season."

There was something about baseball that turned cerebral judges into pennant-waving schoolboys; that caused them to lose their judicial bearings, to twist precedents, and to jeopardize the dignity of the federal courts; and that made it nearly impossible for any litigant to defeat the baseball establishment. This case was about more than *Federal Baseball* and *Toolson* or Justice Holmes and *stare decisis*; it was about the grip of the national pastime on the minds of the men in black robes. This was what Flood was up against as his lawsuit made its way to the Supreme Court.

In Baltimore, Flood downplayed the news of the Second Circuit's decision. "We knew nothing would get resolved in the lower courts," he said. "The Supreme Court chooses the cases it wants to hear. I just hope that ours will be one of them." He sounded more like a lawyer and played less like a ballplayer.

After a 2-for-8 start, Flood managed only a bunt single in three home games against the Yankees. His bat had slowed so much, Detroit Tigers chief scout Rick Ferrell noted, that the Yankees were "not even bothering to curve him." Williams, who noticed that Flood hit only five balls in the air during his first 20 at-bats, thought that he had lost the snap in his swing.

Flood's fielding also betrayed him during the first game of a doubleheader against the Yankees on April 11. In the second inning, he failed to pick up Curt Blefary's sinking line drive off Senators ace Dick Bosman. As the ball sliced to Flood's right, he dived instead of getting in front of it, missing the ball by three feet. It rolled all the way to the 410-foot sign on the RFK Stadium wall for an inside-the-park home run. The Senators lost, 1–0.

Williams did not yell at Flood; he humiliated him. At the end of the eighth inning, Flood grounded out for the fourth time that day. He trotted past first base, removed his batting helmet, and peered into the dugout for a teammate to bring him his cap, glove, and sunglasses. Williams sent Richie Scheinblum, a pinch hitter in the eighth, into right field and shifted Unser into center. He let Flood die out there on the field.

Few players noticed the tension between Williams and Flood, but the way Williams pulled Flood for a defensive replacement was hard to miss. "You can't handle a seven-time Gold Glove winner like Curt Flood like you handle a Tom McCraw," Senators first baseman–outfielder Tom McCraw said. "You've got to give him a certain amount of respect, too."

Williams again said all the right things to the press after the game but privately seethed about being stuck with a no-hit, no-field center fielder. "Syphilitic Jesus Christ," Williams told Shelby Whitfield, "that guy can't play a lick."

Williams benched Flood only five games into the season. Flood's fielding gaffe and 3-for-20 start (two of the three hits being bunt singles) gave him just cause. Flood sat out the second game of the doubleheader against the Yankees as well as the first of three home games against Boston. He made a pinch-running and a pinch-hitting appearance during the last two games. "I told him the way we were going we just couldn't afford to carry him unless he gave us more hits," Williams told the *Boston Herald Traveler*. Flood accepted the manager's decision like a professional, cheering on his teammates from the dugout, but he refused to talk with members of the Boston press corps about his lack of playing time.

As badly as he had played, Flood was a 12-year veteran and one of the team's highest-paid players. He could have received more than five games to play his way back into shape. "I'm not sure Flood ever got a real square deal with Ted," Whitfield said. "Williams felt all along that Flood was finished. . . . I knew that Flood wasn't going to get a fair shake with Ted."

"Ted fucked him," McLain said. No Senators player hated Williams more than McLain. The 1968 and 1969 American League Cy Young Award winner constantly clashed with Williams, challenging his manager's authority. McLain insisted that Williams never wanted Flood on the team in the first place and never showed Flood the proper respect. "Ted's main goal in life that season was to see Curt Flood fail and to see Denny McLain fail," McLain said. "I told him that to his face in '72."

According to McLain, Short was "sideways livid" that Flood was not in the lineup. The owner, however, was at a loss about what to do about the tension between Williams and Flood. "All Bob Short kept saying was, 'I don't know what to do. I don't know what to do,'" McLain said. Short asked McLain: "Do you have any solutions to this problem?" McLain never offered any but knew it was not just going to go away. "There was a terrible strain," McLain said.

The benching gave Flood more time to think about his off-field problems. He had bigger things to worry about than Ted Williams pulling him for a defensive replacement and benching him. "That was the knife going in," Maddox said. "You knew he wasn't going to last much longer. That was the final nail in the coffin."

On the team's first extended road trip, Flood roomed with Maddox during the first two games in Cleveland. Maddox tried to get Flood to join him for breakfast. Flood said he preferred room service. He refused to leave the room except for games. He drank all night after games, slept it off all morning and afternoon, and then got dressed just in time to get to the ballpark. After the games, he returned to his room and started the whole cycle again.

One night in Cleveland, Richie Scheinblum saw Flood standing in the lobby of the hotel by himself. He saw how sad Flood looked and asked if there was anything he could do to help. They talked for five to ten minutes. "He felt like he had let a lot of people down," Scheinblum said.

Flood finally returned to the starting lineup April 17 against the Indians and responded after the four-game layoff with two nice catches and an infield single that scored the winning run. He also started the first game of the next day's doubleheader.

After those first two nights in Cleveland, Flood told Maddox: "I'm going to get a room for myself, just keep it quiet." Flood roomed by himself when the team traveled to New York for two games at Yankee Stadium.

Upon arriving in New York, he placed a courtesy phone call to Marvin Miller. Miller had heard reports from other players that Flood could not hit anymore. At one point in the conversation, Miller asked Flood how things were going. "Let's talk about something else," Flood said. Miller was not surprised that Flood was struggling to come back from a one-year layoff at age 33. At the time, Flood kept his off-field problems to himself. "He said he was fine," Miller told the *New York Daily News*. "He always said that." Flood said he would call Miller before he left New York but never did.

Flood was beginning to come mentally unglued. Hate mail about the lawsuit had been pouring in with his return to the game. He recoiled at "freaky letters" like the one that began, "Dear Nigger . . . You're a dead nigger." He tried to ignore the threats in the mail, on the phone, and to his children.

An incident in New York sent Flood over the edge. Arriving at his locker at Yankee Stadium for the team's April 20 afternoon game, Flood discovered a black funeral wreath. This symbol of death was hanging where his uniform was supposed to be. Flood's mind began to race. If someone could get to his locker, then someone could get to him. "Whoever it was had to have some clout to drag this funeral wreath in and put it in my locker," Flood said. "Scared the shit out of me."

How the wreath got there remains a mystery. Flood's teammates insisted that they respected him too much to pull a stunt like that. McLain blamed the person he blamed for everything—Williams—or a member of his coaching staff. It could have been the same person who had written "Fuck you" on Maddox's Angela Davis sticker. Flood kept the news of the black funeral wreath from the rest of his teammates, including the person he was supposed to room with in New York, Tom McCraw.

As a veteran black player, McCraw could relate to Flood better than the 23-year-old Maddox. Like Maddox, McCraw admired Flood's courage for standing up to the baseball establishment. On March 29, the Senators had acquired McCraw in a trade with the White Sox. An eight-year veteran, McCraw had been demanding a trade for several seasons so that he could prove that he was more than a part-time player. "My case bears out what Curt Flood is fighting about," he said after coming over from Chicago.

McCraw could see that the stress of Flood's lawsuit was getting to him. "It's hard to focus and concentrate when you've got such a big burden on your shoulders, that you've jumped out in the deep water here and everybody's shooting at you," he said, "especially the media, feeding off what the owners are telling them, that he was the culprit in this whole mess. He was like a man on an island out there by himself. Everybody's taking potshots."

By choosing to room by himself in New York, Flood was able to hide his drinking from his teammates, including McCraw. "I don't remember ever seeing Curt Flood take a drink of anything," McCraw said. "He was by himself."

Most of Flood's teammates believed that he was unhappy only about his poor and sporadic play. That's the impression he gave Frank Howard. Before a home game against the Milwaukee Brewers, Flood approached Howard in the tunnel at RFK Stadium leading from the clubhouse to the dugout.

"Frank," Flood said in a serious tone of voice, "I've lost it."

Howard told Flood that his skills were not going to come back right away and encouraged him to stick with it. But that was not really what Flood meant. He was losing his mind.

That April 24 night Flood's pinch-hit single scored the game-tying run. The 6,597 fans at RFK Stadium gave him a standing ovation. The next day, he sat on the bench until a ninth-inning pinch-hitting appearance. He walked. Williams had relegated him to being a $110,000 pinch hitter and platoon player who hit only against left-handed pitchers.

Larry Whiteside of the *Milwaukee Journal*, the only black baseball beat writer at the time, landed a rare interview with Flood. "You know, I never thought I'd be back to play baseball again," Flood told Whiteside. "I was away for a year and a half and did nothing. I was up to about 175 pounds. Now I'm back and it's hard." Flood looked like a young player the way he wore his hair in a bushy Afro that poked out of the sides of his cap. He just didn't feel like a young player. He confessed that it felt as if he had been playing baseball for 40 years. He was philosophical about his part-time status and about his lawsuit. "I try not to think about the lawsuit anymore," he said. "It's something that is out of my hands."

Whiteside asked if Flood planned to retire after the season. "I don't know about after this year," Flood said. "It's something I haven't really considered. In fact, the thought frightens me a little. And I've got enough to worry about this year."

Around the batting cage that weekend, Flood could barely keep his emotions in check. He exploded at William Gildea, the *Washington Post* sportswriter who had written some of the earliest articles about Flood's possible move to the Senators and then interviewed Flood in St. Petersburg during his instructional league stint. After the incident around the batting cage, Gildea was so angry and embarrassed that he retreated to the Senators' dugout. A few minutes later, Flood came over and sat at the other end of the dugout. Neither man said a word. It was Flood's way of apologizing. To this day, Gildea regrets not asking Flood what was on his mind.

Flood revealed some of his feelings to one of the team's biggest malcontents, first baseman Mike Epstein. Epstein was one of the few young players with the courage to buck the reserve clause. A former football fullback and baseball star at the University of California at Berkeley, he signed with the Baltimore Orioles in 1964 and found himself stuck behind Boog Powell at first base. In 1966, Epstein was voted the minor league player of the year in Triple-A Rochester. The Orioles had just won their first World Series. Before the 1967 season, they sent Epstein back to Rochester. He refused to report. He went home for a month to Stockton, California, and threatened to hire an attorney. Soon after he said that, Orioles general manager Harry Dalton traded him from the best team in the league to one of the worst, the Senators. "They were trying to say, 'You're not bigger than baseball,'" Epstein said. "I wasn't trying to be bigger than baseball. I was just trying to play."

Williams had given up on Epstein because he believed that the young slugger could not hit left-handed pitching. Epstein had campaigned all spring to be traded. Epstein and Flood bonded over their antipathy for the reserve clause and as outsiders. Epstein never admired another player more than he admired Flood. Flood explained to Epstein that his lawsuit challenged more than the reserve clause and the baseball establishment.

"My problem is I'm black," Flood said.

"How do you think I feel?" Epstein replied. "I'm Jewish."

"We had the common identity," Epstein said. "We both felt persecuted, and it just wasn't going to come out the way it was supposed to."

Flood approached Epstein as they shagged fly balls before Sunday's game against Milwaukee. "Things are closing in on me," Flood said. He was not having any fun playing baseball and his life outside the game was a mess. "Life is like baseball," Epstein told Flood. "You have a slump and you get out of it."

The previous day, Flood had paid the team's clubhouse manager, Fred Baxter, for the extra services Baxter and his assistants provided the players. Baxter thought it was a little strange—players did not usually settle up with the clubhouse guys until they received their paychecks on the 15th or 30th of the month.

On Monday against Minnesota, Flood spent the entire game sitting on the bench wearing big, dark sunglasses. Williams had noticed that the circles under Flood's eyes were even more pronounced. It looked as if he hadn't slept the previous night.

A Minneapolis reporter asked Flood how things were going. "Not too good," he said. Flood limited his answers to the rest of the reporter's questions to "yes" or "no." He elaborated only when asked why he was not playing. "That's up to Ted," Flood replied. "He's the boss."

After the game, Epstein and Flood exchanged what Epstein thought were normal good-byes.

"Take care," Flood said.

"Yeah, I'll see you tomorrow," Epstein said.

Pitcher Denny Riddleberger, whose locker was next to Flood's, knew better. Flood intimated that he was having off-field problems and was going to have to find something else to do. Flood kept a photograph of himself in his locker from a recent issue of *Sports Illustrated.* The photo showed Flood, his brow furrowed and his arms wrapped around a pole in the dugout, deep in thought. To Riddleberger, the photograph captured Flood's state of mind: contemplative, tortured, and hanging on for dear life.

After Monday night's game, Flood said good-bye to Riddleberger.

"Take care," Flood said. "I don't think I'll be seeing you for a while." He left the photograph, his uniform, his cap, and all his other baseball clothes behind.

Flood ate dinner after that night's game with pitcher Casey Cox. Since they both lived at the Anthony House, they often ate meals and rode to the ballpark together. At dinner, Flood complained about the media hounding him about his lawsuit and talked about "some things going wrong" but did not elaborate.

Later that night at Fran O'Brien's, Flood met up with catcher Paul Casanova. "He said everything was good," Casanova recalled. Casanova even asked if Flood wanted to rent an apartment on Rhode Island Avenue. "Cassie," Flood said, "we'll talk about it."

Cox and Flood had agreed to meet the next day in front of the Anthony House at 3:30 p.m. to go to the ballpark. Flood never showed.

Tim Cullen, the team's player representative, discovered just before batting practice that something was amiss. Between 4:30 p.m. and 5 p.m., Fred Baxter called Cullen off the field and into the clubhouse. Bob Short was on the phone.

"Tim," Short said, "do me a favor. Look in Curt's locker and see if his street clothes are in there."

There was nothing in Flood's locker except his baseball gear.

"Thanks," Short said. "That's all I needed to know."

A few moments later, Short came down on the field and sat in the Senators' dugout. One of the coaches waved Cox in from shagging fly balls in the outfield.

"Where's Curt?" Short asked Cox.

"I don't know," Cox said. "We were supposed to meet at 3:30. I thought he was already at the ballpark."

Short called the Anthony House; Flood had checked out.

He then spoke with McLain. "You've got to know where Curt is," Short said.

McLain did not know. He lamely suggested that Flood had changed hotels.

Maddox was worried that Flood had overslept. The Senators' batting practice came and went. As the Twins began to take their batting practice, Maddox went into the clubhouse and checked Flood's locker. He thought that Flood might miss the game.

A *New York Daily News* photographer found Flood first. Wearing sunglasses, a tan leather jacket, and beige bell-bottoms, Flood had purchased a one-way first-class ticket on an 8 p.m. Pan Am flight from New York's John F. Kennedy International Airport to Barcelona, Spain.

"I'll throw you and your blinking camera out that window," Flood reportedly snapped at the *Daily News* photographer who tried to take his picture.

Someone at the *Daily News* tipped Short off that Flood was at JFK and had purchased a one-way ticket to Barcelona. Short hastily called a press conference and alerted the media that Flood had left the team. He was trying to catch up with Flood in New York.

At 4:55 p.m., Flood sent Short a telegram from JFK Airport:

> I TRIED A YEAR AND A HALF IS TOO MUCH VERY SERIOUS PERSONAL PROBLEMS MOUNTING EVERYDAY THANKS FOR YOUR CONFIDENCE AND UNDERSTANDING
> FLOOD

Short posted the telegram on the clubhouse wall. Almost all of Flood's teammates and coaches were shocked. Only Maddox, McCraw, McLain, and Riddleberger were not surprised. They knew that Flood's problems went beyond baseball and that his heart was no longer in the game.

Maddox felt guilty as he started the next night in center field in Flood's place, but he was relieved to see his troubled friend go. He would not have tried to talk him into coming back. He was sorry that he never had the chance to say good-bye.

Short, however, was not giving up so easily. He first tried, unsuccessfully, to reach Arthur Goldberg. He learned the next day that Goldberg was vacationing in Hawaii. Then, between 6:15 and 6:30 on the night of Flood's departure, Short called Joe Reichler, the assistant to commissioner Bowie Kuhn. A longtime AP reporter, Reichler had printed Bill White's remarks in 1961 about the St. Petersburg Chamber of Commerce breakfast and the Cardinals' segregated spring training facilities. Short asked Reichler to go to Kennedy Airport to talk Flood out of leaving.

Reichler arrived at Kennedy Airport at 7:15 p.m. and found Flood sitting at an airport bar. Flood said he was in a hurry to catch an 8 p.m. flight back to Washington.

"By way of Barcelona?" Reichler asked.

Flood laughed. "It's not baseball I'm worried about but other things," he said. "I just can't cut it anymore. The problems are mounting and I'm going crazy thinking about them." Flood told Reichler he had been thinking for a month and a half about leaving.

For 20 minutes, Reichler tried to persuade Curt to stay. He told him that he was not a quitter. Then Reichler shifted tactics and said Flood owed it to Short to come back.

"I know I owe Bob Short a great deal," Flood said. "He stuck his neck out for me. All right, I'll give it some thought."

Reichler thought he had persuaded Flood to stay. He suggested that Flood take a few days off in New York City to think things over. Suddenly, Flood regained his resolve.

"No, no," Flood said. "I'm not going to do it. I've reached the end. I'll go crazy if I don't get out. I'll go crazy, if I don't get out."

Flood boarded Pan Am flight 154 for Barcelona and settled into seat 3-F, refusing a request to step off the plane to speak to the press before takeoff. When his flight touched down at 5:15 a.m. in Barcelona, however, Flood did not disembark. He might have slipped away three hours earlier when the plane stopped in Lisbon, but no one knew for sure where he was.

Short told the press that he hoped Flood would return. Williams publicly praised Flood as "big league all the way," but privately, Whitfield said, "it was good riddance."

Most of the press hammered Flood for jumping ship after just 18 games, especially after collecting close to half a season's salary from Short. Flood's lawsuit, according to *New York Post* columnist Larry Merchant, "was an act of desperation by a deeply troubled and disturbed man." *New York Daily News* columnist Dick Young wrote that the players' continued support for Flood's lawsuit would break down along racial lines. "[I]f you have to feel sorry for someone," Young wrote, "try the people who put their faith in him, and are left holding the bills." "The

Flood sympathizers said he had problems," *Washington Evening Star* columnist Merrell Whittlesey wrote, "but we all have problems."

Red Smith was one of the few writers who understood the reality of Flood's situation: "If he wins his suit, everybody else will benefit. The fetters will be eased for all other players present and future. Baseball will gain respectability as an American institution. The only one who has nothing to gain is Curtis Charles Flood."

Lieutenant Fred Grimes, a black St. Louis police officer and friend of Flood's, implored *St. Louis Post-Dispatch* columnist Bob Broeg not to write another negative column. "He's running away from himself," Grimes said, "so don't be hard on him. This man's personal life is as unpleasantly involved as a soap opera."

Flood left the country for parts unknown not because he had lost a step or two, or even three, or because he no longer had any desire to play baseball, though both were true, but because leaving was the only way to preserve his sanity and his lawsuit.

Flood's "personal problems mounting every day" were mostly financial. Two days before he left, Beverly filed a lawsuit seeking back alimony and child support even though she had married a St. Louis attorney, Richard L. Johnson. The debts and legal fallout from his photography business had not gone away. Creditors had been hounding Flood from the moment the season began. They called him day and night and drove him to distraction. He avoided them by refusing to cash his last few paychecks until he left for Barcelona.

Flood had been receiving paychecks since November and had collected between $50,000 and $60,000. He could have collected the rest of his $110,000 salary, according to his oral agreement with Short, by playing until June 15. Flood, however, had too much pride merely to hang on for a paycheck. His hitting was anemic (7-for-35 with no extra-base hits), his fielding was not much better, and his manager had relegated him to the bench. He refused to embarrass himself any longer.

A week before he left, Flood's personal attorney, Allan Zerman, had advised him that filing for bankruptcy protection was his best option. Short agreed that bankruptcy was the only way to shield Flood's salary from his creditors and his ex-wife. Otherwise, Flood could not have become solvent even if his paychecks had continued for another five to ten years.

Bankruptcy, however, came with an unbearable cost: the end of his lawsuit. Had Flood declared bankruptcy, a court-appointed receiver could have settled his lawsuit for money damages and distributed them among Flood's creditors. Paul Porter had met three times with Goldberg about a possible settlement. Goldberg wanted the reserve clause modified and Flood's lost salary in 1970 and his legal fees reimbursed. There was no deal. If Flood declared bankruptcy, the decision to settle would no longer have been up to Flood, Goldberg, or the Players Association.

Flood remembered his promise to the player representatives in Puerto Rico to see his lawsuit through to the end. In the minutes from the union's July 12, 1971, executive board meeting, Miller and Moss explained to the players: "It seems clear that rather than letting down the players, as many members of the press have reported, Curt's problems were compounded because of his awareness of his responsibilities to the rest of the players."

Flood refused to declare bankruptcy because he wanted his shot before the Supreme Court of the United States. He sacrificed everything to get it.

CHAPTER FOURTEEN

Arthur Goldberg returned to Washington just a few months after Flood's sudden departure. Goldberg had lost his bid to unseat Nelson Rockefeller as governor of New York the previous November. Rockefeller's political machine had targeted white ethnic voters en route to an easy victory. It was later revealed that Rockefeller had paid a right-wing publishing house $60,000 to publish 100,000 paperback copies of an anti-Goldberg biography that was distributed as campaign literature. Goldberg also believed that the key to his campaign's success lay in a book. He forced his campaign staff to prepare a volume about his stances on the various issues. If New Yorkers would read the book, Goldberg believed, he would win the election. At first, no one would publish it. Then, after Goldberg self-published the book, no one read it. He lost by nearly 700,000 votes. Stephen Breyer, a former Goldberg law clerk and future Supreme Court justice, worked on the campaign while teaching at Harvard Law School. "I cannot be terribly sad that you did not [win]," Breyer wrote Goldberg, "for I suspect that you will be happier not being Governor."

Goldberg was not happy at Paul, Weiss, either. On June 16, 1971, he announced that he was leaving the New York law firm after four years to open his own legal practice in Washington. Paul, Weiss support staffers disliked Goldberg so much that they removed his name from the firm's elevator directory at 345 Park Avenue the next day.

Goldberg could not wait to return to Washington, where he had enjoyed his finest hours as Kennedy's secretary of labor and second Supreme Court nominee. He had lived there for 17 years, from 1948 to

1965. His children had grown up there. His country house, a farm once owned by Chief Justice John Marshall, was 30 minutes outside the city in Marshall, Virginia. Goldberg rented office space from Caplin & Drysdale, a law firm started by former IRS commissioner Mortimer M. Caplin. He told Marvin Miller and Dick Moss that he only wanted to represent nations, but he still shared a few clients with his former Paul, Weiss partners, including the erstwhile Washington Senators outfielder living in self-imposed exile somewhere in Europe. Curt Flood's lawsuit provided Goldberg with the perfect vehicle for making a triumphant return to the nation's capital. If only he could persuade the Supreme Court to hear the case.

The Supreme Court spends a lot of time determining what cases it wants to decide. The Court operates under the Rule of Four: Four of the nine justices must agree to hear a given case. Requests typically arrive at the Court in the form of petitions for a writ of certiorari, which are known as cert petitions. The Court responds by either granting or denying cert. Most cert petitions are denied. Of the more than 3,100 cert petitions the Court received during the 1971–72 term, the Court heard oral arguments on 177 and issued 129 opinions. In most cases, the Court denies cert without any comment or indication of how the justices voted. The lower court's opinion is neither affirmed nor reversed; it is simply allowed to stand.

From the moment he agreed to take the case, Goldberg knew that the success or failure of Flood's lawsuit hinged on the Court's decision to grant or deny cert. It all came down to Flood's cert petition and the man Goldberg called on to draft it, a Paul, Weiss associate named Dan Levitt. Levitt knew what a winning cert petition looked like because he had read hundreds of them as a Supreme Court law clerk. A Pittsburgh native who had attended 30 to 40 Pirates games a year at Forbes Field, Levitt tied for sixth in the class of 1964 at Harvard Law School with Stephen Breyer. He then succeeded Breyer in 1965 as one of Goldberg's clerks. That summer, when Goldberg left for the United Nations, Levitt stayed at the Court for an additional two years as a clerk for Goldberg's replacement, Abe Fortas.

Levitt also knew how to write. Goldberg so liked the way Levitt wrote that he had Levitt draft his UN speeches and cautionary letters to President Johnson about Vietnam. As an associate at Fortas's old law firm, Arnold & Porter, Levitt wrote speeches read on the Senate floor defending Fortas's unsuccessful nomination for chief justice. After a few years at Arnold & Porter, Levitt left to join former U.S. attorney general Ramsey Clark at Paul, Weiss's Washington office.

Goldberg often asked Levitt to come to New York to answer mundane legal questions that any associate in the firm's New York office could have researched and answered. Goldberg implicitly trusted his former clerks. They were his boys. After he lost out as governor of New York, he gave a series of lectures at Northwestern law school on the Warren Court, each of which was written by a former clerk. He published the lectures as a 1971 book titled *Equal Justice: The Warren Era of the Supreme Court*. Levitt drafted Flood's cert petition, and Goldberg reviewed it. It was as if they were back at the Court again.

Levitt's Supreme Court expertise and writing talent notwithstanding, a successful cert petition requires a certain amount of luck. The Court generally takes cases for one or more of the following reasons: to resolve conflicting decisions about a federal question among the lower courts; to reverse a lower court opinion in conflict with a Supreme Court decision; or to address an area of federal law of great national interest. "A review on writ of certiorari," the Court's rules stated, "is not a matter of right, but of sound judicial discretion, and will be granted only where there are special and important reasons therefor." It is an inexact science. "Frequently," the second Justice John M. Harlan remarked, "the question whether a case is 'certworthy' is more a matter of 'feel' than of precisely ascertainable rules."

Salerno, the federal lawsuit brought by the two American League umpires allegedly fired for their unionizing activities, did not make the cut. The Court denied the *Salerno* petition and gave no reason for doing so, though red flags abounded. The umpires' petition contained too many disputed facts about why they were fired, none of which had been explored in the courts below because the case had been dismissed before trial. The umpires also had not been subjected to the most pernicious aspect of baseball's legal monopoly—the reserve clause. Nor did they raise state antitrust claims. As a factual and legal matter, *Salerno* represented a poor challenge to *Federal Baseball* and *Toolson*.

Levitt's job was to persuade the Court of the "special and important reasons" why Flood's case was more certworthy. It presented almost no disputed issues of fact and a clear question of law. It affected more than a washed-up ex-ballplayer living out his days in Europe, the 600 ballplayers currently in the major leagues, or even the future of professional sports. Based on the Supreme Court's puzzling interpretation of a congressional statute (the Sherman Antitrust Act), it affected the legitimacy of the Court itself. One of the Court's main functions is to provide guidance to the lower courts, yet the lower courts struggled to reconcile *Federal Baseball* and *Toolson* with antitrust claims brought under state law.

Levitt made his case in the first two and a half pages of Flood's cert petition in a section known as "Questions Presented." Levitt knew that the justices and their law clerks paid a disproportionate amount of attention to these questions. He wrote them in a way that made it difficult for the Court to refuse to hear the case.

The opening paragraph portrayed Judge Waterman's Second Circuit opinion as an invitation to the Court to overrule itself; Levitt quoted Waterman asserting that *Federal Baseball* and *Toolson* created "a most frustrating predicament" and blaming "the vagaries of fate" for the anomalous result in Flood's case. Baseball was immune from federal antitrust law because the game was not interstate commerce, but it was immune from state antitrust law because the Second Circuit found the game to be "so uniquely interstate commerce."

The first of five questions presented challenged the Court to "rectify this bizarre result and thus preserve 'public faith in the judiciary as a source of impersonal and reasoned judgments.'" The second question suggested that the Court's subsequent decisions refusing to extend antitrust exemptions to the theater, boxing, football, and basketball "undermined" *Federal Baseball* and *Toolson*. The third question raised the problem of insulating baseball from state antitrust regulation and "creating a unique 'no man's land.'" The fourth question asked whether the federal courts could usurp all of state antitrust law without examining how the application of state law affected the business of baseball. The fifth and final question was the most damning: It portrayed baseball officials as running from forum to forum contradicting themselves to prevent any governmental regulation of the game and any challenge to the reserve clause.

On July 6, 1971, Flood's legal team filed 40 printed copies of its cert petition with the clerk's office at the Supreme Court. The brief's blue cover listed Goldberg and Topkis, the only two members of the Supreme Court bar, above the addresses of their respective law firms; Levitt, Max Gitter, and Dick Moss were listed as additional counsel.

Major League Baseball officials responded just the way they should have—with a measured, 21-page brief in opposition explaining that the sky was not really falling. Flood, they argued, wanted to overturn two well-established Supreme Court precedents that enabled Major League Baseball to develop and prosper. According to baseball's brief, *Toolson* had made it clear that removing baseball's antitrust exemption was up to Congress, but, after numerous hearings, Congress had failed to act. In light of baseball's antitrust immunity, baseball argued, any changes to the reserve clause should be left to the bargaining table. "The issues raised here are long-settled questions which Petitioner seeks to overturn," baseball's brief concluded. "They are not issues of general importance and there is no conflict among the courts with respect to them." In other words, the Court should not waste its time with baseball.

On September 9, Flood's legal team submitted a four-page reply brief that tried to rebut baseball's arguments. Congress's failure to act—especially on legislation that tried to extend baseball's exemption to all professional sports—could not be read to mean anything. Baseball had failed to respond to Flood's argument that there had been no examination whether state antitrust law interfered with the business of professional baseball. And baseball's "sudden enthusiasm" to negotiate belied its past refusals to agree to even the slightest reserve clause modifications.

The fate of Flood's case now rested with the nine justices and their law clerks. Each justice selected anywhere from two to four recent law school graduates to serve for a year or two as his law clerk. One of the clerks' most important jobs, which began during the summer, was to read each cert petition, summarize the arguments, and recommend whether to grant or deny cert. These recommendations usually came in the form of cert memos.

Shortly after Flood filed his reply brief, the Court lost two of its most respected justices. On September 17, Justice Hugo Black submitted his resignation. Six days later, Justice John Harlan followed suit. Black, 85, suffered a stroke and died two days after Harlan's resignation; Harlan, 72, had been stricken with spinal cancer and would not survive the end of the year.

During his 34 years on the Court, Hugo L. Black recast his legacy from that of a U.S. senator from Alabama who had briefly belonged to the Ku Klux Klan to that of a great constitutional thinker. A staunch New Dealer, Senator Black was nominated to the Court in 1937 by Franklin Roosevelt. As a Supreme Court justice, he emerged as the strongest voice on the Court for freedom of speech and other constitutional rights. He took tremendous heat from his fellow southerners for his support of *Brown v. Board of Education* and other desegregation cases. Despite his status as one of the Court's great civil libertarians, he had grown increasingly conservative in his later years. He had no qualms about abandoning the Court's prior decisions in pushing his Bill of Rights–oriented constitutional agenda, but when it came to reinterpreting the meaning of an old congressional statute, he almost always sided with *stare decisis*. He wrote most of the Court's unsigned opinion in *Toolson*, reaffirming *Federal Baseball* by completely changing its meaning. He also dissented from a 1970 decision reversing the Court's prior interpretation of a piece of congressional legislation. In his final years on the Court, Black had become increasingly infirm.

John M. Harlan had the Court in his blood. His grandfather and namesake, the first Justice John Marshall Harlan, had written a famous dissent objecting to the Court's 1896 *Plessy v. Ferguson* decision upholding a Louisiana law requiring racially separate railroad cars. A former Wall Street lawyer and Eisenhower nominee to the Second Circuit and then to the Supreme Court, the second Justice Harlan was an open-minded judicial conservative. He disagreed with many of the Warren Court's decisions expanding individual rights but based his disagreements on legal principles.

The previous term, Harlan had saved Muhammad Ali from going to prison. Harlan was supposed to write the Court's opinion upholding Ali's draft-evasion conviction, but his law clerks asked him to reconsider and sent him home with Alex Haley's *The Autobiography of Malcolm X* and Elijah Muhammad's *Message to the Blackman in America*. Harlan returned the next day persuaded that Ali objected to all wars, based on bona fide religious beliefs. The other justices agreed to go along with him. In an unsigned opinion, the Court unanimously reversed Ali's conviction on a technicality—the state draft appeal board had failed to specify its reason for rejecting Ali's conscientious objector status. "It's what Justice Harlan called a 'pee-wee,'" Harlan clerk Thomas Krattenmaker told authors Howard L. Bingham and Max Wallace. "It was a way of correcting an injustice without setting a precedent and changing the law."

Harlan staunchly believed in *stare decisis*. He dissented in *Radovich v. NFL* because he saw no distinction between baseball and football. "If the situation resulting from the baseball decisions is to be changed," he wrote, "I think it far better to leave it to be dealt with by Congress than for this Court to becloud the situation further, either by making untenable distinctions between baseball and other professional sports, or by discriminatory fiat in favor of baseball." But Harlan understood that *stare decisis* had its limits. He wrote in 1970 that *stare decisis* promoted "'public faith in the judiciary as a source of impersonal and reasoned judgments.' Woodenly applied, however, it builds a stockade of precedent that confines the law by rules, ill-conceived when promulgated, or if sound in origin, unadaptable to present circumstances. No precedent is sacrosanct."

In Black and Harlan, Flood lost two of the Court's great thinkers. Black would not have voted for Flood, but Harlan—based on his opinion in Ali's case, his dissent in *Radovich*, and his recognition of the limits of *stare decisis*—might have.

Because of Black's and Harlan's sudden retirements, Flood's cert petition reached the Court with only seven justices: three liberals (William Brennan, William Douglas, and Thurgood Marshall), two moderates (Potter Stewart and Byron White), and two recent Nixon appointees (Chief Justice Warren Burger and Harry Blackmun). Levitt and Goldberg knew Flood's petition could not be tailored to the political instincts of the justices as in a criminal or civil rights case. Baseball and antitrust law cut across labels like liberal, moderate, and conservative. That's why, in Flood's petition, Levitt tried to appeal to the Court as an institution to correct its past mistakes and to the justices' common sense. "We tried to shame them into taking the case," Levitt said.

Flood's cert petition received its warmest reception from Douglas's chambers. The only member of the Court remaining from *Toolson*, Douglas regretted his decision to affirm *Federal Baseball*. In January

1971, the Court's standard denial of cert in *Salerno* contained an additional sentence: "Mr. Justice Douglas is of the opinion that certiorari should be granted."

Two months later, Douglas sided with forward Spencer Haywood against the National Basketball Association (NBA). In the middle of the 1970–71 season, Haywood jumped from the American Basketball Association's Denver Rockets to the NBA's Seattle SuperSonics. The NBA, however, threatened to prevent Haywood from playing because of its "four-year rule," which prohibited anyone from playing in the NBA until his college class graduated. The 21-year-old Haywood, whose class had not graduated, sued the NBA and obtained an injunction that kept him on the SuperSonics. In entering the injunction, Judge Warren Ferguson said that "professional athletes cannot be used and treated as merchandise." The Ninth Circuit Court of Appeals, however, lifted Ferguson's injunction. Haywood appealed to Douglas, the supervisory justice of the Ninth Circuit. Douglas reinstated the injunction, which allowed Haywood to compete in the NBA playoffs while his lawsuit continued. In a two-page order, Douglas found the NBA's rules suspect and revealed his feelings about baseball's special status:

> The [NBA's] college player draft binds the player to the team selected. Basketball, however, does not enjoy exemption from the antitrust laws. Thus the decision in this suit would be similar to the one on baseball's reserve clause which our decisions exempting baseball have foreclosed. This group boycott issue in professional sports is a significant one.

Douglas deemed the reserve clause and the NBA draft "group boycotts," which were considered automatic violations of the antitrust laws, because other employers were refusing to negotiate for the athletes' services.

For William O. Douglas, the work of a Supreme Court justice was a four-day-a-week job. He often drafted dissenting opinions while sitting on the bench during oral argument. In his spare time, he wrote dozens of books to augment his salary after three divorces had destroyed him financially. He was 67 when he married his fourth wife, a 22-year-old college student. A Columbia law graduate and a corporate law professor at

Columbia and Yale, Douglas made a name for himself during the New Deal, cleaning up Wall Street as Roosevelt's Securities and Exchange Commission chairman. Roosevelt rewarded Douglas in 1939 by nominating him to the Court. Douglas expected Roosevelt to tap him as his next vice president in 1944 instead of Truman. That call never came. He accepted life as a Supreme Court justice as a consolation prize for failing to become president of the United States. Douglas served longer, 36 years, and wrote more opinions than any other justice in the Court's history.

Douglas stood out as the Court's liberal loose cannon and resident demonic genius. He lived his libertarian ideals. An avid hiker and outdoorsman, he holed himself up in his mountain cabin in Goose Prairie, Washington, until just before the term began and usually returned there before the term ended. There were no phones at his hideaway. The only way to contact him was by mail or at the nearest phone in town. When the Court was not in session, he relied on his law clerks to send him their cert memos and to relay his thoughts to the Court.

On September 23, 1971, one of Douglas's law clerks, Kenneth R. Reed, wrote a one-page, single-spaced typewritten memo to the justice. A recent University of Arizona law graduate, Reed typified the law clerks whom Douglas selected from western law schools to counteract what he perceived to be an East Coast, Ivy League bias among the clerks. Reed's cert memo summarized the history and arguments in Flood's case in six paragraphs of judicial shorthand. The memo's conclusion was telling: "Your dissent of the denial of cert last Term in *Salerno v. Kuhn* would indicate GRANT & DISSENT FROM DENIAL." Based on *Salerno*, Reed understood that Douglas was going to vote to grant Flood's cert petition but that three other votes were not likely to be forthcoming.

Douglas received Reed's memo in Goose Prairie. On September 27, Reed wrote a short letter to Chief Justice Burger on Douglas's behalf. Reed included *Flood v. Kuhn* among a handful of cases that Douglas wanted to discuss with the entire Court, thus placing Flood's petition on the "discuss list." Petitions not placed on the discuss list by any of the justices were automatically denied. Douglas guaranteed that Flood's petition would be discussed and voted on by all the justices at their next private conference. The same day as Reed's letter, Burger circulated a memo to the other justices indicating that, at Douglas's request, Flood's petition would be among the dozens of cases discussed "at Conference the week of October 4."

The conference is the most secretive aspect of the Court's behind-the-scenes decision-making processes. At conference, the justices are supposed to be able to conduct the Court's business without distraction, to discuss cases in private, and to speak their minds without posturing before the press and public. The justices vote on cert petitions and tentatively vote on and discuss recently argued cases.

October 4, 1971, was the first Monday in October—the traditional first day of the Court's term. After a brief Court session in which Burger paid tribute to Black and Harlan, the session was adjourned so the justices could hold the term's first conference. The justices retreated to the oak-paneled conference room behind the courtroom and next to the chief justice's chambers. A portrait of Chief Justice John Marshall adorned the wall above the fireplace. Hardbound copies of the *U.S. Reports* lined the walls. An antique desk, which Burger had added to the room much to some of the justices' consternation, stood off to one side.

The justices shook hands before sitting in green high-backed chairs around a long rectangular table. Burger sat at one end of the table and controlled the agenda. Douglas, as the most senior associate justice, sat at the other end of the table. The others—Brennan, Stewart, White, Marshall, and Blackmun—sat in order of seniority. As the most junior justice, Blackmun sat closest to the double doors. If there was a knock at the door, he was instructed to open it. No secretaries, no law clerks, and no court personnel were allowed in the room. Some justices took notes about what the other justices said about each case. Some returned to chambers and immediately told their law clerks what had happened there, often in entertaining fashion. But what had happened at conference was supposed to stay at conference. Many years later, a television reporter was caught trying to read a document that had been thrown into the conference room's fireplace. The incident reinforced the justices' obsession with secrecy.

Black's and Harlan's retirements had left the justices shorthanded. A seven-member Court cannot perform the work of nine. They tried to delay oral arguments on any controversial cases until the two new justices had been nominated and confirmed. But decisions on 655 cert petitions—about one-fifth of the petitions for the year—could not be delayed. The Court's calendar for the rest of the year depended on the outcome of those petitions.

As promised, Flood's petition came up for a vote. The justices, led by the chief justice, voted on Flood's petition in order of seniority. The three most senior justices, Burger, Douglas, and Brennan, voted to grant cert. Burger's vote was a surprise. Nixon had appointed him to be the antidote to Earl Warren, to be the law-and-order chief justice, not to vote against the baseball establishment. Brennan's vote was unsurprising. One of the Court's liberal voices along with Douglas and Marshall, he had voted to grant cert in *Salerno*. A master of the cert process who skimmed all the petitions that came through his chambers, Brennan could tell by the questions presented whether to grant or deny a petition. He wanted to hear Flood's case.

Stewart, White, Marshall, and Blackmun voted to deny Flood's cert petition. A vote to deny from Marshall—the great oral advocate who had argued the famous *Brown v. Board of Education* case and the first black Supreme Court justice—was even more surprising than Burger's vote to grant. It would be a mistake, however, to read too much into Marshall's vote. He may have believed that there was no chance of *Toolson* and *Federal Baseball* being overturned. Whatever the reason behind it, Marshall's decision was a critical blow. Three justices voted to grant Flood's petition; four justices voted to deny it.

Under the Rule of Four, Flood's petition was dead. He faced the denial of his case without an opinion, a chance to be heard, or even an indication whether the lower courts had been right or wrong. The purpose of the Rule of Four, however, is to allow a minority of the justices to hear a given case. This is particularly important if four justices are voting to grant cert in order to overrule one of the Court's prior decisions. As Brennan said, "five give the four an opportunity to change at least one mind."

Some commentators have suggested that the Rule of Four did not apply with a seven-member Court. According to a private memo from Burger to his fellow justices, however, the Court adhered to the Rule of Four at the beginning of the 1971 term. If there were three votes for cert, then the Court would "relist" the case to discuss it at another conference in a week or two. The idea was to see if another vote for cert emerged.

Douglas assumed that Flood's petition would be denied. In the middle of the October 4 conference, he scrawled the following note on a 4½-by-8-inch piece of white paper:

> No. 71-32
> I'll write on denial of cert.
> (1) *Toolson* was wrong.
> (2) If it's right, how about state anti-trust laws?
> WOD

The note was classic Douglas—terse but right on point. Douglas folded over the note and wrote "Reed" on the front. He then passed the note to the junior justice, Blackmun, who opened the door of the conference room and handed it to one of the Court's pages guarding the door. The page then gave the note to Reed.

Douglas informed the justices that he intended to write a dissent from the denial of cert. This was not to be a single sentence indicating that he disagreed with the decision to deny cert, which Douglas had turned into a common personal practice by the early 1970s, but a short dissenting opinion about why Flood's petition should have been granted. Dissents from denial are sometimes written, but not published, to try to persuade a fourth justice to vote for cert. Douglas asked the justices to "relist" Flood's petition for two weeks. This gave Douglas time to draft his dissenting opinion before the decision to deny cert was made public. It also gave another justice time to change his mind.

Reed immediately began to draft Douglas's dissent from the denial of cert. Douglas usually wrote all his own opinions, but this was more like a mini-opinion. On October 7, Reed turned in a first draft, which Douglas reworked during the next six days before circulating it to the other justices. On the first page, Douglas had inserted October 18 as the date that he believed Flood's petition would be denied. The five-page draft dissent, with citations omitted, began:

> Today, the Court denies certiorari to a man who wanted simply to work for the employer of his choice but who was prevented from doing so by a concerted refusal to deal among his prospective em-

> ployers. This anomaly in our antitrust laws occurs solely because Curtis C. Flood sought to earn his livelihood as a baseball player. Had this same group boycott occurred in another industry, or even another sport, we would have no difficulty in sustaining his claim. The result obtains, however, because of professional baseball's exemption from the antitrust laws—an exemption predicated upon an overly narrow interpretation of Congress' power under the Commerce Clause, which retains its force solely because of judicial paralysis.

Douglas argued that *Federal Baseball* was based on overruled Supreme Court decisions about interstate commerce, and that *Toolson*'s reliance on Congress's failure to act was meaningless because Congress had failed to pass proposed legislation granting all professional sports antitrust exemptions. A footnote offered a personal admission from Douglas: "While I joined the Court's opinion in *Toolson*, I have come to regret that vote and would now correct what I believe to be its fundamental error." Finally, the draft argued that even if federal antitrust law did not apply, state law did. The purpose of the Sherman Antitrust Act was to supplement state law, not to displace it. The draft concluded with a warning to his colleagues not to view this as an inconsequential baseball case:

> The questions raised by petitioner are important ones. They involve the scope of Congress' power under the Commerce Clause and the interrelationship of state and federal antitrust law. I would grant certiorari in this case and set it for oral argument.

Douglas's draft dissent from the denial of cert was never published.

On the morning of October 15, Flood's petition came up for another discussion and vote at conference. There is no indication whether any of the justices corresponded with Douglas about his draft dissent. Nor is there any record of the substantive discussion about Flood's petition that day. It may have been the persuasiveness of Douglas's draft or the mere fact that three of the seven justices had already voted to grant, but one justice changed his mind. Byron White—the former football star,

Rhodes scholar, and Kennedy Justice Department official—switched his vote, giving Flood's petition the four votes it needed for a full Supreme Court hearing.

The Court waited four days to announce its decision, as it had initiated a new practice during the 1971 term of issuing its grants and denials of cert on Tuesdays. On the morning of Tuesday, October 19, the Court granted certiorari in two cases and denied cert in 82 others. Of Flood's petition, the Court issued the following four-line order:

> Certiorari Granted
>
> **No. 71-32.** Curtis C. Flood, petitioner, v. Bowie K. Kuhn et al. Petition for writ of certiorari to the United States Court of Appeals for the Second Circuit granted.

The public did not know how many votes Flood's petition had received, who had voted for it, why the Court had decided to hear the case, or even when it would be heard.

This simple four-line order thrust Curt Flood's name back into the nation's headlines. The *New York Times* and *Washington Post* ran front-page stories about the Court's announcement. All three television networks reported it on the nightly news. Sports columnists from across the country began to predict Flood's Supreme Court victory. "Unless President Nixon appoints Bowie Kuhn and Joe Cronin to the two vacancies on the Supreme Court," *Chicago Tribune* columnist Robert Markus wrote, "the Grand Old Game may be in trouble."

The day after the Court granted Flood's cert petition, Nixon announced on national television his choices to replace Black and Harlan. "Presidents come and go," Nixon told the nation, "but the Supreme Court through its decisions goes on forever." During his presidency, Nixon remade the Court by replacing four of its nine members. He had already installed Burger as chief justice and replaced Abe Fortas, after the Senate had rejected Nixon's first two nominees, with Eighth Circuit judge Harry Blackmun. This time, Nixon surprised the nation with his choices to replace Black and Harlan: Lewis Powell and William Rehnquist.

A former American Bar Association president and rainmaker at the Richmond, Virginia, law firm of Hunton & Williams, Lewis F. Powell

A three-time All-Star and seven-time Gold Glove winner for fielding excellence, Curt Flood (above) played center field for the St. Louis Cardinals for 12 seasons. He and his best friend on the team, Bob Gibson (below, second from left), accept their 1965 Gold Glove awards during a pregame ceremony at Busch Stadium.

Branch Rickey, who finished out his illustrious baseball career as a Cardinal consultant, wrote in a 1964 scouting report that Flood (left) had the "best hitting form of any man on the Cardinal club." Flood (below), known for his acrobatic catches, stretches for a line drive at Chicago's Wrigley Field.

Flood's portrait of Martin Luther King Jr. (above) brought the center fielder national media attention and an appearance on the *Today* show. Although he probably did not paint the portrait of Dr. King, Flood (below) liked to draw and was an accomplished sketch artist.

Flood and Allan Zerman (above) review documents related to Flood's lawsuit. Flood did not initiate legal proceedings against Major League Baseball until consulting with Marvin Miller (left), the executive director of the Major League Baseball Players Association, and after receiving the support of the union's player representatives.

Flood's two biggest childhood mentors were Sam Bercovich (above, standing far left) and George Powles (kneeling far right), the sponsor and coach, respectively, of the Capt. Bill Erwin Post American Legion team that won the 1955 California state championship. Curt (left) shown here sliding into home, was the 1955 Bill Erwin team's star.

Flood (third from right) stood out among his Savannah teammates not only because of his small size but also because of his skin color. Buddy Gilbert (fourth from right) befriended Flood, and Leo Cardenas (second from right) played 16 major league seasons and made five All-Star teams at shortstop.

In the minors and during his first season with the Cardinals, Flood wore number 42 in honor of his hero, Jackie Robinson, then switched to number 21, half of Robinson's number.

In February 1962, Robinson (second from right) brought the 24-year-old Flood (far right) to Jackson, Mississippi, to speak at an NAACP rally along with heavyweight champion Floyd Patterson (far left) and former light-heavyweight champion Archie Moore (second from left). The experience helped Flood get involved in the civil rights struggle.

Flood and his wife, Beverly, sit on the diving board of their backyard pool after integrating a white neighborhood in Alamo, California, in October 1964 with a court order and armed police protection.

As police inspect the house before they allow Flood and his family to enter, Flood talks with supportive neighbors and engages a potential young fan.

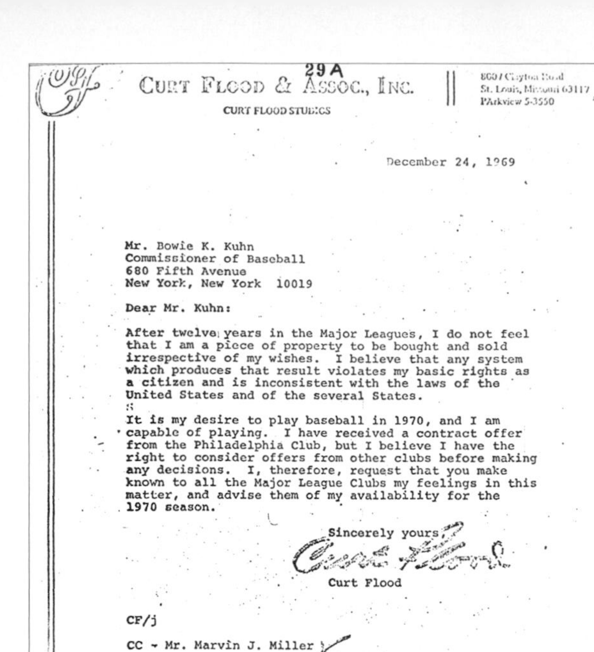

29 A

CURT FLOOD & ASSOC., INC.

CURT FLOOD STUDIOS

860 Clayton Road
St. Louis, Missouri 63117
PArkview 5-3550

December 24, 1969

Mr. Bowie K. Kuhn
Commissioner of Baseball
680 Fifth Avenue
New York, New York 10019

Dear Mr. Kuhn:

After twelve years in the Major Leagues, I do not feel that I am a piece of property to be bought and sold irrespective of my wishes. I believe that any system which produces that result violates my basic rights as a citizen and is inconsistent with the laws of the United States and of the several States.

It is my desire to play baseball in 1970, and I am capable of playing. I have received a contract offer from the Philadelphia Club, but I believe I have the right to consider offers from other clubs before making any decisions. I, therefore, request that you make known to all the Major League Clubs my feelings in this matter, and advise them of my availability for the 1970 season.

Sincerely yours,

Curt Flood

CF/j

CC - Mr. Marvin J. Miller

- Mr. John Quinn

Flood's December 24, 1969, letter to Commissioner Bowie Kuhn asked for his freedom from the reserve clause and has been included in a book about the most famous letters of the 20th century.

During Flood's January 3, 1970, appearance on *ABC's Wide World of Sports,* Howard Cosell asked him what was wrong with a ballplayer making $90,000 a year being traded. Flood replied: "A well-paid slave is nonetheless a slave."

Flood sits in the lobby at the Warwick Hotel in New York on January 16, 1970, the day his lawsuit was filed.

Flood is surrounded by some of his closest friends, including business partner Bill Jones (far left), attorney Allan Zerman (seated second from right), and Marian Jorgensen (standing far right).

Flood (right) walks up the steps of the Foley Square courthouse during his trial with his lawyer Allan Zerman (far left) and Marvin Miller (second from right).

Judge Irving Ben Cooper, shown on March 4, 1970, after denying Flood's request for an injunction to remain with the Cardinals, refused to dismiss Flood's lawsuit and therefore allowed the case to proceed to trial.

Jackie Robinson, shown testifying before the U.S. Senate in January 1970, brought tears to Flood's eyes five months later when he testified against the reserve clause on the second day of Flood's trial. After his trial testimony, Robinson ate lunch with sportswriter Red Smith and pitcher-turned-author Jim Brosnan (right), who also testified for Flood.

Hank Greenberg (left) initially expressed reservations about testifying for Flood, but he may have been persuaded by his good friend and maverick owner Bill Veeck (below). Veeck kept the courtroom in stitches during his testimony as a rebuttal witness for Flood.

Arthur Goldberg (right), leaving the courthouse with Flood on the first day of the trial, was absent for much of the three-week trial while campaigning for governor of New York.

Commissioner Bowie Kuhn (center), throwing out the first ball at a minor league game in August 1972 with Bob Feller (left) and Stan Musial (right), testified at Flood's trial that baseball could not exist without the reserve clause.

Pitcher Denny McLain (center) and a few others insisted that Washington Senators manager Ted Williams (left) did not give Flood a fair shake during his brief comeback attempt in 1971. Flood's financial problems and alcoholism, however, left him a deeply troubled man.

A *Sports Illustrated* photographer captured Flood's state of mind as he hung on to a pole in the Senators dugout. Flood's comeback lasted only a few weeks into the season before he left for Spain. "I TRIED A YEAR AND A HALF IS TOO MUCH VERY SERIOUS PERSONAL PROBLEMS MOUNTING EVERYDAY," he wrote in a telegram to his teammates.

The Supreme Court justices who decided the *Flood v. Kuhn* case: (standing from left to right) Lewis Powell, Thurgood Marshall, Harry Blackmun, William Rehnquist; (sitting from left to right) Potter Stewart, William Douglas, Warren Burger, William Brennan, and Byron White.

Arthur Goldberg stands on the plaza outside the Supreme Court after arguing Flood's case, an unhappy return to the Court for the former justice.

After exiling himself to Majorca, Spain, Flood owned a bar called the Rustic Inn.

At a White House ceremony celebrating Ken Burns's *Baseball* documentary in September 1994, Flood, his second wife, Judy, and her daughter Shawn met President and Mrs. Clinton. After Flood's death, President Clinton signed the Curt Flood Act of 1998 into law, removing a small piece of baseball's antitrust exemption.

Jr. had rejected Nixon's prior overtures to join the Court. The 64-year-old Powell's eyesight was failing, and he did not think he could read for more than 50 hours a week. Nixon persuaded Powell that, even if he served only 10 years, he could make a valuable contribution to the Court. A classic southern gentleman, Powell portrayed himself at his confirmation hearings as a racial moderate. He never endorsed Senator Harry Byrd's advocacy of massive resistance and interposition. Nor did he do anything to further racial progress. He personally opposed *Brown* at the time it was decided. During his time as chairman of the Richmond School Board, from 1952 to 1961, only two of the city's 23,000 black children attended school with whites. Powell voted in favor of giving white parents tuition grants so their children could attend private schools. Powell ignored pressure from white segregationists to close Richmond's public schools and fought to keep them open. His law firm, however, had represented Prince Edward County, Virginia, in its attempt to close its schools rather than integrate. On December 6, the Senate confirmed Powell, 89–1.

First in his class at Stanford Law School, William H. Rehnquist clerked on the Supreme Court from February 1952 to June 1953 for Justice Robert Jackson. As an aide to Barry Goldwater's 1964 presidential campaign, he impressed future Nixon deputy attorney general Richard Kleindienst. Based on Kleindienst's recommendation, Nixon named Rehnquist assistant attorney general in charge of the Office of Legal Counsel (OLC), the executive branch's legal adviser. Rehnquist had vetted Nixon's other Supreme Court nominees and had written memos, including one claiming that it was constitutional to wiretap members of the antiwar movement.

Now that the 47-year-old Rehnquist was a nominee himself, his conservative views created problems for him. The controversy began in early December, after he had testified before the Senate Judiciary Committee and just as the debates began on the Senate floor. *Newsweek* magazine published a memo that Rehnquist had written as a law clerk to Justice Jackson titled "A Random Thought on the Segregation Cases." Rehnquist wrote: "I realize that it is an unpopular and unhumanitarian position, for which I have been excoriated by my 'liberal' colleagues, but I think *Plessy v. Ferguson* was right and should be reaffirmed." Rehnquist told the Senate that the memo expressed Justice Jackson's views, not his own. Rehnquist's actions belied his feeble explanation. As a lawyer in Phoenix, Arizona, he had written editorials and made public statements opposing local antidiscrimination, public-accommodations, and school-desegregation ordinances. He had been accused of intimidating minority voters during the early 1960s at local polling places. In an attempt to save his nomination, Rehnquist sent a letter to Senator James Eastland, the chairman of the Senate Judiciary Committee, disavowing the views in the memo and embracing *Brown v. Board of Education*. On December 10, the Senate voted to confirm Rehnquist, 68–26.

On January 7, Powell and Rehnquist officially joined the Court, tilting it in a decidedly conservative direction. Based on their credentials, neither of Nixon's latest nominees seemed like a potential vote in Flood's favor.

Nixon's Justice Department, one of the chief enforcers of federal antitrust law, remained conspicuously silent about Flood's lawsuit. The Justice Department frequently weighs in on issues of importance that come before the Court through friend of the court, or amicus, briefs, and even during oral argument before the justices. For example, when the Court agreed to hear William Radovich's antitrust lawsuit against the NFL in 1957, Assistant Solicitor General Philip Elman argued the government's position in favor of Radovich. Nixon's Justice Department, however, never came out pro or con on Flood.

Philip Roth imagined Flood's place in the eyes of the Nixon-led establishment in his 1971 novel, *Our Gang*, his follow-up to the bestselling novel *Portnoy's Complaint*. In *Our Gang*, a forgettable but somewhat prescient satirical novel about the Nixon administration, Roth portrayed President Trick E. Dixon and his advisers discussing their enemies list:

> HIGHBROW COACH: To the list then, gentlemen. 1: Hanoi. 2: The Berrigans. 3: The Black Panthers. 4: Jane Fonda. 5: Curt Flood.
>
> ALL: *Curt Flood?*
>
> HIGHBROW COACH: Curt . . . Flood.
>
> SPIRITUAL COACH: But—isn't he a *baseball* player?
>
> TRICKY: *Was* a baseball player. Any questions about baseball players, just ask me, Reverend. *Was* the center fielder for the

> Washington Senators. But then he up and ran away. Skipped the country.

During the Watergate hearings two years later, Nixon's former counsel, John Dean, revealed that the administration had indeed kept an enemies list. Flood was not on it, but Fonda and Joe Namath were.

In *Our Gang*, Trick E. Dixon blames Flood for a Boy Scouts protest about a presidential speech advocating voting rights for the unborn. In a speech to the nation, Roth's Dixon explains:

> In 1970, with no more warning than the Japanese gave at Pearl Harbor, "Curt Flood," as he then called himself, turned upon the very sport that had made him one of the highest-paid Negroes in the history of our country. In 1970, he announced—and this is an exact quotation from his own writings—"Somebody needs to go up against the system," and proceeded to bring a legal action against Organized Baseball. According to the Commissioner of Baseball himself, this action would destroy the game of baseball as we know it, if Flood were to emerge victorious.

Dixon declares war on Denmark and demands that the Danish government "surrender to the proper American authorities the fugitive from the Washington Senators of the American League of Professional Baseball Clubs, the man who fled this country on April 27, 1971, exactly one week to the day before the uprising of the Boy Scouts in Washington—the man named Curtis Charles Flood."

After the real Curt Flood took off for Barcelona on Pan Am flight 154, the media, Bob Short, and the U.S. government hunted him down like a fugitive. The *New York Post* called the Pan Am desk in Barcelona as soon as Flood's flight had landed. Airline officials found no record of his leaving the plane or passing through customs in Barcelona. Only 4 of the 17 first-class passengers remained on the plane during the last leg of the trip. Flood was not one of them. He had gotten off the flight in Lisbon. The *New York Post* repeatedly paged him in the Lisbon airport, but he did not answer.

In Lisbon, Flood purchased a plane ticket to Madrid. On April 28, he registered under Curtis C. Flood in a small Madrid hotel. An enterprising UPI reporter got him on the phone. "I'm sorry, but I cannot make any comment to newsmen," Flood said. Early the next morning, he checked out of the hotel, once again refused to answer the reporter's questions, and jumped into a cab to Madrid's Barajas Airport.

The Senators gave Flood a week to find himself before they tried to find him. Short sought the government's help. On May 6, the State Department sent out a telegram regarding the "Welfare/Whereabouts Curt Flood" to its embassies in Lisbon, Barcelona, Copenhagen, and Madrid. The telegram said:

> 1. ROBERT SHORT, PRESIDENT WASHINGTON SENATORS BASEBALL TEAM, HAS REQUESTED DEPARTMENT'S HELP IN LOCATING CURT FLOOD, SENATORS' PLAYER WHO IS BELIEVED TO BE RESIDING IN ONE OF ADDRESSEE CITIES. FLOOD DEPARTED U.S. APRIL 27, PAA 501, TICKETED FOR BARCELONA BUT REPORTEDLY LEFT FLIGHT AT LISBON. FLOOD HAS PREVIOUSLY RESIDED IN COPENHAGEN.
> 2. ACTION POSTS REQUESTED TO TRY TO LOCATE FLOOD. FLOOD, AN ARTIST, MAY BE RESIDING IN AN ARTIST COMMUNITY. SHORT WISHES FLOOD TELEPHONE HIM COLLECT AT FOLLOWING NUMBERS: (202) 546-2880; (612) 929-1005; (612) 333-6161.

The last line of the memo listed Flood's passport number and date and place of birth.

Actor Yul Brynner, according to gossip columnist Leonard Lyons, called Flood in Madrid to offer him a role in the Spanish Western *Catlow*. "No thanks," Flood reportedly told Brynner. "That cowboy movie stuff is for Jim Brown."

Flood pulled a neat disappearing act. A month after he had left the Senators, he was no longer in Madrid. No one knew exactly where he was. Short claimed to know the general area where he was hiding but was unwilling to send a man over there to find him. The promanagement

Sporting News floated a false rumor that Flood was in Mexico. The Mexico rumor persisted for at least another month.

Flood eventually surfaced on Majorca, an island off the eastern coast of Spain. On May 1, he checked into the $25-a-night Hotel Melia. He did not return two messages that the U.S. embassy had left for him. A few months later, he returned to Denmark. From July 25 to August 1, he stayed at the Sheraton Hotel in Copenhagen. Journalists vacationing in Europe kept searching for him. Jimmie Angelopolous of the *Indianapolis News* contacted the State Department, which had tracked Flood to Majorca in May and Copenhagen in July. Neither Angelopolous nor the State Department could find Flood in Spain in August.

Flood made his permanent home on Majorca. Located between Ibiza and Minorca in the Spanish-owned Balearic Islands in the Mediterranean Sea, Majorca had been the home to writers (author and diarist Anaïs Nin, British poet Robert Graves), artists (Spanish surrealist painter Joan Miró), and musicians (Frédéric Chopin and his lover, novelist George Sand, spent their famous "winter of discontent" there). Beginning in the 1950s, the island became a popular tourist attraction and refuge for Hollywood celebrities. Flood ended up in Majorca somewhat by accident. His friends in Denmark told him about Las Palmas in the Spanish-owned Canary Islands off the coast of Morocco. His travel agent booked him to Palma, the largest city on Majorca, instead. Flood lived in San Augustin, a small coastal town about 10 minutes southwest of Palma.

During the 20th century, racism drove many of black America's brightest stars abroad. They fled unjust criminal convictions (heavyweight champion Jack Johnson) and political persecution (Communist actor-singer Paul Robeson). Many of them sought artistic freedom (writers Richard Wright and James Baldwin, singers Josephine Baker and Nina Simone, and tenor saxophonist Dexter Gordon).

Flood continued the tradition of black expatriates living in Europe, but he left America to escape his profession, not to pursue it. Europeans did not care about baseball. Flood once told a Spanish woman that he had been a baseball player. "Yes," she said, "but what do you do for a living?" Majorca was the perfect place for him. He did not want to deal with his personal and financial problems, to be recognized as a ballplayer, or to answer questions about his lawsuit. He was hiding from all the demons that had haunted him in Washington. "It was kind of fitting he was living on some island because he was on one anyway," his former teammate and sometimes roommate, Elliott Maddox, said. "It was virtually impossible to get through."

Rumors abounded in May that Flood might be returning to the Senators. They lacked any basis in fact. After a few weeks in Spain, Flood knew he had made the right decision. He had felt so much pressure during his two months with the Senators. He realized that physically he could not compete anymore. And, since his paychecks would have gone to his creditors, there was no use trying.

Flood, however, did not sever all his ties to baseball. From Majorca, he called Marvin Miller. He did not explain why he had left the Senators other than to say "the situation had deteriorated." Miller promised to keep him updated about the case. Indeed, the day the Supreme Court granted cert, Miller called Flood with the news. Flood asked Miller what it meant. Ever the pessimist, Miller tried not to give Flood false hope. "I know that it takes just four votes to accept the case, but you shouldn't get too high on this because that doesn't necessarily mean you've got four votes in your pocket," Miller told him. "It just means that it's a case that ought to be heard."

Flood's other legal problems played out at home. On July 29, a federal judge in St. Louis ordered Flood and his business partner, Bill Jones, to pay $27,497 owed to a suburban St. Louis couple for buying their photography shop. Flood escaped liability in another federal lawsuit. On September 1, another federal judge in St. Louis ordered Flood's business partners to repay a North Carolina–based printing company $69,528. Flood was ruled to have invested $20,000 in the photography business and pledged to invest more, but he did not commit fraud against the printing company. He still remained on the hook for half of the first judgment and for the rest of the photography business's unpaid withholding taxes to the IRS.

Flood desperately needed money. Repaying his creditors was the least of his concerns; in Majorca he struggled to live, having apparently spent the last of his Senators paychecks. A few weeks before the Court granted cert in his case, Flood wrote Miller asking for an early severance payment of $10,000. Under the rules of the major league pension plan then negotiated by Miller and the union, a player was allowed to withdraw $1,000 for every year of major league service up to $10,000. Players could withdraw the money early without reducing the rate of their pension benefits as long as the money was repaid with interest before they began collecting their pensions. The purpose of the lump-sum severance payment was to prevent players from ending up destitute before their pensions kicked in—particularly for players whose careers ended suddenly from injuries.

At the time of Flood's request, Miller was out of town. On October 18, Dick Moss wrote Flood and explained that he was not eligible to receive the money until a year after his April 27, 1971, retirement. "I'm sorry that we cannot respond more favorably to you [*sic*] inquiry," Moss wrote. "I do understand the urgency of your request, but unfortunately there is nothing we can do to advance the time of your entitlement." The only way around the rules of the pension plan would have been to ask the players' pension board to vote to change the eligibility requirements. That never happened.

Despite everything he had done for his fellow players, Flood looked elsewhere for money. He could not wait six months for his pension. He wrote a letter to Arthur Goldberg asking for a $10,000 loan that he promised to repay with interest when his severance check arrived April 28. Flood mailed his letter to Goldberg's old suite at the Pierre Hotel. Goldberg did not receive it in Washington until December 21.

Flood's typewritten letter said, in part:

> I hope my letter finds you and your family in the best of health and all going well with our law suit. Marvin has kept me advised of its progress periodically and whatever the outcome, I can't help from feeling quite proud.
>
> You told me once if I ever had any problems to feel free to call upon you. I am, however, quite sure that you meant that professionally and this is very personal.
>
> The enclosed letter will explain half of my problem. The ten thousand dollars mentioned, as the letter from Marvin states, will not be available to me until April. Needless to say I had counted on this money to carry me for a couple of years or at least until I am able to return home. I was unaware of the necessity to wait one

> year for the allowance and, frankly, I wasn't very careful with the money that I had saved. Now I find myself in a [*sic*] extremely tight situation. And if I don't have some cash coming in soon it borders on disaster. . . .
>
> I sincerely hope you do not feel that I am taking advantage of our friendship. But since the ten thousand is there and secure, and I am able to pay current interest rates, our friendship is not in question. It will be handle[d] as a business deal rather then [*sic*] a favor.

Flood asked Goldberg's secretary to telex him yes or no. There is no record of how Goldberg responded.

Goldberg rejoiced when the Court granted cert because he believed that it meant he had won Flood's case. He did not know how the justices had voted, but he figured that they would not have granted cert to review two of the Court's prior decisions unless a majority of the justices favored overruling them. If the Court believed that *Federal Baseball* and *Toolson* were right, it would have denied cert without comment. Little did Goldberg know that he had only three strong votes to hear the case.

Goldberg brimmed with false confidence as his trusted former associate, Levitt, began to prepare Flood's brief. Supreme Court briefs provided both sides with the best opportunity to persuade the justices to vote their way. "[I]t is the brief that does the final job, if for no other reason than that the opinions are often written several weeks or sometimes months after the argument," Justice Marshall, a former Second Circuit judge and solicitor general, said. "The arguments, great as they may have been, are forgotten. In the seclusion of his chambers, the judge has only his briefs and his law books. At that time your brief is your only spokesman."

By the time the Supreme Court briefing began, each side knew what the other was going to say. These issues had already been briefed and argued at trial, briefed and argued before the court of appeals, and briefed in a cert petition. Weaker arguments, such as Flood's slavery and peonage claims, had been eliminated, and stronger arguments had been refined along the way.

Flood's brief argued that, Justice Holmes and *stare decisis* notwithstanding, the Court's two baseball decisions no longer made any sense.

As Judge Waterman's Second Circuit opinion noted, Holmes himself had once written of *stare decisis*:

> It is revolting to have no better reason for a rule of law than that so it was laid down in the time of Henry IV. It is still more revolting if the grounds upon which it was laid down have vanished long since, and the rule simply persists from blind imitation of the past.

The first part of Flood's 45-page brief attacked Holmes's *Federal Baseball* opinion as "moribund." In ruling on President Roosevelt's New Deal legislation, the Court had broadened the definition of interstate commerce beyond Holmes's cases and legal reasoning. Holmes's opinion in *Federal Baseball*, the brief argued, relied on "precedential underpinnings [that] have long since disappeared."

Flood's brief also portrayed *Federal Baseball*, even after *Toolson*, as an outlier. The Court had refused to extend the logic of baseball's exemption to theatrical performances, boxing matches, or professional football. Douglas had widened the breach by adding professional basketball to the mix in the *Haywood* case.

If his lawyers could not persuade the Court to overrule *Federal Baseball* and *Toolson*, Flood had a fallback position in his state antitrust claims. It relied on a literal reading of *Federal Baseball*: If baseball was not interstate commerce subject to federal regulation, then it was intrastate commerce subject to state regulation. Indeed, in their brief nearly 50 years earlier in *Federal Baseball*, baseball officials had conceded that state antitrust laws applied. The state law argument gave the Court a way to avoid overruling *Federal Baseball* and *Toolson*, but it allowed Flood's legal challenge to the reserve clause to continue. It also was designed to appeal to the Court's conservative members, who believed that the Warren Court had expanded federal power to protect civil rights and civil liberties at the expense of the legal authority of the states.

After the Court granted cert, baseball officials tried to present a brave public face. Kuhn said that the decision to grant cert "does not affect the merits of the case. We have complete confidence in the fairness of the court's ultimate decision." Minnesota Twins owner Calvin Griffith, however, hit the panic button. "The reserve clause is the salvation of our sport," he said. "Without it, we can't protect our own players. There will be no competition." The media speculated that the owners might try to settle Flood's case—one of the subjects at their annual winter meeting November 26 in Phoenix. Behind the scenes, the lawyers for each of the clubs were clamoring to baseball's lawyers to settle. Too much was at stake to leave the fate of their legal monopoly in the hands of nine life-tenured jurists. Victor Kramer, who had represented the commissioner at Flood's trial, privately warned his client: "Be prepared to lose."

Lou Hoynes, the lawyer now in charge of the owners' defense, did not share Kramer's pessimism. A high school basketball player from Indianapolis, Hoynes graduated from Columbia and then Harvard Law School. The young Willkie Farr partner who had been sent to Harvard to recruit Hoynes was Bowie Kuhn. Hoynes worked on baseball matters with Kuhn and "The Wise Man" of baseball, Lou Carroll. Carroll and Hoynes were extremely close. Carroll helped Hoynes make partner at Willkie Farr after just six years, a rapid rise at the firm that in turn made Kuhn expendable enough to become the commissioner. On October 25, 1971, Carroll succumbed to cancer after 35 years as the National League's counsel. Hoynes replaced his late mentor, but not before flying out to Los Angeles and spending the day with the real power broker of Major League Baseball, Dodgers owner Walter O'Malley. O'Malley blessed Hoynes's promotion to National League counsel and de facto head of the Flood litigation, but warned him: "Don't embarrass me."

O'Malley, however, wanted Kuhn to make the main argument in the *Flood* case before the Supreme Court. But Kuhn knew he was not up to the task. "I felt we needed a practicing lawyer, which I wasn't at the time," he recalled. Kuhn chose the 36-year-old Hoynes to plead baseball's case. Having worked with Hoynes for years, Kuhn never considered anyone else. "I had very high regard for him," Kuhn said. "I just felt he was the right man for the job."

Hoynes's selection ruffled the feathers of Kuhn's lawyers in the *Flood* case. Paul Porter and Victor Kramer, both senior partners at Arnold & Porter, wanted the assignment. A charmer, raconteur, and Washington insider who knew every politico and journalist in every two-bit town in America, Porter had been representing the commissioner's office on Capitol Hill since Happy Chandler ruled baseball in the late 1940s. In

1950, Porter had argued an antitrust case before the Supreme Court, but he was no longer viewed as an active litigator. Kramer was an antitrust expert but too brash and outspoken for baseball. Earlier in the case, he had clashed with Hoynes over the post-trial brief.

No one was better positioned to argue Flood's case for baseball than Hoynes. He knew the history of the antitrust exemption. He had crafted the legal argument in the Milwaukee case stating that baseball was exempt from the federal antitrust laws because of *stare decisis*, but that federal law preempted state law because baseball was interstate commerce. He had played an active role at Flood's trial—conducting the direct examination of baseball's expert economist, John Clark, and cross-examining Flood's expert economist, Robert Nathan; NFL commissioner Pete Rozelle; NBA commissioner J. Walter Kennedy; and NHL president Clarence Campbell. Hoynes assumed control of the *Flood* case for baseball during the post-trial briefing and considered the owners' 133-page post-trial brief one of the finest documents of his legal career. He directed the writing of the Second Circuit brief and then, after arriving a few minutes late, argued the owners' case there.

Under Hoynes's direction, the owners' 60-page Supreme Court brief refocused the Court's attention on the meaning of *Toolson*. As Hoynes had argued in the Milwaukee case, *Toolson* changed the rationale for baseball's exemption from interstate commerce to *stare decisis*. "Without reexamination of the underlying issues," the *Toolson* Court wrote, it upheld *Federal Baseball* "so far as that decision determines that Congress had no intention of including the business of baseball within the scope of the antitrust laws." *Toolson* also recognized that baseball had relied on this exemption for the last 30 years. In effect, the Court had thrown the ball to Congress to subject baseball to the antitrust laws. The owners' brief contained a history of the subsequent congressional hearings and bills that had failed to become law. It also quoted from the Court's opinions about theatrical performances, boxing matches, and professional football—all of which recognized that baseball's exemption now rested on *stare decisis* and was up to Congress to change.

The owners' key argument grounded baseball's immunity on federal labor law. The Players Association, the owners argued, had agreed to the reserve clause in labor negotiations and therefore could not turn around and sue on antitrust grounds. The owners' brief quoted a dissenting opinion of Justice Goldberg's that a "mandatory subject" of labor negotiations "is not subject to the antitrust laws." Even if the Court overruled its decisions in *Toolson* and *Federal Baseball*, the owners believed, they could win based on this theory, which is referred to as the labor exemption.

The labor-exemption argument troubled Goldberg. As a factual matter, he argued that the owners never negotiated in good faith about the reserve clause. But navigating around some of the Court's decisions and his own opinions on this issue was trickier. Goldberg called David Feller—his former law partner, general counsel to the Steelworkers, and a law professor at Berkeley—for help. Feller critiqued Flood's brief and tried to help Goldberg craft a better response to the labor-exemption argument in Flood's 18-page reply brief. After all the briefs had been filed, Michael Jacobs and Ralph Winter weighed in with a *Yale Law Journal* article arguing that Flood's case was a labor dispute masquerading as an antitrust dispute and that it should be dismissed because the reserve clause was a mandatory subject of labor-management negotiations. The labor-exemption argument was not a clear winner for the owners, but the law seemed to be turning in their favor.

With Powell and Rehnquist not joining the Court until January 7, oral argument on Flood's case was pushed back to March 20. The Court asked both sides to submit the names of the lawyers arguing the case. Attached to the form letter was a list of 11 rules about oral argument. Goldberg did not need to be reminded about the Court's rules. Each side received 30 minutes. As a nod to Paul Porter, baseball gave him five minutes to introduce the commissioner and the remaining 25 minutes to Hoynes. Flood would be represented by Goldberg.

Hoynes exulted over the news that Goldberg, not Jay Topkis, would be arguing Flood's case. Goldberg had been absent from most of the trial while campaigning for governor of New York, and he had not distinguished himself in his brief trial appearances—especially in his direct examinations of Curt Flood and Jackie Robinson—or during his argument before the Second Circuit. No one on Flood's legal team knew the trial record better, had been quicker on his feet in Judge Cooper's courtroom, or was more prepared to argue the case before the Court than Topkis. Hoynes thought Topkis was "one of the smartest lawyers of his time."

Topkis played only a nominal role after the trial. His name was on the Second Circuit and Supreme Court briefs, but he did not help draft them. Miller later admitted that one of his biggest tactical mistakes—apart from not encouraging players to attend Flood's trial—was not tapping Topkis to argue Flood's case "all the way through."

Topkis's involvement in the merits of the case ended soon after a February 16 letter to Goldberg. "Offering you help on a Supreme Court argument is as clear a case of *lèse-majesté* as I can imagine—but if there is anything that Max [Gitter] or I can do, please let us know," Topkis wrote. The two men were no longer law partners and not close friends. Topkis merely extended Goldberg a professional courtesy. Four days later, Goldberg replied: "I believe that you and I have canvassed the ground so extensively that there is little need for a meeting between us on the subject."

Instead, Goldberg's help came from two associates in Paul, Weiss's Washington office, Levitt and Peter Westen. They knew what they were doing. Levitt not only had clerked for Goldberg and Fortas on the Court, but also had written almost every word of the *Flood* briefs. Westen, who had clerked for Douglas during the 1969 term, also contributed to the legal research and Supreme Court briefing. In late February and March, Levitt and Westen wrote Goldberg memos to help him prepare for argument. They offered him hypothetical questions the justices might ask as well as possible answers. Westen discussed the state antitrust claims. Levitt critiqued Jacobs's and Winter's labor-exemption article.

In mid-March, Levitt and Westen met with Goldberg. Goldberg's new office at Caplin & Drysdale at L and 17th was only a block away from Paul, Weiss's Washington office on K and 17th. The two young associates did not formally act as justices and ask Goldberg questions at the podium (a process known among the Supreme Court bar as "mooting" or "moot court"). Having argued before the Court several times, Goldberg did not need or want such practice. Instead, he laid out the argument that he planned to make before the Court. Westen thought he "sounded terrific." That night, Westen came home from work and told his wife that "it would be one of the great arguments of the year."

Hoynes, who unlike Goldberg had never argued before the Court, was not leaving anything to chance. He took the train to Arnold &

Porter's office in Washington for a full moot court session. Hoynes stood at the podium in front of an Arnold & Porter conference table fielding questions from lawyers who had either clerked for or argued before the Court. It was Hoynes's own mock Supreme Court.

There was a special chief justice presiding over Hoynes's moot court session that day: Abe Fortas. Baseball did not retain a former justice to argue on its behalf, but it had one aiding its preparation for oral argument. After resigning from the Court because of a financial conflict of interest, Fortas had found his return to private life difficult. Arnold & Porter—the firm formerly known as Arnold, Fortas & Porter that he had helped build into Washington's second-largest law firm and where his wife worked as a tax partner—did not want him back. An abrasive, take-no-prisoners personality, Fortas had alienated many of the firm's young partners. It took a lot for Fortas, who had opened his own small law office in Georgetown, to return to his old firm's offices.

Fortas attended the moot court session for only one reason—out of loyalty to his former partner and lifelong friend, Paul Porter. In November 1970, Fortas had written Porter a three-page memo evaluating the *Flood* case as only a former justice could. In the memo, Fortas correctly predicted that the Supreme Court would grant cert. He did not think Flood's state antitrust claims or his 13th Amendment and indentured-servitude arguments would carry much weight. Nor did he think much of baseball's labor-exemption argument. *Toolson*, Fortas believed, was on shaky ground. To preserve baseball's antitrust exemption, Fortas suggested that the owners get a member of Congress to introduce legislation protecting baseball's exemption and to negotiate modifications to the reserve clause with the union. Fortas wrote that ultimately "this is one of the relatively unusual cases in which approach and substance of presentation of issues to the Court may be of great significance." The owners' ability to preserve their exemption came down to oral argument. The justices, Fortas wrote, would not be eager to uphold *Toolson* on *stare decisis* grounds. "Reliance upon *stare decisis* will leave the Court (with the possible exception of one Justice) uncomfortable; and this is a dangerous state of mind for Organized Baseball," Fortas concluded in his memo. "Only an appealing presentation of the special equities in this situation can counteract the unease which the *Toolson* result will generate."

At Hoynes's and Porter's moot court session, Fortas brought more than just the ideas in his November 1970 memo and his experiences as a former justice; he also knew how to make a persuasive presentation at oral argument, having argued one of the Supreme Court's landmark constitutional cases. *Gideon v. Wainwright*—prompted by a handwritten cert petition from an indigent inmate named Clarence Earl Gideon—won indigent criminal defendants the right to appointed counsel at felony trials. Fortas had briefed and argued the case *pro bono* at the request of the Court. He undoubtedly used his expertise as a former justice and esteemed oral advocate to grill Hoynes and Porter at their moot court session. Curt Flood may have been the Clarence Earl Gideon of the 1971 term, the lone individual taking on the establishment, but the baseball establishment had Gideon's lawyer on its side.

CHAPTER FIFTEEN

During breakfast with Dan Levitt at the Hay-Adams Hotel on the morning of the Supreme Court argument, Arthur Goldberg revealed his new strategy. Goldberg figured that the Court knew the legal issues and had granted cert in order to reverse *Federal Baseball* and *Toolson*. He decided to step behind the lectern, talk for two or three minutes, and open the floor to questions. If the justices had no questions, he promised, he would sit down.

Levitt thought it was a bold strategy that only a former justice could pull off. The goal of oral argument is to present your best reasons why the Court should vote in your favor. Goldberg's strategy meant that either he was supremely confident about winning, incredibly nervous about his return to the Court, or both.

A lot was riding on Goldberg's argument. This was supposed to be his triumphant return to the Court after resigning in 1965. It also represented his chance to reclaim his position at the pinnacle of the Washington legal establishment. Goldberg's reputation and career were not the only things hanging in the balance. Curt Flood had sacrificed everything—his playing career, his financial well-being, and his life in America—to get his lawsuit to this point. Goldberg needed to make the best possible showing so that Flood's personal sacrifices would not be in vain.

The conventional wisdom is that cases can be lost but not won at oral argument. The Court's earliest advocates, such as Daniel Webster, spoke for as long as they wanted; argument lasted for days. Over the years, the Court gradually reduced the time allotted for each side, from eight hours in 1848 to two hours in 1871, an hour and a half in 1911, one hour in 1925, and finally to a half hour in 1970, when Chief Justice Burger cut the time of oral argument in half so the Court could keep up with its expanding caseload. The justices on the Burger Court disagreed about the importance of oral argument. Brennan wrote that "truly skillful advocacy [makes] a difference only in a handful of cases." Rehnquist opined that during oral argument "you do have an opportunity to engage or get into the judge's mental process." Oral argument does make a difference, particularly in a closely divided case such as Flood's.

After revealing his plan to Levitt, Goldberg drove to National Airport to pick up Max Gitter and headed for the Court. On the way, Goldberg must have gotten himself turned around crossing one of several bridges over the Potomac River into Washington, or ended up on the wrong side of the U.S. Capitol. He started to drive in circles searching for the Court. He was lost. Goldberg eventually found his old workplace, but it was not a good omen.

The Supreme Court building is difficult to miss. The white marble palace stands four stories high behind the Capitol and next to the Library of Congress's Jefferson Building. Television cameras, not allowed in the courtroom, are set up on the 252-foot plaza. Two rows of eight marble columns help form the building's portico. A sculpture, *Liberty Enthroned*, graces the top of the building, with the scales of justice across her lap; she is guarded by *Order* and *Authority*, with three figures on each side representing *Council* and *Research*. Engraved just below the sculpture is the famous phrase "Equal Justice Under Law."

The public lined up on the Court's marble steps for the chance to see Goldberg's argument. The lucky ones walked through two bronze doors, which depict great scenes in legal history and weigh six and a half tons apiece, and down the main corridor, known as the Great Hall. The Great Hall is lined with double rows of marble columns and busts of the chief justices. Two oak doors lead into the courtroom, an expanse of mahogany and marble featuring 44-foot ceilings, 24 giant columns made from the finest Italian marble, and walls and friezes depicting great figures in legal history.

The courtroom filled up quickly on the morning of March 20. With seats for only 355 people, including the press and Supreme Court bar, the Court offered about 200 to 250 seats to the public. The press overflowed its small reserved section on the room's left side. The justices' law clerks scrambled for seats on the far right side. Bowie Kuhn sat among the spectators. Flood's St. Louis attorney, Allan Zerman, also was on hand. They all wanted to see the Court address Flood's case against baseball.

Several key members of Flood's trial team were notably absent from the courtroom. Jay Topkis, who had planned on attending the argument before it was pushed back, was too preoccupied with his own legal practice at Paul, Weiss to watch Goldberg argue what should have been Topkis's case. Marvin Miller was visiting spring training camps to rally his troops during a pension dispute that would lead to the first strike in the union's history.

Miller was too busy with the impending strike to think about the strategic implications of having Flood in the courtroom. Many litigants do not attend oral argument. Muhammad Ali, for example, did not attend his. But there was something obviously personal at stake in Ali's case—imprisonment. As a result of Flood's decisions to return to baseball, quit the Senators, and move to Europe, the outcome of his case appeared to have minimal impact on him personally—other than the highly unlikely recovery of damages if the case was remanded for trial. Flood's presence at the Court that day might have reinforced how his decision to sue had ruined his life. Instead, he was out of sight, out of mind.

In Majorca, Flood reportedly worked part-time as a sports announcer for an English-language radio station. In January 1972, he began working at a bar. Miller did not say anything, but he knew from the trial that the last place Flood needed to spend his time was in a bar. Flood's self-imposed exile had also cost him his true love. In February 1972, Flood's former girlfriend, Judy Pace, married actor Don Mitchell from the television show *Ironside*. Flood was destitute, drinking too much, and in all likelihood still awaiting the $10,000 severance payment due April 28. The last place he wanted to be on the morning of March 20 was in that marble courtroom surrounded by the media, curiosity seekers, and baseball fans.

At 10 a.m., the marshal banged a gavel on a wooden block. The audience rose. The marshal invoked the Court's traditional greeting: "The honorable, the Chief Justice and the Associate Justices of the Supreme Court of the United States. Oyez! Oyez! Oyez! All persons having business before the honorable, the Supreme Court of the United States, are admonished to draw near and give their attention, for the Court is now sitting. God save the United States and this honorable Court!"

The black-robed justices shook hands before walking through the red draperies behind four marble columns. They took their seats on the mahogany bench. At a cost of $8,500, Burger had ordered the bench sawed in three parts and angled. Unveiled the previous month, the new bench allowed the justices to see and hear who had asked a particular question during oral argument.

As the chief justice, Burger sat in the center seat. The associate justices sat in order of seniority with the most junior justices on the ends. The lineup, from left to right facing the audience, was as follows: Powell, Marshall, Stewart, Douglas, Burger, Brennan, White, Blackmun, and Rehnquist.

After four minutes of preliminary proceedings, Burger announced the first case in a clear, stentorian voice: "So first, this morning, in Number 71-32, Curtis C. Flood against Kuhn and others." Burger paused for a moment, almost as if he did not know how to address a former member of the Court. The justices fretted about how to address their former colleague. They did not want to call him Mr. Justice or Arthur because they did not want to show favoritism. Many of them tried to avoid addressing him by name.

"Mr. Goldberg," Burger finally said.

Goldberg was standing at the mahogany lectern only eight feet from the front of the justices' elevated bench. It is impossible, from that position, to see all nine justices without turning one's head. The podium is so close because the idea is to engage the justices in an intimate conversation. What often happens is that the justices end up having an intimate conversation among themselves, using persistent questions to the oral advocate as a conduit. "You have questions by *one* and you have to respond in terms of *nine*," Fortas said after he had left the bench. The justices have often been described as nine separate law offices, or, as Justice Holmes reputedly put it, "nine scorpions in a bottle."

Of the nine scorpions sitting on the bench that day, only four remained from Goldberg's time on the Court: Brennan, Douglas, Stewart, and White. Of those four, he maintained close friendships and a steady stream of correspondence with only his fellow liberals, Brennan and Douglas. Goldberg had made two recent public appearances with the current justices—at Justice Black's funeral on September 28, 1971, at the National Cathedral in Washington and at Justice Harlan's funeral on January 4 in Connecticut.

Responding to Burger's formal greeting at the lectern, Goldberg played it straight by uttering the traditional opening words at oral argument: "Mr. Chief Justice, and may it please the Court." Goldberg briefly summarized Flood's case as attacking the legality of the reserve clause under federal antitrust law, state antitrust law, and common law. He explained that the reserve clause bound players to their teams for life and extended throughout the major and minor leagues in the United States, Mexico, and Japan. Goldberg spoke slowly and haltingly—almost as if he had forgotten what he wanted to do or say. Blackmun, sitting in Goldberg's old seat, thought Goldberg's nasal midwestern monotone was an "unpleasant voice."

Goldberg abandoned the strategy he had laid out at breakfast. Rather than open up the floor to questions (a dubious strategy) or explain to the Court why it should vote in Flood's favor (the soundest strategy), he announced he was going to review the facts of Flood's case. This might have been a good idea given Flood's absence except for one problem: Goldberg knew nothing about Flood. He butchered the facts of Flood's baseball career. He said Flood had signed a contract with the Reds at age 15 (he signed at 18). He said Flood had won "several Golden Gloves competitions," as if Flood were a boxer. He also said Flood had been elected team captain by his teammates (general manager Bob Howsam had appointed him and McCarver).

Goldberg knew he was in trouble because he turned for help to the astonished Levitt and Westen, who were sitting at counsel's table to the right of the podium. "Everybody in that courtroom knew that he froze," Levitt said. "He did not realize how that was going to affect him, appearing before his brethren as a lawyer advocating." Maybe it was his old friends, Brennan and Douglas, sitting on that mahogany bench where he should have been had it not been for Johnson's persistence and

Goldberg's own ego. Maybe it was the knowledge that he was not as prepared as he should have been for oral argument.

Westen thought that Goldberg might have been "overconfident." But when he turned to Levitt and Westen for help, it was clear that confidence was gone. Not having prepared anything about the facts of Flood's case or playing career, they handed Goldberg a few notes in the hope that he would regain his train of thought.

Instead of shifting to the legal argument that he had supposedly practiced, Goldberg began listing Flood's season-by-season batting averages. He repeated that Flood had batted "around .300" and that he had won "several Golden Gloves awards. These are awards given to someone for excellence in fielding." He also repeated that Flood had received a form notice and a telephone call informing him of the trade from the Cardinals to the Phillies.

When Goldberg repeated the information about Flood's Gold Glove awards, Levitt looked up from counsel's table and saw Justice Brennan cringe. Brennan and Goldberg had shared adjoining chambers and had been allies on the Warren Court. Brennan's pained expression indicated just how embarrassed he was for his friend and former colleague.

Goldberg droned on with a desultory discussion of the facts of Flood's case, using up more than half of his time. He read the legal letters between Flood and Kuhn, pointing out the offensiveness of Kuhn's "Dear Curt" opening; he read Judge Waterman's description of the reserve clause; he repeated that it applied to the major leagues, minor leagues, Mexico, and Japan; he listed Flood's federal antitrust, state antitrust, and 13th Amendment claims (even though the last of the three had not been briefed before the Supreme Court); and he mentioned that after sitting out a year, Flood had failed in his comeback attempt with the Senators. Blackmun wrote in his notes about the argument: "too much time on facts." It was the understatement of the year.

Finally, after more than 17 minutes of Goldberg's feeble factual recitation, the justices began to jump in with questions. Stewart asked how much thc Phillies had offered Flood to play for them in 1970. Goldberg said Flood had been offered "an increase to $100,000 with salary and other benefits" (the Phillies had sent him a contract for

$90,000 but originally offered him $90,000 plus $8,000 in spring training expenses). Goldberg then tried to answer the question "'Why this high-paid ballplayer did this?' He did it, as he simply said, out of principle. He no longer wanted to be treated as chattel property. He made that decision on his own, and although he has been supported in this litigation by the Players Association . . . this was his decision. . . . In fact he was told by the director, Mr. Miller, that he had a tough case. Nevertheless, he felt in good conscience he had to pursue it."

Goldberg seemed to steady himself with this decent summation of Flood's motives. The main point of Stewart's question was to inquire about damages, but it painted Flood in an unsympathetic light because he had turned down a $100,000 contract. Goldberg—the driving force behind Flood's 13th Amendment and involuntary-servitude claims—had explained, without using the exact words, why Flood considered himself "a well-paid slave."

Rehnquist, sitting on the far right seat, pointed out that "[a]s a practical matter, though, he had no real chance of remaining in St. Louis and negotiating another contract with the St. Louis club; he would have had to go to one of the other teams, even if it hadn't been for the reserve clause."

Goldberg responded: "That's right, Mr. Justice, provided this clause is legal. And I shall say it is not."

A good oral advocate has to know when to agree with a justice and the implications of agreeing with the justice's question or comment. Even if Flood had been declared a free agent, he would not have signed with the Cardinals, because they had indicated by trading him that they did not want him anymore. He likely would have signed with another team. Goldberg, however, did not get it. Rehnquist reiterated his point. Goldberg still didn't get it. He had been tossed two softball questions and could not answer either of them.

The Supreme Court law clerks, watching from the far right side of the courtroom, were so embarrassed by Goldberg's performance that they refrained from their usual snide comments. This was not the same man who had argued the Steel Seizure cases from federal trial court to the Supreme Court in three weeks. He was like an aging Willie Mays stumbling around in the New York Mets outfield in 1973, except that Goldberg had another 10 minutes left at the lectern to regain his footing. His performance soon moved Brennan and the other justices from pity to disgust.

Brennan asked: "Mr. Justice, may I ask you, suppose [the reserve clause] had been collectively agreed to, would your position be any different?"

Goldberg: "No, and I shall discuss that when I come to the labor exemption."

Brennan was irritated. He had shown Goldberg a high degree of deference by calling him "Mr. Justice." Goldberg had responded by committing one of the cardinal sins of oral argument: refusing to answer a justice's question.

Brennan replied: "I hope you're going to get to that. You're talking rather . . ."

Goldberg: "I will move fast . . ."

The audience laughed.

". . . because of the shortness of time."

They were not laughing with him.

Goldberg had been asked a key substantive question. Even if *Federal Baseball* and *Toolson* were overruled, would Flood still lose because the reserve clause had been part of a labor agreement? Instead of answering it, Goldberg continued with his train of thought. He seemed to be lecturing his former colleagues rather than engaging them in an intimate conversation.

The image in Hoynes's head was of Goldberg flipping pages. Neither Levitt nor Westen had prepared a written script for Goldberg, but he seemed to be reading from some type of outline and did not want to be interrupted. He had now broken a second cardinal rule of oral argument: Don't read your argument. No oral advocate before the Supreme Court gets to march through his or her argument in order. Everyone is interrupted and asked questions. Goldberg was, in effect, asking for special treatment.

Brennan then asked if *Federal Baseball* and *Toolson* had to be overruled.

"They would have to be overruled," Goldberg said. "They should be overruled. They should be overruled for very good reasons."

Brennan then pointed out that *Federal Baseball* and *Toolson* "both dealt with the issue of statutory construction" and "the Court doesn't readily overrule statutory construction cases."

Goldberg responded by alluding to Stewart's unanimous opinion in another case reinterpreting the meaning of civil rights legislation, promising to return to that case "in a moment," then naming the wrong case. Goldberg did return to the case later, but his opportunity to discuss *stare decisis* and several of the Court's recent decisions reinterpreting the meaning of congressional statutes had been lost.

White asked why *Federal Baseball*, which said in effect that labor could not be commerce, was wrong. Goldberg responded that in Flood's case, labor was a commodity. White tried to help Goldberg by reminding him that the Court had already rejected the labor-exemption argument in *Radovich*, its 1957 football decision.

Goldberg did not broach one of his most important arguments—if federal antitrust law did not apply, then state antitrust law did—until he was past the 29-minute mark. Goldberg needed to explain why state law was not preempted by federal law (as Judge Cooper had said) or did not apply because baseball was "so uniquely interstate commerce" (as the Second Circuit had said), but he was almost out of time.

Douglas asked: "Has this man left baseball?"

Goldberg, lost in his state antitrust argument, did not hear the question. "Pardon?"

"Has the petitioner left baseball?"

"Yes." It was a question already addressed in the briefs. Many justices, however, do not read the briefs before oral argument. And some ask questions in order to lead into a more important question. That was the case here.

"Is the case moot?" Douglas asked.

"No, it is not," Goldberg said. He explained that Flood had the right to recover damages from sitting out the 1970 season. Flood also could return to baseball either in the minor leagues or in Japan, places where the reserve clause still applied. These were decent factual answers. But Goldberg should have discussed the Court's decision in *Radovich v. NFL*. In 1946 William Radovich, an all-pro offensive lineman with the Detroit Lions, was blacklisted for five years for breaking the reserve clause in his NFL contract and signing with the Los Angeles Dons of the rival All-America Football Conference. Two years later, the NFL threatened a minor league football team with legal action for trying to sign Radovich as a player-coach, and the team rescinded its offer. Although Radovich did not file suit until after his playing days were over in 1949, the Court ruled that a group boycott could still be challenged because the antitrust laws "protect the victims of the forbidden practices as well as the public."

The justices, by inquiring about mootness for the second time during the course of the argument, seemed to be asking themselves: What are we doing here? Why did we grant cert in the first place? The Supreme Court does not issue advisory opinions. It does not resolve hypothetical conflicts. It decides real disputes brought by real people. Curt Flood, the petitioner in this case, seemed to have nothing left at stake.

That's why Flood's reply brief, at Topkis's urging, concluded with a discussion of the salary dispute between Oakland A's owner Charlie Finley and his 22-year-old Most Valuable Player and Cy Young Award winner, pitcher Vida Blue. Blue made $14,750 for his phenomenal 1971 season, hired a lawyer, and asked for a raise to $92,500. A notorious tightwad, Finley refused to pay him more than $50,000. "I won't trade him and I won't sell him," Finley said. "Either he accepts what we have offered or he's through in baseball." Blue, who wrote the foreword to the paperback edition of Flood's book, *The Way It Is*, announced his retirement. He claimed to have accepted a public relations job with a bathroom-fixtures company. In late April, Kuhn intervened, and Blue returned to the A's in early May with a $63,000 salary. Blue's contract dispute, however, signaled that there would be more Curt Floods.

Goldberg was well informed about Vida Blue. He had spoken on the phone with Blue's attorney, Robert Gerst. Topkis had sent him a Red Smith column about the dispute, which was quoted in Flood's reply brief. "Quite possibly," Topkis wrote Goldberg on February 18, "some members of the Court will have lost enthusiasm for Curt Flood but may be stirred up by Blue."

A good oral advocate would have mentioned Vida Blue's contract dispute. A good oral advocate would have brought up the Court's ruling in *Radovich*. A great oral advocate, one familiar with the trial record and Flood's personal story, could have explained the sacrifices that Flood had made to get the case to this point—how he had left the Senators and refused to declare bankruptcy in part to maintain his lawsuit. Goldberg, however, was unfamiliar with the facts and was neither a great nor even a good oral advocate at this point in his legal career.

After 31 minutes, Goldberg said he would say a few more words and then reserve some time for rebuttal.

Burger cut him off. "Your rebuttal time is used up."

Goldberg did not hear him and kept talking.

"Excuse me. Excuse me," Burger said. "Your time is completely consumed, but we'll extend it three minutes and enlarge yours three minutes, Mr. Porter."

Supreme Court clerks watching the argument thought it was one of the few statesmanlike and magnanimous gestures that Burger had made during the entire term. The extra three minutes allowed Goldberg to preserve a shred of dignity.

Instead of immediately sitting down and saving his newfound rebuttal time, Goldberg continued to discuss the labor exemption. Flood's best arguments—that *Federal Baseball* and *Toolson* were wrongly decided and Flood's state antitrust claims were not preempted by federal antitrust law—fell by the wayside. "He never got to make his argument," Levitt said.

The justices, who had asked Goldberg very few questions compared with other litigants, just let him exhaust himself. Embarrassed and irritated, they knew that he was not up to the task. Goldberg talked about the labor exemption for another three minutes and then sat down.

"Thank you," Burger said. "Mr. Porter."

Paul Porter's job was to introduce himself as the commissioner's lawyer, to explain the commissioner's role in the governance of Major League Baseball, and to hand the case over to Hoynes. Porter was not supposed to answer questions and consume Hoynes's time and argument. In preparing for the argument, one of the lawyers reminded Porter what Bill Veeck had told his midget batsman, Eddie Gaedel—that if he lifted the bat off his shoulder, Veeck would be on the roof with a high-powered rifle and shoot him dead. "If you answer one question," the lawyer joked, "there's a guy with a high-powered rifle in the back of the Supreme Court."

The justices, however, wanted answers. And they had not received any from Goldberg. After Porter intoned in his gravelly voice, "Mr. Chief Justice, may it please the Court," he tried to stay true to his task. He explained his role as the commissioner's lawyer and that Hoynes would discuss why "this litigation involves basically a labor dispute." He tried to explain the commissioner's supposedly neutral position in baseball, but the justices stopped him cold.

Brennan asked if the structure of baseball was different from those of other sports.

Porter explained that the minor leagues, which accounted for 25 percent of baseball's revenues, made baseball unique. He referred to the commissioner's prior testimony that the reserve clause was essential to equalize competition and to ensure the integrity of the game.

White jumped in and asked: "But doesn't this go to whether it would be a violation of the antitrust laws rather than to coverage [whether baseball was subject to federal or state antitrust law]?"

Porter answered that this union-driven lawsuit was really a labor dispute that should be resolved at the bargaining table, as Hoynes intended to explain in his argument. Porter was trying to extricate himself from the lectern. The justices would not let him go.

"But Mr. Porter," Brennan asked, "you just said this litigation was brought by the players union?"

Porter explained that it was financed by the Players Association.

"Are you saying this is their lawsuit, not Flood's?" Brennan asked.

"Absolutely, yes, sir . . . with the exception of the petitioner, Mr. Flood, all the witnesses in support of Mr. Flood's case testified that some form of reserve system was essential."

Porter's response touched on a key theme of baseball's argument—marginalizing Flood's role in the litigation. It also led perfectly into Hoynes's argument that this really was a labor dispute governed by labor law. Even though he had strayed from his task of talking about the commissioner, no one shot Porter down. He had helped baseball's cause. With that, he excused himself and yielded the lectern to Hoynes.

Hoynes wanted to give the justices a better reason to uphold *Federal Baseball* and *Toolson* than just *stare decisis*. He did not want to argue that they had to uphold those decisions even though they made no sense. That's where the labor exemption came in. Hoynes wanted to argue that the reserve clause was part of a labor agreement, would be subject to future negotiations, and therefore was immune from antitrust lawsuits. The labor exemption, Hoynes believed, gave *stare decisis* meaning. It gave the justices a reason for voting his way. If only the justices would give him the opportunity to state his case.

Hoynes's journey to the Supreme Court had not been without incident. He and two young Willkie Farr associates had arrived in Washington the day before by train. They rented a car and piled all their clothes, briefs, case law, argument books, and notes into the trunk. One of the young associates, after being asked whether he had the car keys in his pocket, proceeded to lock the keys in the trunk. It was the night before the biggest argument of his life and Hoynes could not study his notes. Two hours later, the ashen-faced associate had unlocked the trunk and arrived at the hotel with Hoynes's notes.

By the time Hoynes reached the lectern, the justices were salivating for some answers to their questions.

"Mr. Chief Justice, and may it please the Court," Hoynes said. "I am counsel for the National League, and I here represent the 24 major league clubs and the two major leagues. The two issues presented here are—"

The justices, as they typically did with the second person at the podium, cut Hoynes off in midsentence. They wanted answers now.

"It is your position that baseball is not commerce?" Douglas asked.

Hoynes conceded that it was. Baseball had admitted as much in its answer to Flood's initial complaint.

Hoynes stayed on point that this dispute was "much broader than Curt Flood's particular situation" and that the "real protagonists are the players union, the Major League Baseball Players Association, and the major league clubs."

The justices continued to pepper Hoynes with questions.

White asked whether all players belonged to the union. Yes. White asked whether Hoynes's position would be the same if the petitioner were a minor league player. Hoynes conceded that the union did not represent the interests of minor leaguers. But, during an extended colloquy with White, Hoynes maintained his position that any modification to the reserve clause must be resolved in labor-management negotiations.

Of the nine justices on the bench that day, Hoynes tried to make extra eye contact with White. A former All-America halfback at the University of Colorado and runner-up for the Heisman Trophy, Byron "Whizzer" White postponed his Rhodes scholarship in 1938 to play one season with the National Football League's Pittsburgh Pirates (later renamed the Steelers). His $15,800 salary doubled the highest ever paid in the nascent NFL. He passed, punted, kicked, and led the league in rushing. After White returned from Oxford and began his first year at Yale Law School, Pittsburgh sold White's contract to the Detroit Lions for $5,000. White deferred his second year at Yale to play for the Lions. He accepted a more than 50 percent cut in salary to $7,500 and played two seasons for Detroit in 1940 and 1941. One of his teammates on the Lions was William Radovich.

World War II ended White's football career and further interrupted his legal education, but launched his career in politics. As an intelligence officer in the Pacific, he wrote the official report about the mysterious sinking of PT boat 109 manned by Lieutenant John F. Kennedy. The two men had met and become friends while White was at Oxford. White finished at the top of his class at Yale Law School and clerked on the Court during the 1946 term for Chief Justice Fred Vinson. After 14 years at a Denver law firm, he served as the national chairman of Citizens for Kennedy during the 1960 presidential campaign and as deputy to Attorney General Robert Kennedy. In that role, he flew to Alabama to protect the Freedom Riders and negotiate with Governor John Patterson. In April 1962, President Kennedy nominated White to the Court.

White turned out to be far more conservative than the Court's other Democratic nominees. Burger indicated to Nixon that White would be a suitable replacement for him as chief justice. "This guy is our reliable swing man right now," Burger told Nixon in June 1972. "He's the one when we run 5–4, he's the guy who usually saves it."

White was a tough guy. He despised the nickname the sportswriters had foisted on him at the University of Colorado. No one except a few old football teammates called him Whizzer to his face. He never seemed to smile, asked extremely tough questions from the bench, and terrified some of the law clerks with his ferocious play on the Supreme Court's top-floor basketball court (the "highest court in the land"). He had been mentioned in both 1965 and 1969 as a possible replacement for Ford Frick and William Eckert as commissioner of baseball. A few people even tried to draft White as the Democratic presidential candidate in 1972 against Nixon.

Hoynes knew that he needed White. No one else on the Court had experienced life as a professional athlete or been sold like a piece of property. The Court, Hoynes believed, would follow White's lead in a case about sports. He was the ultimate swing vote in Flood's case.

Thurgood Marshall picked up on White's question that a minor leaguer was not protected by the union and therefore baseball could not be immune from all lawsuits under federal labor law. Marshall spoke in a slow southern drawl that he had picked up in the segregated black middle-class Baltimore neighborhood of his youth and from defending blacks in courtrooms throughout the South as the top litigator for the NAACP Legal Defense and Educational Fund. Marshall dismantled the legal justification for racial segregation through a series of cases brought on behalf of black students culminating with his argument in the seminal case of the 20th century, *Brown v. Board of Education*. As an NAACP lawyer, he won 29 of the 32 cases he had argued before the Supreme Court. In 1961, President Kennedy appointed Marshall to the Second Circuit. Four years later, President Johnson made him the first black solicitor general, then nominated him for the Court in 1967.

Marshall's first law clerk on the Second Circuit was Ralph Winter, a Yale law professor (and future Second Circuit judge) and coauthor of the *Yale Law Journal* article about Flood's case and the labor exemption. Winter's article mirrored baseball's argument that since the union had included the reserve clause in the collective bargaining agreement, then one of its members, namely Flood, was not allowed to turn around and sue baseball under the antitrust laws. If Winter wrote it, then Marshall took notice of it. Marshall used Hoynes to denigrate the union.

"Mr. Hoynes," Marshall said, "how far does this representation of Flood go? For example, did the owner consult with the Players Association about this movement?"

Of Flood's trade, Hoynes said it did not. The trade was conducted under the rules of the bargaining agreement.

Marshall was only beginning. "My question was," he said, "how much representation did Flood get from this outfit . . . [a]s to this trade which is the basis of this suit? Now, what position did the union take on that? Or do you call it a union?"

"I call it a union, your Honor," Hoynes said. "The union met with Flood and agreed to finance the litigation. It is quite transparent . . . that the union has controlled this litigation from beginning to end."

Marshall kept on Hoynes: "So you're saying that a union, which says to management, 'You can pick up a man and throw him out the door,' without any recovery, that that's a union?" Hoynes denied that the union had agreed to that or that it had happened that way in this case.

Marshall repeatedly asked Hoynes where the record showed that the union had agreed to the reserve clause. Hoynes kept insisting that the union had agreed to it in collective bargaining. Marshall touched on the most disputed factual issue in the entire case. If Marvin Miller had been arguing for Flood, he would have said that the union had declared the reserve clause illegal during negotiations over the 1968 Basic Agreement and that both sides had agreed to set the reserve clause issue aside for the purposes of the latest agreement. But Miller was not there. And, technically, even though the union had reserved its right to challenge it, the reserve clause was part of the 1968 Basic Agreement governing Flood's lawsuit.

These were questions that Marshall should have asked Goldberg. Goldberg, however, did not answer many of the justices' questions and had not been up to the task of answering the ones he did. So Marshall posed them to Hoynes.

"Well, what good is the union?" Marshall asked. "What has it done concerning individual players' relationships? . . . Wouldn't you say nothing? . . . Wouldn't you say under the reserve clause there was no room for bargaining?"

There was the rub. A clever former criminal defense attorney who had cross-examined many witnesses, Marshall fired off this series of questions, not allowing Hoynes time to answer, to make his point. The labor-exemption argument was predicated on the assumption that both sides had started at an equal place in the negotiations.

Hoynes tried to respond. He argued that Flood's lawsuit prevented negotiations over the reserve clause from taking place.

"How is this union protecting this individual, the named petitioner, Curtis C. Flood?" Marshall asked.

Hoynes said the union bargained for future benefits. He then explained how Flood had returned to baseball with the Washington Senators, but that his poor play on the field and financial and business problems off the field had forced him to leave the team and the United

States. He emphasized that baseball officials wished that Flood had kept playing.

"None of this is in the record?" Marshall asked. "His playing with Washington or any of this other business." Hoynes said it was not, even though both of Flood's briefs acknowledged that he had tried and failed to make a comeback with the Senators.

"That's what I thought," Marshall said. As soon as he said that, Marshall swiveled in his chair and turned his back on Hoynes. Thanks to the Court's new angled mahogany bench, all the justices saw Marshall's rude little display. At that moment, Hoynes knew that he had gained the sympathy of the other justices.

Marshall's antics gave Hoynes time to regroup. Hoynes kept the focus away from *Federal Baseball*, *Toolson*, or, God forbid, Flood's state antitrust claims. He stuck to his strategy of portraying this as a union-driven lawsuit, a glorified labor dispute in which Flood played only a nominal role. "[T]he players union is entirely in control of this litigation, and . . . it is concerned less with remedying any alleged wrong that may have been performed on Mr. Flood than it is trying to reorganize the employment relationships in professional baseball," Hoynes said. "In other words, the union is after larger game here." As proof, Hoynes explained that at trial Flood favored complete elimination of the reserve clause and all the union's other witnesses favored modification. "This testimony represented a repudiation, really, of Mr. Flood's position, and left him the forgotten man for the remainder of the case."

White, perhaps embarrassed by Marshall's behavior, threw what Hoynes described as "hanging curveballs" about the labor exemption. White asked why the union did not negotiate individual salaries (neither the players nor the owners wanted it that way because of the players' vastly different skill levels and salaries). He asked why the reserve clause couldn't apply to some players and not others (it would not be workable). He asked what if the owners suddenly decided to set a maximum salary of $100,000 (such a maximum would have to be negotiated with the union, and unilaterally instituting such a system would be "improper"). He asked if Hoynes opposed a remand to a lower court to consider the labor-exemption issue (Hoynes did not oppose it but thought the record was clear on the issue).

White's line of questioning allowed Hoynes to bring up Jacobs's and Winter's *Yale Law Journal* article. Hoynes's associate, Robert Kheel, held up a copy of it. Hoynes discussed Congress's failure to pass any legislation to take away the exemption. He ended with a nod to *stare decisis* and the Court's decisions in *Federal Baseball* and *Toolson*. With that, Hoynes finished his argument with a minute to spare. He never answered any questions about why the Court should continue to follow the logic of *Federal Baseball* or why Flood did not have valid claims under state antitrust law.

By all accounts, Hoynes had done a masterful job of putting baseball's best foot forward. He engaged the justices, answered their questions, and steered the discussion to the issue he wanted to discuss. "They got my best that day," Hoynes recalled recently. "Thirty years later, I could not have done a better job."

What Flood needed was a strong rebuttal. Goldberg, however, had exhausted all his rebuttal time. That did not stop him from trying.

As Hoynes finished his argument, Goldberg picked up his notes and made his way to the lectern. Solicitor General Erwin Griswold, the dean of Harvard Law School when Hoynes had been a student there, approached from the left to argue the next case. The justices' eyes widened in horror at the thought of Goldberg speaking again. Hoynes kept both hands on the lectern. He then turned around and stepped between the lectern and Goldberg, allowing Griswold to slide by. Griswold winked at Hoynes and grabbed the lectern. It was a perfect pick play. Hoynes's Indiana high school basketball coach would have been proud.

"Thank you, gentlemen," Burger intoned at 11:12 a.m. "The case is submitted."

With that, Griswold said, "May it please the Court," with Goldberg still standing behind him.

After Goldberg gathered his briefcase and made his way out of the courtroom, he told Levitt: "That was the worst argument I've ever made in my life."

Levitt later agreed: "It was one of the worst arguments I'd ever heard—by one of the smartest men I've ever known, in the setting where he should have been a super advocate. It was like he choked."

Goldberg walked through the double oak doors, across the Great

Hall, and down the Court's marble steps. He held an impromptu press conference for the waiting television cameras. After the glare of television lights was gone, an Associated Press photographer caught Goldberg on the Court's plaza near one of the fountains with a downcast look on his face.

If ever a case had been lost at oral argument, Flood's was it.

CHAPTER SIXTEEN

Nearly five hours after Goldberg's argument, the justices met in conference to discuss the four cases argued that day. The conference on the merits of argued cases is more like a straw poll than an extended dialogue. The justices do not usually engage in a back-and-forth discussion. They merely state their views on the case and reveal their tentative votes. This process is important for two reasons: First, it is the last face-to-face meeting of all the justices about the case; and second, it allows the chief justice (or the most senior justice in the majority) to assign a justice to write the majority opinion about the case. Once again, no law clerks, secretaries, or court personnel attend the conference. The justices meet and talk in private. The only record of what is said comes from the justices' handwritten notes.

As the first case argued that day, *Flood v. Kuhn* was the first to be discussed. It was Burger's job, as chief justice, to summarize the issues of the case. The other justices sometimes complained that Burger was ill-prepared for conference and relied too much on his law clerks' memos. They admired the way Burger's predecessor, Earl Warren, whom they referred to as the "Super Chief," had conducted conference. Warren, who would often meet with Brennan the day before conference, would boil a case down to its essence and explain in plain English the moral or practical issues at stake. In contrast, Burger's summaries tended to go off on tangents and often failed to capture the crux of the matter.

Burger's view on Flood's case was simple and straightforward: *Toolson* was wrong. President Nixon's supposedly conservative chief justice had just voted to reverse two Supreme Court precedents. The other justices once again spoke in order of seniority.

Douglas found himself agreeing with Burger. He believed that *Toolson* was out of step with the Court's other commercial decisions and that baseball's antitrust exemption "muddies the waters." Professional baseball, football, and basketball should be treated alike. He voted to reverse and send it back for a new trial.

Brennan explained that he had joined Harlan's dissent in *Radovich* precisely for the reasons articulated by Douglas—baseball, football, and basketball should be treated the same under the antitrust laws. He wanted to overrule *Toolson* and remand the case for a new trial about the labor exemption. Flood's state antitrust claims, Brennan argued, were preempted by federal law. He thought there might be certain advantages to the reserve clause, but the Court did not have to reach that issue. It only had to overrule *Toolson* and send the case back for trial.

Brennan's was the third vote to reverse. Flood 3, Baseball 0. Flood needed only two of the next six votes to win. But, again, these votes were tentative and designed to allow the assignment of the majority opinion. Once the justices read the majority and dissenting opinions, they could switch sides, turning the majority opinion into a dissent and vice versa.

Stewart voted to affirm. He argued that the Court had invited Congress to eliminate baseball's exemption, and Congress, by doing nothing, had implicitly approved the exemption. The exemption, Stewart believed, affected the actual operation of baseball and was best left up to Congress to change. The state antitrust claims were preempted, he said, based on the Milwaukee case.

White voted to affirm. He agreed with Stewart.

Marshall also voted to affirm. This seems shocking in light of Marshall's questions (and behavior) at oral argument. It reflects the adage that it is often a mistake to read too much into a justice's questions and reactions at oral argument. Marshall, straying from fellow liberals Brennan and Douglas, believed that Stewart had made a more compelling argument.

Flood 3, Baseball 3.

Blackmun said that *Federal Baseball* had decided that baseball was a sport, not a business. He had misread *Federal Baseball*, which said baseball was a business but in 1922 was not interstate commerce. Blackmun also said it was "untenable" to apply the state antitrust laws. He viewed this more as a labor dispute than an antitrust problem. He voted to "tentatively affirm."

Powell, who later emerged as one of the Court's moderates, agreed with Burger, Douglas, and Brennan to reverse. It made no sense to have an exemption for baseball but not for football. Congress's failure to act was not equivalent to action. If the Court reversed *Toolson*, then Congress could act.

Before Powell spoke, however, he issued an important disclaimer. He owned stock in Anheuser-Busch and was not sure whether it owned the St. Louis Cardinals, one of the named defendants. If Anheuser-Busch owned the Cardinals, he promised, he would disqualify himself from the case. His views, therefore, were even more tentative than the other justices'.

Flood 4*, Baseball 4.

Rehnquist, the Court's other conservative besides Burger, voted to affirm the exemption—with another important caveat. He agreed with Stewart that the Court had missed its chance to overrule *Federal Baseball* in *Toolson* and that Congress had failed to act. Rehnquist, however, disagreed with the lower courts about the state antitrust claims. He believed that even if Congress had exempted baseball by not acting, the state antitrust laws still applied. He wanted to send the case back for trial on that ground. During his ensuing 33 years on the Court, Rehnquist made it his mission to resurrect the power of the states. The federal courts, he believed, had trampled on state sovereignty. In 1972, however, Rehnquist was in the minority on states' rights issues.

Flood 4*, Baseball 5.

The tentative votes were as follows:

Burger, Douglas, Brennan, and Powell for Flood.

Stewart, White, Marshall, Blackmun, and Rehnquist for Baseball.

Burger reiterated his decision to reverse. That placed him in the minority. The chief justice assigns the majority opinion only when he is in the majority. When he is in the minority, the most senior justice in the majority assigns the opinion. Burger restated his vote to reverse because earlier that term, such as in the abortion cases, he had been accused of assigning opinions when he had voted with the minority.

For the first time in his career, Stewart controlled the assignment of a majority opinion. Even as of the last term, Black, Douglas, Brennan, and Harlan had had more seniority. With Black and Harlan gone and Burger, Douglas, and Brennan in the minority, the opinion assignment in Flood's case fell to Stewart.

Potter Stewart was one of the youngest justices ever named to the Court. Four years after naming him to the Sixth Circuit Court of Appeals, President Eisenhower nominated the 43-year-old Stewart to the Supreme Court in October 1958. A member of a prominent Cincinnati family, Stewart had attended Hotchkiss, Yale, and Yale Law School. He was regarded as one of the most handsome justices and also one of the most open with the press. Richard Nixon believed that Washington's "social and intellectual climate" influenced Stewart; the president told Burger later that term that Stewart attended too many Georgetown dinner parties. At one of those parties in the spring of 1977, Stewart met journalist Bob Woodward and became the impetus and an anonymous source for Woodward's and Scott Armstrong's 1979 Supreme Court exposé, *The Brethren*.

Stewart did not announce his assignment of Flood's case for a few weeks. The assigning justice generally waits a week or two before revealing his opinion assignments. After conference, the justices usually do not discuss cases in face-to-face meetings. They communicate through interoffice memos. During this phase of a Supreme Court case, they really do act like nine separate law offices.

On March 21, the day after conference, Powell circulated a two-paragraph note to his fellow justices:

> I have now verified the fact that the St. Louis Cardinals are owned by a subsidiary of Anheuser Busch.
>
> Accordingly, and regretfully, I am out of the case. Fortunately, this will not affect the result.
>
> L.F.P., Jr.

Powell was out. The press and public would not learn of his decision until after the case had been decided. And even then, they would not know why Powell withdrew. Powell's decision to disqualify himself was the subject of much speculation. Why would a justice withdraw from a case just because he owned stock in a company whose subsidiary owned one of the defendants—particularly if he had decided to vote against that defendant?

The decision to withdraw from a case is entirely up to the individual justice. The justice does not usually disclose why he or she chooses to withdraw, but there are exceptions. For example, Rehnquist participated in a 1972 case about an army surveillance program of suspected radicals despite having testified before the Senate on the issue while working for the Justice Department. He released a memo denying that his past involvement had amounted to a conflict of interest. More than 30 years later, Justice Antonin Scalia refused to withdraw from a case involving the Energy Task Force run by Vice President Dick Cheney even though Scalia had recently flown with the vice president on Air Force Two for a private duck-hunting trip. Scalia released an exhaustive memo explaining his decision not to withdraw.

Powell's decision to withdraw over stock ownership was not surprising in light of his Supreme Court nomination hearings. The biggest issue at Powell's hearings was race. The second biggest issue was his stock ownership. Stock ownership had torpedoed one of Nixon's prior southern Supreme Court nominees, Fourth Circuit judge Clement F. Haynsworth Jr. A well-respected jurist despite his conservative racial views, Haynsworth had voted on several cases involving companies in which he either owned or would later own stock. Haynsworth had been nominated to replace Abe Fortas, whose resignation, triggered by a financial scandal, had made the justices' finances a point of emphasis. The Senate rejected Haynsworth's nomination, 55–45.

Before his own hearings, Powell disclosed that he and his wife owned nearly $1.5 million in stocks, bonds, and other publicly traded securities. That included 880 shares of Anheuser-Busch stock, then worth $44,110. Powell planned to put all the stocks into a blind trust. The ABA, however, issued new ethical guidelines requiring judges to have knowledge of their financial holdings to allow them to avoid conflicts of interest. Powell testified before the Senate Judiciary Committee that he planned to sell most of his stock holdings except those that had increased enormously in valuc. He apparently held on to his Anheuser-Busch stock. Of his remaining stock holdings and former clients, Powell promised the Senate: "If they should be involved in litigation in court—certainly for the foreseeable future—I would not take part in it."

Even with Powell out, Stewart still had to assign the opinion to someone who could maintain a bare five-vote majority. The eight remaining justices had not yet cast their official votes. Powell's withdrawal gave baseball slightly more breathing room, but the tentative 5–3 majority could easily turn into a 4–4 tie if one justice switched his vote.

Stewart could have assigned the opinion to himself. He was a big Cincinnati Reds fan. During oral argument on October 10, 1973, Stewart received inning-by-inning updates of the fifth and deciding game of the National League Championship Series between the Mets and the Reds. One of Stewart's law clerks passed him updates on small Supreme Court note slips. He learned that the Reds had stranded the bases loaded in the first. Then came another update: "Mets 2, Reds 0. V.P. Agnew Just Resigned!!" Two years later, Stewart won $4 in a pool among the justices about the 1975 Reds–Red Sox World Series. He also exchanged notes on the bench with Blackmun about the Reds' fast start during the 1980 season.

Stewart did not take Flood's opinion for himself because he knew the best way to preserve a bare five-vote majority—assign the opinion to a justice on the fence. White and Marshall seemed to be in total agreement with him. Rehnquist also firmly agreed to uphold baseball's exemption, but his views on the state antitrust claims were out of step with those of the rest of the Court and might jeopardize the majority. That left the one justice who had voted to "tentatively affirm"—Harry Blackmun.

Harry A. Blackmun's best childhood friend was Warren Burger. They had grown up together in the same St. Paul neighborhood. Blackmun was the best man at Burger's wedding. They maintained a long-distance friendship for 20 years as lawyers and appeals court judges through extensive correspondence. Upon being confirmed as chief justice, Burger asked Blackmun for suggestions about how to run the Court. The media tagged them with the nickname of Blackmun's favorite baseball team, "the Minnesota Twins."

Blackmun was one of the Court's biggest baseball fans. Growing up in St. Paul, he rooted for the minor league St. Paul Saints and the Chicago Cubs. At a Washington luncheon in August 1970, a Minnesota company presented him with a Senators cap and autographed team baseball. The Twins, however, had become Blackmun's team. The *Sport-*

ing News revealed in May 1970 that Blackmun possessed "'a vast mental storehouse' of baseball records and lore." The publication predicted during Flood's trial that "[t]he presence of Justice Blackmun in Washington should be of significance when Curt Flood's suit against the reserve clause reaches the Supreme Court."

Blackmun needed the *Flood* opinion to boost his confidence. He had only one full Supreme Court term under his belt and was still feeling his way. On paper, he possessed all the right credentials: summa cum laude as a Harvard math major, Harvard Law School, partner at a Minneapolis law firm, counsel to the Mayo Clinic, and 10 years as an Eisenhower-nominated Eighth Circuit judge. Yet he frequently referred to himself as "old number three," Nixon's third choice to replace Fortas after Haynsworth and G. Harrold Carswell. Maybe the Court's cloistered, scholarly environment reminded Blackmun of the academic pressure of Harvard Law School, where he had finished 120th out of 451 students in his class.

Blackmun struggled with an essential part of a Supreme Court justice's job—deciding cases. The stress of decision making had driven Justice Charles Whittaker to physical exhaustion and had forced his retirement from the Court in 1962 after just five years. As an Eighth Circuit judge, Blackmun had felt that the Supreme Court could correct any of his erroneous appeals court opinions. Now he was working without a safety net. Blackmun's problem was that he sought a clear answer to each case as if he were figuring out an algorithm. He wrote opinions that seemed to balance the equities on each side and then announced his decision at the end. A more experienced justice would advocate his position and try to persuade the rest of the Court (and the public) that he was right.

Blackmun's preargument notes on *Flood v. Kuhn* reveal how much he agonized over the case's outcome. On February 28, he received a bench memo from one of his law clerks, John Rich. Blackmun then outlined his thoughts about the case in his distinctive shorthand on blue-lined notebook paper. His notes indicate that he agreed with Flood's position. He was "willing to overrule *Federal Baseball* and *Toolson*" because baseball "cannot escape the interstate commerce aspect today." He described the application of state antitrust laws as a "horror" that should warrant preemption. He wanted to "bring all professional sports into a consistent pattern." As for baseball's arguments, he found its reliance interests "unpersuasive," while the "collective bargaining approach does not appeal to me." He concluded that the reserve clause was a "per se violation of the federal antitrust laws."

The Harvard math major then mapped out the decision's different permutations:

1) Affirm *Federal Baseball* and *Toolson*, refuse to declare baseball interstate commerce or a business, and leave it up to Congress and collective bargaining; or
2) Overrule *Federal Baseball* and *Toolson*, recognize baseball as a business, Congress is never going to fix problem, apply federal antitrust law, and pre-empt state antitrust laws as "insufferable," and avoid collective bargaining.

Blackmun chose option two and reached the following tentative conclusions:

1. Overrule *Federal Baseball* and *Toolson*—"this is desirable."
2. Apply federal antitrust laws per *Radovich*.
3. No labor exemption.

On March 15, five days before oral argument, Blackmun scribbled out two more pages of thoughts about Flood's case. He asked himself what would be the result of overruling *Federal Baseball* and *Toolson*. He believed the rich teams would not acquire all the best players because that did not happen in football. But, he added, "I suspect it would be a disaster and that baseball would protect itself." He described the application of antitrust laws of different states as "intolerable" and an "abomination." He agreed with his law clerk's memo that this was really a labor dispute because the monopoly affected only the players, not consumers. "Cert," Blackmun wrote, "therefore should have been denied. But it was granted."

Blackmun concluded five things about the case:

1. Abandon *Federal Baseball* and *Toolson* in any event.
2. Place it on a labor basis . . .

3. If not, follow *Radovich.*
4. State antitrust law is pre-empted.
5. Hope for the best.

He then wrote down a few possible questions for oral argument. He asked about the institution of baseball's free-agent draft in 1965, which essentially prevented players from ever choosing which team they played for—a fact that Blackmun believed made the reserve clause even more troubling. His switch to "tentatively affirm" at the March 20 conference could be attributed to Hoynes's persuasiveness (or Goldberg's lack of persuasiveness) at oral argument, the comments of more senior justices Stewart, White, and Marshall at conference before Blackmun announced his vote, or Blackmun's chronic indecisiveness.

Stewart thought *Flood v. Kuhn* was an easy case. He described it to Woodward and Armstrong as "a case of *stare decisis* double dipped." He figured that he could assign the *Flood* opinion to Blackmun to build up his confidence. Blackmun, the Court's resident medical expert as the former counsel to the Mayo Clinic, had already been saddled with writing the Court's abortion decisions that term. *Flood v. Kuhn* would be a quick and painless diversion.

On the day of the conference, Stewart asked Blackmun to write the majority opinion in *Flood v. Kuhn* as a one-paragraph unsigned opinion, known as a *per curiam*, along the lines of the Court's opinion in *Toolson*.

"Harry, do it very briefly," Stewart told Blackmun. "Write a *per curiam* and we'll get rid of it."

On April 3, Stewart informed the other justices of his assignment of the *Flood* case to Blackmun.

The press and legal community waited and weighed in with predictions. Before oral argument, Las Vegas prognosticator Jimmy "the Greek" Snyder placed three-to-one odds that the Court would rule against Flood. After the argument, a Flood sympathizer agreed—and not because of Goldberg's performance that day. David Feller, Goldberg's former law partner who had helped craft a response to the labor-exemption argument, told the *Washington Evening Star* that the baseball strike in early April made it less likely that Flood would prevail. The strike cast Flood's lawsuit more as part of an ongoing labor dispute. The reserve clause, Feller said, would be resolved either at the bargaining table or through another strike. Goldberg jokingly chided Feller that his remarks failed to show the proper deference to his former "senior partner." Feller replied in good humor: "I didn't say that Flood would lose in the Supreme Court. What I did say was that I thought the strike had increased the odds in favor of a loss because it made the labor exemption issue much more credible." Feller also believed the strike had made Miller and his union more powerful—powerful enough not to need the Court's help in toppling the reserve clause. Feller confessed to harboring "a somewhat cynical view of the Court's processes and a suggestion that the Court looks at the realities of the power situation in making its decisions rather than the questions of law which in theory govern it."

One of Kuhn's lawyers, Victor Kramer, offered an implausible theory about why the owners would win. "It's in the bag," Kramer told Dan Levitt, one of Flood's lawyers. "Baseball has arranged to let the justices know on the social circuit in Washington that if they come out the right way on this, Washington will get its baseball team back." The Senators had left Washington after the 1971 season to become the Texas Rangers. And even though Kuhn was desperately trying to lure another major league team to his old hometown, there was no evidence to support Kramer's claim. President Nixon had warned his Supreme Court nominees to stay away from the Washington cocktail party circuit. Stewart was a fixture at such parties, but nothing suggests that he or any other justice had spoken with baseball officials. The only justice with the nerve to discuss pending cases with Nixon was Burger. Burger told Nixon on June 14, 1972, about a "capital punishment case coming down in two weeks" and "busing cases next term," but *Flood v. Kuhn* never came up. Burger, moreover, had cast his initial vote in Flood's favor. Kramer's information seemed to be fueled more by bluster, bitterness over not having argued the *Flood* case before the Supreme Court, and Georgetown party gossip than by fact.

Blackmun read some predictions about the case. He clipped an article from the *Washington Evening Star* published the day after the oral argument under the headline: "Remand Likely in Flood Case." That prediction seemed to read too much into some of the justices' questions. He also saved a short item from the April issue of *Sports Illustrated* about Michigan State political scientist Harold J. Spaeth using a computer to predict Flood's victory. Spaeth tallied how the justices had voted in prior antitrust cases. He forecast that baseball's antitrust exemption would be overruled and that the legality of the reserve clause would be decided by a lower court. He predicted that "[t]he vote should be unanimous, with a possible Rehnquist dissent." Spaeth, however, failed to account for the difference between antitrust cases and baseball cases. The justices were not machines; they were men. And baseball turns men—even ones with life tenure—into boys.

An opinion that, in Stewart's view, should have taken Blackmun hours ended up taking him days and weeks. The Court used to be the only branch of government in Washington that did its own work. Many of the justices, however, increasingly turned to their law clerks to write first drafts of their opinions. To his credit, Blackmun tackled his *Flood v. Kuhn* opinion on his own. He holed up in the justices' private library on the second floor of the Supreme Court building and wrote the opinion in longhand on an antique wooden desk. He worked on the opinion from April 14 to early May. No one knew what was taking him so long. The books Blackmun took with him to the library might have provided clues: *The Baseball Encyclopedia*, Lawrence S. Ritter's *The Glory of Their Times*, and Harold Seymour's and David Quentin Voigt's histories of baseball.

On May 4, Blackmun sent Stewart a two-paragraph note:

> Dear Potter:
>
> I have a proposed Per Curiam for this case at the Printer. I must confess to you that I have done more than merely follow *Toolson* with a bare peremptory paragraph. That case, for me, proved to be an interesting one, and I have indulged myself by outlining the background somewhat extensively. As a matter of fact, this has prompted me to conclude that *Federal Baseball* and *Toolson* have a lot to be said for them. When I finally get to the heart of the matter, however, I give it rather summary treatment. The briefs on both sides are good and I rationalize by saying that they deserve at least this much.
>
> Please give the opinion a reading and let me have your general reactions. The case, supposedly, is critical for the baseball world. I am not so sure about that, for I think that however it is decided, the sport will adjust and continue.

The next day, Blackmun circulated the first printed draft of his entire opinion to the rest of Stewart's colleagues.

Part I of Blackmun's opinion, titled "The Game," expounded on baseball's history in three extended paragraphs, mentioning the first recognized official game in 1846 at Hoboken's Elysian Fields, the founding of the Cincinnati Red Stockings in 1869, the creation of the National League, the rise and fall of various rival leagues, the 1919 World Series fix, the shifting and expansion of franchises, the institution of the new player draft in 1965, and the formation of the Major League Baseball Players Association in 1966 (Miller became its first full-time executive director that year, but it had been in nominal existence since 1954).

Blackmun's next paragraph created the most controversy and subjected him to the most ridicule. "Then there are the many names," it began, "celebrated for one reason or another, that have sparked the diamond and its environs and that have provided tinder for recaptured thrills, for reminiscence and comparisons, and for conversation and anticipation in-season and off-season." He then proceeded to list 79 players in baseball history, beginning with Ty Cobb, Babe Ruth, Tris Speaker, and Walter Johnson and ending his original list with Bill Dickey, Zack Wheat, George Sisler, and Charlie Gehringer. "The list seems endless," Blackmun wrote.

Blackmun's list did not consist only of Hall of Famers or players strictly of a certain skill level. It was more eclectic than that. It included all 26 players interviewed by Lawrence S. Ritter for his classic oral history, *The Glory of Their Times: The Story of the Early Days of Baseball Told by the Men Who Played It.* Those players, scattered throughout Blackmun's list, included Hall of Famers Rube Marquard, Wahoo Sam Crawford, Edd Roush (who sat out the entire 1930 season because of a contract dispute), Goose Goslin, and Paul Waner, but also obscure players including Fred Snodgrass (best known for a dropped fly ball in the 1912 World Series) and Bill Wambsganss (who once turned an unassisted triple play). Blackmun's list even included some of the game's great characters merely mentioned in Ritter's book, such as Germany Schaefer. "These are names only from earlier years," Blackmun explained in a footnote. "By mentioning some, one risks unintended omission of others equally celebrated." His criteria for inclusion on the list seemed as idiosyncratic as his vote on Flood's case.

Blackmun followed up his list of players with more useless baseball arcana. He referred to Ring Lardner and the "World Serious," Ernest Lawrence Thayer's poem "Casey at the Bat," and "the ring of 'Tinker to Evers to Chance.'" He included the entire poem about the Chicago Cubs' aforementioned double-play combination—"Baseball's Sad Lexicon" by Franklin Pierce Adams—in a footnote. He also quoted George Bernard Shaw describing baseball as "the great American tragedy." The list of retired baseball greats, however, became Blackmun's obsession and the defining aspect of his opinion.

The rest of Blackmun's opinion was fairly straightforward. Part II discussed the facts of Flood's career and listed his annual salary figures. Flood received less than three printed pages. Part III quoted extensively from the lower court opinions of Judge Cooper and the Second Circuit. Part IV reviewed in detail all the Court's opinions touching on baseball's antitrust exemption, including *Federal Baseball* and its interstate commerce underpinnings; *Toolson* and the cases that followed about theatrical performances, boxing, football, and basketball; and the proposed congressional legislation over the years. Finally, Part V—only 4 of the opinion's 27 pages—provided the reasoning behind his decision.

After conceding that baseball was a "business and it is engaged in interstate commerce," Blackmun characterized baseball's antitrust exemption as an "exception," "anomaly," and "aberration." "Even though others might regard this as 'unrealistic, inconsistent or illogical,' the aberration is an established one. . . . It is an aberration that has been with us now for half a century, one heretofore deemed fully entitled to the benefit of *stare decisis*, and one that has survived the Court's expanding concept of interstate commerce. It rests on a recognition and an acceptance of baseball's unique characteristics and needs."

Recognizing that the Court had refused to grant other professional sports similar immunity, Blackmun placed blame for baseball's exemption on Congress: "We continue to be loath, 50 years after *Federal Baseball* and almost two decades after *Toolson*, to overturn those cases judicially when Congress, by its positive inaction, has allowed those decisions to stand for so long." Never has a Supreme Court opinion turned on a more oxymoronic phrase than "positive inaction." Blackmun passed the buck to a political body that he knew would not remove baseball's exempt status: "If there is any inconsistency or illogic in all this, it is an inconsistency and illogic of long standing that is to be remedied by the Congress and not by this Court." After upholding *Federal Baseball* and *Toolson* on *stare decisis* grounds, Blackmun ruled that Flood's state antitrust claims were preempted by federal law. He found no reason to address baseball's labor-exemption argument.

Blackmun still needed four additional votes for a majority opinion. Stewart read Blackmun's first draft with chagrin. He had instructed Blackmun to write a one-paragraph *per curiam*, and Blackmun had come back with a 27-page ode to baseball. Blackmun's paean to the national pastime was not even original—Judge Moore had already written an even more fawning concurring opinion in the Second Circuit. Instead of addressing Flood's claims in a legally rigorous way, Blackmun's opinion called attention to the Court's past blunders and portrayed the justices as a bunch of sycophantic baseball fans.

Stewart, however, did not want to jeopardize Blackmun's already fragile psyche. He instead called Blackmun and asked him about his list of famous ballplayers.

"I like that history of baseball," Stewart said, "but why didn't you name Eppa Rixey?"

"Didn't I name Eppa Rixey?" Blackmun asked.

"No," Stewart replied. "And you know what a famous player he was for the Cincinnati Reds. If you will add him, I'll join your opinion."

Blackmun agreed to add Eppa Rixey, a big left-handed pitcher who had somehow managed to get into the Baseball Hall of Fame despite marginal credentials (266–251 career record in 21 seasons).

On May 9, Stewart circulated a typewritten letter to his colleagues:

Dear Harry:

I agree with your memorandum in this case and hope it will become a signed opinion for the Court.

Sincerely Yours,
P.S.

The story of how and why Stewart signed on to Blackmun's opinion soon made its way through the law clerk grapevine. The name games—and the battle for the majority opinion in *Flood v. Kuhn*—had only just begun.

Blackmun also received encouragement from an unexpected source: Powell. On May 8, Powell wrote Blackmun:

> Dear Harry:
>
> Although I am "out" of the case, I have read with fascinated interest your splendid opinion.
>
> It is a classic summary of the history of organized baseball which will delight all old fans—as it did me. I had no idea you were such an expert on the game.
>
> If I had participated, I was inclined to overrule *Federal Baseball Club* as an anachronism of antitrust law. Your persuasive opinion might have won me over.
>
> Sincerely,
> Lewis

There was nothing persuasive about Blackmun's baseball blather. Powell may just have been patting Blackmun on the back. But if Blackmun was having any second thoughts about Part I of his opinion, Powell's kind words ended them.

The opposition came soon enough. On May 11, Douglas circulated his draft dissent. He had been working on it ever since he received Blackmun's draft. Douglas, like Blackmun, did his own work. He wrote out the dissent in longhand on a yellow legal pad. His secretary typed it and immediately sent it to the printer, though it went through several drafts before Douglas circulated it among his colleagues. Although he borrowed a few bits and pieces from the dissent from the denial of cert he and his law clerk, Kenneth Reed, had drafted in October, the language was fresh and new and unmistakably Douglas's.

Federal Baseball, Douglas began, "is a derelict in the stream of the law that we, its creator, should remove. Only a romantic view of a rather dismal business account over the last 50 years would keep that derelict in midstream." Douglas's first footnote acknowledged that he had voted to affirm in *Toolson* but had "lived to regret it." He described baseball as "big business" guilty of "predatory practices." "The beneficiaries of the *Federal Baseball Club* decision," he wrote in a snide comment about Blackmun's list of ballplayers, "are not the Babe Ruths, Ty Cobbs, and

Lou Gehrigs." He portrayed these players as the "victims of the reserve clause."

Douglas destroyed the linchpin of Blackmun's argument. "If congressional inaction is our guide," he wrote, "we should rely upon the fact that Congress has refused to enact bills broadly exempting professional sports from antitrust regulation." Douglas appealed to the Court to act: "The unbroken silence of Congress should not prevent us from correcting our own mistakes." Douglas's dissent was six paragraphs of poetry and persuasion. It was everything that Blackmun's opinion was not—straightforward and well reasoned. It reflected the difference between 33 years and 2 years of experience on the Court.

The day Douglas circulated his dissent, Marshall phoned his law clerk to say he was not joining Blackmun's opinion. Marshall's law clerk prepared a dissent overruling *Federal Baseball* and *Toolson* and remanding the case to the trial court to decide the labor-exemption issue. Multiple dissents often arise out of a closely divided case, such as Flood's, in which the justices express different concerns with the majority opinion. Marshall's primary concern, judging from his questions at oral argument, was about the labor exemption. On May 11, he circulated his dissent to the other justices' chambers.

Marshall's dissent was not as well written as Douglas's. Unlike the other opinions, however, it began with Curt Flood's story. "To non-athletes, it might appear that petitioner was virtually enslaved by the owners of major league baseball clubs who bartered among themselves for his services," Marshall's dissent said. "But, athletes know that it was not servitude that bound the petitioner to the club owners; it was the reserve system."

Marshall's dissent characterized the Court as "torn between the principle of *stare decisis* and the knowledge that" *Federal Baseball* and *Toolson* "are totally at odds with more recent and better reasoned cases." It rejected the idea that Congress had endorsed the exemption by failing to act. "The importance of the antitrust laws to every citizen must not be minimized," the dissent said. "They are as important to baseball players as they are to football players, lawyers, doctors, or members of any other class of workers."

Marshall's dissent asserted that overruling *Federal Baseball* and *Toolson* "does not mean that petitioner would necessarily prevail." With a nod to Jacobs's and Winter's *Yale Law Journal* article (cited in a footnote), the dissent launched into a four-page discussion of the labor exemption. Marshall concluded that "none of the prior cases is precisely in point" and "the issue was not squarely faced" at Flood's trial or before the Second Circuit. Marshall, therefore, sought to send Flood's case back for a trial on the labor-exemption issue—just the sort of compromise position that might win over a majority of the justices. Marshall wanted his dissent to become the opinion of the Court.

It was unclear why Marshall switched his vote. Maybe he saw the slavery aspect of Flood's fight for economic freedom in professional baseball. Maybe his liberal law clerk showed him a draft dissent and encouraged him to adopt it. Maybe it was the result of a conversation with his close friend and liberal ally, Justice Brennan. Marshall often voted the way Brennan did.

A small, impish-looking man, William J. Brennan Jr. was one of the Court's judicial giants. The second of eight children born to Irish-Catholic immigrants, he grew up in Newark, New Jersey. His father shoveled coal at a brewery and emerged as a local labor leader. After attending the University of Pennsylvania and Harvard Law School on scholarships, Brennan returned to New Jersey to practice law. From 1949 to 1952, he rose through the state court system as a trial judge, appeals court judge, and state supreme court justice. In 1956, President Eisenhower nominated Brennan, a Democrat, to the Supreme Court of the United States. Eisenhower needed the support of Catholic Democrats during his 1956 reelection campaign, just as he had needed Earl Warren to deliver California in 1952. Much to Eisenhower's dismay, Brennan and Warren ignited an individual-rights revolution.

If anyone could turn a dissent into a majority opinion, it was Brennan. Brennan was the Warren Court's architect and field general. He was not a politician who traded votes like some legislator. He understood the persuasiveness of the written word and the power of different legal arguments to win over colleagues to his point of view. He explained to his law clerks the most important rule of law. He held up his hand and wiggled his fingers. "Five votes," Brennan said. "Five votes can do anything around here."

Brennan's position on Flood's case was clear. He had voted to grant cert in both *Salerno* and *Flood v. Kuhn*, and he had voted for Flood at conference. His voice, however, had not yet been heard. Brennan was focusing his efforts elsewhere. The Court was wrestling with huge issues that term, including the constitutionality of abortion and the death penalty.

On May 12, Brennan circulated a one-sentence letter agreeing to join Douglas's dissent in Flood's case. Joining a dissent was a common practice and clearly showed where Brennan stood. But Flood was going to need more help from Brennan than that. Neither Douglas nor Marshall could muster a five-justice majority in Flood's case on his own. Douglas was not a consensus builder, and his dissent was too short to serve as a majority opinion. Marshall's dissent floated a possible compromise on the labor-exemption issue, but it lacked the power or persuasiveness of a majority opinion. They needed Brennan to rework their dissents and to rally another justice to Flood's side. At the end of the term, however, Brennan was trying to persuade Blackmun to issue two opinions striking down restrictive state abortion laws and to cobble together a majority to strike down state death penalty laws.

With Powell out and Marshall's defection in *Flood v. Kuhn*, the eight justices were locked in a 4–4 tie. In a tie, the Court issues an unsigned *per curiam* opinion upholding the lower court's decision. A 4–4 tie would have been a tough way for Flood to lose, but three justices had not yet cast their official votes: Rehnquist, White, and Burger.

Three days after Brennan had joined Douglas's dissent, Rehnquist announced his decision. Douglas learned from his law clerk that Rehnquist planned to vote to affirm the exemption but not to join Blackmun's opinion. On May 15, however, Rehnquist cast aside any problems with Flood's state antitrust claims or Blackmun's opinion. Rehnquist circulated a one-sentence letter joining Blackmun. Around the same time, Douglas and Marshall circulated revised drafts of their dissents to prepare them for final publication and to fish for additional votes.

Instead of shoring up the reasoning in his opinion, Blackmun spent his time tinkering with his list of famous former ballplayers. Law clerks delighted in calling Blackmun's chambers and proposing additional names. A Rehnquist clerk jokingly suggested former Washington Senators pitcher Camilo Pascual. Blackmun's law clerk took the suggestion seriously. A few minutes later, the Rehnquist clerk received a return phone call from Blackmun's chambers: The justice had looked up Pascual in *The Baseball Encyclopedia*; despite the pitcher's great curveball, his 174 career wins did not meet Blackmun's ambiguous criteria.

Some of the name games may have been overblown. Woodward and Armstrong claimed that Blackmun had added three black players—Satchel Paige, Jackie Robinson, and Roy Campanella—at the behest of Justice Marshall. This story makes no sense for several reasons. Blackmun recalled watching Campanella, who had played for the St. Paul Saints in 1948, "knocking fungoes on the roof of the Coliseum in left field. He had to be on my original list." Indeed he was, as were Robinson and Paige. Marshall circulated his dissenting opinion on May 11 and therefore would have been in no position to make such a trivial request. Over the years, Blackmun often refused to answer letters from reporters about *Flood v. Kuhn* except to deny the Marshall story. Blackmun recalled only one justice's request about baseball names—Stewart's about Eppa Rixey.

That did not stop Blackmun from adding more names to his list. On May 25, he circulated a revised draft of his opinion. He made no improvements or changes to his reasoning in Part V for upholding *Federal Baseball* and *Toolson*. Yet he added an extended footnote in Part I reciting a 1926 poem, "He Never Heard of Casey," by legendary sportswriter Grantland Rice. He also added 12 more players to the list: "Eppa Rixey, Harry Heilmann, Fred Clarke, Dizzy Dean, Hank Greenberg, Pie Traynor, Rube Waddell, Bill Terry, Carl Hubbell, Old Hoss Radbourne [*sic*], Rabbit Maranville, Lefty Grove." He was not done. The name games distracted Blackmun from his primary objective—persuading the last two justices to sign on to his opinion.

The justice most likely to switch sides was Byron White. Douglas's law clerk, Kenneth Reed, believed that the former college and professional football star might change his mind. On March 11, Reed wrote Douglas that "Justice White's clerks indicate that he may be inclined to overrule *National* [*sic*] *Baseball* and *Toolson* and thus reverse the case. Apparently, however, he is in no hurry to vote." Ten days later, Reed wrote Douglas:

> According to rumor, Justice White continues to be the most likely source of a fifth vote to overrule *National Baseball Club* [*sic*] and *Toolson*. According to his clerks, however, he is still in not much of

> a hurry to cast his vote. Justice Powell's clerks apparently sought to get him back into the case since he is opposed to *Toolson*, but they were unsuccessful because of his stock ownership in Anheuser Busch.

With Powell definitely out (and encouraging Blackmun), it was up to White. As a professional football player, he had been sold by Pittsburgh to Detroit for $5,000 and taken a more than 50 percent salary cut to $7,500, so he knew how it felt to be treated like a piece of property. On the other hand, he may not have understood why a ballplayer making $90,000 had quit over a trade.

There was a flicker of hope. One of Marshall's law clerks, according to Woodward and Armstrong, approached Marshall about making a few minor changes suggested by one of White's law clerks. White apparently believed that Flood might have viable state antitrust claims. Marshall refused to make the changes. Informed that the White clerk believed the changes might be necessary to get White's vote, Marshall replied: "He'll never join."

This was where Marshall needed Brennan's help. Brennan had joined Marshall's second draft dissent on May 15, but he never intervened with White. Marshall's prophecy about White turned out to be self-fulfilling—with a catch.

On March 26, the day after Blackmun had circulated his revised draft, White sent him the following note:

> Dear Harry:
>
> Agreeing with the result you reach and preferring the long form to a short *per curiam*, I join your memorandum in this case but with the gentle suggestion that you omit Part I.
>
> Sincerely,
> Byron

With White's vote, there was no way Flood could win. The best he could do was a 4–4 tie, which was a legal defeat for Flood but not a meaningful victory for Major League Baseball. The owners would not have been content with a tie because it has no precedential value. They needed a majority opinion to support their antitrust exemption and maintain their reserve system. Their only hope was that another justice would join Blackmun's opinion.

The 12 players Blackmun had added to the list obviously did not persuade White. His "gentle suggestion" about deleting Part I was more than a gentle suggestion. White, according to one of his law clerks, liked to "cut the corners square." He was a no-nonsense guy who refused to demean an opinion about professional athletes with sports trivia. Blackmun refused to remove Part I. White responded by joining all of Blackmun's opinion except Part I—a fact noted in the final decision.

The fate of Blackmun's opinion came down to Burger. If he voted the way he had at conference, the case would end in a 4–4 tie. Blackmun's opinion would never see the light of day. Instead, baseball would receive a one-paragraph unsigned opinion, an exemption upheld by default, and a hollow victory over Flood.

Burger's views of the *Flood* case can be gleaned only from his lone comment at conference: *Toolson* should be overruled. There had been no noise out of the Burger chambers since the circulation of the Blackmun, Douglas, and Marshall opinions. Burger forbade his law clerks from talking to the other justices' clerks about pending cases. The main source of Court gossip was cut off.

It has often been said that Warren E. Burger, with his white hair and classic good looks, looked like the perfect chief justice but rarely acted like one. To the other justices, particularly those fond of Earl Warren, Burger lacked both the intellectual curiosity and the common touch to lead the Court. Burger reveled in the Court's rituals and traditions rather than its substantive work. He made his biggest impact in his administration of the federal courts and the Supreme Court building rather than with his written opinions.

Burger's path to power was not as smooth as Blackmun's. Burger sold insurance by day and attended the University of Minnesota for two years and St. Paul College of Law for four years at night. He worked for a St. Paul law firm while Blackmun, after seven years at Harvard, joined a more prestigious Minneapolis firm.

Burger's big breaks came through politics. In 1948 and 1952, he served as Minnesota governor Harold Stassen's floor manager at the

Republican National Convention. In 1952, he helped deliver Minnesota's delegates to Dwight Eisenhower, who made Burger the assistant attorney general in charge of the Justice Department's Claims (Civil) Division. Burger earned his stripes by arguing a loyalty case before the Supreme Court (accusing a Yale professor–government consultant of disloyalty to the United States government), a case the solicitor general had refused to argue. Burger lost, but in 1956 Eisenhower nominated him as a federal appellate judge on the D.C. Circuit. Burger caught Nixon's eye with a 1967 speech about criminal law and as a frequent Warren Court critic. Two years later, Nixon nominated him as chief justice. The president consulted with his chief justice about subsequent Supreme Court vacancies and other judicial nominations, allowing Burger to lobby for a place on the Court for his former best man, Harry Blackmun.

Burger had been trying to cultivate Blackmun for months. He had assigned Blackmun the abortion cases and was spending an unusual amount of time in Blackmun's chambers at the end of the term. He frequently sent Blackmun notes of encouragement. Despite Burger's support, Blackmun resented the "Minnesota Twin" moniker. He eventually emerged from Burger's shadow with a different judicial philosophy and as his own man, but in June 1972 he needed Burger to sign on to his *Flood* opinion.

On June 13, Burger finally showed his hand:

> Dear Harry:
>
> After much travail I come out on this case as a "reluctant affirm."
>
> Regards,
WEB

That same day, Burger circulated a concurring opinion revealing the narrowness of baseball's victory:

> [L]ike Mr. Justice Douglas, I have grave reservations as to the correctness of *Toolson* . . . ; as he notes in his dissent, he joined that holding but has "lived to regret it." The error, if such it be, is one on which the affairs of a great many people have rested for a long time. Courts are not the forum in which this tangled web ought to

> be unsnarled. I agree with Mr. Justice Douglas that congressional inaction is not a solid base, but the least undesirable course now is to let the matter rest with Congress; it is time the Congress acted to solve this problem.

The first sentence of Burger's concurrence refused to join Part I of Blackmun's opinion. Blackmun later speculated that Burger and White "thought perhaps it was beneath the dignity of the Court to indulge in a sentimental journey about baseball." He never discussed the issue with either of them. Burger nonetheless represented a fifth vote for Blackmun's opinion and for baseball—but on the narrowest possible grounds. The final score was Baseball 5, Flood 3.

Speculation has been rampant over the years about why Burger changed his vote. Rumors spread among law clerks, according to Woodward and Armstrong, that Burger had agreed to join Blackmun's opinion in exchange for putting off a final decision in the abortion cases until the following term. There is no evidence to support this theory. Blackmun had asked as early as January 18 that the abortion cases be reargued before a full nine-member Court. After circulating a rough draft of his abortion opinions later that term, on May 31 Blackmun renewed his request to have the cases reargued. Ten days later, Blackmun informed his fellow justices at their private conference that "the real reason he wanted [the abortion cases] reargued was that he didn't think the country could stand having the death penalty and abortion laws declared unconstitutional on the same day." The abortion cases were reargued the following term, but not because of *Flood v. Kuhn*.

A simple vote trade between Blackmun and Burger seems far-fetched. It seems more likely that Burger did not want the *Flood* case to end in a 4–4 tie and was simply trying to curry favor with his "Minnesota Twin"—but not enough to join Blackmun's Part I.

Blackmun was not done with his name games. He never circulated another draft to his fellow justices, but before the decision was announced and published, he added two players to the list. He inserted Jimmie Foxx between Rabbit Maranville and Lefty Grove. Foxx, who hit 534 home runs, would have been a glaring omission from any list of baseball greats. On June 1, Blackmun clipped a *New York Times* obituary of Morris "Moe" Berg. A multilingual catcher, Berg attended Princeton, the Sorbonne, and Columbia Law School. He used his gift for languages to sneak behind enemy lines and spy on atomic scientists for the Office of Strategic Services during World War II. He also played 15 undistinguished major league seasons and batted .243. "He can speak ten languages," the joke about Berg went, "but he can't hit in any of them." Blackmun slipped Berg's name into the list between Old Hoss Radbourn and Maranville. The justice's fascination with Berg continued. Twenty-five years later, he read Nicholas Dawidoff's biography of Berg, *The Catcher Was a Spy*. Blackmun gave the book a B—a tough grade considering his own attempt at baseball writing.

On the morning of Monday, June 19, Blackmun placed an arrow in his appointment book next to the date and accompanying note that the first official game of baseball was played on June 19, 1846. The Court convened at 10 a.m. and announced seven decisions. The Court does not provide advance warning about which decisions will be announced, but it was almost the end of the term—decision time for Flood's and other cases. The most junior justices announce their majority opinions first. Powell announced two opinions. The first rejected the Nixon administration's wiretapping of suspected radicals without search warrants—a story that received above-the-fold treatment on the front pages of the *New York Times* and *Washington Post*. The other allowed municipal court clerks to issue search warrants and garnered almost no notice.

Blackmun rose to speak. Justices, particularly in important cases, often summarize and maybe even read a few paragraphs from their decisions. Blackmun read from three typewritten pages. "This case presents an issue that was before the Court first in 1922, then a second time in 1953, namely, whether professional baseball's reserve system is within the reach of the federal antitrust laws," he began.

"This case is one instituted by Curtis Charles Flood, known on the diamond as Curt Flood. . . ."

At that moment, Nina Totenberg, then a reporter for the *National Observer*, broke the Court's usually somber mood by laughing. As Blackmun continued reading, Powell winked at the reporters sitting on the left side of the courtroom. Blackmun concluded by mentioning that Powell "took no part in the consideration or decision of the case." Those same words appeared in the official text of the decision but were not literally true. Powell had participated in oral argument and one private conference and had written Blackmun an encouraging note. Powell represented a possible fifth vote for Flood. More than anything else, his decision to withdraw affected the outcome of Flood's case because otherwise Burger may not have felt the need to break a nonexistent tie.

Blackmun also announced Burger's concurrence, Burger's and White's refusal to join Part I, Douglas's and Marshall's dissents, and Brennan's joining both dissents. The dissenting justices sometimes, but not often, read from their opinions if they feel strongly about a case. Douglas was not in the courtroom that day. He had already made his way back to his Goose Prairie cabin, having asked Burger to announce his dissent. Neither Marshall nor Brennan said a word. The Court announced four more decisions and then adjourned.

The clerk of the Court, Michael Rodak Jr., sent identical six-word telegrams on the afternoon of June 19 to Arthur Goldberg and Lou Hoynes: "JUDGMENT FLOOD AGAINST KUHN AFFIRMED TODAY." It had been exactly nine months since the Court had agreed to take the case.

Goldberg was a bit confused after reading the Court's decision. White and Burger joined only Parts II–IV of Blackmun's opinion. They had forgotten to join Part V, the legal holding of the case. So, technically, without a five-justice majority for Part V, there was no opinion of the Court. Goldberg called Henry Putzel Jr., the Court's reporter of decisions, and pointed out the error. Putzel conferred with the two justices, who agreed to revise the Court's opinion to read that they had joined all but Part I of Blackmun's opinion. Putzel notified Blackmun, who had approved the opinion's syllabus. On July 3, the Court sent a letter to counsel alerting them of the change and revised the paper copy of the *U.S. Reports*. The Court could not even announce its decision properly.

Goldberg indicated that he "was not surprised at the result in Flood's case although I did expect better opinion writing." He agreed with Topkis, who wrote Goldberg that the "Supreme Court screwed us. . . . I am afraid that the sad fact is that nothing today's Court does is terribly likely to surprise me." Some of the blame lay with Goldberg and his awful oral argument. Dan Levitt did not think that Goldberg's argument, as bad as it was, affected the outcome. But Peter Westen, the other associate at counsel's table that day, believed that Flood would have won if the case had been decided on the briefs alone. Goldberg refused to seek an opportunity to redeem himself. He vowed never to argue another case before the Supreme Court.

Even though they were no longer law partners, Goldberg left it up to Topkis to settle the bill with Marvin Miller. Topkis came away from Flood's trial with a deep respect and admiration for Miller. They shared the sting of the Supreme Court defeat and remained friends long after the bill had been settled. The Players Association, Topkis wrote Miller, owed Paul, Weiss $100,000 ($25,000 had already been paid, and Goldberg did not charge the union an additional $34,000 for his billable time). In the last line of his letter to Miller about the bill, Topkis wrote: "The only bad thing about the case from my point of view was losing it—everything else aside, Mrs. Lincoln, how was the show?"

Bowie Kuhn reacted to the decision with a lawyer's caution, describing it as "constructive." "The decision opens the way for renewed collective bargaining on the reserve system after the 1972 season," he said in his prepared statement to the press.

Miller lacked Kuhn's faith that "renewed collective bargaining" would free the players from the reserve clause. "Renewed?" Miller said to Red Smith. "It has never begun." Miller was determined to press the owners for modifications to the reserve clause during the next round of labor negotiations, but he knew from his experiences not to be overly optimistic.

Ever the strategist, Miller hoped "that the Congress will accept the Court's clear invitation to act in this matter and we will be cooperating fully with the Congress to achieve that result." Howard Cosell, testifying before the Senate Commerce Committee the day Flood's decision came down, remarked: "The original reserve clause is so old I think it must have been written by William of Orange." Senator Sam Ervin (D-NC), the future star of the Watergate hearings, expressed similar sentiments before a House subcommittee two months later. "I hope you will all join with me in trying to pass this legislation to help vindicate the courageous sacrifice of Curt Flood so that those athletes that come after can say truthfully and proudly that 'I am not a piece of property,'" Ervin said. It "is easy to become emotional about the plight of American professional athletes . . . even though their numbers are small, they are slaves. Even though many are well-paid slaves." Miller's hope and Cosell's and Ervin's testimony notwithstanding, Congress did nothing. The union was no match for baseball's lobby in Washington. "By the time the gentlemen on Capitol Hill get around to rendering a decision," *Chicago Sun-Times* columnist Bill Gleason wrote, "Curtis Flood will be an old gentleman living in retirement."

The Court's decision landed Flood on the front pages of the *New York Times* and *Washington Post* and on the network news. It was the last time he was foremost on the mind of America. After that day, most of the country forgot about him.

The press ripped into the decision. Red Smith, now writing for the *New York Times*, labeled it a "cop-out" and "a disappointment for several reasons that have nothing to do with Curt Flood's bid for $3-million in damages. . . . It is a disappointment because the highest Court in the land is still averting its gaze from a system in American business that gives the employer outright ownership of his employees. . . . It is a disappointment because this Court appears to set greater store by property rights than by human rights." It was not just Red Smith taking on the establishment. The *New York Times*, *Washington Post*, *Washington Evening Star*, *Baltimore Sun*, *Minneapolis Star Tribune*, and *St. Louis Post-Dispatch* all wrote editorials condemning the decision. Most sports columnists blasted the Court. Only backers of the baseball establishment—the *Sporting News*, Dick Young, Bob Broeg, Joe DiMaggio, and Ted Williams—applauded the ruling.

Over the years, Blackmun's "sentimental journey," as he described Part I, took heat from all corners. It started with the sportswriters. "Presumably," *Los Angeles Times* columnist Jim Murray wrote, "the decision was handed down in the form of bubble-gum cards." Blackmun later said he was "amused" by "the complete antagonism of the sportswriters in Washington and New York. I think they felt I had impinged on their turf." Blackmun's opinion, however, helped turn the conservative sporting press in Flood's favor.

Then came the investigative reporters. Woodward's and Armstrong's book, *The Brethren*, revealed that Stewart had been "embarrassed" about assigning the *Flood* opinion to Blackmun. In December 1979, one of Blackmun's law clerks, Bill Murphy, read excerpts of the book in *Newsweek*. The next morning at breakfast, he alerted Blackmun to Stewart's comments. Murphy also brought in some old baseball cards from his personal collection. During oral argument, Blackmun passed Stewart the cards of several former Reds players, including Gus Bell, Vada Pinson, and Frank Robinson, along with a handwritten note mentioning the book's report that Stewart had been "embarrassed." Stewart replied that it was "nonsense." Blackmun was not so sure. Nearly 10 years later, Woodward revealed Stewart as one of the book's confidential sources. In a September 1995 oral history, Blackmun was asked about Stewart's remark:

> [W]hen I talked to him about it, he was so emphatic in his denial of having made that statement, and I wondered at the time, because it would not have been out of character for him to make that statement. I think Potter was always critical of me from the very beginning, to a degree. I don't know whether he thought I was incapable of being on the Court or shouldn't be there or what, but we were in opposition on a number of occasions, but other times not. We were always very friendly together. I always had to watch the writing, as far as Potter was concerned.

Blackmun and Stewart carried on a friendship through their mutual love of baseball, passing notes about the game while on the bench and lending each other books on baseball history.

Legal scholars picked up where the press and Stewart left off in criticizing Blackmun's *Flood* opinion. Professor William Eskridge called it "an almost comical adherence to the strict rule against overruling statutory precedents." Eskridge was not alone; most scholars blasted Blackmun's opinion. The reason for the Court's decision, according to Eskridge, had nothing to do with its respect for *stare decisis*; it had everything to do with Blackmun's ode to baseball and the list of names in Part I.

The Washington legal community derided Blackmun's list. A former Supreme Court clerk wrote a parody of the opinion, privately circulated among Washington lawyers, titled "Baskin v. Robbins." "There are many great ice cream flavors," the mock opinion began as it listed off flavors from chocolate, vanilla, and strawberry to rocky road. "The list seems endless."

After the Court's decision came out, a law clerk alerted Blackmun to a glaring omission from his list of names—Mel Ott. Blackmun insisted that Ott, the New York Giants right fielder who hit 511 home runs, was on the list. "I shall never forgive myself," Blackmun said. He was so upset that he scribbled "Mel Ott?" in the margin of his copy of the *U.S. Reports* containing the *Flood* decision. Blackmun kept a gift in his chambers from his law clerks—a Mel Ott model Louisville Slugger bat mounted on an engraved plaque bearing the justice's reaction upon learning of Ott's omission. The bat was one of Blackmun's prized possessions.

Blackmun staunchly defended his "sentimental journey" and proclaimed *Flood v. Kuhn* his favorite opinion. "[I]t's been a great conversation piece," he said. "I can go to Chicago, and somebody will come up and say, 'I read your list of the great heroes of baseball, but why didn't you include Joe Zilch?' And then we'd have a conversation going as to why I didn't include Joe Zilch. He didn't bat well enough over ten years or something. Sure." Talking baseball was a welcome respite from the threats and hate mail Blackmun began to receive for writing the majority opinion in the landmark abortion case, *Roe v. Wade*, the following term.

Blackmun enjoyed being viewed as the Court's number one baseball fan. A week after his *Flood* opinion came out, a California man sent Blackmun his article about the connections between the supposed founder of baseball, Alexander Cartwright, and the Freemasons. In 1973, a friend from Minnesota sent him poems he had written about "Casey at the Bat," Blackmun's favorite poem. Two years later, Judge Roger Robb of the D.C. Circuit sent him a *University of Pennsylvania Law Review* article, "The Common Law Origins of the Infield Fly Rule." The 47th member (out of 700) of the Emil Verban Memorial Society, a who's who of Washington, D.C.–based Chicago Cubs fans, Blackmun had grown up rooting for the Cubs before becoming a Twins fan and regularly entertained former Cubs players in his chambers. The criticisms from the press, the legal community, and his fellow justices about his *Flood* opinion left him unperturbed. "I would do it over again because I felt that baseball deserved it," he said.

Blackmun failed to see the consequences of his conversation piece on the Court. More so than with the legislative or executive branches, the Court's legitimacy depends on the people's confidence in the institution's decisions. As Alexander Hamilton, one of the framers of the Constitution, wrote in *The Federalist Papers*, the judiciary "will always be the least dangerous [branch] to the political rights of the Constitution" because it "has no influence over either the sword or the purse. . . . It may truly be said to have neither FORCE nor WILL, but merely judgment." *Flood v. Kuhn* represented a lapse in the Court's judgment. Some of the justices seemed to have bowed to the aura and mystique of baseball as the national pastime rather than striving to correct two of the Court's erroneous decisions. They compounded the errors in those decisions and compromised the Court's integrity. A footnote in Marshall's *Flood v. Kuhn* dissent encapsulates the problem with Blackmun's "sentimental journey": "'[A] decision contrary to the public sense of justice as it is, operates, so far as it is known, to diminish respect for the courts and for law itself.'"

In the years after *Flood v. Kuhn*, Blackmun developed into a confident and extremely liberal justice. He was proud of his reputation as someone who stood up for "outsiders, or the little people"—whether they were women, abused children, homosexuals, Native Americans, or death row inmates. "I think there's a tendency in judicial writings to overlook the human-being factor in almost—well, in most cases," he later said. In writing the majority opinion in *Flood v. Kuhn*, however, Blackmun lost himself in the romance of baseball and forgot about the struggles and sacrifices of Curt Flood.

CHAPTER SEVENTEEN

The day the Court's decision came down, Marvin Miller called Curt Flood in Majorca with the news. Miller had played the role of pessimist in chief about Flood's lawsuit from day one. But Miller still hated to lose, and privately, he was disconsolate. On the phone, Flood tried to cheer Miller up. Flood's few public comments were similarly upbeat. "Baby, I gave them one hell of a fight," he told *Newsweek*.

Curt Flood was not baseball's first free agent. Nor did his lawsuit create free agency. But his legal battle set the stage for free agency in baseball.

Flood's lawsuit helped change public opinion. "What *Flood v. Kuhn* really accomplished," according to Miller, "was . . . raising the consciousness of everyone involved in baseball: the writers, the fans, the players—and perhaps even some of the owners." It certainly helped unite the players. Before the 1969 season, some players had ignored the union's edict to refuse to sign new contracts until the resolution of a pension dispute. Three years later, the players displayed so much unity during pension negotiations that they initiated a 13-day strike that delayed the start of the 1972 season. The change in the media's tone—from its vilification of Flood for his "well-paid slave" remark in 1970 to its outrage over the Supreme Court's decision two years later—was incredibly telling. The Court's weak justifications for baseball's antitrust exemption left the reserve system on shaky ground. Even the owners' chief negotiator, John Gaherin, knew after reading the decision that free agency was inevitable. "After the *Flood* case," Gaherin said, "it wasn't a question of if the reserve structure would be restructured or annihilated, but when." Gaherin tried to explain to the owners that they had won on a technical jurisdictional point, that baseball was immune from antitrust lawsuits, not on the merits of the reserve clause. That point was still up for grabs and, with Marvin Miller on the other side, seemed to be headed in the players' favor.

Flood's lawsuit also made Miller's job easier because the owners kept insisting at trial and on appeal that the reserve clause was a collective bargaining issue. Before the *Flood* case, the owners had refused to entertain any modifications to the reserve clause. Now the pressure was on the owners to negotiate in good faith. They could no longer reject all the players' proposed modifications to the reserve clause without making counteroffers. If the owners failed to negotiate in good faith, they could incur the wrath of the National Labor Relations Board or the federal courts.

This became apparent during negotiations over the 1973 Basic Agreement. Miller and the players agreed to keep the reserve clause in place for three more years but won other critical concessions. Players with two years of continuous major league service and three years of noncontinuous service would be eligible for salary arbitration, meaning they could resolve salary disputes before an independent arbitrator. Salary arbitration would bear enormous fruit in the form of increased players' salaries. Veteran players won their first taste of freedom from unwanted trades because of a rule inspired by Flood's objection to being traded after 12 seasons with the Cardinals. Under the 10-and-5 rule, any player with 10 years of major league service and 5 years with the same team could not be traded without his consent. The 10-and-5 rule would have prevented Flood's trade and is often referred to as the Curt Flood rule.

The Curt Flood rule could no longer help the person who inspired it. In Majorca, Flood worked at the Rustic Inn, a bar he owned with Ann, a woman he referred to as his wife but was only a girlfriend. Decorated with bats, gloves, autographed balls, and photographs, the Rustic Inn developed into a popular hangout for American servicemen from the Sixth Fleet. A picture of Flood from his playing days hung on the wall behind the bar. He spent most of his days drinking with the servicemen and occasionally played softball with them. The servicemen found him charming; he even entertained questions from a few enterprising newsmen.

Flood's Supreme Court defeat was never far from his mind. He told Bob Sheridan, an up-and-coming Miami sportscaster, that he was writing a second book about the Court's decision. Curt expounded on some of his theories about the decision during a January 1973 conversation with Vernon Sherwin, a retired *Baltimore Evening Sun* news editor living in Majorca. Flood pointed out that three of the four Nixon appointees had voted against him and the fourth, Powell, had abstained. "He abstained," Flood said, "but I sometimes wonder when he acquired the stock and whether he just abstained from voting or whether he abstained from discussing the case with the other judges." Powell's comments at conference and his note of encouragement to Blackmun would have sent Flood through the roof.

Flood criticized the new labor agreement during an April 1, 1973, interview with his old friend Howard Cosell. Cosell had befriended Flood when Flood needed friends most, standing by him even after the furor over his lawsuit had subsided. He helped Flood's business by sending him videotapes of major league games and Muhammad Ali fights to show to the American servicemen at the Rustic Inn.

Flood was disappointed because the new labor agreement called for no negotiation over the reserve clause for three more years. "It's been three years since I started to fight it and now three more years will go by and it'll be at least another three years before they do anything about it," Flood told Cosell. "I've given a lot of time and money to do this." The 10-and-5 rule was not enough to mollify Flood; he wanted the end of the reserve clause. "The problem with the reserve clause is that it ties a man to one owner for the rest of his life," he said. "There is no other profession in the history of mankind except slavery in which one man was tied to another for life."

Off camera, Flood and Cosell sat on the roof of the bar with the Mediterranean Sea behind them. Flood looked awful. His receding hair looked wild and unkempt. His face looked fatter. His eyes looked weary and tired. Tears came to his eyes. He touched his head and his heart. "These are mine," he told Cosell. "They belong to me. You can't buy them, you can't sell them, and you sure can't *trade* them." Flood was homesick and, according to Cosell, "[i]n spite of himself, he missed baseball."

Flood had already missed the funeral of the man who had taught him the most about freedom, Jackie Robinson. Before his death, Robinson was honored during an on-field ceremony before Game 2 of the 1972 World Series between the Oakland A's and the Cincinnati Reds. The ceremony marked the 25th anniversary of Robinson's first major league season. "I am extremely proud and pleased to be here this afternoon," a nearly blind Robinson told the crowd, "but must admit I'm going to be tremendously more pleased and more proud when I look at that third base coaching line one day and see a black face managing in baseball." Robinson had been estranged from the game for so long that he may not have realized that most managers no longer doubled as third base coaches. Nine days later, Robinson died of a diabetes-related heart attack at age 53. "Jackie, as a figure in history, was a rock in the water, creating concentric circles and ripples of new possibility," a young, Afro-wearing minister named Jesse Jackson told 2,500 mourners at Manhattan's Riverside Church. Robinson was buried in Brooklyn beneath a gravestone bearing his own words: "A life is not important except in the impact it has on other lives."

In the tradition of his hero, Flood continued to stand up for his convictions, but he may not have been privy to Marvin Miller's incremental approach to attacking the reserve clause. Even though the 1973 Basic Agreement had been signed, Miller was not going to put the fight for free agency on hold for three years. He had at his disposal a new generation of ballplayers and new weapons, foremost among them independent grievance arbitration.

Miller believed that Flood's lawsuit had facilitated the owners' acceptance of an independent arbitrator. Before the union's December 1969 meeting in Puerto Rico, the owners had rejected the idea. Six months later, on the eve of Flood's trial, the owners agreed to the new grievance procedure as part of the 1970 Basic Agreement, which ran for three years. Flood's lawsuit had removed the critical obstacle to the agreement—the reserve clause—from the bargaining table. The lawsuit also struck the fear of God in the owners that they were going to lose their antitrust exemption. In the past, Miller said, the owners had argued that they could self-regulate their business and therefore avoid government intervention. With Flood's lawsuit challenging their autonomy, the owners granted the players a right enjoyed in every other industry by allowing them to have their grievances decided by a neutral party. It turned out to be a costly concession.

The power of an independent arbitrator was illustrated in the case of 1974 American League Cy Young Award winner Catfish Hunter. After the 1974 season, Hunter filed a grievance claiming that A's owner Charlie Finley had reneged on a portion of his contract by refusing to set up a $50,000 annuity in the pitcher's name. The independent arbitrator, Peter Seitz, ruled that Finley had breached Hunter's contract and declared the A's ace pitcher a free agent. After the ruling, teams flocked to Hunter's native North Carolina and began a bidding war for his services. Hunter eventually agreed to a five-year, $3.5 million contract to pitch for the New York Yankees. Hunter's contract opened other players' eyes to what free agency could do for them.

Miller's ultimate goal was to use independent grievance arbitration to test the meaning of the language in the reserve clause, paragraph 10(a) of the Uniform Player Contract. Paragraph 10(a) said that if a player refused to sign his contract, "the Club shall have the right . . . to renew the contract for the period of one year." Read literally, the reserve clause was a one-year option on, not lifetime ownership of, a player's services. In 1967, a California judge interpreted similar language in the NBA contract of forward Rick Barry as a one-year option. Miller believed that an independent arbitrator would say the same thing about paragraph 10(a). He just needed the right test case.

Major league players began testing the meaning of paragraph 10(a) by refusing to sign new contracts and forcing the owners to exercise the renewal provision. The players were essentially working under their previous season's salaries but without signed contracts as they attempted to break the cycle of perpetual options on their services. Nervous about retaining their unsigned players, major league teams tried desperately to sign them to new contracts during the season. The St. Louis Cardinals' young catcher, Ted Simmons, played without a signed contract until July 1972, when he signed a two-year deal worth $75,000. Six players began the 1974 season without signed contracts, but only two made it to the end. Yankees reliever Sparky Lyle pitched without a new contract until the last day of the season and pitched well, earning a retroactive salary of $87,500 for 1974 and $92,500 for 1975. San Diego Padres outfielder

Bobby Tolan, another former Cardinals teammate of Flood's, played the entire 1974 season without a contract, receiving a retroactive raise to nearly $100,000 for 1974 and a similar amount for 1975.

In 1975, Los Angeles Dodgers ace Andy Messersmith became the first player to play an entire season without a signed contract and to challenge the meaning of paragraph 10(a) before an independent arbitrator. When the Dodgers refused to give Messersmith a no-trade clause in his 1975 contract, the two-time 20-game winner refused to sign a new deal. He won 19 games that season with a 2.29 ERA. After the season, Messersmith rejected the Dodgers' last-minute offer of $135,000 retroactively for 1975 and a combined salary of $320,000 for 1976 and 1977. Instead, Messersmith gambled that an arbitrator's decision about paragraph 10(a) would make him a free agent.

Montreal Expos pitcher Dave McNally joined Messersmith's grievance. A four-time 20-game winner with the Baltimore Orioles, McNally had been traded to the Expos before the 1975 season. He could not come to terms with the Expos before the season and played for them without a signed contract until June 8, when the 32-year-old left-hander left the team. The next day, McNally announced his retirement; he planned to open a car dealership. Miller wanted another plaintiff in the case and asked McNally to join Messersmith's challenge to paragraph 10(a). McNally agreed. In November, Expos president John McHale suddenly showed up in McNally's hometown of Billings, Montana, to offer him a $25,000 bonus to go to spring training in 1976 and a $125,000 contract if McNally made the team. McNally turned down an easy $25,000, and, even though he had every intention of retiring, insisted on joining Messersmith's grievance.

The owners attacked Messersmith's and McNally's grievance on multiple fronts. They unsuccessfully tried to get a federal judge to declare that the reserve clause was outside the scope of the grievance procedure because both sides had agreed to set aside the reserve clause as part of the 1970 Basic Agreement. The owners' biggest mistake was not exercising the right that either side had to fire arbitrator Peter Seitz, who had already ruled against them in the Hunter case. Once the arbitration had begun, the owners argued before Seitz that the reserve system consisted of not only paragraph 10(a) but also the Major League Rules—including Rule 3(a) requiring all players to sign the Uniform Player Contract containing the reserve clause, Rule 3(g) against tampering with players under contract, and Rule 4-A about the reserve lists—all of which the players had agreed to obey as part of the Uniform Player Contract. The players simply argued that the reserve system came down to the meaning of paragraph 10(a). Seitz sided with the players, interpreting paragraph 10(a) to be a one-year option and declaring Messersmith and McNally free agents. Messersmith and McNally won the players what Flood had not: freedom. Emboldened by nearly 50 years of courtroom victories, the owners attempted the difficult task of persuading a federal judge to overturn an arbitrator's binding decision. A Kansas City–based federal trial judge and a federal appeals court upheld Seitz's ruling. As baseball's second recent high-profile free agent, Messersmith signed a three-year no-trade contract with the Atlanta Braves worth $1 million. McNally, as he had originally intended, retired.

The Messersmith-McNally decision gave Miller and the Players Association incredible leverage in the ongoing negotiations over the 1976 Basic Agreement. Miller recognized that making all the players immediately eligible for free agency would create an oversupply of free agents and depress the value of their services. Instead, the union negotiated a deal that allowed players to become free agents by continuing to play without signed contracts in 1976, or after their sixth year of major league service. In addition, players with five years of major league service could demand a trade. During the first offseason with multiple high-profile free agents, Reggie Jackson signed the largest free-agent contract by agreeing to a five-year deal worth $3 million with the Yankees.

The gains from the Hunter and Messersmith decisions, according to Miller, could not have been achieved without Flood's struggle and sacrifices. "I can't help but think both Hunter and Messersmith/McNally had to, at the appropriate time, have been influenced by the courage of a Curt Flood," Miller said. "As in any case of an advance that had to be fought for, the struggle of those who came before, including those who didn't succeed, had to have an impact on those who later proved to be successful. In my gut, I feel there was a connection, but I can't prove it."

Miller and Moss tried to educate the players about what Flood had started. In the spring of 1977, they traveled to all the teams' spring training camps. They mentioned Flood's name and told his story at practically every stop. Miller and Moss wanted the union to recognize Flood, but they wanted it to come from the players. The six years that Flood had been away from the game was a baseball lifetime. Many players did not even know who he was.

Flood's last few years in Europe had not been kind. The Spanish police, after seeing servicemen coming and going at all hours, closed his bar. Having lost his only source of income, he gave his World Series rings to a vacationing Texas couple as collateral for a "loan" of a few thousand dollars. Flood packed up his remaining baseball trophies and memorabilia, left some debts behind in Majorca, and sought refuge in Andorra, a tiny country perched in the Pyrenees on the Spanish-French border, with Ann and her teenage son. After Curt and Ann parted ways, he found himself unable to rent an apartment in Andorra because he was black. The Andorran government refused to grant him a work permit. He performed odd jobs to survive, working for a time as a carpet installer and living in a single room above a British-owned pizzeria called Nelson's Tavern. He drank there so frequently that his picture joined those of 40 regulars above the bar. Flood's photo was the only one with a caption: "Super Hermit." Drunk and destitute, Flood sometimes found shelter with friends. His possessions consisted of a dog, a scooter, and a small duffel bag of belongings. "He is said to often voice regret that he ever made his sensational stand and walked out of baseball and turned his back on America," a Spanish correspondent informed *Sports Illustrated* in August 1975.

On October 1, 1975, Flood was arrested outside a well-known Andorran department store. The police broke his left arm, accused him of theft, and threw him into jail. "There have been reports that he has drinking problems," a cable sent from the American consulate in Barcelona to the State Department said. "He had no money when he was detained." Two days later, the local judge decided not to charge Flood with theft because he "was drunk when he attempted to rob a department store" and "no merchandise was stolen." That afternoon, the Andorran government put him on a bus to Barcelona.

About 10 days later, Flood landed in a Barcelona psychiatric hospital and was treated for alcoholism. When the hospital discharged him at the end of October, he could not pay the $300 bill so the city of Barcelona picked up the tab. He wanted to go home to Oakland but could not afford the $330 flight from Barcelona to New York. The State

Department requested financial assistance from the Department of Health, Education, and Welfare and contacted Flood's family. In early November 1975, according to a State Department cable from Henry Kissinger, Flood's father paid for Curt's ticket to Oakland.

Flood arrived at the Oakland airport with only a small duffel bag. He had nothing to show for his playing career. He was almost 38 years old and back at square one. He was not back on Helen Street in a West Oakland ghetto, but he returned home just as poor as he had left. His family and a few friends greeted him. He was a mess. Instead of getting help, he retreated into his own personal prison. He moved in with his 76-year-old mother, Laura, in one of three adjacent apartments that he had originally purchased for her and the rest of his family. She, too, had issues with alcohol and could not rehabilitate her youngest son. Curt's half sister Rickie and his brother Carl lived in the other two apartments.

Curt's relationship with Carl had never recovered from his brother's February 1969 attempted jewelry store robbery and shoot-out with police. Curt believed the resulting bad publicity was the reason the Cardinals had traded him. Carl's crime had attracted the attention of both of the St. Louis daily newspapers. Carl had also stolen money and photographs from people who had prepaid for Flood to paint their portraits. During his prison sentence for the robbery, Carl worked as a part-time staff member for Missouri lieutenant governor William C. Phelps investigating prison-related complaints in an ombudsman program that Carl had devised. In 1974, he presented former Missouri governor Warren E. Hearnes with a portrait that Curt had supposedly painted in 1965. After more than six years in prison, Carl was released on parole in November 1975 and returned to Oakland. The following year, with the help of the local Legal Aid Society and ACLU chapter, Carl sued the Alameda County director of elections to regain his voting rights. He lost because he was on parole until 1982.

Curt detested Carl's presence in those apartments. Carl continued to run scams on his family. He acted like a bedridden invalid around his mother, Laura, so she would take care of him. Then, after she went to bed, he jumped into a waiting convertible to hit the town. In 1980, he wrote a poem about Willie McCovey and published it in the *Oakland Tribune* under Curt's name.

Curt could not evict Carl because the apartments in East Oakland no longer belonged to him. While Curt was in Spain, the IRS continued to pursue his back taxes—perhaps the unpaid withholding taxes from his photography business—and went after the apartments. He instructed Rickie, who had been keeping up the mortgage payments, to do anything to prevent their mother from being evicted. Rickie took title to the property and continued to pay the mortgage. Curt had been so poor while living in Spain that he had asked her to return his $10,000 down payment. She said she had sent him the money.

Back in Oakland, Flood's drinking continued unabated. He nearly died in June 1976 after fracturing his skull. His family says he fell from a ladder onto a concrete patio while trying to fix the antenna on the roof. He told a reporter that he fell down a flight of stairs. Others believed the fall was not accidental. He admitted to having "a couple of beers too many." "They gave me a brain scan," he said of his hospital stay, "and they found nothing."

This was the humorous yet proud public face Flood showed in September 1976 to the *New York Times*'s Murray Chass. Flood smoked cigarettes while discussing his lawsuit (it angered him that no active players had shown up at his trial); his life (he spent his days sitting around and doing nothing); and his desire to get back into baseball. "It's a little difficult to find a job for a used center fielder," he told Chass. "You can't look in the want ads and find a job like that."

All the reporters who interviewed Flood at his mother's apartment asked about his painting career. A portrait of his youngest daughter, Shelly, hung next to the door. Another of his young, beautiful mother adorned the wall over the couch. He parried any questions about making a living as a painter.

Flood desperately wanted to get back into baseball. It was the only thing he knew how to do. Ideally, he wanted a six-week job as a spring training instructor. He hoped to teach young players what he knew about the game. He did not want the job given to several retired black players—first base coach. He refused to spend his life telling players: "Don't get picked off."

Teams were not lining up for Flood's services for a reason: He had sued them all in federal court. If there had been an enemies list in Major League Baseball, Flood would have been on it. Although he denied it at the time, he had been blacklisted. Flood tried to explain why he had sued baseball. "The things that I did, I did for me," he said. "I did that because I thought they were right. I thought I should have some control over what happened to my life."

Flood did not begrudge the million-dollar contracts won by Hunter and Messersmith. He thought it was "cool" that "other people have benefited" from his lawsuit. "These guys are making more money and deservedly so. They're the show. They're it. They're making money because they work hard. Don't you tell me one minute that Catfish Hunter doesn't work his butt off. I know he does and he's the show."

The Messersmith-McNally decision, however, dredged up all the feelings of unfairness about how the Supreme Court had decided his case. "[T]here was no way a black man was going to win that suit," Flood wrote in 1977. "Listen, it eventually took two white guys—Andy Messersmith and Dave McNally—to destroy the reserve clause. Their battles were appreciably the same as mine." If only Flood had won his lawsuit, he might have been able to live in peace. His loss before the nation's highest court gnawed at him.

Flood healed some of his wounds with the help of a friend of his sister, Barbara. Karen Brecher, who had befriended Barbara at a previous job, worked as a supervisor for the Alameda County Welfare Department. Karen came from a middle-class white family. She and Curt started dating and lived together for six years. Flood often referred to her as his wife even though they never married. Curt and Karen joined a bowling league. He occasionally played with Karen's son, Phil, on a slow-pitch softball team. They all lived together in Alameda and later moved to East Oakland not far from Flood's family.

Karen wrote to the Texas couple asking them to return Flood's World Series rings. The couple said they never wanted the rings in the first place and returned them in the same cigar box in which Flood had given them away. The day the rings arrived in the mail, Flood cried. He thought he had lost them forever. Bob Feller, a vocal critic of Flood's lawsuit, called the house and asked if Flood wanted to sell his World Series rings. Flood was not parting with them again. He was poor, but Karen could support him on her welfare supervisor's salary.

Flood missed baseball. He attended Oakland A's games and often hung out with some of the players at an Alameda bar called the 19th Hole. A few players recognized him. Pitcher Mike Torrez, a former Cardinals teammate, gave him the gold chain from around his neck in appreciation for what Flood had done. Flood often kept score at home while watching games on television. There was only one baseball announcer whom he could not bear to watch—Joe Garagiola. Garagiola, who had testified against him at his trial, made Flood's stomach churn.

Flood raised his public profile and fattened his wallet with several media opportunities. He coauthored a first-person article about his life and lawsuit for the November 1977 issue of *Sport* magazine. Howard Cosell conducted another television interview with him on January 22, 1978, for *ABC Sports Magazine*. It was the weekend of Flood's 40th birthday. Cosell flew Curt and Karen out to New York City, put them up at a fancy hotel, gave them theater tickets, and sent a limousine to take Flood to the studio. Nobody treated Flood more like a somebody than Cosell.

Richard Reeves spent a night on Flood's couch for a March 1978 *Esquire* profile titled "The Last Angry Men"—"a search for heroes—for men who stood up to the system." Richard Carter, the collaborator on Flood's book, tried to discourage Reeves from contacting Curt. "Maybe you should leave him alone," Carter told Reeves. "Look, he took on something very big and it broke him." Flood also begged Reeves not to come:

> Please, please don't come out here. Don't bring it all up again. Please. Do you know what I've been through? Do you know what it means to go against the grain in this country? Your neighbors hate you. Do you know what it's like to be called the little black son of a bitch who tried to destroy baseball, the American Pastime?

Flood relented after Reeves agreed to his request for one-third of the money from the article (because Flood was to be one of three people profiled). For the only time in his career, Reeves paid a source; he gave Flood $750.

Reeves admired Flood for taking on the establishment and pitied him for what he had become. Flood could not figure out how to put his life back together without baseball. He had been told that the price for challenging the reserve clause would be high, but he could not have known that he would be paying for that choice for the rest of his life. He drank straight vodka as he and Reeves talked into the night. "He was about the saddest man I ever met," Reeves recalled.

Flood was so desperate for money that he tried to revive his portrait business. He and Karen started Curt Flood Portraits. Oakland furniture store owner Sam Bercovich agreed to show the paintings at E. Bercovich and Sons and even printed up flyers announcing "portraits by Curt Flood painted from your favorite photograph."

The key to the business was reconnecting with Burbank-based artist Lawrence Williams. On January 9, 1978, Flood sent Williams payment for several portraits and thanked him for "whipping out the portraits I ordered on such short notice." Flood also informed Williams of his new portrait business. "I decided that in leiu [*sic*] of a dishwashing job, I will try and sell portraits," he wrote in a letter typed by Karen. "You should do a lot of business up your way," Williams replied the next day by telegram. "I have one former professional football player that has been associated with me for 9–10 years, and he made a little over $80,000 this past year." Williams was alluding to former NFL wide receiver Tommy McDonald.

On March 2, Flood sent Williams a check for another portrait and asked for more paintings. A New York gallery had invited Flood to show some baseball paintings, with part of the commission funding a new Harlem sports complex. Flood was concerned that the gallery would be able to detect the process used to create the portraits, in which Williams would blow up photographs, stretch and mount them on Masonite, and then paint over the blown-up photographs with a palette knife instead of a brush. "Is there any way (short of doing it myself from scratch) to provide them with some paintings to sell, that would not reflect this process?" Flood asked Williams. "Do you know of any galleries that might be able to push your/my work?" Flood inquired. It is doubtful that Curt could have painted a portrait from scratch. Karen once asked him if he could. He said no. He was too drunk most of the time even to try.

Except to Karen and a few family members, Curt kept up the illusion that he was painting the portraits. He even fooled Bercovich, who asked Flood to paint a portrait of Cincinnati Reds second baseman Joe Morgan for a banquet a few days later honoring the East Oakland star.

"Sam Bercovich," Flood said, "you're the only person I can't say no to."

Flood quickly sent the photograph of Morgan off to Williams in Burbank, and a few days later presented Bercovich with a completed portrait. Morgan started to cry when he saw it and later hung it prominently in his home. Flood told Bercovich that he had stayed up all night painting even though he had never touched a brush (or a palette knife) to the canvas. But Flood had stopped signing his name on the portraits, an indication that his conscience had begun to get the best of him.

Bercovich tried to help Flood return to baseball and to his roots. In the fall of 1977, Flood coached the Bercovich-sponsored American Legion team that he had played for as a youngster. He also coached a younger Connie Mack team. Bercovich treated Flood like one of his sons. The bat that Flood had used during the 1964 World Series still hung on the wall of Bercovich's store.

Bercovich's plans for Flood included a return to the major leagues. As a supposed prelude to buying the Oakland A's from Charlie Finley for $12 million, Bercovich purchased the team's radio rights. The A's began the 1978 season without a radio contract; Larry Baer, a student at the University of California at Berkeley (and the future executive vice president and chief operating officer of the San Francisco Giants), broadcast their first 23 games on a 10-watt Cal station that could not be heard beyond the Berkeley hills. One month into the season, Bercovich paid $150,000 for the radio rights and switched the games to KNEW, a 5,000-watt country music station. He chose as his broadcast team legendary Oakland Oaks play-by-play man Bud Foster and Flood.

For the rest of the 1978 season, Flood hit the road as the A's radio color commentator. Bercovich insisted that Finley include Flood on the broadcast team.

"Oh, Curt Flood, he's the guy that cost the owners all this money," Finley said.

"Just think of what Bowie Kuhn would think," came the reply.

"Hired," Finley said.

No one disliked Bowie Kuhn more than Finley. During the 1976 season, he had tried to sell Joe Rudi and Rollie Fingers to the Red Sox and Vida Blue to the Yankees for a total of $3.5 million before they left the A's via free agency. Kuhn had voided the sales as contrary to the best interests of baseball. Finley had called Kuhn "the village idiot," "the nation's idiot," and "his honor, the idiot in charge" and challenged the commissioner's power in court. Finley lost. He constantly battled with his players, particularly at contract time, but Flood said: "You'll never hear negative things about Charlie Finley from me." Giving Flood an open mike was Finley's sweet revenge on Kuhn.

Flood's first night in the broadcast booth attracted camera crews from ABC and CBS and reporters from the *Los Angeles Times* and *New York Times*. He did not say much to entertain the listening audience. He possessed all the tools to be a great announcer—a smooth speaking voice, subtle wit, and years of knowledge about the game. He practiced at home and arrived at the ballpark early. On the air, however, he always seemed to say the wrong thing or nothing at all.

Flood's problem was alcohol. At the ballpark, the writers could smell it on his breath. He announced games drunk. His friends warned him that he was embarrassing himself. Instead of popping off about the players or the owners on the air, he simply clammed up. One night in New York, he refused to announce that night's game. He did not answer the phone in his hotel room. It was as if he were back with the 1971 Senators.

Flood's harsh experiences at Yankee Stadium continued. At a pregame party in George Steinbrenner's office, he ran into his former legal adversary, Bowie Kuhn. Flood walked over and extended his hand.

"I bet you don't know who I am," Flood said, according to Kuhn.

Kuhn said he did.

"Well, I suppose I'm not one of your real favorites," Flood said.

Kuhn said he harbored no hard feelings. They exchanged small talk about Flood's postbaseball life and broadcasting career. Kuhn could not resist a parting shot: "But you were wrong to walk out on Bob Short in 1971 after taking his money."

Kuhn's comments betrayed his ignorance. Flood had collected only about half a season's salary from Short. He could have hung around for a few more weeks until June 15, when, as Short promised, Flood would have been entitled to the other half of his salary. Kuhn showed that even after three years of litigation, he lacked any understanding of what made Flood tick.

That encounter was classic Bowie Kuhn—smug and condescending even about his one moment of victory against Marvin Miller and the union. In November 1982, after a decade of being outmaneuvered by Miller and the Players Association, Kuhn was voted out of office at the end of his term. Two Supreme Court justices who had voted against Flood, Potter Stewart and Byron White, were mentioned as possible successors. The owners replaced Kuhn in October 1984 with the organizer of the 1984 Summer Olympics in Los Angeles, Peter Ueberroth.

Kuhn, like Flood, found adjusting to life outside baseball difficult. After writing a score-settling autobiography, Kuhn returned to his old law firm, Willkie Farr, but spent most of his days sitting around his office doing very little. He had no clients and no desire to practice law. His partners had not wanted him back and were gently pushing him out the door. Against the advice of his longtime friend Lou Hoynes, Kuhn started a new law firm in January 1988 with a lawyer named Harvey Myerson. Under the name of Myerson & Kuhn, Myerson bilked clients and absconded with the firm's assets. Kuhn, who had ignored Myerson's activities, was on the hook for the firm's debts. Two years after starting the firm, Kuhn protected his remaining assets by selling his New Jersey home and purchasing a mansion in Ponte Vedra Beach, Florida, near Jacksonville. He eventually made a lump-sum payment to his creditors of several million dollars and went into business buying and selling minor league franchises—franchises he had said would not exist without the reserve clause. He became reclusive and devoutly religious, joining Opus Dei, a private Catholic sect with more than 3,000 U.S. members. In 2005, he served as the chairman of the Thomas More Law Center, a nonprofit organization founded by conservative Roman Catholics, which litigated an "intelligent design" lawsuit on behalf of a Pennsylvania school board seeking to teach ninth-grade biology students a religion-based alternative to evolution.

Kuhn, who rarely commented about the *Flood* case, said he'd had no choice but to deny Flood's request in December 1969 to become a free agent. Nor did he have any regrets about his handling of the matter. "I don't think I would have done anything differently," Kuhn said. "We were successful."

The clearest indication of how he felt about the whole affair came after the release of his 1987 autobiography, *Hardball.* Kuhn sent a copy to the justice who had switched his vote at the last minute in baseball's favor, recently retired chief justice Warren Burger. Kuhn met Burger for the first time after both men had relinquished their respective offices. In Burger's smaller Supreme Court chambers befitting a retired justice, Kuhn asked Burger to serve as a potential arbitrator in some asbestos litigation. The *Flood* case never came up. Kuhn's handwritten inscription, dated May 27, 1987, read:

> To the Chief Justice:
>
> With fond regards to a great American
>
> Best always,
> Bowie K. Kuhn

Burger saved the book in his personal collection until his death in 1995. He never revealed publicly why he had switched his vote.

Aside from the parting shot from Kuhn, Flood received a warm reception during the 1978 season from an unexpected source—the St. Louis Cardinals. In May, Cardinals general manager Bing Devine—the same man who had traded him to the Phillies in October 1969—called Flood and invited him to St. Louis on June 9 for the 25th anniversary celebration of Anheuser-Busch's ownership of the team. Devine asked Flood to be one of 10 guests of honor. Flood graciously accepted.

Before the lawsuit, Flood had been one of Gussie Busch's favorite players. Busch later blamed Flood for turning baseball into a business for him. Busch, however, let bygones be bygones. So did Flood. On June 9, Gussie greeted Curt warmly. "You were always my favorite center fielder," the beer baron said.

Flood donned a full Cardinals uniform, including a late-1970s pullover jersey with his name and number on the back. He rode through the tunnel at Busch Stadium in a Pontiac Firebird with "Flood 21" on the side. He stood up through one of the T-tops and waved at the adoring 45,487 fans. Nine years after his last at-bat in that ballpark, they gave him a standing ovation. Cardinal Nation loved Flood. And Flood loved the Cardinals. After all, he had sued baseball to stay in St. Louis, not to leave. Upon his return, the team's management treated Flood the same way it treated Bob Gibson, Stan Musial, and Enos Slaughter. A personalized car drove each of the anointed players to a podium in the center of the field.

Gibson playfully pinched the cheek of his good friend and former roommate. Gibson lived in Omaha and had tried to stay in touch with Flood through phone calls and letters. Gibson even gave Flood the Cardinals uniform off his back that day. The two old friends ate dinner together at a St. Louis restaurant. Flood spent that weekend drunk but incredibly happy. It was a grand homecoming to St. Louis and a reminder of the happiest times of his life.

Flood returned from St. Louis euphoric. One afternoon before an A's game, he put on his Cardinals uniform. He lent Gibson's uniform to his 21-year-old radio producer, Larry Baer. Flood and Baer took the field; Flood took batting practice. Baer admired Flood's graciousness and warmth. He was fascinated by the players' reaction to Flood. A few thanked him for what he had done. But many players did not even know who he was. "A lot of people didn't know how to react to him," Baer said. "In a lot of ways, at least for the players, he was a conquering hero. The front office people were polite but not all that respectful."

Flood's return to baseball ended after less than a season of subpar color commentary with the A's. Bercovich lost out on his bid to buy the club from Finley and did not repurchase the radio rights the following season. The best thing about the loss of his radio gig was that it curtailed Flood's inebriated attempts to drive to and from the ballpark. He once lost his car in the stadium's parking lot. Another time, he was pulled over for driving 20 miles per hour in the fast lane of the freeway. The police officers asked for his autograph and sent him on his way without a ticket. After that incident, however, he avoided Oakland's many freeways and stuck to side streets.

Flood tried to earn some extra money in December 1978 by participating in the ABC *Superstars* competition in the Bahamas. There was a problem—he could neither run nor stay sober. Physically unable to compete against other ex-athletes, he dropped out of most of his events with the exception of bowling. In addition to his free trip to the Bahamas, he received the minimum $1,000 appearance fee.

While Flood was in the Bahamas, Pete Rose, the singles hitter often compared to Flood, signed a four-year contract with the Philadelphia Phillies for $800,000 a year. "I guess I thought that something like this might happen," Flood said. "But not to this extreme." Without his $300-a-week radio job, Flood sat in front of the television all day and all night drinking straight vodka. He even slept with the television on. He was afraid of the dark.

Flood's friends believed that he had sacrificed too much to challenge the reserve clause. Reporters frequently asked him, if he had it to do all over again, would he? He usually said yes. The private answer was no. Flood, Karen said, was "not that altruistic." If he had known that he would end up impoverished back in Oakland, he never would have done it. Flood's financial situation forced him to confront that reality. "[O]ver the past seven years I've not made that much money. I've been stripped of my security," he wrote in *Sport* magazine. "You always have a little selfish thing in the back of your mind which asks, 'Did I give up too much to do this?' I'll never know."

Some players acknowledged what he had done for them. Rod Carew, the California Angels' new first baseman in 1979, thanked Flood for his five-year, $4 million contract. "I wanted to bring Curt to my first press conference with the Angels and thank him publicly, but I couldn't find him," Carew said upon arriving at spring training. "The last I heard he was in Oakland, but nobody could find him for me. But sooner or later I'll find him, and when I do I'll thank him." Flood appreciated comments like Carew's. "All around the league last season people were expressing appreciation to me in the same vein, and I always answered, 'Hey, that's cool.' And I mean it." He insisted that he was not "bitter." Other times, Flood sensed a different tone in some people's voices when they realized that he was Curt Flood. "There's a negative undertone to it," he said. "People will nod recognition and say, 'Oh yeah, he's the guy who wanted to ruin baseball.'"

Carew's comments no doubt stemmed from the lessons of Marvin Miller. Joe Morgan said that Miller concluded every discussion with the players in spring training the same way: "Curt Flood got you these things." Miller understood the importance of educating the players about those who had made sacrifices for them.

Yet what Flood really needed from the union was a job. The NFL

Players Association hired Dave Meggyesy—the St. Louis Cardinals linebacker who had quit in 1970 because football was "dehumanizing"—to open its West Coast office in San Francisco. Miller could have done the same thing for Flood, whose pension kicked in no earlier than at age 45. Many baseball players either grew up in or lived in California. Players from both leagues played games in the Bay Area. The job, even a token position that paid him $20,000 a year, would have helped Flood regain his dignity and made him feel that he was still part of the game.

In April 1979, Flood voiced second thoughts about the players' skyrocketing salaries. "When I started my case," Flood said in an interview with *Newsweek*, "we tried to get the owners to agree to a middle ground, where players would have some rights. But now it's swung too far in the other direction." Maybe it was the alcohol talking. Flood's drinking problem, as much as the lingering bitterness from his lawsuit, probably kept him from finding a job in baseball. Before the 1980 season, he wrote Bill Veeck, Charlie Finley, George Steinbrenner, and recently fired Cardinals general manager Bing Devine. He received several nice replies. Veeck, who had repurchased the White Sox in 1975 after testifying against the owners at Flood's trial, wrote "that if anything comes up, I'd be first on his list." Veeck then hired Orlando Cepeda, a close friend of Flood's, recently released from prison after a drug conviction. "I think people in baseball are holding a grudge," Flood said. "It's a very sad and disappointing part of my life."

Flood's biggest disappointment was his strained relationships with his five children. By leaving for Denmark in 1970 and Spain in 1971, Flood had abandoned his children when they needed a father most. Curt Jr., who was 11 when his father left for Denmark, later experienced his own problems with alcohol. Flood felt like a failure as a father. He dreaded Thanksgiving and Christmas. Father's Day was a nightmare. He tried to reconnect with his children, who occasionally came to Oakland to visit him. Flood, however, did not have much to offer them. Alcohol was his escape.

Flood's consumption of straight vodka had begun to take its physical toll in the form of blackouts, hallucinations, and alcoholic seizures. He had to be hospitalized on two or three occasions but never seemed to remember his seizures. Finally, Karen turned on a small tape recorder during one of his seizures. She played it for him the next day. He was shocked to hear himself mumbling and talking in gibberish. He agreed that he needed help.

With Karen's help, he spent 30 days in alcohol rehabilitation in early 1980 at the Alta Bates Medical Center in Berkeley. He later refused to go to Alcoholics Anonymous for fear that people would recognize him, but after 30 days at Alta Bates, he sobered up. A lingering benefit from Flood's season of color commentary was the health insurance he received by joining the American Federation of Television and Radio Artists (AFTRA). Flood had been dropped from the Players Association's health plan after he stopped paying his premiums, but his AFTRA health insurance allowed him to take care of some chronic physical problems. When Andorran police had broken his left arm in 1975, doctors had inserted pins that were never removed. The pins had infected his arm, pushed through the skin, and left him in constant pain. Flood was finally able to get them taken out. He also received a new set of upper teeth.

Flood's sobriety landed him a different type of baseball job—as the commissioner of the youth baseball league for the Oakland Parks and Recreation Department. Bill Patterson, Flood's old friend who ran the De Fremery playground in West Oakland, helped him get the job, provided that he stay sober. Flood served as the first commissioner of the Youth America Baseball program for 3,000 Oakland boys and a few girls. "I'm the Bowie Flood," he said.

His job as youth baseball commissioner enabled him to be Curt Flood the baseball player again. With the city supplying only 60 percent of the league's funds, Flood solicited contributions from famous ballplayers. Joe Morgan donated $4,000 from an award. Reggie Jackson donated $2,000 in equipment. A's pitcher Mike Norris promised to donate $500 for each of his wins. Flood even affiliated himself with the Oakland A's special projects division, which agreed to contribute $30,000 over five years. He showed films of Rod Carew on hitting, Willie Horton on power hitting, and Darrell Johnson on coaching. Children looked up to him.

His new job revived his status as a local hero. The Bay Area Life Membership Committee of the NAACP honored him at a March 8,

1980, banquet before 900 people, including homegrown baseball stars Morgan and Willie Stargell. The Oakland Public Schools declared March 24–29, 1980, "Curt Flood Week." Students from McClymonds and Oakland Technical high schools presented him with a book of tributes and poems.

Flood's newfound sobriety and local celebrity also improved his home life. He helped around the house. He built shelves and decorated them with felt designs. He expertly carved a hiding space for valuables in the pages of a French cookbook. He took spare parts and constructed an Easter egg holder that turned the egg and made it easier to decorate. He liked to construct model airplanes. He drew cartoons. Although he might not have known how to paint portraits, he still possessed an artist's mind and a craftsman's touch.

Aside from his stray comments in *Newsweek*, Flood continued to stand up for his fellow ballplayers. As a potential baseball strike loomed that eventually halted the 1981 season, he predicted that the players would strike and stood behind them 100 percent. "If they backslide now, they'll take the 'free' out of free agent," he said. "Ballplayers got crapped on for a long, long time. It's very hard to say what's fair, but I think the players are now in a place where they're getting an equitable share. And what weapons do they have to keep that share, except a possible strike? How do you threaten a millionaire, with a gun? I also don't think the players should be responsible for keeping the owners honest among themselves."

The owners responded by keeping Flood out of baseball. Some of his longtime friends fared better. Bob Gibson, whose friend and former catcher Joe Torre was managing the New York Mets, landed a job as the Mets' assistant pitching coach. Bill White was broadcasting Yankees games. Flood yearned to join Gibson and White back in the game. His most prized possession, besides his World Series rings, was his leather-bound lifetime pass to any major league ballpark. "I lived for baseball," he said. "There was absolutely nothing to compare to the high I got playing."

Before the 1981 season, Gibson wrote Flood about his new job with the Mets but mostly to reminisce. "I'll never forget the years we spent together as teammates, roommates, and friends," Gibson wrote. Flood,

Gibson, and other black players of their generation never forgot their experiences in segregated southern minor league towns and spring training camps. Those Jim Crow experiences made them feel like outsiders for the rest of their careers. "I saw Bill White in New York at [former Yankees catcher] Elston's [Howard] wake. He's doing pretty well. I often think about the days we spent in the early years in St. Pete, Fla.," Gibson wrote. "Times have really changed. All for the better."

That segregation and discrimination turned Flood against the establishment. It turned him into a fighter. And despite losing the biggest battle of his life, he kept fighting—even if it kept him out of baseball.

Flood began to show signs of losing his daily battle with alcoholism. In January, he flew to New York to be honored as the Cutty Sark Leader of 1982. The scotch maker ran a full-page color advertisement later that year in national magazines. "Some people think you can't beat the system," the headline said. "Here's to those who show the way." Next to a silhouetted photograph of Flood, the advertisement told the story of his lawsuit "that opened doors for every baseball player in America." "So today, a lot of people salute Curt Flood," the ad copy concluded. "Including those who make his favorite Scotch, Cutty Sark." Flood rationalized the advertisement based on the dubious distinction that the ad did not say he drank scotch, only that Cutty Sark was his "favorite." Cutty Sark donated money to Oakland's Little League program and paid Flood for the promotional campaign. Karen knew that Curt was in trouble when he arrived home in January with a case of liquor.

In August 1982, he attended the Baseball Hall of Fame's induction ceremony honoring his former McClymonds High School teammate Frank Robinson. During his playing career, Robinson refused to speak out on racial and social issues. He reacted to Flood's lawsuit with silence. In October 1974, the Cleveland Indians named him baseball's first black manager. After the Indians fired him in 1977, Robinson could not find a job. Flood had fought for Robinson. Picking up the cause championed by Jackie Robinson nine days before his death, Flood spoke out in March 1980 about the "lack of blacks in management." "It is time for the Hank Aarons to speak out about the injustice that has Frank Robinson unable to find a job," Flood said. "That's tragic. Racism is not an undocumented rumor in baseball. It is a malady that permeates our national pastime." The next season, Robinson became the first black manager to be rehired—returning to the Bay Area in 1981 to manage the San Francisco Giants. A few weeks before his Hall of Fame induction, he and Giants second baseman Joe Morgan put on a clinic for Flood's Little Leaguers.

Flood and Robinson were not particularly close, but Flood paid his own way to Robinson's Cooperstown induction ceremony. He wanted to see and be seen. He sat about 100 feet away from the podium in the back of the reserved seating section. Robinson took time out from his speech to acknowledge him. "If Curt Flood is in the audience, please stand up—Curt," Robinson said. Curt stood up to applause. "He wasn't a bad baseball player either . . . ," Robinson said. "I think Curt was the first ballplayer to really make a sacrifice toward free agency, and I don't think he has ever gotten the thanks he so richly deserves for doing that for today's players. I can't say that, Curt, because they don't have free agents for managers." Robinson's last line was a joke, but he still did not get it. Robinson stayed in the game by keeping his mouth shut; Flood was ostracized from it for speaking out.

As soon as he turned 45 in January 1983, Flood took his $2,500-a-month pension and left Karen. It was no way to repay her for years of financial and emotional support. He left with his sobriety and future in question, still searching for happiness, a fresh start, and a job in baseball.

CHAPTER EIGHTEEN

During the mid-1980s, Curt Flood made a comeback—in life—after reconnecting in Los Angeles with his old girlfriend, Judy Pace. Pace's career as an actress had peaked in the late 1960s and early 1970s. Aside from her roles on television's *Peyton Place* and *Brian's Song*, she received positive reviews in Ossie Davis's film *Cotton Comes to Harlem* (1970), and costarred with Jim Brown in *The Slams* (1973). She made a few guest appearances during the 1970s on television shows including *Sanford and Son*, *That's My Mama*, *Good Times*, and *What's Happening!!* Divorced from actor Don Mitchell in 1986, she spent most of her time raising her two daughters.

A friend of Flood's, sportswriter Stu Black, contacted Pace in 1985 about a screenplay he was writing for a proposed movie about Flood's life. Before speaking to Black, however, Pace wanted to talk to Flood. Flood flew to Los Angeles to see her on the way to a San Diego baseball card show. They agreed to meet at a hotel near LAX for lunch. It was the first time they had seen each other in 15 years. Lunch lasted more than five hours. Flood took the last flight out that night to San Diego. The movie plans never materialized, but Curt's relationship with Judy took off. On December 28, 1986, more than 20 years after they had first met, they were married in Las Vegas. "I wasn't going to let her get away again," he said.

Judy helped Curt become a whole person again. In February 1986, he moved into her home in the Baldwin Hills section of Los Angeles. He quit drinking for good (with a public push from Howard Cosell in a July 1986 *San Francisco Chronicle* column). He received a second chance at fatherhood with Judy's two daughters, Shawn and Julia, both of whom went on to graduate from Howard University. Living in Los Angeles also allowed Flood to repair his relationships with his five children from his previous marriage. Curt Jr., who bears a strong resemblance to his father, treasured those days.

Finally at peace, Flood rejected the attempts of writers to turn him into a martyr. "Don't make my life out to be a Greek tragedy," he said. "I live on top of a hill. I'm married to a movie star. I have a wonderful life—though the owners would like me to have a tin cup somewhere." He had grown philosophical about his lawsuit—what he referred to as "the central fact of my life." "I did it because I believed in the American dream," he said. "I believed that if you were right, the nine smart men on the Supreme Court would say that."

He still seethed about the Court's decision after reading about the behind-the-scenes vote switching in *The Brethren*. "I certainly hope that great issues of our time were handled better than that one was," he said. He still believed that his case was not "decided on the merits" but on "jealousy" and "prejudice": "The good old boys got together and decided that this little black kid wasn't going to change the great American game."

From his legal defeat, Flood emerged with a spiritual victory. "I have never felt I gave up too much," he said. "All the things that I got from it, they're intangibles. They're all inside of me. Yes, I sacrificed a lot—the money, maybe even the Hall of Fame—and you weigh that against all the things that are really and truly important that are deep inside you, and I think I succeeded."

The only aspect of his lawsuit that bothered Flood was the lack of support from his fellow players. "I am bitter now because I know in retrospect that we lost because my guys, my colleagues didn't stand up with me," he told filmmaker Ken Burns. "If superstars had stood up and said 'We're with Curt Flood,' if the superstars had walked into the courtroom in New York and made their presence known . . . had we shown any amount of solidarity, I think the owners would have gotten the message very clearly and given me a chance to win that." But as a rededicated family man, he understood why Hank Aaron, Ernie Banks, Willie Mays, and Frank Robinson had not rushed to his defense at the time of his lawsuit. They were afraid of being "guilty by association" and needed their jobs in baseball to support their families.

A job in baseball continued to elude Flood. Cosell wrote in July 1986 that the union should give Flood a job. The union was Flood's only hope. As Bob Gibson said, management still viewed Flood "as a traitor." By this time, Marvin Miller had handed over the reins to Don Fehr. Fehr was too young to have worked on Flood's lawsuit and did not know Flood well, but the new union boss must have been aware of Flood's desire to return to the game.

Flood voiced support for the players during the strikes in 1981 and 1994. "One of the reasons I can't get a job in baseball is I can't keep my mouth shut," he said. He carried on Jackie Robinson's fight for more blacks in management positions—not to find Frank Robinson a job or to lobby for his own, but because of the injustice of it all. In February 1986, he pointed out to the *Sporting News* that "we've only had two black managers. There are none in the front office except for Henry Aaron in Atlanta."

An incident at the beginning of the 1987 season finally gave potential black coaches and executives hope. Al Campanis, a Dodgers executive and a former minor league teammate of Jackie Robinson's, unintentionally helped their cause during an April interview on ABC's *Nightline* on the 40th anniversary of Robinson's first major league season. Blacks, Campanis suggested, "may not have some of the necessities to be" field managers or general managers. Campanis revealed on national television what baseball people had been doing for years: excluding blacks from the hiring process.

Baseball went into damage-control mode. Commissioner Peter Ueberroth hired black sociologist Dr. Harry Edwards and the consulting firm of former secretary of the army Clifford Alexander and Janet Hill (the wife of former NFL running back Calvin and mother of future NBA star Grant) to study the problem, prompting Jesse Jackson to call off a black boycott of major league stadiums scheduled for July 4.

Black former major leaguers, however, felt excluded from the process run by nonbaseball people. Flood was among a group of players who met with Ueberroth and Edwards during the All-Star break, but Flood still could not find a baseball job. "I had written to four or five different clubs with the intent of finding nothing more than a token job," he said. "I only got a response from one of them, and this was 'A.C.'—after Campanis. Honestly, I don't know what their problem is."

In November 1987, Flood and 60 black former players met for three days in Irving, Texas, to discuss their common experiences and to form their own organization, known as the Baseball Network. "Forty years after the debut of Jackie Robinson, bitterness is not what I am," Flood told the *Baltimore Sun*'s Mark Hyman. "But I am a little embarrassed we have not gone further." When asked what kind of job he wanted in baseball, Flood replied that he wanted to be an owner. He believed in the Baseball Network and designed a piece of jewelry in an effort to raise money for the organization. With former scout Ben Moore as executive director, the former players elected five men to a board of directors: Frank Robinson, Ray Burris, Jim "Mudcat" Grant, Willie Stargell, and Flood. Flood was named the board's president, probably because he had nothing left to lose with management.

Flood came close to landing a major league job with his old team, the St. Louis Cardinals. In 1985, the Cardinals had made Flood's former teammate, shortstop Dal Maxvill, the team's general manager. Three years later, Maxvill needed a director of player development. This was not the "token position" that Flood had been seeking, but one of the most integral positions in a team's minor league system. Flood nonetheless applied for the job.

Maxvill flew out to Los Angeles to interview Flood. Maxvill remembered Flood as an outstanding defensive center fielder, a hitter who sacrificed his at-bats to advance leadoff man Lou Brock, a smart ballplayer who squeezed the most out of his 5-foot-9, 165-pound frame, and a great teammate who rooted for his fellow players. During the interview, Flood asked Maxvill a series of questions: Do I know the game? Do I get along with people? Do you think I can do the job? Maxvill found himself answering yes each time. Maxvill was not sentimental about former teammates, having declined to allow Gibson to manage the Cardinals' Triple-A team in Gibson's hometown of Omaha. But, as a former player representative, Maxvill understood the sacrifices that Flood had made for his fellow players. He wanted to hire Flood. Maxvill explained that the position required lots of travel and someone willing to live in St. Louis. Flood wanted to stay in Los Angeles. In June 1988, Maxvill ended up hiring future major league manager Jim Riggleman as director of player development. Neither Maxvill nor any other major league executive ever offered Flood the "token position" he desired. Instead, Flood found jobs and recognition outside the baseball establishment.

Judy helped burnish Curt's public image. For years, she had worked actively for black causes. Along with other black actresses, she helped organize the Kwanzaa Foundation in 1973 to raise scholarship money for black students. She also participated in the efforts of the Beverly Hills–Hollywood NAACP chapter to fight for the inclusion of black actors in the entertainment industry. She volunteered on Jesse Jackson's 1988 presidential campaign. Judy's activism may have led to the NAACP's belated recognition of Flood's fight for freedom. At the NAACP's Image Awards in December 1987, Flood received the first Jackie Robinson Sports Award. Actor George C. Scott presented him with the honor. That same year, Flood was honored in San Francisco by the Instituto Laboral de la Raza in conjunction with the Latino Labor Day festivities. The AFL-CIO named an award after him. Two years later, the city of Oakland dedicated the Curt Flood Park and Sports Complex.

Players, old and new, found their own ways to recognize Flood. Before a 1984 old-timers game at Busch Stadium, relief pitcher Bruce Sutter found Flood and said, "Thanks for all of us." After the 1984 season, Sutter signed a six-year contract with the Atlanta Braves worth nearly $10 million. Five years later during an old-timers game at Fenway Park, opposing pitcher Bill "Spaceman" Lee showed his appreciation by serving up a fat pitch. "I thought, 'Here was the one guy who did as much for baseball as anyone else,' so I just said, 'Here, hit it,'" Lee said. Flood hit a home run.

These were happy times for Flood. He worked at Randy Hundley's fantasy camps, played in old-timers games, and signed autographs at card shows and All-Star Game fan festivals. He drew sports cartoons that he wanted to publish and claimed to be writing a sequel to *The Way It Is*. He also started the Curt Flood Youth Foundation, a nonprofit organization that helped underprivileged youngsters in foster care, with HIV, or simply in need of sports equipment. He invited former major leaguers Ernie Banks and Tommy Davis to serve on the foundation's board.

Flood never forgot where he had come from or who had helped him along the way. In October 1987, his beloved American Legion coach, George Powles, died of a heart attack at age 77. Flood was the only former major leaguer to attend the memorial service. He surprised his coach's family by asking to speak. He related how no one ever gave Powles any trouble when he drove in and out of the ghetto to teach and coach at McClymonds because "he was part of the family." He remembered the hours Powles had spent hitting him ground balls in the school's gymnasium. "I didn't appreciate it until three World Series later all of the things he ingrained in me as a youngster," Flood told the audience. "His legacy will live on. It will live on with me in my heart." Just six years earlier, Flood had been too drunk and destitute to attend Powles's induction into the California Coaches' Hall of Fame in Anaheim. Karen had been forced to send a telegram in his name to the banquet hotel. Flood's heartfelt eulogy showed how far he had come.

In 1989, Flood was named commissioner of the new Senior Professional Baseball Association (SPBA). An eight-team league originally based around Florida's spring training ballparks, the SPBA was supposed to be baseball's version of the senior golf tour for players 35 and over (and catchers over 32). Earl Weaver and Dick Williams managed; Bobby Bonds, Rollie Fingers, Graig Nettles, Tony Perez, and Luis Tiant played.

The person who had recommended Flood as the SPBA's commissioner was Joe Garagiola. Garagiola apologized to Miller for his "terrible mistake" in testifying against Flood. Years later, Garagiola publicly confessed his sins. "I thought if the reserve clause went, baseball was going," he said. "I was so wrong, I can't begin to tell you. It took a lot of guts to do what he did."

Flood's job as SPBA commissioner inspired an old friend to show up at the league's opening press conference at Gallagher's Steak House in New York City—Howard Cosell. After the press conference, Cosell ate lunch with Curt, Judy, Dick Williams, and league founder Jim Morley. Cosell regaled the table with stories about Flood. He said Bowie Kuhn lacked "the balls" to stand behind Flood and make him a free agent.

Flood's senior league commissionership was mostly ambassadorial. The league owners rented him a Miami apartment from September to February and paid him a $60,000 salary. He signed autographs for fans. At Opening Day in Pompano Beach, he ushered Mickey Mantle to the mound to throw out the first ball. He deferred to Major League Baseball commissioner A. Bartlett Giamatti on any major controversies, such as the then-uncertain status of Pete Rose. The senior league struggled to survive beyond that first season. As a cost-cutting measure, the owners decided not to renew Flood's contract, though he received another $60,000 to $65,000 in severance pay. The league limped along for one more season. Some people speculated that Flood's presence hurt the SPBA's standing with Major League Baseball.

Flood never fell out of favor with Marvin Miller. In June 1991, Miller published *A Whole Different Ball Game*, a caustic retort to Kuhn's autobiography. If history is written by the victors, then Miller deserved to tell his version of the players' repeated victories over the owners. Thanks to Miller, baseball players have the strongest union in professional sports. Don Fehr honored Miller that summer by inviting former players to New York for a book party at Mickey Mantle's restaurant. Curt and Judy flew in for the event. They ate breakfast before the party with Marvin; Marvin's wife, Terry; baseball guru Bill James, who had written the introduction to Miller's book; and former union general counsel Dick Moss. After the party, Curt and Judy joined the Millers for dinner. Miller's admiration for Flood ran deep. The two men saw each other for the last time in Colorado Springs in 1992, when Miller accepted an award from the Major League Baseball Players Alumni Association, but they stayed in frequent contact.

Reunited with Moss at Miller's book party, Flood was invited to join an even bigger threat to the baseball establishment than another antitrust lawsuit: a rival league. An August 12 strike and subsequent lockout aborted the 1994 baseball season and canceled the World Series. Baseball's antitrust exemption once again came under attack in Congress. Criticism over the Supreme Court's decision in Flood's lawsuit reached a fever pitch. Even Justice Blackmun began to question the wisdom of his decision. "It may be that had the baseball case gone the other way, in the long run, it would have been just as well, if not better," Blackmun said in April 1995. "But it wouldn't surprise me if baseball were to lose its antitrust exemption."

Rather than try to avenge past legal defeats, Moss, Smith College economics professor Andrew Zimbalist, former representative Bob Mrazek (D-NY), and Representative John Bryant (D-TX) decided to mount an on-field challenge to Major League Baseball—the United Baseball League. They wanted to create a competitive market for the players' services. They promised to field 10 teams in 1996 and named Flood a stockholder and vice president.

On December 6, Flood and Moss met in Atlanta with 80 striking players, including future Hall of Famers Paul Molitor, Eddie Murray, and Kirby Puckett, and other stars including Frank Thomas, Fred McGriff, Orel Hershiser, and David Cone. Moss discussed the proposed league. Flood, wearing large wire-rimmed glasses, balding, about 20 pounds heavier than in his playing days, was unprepared for his reception. The players gave him a standing ovation. He got so choked up that he almost forgot what he was going to say. Silence filled the room as he told the players about his fight against the reserve clause. It had been nearly 25 years since he addressed the player representatives in Puerto Rico. He gave the current group of players lasting advice about dealing with the owners regarding free agency: "Don't let them put the genie back in the bottle." Don Fehr did not think enough of Flood to give him a job with the union but welcomed him as a unifying force during the strike. "Curt Flood remains an extraordinarily powerful symbol even to the players of this generation, many of whom have never seen him before," Fehr said. "The players talked to him and shook his hand, and I suspect they will remember it for some time."

Flood wrote a first-person account of his reasons for backing the new league in the April 1995 issue of *Sport* magazine:

> I'm entering into this venture with goodwill and without malice toward the established leagues. There is no animosity or revenge on my behalf resulting from my 1969 [*sic*] Supreme Court case. However, I must say this: Major league baseball owners have enjoyed unchallenged supremacy for 80 years. In recent memory, despite strong and resilient fan support, the baseball business has been ruptured by [a] succession of destructive crises, culminating in the most recent strike.

Major League Baseball returned in 1995; the United Baseball League never came to fruition.

Ken Burns's nine-part *Baseball* documentary in 1994 reminded fans of Flood's continued significance. With questions prompted by Judy, Burns interviewed Flood at length and made him one of the documentary's featured commentators. Flood discussed the influence of Jackie Robinson, the civil rights movement, the opposition to the Vietnam War, and the assassinations of the Kennedys and Martin Luther King on his decision to sue baseball.

At the documentary's premiere in Washington, D.C., Curt and Judy toured the White House and met President and Mrs. Clinton. The premiere also reunited Flood with other former players interviewed for the project. Tim McCarver watched Flood glide down the red carpet in a sharp-looking suit. McCarver teased his former Cardinals co-captain that he looked regal. "I am in the process of living happily ever after," Flood confessed in a three-page Christmas letter in 1994 to friends and family.

The fairy-tale ending came to an abrupt halt in Flood's Arlington, Texas, hotel room at the 1995 All-Star Game. He fainted and blamed it on the heat. He consulted an ear, nose, and throat doctor about what he thought was a sinus infection. He soon "sounded like Louis Armstrong." At that point, doctors discovered a lump in his throat—throat cancer. They initially gave him a 90 to 95 percent chance of recovery. He had quit smoking in 1979 and drinking in 1986. Over the next year, he underwent chemotherapy, radiation treatment, and operations on nodes on both sides of his throat.

Word leaked out about Flood's illness in October 1995 when he missed the funeral of his good friend Vada Pinson. Pinson was not found for three days after suffering a stroke. Flood still had a message from him on his answering machine. Eight months earlier, Pinson had driven all the way from South Florida to San Francisco to present Flood for induction into the Bay Area Sports Hall of Fame. Flood could not attend Pinson's funeral because of a radiation treatment but made good on his promise to present Pinson for induction a year later.

The Players Association quietly helped Flood with his medical bills. Having been dropped from the players' health plan years earlier, Flood did not have adequate insurance to pay for his cancer treatments. The union dipped into its own coffers to pay about $400,000 of his health care costs. The Baseball Assistance Team (BAT), an organization created to help ex-ballplayers in need and spearheaded by Joe Garagiola, also supported Flood and his family.

The chemotherapy, radiation treatment, and multiple throat operations eventually robbed Flood of his ability to speak. But Bill White made sure that Flood could still be heard. The former Yankees broadcaster had ascended to National League president in 1989, making him baseball's highest-ranking black official. Aside from Gibson, White was Flood's closest former teammate. In 1993, Rawlings discovered that Flood had never received his 1969 Gold Glove Award because he had sat out the following season. White presented the award to Flood at a black-tie event in New York City. After Flood could no longer speak, White arranged for the purchase of a special computer that voiced Flood's typewritten thoughts. White kept his contribution quiet, just as he had downplayed his role in integrating spring training camps in Florida.

Marvin Miller frequently called Flood's home. Like most people, Miller spoke with Judy as Curt typed on his computer or wrote down what he wanted Judy to say. He communicated the same way with filmmaker Spike Lee, whose 15-minute segment on Curt for HBO's *Real Sports* featured Judy reading from Curt's journal and interviews with ballplayers from his era. Flood wanted Lee to make a feature-length film about his life.

Flood did not want anyone's pity. At the end, he instructed Judy not to allow any weepy visitors into his room at UCLA Medical Center. He wanted to enjoy the time he had left. In his one-page Christmas letter to family and friends in 1996, he acknowledged "mixed feelings of joy and sadness" but quoted advice that his late mother, Laura, who had died three years earlier, used to give him: "Start counting your blessings, Squirtis, by the time you finished, you won't have time for anything else!" Flood's iron will and indomitable spirit came from his mother. Even near death, he sounded like a survivor: "Say this: 'Curt accomplished every goal that he set for himself, and simply moved on.'"

Curt Flood passed away on January 20, 1997—Martin Luther King Day. Two days earlier, he had turned 59. He died a proud and happy man.

At his memorial service a week later at First African Methodist

Episcopal Church in downtown Los Angeles, 300 people paid tribute to Flood in what the program called "Curt's 9th Inning." He received two standing ovations. Oscar Brown Jr. sang an original work about his departed friend. President Clinton sent a telegram that was read at the funeral service. Nine baseball people spoke.

One of the toughest and proudest men ever to step on a pitcher's mound struggled with his emotions that day.

"My name is Bob Gibson," he said. "This is not easy.

"I think I knew Curt as well as anyone. We were roommates for ten years, and I knew him for 40 years. And in those 40 years, I could never remember being unhappy or having a mean thought about him. And that's unusual for me. . . . Curt had a way of bringing you back to reality when you got a little too high. When you were down and didn't think anything could be funny, he could make you smile. . . .

"I've been sad for a while, but I'll get over it," Gibson concluded. "When I do, my next thoughts about Curt Flood won't make me sad; they'll make me smile."

Conservative columnist and baseball author George Will also spoke that day. In November 1993, Will had written a glowing *Washington Post* column about Flood. Flood never forgot it and made sure that Will spoke at his funeral. In his eulogy, Will compared Flood to Rosa Parks. He criticized the Supreme Court's decision in Flood's case and analogized it to the infamous 1857 *Dred Scott* decision denying the freedom of a St. Louis slave who had escaped north on a train. "It was one of those rare occurrences," Will recalled, "where George Will and Jesse Jackson were sharing the same podium."

Nearly 25 years after he had eulogized Jackie Robinson, the Reverend Jesse Jackson delivered a spine-tingling eulogy about Flood. Jackson's voice rose as he closed his notes, nodded his head, and concluded: "Don't cry for long, Curt is the winner. The courts lost. Curt won. Baseball is better. And people are better. America is better. Because God sent an instrument his way. Let him rest. Fought the good fight. Finish his race. He kept the faith. Thank God that Curt Flood came this way. We love you, Curt. You are a winner."

Jackson called for Flood to go into the Baseball Hall of Fame. Flood's 1,861 hits, .293 lifetime batting average, seven Gold Gloves, and three All-Star Game appearances alone do not warrant his inclusion, but several sportswriters, including the late Leonard Koppett, have advocated Flood's candidacy based on his status as one of the game's pioneers. Larry Doby, the American League's first black player, was inducted in 1998 in part on this basis. In his final year on the baseball writers' ballot in 1996, Flood received 71 votes, his highest vote total. One of 25 players on the Veterans Committee's 2005 ballot, he received only 10 (out of 80) votes. "You would think that every Hall of Famer who had made millions as a free agent, courtesy of Flood's lawsuit, would have voted for Flood," wrote *New York Times* columnist Dave Anderson. The Hall of Fame, however, is a conservative institution. Bowie Kuhn has been on its board of directors since 1969, and Marvin Miller, whose impact on the game outstrips that of every baseball executive except Judge Landis and Branch Rickey, has still not been inducted. Flood's chances of election by the Veterans Committee remain slim indeed.

Jackson also called for the Players Association to create a Curt Flood Courage Award, and he called on the players who benefited from Flood's lawsuit to endow it. That seems as unlikely as his Hall of Fame induction.

Many former players attended Flood's funeral. Joe Black, Orlando Cepeda, Bob Gibson, Earl Robinson, Bill White, and Maury Wills served as pallbearers; Lou Brock, Lou Johnson, John Roseboro, and Don Newcombe served as honorary pallbearers. Both Black and Newcombe had carried Jackie Robinson's coffin 25 years earlier. Many other former players dotted the audience, including Don Baylor, Doug DeCinces, Al Downing, Tito Fuentes, Steve Garvey, Lee Maye, and Joe Morgan.

Not a single active player attended Flood's funeral. Union reps David Cone and Tom Glavine issued a prepared statement, and Cone gushed about Flood to at least one New York sports columnist. It was the end of January. Cone, Glavine, and other active players, many of whom lived in Southern California, did not have anywhere to be that day. They seemed to have forgotten all about Flood since his 1994 speech in Atlanta. The absence of active players was a sign that the union leadership had stopped educating its members.

Congress, the institution that had done nothing to correct the Supreme Court's baseball decisions, finally came to Flood's aid. Representative John Conyers (D-MI), who had read President Clinton's telegram at Flood's funeral, introduced H.R. 21—in honor of Flood's number—removing baseball's antitrust exemption as it related to labor issues. Senator Orrin Hatch (R-UT) introduced a similar bill in the Senate. Wanting to send a message after the 1994 baseball strike, Congress passed the legislation as the Curt Flood Act of 1998. President Clinton signed it into law. The owners agreed to relinquish a small piece of their exemption—allowing major league players to file antitrust lawsuits about labor issues—because the legislation lacked any teeth. The Supreme Court had ruled in a 1996 case involving the NFL that labor unions and their members could not sue under the antitrust laws because of the labor exemption. The Players Association, therefore, would have to decertify as a union for a major league player to sue under the Curt Flood Act. Baseball's antitrust exemption, for all intents and purposes, remained unscathed. Congress gave Flood a posthumous but hollow victory.

Curt Flood's legacy has nothing to do with congressional legislation or Supreme Court precedents but with starting the fight for free agency in baseball. "Baseball didn't change Curt Flood," Jesse Jackson said during his eulogy. "Curt Flood changed baseball." He changed all professional sports. Flood's lawsuit sounded the alarm about the players' lack of economic freedom. Curt may not have won a single player free agency, but he exposed baseball's system of perpetual player-ownership as exploitative and un-American. He helped usher in a new era that allowed the players to exercise greater control over their careers and to share in the owners' economic prosperity.

Free agency, despite the yearnings of some sentimentalists, has been good for baseball. Competitive balance has improved. The Yankees, Cardinals, or Dodgers do not win the pennant every year. Nine different teams won the World Series during the 1980s, six different teams won during the 1990s (with no winner in 1994), and six different teams won from 2000 to 2005. Attendance has increased dramatically. Television revenue has soared. Free-agent signings have only heightened fan interest during the winter months. Players shift teams no more now than they did before free agency. The difference is that the players of today do not always change teams because they have to, but because they want to.

Flood cannot be blamed for the real source of the average fan's discontent: the players' skyrocketing salaries. The average major league salary has increased from $29,303 in 1970 to $371,571 in 1985 to $2,632,655 in 2005. The largest free-agent contract of 25 years ago,

Dave Winfield's 10-year deal eventually worth $18 million, pales in comparison to Alex Rodriguez's 10-year, $252 million contract. Flood, however, would have applauded Rodriguez's riches. He understood that the players' salaries are the outgrowth of America's obsession with celebrity and entertainment. "Sylvester Stallone got $30 million for *Rocky II*. He said 30 words you could understand in the whole movie. Nobody seems to mind that," Flood said in 1989. "But does Sylvester Stallone do more relevant things than Roger Clemens? Isn't baseball show business?" Flood also recognized that the owners have no more right to the almighty entertainment dollar in sports than the players. "If the owners put a cap on their own salaries, then we'll agree to put a cap on our salaries," Flood said before the 1994 strike. "If George Steinbrenner—particularly George Steinbrenner—has a cap, then we'll all have a cap." After more than three decades of fighting free agency tooth and nail, the owners finally seem to be at peace with paying the players what they are worth. The owners' only lingering issue is how to divide baseball's enormous revenues among themselves.

Curt Flood's lawsuit was about an idea much more basic in our society than free agency in baseball—it was about the freedom to choose where to work. He helped destroy the myth of employer or employee loyalty. The boss will reassign you, fire you, or lay you off in a heartbeat if it will help the bottom line. The days when people worked for the same company or even in the same occupation for their entire lives are long gone. People are always on the lookout for a better job or a better deal. "We may not want to admit it, but there's a little Curt Flood in all of us," *Houston Chronicle* business columnist Loren Steffy wrote during the 2005 World Series. "If baseball is an analogy for life, then we have become a society of free agents."

Flood was willing to sacrifice his playing career, his earning power, and his future in the game, all for a lawsuit that he knew was going to benefit only future generations of professional athletes, because freedom meant more to him than money or fame. Segregation and discrimination imbued Flood and other black athletes of his generation with a heightened sensitivity to injustice. As Flood often said, he came of age during the civil rights movement. The money in professional sports at the time was not so great as to prevent him from standing up for his principles.

His life and lawsuit amounted to more than collecting a paycheck; they were about personal freedom. "What about freedom makes us march and picket and sometimes die?" Flood said in 1980. "It is the right to choose. To me, freedom means simply I belong to me."

Flood paid a terrible price for taking on the establishment and served as a cautionary tale for the modern professional athletes whom he helped enrich. Michael Jordan, Derek Jeter, and LeBron James could never have obtained their multimillion-dollar salaries and endorsement deals without the right to sell their services to the highest bidders. Yet they depend so much on corporate America that political or social activism would be career suicide. Speaking out is not part of the equation. As Jordan reportedly told a friend who asked him to campaign in his home state of North Carolina against Republican senator Jesse Helms, "Republicans buy shoes, too."

Jackie Robinson, a black man who often voted Republican, started it all. Of everything Flood had accomplished in baseball, nothing gave him more joy than standing on first base at Ebbets Field on September 16, 1956, two bases away from his hero, appearing at a 1962 NAACP rally with him in Mississippi, and watching Robinson testify on his behalf at his trial. It pained Flood that many modern players had no idea who Robinson was.

Even fewer of today's athletes know the name Curt Flood. *Sport* magazine asked 10 major leaguers in 1994 about what Curt Flood meant to them; only a few recognized his name. If Yankees manager Joe Torre senses his players' taking the game for granted, he tells them about Flood. "I just want players to understand the reason that they're doing pretty well and they have a lot of rights and that's because of what Curt Flood gave up," Torre said. Outspoken former NBA star Charles Barkley has tried to make Flood's name resonate with the next generation of professional athletes. "How can anybody drawing a paycheck in sports today not know about Curt Flood?" Barkley wrote. "How did his contributions get so overlooked? Athletes had no say in where they played until Curt Flood stood up and refused to be traded." In 1999, *Time* magazine named Flood "one of the ten most influential athletes of the century."

Robinson and Flood took professional athletes on an incredible journey—from racial desegregation to well-paid slavery to being free and extremely well paid. Robinson started the revolution by putting on a uniform. Flood finished it by taking his uniform off. Robinson fought for racial justice. Flood fought the less-sympathetic fight for economic justice. They never stopped fighting for freedom. The struggle took years off their lives. Neither man lived into his 60s. Curt Flood dedicated his life to making Jackie Robinson proud.

ACKNOWLEDGMENTS

Some people thought I was crazy when I quit my job practicing law at a prominent Washington, D.C., firm to write this book. I had no book deal and no agent. A lawyer advised me that I would be labeled a dilettante. My friends teased me that I needed to get a real job. Maybe they were both right, but I have never regretted my decision to write full-time and to tell the story of Curt Flood and his lawsuit.

My acknowledgments may seem longer and more tedious than Justice Blackmun's list of baseball greats in his *Flood v. Kuhn* opinion, but many people deserve credit for helping me with this project. All the book's errors and omissions are entirely my own.

I am indebted to all the people who agreed to be interviewed for this book. Almost all of the interviewees are listed in my bibliography, but a few people (usually former Supreme Court law clerks) did not want their names mentioned. I learned so much from all of you and appreciate your time, insights, and patience. Some people have put up with multiple interviews, phone calls, and e-mails. In this regard, Sam Bercovich, Herman Flood, Lou Hoynes, Marvin Miller, Iola "Rickie" Riley, Jay Topkis, and Allan Zerman deserve special mention. I am also grateful to Judy Pace Flood for agreeing to speak with me despite her desire to write a book about her late husband.

Equally important are people whose names do not show up in either the text or bibliography but who facilitated many of my interviews and research requests.

The following people helped me from Major League Baseball: Rick Cerrone and Stephanie Hall of the New York Yankees, John Dever and

Lars Thorn of the Washington Nationals, Lorrie Platt of the Cincinnati Reds, Greg Rhodes of the Cincinnati Reds Museum, Larry Shenk of the Philadelphia Phillies, Bill Stetka of the Baltimore Orioles, Melody Yount and Mark Murray of the St. Louis Cardinals, and Larry Baer of the San Francisco Giants.

Many others in academia, law, journalism, and government also helped me with source material. The following people provided me with documents, unpublished manuscripts, phone numbers of sources, access to newspaper archives, videotapes, or simply their professional expertise: Bruce Adelson, Perry Apelbaum, Joel Boyd, Ken Burns, Joe Camacho, Lou Charlip, Greg Chernack, Stacey Dansky, Ross Davies, Roscoe Dellums, Gerald Early, Ezra Edelman, John Erardi, Chet Fenster, Ron Fimrite, Janet Frankston, Bill Gallo, David Garrow, Abbe Gluck, Jerry Goldman, Peter Golenbock, Teddy Greenstein, Tom Holster, Rick Hummel, Dennis Hutchinson, Roger "Mud" Kaplan, Bob Kheel, Barry Klein, Chuck Korr, David Lipman, John Lowe, Brent McIntosh, Dave McKenna, David Maraniss, Bill Mead, Leigh Montville, Craig Mortali, Dave Newhouse, Erika Peterman, Gary Poole, Josh Prager, Marty Price, Arnold Rampersad, Bob Ridlon, Bob Rose, Mike Rosenberg, Tom Shakow, Eric Shumsley, Harold Spaeth, Susanna Steisel, Joe Strauss, Michael Sundermeyer, John Thorn, Jack Vardaman, Peter Wallsten, Matt Waxman, George Will (and his assistant Sarah Moeschler), Phil Wood, and Richard Zamoff.

A special thanks to David Hardy, Richard Huff, Wanda Hunt, and Priscilla Jones of the Office of Information and Privacy at the Federal Bureau of Investigation; and Charlotte Duckett, Margaret Grafield, Lori Hartmann, Francis Terry McNamara, and Katrina Wood of the Office of Information Programs and Services at the State Department.

Archivists and librarians around the country tracked down articles and documents for me and guided me to research collections I never would have found without their assistance. In that regard, I'd like to thank the following people and institutions: Jeff Flannery, Ernie Emrich, Patrick Kerwin, Joseph Jackson, and Michael Spangler at the Library of Congress Manuscript Division; the law library and newspaper and microfilm staffs at the Library of Congress; Shannon Boyd, Bonita Carter, Shirley Ito, Michael Salmon, and Wayne Wilson at the Amateur

Athletic Foundation of Los Angeles library; Steve Gietschier of the *Sporting News*; Gabriel Schechter at the National Baseball Hall of Fame Library; John Esquivel at the *Alameda Times-Star*; Alice Wertheim at the *Atlanta Journal-Constitution*; Paul McCardell and Jean Packard at the *Baltimore Sun*; Deborah Bade at the *Chicago Tribune*; Michael Panzer at the *Philadelphia Inquirer* and *Daily News*; Matthew Fernandez at the *St. Louis Post-Dispatch*; Charles Brown at the St. Louis Mercantile Library; John Martin at the *St. Petersburg Times*; Judy Canter at the *San Francisco Chronicle*; the staff at the King Center; Laura Harmon at the LBJ Library; John Jacob of the Lewis F. Powell Jr. Archives at Washington & Lee University School of Law; Steve Lavoie of the Oakland Public Library; Robert Ellis, Greg Plunges, Marvin Russell, Steve Tilly, and John Vernon at the National Archives; Bill Marshall and Jeff Suchanek at the University of Kentucky; Steve Kinsey at Morgan State University library; Marge McNinch at the Hagley Museum & Library; Diane Kaplan and her staff at the Yale University Manuscript & Archives; the U.S. Supreme Court library staff; the Newspaper and Microfilm Center at the Philadelphia Free Library; Randy Gue and Susan McDonald in the special collections division of Emory University's Woodruff Library; Gail Malmgreen and the staff at the Robert F. Wagner Labor Archives at New York University; Jennifer Burns at the High Point Museum.

In my humble opinion, Dave Kelly at the Library of Congress is the world's greatest librarian. He knows a ton about sports, music, history, politics, and everything else in between. He always responds to my research questions, even the stupid ones and sometimes ones I have already asked him. During the last few years, he has become not only one of my best sources of information and inspiration but also a trusted friend. Thanks, Dave.

Another good friend (and my favorite law firm librarian), Caitlin Lietzan, provided me with invaluable suggestions, professional expertise, and encouragement.

The following people lent me photographs out of the goodness of their hearts: Marge Brans, John Engels, Buddy Gilbert, Marian Jorgensen, and Allan Zerman. Others facilitated the use of images from their respective institutions: Kim Apley at Corbis, Pat Kelly and Bill Burdick at the National Baseball Hall of Fame Library, John Keller and

Bruce Lindsey at the William J. Clinton Presidential Library, Trish Murphy and Camilla Zenz at Zuma Press, Richard Anastasio at *Sports Illustrated*, and Marilyn Rader at AP/World Wide Photos.

Many friends opened their homes and apartments to me, some of them on multiple occasions and for days at a time: Phil and Sandy Brooks, Jan Ewald and John Thompson, David and Katherine Fierson, Charles Katz, Peggy Krendl, Cade and Taylor Metz, Peter and Kate Ocko, Darren Reisberg, Clara Shin, and Dan and Wendy Stein. I hope I was not the world's worst house guest. Your words of encouragement meant as much to me as your hospitality.

Other friends did not contribute a single thing to this book other than listening to me complain about some aspect of it. You know who you are. I'm not going to try to list everyone.

I cannot begin to thank the following people who read all or part of this manuscript prior to publication: Flip Brophy, Richard Ben Cramer, Lou Hoynes, Ben Kerschberg, Chris Klatell, Anthony Lewis, Kevin McDonald, Marvin (and Terry) Miller, John Thompson, Jay Topkis, and Jules Tygiel. Some of you spent hours giving me comments about the manuscript. Others responded to my panicked phone calls with words of wisdom. I hope I can return the favor to you some day.

Extra special thanks go to Andy Knobel, the deputy copy chief at the *Baltimore Sun* sports department and my official safety net. Andy has fact-checked both of my books, and he has saved me from more embarrassing errors than anyone will ever know. Andy's fertile baseball mind made this a better book.

My editors at Viking, Wendy Wolf and Cliff Corcoran, made this book a reality. I am indebted to Wendy for buying this book. She had a clear vision for the book and lent her experience and wisdom at critical junctures. Cliff is everything a great editor should be: meticulous, opinionated, and dedicated as hell. He read this book multiple times and each time attacked the book's weaknesses through his comments and suggestions. Cliff edited this book as if it were his own; he helped me take it to another level. I really appreciate his pushing and prodding and admire him greatly. He is also one of the nicest Yankees fans I have ever met.

Others deserving of thanks include copy editor Adam Goldberger, production editor Sharon Gonzalez, designers Daniel Lagin and Jesse Reyes, and publicist Shannon Twomey. Roy Jacobs and John Pelosi also provided valuable legal expertise.

I would be remiss if I did not thank many longtime mentors and unofficial advisers, including the following current and former *Baltimore Sun* sportswriters: John Eisenberg, Mark Hyman, Paul McMullen, Buster Olney, Ken Rosenthal, and Peter Schmuck.

John Feinstein has been giving me great career advice since I was a 17-year-old kid; his words of wisdom spurred me to write this book sooner rather than later. Paul Dickson also gave me advice and encouragement along the way, as did his friend George Gibson of Walker & Company.

It is rare that meeting one of your literary heroes becomes a life-changing event. I first met author Richard Ben Cramer when I was a young reporter covering the Orioles and he was writing a *Sports Illustrated* profile on Cal Ripken Jr. Ten years later, a chance encounter with Richard at a book signing at the Smithsonian changed the course of my life. He thought it was "unacceptable" that I had no publisher and no agent for my Curt Flood book. Since then, Richard has done everything in his power to help me succeed. I'll never be able to repay him for his kindness and generosity.

Because of Richard, I now have the world's greatest agent, Flip Brophy. Her enthusiasm for this project has made everything possible. She has kept me from becoming a truly starving artist, she has fought for me at every turn, and she cares about how each decision affects my career. I tell people that Flip is like my guardian angel. Every day I count my blessings that I have her in my corner.

Flip's assistants, Cia Glover and Sharon Skettini, deserve special mention for fielding my annoying phone calls, responding to some of my more foolish requests, and treating me like a somebody.

I often tell people that when I quit my job as a lawyer, my parents wondered where they had gone wrong in life. In truth, it did not matter whether they agreed with my decision. Their belief in me has been unwavering. I hope they realize how much their love and friendship have meant to me. They have influenced me as much as anyone. I hope I can continue to make them proud.

My brother Ivan and his wife Tamara also have been sources of emotional support and comic relief. On a weekly basis, my brother would call me and ask: "Is the book done yet?" I can finally say, yes, Ivan, it is.

Finally, I'd like to thank Curt Flood. I never had the chance to meet Curt or even speak to him on the phone, but my admiration for him runs deep. His guts and courage made me want to write this book. I hope I have done his story justice.

NOTES

KEY

AC	*Augusta* (GA) *Chronicle*
AJ	*Atlanta Journal*
AN	*Amsterdam* (NY) *News*
BAA	*Baltimore Afro-American*
BES	*Baltimore Evening Sun*
BG	*Boston Globe*
BHT	*Boston Herald-Traveler*
BMS	*Baltimore Morning Sun*
BN	*Birmingham News*
BRA	*Boston Record-American*
BS	*Baltimore Sun*
CA	*Chicago American*
CDEF	*Chicago Defender*
CDN	*Chicago Daily News*
CE	*Cincinnati Enquirer*
CP	*Cincinnati Post*
CPD	*Cleveland Plain Dealer*
CST	*Chicago Sun-Times*
CT	*Chicago Tribune*
CTS	*Cincinnati Times-Star*
DS	*Durham* (NC) *Sun*
GDN	*Greensboro Daily News*
HC	*Houston Chronicle*
HP	*Houston Post*
HPE	*High Point* (NC) *Enterprise*
JCL	*Jackson* (MS) *Clarion-Ledger*
KDFP	*Kinston* (NC) *Daily Free Press*
LAT	*Los Angeles Times*
MJ	*Milwaukee Journal*
MMNG	*Martinez* (CA) *Morning News-Gazette*
MS	*Minneapolis Star*
MST	*Minneapolis Star-Tribune*
NARA	*National Archives and Records Administration*
NSD	*National Sports Daily*
NYDN	*New York Daily News*
NYLJ	*New York Law Journal*
NYP	*New York Post*
NYT	*New York Times*
NYTM	*New York Times Magazine*
OS	*Orlando Sentinel*
OT	*Oakland Tribune*
PC	*Pittsburgh Courier*
PDN	*Philadelphia Daily News*
PEB	*Philadelphia Evening Bulletin*
PI	*Philadelphia Inquirer*
PP	*Pittsburgh Press*
PPG	*Pittsburgh Post-Gazette*
PT	*Philadelphia Tribune*

RAA	*Richmond* (VA) *Afro-American*	*SPD*	*St. Louis Post-Dispatch*
RI	*Richmond* (CA) *Independent*	*SPT*	*St. Petersburg Times*
RNO	*Raleigh News and Observer*	*TSN*	*The Sporting News*
SA	*St. Louis American*	*Tr.*	*Pretrial transcript*
SFC	*San Francisco Chronicle*	*TT*	*Trial transcript*
SFE	*San Francisco Examiner*	*TW*	*Tulsa World*
SGD	*St. Louis Globe-Democrat*	*WDN*	*Washington Daily News*
SI	*Sports Illustrated*	*WES*	*Washington Evening Star*
SMN	*Savannah Morning News*	*WP*	*Washington Post*
		WSJ	*Wall Street Journal*

CHAPTER ONE

Page

1 at 4 a.m.: Herman Flood Jr. interview. There is some dispute as to whether Flood first heard about the trade from a newspaper reporter or from Toomey. Curt's oldest brother, Herman, who was living with Flood in St. Louis at the time, distinctly recalls Curt being woken up by a baseball writer. "Herm," Curt said after waking up his brother, "I've just been traded." Ibid. Marvin Miller also said that a newspaper reporter contacted Flood first. Marvin Miller interview; Miller, *A Whole Different Ball Game*, 172. Finally, in an interview with Ken Burns, Flood confirmed that a "sportswriter" called him first, then Toomey. Burns/Flood Transcript, 8–9. A sportswriter could have called him first. The *St. Louis Post-Dispatch* was an afternoon paper with early-morning deadlines. It ran a brief, unsigned article on the day of the trade. *SPD*, 10/8/69, 4E. *Post-Dispatch* sports columnist Bob Broeg was a close friend of Cardinals general manager Bing Devine and was probably the first reporter to learn about the trade. Broeg, however, did not remember calling Flood. Bob Broeg interview. And the sportswriter closest to Flood was Jack Herman of the *St. Louis Globe-Democrat*.

In the weeks and months after the trade, however, Flood never mentioned the sportswriter, only Toomey. During his trial testimony (under oath), he said he first learned about the trade in a phone call from Toomey. He said the same thing in a magazine article five months after the trade and in his autobiography written two years later. TT, 43:3–14; Flood, "Why I Am Challenging Baseball," *Sport*, 3/70, 10, in Thorn, ed., *The Armchair Book of Baseball*, 130; Flood, *The Way It Is*, 185, 187.

1 The voice: Flood, "Why I Am Challenging Baseball," *Sport*, 3/70, 10, in Thorn, ed., *The Armchair Book of Baseball*, 130.

1 "Hello, Curt?": Flood, *The Way It Is*, 185.

1 "middle-echelon coffee drinker": Ibid., 187.

2 Under the major league rules: Major League Rule 4-A in 1969 *Blue Book.*

2 "[T]he Club shall have the right": TT, 25A. Prior to the 1968 Basic Agreement, a player's salary could be reduced by a maximum of 25 percent.

3 The morning of Toomey's: Herman Flood Jr. interview; Flood, *The Way It Is*, 185–86.

3 "When Bob and I were reading": *SPD*, 1/28/97, 1C.

3 One of Flood's favorite authors: *CP*, 9/22/99, 1B.

4 "the relatively conscious whites"; "God gave Noah": Baldwin, *Collected Essays*, 346–47.

4 A few hours after: TT, 45:12–46:22 (Flood); Flood, *The Way It Is*, 188.

4 so Flood left a message: TT, 1134:18–25 (Devine).

4 At 9:30 a.m., Devine explained: TT, 1130:18–22, 1134:11–16, 18–23 (Devine).

4 As soon as it was over: TT, 1134:18–23 (Devine).

4 Devine had wanted: TT, 1131:8–24 (Devine).

4 least respected: Tim McCarver interview.

4 On the last night: *SPD*, 1/29/67, 7B. See also Devine, *The Memoirs of Bing Devine*, 83–85; Halberstam, *October 1964*, 28–30; *TSN*, 5/9/62, 10; *SGD*, 12/6/57, 21.

5 The Cardinals' manager: *SGD*, 2/11/58, 17; *TSN*, 2/19/58, 22; *TSN*, 3/5/58, 21.

5 At the time: *TSN*, 11/13/57, 23; *SGD*, 2/11/58, 17; Flood, *The Way It Is*, 45–47.

5 He was sitting: Flood, "Why I Am Challenging Baseball," *Sport*, 3/70, 10, in Thorn, ed., *The Armchair Book of Baseball*, 126–27; Flood, *The Way It Is*, 47.

5 For 30 minutes: Flood, "Why I Am Challenging Baseball," *Sport*, 3/70, 10, in Thorn, ed., *The Armchair Book of Baseball*, 126; *TSN*, 10/30/65, 8.

5 He vowed: *WP*, 1/2/70, D6.

5 Twelve years later: TT, 45:12–46:22 (Flood); TT, 1135:6–14 (Devine); *SPD*, 10/8/69, 4E; *SPD*, 10/9/69, 4D; Flood, *The Way It Is*, 188.

5 He was physically and mentally: TT, 1135:6–14 (Devine); *SPD*, 10/9/69, 6D.

5 Toomey had insulted him: *SPD*, 2/25/69, 1B; *SPD*, 2/27/69, 1C; *SGD*, 2/27/69, 1D; TT, 1138:14–17 (Devine); Flood, *The Way It Is*, 172.

5 "Baseball's Best Centerfielder": Leggett, "Not Just a Flood, but a Deluge," *SI*, 8/19/68, 1, 18–24. According to the "Win Shares method" conceived by statistical guru Bill James, Flood was the best defensive outfielder in baseball history. James, however, concedes that Flood's early exit from the game inflated his overall ranking. James, *The New Bill James Historical Baseball Abstract*, 747–48.

5 The press predicted: *NYP*, 3/20/69, 104.

6 Flood believed that: *SPD*, 3/4/69, 3C (Flood: "If I don't get it after the year I had, I never will").

6 "If you don't pay me": TT, 69:11–12 (Flood); *SPD*, 3/2/69, 1F; *TSN*, 3/15/69, 8 (reporting that one player threatened to quit, believing it to be Flood).

6 "At this moment": *SGD*, 3/3/69, 1B. For similar quotes, see *SPD*, 2/27/69, 1C (reporting that Flood is asking for $100,000); *SGD*, 2/27/69, 1D ("If Lou [Brock] gets $100,000, there will be three of us," Flood said. Gibson was already making more than $100,000. Brock settled for $88,000); Flood, *The Way It Is*, 172 (Flood incorrectly later wrote that he demanded $90,000, not $100,000).

6 Devine explained: *SPD*, 3/4/69, 1C; TT, 69:2–14 (Flood).

6 "I'm making $90,000 now": *NYP*, 3/20/69, 104.

6 The ball sailed: *SPD*, 10/11/68, 1B, 2B; *SGD*, 10/11/68, 1B, 2B; *PI*, 10/11/68, 34; *WP*, 10/11/68, E1, E2; *TSN*, 10/26/68, 8. Flood lost a ball in the white shirts earlier in the Series, breaking late in Game 2 on Dick McAuliffe's sinking bases-loaded liner. The ball went off Flood's glove and two runs scored. *SPD*, 10/4/68, 6C; *TSN*, 10/19/68, 7, 8.

6 Flood accepted full responsibility: *SPD*, 10/11/68, 1B; *SGD*, 10/11/68, 1B, 2B; *PI*, 10/11/68, 34.

7 During spring training: Flood, *The Way It Is*, App. B, 228–36; *SPD*, 3/23/69, 1A, 9A, 1B; *SGD*, 3/24/69, 1B; *SGD*, 3/25/69, 3B; *SPD*, 3/24/69, 2C; *TSN*, 4/5/69, 3.

7 Busch's favorite player: *SPD*, 5/21/65, 4B; Hernon and Ganey, *Under the Influence*, 244.

7 In May 1969: TT, 41:8–14, 23–25 (Flood); *SGD*, 4/26-27/69, 6H; Flood, *The Way It Is*, 85–86; Flood, "Why I Am Challenging Baseball," *Sport*, 3/70, 10, in Thorn, ed., *The Armchair Book of Baseball*, 127–28.

7 His bat orders; He discovered; "Something is happening"; "They're either going"; "Yes": Jim "Mudcat" Grant interview.

7 In May 1969, the newspapers: *SPD*, 5/21/69, 4C; *SGD*, 5/22/69, 1D; *BES*, 5/21/69, D2.

7 anonymous comments: *SGD*, 9/9/69, 1C.

7 Devine responded: *SGD*, 9/10/69, 2B; Flood, *The Way It Is*, 184.

7 "If they trade me": *PEB*, 10/9/69, 29; *PI*, 11/14/69, 37.

7 the same mental and physical: TT, 1135:6–14 (Devine); *SPD*, 10/9/69, 6D.

7 "shot me down": TT, 1136:23–25, 1137:2–18 (Devine).

7 "emotional reaction": TT, 1135:16–24 (Devine).

7 The Cardinals general manager believed: TT, 1135:25–1136:13 (Devine).

8 "Well, there's not much use": TT, 1136:3–4 (Devine).

8 He then offhandedly: TT, 1136:11–17 (Devine).

8 Flood sat in a chair: Flood, *The Way It Is*, 185–86.

8 Quinn called: *PDN*, 10/9/69, 67.

8 "comes as a surprise"; "For the past two years"; "I then told": *SPD*, 10/8/69, 4E; *SPD*, 10/9/69, 6D.

9 "unless he's better": *SPD*, 10/12/69, 7B. For variations of this quote, see *SPD*, 1/4/70, 3D; *WP*, 1/2/70, D6.

9 In March 1967, he had presented: *SPD*, 3/10/67, 1E; *SGD*, 3/10/67, 1B.
9 Busch was so enamored: *SPD*, 3/10/67, 1E; *SPD*, 10/1/67, 29J.
9 the governors of Illinois and Missouri: *SGD*, 2/22/68, 1D (Illinois); *SGD*, 9/26/68, 8D (Missouri); *SGD*, 8/22/69, 3B (Pope).
9 Leukemia Guild of Missouri: *SPD*, 12/21/67, 9C; "Oil in the Outfield," *Sport*, 3/68, 8; *SPD*, 9/6/68, 2D.
9 he had made an extra $15,000: "Oil in the Outfield," *Sport*, 3/68, 8.
9 "Rembrandt": *SGD Magazine*, 3/31/68, 4, in *TSN*, 4/20/68, 9; Gross, "Curt Flood—Ballplayer and Artist," *SGD Sunday Magazine*, 3/31/68, 4, reprinted in *TSN*, 4/20/68, 9, and *Ebony*, 7/68, 70.
9 *Today* show: Flood, *The Way It Is*, 130.
9 above her desk: King, "Martin's Legacy," *Ebony*, 1/86, 108 (photograph).
9 "Your painting": *SPD*, 9/6/68, 2D.
9 White House: *NYT*, 1/22/02, A15; *WP*, 1/22/02, A2; Judy Pace Flood interview.
9 Yes, he had been drawing: *SPD*, 9/11/67, 2D; Gross, "Curt Flood—Ballplayer and Artist," *SGD Sunday Magazine*, 3/31/68, 4, reprinted in *TSN*, 4/20/68, 9, and *Ebony*, 7/68, 70; Flood, *The Way It Is*, 21, 30.
9 During the fall of 1959: *TSN*, 4/20/68, 9; Gross, "Curt Flood—Ballplayer and Artist," *SGD Sunday Magazine*, 3/31/68, 4, reprinted in *TSN*, 4/20/68, 9, and *Ebony*, 7/68, 70.
10 His sketches of teammate: *SPD*, 9/8/63, 4F; *TSN*, 9/7/63, 4.
10 watched him unpack the paintings: Bill Jones interview.
10 The day after the trade: Flood, *The Way It Is*, 185–86, 188.
10 "Notice to player number 614"; "Best of luck": TT, 48–49 (Flood).
10 "If I had been": Flood, *The Way It Is*, 187.
10 Flood was so depressed: Ibid., 189.
10 Few people understood; "that white lady": Ibid., 124.
10 mother hen: Marian Jorgensen interview; Jim "Mudcat" Grant interview.
10 Mean and sometimes Machiavellian: Marian Jorgensen interview; Bill Jones interview.
10 Flood met Marian: Flood, *The Way It Is*, 113–19.
11 "humanists": Ibid., 115.
11 The Jorgensens became: Ibid., 113–19.
11 The owner of an Oakland engraving: Ibid., 118–19.
11 the Lord's Prayer: Stump, "Curt Flood in the Midnight League," *Sport*, 3/65, 79.
11 Johnny made Curt a partner: *TSN*, 9/14/63, 7; *TSN*, 1/25/64, 9.
11 Johnny was stabbed: *OT*, 12/15/66; *OT*, 12/16/66, 1, 8; *OT*, 12/17/66, 25; Ancestry.com *California Death Index*, 1940–1997.
11 Oakland police detectives: Jack Richardson interview; *OT*, 12/20/66, 16; Flood, *The Way It Is*, 122.
11 In 1967, Curt begged Marian: Flood, *The Way It Is*, 122–24.

11 Marian had taken: Ibid., 125–29.

11–12 Carl had begun pocketing: Karen Brecher interview.

12 $300-a-day: *SGD*, 3/18/69, 1A, 8A; *SPD*, 3/17/69, 1A, 5A. Flood claimed that Carl was addicted to morphine, not heroin. Flood, *The Way It Is*, 131.

12 Carl and a convicted: *SGD*, 3/18/69, 1A, 8A; *SPD*, 3/17/69, 1A, 5A; Flood, *The Way It Is*, 131–32.

12 Carl's arrest: *SPD*, 4/8/69, 2C.

12 she could drink, swear: Allan Zerman interview.

12 Some people thought: Bill Jones interview; Rickie Riley interview.

12 Two days after the trade: Flood, *The Way It Is*, 189.

12 Even before his trade: Katz, "Life with the Cardinals," *Sport*, 7/68, 57; *SPT*, 4/25/68, 1-C; Olsen, "In the Back of the Bus," *SI*, 7/22/68, 34 (anonymous quotes criticizing reserve clause which appear to be from Flood, who was quoted earlier in the article).

12 Curt pondered: Flood, *The Way It Is*, 189.

12 "I went to Europe": *NYP*, 3/20/69, 104.

12 Club 6: Ibid.; *Footwear*, 5/1/69, 27, *Independent*, 3/6/69, in Curt Flood *TSN* file; *SPD*, 3/2/69.

13 Even in Copenhagen: *PI*, 10/13/69, 25; *TSN*, 11/1/69, 17; TT, 56:3–57:9 (Flood); Flood, *The Way It Is*, 189.

13 Flood reiterated: *PI*, 10/13/69, 25; TT, 57:2–9 (Flood).

13 On November 7: TT, 57:19–58:18 (Flood); *PDN*, 11/8/69, 29; *PEB*, 11/9/69, sec. 3, 5.

13 They treated their players; "northernmost southern city": Flood, *The Way It Is*, 188.

13 "the nigger here": Parrott, *The Lords of Baseball*, 242. Parrott, the Dodgers' traveling secretary and publicist, is the only source for this allegation. He claims to have been on the phone with Branch Rickey during Rickey's conversation with Pennock.

13 Phillies owner Bob Carpenter: Robinson, "A Kentucky Colonel kept me in baseball," *Look*, 2/8/55, 86.

13 Philadelphia manager Ben Chapman: Robinson, *Jackie Robinson: My Own Story*, 128, 145; Robinson, "A Kentucky Colonel kept me in baseball," *Look*, 2/8/55, 86–87.

13 The Ben Franklin: Parrott, *The Lords of Baseball*, 243–45; Robinson, "A Kentucky Colonel kept me in baseball," *Look*, 2/8/55, 87.

14 Quinn explained: *PDN*, 11/8/69, 29; *PEB*, 11/9/69, sec. 3, 5; TT, 57:19–58:18 (Flood).

14 Flood insisted: *PDN*, 11/8/69, 29; *PEB*, 11/9/69, sec. 3, 5; TT, 57:19–58:18 (Flood).

14 "It may be": *PEB*, 11/9/69, sec. 3, 5; *TSN*, 11/29/69, 30.

14 "keep an open mind": *PEB*, 11/9/69, sec. 3, 5.

14 "I don't think": TT, 58:15–16 (Flood).
14 "Curt Nearly a Phil": *PDN*, 11/8/69, 29.
14 if he had $1,000: *PEB*, 11/9/68, sec. 3, 5.
14 Two of Flood's former teammates; "the money": *PDN*, 11/19/69, 61.
14 Flood liked Quinn: Flood, *The Way It Is*, 189–90; *PDN*, 11/19/69, 61.
14 Soon after he had returned: Allan Zerman interview; Flood, *The Way It Is*, 190.
15 Zerman had never seen: Allan Zerman interview.
15 "There is one other alternative": Flood, "Why I Am Challenging Baseball," *Sport*, 3/70, 10, in Thorn, ed., *The Armchair Book of Baseball*, 130.
15 Flood was startled: Ibid.; Allan Zerman interview.

CHAPTER TWO

Page

16 Marvin Miller was not expecting: Marvin Miller interview; *PEB*, 1/6/70, 49, in *TSN*, 1/24/70, 38; Miller, *A Whole Different Ball Game*, 169, 173–74.
16 Miller did not know: Miller, *A Whole Different Ball Game*, 170–71; Marvin Miller interview; *BAA*, 2/25/69, 14.
16 Miller could tell: Marvin Miller interview; Miller, *A Whole Different Ball Game*, 173–74.
16 "wouldn't bet": Marvin Miller interview.
16 Flood asked Miller: *PEB*, 1/6/70, 49, in *TSN*, 1/24/70, 38; Flood, *The Way It Is*, 190; Miller, *A Whole Different Ball Game*, 169.
17 "J.C." or "Don Quixote"; "He likes the impossible": *NYP*, 2/26/69, 93.
17 The son of a ladies' garment: Miller, *A Whole Different Ball Game*, 11–18.
17 Giants public relations man: Ibid., 51–52; Boyle, "This Miller Admits He's a Grind," *SI*, 3/11/74, 23. For the best profile of Miller, see Fimrik, "Marvin Miller," *SI*, 3/3/80, 56–70.
17 He then began taking prelaw: Marvin Miller interview.
17 Miller spent the first 12 years: Ibid.; Boyle, "This Miller Admits He's a Grind," *SI*, 3/11/74, 23, 25; Helyar, *Lords of the Realm*, 17–18; Miller, *A Whole Different Ball Game*, 19–21.
17 rudderless: Helyar, *Lords of the Realm*, 18.
18 Steelworkers Union: Its official name is the United Steelworkers of America, but it is commonly referred to as the Steelworkers Union.
18 For years: For the early history of the union, see Korr, *The End of Baseball As We Knew It*, 15–34; Lowenfish, *The Imperfect Diamond*, 139–53, 183–92; Helyar, *Lords of the Realm*, 9–14; Miller, *A Whole Different Ball Game*, 6–7, 40.
18 Miller came: Miller, *A Whole Different Ball Game*, 4, 31; Roberts, "The Game Deserves the Best," *SI*, 2/24/69, 45–46.
18 "a strong man": Boyle, "This Miller Admits He's a Grind," *SI*, 3/11/74, 25.

18 Cannon balked: Dolson, *Jim Bunning*, 104–9; Korr, *The End of Baseball As We Knew It*, 28–31; Helyar, *Lords of the Realm*, 17.
18 "pencil-thin"; "shimmering blue": Fimrik, "Marvin Miller," *SI*, 3/3/80, 64.
18 Roberts begged: Miller, *A Whole Different Ball Game*, 40–41.
18 Miller denied: Marvin Miller interview.
18 the players voted, 489–136: The voters also included 120 coaches, managers, and trainers, who were not part of the association but were included in the pension plan. Ibid.
18 The player representatives informed Miller: Ibid.; Miller, *A Whole Different Ball Game*, 68–72; Korr, *The End of Baseball As We Knew It*, 47–50.
18 $344 in annual union dues: Prior to Miller's election, the players had been paying $344 a year to fund the pension plan until the owners agreed to fund it for them. The annual pension contribution became the players' union dues. The union dues were tax deductible, but the pension contribution was not, so Miller ended up saving the players money on the deal. Marvin Miller interview.
19 The 49-year-old Miller: Miller, *A Whole Different Ball Game*, 143.
19 He tackled issues: Ibid., 95–97; Helyar, *Lords of the Realm*, 29, 36; Korr, *The End of Baseball As We Knew It*, 68–75; "At Last, Professional Bargaining in Baseball," *Sport*, 10/67, 98.
19 he showed the players: Helyar, *Lords of the Realm*, 91–101; Korr, *The End of Baseball As We Knew It*, 75–76; Miller, *A Whole Different Ball Game*, 99–101.
19 The promanagement sporting press: The leaders of the anti-Miller faction were the *Atlanta Journal*'s Furman Bisher and the *New York Daily News*'s Dick Young. *See AJ*, 2/25/69, 1-C; *NYDN*, 4/14/72, 81; Korr, *The End of Baseball As We Knew It*, 43–45. They later led the charge against Flood's lawsuit.
19 Miller's mission: Marvin Miller interview; Allan Zerman interview; Miller, *A Whole Different Ball Game*, 174–81.
19 Flood began: Miller, *A Whole Different Ball Game*, 174–75.
20 "[e]very contract, combination"; "trade or commerce": 15 U.S.C. sec. 1. The Sherman Act also provides for triple damages and attorneys' fees. 15 U.S.C. sec. 15. In 1924, Congress supplemented the enforcement of the Sherman Act with the Clayton Act. 29 U.S.C. sec. 52.
20 The U.S. Constitution: This is known as the "Commerce Clause." U.S. Const., art. I, sec. 8, cl. 3.
20 A District of Columbia jury: The jury verdict was $80,000. The jury also awarded the owners of the Baltimore Terrapins $24,000 in attorneys' fees. See Supreme Court Brief on Behalf of Plaintiff in Error in *Federal Baseball*, 2.
20 A federal appeals court: For the best explanation of the appeals court's decision, see White, *Creating the National Pastime*, 71–81.
20 "The business is giving": *Federal Baseball Club of Baltimore, Inc. v. National League of Professional Baseball Clubs*, 259 U.S. 200, 208 (1922). For additional facts about *Federal Baseball*, see Supreme Court Records and Briefs for *Federal*

Baseball (on file with author); 269 F. 681 (D.C. Cir. 1921) (Court of Appeals decision).

20 The Court said that the transportation: *Federal Baseball*, 259 U.S., 208–9.

21 "loathe[d] and despise[d]"; "foolish law": Howe, ed., *Holmes-Laski Letters*, 249, 719.

21 A bookish, unathletic child: White, *Creating the National Pastime*, 80. A Holmes biographer described him as a "thin and awkward" child who "shrank from new things" and "did not learn how to skate or to ride." Novick, *Honorable Justice*, 13. Another biographer said that Holmes "rowed 'a good deal,' swam, shot, and fished." Baker, *The Justice from Beacon Hill*, 56.

21 In Holmes's defense: McDonald, "Antitrust and Baseball: Stealing Holmes," *J. of Sct. Hist.*, vol. 2 (1998), 107–15. McDonald's article is the best defense of Holmes.

21 a 29-year-old pitcher: *LAT*, 5/2/51, C2; *NYT*, 12/6/51, 56; *NYT*, 5/26/53, 1, 25; *NYT*, 10/11/53, E10; *NYT*, 10/14/53, 37; *NYT*, 11/10/53, 1, 40; *TSN*, 12/14/87, 60; *Toolson v. New York Yankees, Inc.*, 101 F. Supp. 90 (D.C. Cal. 1951); 200 F.2d 198 (9th Cir. 1952); 346 U.S. 356 (1953).

21 Toolson had signed: *SFC*, 2/16/70, 46.

21 ineligible list: 101 F. Supp., 93.

21 two other unsuccessful: *NYT*, 10/11/53, E10; *TSN*, 10/14/53, 21; *Kowalski v. Chandler*, 202 F.3d 413 (6th Cir. 1953); *Corbett v. Chandler*, 202 F.2d 428 (6th Cir. 1953).

22 "underlying issues": *Toolson*, 346 U.S., 357.

22 "the greatest bait-and-switch": McDonald, "Antitrust and Baseball: Stealing Holmes," *J. of Sct. Hist.*, vol. 2 (1998), 100.

23 "Without reexamining": *Toolson*, 346 U.S., 357 (emphasis added).

23 The second half of this final sentence; "to make it clear": Warren asked Black to include the sentence instead of publishing a concurring opinion. Memo Warren to Black, 10/23/53, Warren Papers, Box 631, Folder "Per Curiam Nos. 18, 23, and 24"; Black Papers, Box 321, "Folder Nos. 18, 23, & 25 Oct. Term 1953 *Toolson v. New York Yankees*." See also Memo Black to Conference, 10/24/53 (informing the justices of the addition), ibid.; Burton Papers, Box 245, Folder 3.

23 as Justice Harold Burton: *Toolson*, 346 U.S., 357–65 (Burton J., dissenting).

23 Before and even after: *Philadelphia Ball Club v. Lajoie*, 202 Pa. 210, 51 A. 973 (1902); *American League Baseball Club v. Chase*, 86 Misc. 441, 149 N.Y.S. 6 (Sup. Ct. 1914); *Gardella v. Chandler*, 172 F.2d 402 (2d Cir. 1949); McDonald, "Antitrust and Baseball: Stealing Holmes," *J. of Sct. Hist.*, vol. 2 (1998), 120–21.

23 Miller was not a lawyer: Marvin Miller interview.

23–24 Dick Moss, who had examined: Dick Moss interview.

24 A former assistant: Korr, *The End of Baseball As We Knew It*, 50–53; Helyar, *Lords of the Realm*, 32–33.

24 theatrical performances: *United States v. Shubert*, 348 U.S. 222 (1955) (the-

ater); *United States v. International Boxing Club*, 348 U.S. 236 (1955) (boxing); *Radovich v. National Football League*, 352 U.S. 445 (1956) (football).

24 "was at best": 352 U.S., 450.

24 "If this ruling": Ibid., 452.

24 Miller predicted; "It's a million"; "But it would benefit"; "That's good enough": Marvin Miller interview.

24 devil's advocate: Marvin Miller interview; Allan Zerman interview; Dick Moss interview. For other accounts of Miller's and Moss's initial meeting with Flood, see *PEB*, 1/6/70, 49, in *TSN*, 1/24/70, 38; Flood, "Why I Am Challenging Baseball," *Sport*, 3/70, 10, in Thorn, ed., *The Armchair Book of Baseball*, 130; Miller, *A Whole Different Ball Game*, 174–82; Flood, *The Way It Is*, 190–91; Golenbock, *The Spirit of St. Louis*, 510.

25 "You're not telling": *PEB*, 1/6/70, 49, in *TSN*, 1/24/70, 38.

25 Flood had not thought: Miller, *A Whole Different Ball Game*, 181.

25 Miller then pressed: Miller, *A Whole Different Ball Game*, 176–81; *PEB*, 1/6/70, 49, in *TSN*, 1/24/70, 38; Flood, *The Way It Is*, 190–91.

25 A stocky, muscular man: *NYT*, 1/21/64, 34; Smith, "Gardella Hales Baseball into Court," *SI*, 3/49, 71. For more on Gardella, see *LAT*, 10/22/94, C1; *SGD*, 2/27/66, 4C; *NYT*, 6/21/50, 38; *WP*, 3/11/49, B4; Lowenfish, *The Imperfect Diamond*, 155–68.

25 Gardella showed up: Smith, "Gardella Hales Baseball into Court," *SI*, 3/49, 71; *NYT*, 2/13/49, 33.

26 Chandler sent a telegram: Danny Gardella interview, Chandler Collection; *LAT*, 10/22/94, C1.

26 On appeal: *Gardella v. Chandler*, 172 F.2d 402 (2d Cir. 1949).

26 Hand wrote: Ibid., 408.

26 "impotent zombi": Ibid., 409, 412 (Frank, J., concurring).

26 "avowed communist tendencies": *NYT*, 4/14/49, 33.

26 Bob Feller: *NYT*, 2/15/49, 31.

27 received half: It may have been $31,000, or slightly more than half. Danny Gardella interview, Chandler Collection.

27 A few years later, Johnson represented: *NYT*, 10/14/53, 37.

27 $36 a week: Danny Gardella interview, Chandler Collection.

27 On April 25, the Cardinals sold: *NYT*, 4/26/50, 46.

27 Gardella struggled: *NYT*, 6/21/50, 38; *NYT*, 6/22/50, 35.

27 "feel like a Judas": Danny Gardella interview, Chandler Collection.

27 Miller continued to grill: Miller, *A Whole Different Ball Game*, 175; TT, 181:12–13 (Miller).

27 During the course: Marvin Miller interview; TT, 180:23–182:18 (Miller); Miller, *A Whole Different Ball Game*, 181; Golenbock, *The Spirit of St. Louis*, 510; Flood, *The Way It Is*, 191; *PEB*, 1/8/70, 23, 26.

27 Miller had heard rumors: Marvin Miller interview.

27 Flood volunteered: Marvin Miller interview; Golenbock, *The Spirit of St. Louis*, 510. Miller said the owners had made Carl's drug conviction public, but the connection to Curt had been made long before Flood's decision to sue. *NYT*, 3/19/69, 32; *CT*, 3/19/69, 12; *SPD*, 4/8/69, 2C.

27 "Nothing you've said": *PEB*, 1/6/70, 49, in *TSN*, 1/24/70, 38. For a slight variation on this quote, see Flood, *The Way It Is*, 191.

28 Miller tactfully: Marvin Miller interview; Allan Zerman interview; Miller, *A Whole Different Ball Game*, 175.

28 Sitting at Flood's side: Allan Zerman interview.

28 Flood expressed concern: Miller, *A Whole Different Ball Game*, 175.

28 At some point: Marvin Miller interview; *PEB*, 1/6/70, 49, in *TSN*, 1/24/70, 38.

28 Both Miller and Flood would repeat: Red Smith was the first to circulate this story in his syndicated column. See *PI*, 12/31/69, 27; *WP*, 1/2/70, D6. Sandy Grady, in his wonderful *Philadelphia Evening Bulletin* interview with Miller, also repeated it. *PEB*, 1/6/70, 49, in *TSN*, 1/24/70, 38. So did the *Philadelphia Daily News*'s Bill Conlin. *PDN*, 1/23/70, 59. Flood gave it the widest circulation in his first-person account in the March 1970 edition of *Sport* magazine. Flood, "Why I Am Challenging Baseball," *Sport*, 3/70, 10, in Thorn, ed., *The Armchair Book of Baseball*, 126; *PI*, 3/1/70, sec. 3, 2; *AJ*, 3/8/70, 1-C, 6-C.

28 After four hours of interrogation: Miller, *A Whole Different Ball Game*, 181–82; Flood, *The Way It Is*, 191.

28 Flood did not immediately: TT, 59:13–60:17 (Flood); Flood, *The Way It Is*, 191–92; *PEB*, 1/8/70, 23; *NYP*, 12/30/69, 77.

28 Flood broached: Flood, *The Way It Is*, 192 (saying it was "above $100,000"). He initially testified that he was offered $90,000 plus $8,000 in spring training expenses. TT, 59:13–60:17 (Flood). However, on cross-examination, Flood was presented with a transcript from his January 20, 1970, appearance on *The Dick Cavett Show*, where he said he was offered in excess of $100,000. TT, 107:12–108:14 (Flood). Philadelphia papers reported that Flood was offered $106,000. Speers, "Why Curt Flood Won't Play for the Phillies," *PI Magazine*, 5/17/70, 10.

28 Money, however, was not: *NYP*, 12/30/69, 77.

29 "I know you"; "No, I'm Curt": Flood, *The Way It Is*, 191–92. For other accounts of this incident, see *WP*, 1/8/70, E5; Speers, "Why Curt Flood Won't Play for the Phillies," *PI Magazine*, 5/17/70, 12; *PEB*, 1/8/70, 23.

29 He told several: *PI*, 12/5/69, 39 (describing it as "any day now"); *PT*, 12/30/69, 15.

29 Flood agreed to call: TT, 104:25–105:5 (Flood); *NYP*, 12/30/69, 80.

29 On November 25, the day after dining: Speers, "Why Curt Flood Won't Play for the Phillies," *PI Magazine*, 5/17/70, 12. Flood had been contacted at least by November 18. *PDN*, 11/19/69, 61 (Flood discusses an offer from Gault Galleries).

29 He even took home: Karen Brecher interview.

29 During those seven hours: Speers, "Why Curt Flood Won't Play for the Phillies," *PI Magazine*, 5/17/70, 12.

29 Flood returned to St. Louis: Flood, *The Way It Is*, 192.

29 He and Zerman huddled: Flood, "Why I Am Challenging Baseball," *Sport*, 3/70, 10, in Thorn, ed., *The Armchair Book of Baseball*, 131.

30 Miller and Moss had begun talking: Miller, *A Whole Different Ball Game*, 182–83; Marvin Miller interview.

30 Flood and a female companion: Marvin Miller interview; Terry Miller interview; Miller, *A Whole Different Ball Game*, 185.

30 He was still curious: Marvin Miller interview.

CHAPTER THREE

Page

31 *"To find a deeper reason":* Lee, "The Curt Flood Story," *Real Sports*, 3/10/97.

31–32 Laura's first husband; "Laura"; "I don't know"; The woman slapped; With the mill workers; Laura and her children; During one of those: Rickie Riley interview.

32 Herman Flood left: 1928 Houston City Directory, 808; Rickie Riley interview. Herman's family was from a small southeast Texas town called Goliad. His father, Riley, was a professional musician who played the violin. 1900 Census, Goliad, Texas, Series T623, E.D. 47, roll 1638, p. 92, line 28; Herman Flood Jr. interview.

32 He found a job: Herman Flood Jr. interview; Judy Pace Flood interview; 1930 Census, Oakland, California, E.D. 1–11, roll 1729, p. 11-A, lines 43–44.

32 Herman and Laura Flood moved back: Rickie Riley interview.

32 Herman Sr. worked two jobs: 1936 Houston City Directory, 568.

32 never saw a dime: Rickie Riley interview.

32 They moved frequently: Ibid.; 1934 Houston City Directory, 579 (Calhoun St.); 1936 Houston City Directory, 568 (Webster Ave.); 1937–38 Houston City Directory, 538, 1929 (Elgin St.); 1939 Houston City Directory, 561, 1829 (Elgin St.); 1940 Houston City Directory, 357, 1433 (Stonewall Ave.); 1941 Houston City Directory, 369, 1487 (Stonewall Ave.).

32 "We have moved": Rickie Riley interview.

33 Jefferson Davis Hospital; take to baseball: Rickie Riley interview.

33 two years old: Curt said his family left Houston for Oakland when he was "about two years old." Flood, *The Way It Is*, 19. Curt's oldest brother, Herman Jr., remembered arriving in Oakland when he was nine years old. Herman Flood Jr. interview. Herman was born in 1931 and was seven years older than Curt. Their half sister Rickie Riley arrived in Oakland a few years ahead of her

family and remembered their arrival as being before Pearl Harbor Day (December 7, 1941). Rickie Riley interview.

The Houston and Oakland city directories, however, paint a slightly different picture, indicating that the Floods left Houston somewhere in 1942 or 1943. 1942 Houston City Directory, 368 (Herman and Laura Flood not listed); 1943 Oakland City Directory, 339 (listed). But there may have been a lag as far as the city directories were concerned.

33 Helen Street: Flood, *The Way It Is*, 20; Rickie Riley interview; Herman Flood Jr. interview.

33 "Second Gold Rush": Johnson, *The Second Gold Rush*, 30 (citing *San Francisco Chronicle* series on the "Second Gold Rush" from April 25 to May 20, 1943).

33 dockworker: 1943 Oakland City Directory, 339.

33 60-hour shifts: Flood, *The Way It Is*, 19–20; Rickie Riley interview; Herman Flood Jr. interview.

33 Texas-style blues: Herman Flood Jr. interview; Johnson, *The Second Gold Rush*, 139–41 (discussing the unique brand of blues blacks brought to Oakland from Texas and Louisiana).

33 1430 Club: Herman Flood Jr. interview.

33 People too poor: Rickie Riley interview; "Curt Flood," *ESPN SportsCentury* (Pace).

33 trumpet: Herman Flood Jr. interview; *PDN*, 6/25/62, 54.

33 play the piano by ear: Rickie Riley interview.

33 fruit; sketch pads: Flood, *The Way It Is*, 21.

34 "righteousness and fairness": *OT*, 7/10/94, B-1.

34 Curt and Carl: Herman Flood Jr. interview; Flood, *The Way It Is*, 25–26.

34 Curt wanted so badly to join: Herman Flood Jr. interview; Flood, *The Way It Is*, 22–23.

34 George Powles: Noble, "The Coach Nobody Wanted," *Saturday Evening Post*, 5/10/58, 118; Laurie Powles interview; Marge Brans interview.

34 Powles arranged: Flood, *The Way It Is*, 30.

34 Curt played catcher: Jethro McIntyre interview; *SFC*, 9/29/68, Oakland Public Library file.

35 He, his wife: Laurie Powles interview.

35 He provided the boys: J. W. Porter interview.

35 he often pitched: Noble, "The Coach Nobody Wanted," *Saturday Evening Post*, 5/10/58, 116.

35 Winifred served: J. W. Porter interview; Jethro McIntyre interview; Flood, *The Way It Is*, 26–27.

35 George talked baseball: J. W. Porter interview; Marge Brans interview; Robinson, *My Life Is Baseball*, 33.

35 He taught them: J. W. Porter interview.

35 "Don't give somebody": *OT*, 1/19/81, C-1.

35 Powles made them: Flood, *The Way It Is*, 26–27.

35 In 1943: Noble, "The Coach Nobody Wanted," *Saturday Evening Post*, 5/10/58, 118.

35 Most whites: Russell and Branch, *Second Wind*, 53, 60–61.

35 he rescued: Ibid., 61; Russell, *Go Up for Glory*, 26–27; Noble, "The Coach Nobody Wanted," *Saturday Evening Post*, 5/10/58, 118.

35 "By that one gesture": Russell, *Go Up for Glory*, 27–28.

36 court-martial: Tygiel, "The Court-Martial of Jackie Robinson," *American Heritage*, August-September 1984, 34–39, in Tygiel, *The Jackie Robinson Reader*, 39–51; Rampersad, *Jackie Robinson*, 102–9.

36 "There was a feeling": Burns, *Baseball*, vol. 6 (1940s); Burns/Flood interview, 2.

36 He sent 17 players: *OT*, 1/19/81, C-1.

36 The best: Robinson, *My Life Is Baseball*, 32–33; Robinson, *Extra Innings*, 25; *TSN*, 6/10/67, 25–26; Bobby Mattick interview.

36 "He was terrific": Robinson, *My Life Is Baseball*, 41; see also Robinson with Anderson, *Frank*, 43. He described Powles as "the man who really got me into playing baseball. Not only playing baseball—but *thinking* it."

36 .429 to Robinson's .424: Robinson, *My Life Is Baseball*, 40.

36 "the trumpet or the bat": Marge Brans interview.

36 In 1949 and 1950, he served: J. W. Porter interview; Flood, *The Way It Is*, 30.

37 "We'd put on a little show": Leggett, "Not Just a Flood, but a Deluge," *SI*, 8/19/68, 21.

37 "George was the coach": Jesse Gonder interview.

37 Curt made extra money: Flood, *The Way It Is*, 30; *OT*, 12/26/54, 5C; Sam Bercovich interview.

37 "Where is"; "We don't": Sam Bercovich interview.

37 "To Sam": Sam Bercovich interview.

37 The Oakland high schools: *TSN*, 6/6/51, 5 (Junior baseball edition).

37 Curt joined: *OT*, 7/27/55, 51.

37 Powles and Bercovich hatched: Rickie Riley interview; Jesse Gonder interview; Jethro McIntyre interview; Joe Gaines interview.

37 Bercovich bought: Sam Bercovich interview.

37 Barbara and Curt: Rickie Riley interview.

38 Curt moved into: Compare Flood, *The Way It Is*, 30 (Flood offers the babysitting explanation) with 31 (Flood says of Oakland Tech, "to which I had been required to transfer when I moved to Barbara's").

38 "I recall": Flood, *The Way It Is*, 25.

38 He thrived; Art Club: Marge Brans interview; Oakland Tech 1956 Yearbook.

38 "fooled around": *SPD*, 6/26/58, 2E.

38 close as brothers; enduring racial slights: Dave Draheim interview; Dale Powers interview; John Engels interview.

38 In 27 Legion games: *HPE*, 3/31/56, 7.
39 "He had immense": Bobby Mattick interview.
39 An infielder: Bobby Mattick interview; *TSN*, 11/6/71, 44; Keith, "Someone Old, Someone New," *SI*, 4/26/80, 46, 49.
39 Hot after Robinson: Bobby Mattick interview; J. W. Porter interview; Marge Brans interview; Lauric Powles interview; Robinson, *My Life Is Baseball*, 39–40, 42–43.
39 Mattick persuaded: Bobby Mattick interview. Powles remained on the Reds' payroll until 1960. *TSN*, 2/17/60, 18. When Mattick moved to the Astros, Powles helped Houston sign Bay Area product Joe Morgan even though Morgan had never even played for Powles. *TSN*, 3/13/65, 24.
39 "Everybody signed": Joe Gaines interview.
39 After Curt graduated: Flood, *The Way It Is*, 32–33; *OT*, 1/31/56, 33. Oakland Tech was divided into January and June classes.
39 "We were prepared": *OT*, 1/31/56, 33.
39 "that all 16": *CE*, 2/1/56, 30.
39 "no less than 11"; "around $25,000": *OT*, 1/31/56, 33.
39 In truth: Flood, *The Way It Is*, 32; Bobby Mattick interview.
39 In part because: *OT*, 1/31/56, 33; *TSN*, 2/15/56, 2.
40 standard team questionnaire: Flood file, Reds Museum.
40 The only one not enjoying: Herman Flood Jr. interview.
40 lengthy criminal record: Carl Flood FBI file.
40 "The three hits": Thomas Johnson interview.
40 "He turned it": Herman Flood Jr. interview. Mattick said he did not recall seeing him play, much less making him an offer. Bobby Mattick interview.
40 a tailor's assistant: Garrow, *Bearing the Cross*, 11–22.
40 a 14-year-old Chicago boy: *WP*, 9/1/55, 2; *NYT*, 9/4/55, S9; *NYT*, 9/18/55, E7; *NYT*, 9/22/55, 64; *WP*, 5/11/2004, A3.

CHAPTER FOUR

Page

42 *"I am pleased"*: Flood, *The Way It Is*, 18.
42 "White"; "Colored"; "For a wild": Ibid., 34.
42 Flood could not wait: Ibid., 34–35.
42 Chuck Harmon: Chuck Harmon interview.
43 he impressed: *CTS*, 3/5/56, 18.
43 flailed at the plate: Stump, "Curt Flood in the Midnight League," *Sport*, 3/65, 79.
43 His lone highlight: *NYT*, 4/1/56, 161; *CE*, 4/1/56, 45; *TSN*, 4/11/56, 32.
43 "after ten years": *TSN*, 6/6/56, 9; Tygiel, *Baseball's Great Experiment*, 314.
43 Immediately after: *CE*, 4/1/56, 46; *CST*, 3/31/56, 14.

43 The players lived in barracks: Flood, *The Way It Is*, 36; *HPE*, 3/29/56, 3D.
43 He and the other black players: Karl Kuehl interview; Flood, *The Way It Is*, 36.
43 At night: Flood, *The Way It Is*, 36–37.
43 "looked miserable": *HPE*, 4/11/56, 7B.
43 60,000: *Baseball Blue Book 1956*, 32.
43 "I was ready": Flood, *The Way It Is*, 37.
44 Whites rioted: *NYT*, 2/5/56, 60; Branch, *Parting the Waters*, 167–68; Patterson, *Grand Expectations*, 396.
44 In March, 100: *NYT*, 3/13/56, 1, 14; Patterson, *Grand Expectations*, 398; Branch, *Parting the Waters*, 183.
44 Dr. King's Montgomery bus boycott: Garrow, *Bearing the Cross*, 76–82; Branch, *Parting the Waters*, 186–96; *Gayle v. Browder*, 352 U.S. 903 (1956); *NYT*, 11/14/56, 1, 22; *NYT*, 12/22/56, 1, 11.
44 The Carolina League's: Adelson, *Brushing Back Jim Crow*, 39–46.
44 Two years later: *NYTM*, 10/13/91, 53; Robinson, *Baseball Has Done It*, 136; Adelson, *Brushing Back Jim Crow*, 70.
44 "peckerwood league": Flood, *The Way It Is*, 39.
44 "One of my first": Ibid., 37.
44 During the first few: Ibid., 38–39.
44 "It's hell down": Stump, "Curt Flood in the Midnight League," *Sport*, 3/65, 79.
44 "I felt too young": Flood, *The Way It Is*, 38–39.
45 "His sister called": Bobby Mattick interview.
45 "What had started": Flood, *The Way It Is*, 38.
45 "We were Jackie's": Ed Charles interview. See also Adelson, *Brushing Back Jim Crow*, 16–17.
46 "considerable amount": *HPE*, 7/20/56, 6B.
46 "There's a goddamned": Flood, *The Way It Is*, 37–38.
46 yelled "Run, nigger": John Ivory Smith interview.
46 until he was transferred: *HPE*, 5/12/56, 7.
46 A month later: *HPE*, 6/11/56, 4B.
46 White teammates saw: Amiel Solomon interview.
46 He once ate: Stump, "Curt Flood in the Midnight League," *Sport*, 3/65, 79.
46 Flood had to ask: Flood, *The Way It Is*, 38.
46 His manager: Karl Kuehl interview; Ibid., 38.
47 "attitude"; "courage"; "They keep": *DS*, 8/1/56, D1.
47 "The manager": Carl Long interview. On July 27, Flood homered in the ninth off Paepke. He also doubled twice, tripled, and drove in a run with a sacrifice fly. There is no record of any stolen bases. *HPE*, 7/28/56, 7; *KDFP*, 7/28/56, 2. The Carolina League box scores did not record hit batsmen, but Paepke "walked" four.
47 singer Nat King Cole: *NYT*, 4/11/56, 1; *LAT*, 4/12/56, 2.
47 "[A] guy was hiding": *TSN*, 4/20/68, 8.

47 128 RBIs: *TSN*, 1/9/57, 8. There is some confusion over Flood's RBI total. Unofficial records immediately after the season credited him with 123. *TSN*, 9/12/56, 38; *RNO*, 9/9/56, II-3. Other sources said 120. *TSN*, 9/19/56, 7; *GDN*, 9/4/56, sec. 2, 4 (just over 120). That number, however, was eventually updated to 128.

47 He dazzled teammates: Nelvin Cooper interview; Haven Schmidt interview; Amiel Solomon interview.

47 Pesky proclaimed: *DS*, 8/1/56, D1.

47 The Carolina League named: *RNO*, 9/6/56, 18.

47 "I lit up": Stump, "Curt Flood in the Midnight League," *Sport*, 3/65, 79.

48 "Pride was my": Flood, *The Way It Is*, 39.

48 Flood was excluded: Sam Bercovich interview.

48 135 pounds: Flood, *The Way It Is*, 39.

48 "I believe": Ibid., 40.

48 He had never been: Burns/Flood interview, 3.

48 On the plane: *TSN*, 9/19/56, 7.

48 number 27: The *Baseball Almanac* lists Flood as wearing number 27 in 1956. See http://www.baseballalmanac.com/players/player.php?p=floodcu01. So does the 1956 Reds yearbook. E-mail, May 13, 2004, with Greg Rhodes, curator of the Reds Museum. Outfielder Al Silvera wore number 27 in 1955 and 1956 until the Reds released him on May 15, 1956. *NYT*, 5/16/56, 41. Reds pitcher Hal Jeffcoat already had number 42. The following year, Flood wore number 21 at spring training and in September. *CE*, 4/4/57, 46; *SMN*, 4/13/57, 46. Flood was not listed in the 1957 Reds yearbook. He wore number 21 for his entire career with the Cardinals except his rookie season in 1958, when he wore Robinson's number 42.

48 A week after joining: *NYT*, 9/17/56, 30; *WP*, 9/17/56, 15, 19; *CE*, 9/17/56, 1.

49 After the season: Rampersad, *Jackie Robinson*, 303–9; TT, 195:12–196:9 (Robinson).

49 The Reds, who regarded: Undated article, Curt Flood file, Reds Museum; *CE*, 9/10/56, 39; *CE*, 9/12/56, 34; *TSN*, 10/17/56, 32; Flood, *The Way It Is*, 42.

49 "wasn't prepared": Adelson, *Brushing Back Jim Crow*, 88. See Aaron with Wheeler, *I Had a Hammer*, 55–76; Aaron with Bisher, *Aaron*, 30–38.

49 the Georgia Senate: *CE*, 2/15/57, 36; Adelson, *Brushing Back Jim Crow*, 202–7.

49 "I think it's": Adelson, *Brushing Back Jim Crow*, 206.

49 That same year: Branch, *Parting the Waters*, 220.

49 Arkansas governor Orval Faubus: Ibid., 222–25.

50 *Savannah Morning News*: *SMN*, 9/4/57, 1; *SMN*, 9/5/57, 1; *SMN*, 9/6/57, 1.

50 "The Georgia city": Flood, *The Way It Is*, 42.

50 in between games: Burns/Flood interview, 6; Lee, "The Curt Flood Story," *Real Sports*, 3/10/97.

50 He could not even wait: Flood, *The Way It Is*, 43; "Curt Flood," *ESPN SportsCentury* (Pace); Ed Charles interview. Flood's white Savannah teammates did not remember his dressing in a separate area. Buddy Gilbert interview; Haven Schmidt interview; Glenn Isringhaus interview. Neither did his black teammate, John Ivory Smith. John Ivory Smith interview.

50 He could not find: Flood, *The Way It Is*, 42–43; Stump, "Curt Flood in the Midnight League," *Sport*, 3/65, 79.

50 Savannah center fielder Buddy Gilbert: Buddy Gilbert interview; Halberstam, *October 1964*, 113–14.

50 "Poor Gilbert's": Flood, *The Way It Is*, 44.

50 "He took a lot": Buddy Gilbert interview.

50 In August, he injured: *SMN*, 8/25/57, sec. 3, 22.

51 His .299 average: *AC*, 9/15/57, 9-B. Fourth among hitters with more than 400 at-bats.

51 He finished: Including 24 doubles (third), 8 triples, 14 home runs, 82 RBIs (fourth), 97 runs (first), 170 hits (tied second), 252 total bases (tied second), 80 walks, and 53 strikeouts. *AC*, 9/15/57, 9-B; *SMN*, 9/15/57, 23.

51 He made two: *SMN*, 7/14/57, sec. 3, 25; *SMN*, 8/18/57, 26; *AC*, 8/18/57, 3-B.

51 His first major league: *CE*, 9/26/57, 37; *SPD*, 4/10/68, 4C.

51 He was sent: *CE*, 3/3/58, 34; Flood, *The Way It Is*, 45; *TSN*, 10/9/57, 33.

51 "a flock of nobodies": *LAT*, 7/5/68, D1.

51 Cincinnati was not ready: Flood, *The Way It Is*, 47.

51 After tearing up: *CE*, 3/4/58, 27; *CE*, 3/24/58, 25; *CE*, 3/30/58, 30. Pinson's numbers in Visalia: .367, 20 HR, 97 RBI, 165 runs, 209 hits, 349 total bases, 40 doubles, 20 triples, and 53 stolen bases.

52 Mattick pointed out; too small: Bobby Mattick interview.

52 Tebbetts denied: Pepe, "How Flood Finally Made It," *Sport*, 11/62, 45; Stump, "Curt Flood in the Midnight League," *Sport*, 3/65, 78; Flood, *The Way It Is*, 62.

52 including Frank Robinson: Bobby Mattick interview; Robinson, *Baseball Is My Life*, 49–50.

52 "There was a quota": "Curt Flood," *ESPN SportsCentury* (Robinson). In addition to Robinson, Pinson, Crowe, and Thurman, the 1958 Reds also opened the season with black pitchers Brooks Lawrence and Joe Black.

52 In 1947, several southern: Rampersad, *Jackie Robinson*, 174–75; Tygiel, *Baseball's Great Experiment*, 185–88; Allen, *Jackie Robinson*, 135–44 (interviews Cardinals players dismissing the story); Kahn, *The Era*, 341–42 (characterizing the denials of the Cardinals players as weak); Red Smith interview, Chandler Collection (explaining how the *New York Herald Tribune*'s Stanley Woodward broke the story and why the denials are wrong).

52 On the Garagiola incident: *TSN*, 9/24/47, 6; *CT*, 9/12/47, 32; *NYT*, 9/12/47,

39; Robinson, *My Own Story*, 129, 158–59; Tygiel, *Baseball's Great Experiment*, 204; Rampersad, *Jackie Robinson*, 184–85.

52 On the Slaughter incident: *CT*, 8/21/47, 27; *NYT*, 8/21/47, 21; *RAA*, 8/30/47, 12; *RAA*, 9/20/47, 15; *TSN*, 8/27/47, 4; Robinson, *My Own Story*, 158; Roeder, *Jackie Robinson*, 136–37; Robinson, "A Kentucky Colonel kept me in baseball," *Look*, 2/8/55, 84. Cardinals outfielder Joe Medwick also collided with Robinson and spiked him at first base. *RAA*, 8/30/47, 12. But that appears to have been accidental. Robinson credited Medwick as one of the players who, like Greenberg, tried to help him out. Robinson, "A Kentucky Colonel kept me in baseball," *Look*, 2/8/55, 87.

52 A few years later: Rampersad, *Jackie Robinson*, 246–47; Golenbock, *Bums*, 428–29 (Roger Kahn recalling Cardinals bench jockeying in 1953 that included epithets such as "nigger" and "black bastard").

52 The Chase Hotel: *PC*, 5/8/54, 14; Robinson, "A Kentucky Colonel kept me in baseball," *Look*, 2/8/55, 87; Campanella, *It's Good to Be Alive*, 193–94; Tygiel, *Baseball's Great Experiment*, 312–13. For sportswriter Wendell Smith's recollections about the Chase Hotel, see *CA*, 1/23/61, 18; *PC*, 2/4/61, sec. 2, 27. Dick Gregory was denied service there as late as 1961. *SA*, 5/12/61, 1A.

52 Flood's first apartment: Flood, *The Way It Is*, 78; Burns/Flood interview, 6.

52 replaced manager Fred Hutchinson: Devine, *The Memoirs of Bing Devine*, 88–90.

53 A diminutive: *SPD*, 9/15/58, 4-B; Devine, *The Memoirs of Bing Devine*, 89–90; Bingham, "Frolic in the Spring," *SI*, 3/9/59, 58–59.

53 White nearly killed: *SGD*, 9/22/59, 19; *SPD*, 4/13/60, 1E.

53 Hemus also refused: Gibson, *From Ghetto to Glory*, 47–49; Gibson, *Stranger to the Game*, 53–55; *SPD*, 6/17/60, 4C (describing Gibson as "bouncing like a 'yo-yo' between Rochester and St. Louis").

53 Hemus believed: Gibson, *From Ghetto to Glory*, 49; Gibson, *Stranger to the Game*, 52–53; Flood, *The Way It Is*, 69; Tim McCarver interview.

53 Flood and Gibson believed: Gibson, *Stranger to the Game*, 54; Flood, *The Way It Is*, 67–68; Halberstam, *October 1964*, 108; Golenbock, *The Spirit of St. Louis*, 434. Bill White, however, thought that Hemus was just bad at managing people. Halberstam, *October 1964*, 108; Golenbock, *The Spirit of St. Louis*, 434. This is supported by Hemus's benching of Stan Musial (see Golenbock, *The Spirit of St. Louis*, 432–33), moving slugging third baseman Ken Boyer to center field and ordering him to hit behind base runners (Gibson, *Stranger to the Game*, 52), and alienating pitcher Jim Brosnan (Golenbock, *The Spirit of St. Louis*, 427–28; Brosnan, *The Long Season*, 206–7, 224). Devine believed that Hemus came into the job with too many preconceived ideas about his players for a first-time manager. Hemus saw taking anyone's advice as a sign of weakness. Bing Devine interview; Devine, *The Memoirs of Bing Devine*, 91.

53 "Hemus acted": Flood, *The Way It Is*, 67–68.

53 "Midnight League": Stump, "Curt Flood in the Midnight League," *Sport*, 3/65, 33.

53 He had already been smoking: Stump, "Curt Flood in the Midnight League," *Sport*, 3/65, 78.

53 Now insomnia and indigestion: Flood, *The Way It Is*, 68.

53 1962 expansion draft: *SGD*, 7/30/61, 1C.

53 Hemus revealed: *SPD*, 5/4/59, 4B; *PPG*, 5/4/59, 22, 24; *PP*, 5/4/59, 24; *PP*, 5/5/59, 31; *TSN*, 5/13/59, 23; *NYT*, 5/4/59, 40; *LAT*, 5/4/59, C1.

53 "You black bastard!": Pitcher Jim Brosnan wrote in 1960 that Hemus called Daniels a "black bastard." Brosnan, *The Long Season*, 115. Gibson wrote in his autobiography that Hemus confessed in the locker room to calling Daniels a "black bastard." Gibson, *Stranger to the Game*, 53 (also claiming that Hemus referred to Daniels as a "nigger" in the team meeting). Gibson, however, was not even there. The previous week, he had been sent down to Triple-A Omaha. *SPD*, 4/28/59, 1C; *TSN*, 5/6/59, 17, 36. Two other subsequent accounts claimed that Hemus said "black bastard." Boyle, "The Private World of the Negro Ballplayer," *SI*, 3/21/60, 78; Halberstam, *October 1964*, 109–10. Flood said Hemus called Daniels a "black son-of-a-bitch." Flood, *The Way It Is*, 70. Daniels, for his part, cannot remember exactly what Hemus called him. "I know it wasn't the n-word," Daniels said. "It was black-something." Bennie Daniels interview.

53 Hemus held a closed-door: *SPD*, 5/4/59, 4B (Hemus locked the clubhouse door after the game, indicating a team meeting free from the press); *PP*, 5/4/59, 24 (claiming that Hemus closed the locker room to dress down his players about their "sloppy play"). Flood said Hemus revealed to the players what was said. Flood, *The Way It Is*, 70. Hemus later went out of his way to compliment Daniels, who supposedly said: "Thank you, little Faubus"—a reference to the segregationist Arkansas governor. Boyle, "The Private World of the Negro Ballplayer," *SI*, 3/21/60, 78; Halberstam, *October 1964*, 110.

54 "Until then": Flood, *The Way It Is*, 70.

54 Johnny Keane: *SPD*, 7/6/61, 1E; *SPD*, 7/7/61, 4B; *SPD*, 4/24/62, 4B.

54 A month later, Keane: It is often asserted that Keane immediately made Flood his starting center fielder. Flood, *The Way It Is*, 72; Gibson, *Stranger to the Game*, 65–66; Rains, *The St. Louis Cardinals*, 174; Golenbock, *The Spirit of St. Louis*, 446; Halberstam, *October 1964*, 113; Craft and Owens, *Redbirds Revisited*, 76; Pepe, "How Flood Finally Made It," *Sport*, 11/62, 45; Stump, "Curt Flood in the Midnight League," *Sport*, 3/65, 78; Leggett, "Not Just a Flood, but a Deluge," *SI*, 8/19/68, 20; Vecsey, "How Curt Flood Inspires the Cardinals," *Sport*, 10/68, 68. Keane, however, used several other players there; Flood did not take over the position until nearly a month after Keane became manager. *SPD*, 8/5/61, 6A; *SGD*, 8/5/61, 9.

54 He could read: Stump, "Curt Flood in the Midnight League," *Sport*, 3/65, 78.
54 Flood first met Bob Gibson: *SMN*, 9/2/57, 12.
54 The segregation and discrimination: Gibson, *Stranger to the Game*, 44–46.
54 One of seven: Gibson, *From Ghetto to Glory*, 5–14, 25, 39–40; Gibson, *Stranger to the Game*, 10–17; *SGD*, 2/16/58, 4E; *SPD*, 6/15/61, 1E.
55 Gibson arrived in St. Petersburg: Gibson, *From Ghetto to Glory*, 41–42.
55 Bill White: Smith, "Baseball's Angry Man," *NYTM*, 10/13/91, 53, 56; *SPD*, 6/7/59, 2C; *NYT*, 3/30/60, 45; *TSN*, 12/18/65, 3–4.
55 One weekend: Only Flood and White attended the Nation of Islam meeting, driving down from Homestead, according to White's 1965 account. *TSN*, 12/18/65, 4. But Flood later said it was he and Gibson. Flood, *The Way It Is*, 28–29. Beginning in mid-February, Flood and White were in Homestead getting extra hitting instruction from coach Harry "the Hat" Walker. *SGD*, 2/12/61, 1E; *SPD*, 2/14/61, 5C. Gibson, however, was not there. *SPD*, 2/24/61, 4B; *SGD*, 2/24/61, 1C; *SPD*, 2/25/61, 4B (reporting that Gibson was due to join the team in St. Petersburg at the start of spring training and he was not in Homestead). Gibson was pitching his team to the Venezuelan league championship until the middle of February. *SPD*, 2/15/61, 4D (the Cardinals received Gibson's signed contract in the mail from Venezuela); *TSN*, 2/15/61, 23; *TSN*, 2/22/61, 27. He then went home to Omaha. Gibson, *Stranger to the Game*, 63–64. Flood was wrong; Gibson was not there.
55 The Louisville Lip: Flood, *The Way It Is*, 28–29.
55 During a two-week: *NYT*, 2/8/61, 39 (Jim Robinson); *LAT*, 2/8/61, C1 (same); *NYT*, 2/22/61, 32 (Donnie Fleeman).
56 "I'll go dancin'": Remnick, *King of the World*, 118; *WP*, 2/5/61, C3 (sparring session); *NYT*, 2/7/61, 44 (sparring session).
56 Clay invited: *TSN*, 12/18/65, 4. Clay's education about the Nation of Islam began in the spring of 1961 in Miami. Remnick, *King of the World*, 127–29.
56 "Sounds as if": Flood, *The Way It Is*, 29.
56 That year, an incident: *SPT*, 3/9/61, C1; Smith, "Baseball's Angry Man," *NYTM*, 10/13/91, 56; Gibson, *Stranger to the Game*, 57–58.
56 At 5:20 p.m.: *SPT*, 3/9/61, 1-C.
56 "When will we be": *SPT*, 3/9/61, 1-C. Also quoted in *PC*, 3/18/61, 30.
56 Cardinals public relations director: *NYT*, 3/9/61, 34; *SPD*, 3/9/61, 2E; *SGD*, 3/9/61, 1D; *CA*, 3/10/61, 13.
57 "The rookie": *PC*, 2/11/61, sec. 2, 28.
57 At spring training; "Do you mean"; "Mr. Busch": Burns, *Baseball*, vol. 8; Burns/Flood interview transcript, 5.
57 Devine called Flood: Flood, *The Way It Is*, 78–79.
57 Wendell Smith: *CA*, 1/23/61, 1, 18. Smith's articles ran in the *Pittsburgh Courier* and the *Chicago American*. Carroll, "Wendell Smith's Last Crusade," 123; Snyder, *Beyond the Shadow of the Senators*, 186–89 (Smith biographical info).

57 "Fat Cats" and "Uncle Toms": *PC*, 1/28/61, sec. 2, 27.

57 A week after: *SPT*, 2/1/61, 1-C; *CA*, 2/1/61, 26; *NYT*, 2/2/61, 33; *NYT*, 2/3/61, 186–90; *NYT*, 2/4/61, 11; *NYT*, 2/19/61, 179; *PC*, 3/18/61, sec. 2, 28; Howard with Wimbish, *Elston and Me*, 99–103; Davis, "Baseball's Reluctant Challenge," 148.

58 Wimbish's wife: Ralph Wimbish Jr. interview.

58 "After dinner": *SPT*, 3/9/98, 1D.

58 White received: *NYP*, 1/28/97, 64.

58 "Curt thought it": Ibid.

58 48 Cardinals and Yankees players: *SPT*, 3/10/61, 1-C.

58 "help to break down": *PC*, 3/18/61, sec. 2, 30; Howard with Wimbish, *Elston and Me*, 102 (claiming that someone from the Yankees front office "insisted" that Howard attend).

58 White, Flood, and the other: *PC*, 3/18/61, sec. 2, 30; *NYP*, 1/28/97, 72, 64; Smith, "Baseball's Angry Man," *NYTM*, 10/13/91, 56. For White's slightly flawed account, see Aaron, *I Had a Hammer*, 153–54. For Gibson's account, including comments from White, see Gibson, *Stranger to the Game*, 57–59.

58 "It was our own": Gibson, *Stranger to the Game*, 59.

58 The sit-ins swept: *NYT*, 5/7/61, E10.

58 Integrated groups: *NYT*, 6/15/61, 38; *NYT*, 6/17/61, 12; Branch, *Parting the Waters*, 412–91; Garrow, *Bearing the Cross*, 154–57, 159–61, 171–72.

59 On July 31; "first class citizens": *CA*, 8/1/61, 18.

59 When the owners: *CA*, 11/9/61, 23.

59 The White Sox: *PC*, 3/3/62, sec. 2, 30; *CA*, 11/9/61, 23; *CA*, 7/31/61, 13; *CA*, 2/4/61, 13; *CA*, 12/1/61, 23.

59 The Cardinals reacted: *SA*, 4/7/61, 1A, 4A; *SA*, 3/16/62, 5A; Smith, "Baseball's Angry Man," *NYTM*, 10/13/91, 56.

59 Rumors surfaced: *SPT*, 4/12/61; Aaron, *I Had a Hammer*, 154.

59 During spring training in 1961: *SPT*, 4/12/61; *SPT*, 5/18/61.

59 A businessman: *SPD*, 2/25/62, 3B; Bing Devine interview.

59 Twenty-nine of the 32: *SPD*, 2/25/62, 3B; *SPD*, 3/15/62, 1E; *SA*, 3/16/62, 5A.

59 The motel's food: Tim McCarver interview.

59 Cardinals players: Smith, "Baseball's Angry Man," *NYTM*, 10/13/91, 56; Gibson, *Stranger to the Game*, 58.

59 Players, front-office: *SPD*, 2/25/62, 3B; *SPD*, 3/15/62, 1E; *BAA*, 3/24/62, 19.

60 In February 1962: 3/23/62 letter from Roy Wilkins to Jackie Robinson, NAACP Collection, B:III C173; Robinson, *Baseball Has Done It*, 13 (incorrectly placing the NAACP rally in January 1963). Several athletes and entertainers, including Bill White, Elston Howard, Roy Campanella, Jim Brown, Dick Gregory, and Harry Belafonte, were unable to attend. Gregory and Howard were listed on the program. Souvenir Program, Tenth Anniversary

Southeast Region Conference NAACP, Sovereignty Commission Online, SCR ID # 10-35-2-17-1-1-1. Belafonte and Campanella declined Robinson's invitation. 2/14/62 telegram from Jackie Robinson to Gloster Current, NAACP Collection, B:III C173. White could not rearrange his schedule, and Brown had a "job commitment." 1/25/62 letter from Ruby Hurley to Gloster Current, NAACP Collection, B:III C273, F "Southeast Regional Office Correspondence 1962."

60 "to let you know": *JCL*, 2/26/62, 1. All of the national and local news accounts were based upon wire reports. See also *NYT*, 2/26/62, 21; *WP*, 2/26/62, A2; *CT*, 2/26/62, C8.

60 swelled with pride: *CDEF*, 3/10/62, 2; *AN*, 3/10/62, 11; *CDEF*, 8/24/63, 8.

60 "Our admiration": *CDEF*, 3/10/62, 2; *AN*, 3/10/62, 11.

60 In Mississippi, Flood: Aurela Norris Young interview, 4/29/83, 9, Southern Regional Council, "Will the Circle Be Unbroken?" program files.

60 "People felt relaxed": Moody, *Coming of Age in Mississippi*, 262.

60 Medgar Evers: 2/9/62 telegram from Current to Robinson, NAACP Collection, B:III C273, F "Southeast Regional Office Correspondence 1962" (instructing Robinson to inform Evers of Robinson's itinerary); Aurela Norris Young interview, 4/29/83, 9, Southern Regional Council, "Will the Circle Be Unbroken?" program files.

60 "do and perform": http://mdah.state.ms.us/arlib/contents/er/scagency/casehistory.html (quoting General Laws of the State of Mississippi, 1956, Chapter 365, 520–524).

60 "Patterson and the other": 2/28/62 report by A. L. Hopkins, investigator, 1–2, Sovereignty Commission Online, SCR ID # 2-55-7-62-1-1-1, www.mdah.state.ms.us/arlib/contents/er/sovcom.

61 By virtue: "Flood, Curtis 2-55-418," at SCR ID # 98-6-3-33-1-1-1, www.mdah.state.ms.us/arlib/contents/er/sovcom.

61 Flood told: *CDEF*, 3/10-16/62, 2.

61 thank-you note: 3/23/62 letter from Roy Wilkins to Flood, NAACP Collection, B:III C173.

61 Frank Robinson and Willie Mays: The Reds paid Robinson's NAACP dues early in his career, but he refused to be active in the organization. A letter from Jackie Robinson encouraged him to speak out on civil rights issues. Jackie charged that Frank was more interested in becoming the first black manager (which he became with the Indians in October 1974) than in speaking out on issues. *BAA*, 5/12/70, 17. Frank later said he was "afraid." Robinson, *Extra Innings*, ix. Jackie also described Mays as a "do-nothing Negro" when it came to the civil rights movement. *LAT*, 3/16/68, A1.

61 "went to": Robinson, *Baseball Has Done It*, 142.

61 President Kennedy: Branch, *Parting the Waters*, 386, 647–53, 656–72.

61 On thc day of King's: *SPD*, 8/29/63, 4D.

61 It tore Flood; "I should be there": Maury Allen interview.
61 During the offseason: *BAA*, 11/3/64, 13.
62 "What are you": Bill Patterson interview.
62 "best hitting": Branch Rickey Papers, Box 51, Folder 2.
62 Cardinals broadcaster Harry Caray: *CT*, 5/1/71, F4.
62 In October 1963, Beverly filed: *OT*, 10/8/63, 36.
62 "inadequate and inferior": *OT*, 2/28/64, 50.
62 On February 27, 1964: *OT*, 2/28/64, 50; *TSN*, 3/14/64, 28; *SGD*, 2/29–3/1/64, 3G.
62 She also received: *LAT*, 2/28/64, B6.
63 By the time Curt and Beverly: *SFC*, 10/27/64, 1, 10; *SFE*, 10/27/64, 1, 16.
63 "No niggers": *SFC*, 10/27/64, 1.
63 The law did not concern: *OT*, 12/25/72, 40.
63 Immediately after receiving: *SFE*, 10/27/64, 1; Rickie Riley interview.
64 They reconvened: *SFE*, 10/27/64, 16; Flood, *The Way It Is*, 119.
64 Beverly was intent: Rickie Riley interview.
64 Marian turned: Flood, *The Way It Is*, 119.
64 On October 26, Condon filed: *OT*, 10/26/64, 11; *OT*, 10/27/64, 1; *RI*, 10/26/64, 1, 2; Flood, *The Way It Is*, 119–20.
64 Backed by: *LAT*, 10/28/64, 2; *SFC*, 10/28/64, 3.
65 "Yes, we thought": *SFC*, 10/28/64, 3.
65 Flood was eventually forced: *OT*, 11/10/64, 40; *OT*, 11/2/64, 19; *NYT*, 11/10/64, 51.
65 "You don't do": *BAA*, 11/3/64, 13.
65 The housing ordeal: *SFE*, 10/27/64, 1, 16; *SFC*, 10/27/64, 1; *SFC*, 10/28/61, 1; *RI*, 10/26/64, 1; *MMNG*, 10/27/64, 1; *MMNG*, 10/28/64, 1.
65 The *Washington Post*: *WP*, 11/2/64, A16.
65 Six women: *SFC*, 10/28/64, 3; *SFE*, 10/28/64, 3; *BAA*, 11/3/64, 13.
65 The men invited: *BAA*, 11/3/64, 13.
65 The Floods' children: *LAT*, 1/24/65, J2.
65 Debbie . . . was excluded: Flood, *The Way It Is*, 120.
65 Racists phoned; The police; Both; "I have no": *LAT*, 1/24/65, J2.
65 A few of Flood's: Earl Robinson interview.
66 "immediately [to]": Memo from FBI Director to SAC, San Francisco, 10/30/64, Flood FBI File, SF office.
66 The San Francisco office: Flood FBI file, SF office.
66 "recent notoriety": Memo from FBI Director to SAC, San Francisco, 10/30/64, Flood FBI file, FOIA appeal, 1/25/05.
66 In October 1963, Hoover: Garrow, *Bearing the Cross*, 303–4, 323, 372–74.
66 The New York Mets players: *NYT*, 6/8/68, 34.
66 Milt Pappas: *SPD*, 6/9/68, 1D, 4D; *SPD*, 6/12/68, 3E; Pappas, *Out at Home*, 189–91; *NYT*, 6/10/68, 60; *Sport*, 8/69, 82.

66–67 "When something happens"; "the best work": *WP*, 8/4/68, C2.

67 Like Flood, McDonald also placed: Tommy McDonald interview.

67 In a 1967 *Los Angeles Times*: *LAT*, 5/23/67, C3.

67 "I guess": Burns, *Baseball*, vol. 8; Burns/Flood interview, 8. For a similar quote, see Curran, "Curt Flood and the Baseball Revolution," *L.A. Weekly*, 4/1–7/94, 24.

CHAPTER FIVE

Page

69 he saw: Dal Maxvill interview.

69 A Washington University: Ibid.; *SGD*, 5/9–10/64, 2G; *SPD*, 5/11/64, 4C; *SPD*, 10/5/64, 4B; Craft and Owens, *Redbirds Revisited*, 147–53.

69–70 Maxvill had no idea; "How can"; "It's just"; "Everybody"; "You haven't"; "It's early"; "Why are": Dal Maxvill interview.

70 "Do you know": Korr, *The End of Baseball As We Knew It*, 87 (Maxvill).

70 While waiting: Ibid.; Tim McCarver interview; McCarver, *Few and Chosen*, 95–96 (recalling they waited in the Atlanta airport). Maxvill insists it was Miami, which makes sense for a flight to Puerto Rico. Dal Maxvill interview.

70 McCarver once walked: Gibson, *Stranger to the Game*, 60; McCarver, *Oh, Baby, I Love It!*, 61; Halberstam, *October 1964*, 220–21.

70 Another time: Halberstam, *October 1964*, 221.

70 At spring training: Gibson, *Stranger to the Game*, 60; Halberstam, *October 1964*, 221.

71 "Tim McCarver was a rugged": Flood, *The Way It Is*, 87–88.

71 "everybody but": *SPD*, 4/12/66, 4C.

71 "complete shock": Tim McCarver interview.

71 "Curt, do you really": "Curt Flood," *ESPN SportsCentury* (McCarver).

71 McCarver soon realized: Tim McCarver interview; McCarver, *Few and Chosen*, 95; "Curt Flood," *ESPN SportsCentury*.

71 McCarver still believed: Tim McCarver interview.

71 Flood had another: Judy Pace Flood interview; Dick Moss interview.

72 The daughter: *BAA*, 8/28–9/1/73, 15.

72 Flood first noticed: Judy Pace Flood interview.

72 "That's awful": Dick Moss interview.

72 For nearly a year; Flood clamored; "[Curt] thought"; "Now you can": Judy Pace Flood interview.

72 The following year: Flood, *The Way It Is*, 178.

72 Over the years, Flood visited: Judy Pace Flood interview; Lisanti, *Fantasy Femmes of Sixties Cinema*, 215.

72 Flood and Pace shared: Judy Pace Flood interview.

73 Before the meeting: Marvin Miller interview.

73 "Why is it": Miller, *A Whole Different Ball Game*, 186.

73 Instead, the owners offered: MLBPA Memo from Miller to All Major League Players, 12/26/69, 1–2; "Minutes of Executive Board Meeting," 12/13–14/69, 1–2 (on file with author).

73 The players also reviewed: "Minutes of Executive Board Meeting," 12/13–14/69, 3; MLBPA Memo, "Discussions with the Owners' Representatives Regarding the Reserve Rules," 1–3 (on file with author).

73 "If you want to change": *SGD*, 1/1/70, E2.

73 Miller spoke first: Marvin Miller interview.

74 "third degree": Handwritten Meeting Notes, 12/13/69, 6 (on file with author).

74 The players were skeptical: Dick Moss interview; Tim McCarver interview; Dal Maxvill interview; MLBPA Memo, "Discussions with the Owners' Representatives Regarding the Reserve Rules," 3.

74 Donn Clendenon: *TSN*, 3/15/69, 17, 20; Gross, "The Ballplayers' Drive for Independence," *Sport*, 8/69, 82.

74 The Expos coaxed: *NYT*, 3/19/69, 53; *NYDN*, 3/25/69, 88; Holtzman, "Two Divisions, Rules, Player Demands, Etc.," 271–75.

74 shaggy-haired, mod-dressing: Harrelson, *Hawk*, 224–44.

74 dark glasses: Ibid., 231.

74 $75,000 plus $25,000: Holtzman, "Two Divisions, Rules, Player Demands, Etc.," 277; Kuhn, *Hardball*, 50; Briley, "Baseball and America in 1969," 274. Compare Gross, "The Ballplayers' Drive for Independence," *Sport*, 8/69, 15 (claiming that Harrelson's salary was $50,000 annual contract plus $25,000 for promotional services).

74 Maury Wills: *TSN*, 6/14/69, 18; *TSN*, 6/28/69, 26.

75 *caveat emptor:* *TSN*, 12/20/69, 28; Holtzman, "Two Divisions, Rules, Player Demands, Etc.," 277–78.

75 After Miller spoke: Marvin Miller interview; "Minutes of Executive Board Meeting," 12/13–14/69, 3–4.

75 "under the same yoke": Handwritten Meeting Notes, 12/13/69, 6; Korr, *The End of Baseball As We Knew It*, 88. See also Flood, *The Way It Is*, 193 (Flood's recollection).

75 After Flood finished: Handwritten Meeting Notes, 12/13/69, 6; Marvin Miller interview.

75 The player representatives questioned: Handwritten Meeting Notes, 12/13/69, 6–11; "Discussions with the Owners' Representatives Regarding the Reserve Rules," 3; Marvin Miller interview; Tim McCarver interview; Dal Maxvill interview.

75 "A lot of people think": *SPD*, 1/27/70, 3B.

76 Tom Haller: Handwritten Meeting Notes, 12/13/69, 7 ("with today's social situation, is being black a motivation"); Flood, *The Way It Is*, 17 ("This is a period of black militance. Do you feel that you're doing this as part of a move-

ment? Because you're black?"); Miller, *A Whole Different Ball Game*, 185 ("He mentioned first the turbulence of the 1960s, the struggle over civil rights and black power, a new consciousness about race relations and past injustices and the righting of wrongs. Haller's question then was: 'Are you doing this simply because you're black and you feel that baseball has been discriminatory?'"); Holtzman, "Two Divisions, Rules, Player Demands, Etc.," 304.

76 Haller's question: Miller, *A Whole Different Ball Game*, 185–86; Marvin Miller interview.

76 But the question was: Tim McCarver interview; Tom Haller interview; Ron Brand interview; Miller, *A Whole Different Ball Game*, 185–86.

76 "I didn't want": Tom Haller interview.

76 "I wanted to make": Ron Brand interview.

76 "fascinating question": Flood, *The Way It Is*, 17.

76 Flood explained: Handwritten Meeting Notes, 12/13/69, 7; Flood, *The Way It Is*, 17–18, 195; Miller, *A Whole Different Ball Game*, 186; Marvin Miller interview; Tom Haller interview.

77 Flood knew: Flood, *The Way It Is*, 17–18.

77 Not even McCarver: Tim McCarver interview.

77 Jim Bunning; Reggie Jackson . . . asked; Haller asked; McCarver asked: Handwritten Meeting Notes, 12/13/69, 7.

77–78 Moe Drabowsky; Bob Locker; Several players; Roberto Clemente; Reggie Jackson: Ibid., 8.

78 Steve Hamilton; Bunning asked: Ibid., 9; Jim Lonborg interview.

78 Drabowsky asked: Handwritten Meeting Notes, 12/13/69, 9.

79 With Miller's support: Korr, *The End of Baseball As We Knew It*, 95.

79 Clemente took up: Handwritten Meeting Notes, 12/13/69, 10.

79 In February 1954: There is some dispute about when Clemente was signed. Some sources say 1952, and Clemente claimed in that union meeting that he was 17. Ibid. That may have been the date of his first tryout, but Clemente was not officially signed until February 1954, when he was 19. *TSN*, 3/3/54, 26.

79 $10,000 bonus (and $5,000 salary): According to Clemente biographer David Maraniss, Clemente received a $10,000 bonus from the Dodgers and $5,000 for the 1954 season. E-mail from David Maraniss, 12/15/05. Compare Handwritten Meetings Notes, 12/13/69, 10 (mentioning only $10,000) with *TSN*, 3/3/54, 26 (reporting that the Dodgers signed him for $15,000).

79 $4,000: Clemente said it was $5,000 (Handwritten Meetings Notes, 12/13/69, 10), but it was actually $4,000. *TSN*, 12/1/54, 26; *TSN*, 12/8/54, 20; *NYT*, 11/23/54, 28. Clemente was available for $4,000 instead of $10,000 for the typical Triple-A player because he was considered a bonus player. Branch Rickey, having left the Dodgers for the Pirates, knew this and stuck it to his nemesis, Dodgers owner Walter O'Malley, by grabbing Clemente for $4,000.

79 "He had me"; "made $300,000": Handwritten Meetings Notes, 12/13/69, 10.

79 Max Alvis; Jackson asked; Drabowsky said: Ibid.
80 "(1) to take": MLBPA Memo, "Discussions with the Owners' Representatives Regarding the Reserve Rules," 3.
80 Joe Torre: Handwritten Meeting Notes, 12/13/69, 10.
80 $5,000; complimentary Cadillac: *NYT*, 3/18/69, 52; *NYT*, 3/17/69, 52; *TSN*, 3/29/69, 12.
80 "I don't care": *TSN*, 3/15/69, 17.
80 "Knowing how"; "I knew Curt": Joe Torre interview.
80 Bunning said; Alvis said: Handwritten Meeting Notes, 12/13/69, 11.
81 A question then arose: Ibid., 10–11; Marvin Miller interview; "Minutes of Executive Board Meeting," 12/13–14/69, 4; Miller, *A Whole Different Ball Game*, 187.
81 $195,000: "Minutes of Executive Board Meeting," 12/13–14/69, 3.
81 When Miller returned: Marvin Miller interview.
81 Miller then asked: Handwritten Meeting Notes, 12/13/69, 11; "Minutes of Executive Board Meeting," 12/13–14/69, 4; TT, 183:7–12 (Miller).

CHAPTER SIX

Page

82 The nameplate: *NYT*, 4/26/91, B9.
82 His partners: *NYT*, 12/19/76, F1.
82 Yet Arthur Goldberg: *WP*, 3/20/69, F7; Reeves, "Goldilocks . . . ," *NYTM*, 6/14/70, 7.
82 Miller knew him: Miller, *A Whole Different Ball Game*, 187.
82 He also worked: Ibid., 187–88; Marvin Miller interview.
82 Goldberg raised Miller's: Marvin Miller interview.
82 He selected Miller: Ibid.; Helyar, *Lords of the Realm*, 18–20.
82 When Goldberg left: *NYT*, 1/14/61, 24; *WSJ*, 1/16/61, 4.
83 Miller called Goldberg: Miller insisted that he initially phoned Goldberg *after* the December 13 meeting between Flood and the player representatives. Marvin Miller interview; Miller, *A Whole Different Ball Game*, 187. Goldberg's phone records, however, indicate that Miller initially called him at Paul, Weiss on December 3. Goldberg Papers, Box I-135, Folder 3. Miller, moreover, claims that the morning they had breakfast, Goldberg appeared on page 1 of the *New York Times* in a story about the Democrats wanting him to run for office. Marvin Miller interview; Miller, *A Whole Different Ball Game*, 188–89; *NYT*, 12/5/69, 1 ("21 Leaders Urge Race by Goldberg"); *NYT*, 12/10/69, 1 (when he announced that he would not run). It is extremely unlikely that upon returning from Puerto Rico on December 15 Miller would have asked Goldberg about running for office, because Goldberg had already announced that he would not be running. *NYT*, 12/13/69, 1; *NYT*, 12/14/69, 71. Miller spe-

cifically remembered the story appearing on page 1 and in the same day's paper (and he was still in Puerto Rico on December 13 and 14). Marvin Miller interview; Miller, *A Whole Different Ball Game*, 188–89. Thus, Miller must have spoken with Goldberg before the meeting in Puerto Rico and then after Puerto Rico arranged a meeting between Goldberg and Flood.

83 On the way to breakfast: Miller, *A Whole Different Ball Game*, 188–89.

83 There was Goldberg: *NYT*, 12/5/69, 1.

83 In the 1966 gubernatorial: Reeves, "This Is the Battle of the Titan?" *NYTM*, 11/1/70, 224.

83 An October 1 poll: *WP*, 11/16/69, 2.

83 Before they began discussing: Marvin Miller interview; Miller, *A Whole Different Ball Game*, 188–89.

83 *When* he won: Miller, *A Whole Different Ball Game*, 188–89.

83 "I took myself": Goldberg Press Conference, 4/25/68, 4, Goldberg Papers, Box I:48, Folder 2. Goldberg repeated this on several occasions, including his speech to the Johnson cabinet meeting announcing his resignation as UN ambassador. Cabinet Speech, 4/23/68, 1, Goldberg Papers, Box I:33, Folder 12.

83 "I personally": Goldberg Press Conference, 4/25/68, 4.

84 With this in mind: Marvin Miller interview; Miller, *A Whole Different Ball Game*, 188–89.

84 "This decision is final": *NYT*, 12/10/69, 1.

84 With Dick Moss at his side: Marvin Miller interview; Miller, *A Whole Different Ball Game*, 189–90.

84 He had seen Goldberg: Miller, *A Whole Different Ball Game*, 188.

84 Although Goldberg was unsuccessful: Shaplen, "Peacemaker-I," *New Yorker*, 4/7/62, 90.

84 In the span of three weeks: Shaplen, "Peacemaker-I," *New Yorker*, 4/7/62, 90, 95; Stebenne, *Arthur J. Goldberg*, 210.

84 "[i]t was the overwhelming": Mikva, "In Memoriam—Arthur Goldberg, the Practitioner," *Supreme Court Historical Society 1990 Yearbook*, 1; *Youngstown Sheet & Tube Co. v. Sawyer*, 343 U.S. 579 (1952).

84 In 1957 he argued: Stebenne, *Arthur J. Goldberg*, 177, 220; Marvin Miller interview; *Textile Workers Union v. Lincoln Mills*, 353 U.S. 448 (1957); *United Steelworkers of Am. v. Am. M'frg Co.*, 363 U.S. 564 (1960).

84 He educated: Stebenne, *Arthur J. Goldberg*, 172, 174; Halberstam, *The Best and the Brightest*, 71.

85 Goldberg could see: Shaplen, "Peacemaker-I," *New Yorker*, 4/7/62, 110, 112; Stebenne, *Arthur J. Goldberg*, 174, 216–19.

85 After accepting: Shaplen, "Peacemaker-II," *New Yorker*, 4/14/62, 68.

85 One of the most visible: Ibid., 49.

85 "I gave": Goldberg, *A Private View of a Public Life*, 132. Kennedy was reluctant

to send Goldberg to the Supreme Court because of Goldberg's value to the administration. Schlesinger, *Robert Kennedy and His Times*, 379; Schwartz, *Super Chief*, 447. On the process of selecting Goldberg for the Supreme Court, see Guthman and Shulman, eds., *Robert Kennedy in His Own Words*, 115–18; Schwartz, *Super Chief*, 446.

85 Arthur Joseph Goldberg: Stebenne, *Arthur J. Goldberg*, 3–6; Shaplen, "Peacemaker-I," *New Yorker*, 4/7/62 58, 60, 63.

85 Frankfurter believed: Schwartz, *Super Chief*, 446; Lewis, *Gideon's Trumpet*, 155.

85 Goldberg and fellow liberals: Rodell, "The 'Warren Court' Stands Its Ground," *NYTM*, 9/27/64, 120; Horwitz, *The Warren Court and the Pursuit of Justice*, 11–12.

86 They protected: *Reynolds v. Sims*, 377 U.S. 533 (1964) ("one person, one vote" in state legislative districts); *Engel v. Vitale*, 370 U.S. 421 (1962) (church and state); *New York Times v. Sullivan*, 376 U.S. 254 (1964) (constitutional libel standard); *Gideon v. Wainwright*, 372 U.S. 335 (1963) (right to counsel for indigent felony defendants); *Bell v. Maryland*, 378 U.S. 226 (1964) and *Cox v. Louisiana*, 379 U.S. 536 (1965) (civil rights demonstrators).

86 not a gifted writer: Dan Levitt interview.

86 He circulated: Van Tassel, "Justice Arthur J. Goldberg," 91–92, in Lowe, ed., *The Jewish Justices of the Supreme Court Revisited*. Goldberg published the memorandum in a law review article. Goldberg, "Memorandum Conference Re: Capital Punishment—October 1963 Term," 27 *South Tex. L. Rev.* 493 (1986).

86 Goldberg made his views: *Rudolph v. Alabama*, 375 U.S. 889 (1963) (Goldberg, J., dissenting from the denial of certiorari).

86 The law clerk: Goldberg and Dershowitz later wrote two articles on the unconstitutionality of capital punishment. Goldberg and Dershowitz, "Declaring the Death Penalty Unconstitutional," 83 *Harv. L. Rev.* 1773 (1970); *NYT*, 1/16/71, E15.

86 In *Griswold v. Connecticut*: 381 U.S. 479, 486 (1965) (Goldberg, J., concurring).

86 He wrote: *Escobedo v. Illinois*, 378 U.S. 478 (1964).

86 Goldberg reveled: *NYTM*, 8/8/65, 62.

86 three-piece suit: Peter Edelman interview.

86 "He was happy": Breyer, "Clerking for Justice Goldberg," *Supreme Court Historical Society 1990 Yearbook*, 4.

86 "three years": Goldberg, *A Private View of a Public Life*, 195.

87 "The [labor] secretary's": Kahn, " 'I'm not discouraged either. Got it?' " *Saturday Evening Post*, 1/29/66, 86.

87 Goldberg and his wife: Goldberg, *A Private View of a Public Life*, 148–50.

87 John Kenneth Galbraith: "Summary of Conversation with Arthur Goldberg,"

2–4, Box 5, Office of President Files, LBJ Library; Galbraith, *A Life in Our Times*, 456–57; Parker, *John Kenneth Galbraith*, 420.

87 Goldberg later denied: In his memoirs, President Johnson gave credence to those rumors by claiming that Goldberg was "restless" on the Court and sought out the UN position. Johnson, *The Vantage Point*, 543–44. Goldberg was so angry over the memoir that he called Johnson on the phone and said he never wanted that untruth repeated again. Goldberg-LBJ Oral History, 1–2, LBJ Library; Goldberg, *A Private View of a Public Life*, 193. He also lashed out at the untruths about him in the president's memoir in a public statement. *WP*, 10/27/71, A10. His denials about being bored on the Court began almost from the moment he resigned. Raskin, "A Conciliator Goes to the U.N.," *NYTM*, 8/8/65, 62.

87 While Goldberg waited: Goldberg-LBJ Oral History, 2; Goldberg, *A Private View of a Public Life*, 193–94; *WP*, 10/27/71, A10.

87 attorney general: Goldberg-LBJ Oral History, 1; *WP*, 10/27/71, A10.

87 "I'm not": Goldberg, *A Private View of a Public Life*, 194. For a similar account of the Valenti-Goldberg confrontation, see Goldberg-LBJ Oral History, 2. These accounts are confirmed by contemporaneous notes, probably Valenti's, of a White House conversation with Goldberg. The notes say: "He is happy on the Court, but if the President wants him in UN, he will do it." "Summary of Conversation with Arthur Goldberg," 1.

87 In the Oval Office: Raskin, "A Conciliator Goes to the U.N.," *NYTM*, 8/8/65, 10.

87 Two days later, Goldberg: "Summary of Conversation with Arthur Goldberg," 3; *WP*, 7/21/65, A1; Raskin, "A Conciliator Goes to the U.N.," *NYTM*, 8/8/65, 10.

87 During the plane ride: Peter Edelman interview; Goldberg-LBJ Oral History, 1–2.

88 Finally, Johnson appealed: Dan Levitt interview; Murphy, *Fortas*, 170–71; *WP*, 8/2/65, A15. Goldberg denied that the vice presidency was a factor in his decision. Kahn, " 'I'm not discouraged either. Got it?' " *Saturday Evening Post*, 1/29/66, 87.

88 That night: Peter Edelman interview; *WP*, 7/21/65, A1.

88 aged him 30 years: Barbara Goldberg Cramer once went looking for her father in 1967 on the floor of the UN General Assembly and did not even recognize him—his hair had turned completely white. *LAT*, 1/20/90, A1.

88 "a lawyer with 116 clients": Kahn, " 'I'm not discouraged either. Got it?' " *Saturday Evening Post*, 1/29/66, 87.

88 Syndicated columnist Joseph Alsop: *WP*, 8/2/65, A1.

88 In cabinet meetings: Goldberg-LBJ Oral History, 2–9.

88 On April 23: Typewritten remarks to the Cabinet, Goldberg Papers, Box I:33, Folder 12 (attached to Dorothy Goldberg Journal Entry, 4/23/68); Letter from Goldberg to Johnson, 4/23/68, Goldberg Papers, Box I:48, Folder 2.

88 Two days later: Letter from Johnson to Goldberg, 4/25/68, Goldberg Papers, Box I:48, Folder 2.

88 It was not a warm: *NYT*, 4/29/68, 1, 3.

88 "I don't want": Typewritten remarks to the Cabinet, 2, Goldberg Papers, Box I:33, Folder 12.

89 Although Goldberg denied: Goldberg-LBJ Oral History, 19; Peter Edelman interview; Dan Levitt interview.

89 Ten days before; "nothing later": Dorothy Goldberg Journal, 3/21/68, 1–3, Goldberg Papers, Box I:33, Folder 10. Warren apparently also told William Brennan that he wanted Brennan as his successor but knew that would never happen. Schwartz, *Super Chief*, 720.

89 Goldberg knew: Dorothy Goldberg Journal, 3/21/68, 2, Goldberg Papers, Box I:33, Folder 10.

89 Syndicated columnist Drew Pearson: Goldberg-LBJ Oral History, 19; Dorothy Goldberg Journal, 6/27/68, 15–16, Goldberg Papers, Box I:176, Folder 2.

89 Johnson told; "I'll ask him": Dorothy Goldberg Journal, 6/27/68, 15–16, Goldberg Papers, Box I:176, Folder 2.

89 $20,000-a-year lifetime salary: Kalman, *Abe Fortas*, 323–24. The salary was not just for Fortas's lifetime but also that of his wife.

89 Goldberg had turned down: Goldberg, *A Private View of a Public Life*, 197–98; *WP*, 5/21/69, A2.

89 recess appointment: Goldberg-LBJ Oral History, 19.

90 On December 11, 1946, Mikan: *CT*, 12/12/46, 59.

90 Mikan, who was pursuing: *CT*, 12/13/46, 39; Mikan, *Unstoppable*, 74; Mikan, *Mr. Basketball*, 46; Peterson, *Cages to Jump Shots*, 160.

91 The day after: *CT*, 1/21/47, 24. Mikan's personal attorney, Stacy Osgood, was a partner in Goldberg's law firm, Goldberg, De Voe, and Brussel. Goldberg, however, mostly took the lead in arguing Mikan's case.

91 As proof : *CT*, 1/17/47, 26.

91 The Cook County judge: *CT*, 1/29/47, 25; *CT*, 1/31/47, 24. The following season, the American Gears pulled out of the NBL, and Mikan's contract was assigned to the Minneapolis Lakers. The NBL merged with the Basketball Association of America (BAA) in 1949 to form the NBA. Peterson, *Cages to Jump Shots*, 162, 166.

91 Thanks to the Mikan case: Miller, *A Whole Different Ball Game*, 188.

91 A former Wrigley Field: Stebenne, *Arthur J. Goldberg*, 5.

91 Goldberg saw the need: Miller, *A Whole Different Ball Game*, 188.

91 Goldberg regarded; "an important case": TT, 183:22–184:3 (Miller); Miller, *A Whole Different Ball Game*, 189.

91 "Arthur Goldberg for": Miller, *A Whole Different Ball Game*, 189.

91 Goldberg's giveaways: Jay Topkis interview.

92 A few days after Flood: Miller, *A Whole Different Ball Game*, 190 (placing the meeting around December 15); TT, 110:2–13 (Flood) (recalling meeting Goldberg with Miller and Moss in mid-December).
92 Flood was nervous: Allan Zerman interview; Flood, *The Way It Is*, 194.
92 his gray and white; The blond wood: Allan Zerman interview; *Esquire*, 9/70, 146; *Village Voice*, 3/12/70, 13.
92 "When he talks": *SGD*, 1/24–25/70, 3E.
92 Goldberg put; "I won't be treated"; "All right"; "the most famous": Flood, *The Way It Is*, 194.
92 Incensed: Typewritten transcript of meeting with Kuhn, 12/14/69, 2, in Flood, *The Way It Is*, 221.
92 Sportswriters attended: *TSN*, 12/6/69, 40.
93 Miller clued in: Marvin Miller interview.
93 book about the best letters: Grunwald and Adler, *Letters of the Century*, 493–94.
93 Miller and Moss wrote the letter: Marvin Miller interview; Dick Moss interview; Miller, *A Whole Different Ball Game*, 190 (indicating that he and Moss "worked on the letter with Curt and reviewed it with Arthur, and Curt signed it"). Flood, however, claimed during trial to have written it. TT, 130:2–11 (Flood). Moss also claimed to have written it. Dick Moss interview.
93 "The idea that": *NYT*, 2/12/67, 183.
93 For Goldberg: Miller says the idea for the letter was Goldberg's. Marvin Miller interview. Flood, however, had mentioned the idea of the letter in Puerto Rico. Handwritten Meeting Notes, 12/13/69, 9. This might not be inconsistent given that Miller met with Goldberg prior to the Players Association meeting in Puerto Rico.
94 He had told: Handwritten Meeting Notes, 12/13/69, 9.
94 "I'm free, black": Marvin Miller interview; Miller, *A Whole Different Ball Game*, 190.
94 the two-paragraph: Miller, *A Whole Different Ball Game*, 190.
94 Fear swept through: Curran, "Curt Flood and the Baseball Revolution," *LA Weekly*, 4/1–7/94, 17.
94 Dear Mr. Kuhn: TT, 29A.
95 Flood's letter miffed: Bowie Kuhn interview; Kuhn, *Hardball*, 80–82.
95 The commissioner had met: "Discussion with Commissioner Kuhn at the Executive Board Meeting of December 14, 1969," MLBPA files, in Flood, *The Way It Is*, App. A, 219–36.
95 Kuhn attributed: Kuhn, *Hardball*, 80–82.
95 Indeed, Kuhn's legal advisers: Lou Hoynes interview.
95 He had even confided: *PT*, 12/30/69, 15.
95 "I feel": TT, 104:25–105:2 (Flood).
95 Quinn's secretary: *NYP*, 12/30/69, 77.

95 Like the commissioner: *PEB*, 1/6/70, 49.

96 His first memories: Kuhn, *Hardball*, 15.

96 He started: TT, 644:6–13 (Kuhn).

96 His first Social Security card: Kuhn, *Hardball*, 15. For background information on Kuhn, see Kuhn, *Hardball*, 12–17; *NYT*, 2/6/69, 45; Leggett, "The Big Leagues Select a Fan," *SI*, 2/17/69, 16–17; Deford, "Heirs of Judge Landis," *SI*, 9/30/74, 94, 96.

96 At Theodore Roosevelt: Kuhn, *Hardball*, 14; *NYT*, 2/6/69, 45; Deford, "Heirs of Judge Landis," *SI*, 9/30/74, 96.

96 In September 1950, he joined: Kuhn, *Hardball*, 16–17; Deford, "Heirs of Judge Landis," *SI*, 9/30/74, 96.

97 Shortly after joining: Kuhn, *Hardball*, 18–19.

97 "What does": Ibid., 18.

97 Along the way: Ibid., 19.

97 Kuhn earned: Lou Hoynes interview; *State v. Milwaukee Braves, Inc.*, 144 N.W.2d 1 (Wis. 1966).

97 Kuhn and his colleagues conceded: Lou Hoynes interview.

98 Agreeing on the result: *State v. Milwaukee Braves, Inc.*, 144 N.W.2d 1 (Wis. 1966).

98 "Bowie Kuhn is": Lou Hoynes interview.

98 Miller's first impression of Kuhn: Marvin Miller interview; Miller, *A Whole Different Ball Game*, 74–76.

98 Five months later: Kuhn, *Hardball*, 75–77.

98 "pedantic": Ibid., 76.

99 Kuhn's Willkie Farr partners: Lou Hoynes interview.

99 "the shadow commissioner"; "Bowie Kuhn's brains": Helyar, *Lords of the Realm*, 110.

99 Kuhn was a compromise: Holtzman, "Expansion, Canadian Club, Feature 1968," 185–89; Kuhn, *Hardball*, 31–36; Burke, *Outrageous Good Fortune*, 282–84; MacPhail, *My Nine Innings*, 111–13; Helyar, *Lords of the Realm*, 97–99.

99 He was a leading force: Snyder, *Beyond the Shadow of the Senators*, 177–80, 214–15. Landis supposedly blocked Bill Veeck's attempt to buy the Phillies in 1942 and stock the team with black players. See *A Well-Paid Slave*, 183, 407.

100 He declared outfielder: Pietrusza, *Judge and Jury*, 349–51, 364, 367.

100 Browns owner Phil Ball: *Milwaukee American Ass'n v. Landis*, 49 F.2d 298 (N.D. Ill. 1931).

100 Landis also freed: Lowenfish, *The Imperfect Diamond*, 120–21.

100 The commissioner crusaded: The numbers vary slightly depending on the source. Compare *TSN*, 4/7/38, 7 (91 Cardinals) and *CT*, 1/15/40, 17 (87 Cardinals and 5 Tigers) with *TSN*, 1/18/40, 1 (91 Tigers) and Lowenfish, *The Imperfect Diamond*, 121–22 (91 Cardinals and 91 Tigers).

100 "the game's upright": Smith, *The Red Smith Reader*, 119.
100 "the ultimate stuffed": Kuhn, *Hardball*, 275.
100 "any act, transaction": Major League Agreement, Art. I, sec. 2(a). For the power to punish, see Art. I, sec. 2(b) and (3).
101 He won praise: *NYP*, 2/26/69, 88, 85; Miller, *A Whole Different Ball Game*, 166–67.
101 He talked Donn: Kuhn, *Hardball*, 45–50.
101 "Baseball": Axthelm, "Let's Make a Deal," *Newsweek*, 11/15/82, 96.
101 In late May, the owners: *NYT*, 5/25/69, sec. 5, 1, 3.
101 Dear Curt: TT, 30A, 135:22–24 (Flood).
102 After Kuhn finished: *WP*, 12/31/69, D2; TT, 135:22–24 (Flood).
102 He then released: *SPD*, 12/31/69, 1C.
102 The next day: *NYT*, 12/30/69, 42; *NYP*, 12/30/69, 80, 77. Koppett said he had learned about Flood's lawsuit on December 2 when Miller sent all the players an MLBPA bulletin. *TSN*, 1/17/70, 33. In truth, however, he had learned about the lawsuit a few weeks earlier from Miller. Marvin Miller interview.
102 "Run along, sonny": *PI*, 12/31/69, 27; *WP*, 1/2/70, D6.
102 "I think the owners": *WP*, 1/3/70, 54; *PI*, 1/4/70, sec. 3, 5.

CHAPTER SEVEN

Page

103 Cosell, who saw: Cosell, *Cosell*, 379.
103 "I don't think": "Curt Flood," *ESPN SportsCentury*; *NYP*, 1/4/70, 143.
104 "It's been written": "Curt Flood," *ESPN SportsCentury*.
104 "A well-paid slave": Ibid.; *NYDN*, 1/4/70, 143.
104 "If people think": *NYDN*, 1/4/70, 143.
104 "through"; "We're just like": Ali, "I'm sorry, but I'm through fighting now," *Esquire*, 5/70, 120–21; "The Black Scholar Interviews: Muhammad Ali," *Black Scholar*, 6/70, 33; Early, "Curt Flood, Gratitude, and the Image of Baseball," 10–11.
104 "Pro football is a silly": *NYT*, 5/30/70, 28.
104 "What is wrong": Meggyesy, *Out of Their League*, 212; Dave Meggyesy interview.
105 "Like a fugitive-slave": Ward, "Is the Base-Ball Player a Chattel?" *Lippincott's Monthly*, 8/1887, 312; Di Salvatore, *A Clever Base-Ballist*, 189, 192–93.
105 "system of servitude"; "the purchase": *American League Baseball Club v. Chase*, 86 Misc. 441, 465, 149 N.Y.S. 6, 19 (1914).
105 "results in something"; "possesses characteristics": *Gardella v. Chandler*, 172 F.2d 402, 409 (2d Cir. 1949) (Frank, J., concurring).
105 "if the players": Ibid., 410.
105 During the 1960s: "Needed—Abe Lincoln of Baseball," *Ebony*, 4/64, 110;

Olsen, "In the Back of the Bus," *SI*, 7/22/68, 28; Early, "Curt Flood, Gratitude, and the Image of Baseball," 9–10.

106 At least one member: Bill Iverson interview.

107 Zerman and Max Gitter: Allan Zerman interview.

107 "Sometimes money's": *SGD*, 1/6/70.

107 The owners received: Marvin Miller interview; TT, 1942:24–1943:5 (Miller); TT, 1610:17–18 (Gaherin).

107 "I just wanted": TT, 1942:8–10 (Miller).

107 Miller realized: Ibid.; Marvin Miller interview.

108 "Baseball Is Sued": *NYT*, 1/17/70, 1.

108 "the reserve clause is part": *NYDN*, 1/4/70, 143.

108 "chaotic results"; "Without the"; "impossible"; "Professional baseball": Press statement of Major League presidents Joseph E. Cronin and Charles S. Feeney, 2, Curt Flood *TSN* file; *TSN*, 1/31/70, 35; *NYT*, 1/18/70, sec. 5, 1, 2; *WP*, 1/18/70, C1.

108 "highly paid star"; "permitted players": Press statement of Major League presidents Joseph E. Cronin and Charles S. Feeney, 1, Curt Flood *TSN* file; *NYT*, 1/18/70, sec. 5, 1.

109 Two days later, Miller charged: *WP*, 1/20/70, D1; *NYDN*, 1/20/70, 67; *NYT*, 1/20/70, 36; *TSN*, 1/31/70, 36.

109 "Curt Win": *NYDN*, 1/18/70, 128.

109 In the *New York Times*, Leonard Koppett: *NYT*, 1/18/70, sec. 5, 2.

109 "occupie[d] a judicial position": *NYDN*, 1/4/70, 143.

109 "I could not communicate": Kuhn, *Hardball*, 83.

109 "You mean"; "If you want": Flood, *The Way It Is*, 197.

110 On January 8, Phillies: TT, 128:19–129:22 (Flood).

110 Flood announced: Ibid.; *SGD*, 1/9/70, 1B; *WP*, 1/10/70, E1.

110 "Is it true"; "You have a terrible": Flood, *The Way It Is*, 197.

110 In one of his few public: *PEB*, 1/8/70, 23; *PDN*, 1/8/70, 49.

110 "What age": TT, 1896:10–13, 1894:12–16 (Miller); Jim Bouton interview; Dick Moss interview; Marvin Miller interview; Miller, *A Whole Different Ball Game*, 193.

110 There was some subsequent: TT, 1893–96 (Miller); TT, 1627:12–1628:24 (Gaherin).

110 "disturb the entire": TT, 1894:21–24 (Miller).

111 "That's exactly what": *NYT*, 1/21/70, 50; *WP*, 1/21/70, D2.

111 "at least $100,000": TT, 107:12–108:14 (Flood); Allan Zerman interview; *PI*, 1/21/70.

111 "Curt Flood isn't helping": *NYDN*, 1/18/70, 113.

111 "That's where I stop": *PEB*, 12/31/69, 18; *SPD*, 1/4/70, 3D.

112 "Flood may become": *PDN*, 1/23/70, 59.

112 Broeg had bristled: Bob Broeg interview.

112 "not a matter"; "If the legality": *SPD*, 1/25/70, 2B.
112 Burnes made no secret: *SGD*, 1/6/70, 2C.
112 "inside and out"; In reality: Flood, *The Way It Is*, 91–93.
113 "He was reading": Hemingway, *Across the River and into the Trees*, 155.
113 Smith despised: Berkow, *Red*, 203.
113 racial issues; remained silent: Ibid., 108–9; Red Smith interview, 31–34, Chandler Collection.
113 "borderline racist": Robert Lipsyte interview.
113 But in November 1968: Ibid.; Berkow, *Red*, 185–93; *NYT*, 11/3/68, 90.
113 He introduced readers: *WP*, 1/2/70, D6; *WP*, 2/8/70, 43; *PI*, 2/8/70, sec. 3, 5.
113 "Curtis Charles Flood": *WP*, 1/2/70, D6.
113 "because Flood earned": *WP*, 2/8/70, 43.
113 "just a fancy name"; "It is pretty late": *LAT*, 1/21/70, C1, C6; *SGD*, 1/26/70, 3C; *TSN*, 2/7/70, 45.
114 There were a few others: Flood, *The Way It Is*, 198.
114 "We think Flood": *HC*, 2/7/70, sec. 1, 10.
114 had railed against: Gerald Early interview.
114 "The Man Who Fights": Thompson, "Man Who Fights Power Structure of Baseball," *Jet*, 2/12/70, 1.
114 "It will be a bit": "Found—An Abe Lincoln of Baseball," *Ebony*, 3/70, 110.
114 "Even if you": *PC*, 3/21/70, 15.
114 Lacy had led the fight: Snyder, *Beyond the Shadow of the Senators*, 177–201.
115 "Flood's decision": *BAA*, 1/6/70, 16.
115 Rustin was relegated: D'Emilio, *Lost Prophet*, 475–77.
115 "Flood stands": *PT*, 2/17/70, sec. 2, 15.
115 "Flood is fighting": Edwards, *Revolt of the Black Athlete*, xix.
115 Many of them threw: Sammons, *Beyond the Ring*, 206.
116 But, as heroic as Ali; Flood, by contrast: Gerald Early interview.
116 They wrote angry letters: *TSN*, 1/31/70, 4; *TSN*, 2/7/70, 4; *TSN*, 2/14/70, 4; *CT*, 1/21/70, C3; *CT*, 1/23/70, C3; *CT*, 2/19/70, C3; *CT*, 5/26/70, C3; *CT*, 11/9/71, C3; *BRA*, 1/27/70, in Miller Papers, Box 3, Folder 9.
116 Soon after Flood's lawsuit: Ron Jacober interview.
116 "Once you were"; "is making it"; "I'm not trying": *SGD*, 1/24–25/70, 1E.
117 "If I had 600 players": *WP*, 4/2/73, D4; *LAT*, 4/2/73, E2; *BES*, 4/5/73, D11.
117 One of the game's: Carl Yastrzemski interview.
117 "That backing": *CST*, 1/20/70, 80; *NYT*, 1/20/70, 36.
117 On January 22, he sent: Letter from Miller to Yastrzemski, 1/22/70, Letter from Yastrzemski to Miller, 1/15/70, Miller Papers, Box 8, Folder 20; *BG*, 1/30/70, 21–22; *TSN*, 1/31/70, 36.
117 "yo-yo"; "If Yastrzemski": *SGD*, 1/30/70, C1.
118 "As far as I'm concerned": *SPD*, 1/28/70, 3E; *PDN*, 1/28/70, 58; *TSN*, 1/24/70, 35.

118 "I can't speak": *BG*, 1/30/70, 21.
118 A few months later, Howard signed: *SPD*, 3/11/70, 4E.
118 Howard said: *BG*, 1/30/70, 21.
118 Years later: Frank Howard interview.
118 "We played": Cal Yastrzemski interview.
118 Ted Williams: *WP*, 1/23/70, B2.
118 Joe DiMaggio; Ralph Kiner: *SFE*, 2/8/70, C3.
118 Robin Roberts: *TSN*, 1/24/70, 38; *PEB*, 1/6/70, 49.
118 Bob Feller: *WP*, 9/13/70, 41.
118 Gil Hodges: *PI*, 6/16/70.
119 Gaylord Perry: *OT*, 2/19/70, 39.
119 Ron Santo: *CT*, 1/22/70, sec. 3, 2.
119 Even Harrelson: *TSN*, 2/7/70, 38.
119 Hank Aaron: "left out": *TSN*, 2/7/70, 6.
119 Soon after those comments: *SPD*, 2/20/70, 2C.
119 "If Curt": *OT*, 2/10/70, 34.
120 "do-nothing": *LAT*, 3/16/68, A1.
120 With his salary approaching $150,000: From 1966 to 1969, Mays made $125,000 per season. *NYT*, 2/28/69, 69. The reports on Mays's salary for 1970 vary. Mays, *Say Hey*, 244 (claiming he made $160,000); Einstein, *Willie's Time*, 328 (putting Mays "in the $150,000 bracket" around 1972); *NYT*, 1/15/70, 73 (Mays as highest salary in majors); *NYT*, 2/14/70, 17 ($150,000); *NYT*, 7/19/70, 137 ($130,000 plus endorsements); *WP*, 3/2/71, D1 ($135,000 in 1970). The following year, Mays signed a two-year contract that paid him $155,000 to $160,000 for 1971. *WP*, 3/2/71, D1.
120 "I can understand": *OT*, 2/10/70, 34.
120 "Willie Mays, Ernie Banks, and Henry Aaron": *CT*, 1/22/70, sec. 3, 2.
120 Billy Williams: Ibid., 4.
120 "To me": *BAA*, 5/12/70, 17.
120 Oscar Robertson: *BAA*, 6/11/66, 27.
121 "We hope": *PI*, 1/21/70, 26.
121 "I'm certainly": *WP*, 1/21/70, D2.
121 "It's going to": *SGD*, 1/20/70, 2C; *WP*, 1/21/70, D2.
121 Hockey players: *NYT*, 1/21/70, 52.
121 "You're crazy"; "a few hundred paces": "Curt Flood," *ESPN SportsCentury*.
121 "Guys who come"; "If he succeeds": Speers, "Why Curt Flood Won't Play for the Phillies," *PI Magazine*, 5/17/70, 7–8.
121 "Something had to be done": *OT*, 3/8/70, 5C; *TSN*, 2/7/70, 38.
121 "Flood is going to go"; "You have to understand Curt": *CPD*, 3/8/70, 2-C.
122 "Curt Flood, my hat's": *NYDN*, 3/14/70, G26; *SPD*, 3/13/70, 6B.
122 "If you want to": Thompson, "Man Who Fights Power Structure of Baseball," *Jet*, 2/12/70, 53.

122 Before the 1966 season: Leavy, *Sandy Koufax*, 201–12.
122 "I have to give": *LAT*, 4/11/70, C3.
122 "We just feel": *WP*, 12/30/69, D1.
122 "We're not interested": *NYP*, 1/2/70, 72.
122 "I think he's right": *BAA*, 1/24/70, F-19.
122 "The way I feel": *TSN*, 1/24/70, 35.
122 Cardinals player representative: *SPD*, 1/27/70.
123 "Maybe I": *NYP*, 1/17/70, 63.
123 "[a]s far as I'm concerned": *TSN*, 2/21/70, 14.
123 "I'd play in"; "I can't understand"; "the wrong guy": *AJ*, 1/20/70, 1C.
123 "I remember Gene Mauch": Ron Brand interview.
123 "the Pope burning down"; "If they wipe": *TSN*, 2/7/70, 45.
123 Richards explained: *AJ*, 1/21/70, 1-D, 7-D; *TSN*, 1/24/70, 14.
123 "Realistically": *TSN*, 3/7/70, 7.
124 "Instead of a sport": *TSN*, 3/28/70, 16; *SPD*, 3/11/70, 1E.
124 "We're much better"; "How good": *PDN*, 4/1/70, 47.
124 "I can only believe": *TSN*, 1/24/70, 38; *PEB*, 1/6/70, 49.
124 "I'm certain that Miller": *CT*, 3/26/70, F4.
124 "I think Curt": *OT*, 3/8/70, 5C.

CHAPTER EIGHT

Page

126 Jay Topkis hoped: Jay Topkis interview.
126 "emotionally unstable": Cooper Nomination Hearing (Cooper Hearing), 43; *NYT*, 3/20/62, 1.
126 He berated: Cooper Hearing, 102, 108, 124.
126 In April 1955: Ibid., 202–5.
126 "an apology": Ibid., 205.
127 "personal wear"; "constant anxiety, irritation": *NYT*, 3/20/62, 33.
127 "like a baby"; "a crummy": "The Judge Takes the Stand," *Time*, 8/17/62, 16.
127 "Bellevue Ben": Goulden, *The Benchwarmers*, 65.
127 "a persecution complex"; Cooper was the most controversial: "Day in Court," *Time*, 3/30/62, 16.
128 "screamed at me": Brill, "Benching of Bad Judges," *Esquire*, 4/10/79, 22.
128 The firm's lead partner: Cooper Hearing, 27–28; Jay Topkis interview; *NYT*, 3/20/62, 33.
128 Cooper reportedly: Brill, "Benching of Bad Judges," *Esquire*, 4/10/79, 22.
128 "We got the madman": Lou Hoynes interview.
128 During his own testimony: Cooper Hearing, 353–54.
128 The vice chairman: *NYT*, 7/9/61, 79; *NYT*, 7/8/62, 56; Jay Topkis interview.
129 In requesting an injunction: 2/3/70 Tr., 19–20, NARA, NY.

129 "The fact that": Ibid., 26:11–16.
129 "counteroffer": Ibid., 30:5–15.
129 "The Court announces": 2/3/70 Tr., 30:17; *NYT*, 2/4/70, 50.
129 When the hearing resumed: 2/3/70 Tr., 32–35.
129 "It is very difficult": Ibid., 50:18–25.
130 "business may fail": Flood Affidavit, para. 9 (on file with author), NARA, NY.
130 "fledgling business": 2/3/70 Tr., 54:14–21.
130 Hughes also read: Ibid., 55; Devine Affidavit, para. 4 and Exh. A, NARA, NY.
130 "if this system": 2/3/70 Tr., 56:13–17; *NYP*, 2/4/70, 100.
130 Porter briefly added: 2/3/70 Tr., 58–63.
130 "You have thrown": Ibid., 67:25–68:2.
130 "You do": Ibid., 68:5–11.
131 "having second thoughts": *TSN*, 2/14/70, 14.
131 Flood's world: Flood, *The Way It Is*, 200–203.
131 "Why I Am": Flood, "Why I Am Challenging Baseball," *Sport*, 3/70, 10, in Thorn, ed., *The Armchair Book of Baseball*, 130.
131 Dave Oliphant: Dave Oliphant interview; Flood, *The Way It Is*, 199–200.
131 In late February: Dave Oliphant interview; Flood, *The Way It Is*, 202–3.
132 "I read them"; "The book's gone"; That same afternoon; "Curt was addicted"; "I really thought": Dave Oliphant interview.
132 Baseball's status: *Flood v. Kuhn*, 309 F. Supp. 793, 797 (S.D.N.Y. 1970).
133 "[f]or years": Ibid., 809.
133 Flood called Zerman: Allan Zerman interview.
133 "The failure": *NYT*, 3/5/70, 49.
133 Flood told Jorgensen: Flood, *The Way It Is*, 200–201.
133 "I'm a baseball player"; He decided: Ibid., 201.
134 "It's my life"; "Let's face it"; "And besides": *SGD*, 3/6/70, 2B.
134 "I'm not a millionaire"; "It's just": Ibid.; *SPD*, 3/6/70, 2C.
134 Flood felt better: Flood, *The Way It Is*, 202.
134 The day after Judge Cooper's decision: *NYT*, 3/4/70, 1; *NYT*, 3/6/70, 22.
135 *New York Post* columnist Pete Hamill: *NYP*, 12/8/69, 49.
135 "I don't want"; "How can you": *NYT*, 3/6/70, 22.
135 "Meanwhile, goddamnit": *Village Voice*, 3/12/70, 13 (emphasis in original).
135 At least one newspaper columnist: *Hudson* (N.J.) *Dispatch*, 1/19/70, Goldberg Papers, Box II-81, Folder 6; *TSN*, 2/7/70, 4.
135 Miller called Goldberg: Phone log, Goldberg Papers, Box I-135, Folder 4.
135 He did not have: Marvin Miller interview.
136 Topkis had played a major: "1969 Report," Goldberg Papers, Box I-76, Folder 3.
136 "Topkis will do": William Sloane Coffin Jr. interview.
136 Goldberg's decision to run: Jay Topkis interview.
136 As a Yale law student: Jay Topkis interview.
136 "Monopoly in Professional Sports": 58 *Yale L.J.* 691 (1949).

136 "It is of great importance": 3/24/70 Tr. 15:12–14, NARA, NY.
136 "We are ready": Ibid., 20:24–25, 21:2–3.
137 Carroll said the Phillies: Ibid., 26:23–24.
137 "Mr. Flood": Ibid., 27:17–18.
137 "But I can tell": Ibid., 28:16–17.
137 "Because speaking": Ibid., 29:2–6.
137 "Flood is a mature man": Ibid., 30:13–21.
137 A week later in Cooper's chambers: 3/31/70 Tr., 26:22–27:6, Hagley Museum, Accession 1352, Box 9.
138 The owners wanted: Ibid., 29:19–20.
138 But, realizing: Ibid., 29:24–30:6, 36:3.
138 "what the rush is": Ibid., 43:9–10.
138 "Mr. Flood has waited": Ibid., 48:9–11.
138 Goldberg wanted: Ibid., 33:3–4.
138 "The rush is": Ibid., 45:13–15.
138 "Our posture": Ibid., 47:23–48:4.
138 "I was told": Ibid., 39:7–14.
138 The next day at Grossinger's: *NYT*, 4/2/70, 1, 32; *WP*, 4/2/70, A1, A6.
139 At Hughes's request: Letter from Cooper to Hughes, 4/1/70, Letter from Hughes to Cooper, 4/1/70, NARA, NY, SDNY.
139 "I think it would": 3/31/70 Tr. 51:11–12.
139 As the commissioner: *PI*, 2/24/70, 19; *BMS*, 4/5/70, A-1.
139 "farce"; "The 'Alice in Wonderland'": Axthelm, "Slap on the Wrist," *Newsweek*, 4/13/70, 48.
139 He thought he could: Kuhn, *Hardball*, 85.
140 "I don't owe"; "Jackie was great": Monte Irvin interview.
140 Irvin called: Flood, *The Way It Is*, 203; Irvin, *Nice Guys Finish First*, 198.
140 The commissioner offered: Kuhn, *Hardball*, 85.
140 Irvin promised: Monte Irvin interview.
140 "Damnit, Monte"; "He'd": Flood, *The Way It Is,* 203.
140–41 "Listen, Curt"; "I don't have"; "I think"; "disgusted": Monte Irvin interview.
141 "a feather": Irvin, *Nice Guys Finish First*, 198.
141 "I thought"; "was in love": Monte Irvin interview.
141 "The commissioner"; "Oh, come on"; "He's a very": Flood, *The Way It Is,* 203–4.
141 League lawyers: Lou Hoynes interview.
141 AM DISAPPOINTED: Kuhn, *Hardball*, 85; Flood, *The Way It Is,* 204.
142 As the commissioner and a fan: TT, 667:7–13 (Kuhn).
142 Kuhn spoke with: *PDN*, 3/12/70, 61; *PDN*, 3/17/70, 72.
142 Even owners Gussie Busch and Bob Carpenter: *PI*, 3/20/70, 27; *PDN*, 3/28/70, 30.
142 Mike Shannon: Mike Shannon interview; *TSN*, 4/4/70, 21.
142 not a single major leaguer: *PDN*, 3/23/70, 60; *PI*, 3/20/70, 27.

143 On March 4: TT, 128:19–129:22 (Flood).

143 This prevented: *SPD*, 4/8/70, 2C; *WP*, 4/8/70, D4.

143 Part of the reason: TT, 667:7–13 (Kuhn).

143 "[a] player on the Restricted List": Rule 15(a), 1969 *Baseball Blue Book,* Ex. A, NARA, NY, SDNY.

143 Although Flood or the Phillies: Rules 18(a) and (b), ibid.

143 Danny Gardella; George Toolson: *NYT*, 6/6/49, 24; *Toolson v. New York Yankees*, 101 F. Supp. 93, 93 (S.D. Cal. 1951).

143 On April 23, Cooper issued: *Flood v. Kuhn*, 312 F. Supp. 404 (S.D.N.Y. 1970); TT, 108A–126A.

CHAPTER NINE

Page

145 He received; Flood and his trial team: *TSN*, 6/6/70, 4.

145 Kuhn sat: *NYP*, 5/20/70, 100.

145 The court clerk: *TSN*, 6/6/70, 4.

145 Members of the press: *TSN*, 6/6/70, 4.

146 "Howard Cosell's big beak": Douglas Robinson interview.

146 "A great day": Bill Iverson interview.

146 "We are not ready": TT, 3:8–10 (Hughes).

147 "Then I told": Reeves, "This Is the Battle of the Titans?" *NYTM*, 11/1/70, 224.

147 He insisted: Richard Reeves interview.

147 "I spent a month": "Mr. Goldberg Runs for Office," *New Yorker*, 6/13/70, 28.

147 Topkis, Bill Iverson: Phone Logs, 5/6/70, 5/14/70, Goldberg Papers, Box I-135, Folder 4.

147 Goldberg's schedule; The morning of Flood's trial: Campaign Schedules, Goldberg Papers, Box I-65, Folder 1.

147 "I would like to": TT, 8:23 (Goldberg).

148 "Mr. Justice Goldberg": TT, 8:24 (Hughes).

148 Cooper refused: TT, 9:10.

148 "Very well"; "Mr. Curtis": TT, 10:15–16 (Goldberg).

148 "I've really got": *CST*, 5/18/70, 91.

148 Gibson, off to a slow: *NYT*, 5/19/70, 50.

148 On April 29: *SPD*, 4/29/70, 25A.

148 He did not know: Flood, "The Legacy of Curt Flood," *Sport*, 11/77, 39.

148 The day before Flood's trial: Allan Zerman interview.

149 it seemed huge: Whitford, "Curt Flood," *Sport*, 12/86, 106.

149 The benches: *TSN*, 6/6/70, 4.

149 First, he said: TT, 12:15–21, 13:11–16 (Flood).

149 He sat hunched: *NYP*, 5/20/70, 104; *NYDN*, 5/20/70, 118; *WP*, 5/20/70, D1; "Curt Flood's Complaint," *Newsweek*, 6/1/70, 85.

149 Goldberg gently: TT, 25:10–14, 21–23 (Flood).
149 he was so afraid: Whitford, "Curt Flood," *Sport*, 12/86, 106.
149–50 Bill Iverson; "because he": Bill Iverson interview.
150 "What are you"; "A baseball card": TT, 25:21–24 (Flood).
150 Flood used: TT, 25:17–26:17, 35:17–36:13 (Flood).
150 Goldberg asked: TT, 30–33 (Goldberg).
150 "I state"; "I would state": TT, 30:18 (Flood).
150 "Now, Mr. Flood"; "No sir": TT, 33:5–7 (Cooper and Flood).
150 "I want you": TT, 33:8–10 (Cooper).
151 "I guess that they": Whitford, "Curt Flood," *Sport*, 12/86, 106.
151 Flood used the baseball card: TT, 35:23–25 (Flood).
151 Goldberg read: TT, 37–38; *NYT*, 5/21/70, 48.
152 receiving $500: TT, 40:17–23, 41:8–14, 23–25 (Flood).
152 "Why did you"; "I didn't think": TT, 63:9–11 (Flood).
152 "[i]f I had": TT, 64:8–9 (Flood).
152 "could play another": TT, 64:10 (Flood).
152 Mark Hughes began by: TT, 107:12–108:14 (Flood).
152 "The trial is": TT, 114:8–15 (Cooper).
153 "[W]e, in conversation"; "I'm sorry"; "That is": TT, 115:20–25 (Flood).
153 "I think some": TT, 118:18 (Flood).
153–54 "Well, which is"; "I would like": TT, 118:19–23 (Flood).
154 "Any revision": TT, 122:17–19 (Flood).
154 "Well, I feel": TT, 121:9–10 (Flood).
154 "Mr. Flood": TT, 125:11–13 (Flood).
154 Goldberg objected: TT, 125:14–17 (Goldberg).
154 "I think": TT, 126:9–10 (Flood).
154 "Do you want"; "No, I like": TT, 126:12–14 (Cooper and Goldberg).
154 "Engraved": This answer was not recorded on the transcript, but picked up by the press. *NYP*, 5/20/70, 100, and *PDN*, 5/20/70, 60 (attributing it to one of Goldberg's associates); *BES*, 5/20/70, D1 (attributing it to Goldberg). Topkis, however, referenced his earlier line in a colloquy with Judge Cooper later in the trial. TT, 1318:11–12 (Topkis) ("As I said before, your Honor, engraved in gold").
155 Miller also detailed: TT, 183:22–184:10 (Miller).
155 Cooper granted: TT, 187a (Cooper).
155 Flood was done: TT, 187 (Cooper).
155 "On the surface": *NYP*, 5/20/70, 100.
155 "trailed on several": *PDN*, 5/20/70, 60.
156 "Lindsay for Mayor": *NYT*, 5/21/70, 1.
156 Every time Kramer hopped; "Some of that": Douglas Robinson interview.
156 one former player: Jay Topkis interview; Bill Iverson interview.
156 "If ever there": Bill Iverson interview.

156 In response to questions: Study of Monopoly Power, Pt. 6, Organized Baseball, 82d Cong., 1st Sess., 10/16/51, 601–2.
157 The Associated Press: *SPD*, 5/20/70, 26.
157 Iverson called; "None of them": Bill Iverson interview.
157 The media: *WP*, 5/21/70, G3.

CHAPTER TEN

Page

158 He had suffered: Rampersad, *Jackie Robinson*, 429; Kahn, *Boys of Summer*, 398–99.
158 His doctor: Rampersad, *Jackie Robinson*, 441.
158 Robinson walked: Burns, *Baseball* documentary, vol. 9 (Flood); Burns/Flood interview, 11.
158 He shook; Tears welled: Flood, *The Way It Is*, 204–5; Flood, "The Legacy of Curt Flood," *Sport*, 11/77, 38–39.
158 A hush fell: Burns, *Baseball* documentary, vol. 9 (Flood); Burns/Flood interview, 11.
159 He criticized: *BAA*, 5/12/70, 17 (Frank); *LAT*, 3/16/68, A1 (Willie); *BAA*, 2/21/67, 13 (Willie); *BAA*, 3/19/68, 12 (Willie); *BAA*, 4/2/68, 12 (Willie). See *A Well-Paid Slave*, 120, 396.
159 He clashed: *LAT*, 7/25/69, B10; *BAA*, 8/5/69, 15; Cosell, *Cosell*, 73–74.
159 "I don't know": "Where the Negro Goes from Here in Sports," *Sport*, 9/66, 57.
159 "when there's an issue": Ibid., 59.
159 "I think Curt is doing": Thompson, "Man Who Fights Power Structure of Baseball," *Jet*, 2/15/70, 52–53.
159 A registered independent: Rampersad, *Jackie Robinson*, 340–41. Rampersad described Robinson as "a Republican at heart, albeit a liberal Republican on the key matter of civil rights." Ibid., 341.
160 Iverson thought: Bill Iverson interview.
160 In July, the company: Rampersad, *Jackie Robinson*, 420–21, 440.
160 "It had seemed": Bill Iverson interview.
160 "thought Flood": Marvin Miller interview.
160 "I was young": Miller, *A Whole Different Ball Game*, 366.
161 Even lawyers: Douglas Robinson interview.
161 "You don't"; "No": TT, 192:6–7 (Robinson).
161 Judge Cooper tried; "Well, sir": TT, 192:8–19 (Robinson).
161 "because in my view": TT, 195:13–18 (Robinson).
162 After the trade: TT, 195:20–196:9 (Robinson).
162 $35,000 to 50,000 or more: On December 13, 1956, the Giants sent Robinson a contract for $35,000, but an accompanying letter from Chub Feeney made it

clear that the financial terms were open to discussion. Jackie Robinson Papers, Box 2, Folder 16. The amount of the Giants' final offer, generally believed to be $50,000, varies depending on the source. *NYT*, 1/10/57, 49 ($50,000 or more); *LAT*, 1/10/57, C1 ($50,000); *WP*, 1/10/57, A20 ($70,000); *CT*, 1/11/57, B3 ("around $50,000"); *TSN*, 1/16/57, 3, 6 ($50,000); *CDEF*, 1/19/57, 18 ($50,000); Rampersad, *Jackie Robinson*, 307 (citing Associated Press source of $65,000); Kahn, *The Boys of Summer*, 388–89 (initial offer of $40,000 plus two years as a scout at $20,000 per season; then the Giants called to up their offer).

162 $42,500: *NYT*, 1/8/57, 35 (reporting $42,500 figure for 1953 and 1957 salary of $33,000); *TSN*, 1/16/57, 4 ($42,500 in 1952); Rampersad, *Jackie Robinson*, 245, 255 ($42,000 in 1952 and possibly 1953).

162 "statement": TT, 196:5–9 (Robinson).

162 During the 1949 season: Rampersad, *Jackie Robinson*, 207.

162 "[A]nything that is": TT, 198:3–11, 17–20 (Robinson); *NYT*, 5/22/70, 22; *NYP*, 5/21/70, 84, 72; *NYP*, 5/22/70, 80; *NYDN*, 5/22/70, 87.

162 younger players: TT, 198:15–17 (Robinson).

162 "the reserve clause": TT, 199:11–13 (Robinson).

162–63 Robinson discussed; "hurt his chances": TT, 200:9–20 (Robinson).

163 "I would like to say": TT, 202:18–20 (Robinson).

163 Hughes objected: TT, 202:21 (Hughes).

163 "that is the issue": TT, 203:21–22 (Cooper).

163 On cross-examination; "I am highly"; "I could have said": TT, 210:2–213:19 (Robinson).

163 Goldberg finally objected: TT, 213:20–214:21 (Goldberg).

163 Robinson indicated: TT, 214:22–215:3 (Robinson).

164 I think they should: TT, 288:6–19 (quoting Organized Professional Team Sports, 85th Cong., 2nd Sess., 295).

164 "Could I have": TT, 288:21 (Hughes). Both Hughes and Goldberg failed to discover Robinson's April 14, 1957, comments about the reserve clause on *Meet the Press*. In that interview, as in his Senate testimony, Robinson both defended and criticized the reserve clause. At one point, he told moderator Lawrence Spivak: "Mr. Spivak, I don't know why I'm defending this reserve clause; really I don't know why I am doing it, so, I will just say here, for the players' benefit certainly something should be done, but I hope it doesn't have to be done through the courts. I hope that the baseball owners will think enough of the ballplayers themselves to say, 'Well, I'm going to do something for the players besides selling them whenever I can—maybe giving them a piece of the money when they are sold.' I hope it's done that way rather than through the courts." *Meet the Press* transcript, 4/14/57, 9, Lawrence Spivak Papers. Thirteen years later, the only thing that had changed was Robinson's willingness to stand up in court against the reserve clause.

164 Robinson had testified: Organized Professional Team Sports, 85th Cong., 2nd Sess., 294–95.
164 "So I believe": Ibid., 296.
164 "It means to me": TT, 217:11–12 (Robinson).
164 "after a certain number": TT, 221:23–24 (Robinson).
165 "It takes a tremendous": TT, 222:4–12 (Robinson).
165 "soliloquy . . . sent chills": Burns, *Baseball*, vol. 9 (Flood); Burns/Flood interview, 11.
165 Instead, Cooper requested: Douglas Robinson interview.
165 "Mr. Greenberg": TT, 224:4–5 (Goldberg).
166 "Stick in there"; "Class tells": Greenberg, *My Life in Baseball*, 189–91; *NYT*, 5/18/47, sec. 5, 5; *TSN*, 05/28/47, 20; Robinson, *My Own Story*, 146–47.
166 Greenberg heard: Greenberg, *The Story of My Life*, 176.
166 "Mr. Galbreath": Ibid., 181.
167 Greenberg, knowing: Stephen Greenberg interview.
167 "Greenberg said": Memo, Gitter and Topkis to Goldberg, 5/7/70, Telephone Logs—1970, Goldberg Papers, Box I:135, Folder 4.
167 physically imposing: Jay Topkis interview.
167 calm, reserved, and almost aloof: Bill Iverson interview.
167 "the reserve clause": TT, 230:18–19–231:15 (Greenberg).
167 Judge Cooper asked: TT, 232:5–18 (Cooper and Greenberg).
167 "[I]t's a unilateral contract": TT, 232:22–24 (Greenberg).
167 "I think": TT, 235:9–21 (Greenberg).
167 "That is the kind": TT, 235:22–24 (Cooper).
168 Greenberg, who believed: TT, 239–40 (Greenberg).
168 Greenberg, however, added: TT, 247:18–19 (Greenberg).
168 Greenberg also admitted: TT, 247:17–18 (Greenberg).
168 peak form: TT, 243:11–15 (Greenberg).
168 "I would be perfectly": TT, 241:12–14 (Greenberg).
168 Marvin Miller retook: TT, 250–84 (Miller).
168 "tried too hard": Brosnan, *The Long Season*, 224.
168 "He's the first pitcher": *WP*, 4/19/66, C4.
169 DeWitt demanded prior: Jim Brosnan interview; TT, 331–33 (Brosnan); Golenbock, *The Spirit of St. Louis*, 430.
169 The Player further: Uniform Player Contract, para. 3(c).
169 DeWitt withheld: TT, 332–33 (Brosnan).
169 "You're being censored": *SGD*, 3/27/63, 3C.
169 "You can't write here": Jim Brosnan interview.
169 $32,000 to $25,000: *LAT*, 3/11/64, B1.
169 "Brosnan can be had": TT, 323:18 (Brosnan).
169 Europe: *TSN*, 12/7/63, 37, 42.
169 "Situation Sought"; "Free Agent": *TSN*, 3/7/64, 21.

169–70 Only the unconventional; Brent Musburger: Jim Brosnan interview.
170 The American Civil Liberties Union: *NYT*, 3/8/64, sec. 5, 3.
170 Bill Iverson called; "Why am I": Ibid.; TT, 348–49.
170 "I didn't perceive": Jim Brosnan interview.
170 Brosnan spent two: Ibid.; TT, 348–49 (Brosnan).
170 On the day of his testimony: Jim Brosnan interview.
170 "fiercely racist": Red Smith interview, 35, Chandler Collection.
170–71 The two men; Brosnan was eager; "What has": Jim Brosnan interview.
171 "He is a large": *WP*, 4/19/66, C4.
171 Brosnan explained: TT, 299:7–301:21.
171 "My wife threatened"; "She gave": TT, 301:22–302:11 (Brosnan).
171 Paul Menking: Jim Brosnan interview; *TSN*, 6/13/70, 8.
171 36 cents postage due: TT, 324:3 (Brosnan).
171 "This is your testimony": TT, 324:18–24 (Cooper).
172 On the reserve clause, Brosnan mentioned: TT, 340–43 (Brosnan).
172 "When a ballplayer": TT, 346:24–347:14 (Brosnan).
172 Brosnan never; "Why was"; "There's a time"; "We don't seem"; "When your": Jim Brosnan interview.

CHAPTER ELEVEN

Page

173 "blur": Flood, "The Legacy of Curt Flood," *Sport*, 11/77, 38.
173 He shared a suite: Allan Zerman interview.
173 Flood also went out for drinks: Max Gitter interview; Bill Iverson interview.
173 One afternoon: Ibid.; Jay Topkis interview.
174 *If you're expecting: NYTM*, 11/30/69, 134.
174 Brown even came: Judy Pace Flood interview.
174 His Warwick Hotel suite: Interview (anon.) by author.
174 The secretaries at Paul, Weiss: Bill Iverson interview.
174 Feeling the pressure: *Sport*, 11/77, 39.
174 The rest of the trial: Flood, *The Way It Is*, 204–5.
175 "Did you ever have": TT, 511:22–25 (Cooper).
175 a move that must have: Robert Kheel interview.
175 "So far as I know": *CST*, 6/2/70, 82.
175 "Some of Curt's friends": Ibid.
175 Flood and Zerman: Allan Zerman interview; *SGD*, 5/29/70, 2B.
175 "Curt Flood still likes": *LAT*, 5/30/70, C4.
175 The night before he pitched: Allan Zerman interview.
176 "I know we talked": Joe Torre interview.
176 "[I]f I had it": Miller, *A Whole Different Ball Game*, 197 (emphasis in original).
176 "obviously not"; "was free": TT, 601:2–9, 602–3 (Hughes).

176 All of Flood's witnesses: TT, 614:6–11, 616:22–25 (Hughes).
177 "we are fortunate": TT, 622:9–25 (Topkis).
177 it was time for *Toolson*: TT, 624–25 (Topkis).
177 insurance companies: TT, 629–31 (Topkis).
177 "The only difference": TT, 632:15–24 (Topkis).
177 "I would ask": TT, 633:6–11 (Topkis).
177 "high moral tone"; "I think": Kuhn, *Hardball*, 70.
178 Kuhn acceded: Marvin Miller interview.
178 "[T]he Lords of Baseball": *NYDN*, 5/17/70, 141.
178 "decorated in Early Authority": Bouton, *Ball Four*, 416.
178 Kuhn tried: Ibid.; Holtzman, "Attendance and Litigation Were Up in 1970," 302; *CST*, 6/2/70, 82.
178 The commissioner viewed: Kuhn, *Hardball*, 86.
179 that "baseball as we know it": TT, 717:17–18 (Kuhn).
179 "Baseball as we know"; "The only aspect": *NYT*, 6/14/70, 3.
179 Without the reserve clause; "exhibition business": TT, 717:4–16 (Kuhn).
179 "chaotic conditions": TT, 680:20–681:4 (Kuhn).
179 Topkis countered: TT, 817 (Topkis and Kuhn).
179 Four teams: TT, 906 (Topkis and Kuhn).
179 Both Kuhn: TT, 741:16–742:2 (Kuhn); TT, 963:23–24, 984:12–16, 1078–80 (Feeney).
179 Feeney raised: TT, 963:22–24 (Feeney).
180 "the public's confidence": TT, 1080:13–18 (Feeney).
180 Kuhn made an equally: TT, 660:7–8, 693 (Kuhn).
180 During a routine double play: *TSN*, 9/24/47, 6; *CT*, 9/12/47, 32; *NYT*, 9/12/47, 39; Robinson, *My Own Story*, 129, 158–59; Tygiel, *Baseball's Great Experiment*, 204; Rampersad, *Jackie Robinson*, 184–85. On the Robinson-Slaughter incident, see *A Well-Paid Slave*, 52, 377.
180 "made a crack": Robinson, *My Own Story*, 129, 158.
180 Garagiola spent: Kahn, *The Era*, 96–98; Allen, *Jackie Robinson*, 138–39; Garagiola, *It's Anybody's Ballgame*, 160.
180 Garagiola spelled: *NYT*, 6/3/70, 35.
180 "Do you always": TT, 1176:23–25 (Cooper and Garagiola).
180 "I wish you": TT, 1177:12–13 (Garagiola).
180 "To me": TT, 1183:17–19 (Garagiola).
180 Topkis declined: Jay Topkis interview.
181 "Being traded": Thorn, et. al., eds., *Total Baseball*, 6th ed., 2505.
181 "one of the finest": TT, 1219:10–19 (Cronin).
181 "Didn't he attain"; "That I don't": TT, 1220:15–17 (Topkis and Cronin).
181 "jumped his reserve clause": TT, 1221:2–3 (Topkis).
182 Kauffman said $125,000: TT, 1513:6–7, 11–14 (Kauffman).
182 "How much"; "I don't know": TT, 1513:19–22 (Topkis and Kauffman).

182 "Eddie": Veeck, *Veeck As in Wreck*, 14.
183 "discriminate[d] against"; "a short ballplayer": Ibid., 21.
183 As the owner; In Cleveland: Ibid., 60, 159.
183 "I have tried": TT, 2037:6–7 (Veeck).
183 Although disputed: Compare Veeck, *Veeck As in Wreck*, 171–72, with Jordan et al., "A Baseball Myth Exploded," 3–13. Historians have given more credence to Veeck's story with the discovery of more contemporaneous references to his alleged plot to stock the Phillies with black players. Lanctot, *Negro League Baseball*, 444 n. 41.
184 "After all": TT, 1984:6–7 (Veeck).
184 After Veeck received: TT, 2018–19 (Veeck); Veeck, *Veeck As in Wreck*, 275–77.
184 "legally and morally"; "Some very knowledgeable": *NYP*, 6/11/70, 91; *CST*, 6/25/72, 141; *NYT*, 2/3/81, B18; *WP*, 5/31/81, D4.
184 During a three-hour dinner: Miller, *A Whole Different Ball Game*, 365–67.
184 "I was prepared": Jay Topkis interview.
185 Veeck initially agreed: Memo, Gitter and Topkis to Goldberg, 5/7/70, Telephone Logs 1970, Goldberg Papers, Box I:135, Folder 4.
185 The owners' lawyers: TT, 919–26.
185 where they ate salmon: Bill Iverson interview.
185 Iverson was concerned: Ibid.
185 Tribute to Bill Veeck: TT, 1959:20–1960:9 (Topkis and Veeck).
185 The owners: Bill Iverson interview; *WP*, 5/31/81, D4.
185 Doctors at the Mayo Clinic: Veeck, *Veeck As in Wreck*, 378–79.
186 Miller sat there; "Bill": Miller, *A Whole Different Ball Game*, 367.
186 "Well, I presume": TT, 1959:12–14 (Veeck).
186 Topkis then read: TT, 1959:15–1960:9 (Veeck).
186 "he had thought": Jay Topkis interview.
186 "wouldn't dislocate": TT, 1965:25 (Veeck).
186 Veeck advocated: TT, 1967:10–11, 1967–69 (Veeck).
186 "though it grieves me": TT, 1971:23–1972:3 (Veeck).
186 "not a question": TT, 1972:11–13 (Veeck).
187 "Everyone should once": TT, 1974:6–13 (Veeck).
187 He believed that teams: TT, 1977, 1981 (Veeck).
187 "I think that it would": TT, 1976:2–4 (Veeck).
187 "I would say": TT, 1988:7–8 (Kramer).
187 Goldberg: TT, 1999–2001 (Goldberg).
187 Cooper asked; "I know": TT, 2008:18–20 (Cooper).
188 "I'm sorry": TT, 2008:25 (Veeck).
188 "I find that question": TT, 2023:24–2024:3 (Veeck).
188 "I think it is": TT, 2035:22–23 (Veeck).
188 "intractable minds": *NYT*, 6/11/70, 59.
188 He walked out: *NYP*, 6/10/70, 112.

188 "necessary": *WP*, 10/9/70, D2.
188 15 trial days: Major League Baseball Post-trial Brief, 4 (on file with author).
188 "leadership"; "exemplary": TT, 2274:25–2275:2 (Cooper).
188 "your hair-trigger": TT, 2275:5–7 (Cooper).
188 "As to the case": TT, 2075:16–23 (Cooper).
189 "The law doesn't"; "'Only death'"; "'Much harm'": TT, 2076:6–12 (Cooper), quoting *In re J. P. Linahan*, 138 F.2d 650, 652, 652–53 (2d Cir. 1943).
189 "That is the effect": TT, 2076:13–14 (Cooper).
189 Flood was not present: *NYT*, 6/11/70, 59.
189 Nor was he: *WP*, 6/9/70, D2; *WP*, 5/27/70, F3.
189 "bedding and boozing": Flood, *The Way It Is*, 207.
189 Members of Flood's legal team: Interview (anon.) by author.
189 Carter's 12-year-old son, John: John Carter interview.
190 The IRS was on his tail: *SGD*, 8/4/70, 3B.
190 In early August, Marian: Flood, *The Way It Is*, 207–8.
190 The failure to file: Letter from Missouri Secretary of State to Allan Zerman, 1/1/71, on file with author.
190 She never remarried: Marian Jorgensen interview; Judy Pace Flood interview.
190 He initially checked into: Flood, "The Legacy of Curt Flood," *Sport*, 11/77, 39.
191 He checked out: Ibid.; Flood, *The Way It Is*, 209.
191 "In Denmark": *WP*, 10/15/70, G1.
191 In *Federal Baseball* and *Toolson*: Flood Post-trial Brief, 58 (on file with author).
191 "Who is the real": Owners' Post-trial Brief, 5–7.
191 Cooper's 47-page typewritten: *Flood v. Kuhn*, 316 F. Supp. 271, 277 (S.D.N.Y. 1970).
192 He rejected: Ibid., 279–80.
192 He found: Ibid., 278.
192 "has the right": Ibid., 281.
192 "To the Four Freedoms": *BES*, 8/19/70, C4.
192 Prior to the trial: *Flood v. Kuhn*, 316 F. Supp., 276.
192 Cooper also predicted; "the reserve clause": Ibid., 283–84.
192 "We are bound": Ibid., 285.
192 "I am particularly pleased"; "Judge Cooper only": *NYT*, 8/13/70, 53.
193 Miller chided: *NYDN*, 8/15/70, 31.
193 Arthur Goldberg heard the news: *NYT*, 8/13/70, 23, 53.
193 He won over a few reporters: *NYTM*, 11/1/70, 25, 59.
193 "This is the end": *NYT*, 8/13/70, 53.
193 "wants to come back": *WP*, 8/13/70, H1.
193 On August 31: *SPD*, 9/1/70, 1C, 2C; *SGD*, 9/1/70, 3B; *PI*, 9/1/70, 22; *NYT*, 9/1/70, 40; *WP*, 9/1/70, 46. Retrosheet and baseballreference.com place the date of the transaction as August 30.

193 *International Herald Tribune*: Flood, "The Legacy of Curt Flood," *Sport*, 11/77, 39; *BMS*, 4/26/81, C10. Compare Flood, *The Way It Is*, 209 (Flood says he heard about the decision "by mail").
193 "permanent home"; He had begun: *NYP*, 10/29/70, 72.
193 His only American visitor: Judy Pace Flood interview.
193 American soldiers: Flood, *The Way It Is*, 209; *NYP*, 10/29/70, 72.
194 "a vacation resort": Flood, *The Way It Is*, 209.

CHAPTER TWELVE

Page

195 *Washington Post* sportswriter Leonard Shapiro: *WP*, 10/15/70, G1. The article was written by William Gildea, but he distinctly remembers another *Post* reporter conducting the initial interview. William Gildea interview. The reporter was almost certainly Shapiro, who remembered calling overseas and interviewing Flood as a young reporter. Leonard Shapiro interview; e-mails from Shapiro to author, November 22 and 23, 2005. Gildea mentioned the phone number in a subsequent article. *WP*, 11/8/70, 46.
195 "This is"; "If I signed": *WP*, 10/15/70, G1.
195 A few moments: *NYT*, 10/17/70, 34; Flood, *The Way It Is*, 210.
196 Instead, Flood agreed: Linn, "The Man Who Begs, Buys, and Borrows Trouble," *Sport*, 5/71, 94.
196 Flood sent a telegram: Flood, *The Way It Is*, 211.
196 A Georgetown law graduate: Blount, "Birds of a Feather Flock to Bob," *SI*, 11/2/70, 27–28; Linn, "The Man Who Begs, Buys, and Borrows Trouble," *Sport*, 5/71, 91–92.
196 He wanted: Blount, "Birds of a Feather Flock to Bob," *SI*, 11/2/70, 28.
197 "faces": Underwood, "They're Ho-Hummers No More," *SI*, 3/15/71, 28; Linn, "The Man Who Begs, Buys and Borrows Trouble," *Sport*, 5/71, 67.
197 "I think Flood": *WP*, 10/14/70, D1.
197 Rumors surfaced: *TSN*, 6/20/70, 16; *TSN*, 8/1/70, 16; *WP*, 8/9/70, 45 (rumors continued after meeting); *TSN*, 8/15/70, 5 (no settlement talk reported); *TSN*, 8/22/70, 8 (Holtzman disbelieves settlement rumors).
197 Short was: *TSN*, 8/1/70, 21.
197 After the meeting: Linn, "The Man Who Begs, Buys and Borrows Trouble," *Sport*, 5/71, 94.
197 During the World Series: *PI*, 10/14/70, 33, 37; *PDN*, 10/14/70, 55.
197 Later that week; "What the"; "I'm going": *PI*, 10/18/70, sec. 3, 1, 14.
198 On October 22: Phone Logs, 10/20/70, Goldberg Papers, Box I:135, Folder 4.
198 Goldberg trailed badly: *NYT*, 10/26/70, 42.
198 Miller had reluctantly: Marvin Miller interview.
198 Breslin talked: *NYTM*, 11/1/70, 59.

198 "It wasn't supposed": Marvin Miller interview.
198 "In my mind's eye": Marvin Miller interview.
198 Goldberg handed Short: "Proposals for Uniform Contract Between Curt Flood and the Washington Senators," Miller Papers, Box 3, Folder 9; Linn, "The Man Who Begs, Buys and Borrows Trouble," *Sport*, 5/71, 94.
199 Short agreed: Flood, *The Way It Is,* 211–12; Linn, "The Man Who Begs, Buys and Borrows Trouble," *Sport*, 5/71, 94.
199 the money: *NYP*, 10/29/70, 72.
199 "Commissioner Kuhn": Flood, *The Way It Is,* 212.
199 The only thing: Ibid., 212–13.
199 farce: *PI*, 11/1/70, sec. 3, 1, 15; *WP*, 11/4/70, B1; *TSN*, 11/21/70, 56, 54.
199 Kuhn was determined: *WP*, 10/29/70, H1; *NYT*, 10/30/70, 49.
199 "Then there's": Linn, "The Man Who Begs, Buys and Borrows Trouble," *Sport*, 5/71, 94.
199 He advised: *PDN*, 11/6/70, 64.
199–200 "In effect": Marvin Miller interview.
200 "If you think": Linn, "The Man Who Begs, Buys and Borrows Trouble," *Sport*, 5/71, 94.
200 If Flood had: *NYT*, 12/19/70, 36.
200 "Do you think": Linn, "The Man Who Begs, Buys and Borrows Trouble," *Sport*, 5/71, 94.
200 "Well, I understand": Miller, *A Whole Different Ball Game*, 201; Marvin Miller interview.
200 "And if anybody": *SPD*, 12/16/70, 3G; *WP*, 12/17/70, E1; *CST*, 1/4/71, 82.
200 Finally, at Goldberg's: *HP*, 3/15/70, 2/D; *NYT*, 12/19/70, 36.
200 He even met: Marvin Miller interview.
200 "You're going": *PI*, 11/1/70, sec. 3, 1, 15.
201 Instead, they selected: Whitfield, *Kiss It Goodbye*, 157–59.
201 "You're not going"; "Of course"; "I wouldn't": Marvin Miller interview.
201 "I'll do it": Linn, "The Man Who Begs, Buys and Borrows Trouble," *Sport*, 5/71, 94, 96.
201 Some of Flood's: *TSN*, 12/26/70, 36.
201 At their winter meeting: Ibid., 40, 42.
201 "The Players Association": Ibid., 40.
202 "a list of all": White, "Baseball's Roaming Son Back at 'Kid's Game' and Liking It," *WES Sportsweek*, 11/22/70, S-14.
202 "Baseball": *WP*, 11/8/70, 46.
202 "by chasing": *WP*, 11/19/72, E2.
202 Flood pointed to Muhammad Ali: *NYP*, 10/29/70, 72.
202 He told: White, "Baseball's Roaming Son Back at 'Kid's Game' and Liking It," *WES Sportsweek*, 11/22/70, S-14.
202 "I feel like": Ibid., S-6.

202 After changing: *WP*, 11/18/70, C1; White, "Baseball's Roaming Son Back at 'Kid's Game' and Liking It," *WES Sportsweek*, 11/22/70, S-7; *WDN*, 11/18/70, 71.
202 "There was": William Gildea interview.
203 "God": White, "Baseball's Roaming Son Back at 'Kid's Game' and Liking It," *WES Sportsweek*, 11/22/70, S-7.
203 "stiff": *WP*, 11/25/70, D1.
203 They made it: *SPT*, 11/18/70, 1-C, 3-C.
203 He spoke with Gildea: William Gildea interview; *WP*, 11/18/70, C1; *WP*, 11/19/70, E2.
203 He opened up: Russ White interview.
203 "Are you writing": *WDN*, 11/18/70, 71.
203 He stayed; He also read: White, "Baseball's Roaming Son Back at 'Kid's Game' and Liking It," *WES Sportsweek*, 11/22/70, S-7.
203 "a rather"; "I'm concerned": *WP*, 11/18/70, C1.
203 Flood had visited: White, "Baseball's Roaming Son Back at 'Kid's Game' and Liking It," *WES Sportsweek*, 11/22/70, S-14.
203 Before the Reds: *CE*, 4/12/57, 26; *CE*, 4/13/57, 11; *NYT*, 4/13/57, 14. Flood mistakenly remembered being with the Cardinals in 1958, but, before the 1958 regular season, the Cardinals traveled through Texas, Oklahoma, Kansas, Colorado, and Nebraska. *SPD*, 3/31/58, 4C. The 1957 Reds played their next game in Baltimore, just as Flood remembered. Compare *CE*, 4/13/57, 11, with White, "Baseball's Roaming Son Back at 'Kid's Game' and Liking It," *WES Sportsweek*, 11/22/70, S-14.
203 Williams claimed: *TSN*, 12/12/70, 57.
204 "Short's a star": Shelby Whitfield interview.
204 "I just want"; "A trade": *WP*, 11/25/70, D1.
204 "I can't think": *WDN*, 11/25/70, 55.
204 "How good"; "I don't know": *TSN*, 12/12/70, 57.
204 A few days earlier: *SPT*, 11/18/70, 3-C.
204 He lived for much: Judy Pace Flood interview.
204 "Right now": *SPT*, 11/18/70, 3-C.
204 "Of course America": *WP*, 11/25/70, D1; *TSN*, 12/12/70, 16.
204 He appeared January 18: *WP*, 1/19/71, C1; *WP*, 1/17/71, 39.
204 Ted Williams skipped: *WP*, 1/24/71, 50; *NYT*, 1/24/71, 56; *WP*, 2/3/71, D1; *TSN*, 2/6/71, 44.
205 "chief masquerade": *NYT*, 2/1/71, 40.
205 Maury Allen: *NYP*, 2/1/71, 49.
205 Allen, as Flood: *NYT*, 2/1/71, 40.
205 "We know": *NYP*, 2/1/71, 49.
206 dismissed before trial: *Salerno v. American League of Professional Baseball Clubs*, 310 F. Supp. 729 (S.D.N.Y. 1969).

206 Before the appeals court's: Holtzman, "Attendance and Litigation Were Up in 1970," 286–87.
206 We freely acknowledge: *Salerno v. American League of Professional Baseball Clubs*, 429 F.2d 1003, 1005 (2d Cir. 1970) (citations omitted).
207 On January 11: *Salerno v. Kuhn*, 400 U.S. 1001 (Jan. 11, 1971).
207 "may not have": Flood Second Circuit Brief, 2.
207 "If Curt Flood": Ibid., 14.
207 *Salerno* did not address: Ibid., 16.
207 Flood's brief: Ibid., 13.
207 They used a large chunk: Owners Second Circuit Brief, 16–27.
207 The owners' lawyers figured: Douglas Robinson interview.
207 They rebutted: Owners Second Circuit Brief, 28–29.
208 They also informed: Ibid., 4–5.
208 "run from one": Flood Second Circuit Reply Brief, 5.
208 In *Federal Baseball*: Ibid., 5–8.
208 did not receive: *NYT*, 1/28/71, 28; *WP*, 1/28/71, F1; nothing in the *New York Law Journal* or *New York Post*; a single paragraph in the *Daily News*, *NYDN*, 1/28/71, 100.
208 On the day of the argument: Lou Hoynes interview.
208 fifth and final: *NYLJ*, 1/27/71, 71.
209 Even so, Hoynes slipped: Lou Hoynes interview.
209 After 90 minutes, the three judges: *NYLJ*, 1/28/71, 16.
209 "The book": *LAT*, 2/23/71, pt. 3, 1.
209 "as randy as": Flood, *The Way It Is,* 100.
209 Flood told tales: Ibid., 104–6.
209 "swapped booze": Ibid., 88.
209 "In case any": Ibid., 101–2.
209 "As a star, a black man": *CST*, 2/8/71, 90.
210 Bowie Kuhn: *WP*, 2/7/71, 93.
210 Kuhn got his revenge: *WP*, 3/12/71, D1.
210 "tripe"; "Mr. Busch pets"; "Philadelphia offered": *BN*, 2/3/71, 15.
210–11 "emerges as a cynic"; "He's the"; "I want"; "Curt is": *SPD*, 3/4/71, 2C; *TSN*, 3/27/71, 26.
211 Flood described: Flood, *The Way It Is,* 76–77.
211 "was a long": *SGD*, 2/24/71, 3B; *TSN*, 3/13/71, 37.
211 Flood said Musial: Flood, *The Way It Is,* 64.
211 simpleminded company man; "wunnerful": Ibid., 52–53.
211 Musial was deeply hurt: *SGD*, 2/24/71, 3B; *TSN*, 3/13/71, 37.
211 "a great American"; "it would appear"; "The one common": *SGD*, 2/24/71, 3B; *TSN*, 3/13/71, 37.
211 "Curt's public disclosure": Whitfield, *Kiss It Goodbye*, 159.
211 "ill-advised"; "Baseball has": *WP*, 1/23/70, B2.

212 "Tell you this"; "Like Curt"; "No, he's entitled": *NYT*, 4/22/71, 49.
212 Even one of Flood's biggest boosters: Whitfield, *Kiss It Goodbye*, 159.

CHAPTER THIRTEEN

Page

213 He had vowed: *WES*, 11/24/70, A-22.
213 He quietly passed: *WES*, 3/14/71, E-2.
213 He did not hold: *TSN*, 4/10/71, 33, 44.
213 "Free Angela Davis": Elliott Maddox interview.
213 "Fuck you": *WP*, 6/30/74, D3.
214 Flood walked; "I like"; Maddox idolized; One baseball subject: Elliott Maddox interview.
214 "I have one": *WP*, 2/23/71, D1.
214 He later claimed: *TSN*, 4/10/71, 33.
214 Back in the room: Elliott Maddox interview.
214 "He's out there"; "Curt came back": *NYP*, 3/8/71, 46.
214 Maddox knew: Elliott Maddox interview.
215 "Ted is a nonconformist": White, "Baseball's Roaming Son Back at 'Kid's Game' and Liking It," *WES Sportsweek*, 11/22/70, S-14.
215 Williams recalled: *WP*, 12/29/70, F1.
215 Flood recalled: White, "Baseball's Roaming Son Back at 'Kid's Game' and Liking It," *WES Sportsweek*, 11/22/70, S-14.
215 "I'm glad you're": *SI*, 3/15/71, 33.
215 Williams indoctrinated; "I thought so": *TSN*, 3/13/71, 41.
216 "the Underminers Club": Denny McLain interview; Whitfield, *Kiss It Goodbye*, 102.
216 "because they were not": *NYT*, 7/26/66, 28; *TSN*, 8/6/66, 5.
216 Mexican mother and his childhood: Montville, *Ted Williams*, 19–23, 35–37, 39.
216 During the 1971 season: Elliott Maddox interview.
216 "As good a player": *NYT*, 2/23/71, 44.
216 Privately, Williams: Shelby Whitfield interview.
216 "Sure, I lived": *OT*, 4/5/71, 37.
216 "Flood has to have": *SPD*, 3/24/71, 18A.
216 Team trainer: Bill Zeigler interview.
217 "aged ten years": *CT*, 5/1/71, F4.
217 During his first time: *WP*, 2/23/71, D1; *WDN*, 2/23/71, 36; *WES*, 2/23/71, A-11.
217 He failed: *WP*, 3/4/71, 97; *WDN*, 3/4/71, 60.
217 "They don't know": *WDN*, 2/23/71, 46.
217 He finally got: *WP*, 3/9/71, D4; *WES*, 3/12/71, A-14.
217 "The toughest thing": *NYT*, 3/28/71, sec. 5, 3.

217 His throw: *WP*, 3/17/71, C1; *WP*, 3/16/71, D1; *WES*, 3/16/71, A-12.
217 Williams later criticized: *WP*, 3/26/71, D1; *TSN*, 4/10/71, 33.
217 Flood even took: *NYT*, 3/28/71, sec. 5, 3.
218 After the first few days; Maddox was constantly; During the nights when; "I've got"; "No": Elliott Maddox interview.
218 "He is in baseball": *LAT*, 3/26/71, pt. 3, 1, 12.
218 "One gained": *WDN*, 4/29/70, 70.
218 "tarnished goods": *BAA*, 2/20/71, 17.
218 "stormy petrel": White, "Baseball's Roaming Son Back at 'Kid's Game' and Liking It," *WES Sportsweek*, 11/22/70, S-14.
219 "What's it gotta"; "Don't you know": Mann, "Ted Williams and Bob Short," *Look*, 5/4/71, 72.
219 Flood met Mann; "[I] better": Ibid., 72, 74.
219 he turned down: *WES*, 3/9/71, A-12.
219 "As long as": Mann, "Ted Williams and Bob Short," *Look*, 5/4/71, 72.
219 "They all": Bernie Allen interview.
219 "Look!": *LAT*, 3/26/71, pt. 3, 1, 12.
219 Flood read books: Paul Casanova interview.
220 "I was expecting": Dick Billings interview.
220 "He was a speed": Del Unser interview.
220 "You hear about": Dick Bosman interview.
220 The day before the season: Orlando Cepeda interview.
220 "Hell, in those days"; A month before spring training: Frank Howard interview.
220 "He didn't spend"; Williams disapproved: Shelby Whitfield interview.
221 Williams also once spied: Bill Zeigler interview.
221 Flood's hitting: *WP*, 3/20/71, D1; *WP*, 3/22/71, D1; *WP*, 3/31/71, D1; *WP*, 4/1/71, K1.
221 He batted only: *WP*, 4/5/71, D5.
221 "I have a feeling": *WDN*, 4/5/71, B-5.
221 "He's the guy": *WP*, 4/6/71, D4.
221 "I'm just the same"; "was not out": *BAA*, 4/10/71, 16.
221 the three-judge panel had affirmed: *Flood v. Kuhn*, 443 F.2d 264 (2d Cir. 1971).
222 "We readily acknowledge"; "so uniquely"; "[W]e do not consider": Ibid., 268.
222 Moore had won: *NYT*, 2/18/57, 16; Gunther, *Learned Hand*, 648–49.
222 "impotent"; "it is of no moment": *Gardella v. Chandler*, 172 F.2d 402, 409–10 (2d Cir. 1949) (Frank, J., concurring).
222 "In my opinion": *Flood v. Kuhn*, 443 F.2d 272 (Moore, J., concurring).
222 "Baseball for almost": Ibid., 268.
223 The Supreme Court in 1922: Ibid., 272.
223 "reservations"; "would limit": Ibid., 273.

223 "We knew nothing": *WP*, 4/8/71, C1.
223 "The Supreme Court": *OT*, 4/8/71, 38.
223 "not even bothering": *WP*, 4/15/71, D1; *CPD*, 4/16/71, 2-C.
223 lost the snap: *WES*, 4/12/71, A-23; *CPD*, 4/16/71, 2-C.
224 In the second inning: *WP*, 4/12/71, D1, D5; *NYT*, 4/12/71, 50; *WES*, 4/12/71, A-23; Dick Bosman interview.
224 Williams did not yell: *WES*, 4/12/71, A-23.
224 "You can't handle": Tom McCraw interview.
224 Williams again said: *WP*, 4/12/71, D1, D4.
224 "Syphilitic": Shelby Whitfield interview.
224 "I told him": *BHT*, 4/14/71, 43.
224 but he refused: *BG*, 4/13/71, 26.
224 "I'm not sure": Shelby Whitfield interview.
225 "Ted fucked"; "Ted's main goal"; "sideways livid"; "All Bob Short"; "Do you have"; "There was": Denny McLain interview.
225 "That was the knife"; On the team's first extended road trip: Elliott Maddox interview.
225 One night in Cleveland; "He felt like": Richie Scheinblum interview.
225 Flood finally returned: *WP*, 4/18/71, 41.
226 "I'm going": Elliott Maddox interview.
226 Upon arriving in New York; "Let's talk": Marvin Miller interview.
226 "He said": *NYDN*, 4/29/71, 113.
226 Hate mail; "freaky letters"; "Dear Nigger": Whitford, "Curt Flood," *Sport*, 12/86, 106; Flood, *The Way It Is*, 18; Curran, "Curt Flood and the Baseball Revolution," *L.A. Weekly*, 4/1–7/94, 25; "Curt Flood," *ESPN SportsCentury* (Pace).
226 "Whoever it was": Whitford, "Curt Flood," *Sport*, 12/86, 106.
226 McLain blamed: Denny McLain interview.
227 "My case bears": *WP*, 5/2/71, 42.
227 "It's hard to focus"; "I don't remember": Tom McCraw interview.
227 Before a home game; "Frank"; Howard told: Frank Howard interview.
227 The 6,597 fans: *WP*, 4/25/71, C1.
227–28 "You know"; "I try not"; "I don't know": *MJ*, 4/25/71, sports sec., 3, 6.
228 He exploded: William Gildea interview.
228–29 Soon after he said; "They were trying"; "My problem is": ; "How do"; "We had the": Mike Epstein interview.
229 "Things are"; "Life is like": *WES*, 4/28/71, C-1.
229 Baxter thought: *WP*, 4/28/71, D1; ibid.
229 dark sunglasses: *WP*, 4/28/71, D1.
229 Williams noticed: Ibid.; *BES*, 4/28/71, C10; *WDN*, 4/28/71, 72; *WES*, 4/28/71, C-1.
229 "Not too"; "yes"; "That's up to Ted": *MS*, 4/28/71, 4D.

229 "Take care"; "Yeah": Mike Epstein interview.
229 Flood intimated: Denny Riddleberger interview.
229 Flood kept: Ibid.; *SI*, 3/15/71, 26.
229 To Riddleberger; "Take care": Denny Riddleberger interview.
230 Flood ate dinner; "some things": *WP*, 4/28/71, D1; *WP*, 10/1/71, D1.
230 "He said everything"; "Cassie": Paul Casanova interview.
230 Cox and Flood had agreed: Casey Cox interview. Cox now claims that it was lunch the next day, not dinner. Ibid.; McKenna, "The Forgotten Flood of 1971," *Washington City Paper*, 4/30/04. His quotes at the time are to the contrary. *WP*, 4/28/71, D1; *BES*, 4/28/71, C10; *WP*, 10/1/71, D1.
230 Tim Cullen; "Tim"; "Thanks": Tim Cullen interview.
230 "Where's Curt"; "I don't know": Casey Cox interview.
230 Short called; "You've got": Denny McLain interview.
230 McLain did not: *BES*, 4/28/71, C10.
230 Maddox was worried: Elliott Maddox interview.
231 A *New York Daily News*; "I'll throw you": *NYDN*, 4/28/71, 100.
231 Short hastily called: *WP*, 4/28/71, D1.
231 At 4:55 p.m.; I TRIED: Telegram, Flood to Short, 4/27/71 (on file with author).
231 Short posted: Joe Camacho interview.
231 Only Maddox: Elliott Maddox interview; Tom McCraw interview; Denny McLain interview; Denny Riddleberger interview.
231 Maddox felt: Elliott Maddox interview.
231 He first tried: Phone Log, 4/28/71, Goldberg Papers, Box I-135, Folder 5.
231 Then, between 6:15 and 6:30: *PI*, 4/29/71, 31.
232 Reichler arrived; "By way": *NYT*, 4/29/71, 53; *WP*, 4/29/71, D1.
232 "It's not baseball": "Curt Flood's Troubles," *Newsweek*, 5/10/71, 67; *NYDN*, 4/28/71, 100.
232 Flood told Reichler he had been thinking: *NYDN*, 4/28/71, 104.
232 For 20 minutes: *PI*, 4/29/71, 31.
232 "I know"; "No, no": *NYT*, 4/29/71, 53.
232 settled into seat 3-F: *NYP*, 4/28/71, 86.
232 refusing a request: *WP*, 4/28/71, D1.
232 "big league": *WES*, 4/28/71, C-3; *WDN*, 4/28/71, 72.
232 "good riddance": Shelby Whitfield interview.
232 "was an act": *NYP*, 4/29/71, 68.
232 racial lines; "[I]f you have": *NYDN*, 4/29/71, 113.
232–33 "The Flood sympathizers": *WES*, 4/29/71, E1.
233 "If he wins": *WP*, 5/5/71, D1; *CST*, 5/5/71, 114.
233 Lieutenant Fred Grimes; "He's running": *SPD*, 5/3/71, 2B.
233 mostly financial: *WP*, 5/5/71, D1; *CST*, 5/5/71, 114.
233 Two days before he left: *SPD*, 5/25/71, 2C.

233 Creditors had been hounding: *CT*, 5/12/71, F4.
233 He avoided them: Charlie Wangner interview.
233 Flood had been receiving: *WDN*, 4/29/71, 70; *NYDN*, 4/29/71, 113; *TSN*, 5/15/71, 5. Compare *TSN*, 8/4/73, 33 (placing the figure at "more than $40,000").
233 A week before he left: *CDN*, 8/19/71, sec. 4, 45.
233 Short agreed: *OT*, 5/5/71, sports sec., 1, 45; *CT*, 5/12/71, F4.
233 Otherwise, Flood: *WP*, 5/5/71, D1; *CDN*, 8/19/71, sec. 4, 45.
234 Paul Porter had met: *TSN*, 4/17/71, 23.
234 Flood remembered; "It seems clear": *CDN*, 8/19/71, sec. 4, 45. An exception to Miller's comment was Dick Young, who acknowledged that Flood had refused to declare bankruptcy to preserve his lawsuit. *TSN*, 5/22/71, 14.

CHAPTER FOURTEEN

Page

235 It was later: *NYT*, 10/11/74, 1; *WP*, 10/13/74, A1; *WSJ*, 11/14/74, 8.
235 He forced: Peter Edelman interview; "Arthur J. Goldberg's Legacies to American Labor Relations," 32 *J. Marshall L. Rev.* 667, 679–80 (1999).
235 "I cannot be terribly": Letter, Breyer to Goldberg, 11/30/70, Goldberg Papers, Box I-62, Folder 2.
235 Paul, Weiss support staffers: *NYT*, 12/19/76, F11; Jay Topkis interview.
236 Goldberg rented: *WP*, 8/4/71, C1.
236 He told Marvin: Dick Moss interview.
236 Of the more than 3,100: Report of the Study Group on the Caseload of the Supreme Court (Freund Report), 57 F.R.D. 573, 613 tbls. III & IV (1972). The number of cert petitions and cert grants excludes 133 death penalty petitions, all of which were granted because of the Court's 1972 decision declaring capital punishment unconstitutional.
236–37 Levitt knew; Levitt also knew; Goldberg often asked: Dan Levitt interview.
237 "A review": Supreme Court Rule, 19(1), 398 U.S. 1009, 1030 (1970).
237 "Frequently": O'Brien, *Storm Center*, 236, quoting T. Clark, "Internal Operations of the United States Supreme Court," 43 *Judicature* 45, 48 (1959).
238 "a most frustrating"; "the vagaries"; "so uniquely": *Flood v. Kuhn*, 443 F.2d 264, 268 (2d Cir. 1971).
238 "rectify": Flood Cert Petition, 2, quoting *Moragne v. State Marine Lines, Inc.*, 398 U.S. 375, 403 (1970).
238 "undermined"; "creating": Flood Cert Petition, 2–3.
239 "The issues": Baseball Cert Opposition, 20.
239 no examination; "sudden": Flood Reply Petition, 3.
239 These recommendations: During the 1971 term, one law clerk in each chamber wrote a cert memo about every case. The following year, six of the justices

began to divide the cert petitions among themselves in what became known as the cert pool.

240 He wrote most of: Warren Papers, Box 631, Folder "Per Curiam Nos. 18, 23, and 24"; Burton Papers, Box 245, Folder 3.

240 He also dissented: *Boys Markets, Inc. v. Retail Clerks Union, Local 770*, 398 U.S. 235, 257–61 (1970) (Black, J., dissenting).

240 In his final years: Garrow, "Mental Decrepitude on the U.S. Supreme Court," 67 *U. Chi. L. Rev.* 995, 1050–52 (2000).

240 Harlan had saved Muhammad Ali: Woodward and Armstrong, *The Brethren*, 136–39.

240 In an unsigned opinion: *Clay v. United States*, 403 U.S. 698 (1971) (per curiam). Thurgood Marshall, as a former lawyer for the NAACP Legal Defense and Educational Fund (which represented Ali), took no part in Ali's decision.

241 "It's what Justice Harlan": Bingham and Wallace, *Muhammad Ali's Greatest Fight*, 249.

241 "If the situation": *Radovich v. NFL*, 352 U.S., 445, 456 (1957) (Harlan, J., dissenting).

241 "'public'": *Williams v. Florida*, 399 U.S. 78, 127 (1970), quoting another Harlan opinion, *Moragne v. State Marine Lines, Inc.*, 398 U.S. 375, 403 (1970) (citations omitted).

241 "We tried to shame": Dan Levitt interview.

242 "Mr. Justice Douglas": 400 U.S. 1001, 91 S. Ct. 462 (1971).

242 "professional athletes": *NYT*, 1/19/71, 43.

242 The [NBA's] college player draft: *Haywood v. Nat'l Basketball Ass'n*, 401 U.S. 1204, 1205–6, 91 S. Ct. 672, 673–4 (1971) (citations omitted).

242–43 On Douglas, see Murphy, *Wild Bill*.

243 "Your dissent": Memo, Reed to Douglas, 9/23/71, Douglas Papers, Box 1561, Folder 71–32(d) "Law Clerk."

243 Reed included: Memo, Reed to Burger, 9/27/71, Douglas Papers, Box 1522, Folder "O.T. 1971 Administrative Conf. Lists."

244 "at Conference": Memo, Burger to Conference, 9/27/71, ibid. Conference is usually capitalized to refer to the nine justices collectively, but "conference" refers to the justices' private meetings.

244 October 4, 1971; The justices retreated: Memo, Burger to Conference, 9/24/71, ibid.

244 They tried to delay: Blackmun Oral History, 4/24/95, 181.

245 But decisions on 655: "Statistical Comparison of the Agenda for Conferences for the First Week of the Term for the Years Shown," Douglas Papers, Box 1522, Folder "Administrative Conf. Lists."

245 The three: Douglas Papers, Box 1484, Folder "Administrative Docket Book #676–980."

245 A master of the cert process: Perry, *Deciding to Decide*, 67–69.

245 "five give the four": *Straight v. Wainwright*, 106 S. Ct. 2004, 2006 (1986) (Brennan, J., dissenting), quoted in Revesz and Harlan, "Nonmajority Rules and the Supreme Court," 136 *U. Pa. L. Rev.* 1067, 1099 (1988).

245 According to a private memo: Memo, Burger to Conference, 11/4/71, Douglas Papers, Box 1522, Folder "Administrative Memoranda by Court."

246 In the middle: Douglas Papers, Box 1561, Folder 71–32(d) "Law Clerk"; Law Clerk interview, 3/23/05.

246 common personal practice: Perry, *Deciding to Decide*, 182; O'Brien, *Storm Center*, 252; Douglas, *Go East Young Man*, 452.

246 Dissents from denial: Perry, *Deciding to Decide*, 170–74.

246 Douglas asked: Docket Sheet, Brennan Papers, Box I:253, Folder 8.

246 On October 7: Douglas Papers, Box 1561, Folder 71–32(d) "Law Clerk."

246 Today, the Court: Draft Dissent, 1 (citations omitted), Douglas Papers, Box 1561, Folder 71–32(d) "Law Clerk."

247 Douglas argued: Draft Dissent, 3–4.

247 "While I joined": Ibid., 4 n.3.

247 Finally, the draft; The questions: Ibid., 4 (citations omitted).

247 On the morning: Conference began that Friday at 9:15 a.m. so the justices could attend the funeral of former secretary of state, and two-year law clerk to Justice Louis Brandeis, Dean Acheson. Memo, Burger to Conference, 10/13/71, Thurgood Marshall Papers, Box 78, Folder 8.

248 Certiorari Granted: Court Journal, 10/19/71, 129, Thurgood Marshall Papers, Box 79, Folder 3.

248 The *New York Times*: *NYT*, 10/20/71, 1, 57; *WP*, 10/20/71, A1, A9.

248 All three television networks: Vanderbilt University Television News Archive, 10/19/71, ABC, CBS, and NBC, record numbers 12941, 213380, and 454349.

248 "Unless President Nixon": *CT*, 10/21/71, F4.

248 "Presidents come": *NYT*, 10/22/71, 24.

248–49 On Powell's background: Jeffries, *Justice Lewis F. Powell, Jr.*, 139–141, 145–50, 174–76.

249 "A Random"; "I realize": 117 *Cong. Rec.* 44,800 (1971); "Supreme Court: Memo from Rehnquist," *Newsweek*, 12/13/71, 32–37.

249–50 On Rehnquist's background: Snyder, "How the Conservatives Canonized *Brown v. Board of Education*," 431–37.

250 Assistant Solicitor General Philip Elman: *WP*, 1/18/57, A22.

250 HIGHBROW COACH: Roth, *Our Gang*, 57.

251 two years later: *NYT*, 6/28/73, 38.

251 In 1970: Roth, *Our Gang*, 95.

251 "surrender": Ibid., 94.

251 The *New York Post*: *NYP*, 4/28/71, 86.

252 In Lisbon; "I'm sorry": *WP*, 4/29/71, D1.

252 Early the next morning: *NYT*, 4/30/71, 29; *CT*, 4/30/71, H1.

252 "Welfare/Whereabouts"; 1. ROBERT SHORT: Telegram, 5/6/71, State Department Records, NARA, College Park, Maryland, R6 59, State Central Files, 1970–1973, Box 326.

252 Actor Yul Brynner; "No thanks": *NYP*, 5/8/71, 27; *SI*, 5/17/71, 66.

252 Short claimed: *WP*, 5/23/71, C4.

252–53 The promanagement *Sporting News*: *TSN*, 6/19/71, 33.

253 The Mexico rumor: *TSN*, 7/24/71, 14.

253 On May 1; Jimmie Angelopolous: Letter, Jimmie Angelopolous to Ted Williams, 8/7/71, *TSN* Archives, Curt Flood File; Jimmie Angelopolous interview.

253 Flood ended up: BMS, 1/6/73.

253 Flood once told; "Yes": *SFC*, 3/19/79, 50.

254 "It was kind": Elliott Maddox interview.

254 Rumors abounded: *WP*, 5/9/71, C3; *WP*, 6/27/71, E1.

254 Flood knew: *WP*, 4/4/79, D4.

254 "the situation"; "I know": Marvin Miller interview.

254 On July 29: *SPD*, 7/29/71, 10D; *CT*, 7/30/71, F3; *CDN*, 7/30/71, 36; *TSN*, 8/14/71, 36.

254 On September 1: *SPD*, 9/1/71, 12A.

254–55 A few weeks; At the time; "I'm sorry": Letter from Moss to Flood, 10/18/71, Goldberg Papers, Box I-94, Folder 11.

255 The only way: Marvin Miller interview.

255–56 He wrote a letter; I hope; Flood asked: Letter from Flood to Goldberg, postmarked 12/21/71, Goldberg Papers, Box I-94, Folder 11.

256 Goldberg rejoiced: Dan Levitt interview.

256 "[I]t is the brief": Winkelman, "Just a Brief Writer," *Litigation*, Summer 2003, 52, quoting Thurgood Marshall, "The Federal Appeal," in Charpentier, ed., *Counsel on Appeal* (1968), 139, 146.

257 It is revolting: Holmes, "Path of the Law," 10 *Harv. L. Rev.* 457, 469 (1897), quoted in *Flood v. Kuhn*, 443 F.2d 264, 268 n.7 (2d Cir. 1971).

257 "moribund": Flood Supreme Court Brief, 18.

257 "precedential underpinnings": Ibid., 19.

257 "does not affect": *WP*, 10/20/71, A9.

257 "The reserve clause": *WP*, 10/20/71, C1; *NYT*, 10/20/71, 57.

258 The media speculated: *TSN*, 11/6/71, 40; *TSN*, 12/4/71, 32.

258 Behind the scenes: Lou Hoynes interview.

258 "Be prepared": Bill Eskridge interview; Douglas Robinson interview.

258 The young Willkie Farr: Bowie Kuhn interview.

258 On October 25, 1971: *NYT*, 10/26/71, 45; *TSN*, 12/11/71, 48.

258 Hoynes replaced; "Don't embarrass": Lou Hoynes interview; Robert Kheel interview; Helyar, *Lords of the Realm*, 110.

258 O'Malley, however, wanted Kuhn: Bowie Kuhn interview; Kuhn, *Hardball*, 88.
258 "I felt"; "I had very high": Bowie Kuhn interview.
259 considered the owners' 133-page : Lou Hoynes interview.
259 "Without reexamination": *Toolson*, 346 U.S., 356–57, quoted in Owners' Brief, 26.
259 The owners' brief: Owners' Supreme Court Brief, 27–28.
260 "mandatory subject": Owners' Supreme Court Brief, 49, quoting 381 U.S. at 710 (Goldberg, J., dissenting).
260 Goldberg called David Feller: Letter from Goldberg to Feller, 12/31/71, Goldberg Papers, Box I-94, Folder 11, Letter from Feller to Goldberg, 1/5/72, Letter from Goldberg to Feller, 1/25/72, and Letter from Goldberg to Feller, 2/28/72, Goldberg Papers, Box I-94, Folder 12.
260 After all the briefs: Jacobs and Winter, "Antitrust Principles and Collective Bargaining by Athletes," 81 *Yale L.J.* 1 (1971–72).
260 The Court asked: Letter from Seaver to Goldberg, 1/28/72, Goldberg Papers, Box I-94, Folder 12.
260 Flood would be represented: Letter from Seaver to Goldberg, 2/1/72, ibid.
260 Hoynes exulted; "one of the": Lou Hoynes interview.
261 Miller later admitted; "all the way": Miller, *A Whole Different Ball Game*, 198.
261 "Offering you help": Letter from Topkis to Goldberg, 2/16/72, Goldberg Papers, Box I-94, Folder 12.
261 "I believe": Letter from Goldberg to Topkis, 2/22/72, ibid.
261 In late February and March: Memo from Levitt to Goldberg, 2/28/72, Memo from Westen to Goldberg, 2/28/72, Memo from Levitt to Goldberg, 3/3/72, Memo from Levitt to Goldberg, 3/17/72, and Memo from Westen to Goldberg, 3/17/72, ibid.
261 In mid-March; "sounded terrific"; "it would be": Peter Westen interview.
261–62 He took the train; There was a special chief justice: Lou Hoynes interview.
262 An abrasive: Kalman, *Abe Fortas*, 380–82.
262 In November 1970, Fortas: Memo from Fortas to Porter, 11/30/70, 1–3, Fortas Papers, Box 120, Folder 331.
262 "this is one"; "Reliance upon *stare decisis*": Ibid., 3.
263 *Gideon v. Wainwright*: 372 U.S. 335 (1963).
263 Fortas had briefed and argued: Lewis, *Gideon's Trumpet*, 161–81.

CHAPTER FIFTEEN

Page

264 During breakfast; Levitt thought: Dan Levitt interview.
265 "truly skillful": *Jones v. Barnes*, 463 U.S. 745, 762 (1983) (Brennan, J., dissenting).
265 "you do have": Bright, "The Power of the Spoken Word: In Defense of Oral Argument," 72 *Iowa L. Rev.* 35, 36–37 (1986).

265 Goldberg drove: Interview (anon.) by author.
265 The white marble: *NYT*, 12/8/34, 1, 3.
266 Jay Topkis: Jay Topkis interview.
266 Marvin Miller: Marvin Miller interview.
266 Miller was too busy: Marvin Miller interview.
266 Muhammad Ali: *NYT*, 4/20/71, 24.
266 Miller did not say: Marvin Miller interview.
267 At a cost of $8,500: *WES*, 2/19/72, A-17.
267 "So first": Supreme Court transcript, 3 (Burger). All oral argument quotations are taken directly from the Court's audiotape. *Flood v. Kuhn* Supreme Court Oral Argument Tape, 71-32, NARA, College Park, Maryland. I have cited only the written transcript, though not entirely complete and accurate, because it is more widely accessible and easier to cite than the audiotape. *Flood v. Kuhn* Supreme Court Oral Argument Transcript (Supreme Court transcript), Law Library, Library of Congress. Neither the audio nor the transcript identifies which justice is speaking. Professor Jerry Goldman of Northwestern University's Oyez Project was extremely helpful in assisting me to identify the justice asking a particular question. In a few instances, Professor Goldman and I resorted to our best guesses.
267 The justices fretted: Blackmun Oral History, 4/24/95, 184–85.
267 "Mr. Goldberg": Supreme Court transcript, 3 (Burger).
267 "You have questions": *NYTM*, 8/1/71, 25.
268 Justice Black's funeral: *NYT*, 9/29/71, 37.
268 Justice Harlan's funeral: Douglas Papers, Box 1522, Folder "Administrative Conference Lists."
268 "Mr. Chief Justice": Supreme Court transcript, 3 (Goldberg).
268 "unpleasant voice": Handwritten Notes, 3/20/72, Blackmun Papers, Box 145, Folder 2.
268 He said Flood had signed: Supreme Court transcript, 4 (Goldberg).
268 astonished Levitt and Westen: Dan Levitt interview; Peter Westen interview.
268 "Everybody in that courtroom": Dan Levitt interview.
269 "overconfident"; they handed: Peter Westen interview.
269 Goldberg began listing: Supreme Court transcript, 6.
269 Levitt looked: Dan Levitt interview.
269 He read the legal letters: Supreme Court transcript, 7–10 (Goldberg).
269 "too much time": Handwritten notes, 3/20/72, Blackmun Papers, Box 145, Folder 2.
269 Stewart asked how much: Supreme Court transcript, 10–11.
269 "an increase": Ibid., 11 (Goldberg).
270 "'Why this high-paid ballplayer'": Ibid., 11–12 (Goldberg).
270 "[a]s a practical matter": Ibid., 12 (Rehnquist).
270 "That's right": Ibid. (Goldberg).

270 The Supreme Court law clerks: Law Clerk interviews, 1/13/04, 3/23/05.

271 "Mr. Justice, may I ask you"; "No"; "I hope you're going"; "I will move": Supreme Court transcript, 13–14 (Brennan and Goldberg).

271 The image in Hoynes's: Lou Hoynes interview.

271 Neither Levitt nor Westen: Dan Levitt interview; Peter Westen interview.

271–72 Brennan then asked; "They would have"; "both dealt"; "the Court doesn't"; Goldberg responded: Supreme Court transcript, 14 (Brennan and Goldberg).

272 White asked; White tried: Supreme Court transcript, 16.

272 "Has this man"; "Pardon"; "Has the petitioner"; "Yes"; "Is the case moot": Supreme Court transcript, 19 (Douglas and Goldberg).

272–73 William Radovich; "protect the victims": *Radovich*, 352 U.S., 448, 454. On Radovich, see also *Radovich v. NFL*, 230 F.2d 620 (9th Cir. 1956); *CT*, 7/6/49, C2.

273 "I won't trade him": Flood Supreme Court Reply Brief, 17, quoting, *NYT*, 2/18/72, 29.

273 He had spoken: Letter from Gerst to Goldberg, 2/25/72, and Letter from Goldberg to Gerst, 2/28/72, Goldberg Papers, Box I-94, Folder 12.

273 "Quite possibly": Letter from Topkis to Goldberg, 2/18/72, ibid.

274 "Your rebuttal time"; "Excuse me": Supreme Court transcript, 19–20 (Burger).

274 Supreme Court clerks: Law Clerk interviews, 1/13/04, 3/23/05.

274 Instead of immediately sitting: Supreme Court transcript, 20–21.

274 "He never got": Dan Levitt interview.

274 "Thank you": Supreme Court transcript, 21 (Burger).

274 Paul Porter's job; In preparing; "If you answer": Lou Hoynes interview.

274 "Mr. Chief Justice, may it please"; "this litigation involves": Supreme Court transcript, 21 (Porter).

275 Brennan asked; Porter explained: Ibid., 22–24 (Brennan and Porter).

275 White jumped in; "But doesn't"; Porter answered: Ibid., 24 (White and Porter).

275 "But Mr. Porter"; Porter explained; "Are you saying"; "Absolutely, yes": Ibid., 24–25 (Brennan and Porter).

275 Hoynes wanted: Lou Hoynes interview.

276 Hoynes's journey: Robert Kheel interview.

276 "Mr. Chief Justice"; "I am counsel": Supreme Court transcript, 25 (Hoynes).

276 "It is your position"; Hoynes conceded: Ibid. (Douglas and Hoynes).

276 "much broader"; "real protagonists": Ibid., 25–26 (Hoynes).

276 White asked: Ibid., 26–28 (White and Hoynes).

276 Hoynes tried to make: Lou Hoynes interview.

277 Pittsburgh sold: Hutchinson, *The Man Who Was Once Whizzer White*, 158.

277 As an intelligence officer: Ibid., 175–78.

277 "This guy": Nixon Tapes, 733–10, 6/14/72, NARA, College Park, Maryland.

277 He despised: Hutchinson, *The Man Who Was Once Whizzer White*, 447–48.

277 terrified: Law Clerk interview, 3/23/05.

277 Ford Frick: Hutchinson, *The Man Who Was Once Whizzer White*, 378.
277 A few people: Ibid., 377–79.
277 Hoynes knew: Lou Hoynes interview.
278 Thurgood Marshall picked up: Supreme Court transcript, 28 (Marshall).
278–79 "Mr. Hoynes"; Of Flood's trade; "My question was"; "I call it a union"; "So you're saying": Ibid., 28–30 (Marshall and Hoynes).
279 Marshall repeatedly asked Hoynes: Ibid., 30–31 (Marshall and Hoynes).
279 "Well, what good"; "What has it done"; "Wouldn't you say nothing"; "Wouldn't you say under": Ibid., 31 (Marshall).
279 Hoynes tried to respond: Ibid., 31–32 (Hoynes).
279 "How is this union": Ibid., 32 (Marshall).
279 Hoynes said the union: Ibid., 32–33 (Hoynes).
280 "None of this"; "His playing"; "That's what I thought" (on audio only): Ibid., 33–34 (Marshall and Hoynes).
280 Marshall swiveled in his chair: Lou Hoynes interview; Robert Kheel interview.
280 "[T]he players union"; "This testimony": Supreme Court transcript, 34 (Hoynes).
280 "hanging curveballs": Lou Hoynes interview.
280 White asked: Supreme Court transcript, 42–48 (White and Hoynes).
281 White's line of questioning allowed: Ibid., 47 (White and Hoynes).
281 Hoynes's associate: Robert Kheel interview.
281 Hoynes discussed: Supreme Court transcript, 49–50 (Hoynes).
281 "They got my best": Lou Hoynes interview.
281 As Hoynes finished: Ibid.; Robert Kheel interview.
281 "Thank you, gentlemen": Supreme Court transcript, 50 (Burger).
281 "That was the worst"; "It was one": Dan Levitt interview.
282 After the glare: *NYT*, 3/21/72, 49.

CHAPTER SIXTEEN

Page

283 Nearly five hours: The conference began at 3:15 p.m. 1972 Appointment Book, Blackmun Papers, Box 60, Folder 9, and handwritten conference notes, Box 145, Folder 2; handwritten conference notes, Douglas Papers, Box 1561, Folder 71-32(d), "Misc. Memos, Cert Memos, Vote of Court."
283 The only record: The dialogue at conference is reconstructed from handwritten notes of three justices: Blackmun Papers, Box 145, Folder 2; Douglas Papers, Box 1561, Folder 71-32(d), "Misc. Memos, Cert Memos, Vote of Court"; Brennan Papers, Box I:253, Folder 8. The votes, but not what was said, were confirmed by Powell's papers, Box 148.
283 The other justices sometimes: Schwartz, *The Ascent of Pragmatism*, 12.
283 *Toolson* was wrong: Douglas Papers, Box 1561, Folder 71-32(d), "Misc. Memos, Cert Memos, Vote of Court"; Brennan Papers, Box I:253, Folder 8.

284 "muddies the waters": Blackmun Papers, Box 145, Folder 2.
284 Professional baseball: Douglas Papers, Box 1561, Folder 71-32(d), "Misc. Memos, Cert Memos, Vote of Court."
284 Brennan explained: Ibid.; Blackmun Papers, Box 145, Folder 2.
284 Stewart voted: Blackmun Papers, Box 145, Folder 2; Brennan Papers, Box I:253, Folder 8; Douglas Papers, Box 1561, Folder 71-32(d), "Misc. Memos, Cert Memos, Vote of Court."
284 He agreed with Stewart: Brennan Papers, Box I:253, Folder 8.
284 believed that Stewart: Blackmun Papers, Box 145, Folder 2; Brennan Papers, Box I:253, Folder 8; Douglas Papers, Box 1561, Folder 71-32(d), "Misc. Memos, Cert Memos, Vote of Court."
285 "untenable": Douglas Papers, Box 1561, Folder 71-32(d), "Misc. Memos, Cert Memos, Vote of Court."
285 He viewed: Brennan Papers, Box I:253, Folder 8.
285 "tentatively affirm": Douglas Papers, Box 1561, Folder 71-32(d), "Misc. Memos, Cert Memos, Vote of Court."
285 It made no sense: Blackmun Papers, Box 145, Folder 2; Brennan Papers, Box I:253, Folder 8; Douglas Papers, Box 1561, Folder 71-32(d), "Misc. Memos, Cert Memos, Vote of Court."
285 Before Powell spoke: Douglas Papers, Box 1561, Folder 71-32(d), "Misc. Memos, Cert Memos, Vote of Court."
285 He agreed with Stewart; state antitrust claims: Ibid.; Blackmun Papers, Box 145, Folder 2; Brennan Papers, Box I:253, Folder 8.
285 Burger reiterated: Blackmun Papers, Box 145, Folder 2; Douglas Papers, Box 1561, Folder 71-32(d), "Misc. Memos, Cert Memos, Vote of Court."
286 "social and intellectual": Nixon Tapes, 733–10, 6/14/72.
286 At one of those parties: Lukas, "Playboy Interview: Bob Woodward," *Playboy*, 2/89, 62–63.
286 They communicate: Perry, *Deciding to Decide*, 148–49.
286 I have now verified: Douglas Papers, Box 1561, Folder 71-32(d), "Misc. Memos, Cert Memos, Vote of Court."
287 Rehnquist participated: *WP*, 6/29/72, A21.
287 He released a memo: *NYT*, 10/18/72, 1, 47.
287 Scalia released: *Cheney v. U.S. District Court,* 124 S. Ct. 1391 (March 18, 2004) (Scalia, J., denying motion to recuse).
287 That included 880; The ABA: *NYT*, 10/30/71, 12.
287 "If they should": Nominations of Rehnquist and Powell, 92nd Cong., 1st Sess., 11/8/71, 204; *NYT*, 11/9/71, 19; Jeffries, *Lewis F. Powell, Jr.*, 237.
288 "Mets 2, Reds 0": Blackmun Papers, Box 116, Folder 1.
288 Two years later; He also exchanged notes: Ibid., Folder 2.
288 They maintained: Greenhouse, *Becoming Justice Blackmun*, 20–41.
288 Upon being confirmed: Ibid., 42–43.

288 At a Washington luncheon: *Rochester Post-Bulletin*, 8/14/70, 10, in Blackmun Papers, Box 1436, Folder 10.

289 "'a vast mental storehouse'"; "[t]he presence": *TSN*, 5/30/70, 16.

289 "old number three": Greenhouse, *Becoming Justice Blackmun*, 51, 189.

289 where he had finished 120th: Ibid., 12.

289 "willing to overrule": Handwritten Notes, 2/72, 1, Blackmun Papers, Box 145, Folder 2.

290 1) Affirm *Federal Baseball*: Ibid., 2.

290 "I suspect it": Handwritten Notes, 3/15/72, 1, ibid.

290 1. Abandon *Federal Baseball*: Ibid., 2.

291 "a case of *stare decisis*": Woodward and Armstrong, *The Brethren*, 190.

291 "Harry, do it": Blackmun Oral History, 12/13/95, 473.

291 Jimmy "the Greek": *WP*, 2/26/72, D3.

291 David Feller: *WES*, 4/14/72, F-4.

292 "senior partner": Letter from Goldberg to Feller, 5/1/72, Goldberg Papers, Box I-70, Folder 4.

292 "I didn't say"; "a somewhat cynical": Letter from Feller to Goldberg, 5/12/72, ibid.

292 "It's in the bag": Dan Levitt interview.

292 "capital punishment": Nixon Tapes, 733-10, 6/14/72.

292 "Remand Likely": *WES*, 3/21/72, C1, in Blackmun Papers, Box 145, Folder 3.

292–93 Harold J. Spaeth; "[t]he vote": *SI*, 4/24/72, 9, in Blackmun Papers, Box 145, Folder 3; *Los Angeles Herald Examiner*, 4/16/72, E-6.

293 The Court used to be: Lewis, *Gideon's Trumpet*, 29.

293 He worked: 1972 Appointment Book, Blackmun Papers, Box 60, Folder 9.

293 The books: *Flood v. Kuhn*, 407 U.S. 258, 262 n. 2 (1972).

293 Dear Potter: Memo from Blackmun to Stewart, 5/4/72, Blackmun Papers, Box 145, Folder 2.

294 "Then there are"; "The list": 5/5/72 Draft, 4–5, Blackmun Papers, Box 145, Folder 2; *Flood,* 407 U.S. at 262–63.

294 "These are names": 5/5/72 Draft, 5 n. 3; *Flood*, 407 U.S. at 263 n. 3.

295 He referred to: 5/5/72 Draft, 5 and nn. 4–5; *Flood*, 407 U.S. at 263–64 and nn. 4–6.

295 "business"; "exception"; "Even though": 5/5/72 Draft, 23–24; *Flood*, 407 U.S. at 282 (citation omitted).

295 "We continue to be": 5/5/72 Draft, 25; *Flood*, 407 U.S. at 283–84.

295 "If there is any": 5/5/72 Draft, 25; *Flood*, 407 U.S. at 284.

296 chagrin: Woodward and Armstrong, *The Brethren*, 191.

296 "I like that"; "Didn't I"; "No": Blackmun Oral History, 4/24/95, 184.

296 Eppa Rixey: Bill James, using a statistical formula to translate a pitcher's win-loss record into "win points," found that Rixey had the second-lowest total of any starting pitcher in the Hall of Fame. James, *The Politics of Glory*, 269.

296 On May 9, Stewart: Memo from Stewart to Conference, 5/12/72, Marshall Papers, Box 87, Folder 10.

297 On May 8, Powell: Memo from Powell to Blackmun, 5/8/72, Blackmun Papers, Box 145, Folder 2; Powell Papers, Box 148.

297 On May 11, Douglas: Douglas Papers, Box 1561, Folder 71-32(d) "Typed draft, Penciled draft, Riders."

297 "is a derelict": *Flood*, 407 U.S. at 286 (Douglas, J., dissenting).

297 "lived": Ibid., n.1.

297–98 "big business"; "The beneficiaries"; "victims of"; "If congressional": Ibid., 287.

298 "The unbroken silence": Ibid., 288.

298 The day Douglas circulated: Letter from Reed to Douglas, 5/11/72, Douglas Papers, Box 1561, Folder 71-32(d), "Law Clerk."

298 "To non-athletes": *Flood*, 407 U.S. at 289 (Marshall, J., dissenting).

298 "torn between"; "are totally": Ibid., 290.

298 "The importance": Ibid., 292.

298 "does not mean": Ibid., 293.

299 "none of the prior"; "the issue": Ibid., 294–95.

299 "Five votes": Hentoff, "Profile: The Constitutionalist," *New Yorker*, 3/12/90, 60.

300 On May 12, Brennan: Marshall Papers, Box 87, Folder 10.

300 At the end of the term: 1971 Case History, Brennan Papers, Box II-6, Folder 14, 15.

300 Douglas learned: Letter from Reed to Douglas, 5/11/72, Douglas Papers, Box 1561, Folder 71-32(d) "Law Clerk."

300 On May 15, however, Rehnquist: Marshall Papers, Box 87, Folder 10.

300 Around the same time: Ibid.; Douglas Papers, Box 1561, Folder 71-32(d) "Final Gallery—galley proofs."

300 A Rehnquist clerk; Blackmun's law clerk: Law Clerk interview, 5/19/05; Law Clerk interview, 3/23/05; Woodward and Armstrong, *The Brethren*, 190.

301 Woodward and Armstrong: Woodward and Armstrong, *The Brethren*, 191.

301 "knocking fungoes": Letter from Blackmun to Daniel Crystal, 10/9/80, Blackmun Papers, Box 145, Folder 3.

301 Indeed he was: 5/5/72 Draft, 4–5, Blackmun Papers, Box 145, Folder 2.

301 Blackmun recalled only one justice's: Ibid.; Letter from Blackmun to Jim Caple, 2/11/97, Blackmun Papers, Box 145, Folder 4.

301 On May 25, he: 5/25 Draft, 5, Blackmun Papers, Box 145, Folder 2; *Flood*, 407 U.S. at 263.

301 On March 11, Reed; "Justice White's clerks": Letter from Reed to Douglas, 5/11/72, Douglas Papers, Box 1561, Folder 71-32(d) "Law Clerk."

301 Ten days later; According to rumor: Letter from Reed to Douglas, 5/21/72, ibid.

302 One of Marshall's law clerks; "He'll never join": Woodward and Armstrong, *The Brethren*, 191.

302 On March 26; Dear Harry: Memo from White to Blackmun and Conference, 5/26/72, Marshall Papers, Box 87, Folder 10.

303 "cut the corners": Law Clerk interview, 1/13/04.

304 allowing Burger to lobby: Greenhouse, *Becoming Justice Blackmun*, 46.

304 was spending an unusual: Law clerk interview, 3/23/05.

304 He frequently: Blackmun Papers, Box 1403, Folders 4 and 5.

304 On June 13, Burger: Marshall Papers, Box 87, Folder 10.

304 [L]ike Mr. Justice Douglas: *Flood*, 407 U.S. at 285–86 (Burger, C. J., concurring).

305 "thought perhaps": Blackmun Oral History, 7/6/94, 18.

305 He never discussed: Ibid., 4/24/95, 184.

305 Rumors spread: Woodward and Armstrong, *The Brethren*, 192.

305 Blackmun had asked: Letter from Blackmun to Burger, 1/18/72, Douglas Papers, Box 1522, Folder "Administrative Memoranda by Court"; Garrow, *Liberty and Sexuality*, 537–38.

305 "the real reason": 1971 Case History at CXLVI, Brennan Papers, Box II-6, Folder 15. Blackmun expressed similar concerns to Justice Powell in private. Ibid., CXLVI-VII. See also ibid., LI, Brennan Papers, Box II-6, Folder 14 (repeating Blackmun's statement at conference).

305 He inserted Jimmie Foxx: *Flood*, 407 U.S. at 263.

305 On June 1, Blackmun: Blackmun Papers, Box 145, Folder 2.

306 "He can speak": *NYT*, 6/1/72, 46.

306 Blackmun slipped: *Flood*, 407 U.S. at 263.

306 Blackmun gave the book: Blackmun Papers, Box 1374, Folder 4.

306 Blackmun placed an arrow: 1972 Appointment Book, Blackmun Papers, Box 60, Folder 9.

306 "This case presents"; "This case is one": Flood Announcement, 6/19/72, 1, Blackmun Papers, Box 145, Folder 2.

306 At that moment, Nina Totenberg; Powell winked: *LAT*, 6/20/72, E5; MJ, 6/20/72, in Blackmun Papers, Box 145, Folder 3.

306 "took no part in": Flood Announcement, 6/19/72, 3, Blackmun Papers, Box 145, Folder 2.

307 He had already made: Letter from Douglas to Burger, 6/15/72, Douglas Papers, Box 1524, Folder 1.

307 "JUDGMENT FLOOD": U.S. Sct. Appellate Case Files, 71-32 to 71-36, NARA, Washington, D.C., Box 87; Goldberg Papers, Box I-94, Folder 12.

307 Goldberg called Henry: Letter from Goldberg to Levitt, 7/12/72, Goldberg Papers, Box I-94, Folder 12.

307 Putzel conferred: Letter from Putzel to Burger and White, 6/26/71, U.S. Sct. Appellate Case Files, NARA, Washington, D.C., Box 87.

307 Putzel notified Blackmun: Letters from Putzel to Blackmun, 6/14/72, 6/16/72, 6/26/72, Blackmun Papers, Box 145, Folder 2.

307 "was not surprised": Letter from Goldberg to Topkis, 7/12/72, Goldberg Papers, Box I-94, Folder 12.

307 "Supreme Court screwed us": Letter from Topkis to Goldberg, 6/30/72, Goldberg Papers, Box I-94, Folder 12.

307 Dan Levitt did not think: Dan Levitt interview.

307 But Peter Westen: Peter Westen interview.

308 The Players Association; "The only bad thing": Letter from Topkis to Miller, 8/2/72, Goldberg Papers, Box I-94, Folder 12.

308 "constructive"; "The decision": *NYT*, 6/20/72, 45.

308 "Renewed?": *NYT*, 6/21/72, 33.

308 "that the Congress": *WP*, 6/20/72, D1.

308 "The original reserve": *WES*, 6/19/70, C-1.

308 "I hope you": *SFC*, 8/10/72.

309 "By the time": *CST*, 6/23/72, 126.

309 "cop-out"; "a disappointment": *NYT*, 6/21/72, 33.

309 The *New York Times*: *NYT*, 6/23/72, 36; *WP*, 6/21/72, A22; *WES*, 6/21/72, A-14; *BMS*, 6/23/72, A-14; *MST*, 6/21/72, 8A; *SPD*, 6/22/72, 2E.

309 the *Sporting News*, Dick Young: *TSN*, 7/3/72, 4; *NYDN*, 6/21/72, 115; *TSN*, 7/8/72, 4; *SGD*, 10/17/72, 2C; *BRA*, 6/21/72, in Miller Papers, Box 3, Folder 9.

309 "sentimental journey": Blackmun Oral History, 4/24/95, 184.

309 "Presumably": *LAT*, 6/22/72, pt. III, 1.

309 "amused"; "the complete antagonism": Harry Blackmun interview with Bill Moyers.

309 "embarrassed": Woodward and Armstrong, *The Brethren*, 191.

309–10 In December 1979; The next morning; During oral argument: William Murphy interview; Note from Blackmun to Stewart, 12/5/79, Blackmun Papers, Box 116, Folder 2.

310 "embarrassed"; "nonsense": Note from Blackmun to Stewart, 12/5/79, Blackmun Papers, Box 116, Folder 2.

310 Nearly 10 years later, Woodward: Lukas, "Playboy Interview: Bob Woodward," *Playboy*, 2/89, 62–63.

310 [W]hen I talked to him: Blackmun Oral History, 9/18/95, 292.

310 lending each other: In 1979, for example, Blackmun borrowed Stewart's copy of Robert W. Creamer's seminal Babe Ruth biography, *Babe*. Blackmun Papers, Box 1408, Folder 13.

310 "an almost comical adherence": Eskridge, "Overruling Statutory Precedents," 76 *Geo L.J.* 1361, 1381 (1988).

310 most scholars: Ross, "Reconsidering *Flood v. Kuhn*," 12 U. *Miami Ent. & Sports L. Rev.* 169, 171–72 (1995) (cataloging the reasons why scholars have agreed or disagreed with Blackmun's decision).

310 The reason for the Court's decision: Bill Eskridge interview.

310 "Baskin v. Robbins"; "There are many": Bill Iverson interview.
311 "I shall never"; "Mel Ott?": Bill Murphy interview; Lazarus, *Closed Chambers*, 21–22; Woodward and Armstrong, *The Brethren*, 192.
311 "[I]t's been": Blackmun Oral History, 7/6/94, 18; see also ibid., 4/24/95, 184.
311 A week after; In 1973, a friend; Two years later: Letter from Jerry R. Erickson to Blackmun, 6/21/72; Letter from W. W. Baade to Blackmun, undated; Letter from Judge Robb to Blackmun, 7/21/75, Blackmun Papers, Box 145, Folder 3.
311 The 47th member: Bruce Ladd interview.
311 "I would do it": Harry Blackmun interview with Bill Moyers. See also Blackmun Oral History, 9/18/95, 295 ("I think it was a good opinion. I'm glad that history is there").
311 "will always be": *The Federalist* no. 78.
312 "'[A] decision'": *Flood v. Kuhn*, 407 U.S. 258, 293 n. 4 (1972) (Marshall, J., dissenting), quoting Peter L. Szanton, "*Stare Decisis*: A Dissenting View," 10 *Hastings L.J.* 394, 397 (1959) (internal quotation marks omitted).
312 "outsiders": Blackmun Oral History, 9/18/95, 294.
312 "I think": Ibid., 12/13/95, 474.

CHAPTER SEVENTEEN

Page

313 Marvin Miller called Curt: Marvin Miller interview.
313 "Baby, I gave them": "A Loss for Curt Flood," *Newsweek*, 7/3/72, 67.
313 "What *Flood v. Kuhn* really accomplished": Miller, *A Whole Different Ball Game*, 195. See also ibid., 196.
313 Even the owners' chief negotiator: Helyar, *Lords of the Realm*, 134–35; *NYT*, 12/22/85, sec. 5, 3.
313 "After the *Flood* case": *NYT*, 12/22/85, sec. 5, 3.
314 Now the pressure: Miller, *A Whole Different Ball Game*, 239.
314 The servicemen found: *TSN*, 9/9/72, 6, 8.
315 He told Bob Sheridan: Bob Sheridan interview; *NYT*, 7/1/72, 14; *WES*, 7/1/72, A-14.
315 "He abstained": *BMS*, 1/6/73.
315 sending him videotapes: Flood, "The Legacy of Curt Flood," *Sport*, 11/77, 40; *SFC*, 9/4/79, 20.
315 "It's been three years"; "The problem": *WP*, 4/2/73, D4. For similar quotes, see *BES*, 4/5/73, D11; *NYT*, 4/2/73, 54; *SGD*, 4/2/73, 1C.
315 Off camera; "These are mine"; "[i]n spite of himself": *SFC*, 7/18/86, 89.
316 "I am extremely proud": Burns, *Baseball*, vol. 9.
316 "Jackie, as a figure": Ibid.; Rampersad, *Jackie Robinson*, 459–61; *NYT*, 10/29/72, 61.
316 "A life": Burns, *Baseball*, vol. 9.

316 Miller believed: Marvin Miller interview; Marvin Miller interview by Gabriel Schechter, 3/24/92, 18.

316 Six months later: *WP*, 5/6/70, D3.

316 In the past: Marvin Miller interview; Marvin Miller interview by Gabriel Schechter, 3/24/92, 18.

317 On Catfish Hunter: Helyar, *Lords of the Realm*, 141–59.

317 "the Club shall have the right": TT, 25A.

317 In 1967, a California judge: *NYT*, 8/9/67, 31.

317–18 On Simmons, Lyle, and Tolan: Helyar, *Lords of the Realm*, 130–36.

318–19 On Messersmith and McNally: Ibid., 162–80; Rovell, "The Early Days of Free Agency"; Stark, "The Decision That Changed the Game"; *WP*, 6/10/75, D1; *NYT*, 10/26/75, 221; *LAT*, 11/20/75, E1.

318 The owners attacked: Lou Hoynes interview.

319 "I can't help but think": Marvin Miller interview.

319 Miller and Moss wanted: *TSN*, 4/16/77, 8.

320 The six years: Flood, "The Legacy of Curt Flood," *Sport*, 11/77, 40.

320 Having lost his only: Karen Brecher interview.

320 Flood packed up; "Super Hermit": "Ebbing Flood," *SI*, 8/11/75, 6, 8.

320 His possessions: Rickie Riley interview.

320 "He is said": "Ebbing Flood," *SI*, 8/11/75, 6, 8.

320 "There have been reports": State Department Document E1, from American Consulate in Barcelona to Secretary of State, 10/2/75.

320 Two days later; "was drunk": State Department Document E2, ibid., 10/3/75.

320 About 10 days later: State Department Document E3, ibid., 10/29/75.

321 In early November 1975: State Department Document E4, from Secretary of State to American Consulate in Barcelona, 11/3/75. Flood's half sister, Rickie Riley, said she paid for his flight home. Rickie Riley interview.

321 Curt believed the resulting bad: Karen Brecher interview.

321 In 1974, he presented: *SPD*, 9/5/74.

321 The following year: *SFC*, 5/4/76, 10.

321 Curt detested: Karen Brecher interview.

321 In 1980, he wrote: Ibid.; *OT*, 7/4/80, D-12.

322 While Curt was in Spain; His family says: Rickie Riley interview.

322 "a couple"; "They gave me"; Flood smoked cigarettes; "It's a little difficult"; Ideally, he wanted; "Don't get picked": *NYT*, 9/9/76, 55.

322 Although he denied it: *OT*, 10/28/76, 39.

323 "The things that I did"; "cool"; "These guys": *NYT*, 9/9/76, 55.

323 "[T]here was no way": Flood, "The Legacy of Curt Flood," *Sport*, 11/77, 39.

323 Flood healed; Karen wrote; Bob Feller; Flood missed: Karen Brecher interview. Feller, according to biographer John Sickels, fell on hard times and drove around the country in his 1974 Ford Maverick selling memorabilia. "At times, his attempts to bring in money and regain financial stability," Sickels wrote,

"took on overtones, that depending on your point of view, were either unsavory or tragic." Sickels, *Bob Feller*, 263.

324 He coauthored: Flood, "The Legacy of Curt Flood," *Sport*, 11/77, 34, 37–40.

324 Howard Cosell conducted: *SPD*, 1/22/78, ed. *3, 6G.

324 It was the weekend: Karen Brecher interview.

324 Richard Reeves spent; "Maybe you should": Reeves, "The Last Angry Men," *Esquire*, 3/1/78, 41.

324 Please, please don't come: Ibid., 42.

324 Flood relented: *BS*, 1/27/97, 9A.

324–25 Reeves admired; "He was about": Richard Reeves interview; *BS*, 1/27/97, 9A.

325 "portraits by Curt Flood": E. Bercovich and Sons Advertisement (on file with author).

325 "whipping out"; "I decided": Letter from Flood to Williams, 1/9/78 (on file with author).

325 "You should do": Telegram from Williams to Flood, 1/10/78 (on file with author).

325 Williams would blow: Barbara Williams interview.

325 "Is there any"; "Do you know": Letter from Flood to Williams, 3/2/78 (on file with author).

325 Karen once: Karen Brecher interview.

326 "Sam Bercovich"; Morgan started to cry: Sam Bercovich interview.

326 But Flood had stopped: Karen Brecher interview.

326 In the fall of 1977, Flood: *SPD*, 10/16/77, ed. *3, 4F; Flood, "The Legacy of Curt Flood," *Sport*, 11/77, 40.

326 The bat that Flood: *OT*, 10/29/76, 47.

326 As a supposed prelude: Sam Bercovich interview; *TSN*, 12/9/78, 34.

326 One month into the season: *NYT*, 4/29/78, 17; *OT*, 5/4/78, 43; *LAT*, 5/7/78, pt. III, 1, 6.

326 "Oh, Curt Flood"; "Just think"; "Hired": Larry Baer interview.

327 "You'll never hear": *OT*, 6/12/78.

327 Flood's first night: *NYT*, 4/28/78, 17; *OT*, 5/4/78, 43; *LAT*, 5/7/78, pt. III, 1, 6.

327 At the ballpark, the writers: Ron Bergman interview.

327 His friends warned him: Jethro McIntyre interview.

327 One night in New York: Larry Baer interview; Ed Bercovich interview; Karen Brecher interview.

327 At a pregame party; "I bet"; "Well, I suppose"; "But you were wrong": Kuhn, *Hardball*, 90.

328 Two Supreme Court justices: Ibid., 373, 376.

328 Against the advice: Lou Hoynes interview.

328 Under the name: *NYT*, 5/12/91, sec. 8, 3; *NSD*, 9/12/90, 6–7; *NYT*, 2/25/90, F6; *NYT*, 2/9/90, D1, D12; Brill, "How Could Anyone Have Believed Them?" *The American Lawyer*, 11/89, 34–35.

328 In 2005, he served as the chairman: *NYT*, 11/4/05, A16.

328 said he'd had no choice: "Curt Flood," *ESPN SportsCentury*.
328–29 "I don't think"; In Burger's: Bowie Kuhn interview.
329 To the Chief Justice: Kuhn, *Hardball* (signed copy) (on file with author).
329 In May, Cardinals general manager: *OT*, 6/12/78.
329 "You were always": Karen Brecher interview.
329 Flood donned: *SPD*, 6/10/78, 1B; *SPD*, 6/11/78, 3F; *OT*, 6/12/78.
330 Gibson playfully pinched: *SPD*, 6/11/78, 3F.
330 The two old friends; Flood spent: Karen Brecher interview.
330 One afternoon; "A lot of people": Larry Baer interview.
330 The best thing: Karen Brecher interview.
330 Flood tried to earn: Ibid.; *CE*, 12/7/78, D-1.
331 "I guess": *CE*, 12/7/78, D-1.
331 Without his $300; "not that altruistic": Karen Brecher interview.
331 "[O]ver the past seven years": Flood, "The Legacy of Curt Flood," *Sport*, 11/77, 40.
331 "I wanted to bring": *NYT*, 3/1/79, B9; "Thanks, Curt," *SI*, 3/12/79, 13; *SFC*, 3/19/79, 50.
331 "All around"; "bitter": "Thanks, Curt," *SI*, 3/12/79, 13.
331 "There's a negative undertone": *SFE*, 5/11/80, B1.
331 "Curt Flood got you": *SFC*, 3/8/80, 44.
332 "When I started my case": "Baseball's Forgotten Man," *Newsweek*, 4/2/79, 18.
332 Before the 1980 season; "that if anything": *SFC*, 3/8/80, 44.
332 "I think people": *TSN*, 4/5/80, 32.
332 Flood's biggest disappointment: Karen Brecher interview; Jesse Gonder interview.
332–33 Flood's consumption; With Karen's help: Karen Brecher interview.
333 Flood's sobriety: Bill Patterson interview.
333 "I'm the Bowie": "Whatever Happened to . . . Curt Flood," *Ebony*, 3/81, 56.
333 His job as youth baseball commissioner: *NYT*, 5/26/81, B9, B12; *OT*, 6/14/81, D1, D4; *SGD*, 5/26/82, 6D; "Whatever Happened to . . . Curt Flood," *Ebony*, 3/81, 56.
333 The Bay Area Life Membership: *OT*, 3/9/80, A-3.
334 The Oakland Public Schools: Tribute book (on file with author).
334 "If they backslide": *SFE*, 5/11/80, B1.
334 "I lived": *SFC*, 9/4/79, 20.
334–35 "I'll never forget"; "I saw Bill White"; "Times": Letter from Gibson to Flood, 1/12/81 (on file with author).
335 "Some people"; "that opened"; "So today": *TSN*, 4/24/82, 8; *Newsweek*, 10/11/82, 85.
335 Flood rationalized: *Utica Press*, 8/2/82, 19.
335 Cutty Sark donated: Ibid.; *NYDN*, 1/8/82, C32.
335 Karen knew that Curt: Karen Brecher interview.
335 "lack of blacks"; "It is time": *OT*, 3/9/80, A-3.

336 A few weeks before: *Utica Press*, 8/2/82, 19.

336 Flood paid his own way: Karen Brecher interview.

336 "If Curt Flood": Frank Robinson Hall of Fame speech transcript, 33, Baseball Hall of Fame; for variations of this quote, see *Utica Press*, 8/2/82, 15; *NYT*, 8/2/82, C7.

CHAPTER EIGHTEEN

Page

337 A friend of Flood's: Judy Pace Flood interview.

337 The movie plans: *SFE*, 9/1/87, F7; Craft, "Curt Flood," *Baseball Cards*, 9/88, 74.

337 "I wasn't going": *SFE*, 9/1/87, F7.

337 with a public push: *SFC*, 7/18/86, 89.

338 Curt Jr., who bears: *Newark Star-Ledger*, 8/7/2002, 49.

338 Flood rejected: *NYT*, 5/26/81, B9; *SPD*, 10/30/89, 3C; *SFC*, 2/14/95, D1.

338 "Don't make my life": *OT*, 7/10/94, B-1.

338 "the central fact": *Sport*, 12/86, 106.

338 "I did it because": *SFC*, 2/14/95, D1.

338 "I certainly hope": *OT*, 6/14/81, D-1.

338 "jealousy"; "prejudice"; "The good old boys": Whitford, "Curt Flood," *Sport*, 12/86, 106.

338 "I have never felt": *SFC*, 2/14/95, D1.

338–39 "I am bitter now"; he understood why Hank Aaron; "guilty by association": Burns/Flood interview transcript, 10.

339 Cosell wrote: *SFC*, 7/18/86, 89. In 1986, only one former player worked for the Players Association: Former Baltimore Orioles shortstop and union executive board member Mark Belanger was hired at the behest of the players when he retired after the 1982 season. In 1993, former second baseman Tony Bernazard was hired to help the association communicate with Latin players. Belanger and Bernazard were the only two former players hired by the union during Flood's lifetime. Interview (anon.) by author.

339 "as a traitor": *Seattle Times*, 2/3/86, C3.

339 "One of the reasons": *OT*, 6/5/94, B-9.

339 "we've only": *TSN*, 2/17/86, 41.

339 "may not have some": *NYT*, 4/8/87, B10.

339 Black former major leaguers: *BMS*, 11/10/87, 3G; Robinson, *Extra Innings*, 1–22.

339 Flood was among: *NYT*, 12/8/87, D25.

339 "I had written": *CT*, 6/30/87, sec. 4, 4.

340 In November 1987, Flood and 60: *BMS*, 11/10/87, 3G; *BG*, 11/28/87, 25; *LAT*, 12/9/87, S3.

340 "Forty years"; owner: *BMS*, 11/10/87, 3G.

340 designed a piece: Jim "Mudcat" Grant interview.
340 Flood came close; Maxvill flew out; During the interview: Dal Maxvill interview.
341 At the NAACP's Image Awards: Craft and Owens, *Redbird Revisited*, 81–82; Craft, "Curt Flood," *Baseball Cards*, 9/88, 74; *SPT*, 12/15/87, 2D.
341 That same year: *OT*, 9/3/87, D-4; *SFE*, 9/1/87, F7.
341 Two years later: *OT*, 10/27/89, F-6.
341 "Thanks for all": *SFC*, 5/24/84, 78; Dickey, "Curt Flood," *Inside Sports*, 8/85, 77.
341 "I thought": *TSN*, 6/19/89, 10.
341 He drew sports cartoons: Curran, "Curt Flood and the Baseball Revolution," *LA Weekly*, 4/1–7/94, 27.
341 He also started: Ibid.; *OT*, 2/4/94, B-8.
342 He surprised: Marge Brans interview.
342 "he was part"; "I didn't appreciate": Ibid. (quoting Memorial Service video).
342 Karen had been: Mailgram, 1/30/81, Karen Brecher to Toastmaster, California Coaches' Association (on file with author).
342 The person who had recommended: Joe Garagiola interview; Jim Morley interview.
342 Garagiola apologized: Whitford, *Extra Innings*, 83.
342 "I thought if the": *NYT*, 1/21/97, B10; *PDN*, 1/22/97, 72.
342 Flood's job: Jim Morley interview; *NYP*, 6/1/89, 85.
342 At Opening Day in Pompano Beach: Paul Casanova interview.
343 He deferred: *Orlando Sentinel*, 7/9/89, C13; *TSN*, 9/18/89, 25.
343 As a cost-cutting measure: Jim Morley interview.
343 Some people speculated: Golenbock, *The Forever Boys*, xi.
343 Don Fehr honored Miller; Miller's admiration: Marvin Miller interview.
343 "It may be": Blackmun Oral History, 4/24/95, 185.
344 Flood, wearing: *PT*, 12/13/94, 7C.
344 "Don't let them": *NYP*, 1/21/97, 75.
344 "Curt Flood remains": *CT*, 12/7/94, S3. For similar quotes see *PI*, 12/7/94, D6; *USA Today*, 12/7/94, 6C.
344 "I'm entering": Flood, "A New Idea," *Sport*, 4/95, 43.
345 Tim McCarver watched: Tim McCarver interview.
345 "I am in the process": 1994 Christmas Letter, 2 (on file with author).
345 The fairy-tale ending; "sounded like"; doctors discovered: *OT*, 2/16/96, B-2.
345 Word leaked out: *CT*, 10/25/95, sec. 4, 3; "Curt Flood, Featured in *Ebony*'s 50th Anniversary Issue, Battles Cancer," *Jet*, 11/13/95, 51; *OT*, 2/15/96, B-2; *OT*, 2/16/96, B-2; *SFC*, 2/15/96, E3.
345 The union dipped: Marvin Miller interview; interview (anon.) by author.
346 The Baseball Assistance Team: Marvin Miller interview; Joe Garagiola interview.
346 In 1993, Rawlings: *USA Today*, 11/18/93, 2C; *SPD*, 11/19/93, 2D.
346 After Flood could no longer speak: Earl Robinson interview.
346 Marvin Miller: Marvin Miller interview.

346 He communicated: *USA Today*, 1/31/97, 2C; Lee, "The Curt Flood Story," *Real Sports*, 3/10/97.

346 "mixed feelings"; "Start counting"; "Say this": 1995 Christmas Card (on file with author); *NYT*, 1/21/87, B10.

347 "Curt's 9th Inning": Funeral Program (on file with author); *LAT*, 1/28/97, B-1; *SPD*, 1/28/97, 1C.

347 "My name is"; "I think I knew"; "Curt had a way"; "I've been sad": *SPD*, 1/28/97, 1C.

347 Flood never forgot: Dick Moss interview.

347 In his eulogy, Will: George Will eulogy (on file with author).

347 "It was one of those": George Will interview.

347 Jackson's voice rose; "Don't cry"; Jackson called: Lee, "The Curt Flood Story," *Real Sports*, 3/10/97.

348 Leonard Koppett: *OT*, 12/14/94, B-2.

348 "You would think": *NYT*, 3/3/05, D1.

348 Jackson also called for the Players Association: Lee, "The Curt Flood Story," *Real Sports*, 3/10/97.

348 Joe Black, Orlando Cepeda: Funeral Program.

348 Both Black and Newcombe had carried: *NYT*, 10/28/72, 25.

348 Union reps David Cone: *NYP*, 1/21/97, 75.

349 "Baseball didn't change": *SPD*, 1/28/97, 1C.

349 Players shift teams: Stark, "Part III: Player Movement Part of Life" (showing that in 1975 only 15 players had been playing for the same team for 10 consecutive years and in 2000 only 15 players had been playing for the same team for 10 consecutive years).

349 The average major league: http://www.baseball-almanac.com/charts/salary/major_league_salaries.shtml.

350 $18 million: Winfield's contract was originally thought to be worth $23 million or $24 million because of confusion over the cost-of-living increase in the deal. The contract, however, was ultimately worth $18 million. *NYT*, 5/17/90, B13.

350 "Sylvester Stallone": *SPD*, 9/30/89, 3C. For a similar quote, see *OS*, 2/27/89, D5.

350 "If the owners": *OT*, 6/5/94, B-9.

350 "We may not want": *HC*, 10/25/05.

351 "What about freedom": *OT*, 3/9/80, A-3.

351 "Republicans buy": Smith, *Second Coming*, xix; *NYT*, 10/31/99, sec. 8, 3; Robert Lipsyte interview.

351 Of everything Flood had accomplished in baseball: *TW*, 3/15/93, B1.

351 *Sport* magazine asked: "Flooding the Market," *Sport*, 1/94, 12.

351 "I just want players": Joe Torre interview.

351 "How can anybody": Barkley, *I May Be Wrong but I Doubt It*, 159.

351 In 1999, *Time* magazine: Okrent, "The 10 Most Influential Athletes of the Century," *Time*, 6/14/99, 93.

BIBLIOGRAPHY

MANUSCRIPT COLLECTIONS

Harry A. Blackmun Papers, Manuscript Division, Library of Congress, Washington, D.C.

William J. Brennan Papers, Manuscript Division, Library of Congress, Washington, D.C.

Harold H. Burton Papers, Manuscript Division, Library of Congress, Washington, D.C.

Albert B. "Happy" Chandler Oral History Collection, University of Kentucky, Lexington, Kentucky.

William O. Douglas Papers, Manuscript Division, Library of Congress, Washington, D.C.

Abe Fortas Papers, Manuscripts and Archives, Yale University Library, New Haven, Connecticut.

Arthur Goldberg Papers, Manuscript Division, Library of Congress, Washington, D.C.

Lyndon Johnson Papers and Oral History Collection, LBJ Library, Austin, Texas.

Hugo LaFayette Black Papers, Manuscript Division, Library of Congress, Washington, D.C.

Thurgood Marshall Papers, Manuscript Division, Library of Congress, Washington, D.C.

Marvin Miller Papers, New York University Library, New York, New York.

Mississippi State Sovereignty Commission Online, Mississippi Department of Archives and History, Jackson, Mississippi.

NAACP Collection, Manuscript Division, Library of Congress, Washington, D.C.

Philadelphia National League Club Collection, Hagley Museum and Library, Wilmington, Delaware.

Lewis F. Powell Jr. Archives, Washington and Lee University, Lexington, Virginia.

Stanley Reed Collection, Margaret L. King Library, University of Kentucky, Lexington, Kentucky.

Branch Rickey Papers, Manuscript Division, Library of Congress, Washington, D.C.

Jackie Robinson Papers, Manuscript Division, Library of Congress, Washington, D.C.

St. Louis Globe-Democrat Collection, St. Louis Mercantile Library, University of Missouri at St. Louis, St. Louis, Missouri.

Lawrence Spivak Papers, Manuscript Division, Library of Congress, Washington, D.C.

Southern Regional Council, "Will the Circle Be Unbroken?" program files, Special Collections and Archives Division, Robert W. Woodruff Library, Emory University, Atlanta, Georgia.

Earl Warren Papers, Manuscript Division, Library of Congress, Washington, D.C.

The *Washington Star* Collection, Washingtoniana Division, Martin Luther King Library, Washington, D.C.

PUBLIC DOCUMENTS

Bureau of the Census, *Ninth, Tenth, Twelfth, Thirteenth, Fourteenth, and Fifteenth Census of the United States—Population*. California, Louisiana, and Texas.

Curt Flood, State Department Files, 1971–1973, National Archives, College Park, Maryland.

Flood v. Kuhn, Second Circuit Briefs and Records, Law Library, Library of Congress, Washington, D.C.

Flood v. Kuhn, Second Circuit Briefs and Records, National Archives, New York, New York.

Flood v. Kuhn, Supreme Court Briefs and Records, Law Library, Library of Congress, Washington, D.C.

Flood v. Kuhn, Supreme Court Briefs and Records, National Archives, Washington, D.C.

Flood v. Kuhn, Trial Court Briefs and Records, National Archives, New York, New York.

Houston, Texas, City Directories.

Richard Nixon, Presidential Tapes, National Archives, College Park, Maryland.

Oakland, California, City Directories.

U.S. Congress, House of Representatives, Judiciary Committee, Study of Monopoly Power, Pt. 6, *Organized Baseball*. Hearings Before the Subcommittee on the Study of Monopoly Power. 82nd Cong. 1st sess., October 16, 1951. Washington, D.C.: GPO, 1951.

U.S. Congress, Senate, Judiciary Committee, Nomination of Irving Ben Cooper, 87th Cong., 2nd Sess., March 19 and 20, June 22, July 11 and 24, August 7, 1962. Washington, D.C.: GPO, 1962.

U.S. Congress, Senate, Judiciary Committee, Nominations of William H. Rehnquist and Lewis F. Powell, 92nd Cong., 1st Sess., November 3, 4, 8, 9, 10, 1971. Washington, D.C.: GPO, 1971. Reprinted in Mersky, Roy M., and J. Myron Jacobstein, eds. *The Supreme Court of the United States: Hearings and Reports on Successful and Unsuccessful Nominations of Supreme Court Justices by the Senate Judiciary Committee, 1916–1975*, vol. 8 (Nominations of Blackmun, Rehnquist, and Powell). Buffalo: William S. Hein, 1977.

U.S. Congress, Senate, Judiciary Committee, *Organized Professional Team Sports.* Hearings Before the Subcommittee on the Study of Monopoly Power. 85th Cong., 2nd Sess., July 9, 15, 17, 18, 22, 23, 24, 28, 29, 30, and 31, 1958. Washington, D.C.: GPO, 1958.

NEWSPAPERS

Atlanta Daily World
Atlanta Journal-Constitution
Augusta Chronicle
Baltimore Afro-American
Baltimore Evening Sun
Baltimore News American
Baltimore Sun
Birmingham News
Boston Globe
Boston Herald-Traveler
Charlotte Observer
Chicago American
Chicago Daily News
Chicago Defender
Chicago Sun-Times
Chicago Tribune
Cincinnati Enquirer
Cincinnati Times-Star
Cleveland Plain Dealer
Cleveland Press
Dallas Morning News
Durham (NC) *Morning Herald*
Durham (NC) *Sun*
Fayetteville (NC) *Observer*
Florida Times-Union
Greensboro Daily News
Houston Chronicle
Houston Post
Jackson Clarion-Ledger
Kinston (NC) *Daily Free Press*
Knoxville Journal
Knoxville News-Sentinel
Los Angeles Times
Martinez (CA) *Morning News-Gazette*
Milwaukee Journal
Milwaukee Sentinel
Minneapolis Star
Newark Star-Ledger
Newsday
New York Daily News
New York Herald Tribune
New York Law Journal
New York Post
New York Times
Oakland Tribune
Orlando Sentinel
Philadelphia Daily News
Philadelphia Evening Bulletin
Philadelphia Inquirer
Philadelphia Tribune
Pittsburgh Courier
Pittsburgh Post-Gazette
Pittsburgh Press
Raleigh News and Observer
Richmond Afro-American
Rocky Mount Sunday Telegram
San Francisco Chronicle
San Francisco Examiner
Savannah Morning News
St. Louis Argus
St. Louis Globe-Democrat
St. Louis Post-Dispatch
St. Paul Pioneer Press
St. Petersburg Times
Seattle Times

The Sporting News
The State (SC)
The Village Voice
Thomasville (NC) *Tribune*
Tulsa World
USA Today
Utica Press
Washington Daily News
Washington Evening Star
Washington Post
Washington Times

INTERVIEWS WITH AUTHOR

Charles Aikens, telephone interview, Oakland, California, March 24, 2004
Bernie Allen, telephone interview, Carmel, Indiana, November 3, 2004
Maury Allen, telephone interview, Cedar Grove, New Jersey, May 12, 2005
William Allman, telephone interview, Washington, D.C., June 30, 2005
Jimmie Angelopolous, telephone interview, Indianapolis, Indiana, December 14, 2004
Kenneth Bachman, Washington, D.C., February 24, 2004
Larry Baer, telephone interview, San Francisco, California, May 23, 2005
Ed Bercovich, telephone interview, Oakland, California, April 4, 2005
Sam Bercovich, Walnut Creek, California, March 18, 2004, and October 14, 2004
Ron Bergman, telephone interview, Oakland, California, October 17, 2004
Dick Billings, telephone interview, Arlington, Texas, November 1, 2004
Dick Bosman, Washington, D.C., April 13, 2005
Jim Bouton, New York, New York, January 28, 2004
Ron Brand, telephone interview, Mesa, Arizona, February 17, 2004
Marge Brans, telephone interview, Castro Valley, California, April 18, 2004, and in person, November 5, 2004
Karen Brecher, Oakland, California, October 13, 2004, and telephone interview, April 27, 2005
Nellie Briles, telephone interview, Pittsburgh, Pennsylvania, October 4, 2004
Bob Broeg, St. Louis, Missouri, August 23, 2004
Jim Brosnan, Morton Grove, Illinois, September 21, 2004, and telephone interview, September 19, 2004
Joe Camacho, telephone interview, Fairhaven, Massachusetts, November 3, 2004, and November 22, 2004
John Carter, telephone interview, Stony Point, New York, September 12, 2004
Paul Casanova, telephone interview, Opa-locka, Florida, April 14, 2005
Orlando Cepeda, telephone interview, Fairfield, California, October 14, 2004
Ed Charles, Queens, New York, May 7, 2004
Murray Chass, telephone interview, Fair Lawn, New Jersey, April 2, 2005
William Sloane Coffin Jr., telephone interview, Strafford, Vermont, February 19, 2004
Nelvin Cooper, telephone interview, Cary, North Carolina, April 25, 2004
Casey Cox, telephone interview, Clearwater, Florida, October 31, 2004
Tim Cullen, telephone interview, Benicia, California, October 31, 2004

Bennie Daniels, telephone interview, Compton, California, June 6, 2004
Richard Danzig, telephone interview, Washington, D.C., February 9, 2005
Tommy Davis, Arcadia, California, March 12, 2004
Dominic DeFraia, telephone interview, Reno, Nevada, February 7, 2005
Bing Devine, St. Louis, Missouri, August 20, 2004
Moe Drabowsky, telephone interview, Sarasota, Florida, February 17, 2005
Dave Draheim, telephone interview, Oakland, California, January 29, 2005
Gerald Early, St. Louis, Missouri, August 23, 2004
Peter Edelman, Washington, D.C., February 17, 2004
John Engels, telephone interview, Reno, Nevada, January 29, 2005
Mike Epstein, telephone interview, Denver, Colorado, March 8, 2004
William Esteridge, Washington, D.C., March 5, 2004
Don Fehr, telephone interview, New York, New York, December 27, 2005
Herman Flood Jr., Oakland, California, March 20–21, 2004, October 12, 2004, and telephone interview, December 13, 2005
Judy Pace Flood, telephone interview, Baldwin Hills, California, May 19, 2005
Joe Gaines, telephone interview, Oakland, California, April 21, 2004
Joe Garagiola, telephone interview, Scottsdale, Arizona, April 5, 2005
Buddy Gilbert, telephone interview, Knoxville, Tennessee, April 25, 2004
William Gildea, Washington, D.C., February 6, 2004
Max Gitter, New York, New York, January 27, 2004
Hank Goldberg, telephone interview, Miami, Florida, April 18, 2005
Jesse Gonder, telephone interview, Oakland, California, April 14, 2004
Jim "Mudcat" Grant, telephone interview, Los Angeles, California, May 20, 2005
Steve Greenberg, telephone interview, New York, New York, April 4, 2005
Joe Grzenda, Washington, D.C., April 13, 2005
Fran Guilberg, telephone interview, McLean, Virginia, August 15, 2004
Sandy Hadden, telephone interview, Otis, Vermont, October 5, 2004
Tom Haller, Indian Wells, California, March 13, 2004
Larry Hammond, telephone interview, Phoenix, Arizona, April 23, 2005
Chuck Harmon, telephone interview, Cincinnati, Ohio, April 25, 2004
Toby Harrah, telephone interview, Azle, Texas, April 14, 2005
Arlene Howard, telephone interview, Teaneck, New Jersey, February 5, 2005
Frank Howard, Lenah, Virginia, November 4, 2004
Louis Hoynes, Sands Point, New York, February 27, 2004, and telephone interview, November 29, 2005
Sid Hudson, telephone interview, Waco, Texas, November 3, 2004
Monte Irvin, telephone interview, Homosassa, Florida, February 1, 2005
Glenn Isringhaus, telephone interview, East Wenatchee, Washington, April 26, 2004
Bill Iverson, Washington, D.C., February 4, 2004
Ron Jacober, telephone interview, St. Louis, Missouri, August 23, 2004
William Jeffress, telephone interview, Washington, D.C., March 21, 2005

Thomas Johnson, Oakland, California, March 21, 2004
Bill Jones, telephone interview, Fort Worth, Texas, November 19, 2004, and in person, New York, New York, November 29, 2004
Marian Jorgensen, telephone interview, Vacaville, California, February 8, 2005, and August 4, 2005
Robert Kheel, New York, New York, February 28, 2004
Victor Kramer, Washington, D.C., February 5, 2004
Karl Kuehl, telephone interview, Buffalo, New York, April 29, 2004
Bowie Kuhn, telephone interview, Ponte Vedra, Florida, March 18, 2005, and May 31, 2005
Bruce Ladd, telephone interview, Chapel Hill, North Carolina, April 6, 2005
Law Clerk interview, Washington, D.C., January 13, 2004.
Law Clerk interview, Washington D.C., March 23, 2005
Law Clerk, telephone interview, Washington, D.C., May 19, 2005
Denny Lemaster, telephone interview, Lilburn, Georgia, February 17, 2005
Dan Levitt, New York, New York, October 8, 2003
David Lipman, St. Louis, Missouri, August 23, 2004
Robert Lipsyte, telephone interview, New York, New York, January 28, 2004
Bob Locker, telephone interview, Lafayette, California, February 21, 2005
Jim Lonborg, telephone interview, Scituate, Massachusetts, February 26, 2005
Carl Long, telephone interview, Kinston, North Carolina, May 17, 2004
Tim McCarver, Siesta Key, Florida, March 23, 2004
Mike McCormick, telephone interview, Pinehurst, North Carolina, February 26, 2005
Tom McCraw, Philadelphia, Pennsylvania, April 16, 2004, and Viera, Florida, February 22, 2005
William J. McDaniel, telephone interview, Baltimore, Maryland, March 28, 2005
Tommy McDonald, telephone interview, King of Prussia, Pennsylvania, January 29, 2005
John McHale, telephone interview, Palm City, Florida, April 5, 2005
Jethro McIntyre, Pittsburg, California, March 18, 2004
Denny McLain, telephone interview, Brighton, Michigan, December 15, 2004
Elliott Maddox, telephone interview, Coral Springs, Florida, November 12, 2004
Ken Mallory, telephone interview, Saint Simons Island, Georgia, February 9, 2005
Bobby Mattick, telephone interview, Scottsdale, Arizona, April 17, 2004
Dal Maxvill, Chesterfield, Missouri, August 20, 2004
Dave Meggyesy, San Francisco, California, March 18, 2004
Ron Menchine, telephone interview, Columbia, Maryland, November 4, 2004
Marvin Miller, New York, New York, May 28, 2003, and December 1, 2004, and telephone interviews, November 15, 2005, and December 30, 2005
John Moore, telephone interview, Ventura, California, December 9, 2005
Jim Morley, telephone interview, Colorado Springs, Colorado, April 11, 2005
Dick Moss, New York, New York, January 27, 2004
Dave Nelson, telephone interview, Bradenton, Florida, November 4, 2004
Dave Newhouse, Oakland, California, March 17, 2004

Bill Nunn Jr., telephone interview, Pittsburgh, Pennsylvania, September 19, 2004
Bob Nuxhall, telephone interview, Hamilton, Ohio, May 3, 2004
Dave Oliphant, telephone interview, Milford, Connecticut, July 16, 2005
Jose Pagan, telephone interview, Sebring, Florida, May 16, 2004
Milt Pappas, telephone interview, Beecher, Illinois, February 16, 2005
Wes Parker, Los Angeles, California, March 15, 2004
Bill Patterson, Oakland, California, March 19, 2004
J. W. Porter, telephone interview, Palm Beach Gardens, Florida, April 14, 2004
Dale Powers, telephone interview, Hillsborough, Oregon, February 8, 2005
Laurie Powles, telephone interview, El Cerrito, California, April 13, 2004
Richard Reeves, telephone interview, Palm Springs, California, February 5, 2005
John Rich, Washington, D.C., March 28, 2005
Jack Richardson, telephone interview, Oakland, California, February 3, 2005
Denny Riddleberger, telephone interview, Westland, Michigan, November 16, 2004
Iola "Rickie" Riley, Oakland, California, March 20–21, 2004, October 12, 2004, and telephone interview, December 13, 2005
Brooks Robinson, New York, New York, January 28, 2004
Douglas Robinson, telephone interview, Hamilton, Montana, September 24, 2004
Earl Robinson, Berkeley, California, March 19, 2004
Ted Savage, St. Louis, Missouri, August 21, 2004
Richie Scheinblum, telephone interview, Palm Harbor, Florida, December 4, 2004
Haven Schmidt, telephone interview, Maquoketa, Iowa, April 25, 2004
Red Schoendienst, St. Louis, Missouri, August 22, 2004
Mike Shannon, St. Louis, Missouri, August 22, 2004
Leonard Shapiro, telephone interview, Washington, D.C., November 19, 2005, and e-mails November 22–23, 2005
Bob Sheridan, telephone interview, Miami, Florida, April 17, 2005
Irwin Smallwood, telephone interview, Greensboro, North Carolina, May 3, 2004
John Ivory Smith, telephone interview, Columbia, South Carolina, August 15, 2004
Wyonella Smith, telephone interview, Chicago, Illinois, December 13, 2005
Amiel "Lefty" Solomon, telephone interview, Murfreesboro, Tennessee, May 13, 2004
Harold Spaeth, telephone interview, Lansing, Michigan, December 3, 2004
Eddie Takei, telephone interview, Costa Mesa, California, February 2, 2005
Tony Taylor, telephone interview, Miami Lakes, Florida, May 22, 2004
Wayne Terwilliger, telephone interview, Arlington, Texas, November 3, 2004
Jay Topkis, New York, New York, October 8, 2003, and December 1, 2004, and telephone interview, September 13, 2004
Joe Torre, Tampa, Florida, February 24, 2005
John Underwood, telephone interview, Palmetto Bay, Florida, April 4, 2005
Del Unser, telephone interview, Scottsdale, Arizona, November 5, 2004
George Vecsey, telephone interview, New York, New York, March 7, 2005
Charlie Wangner, telephone interview, Arlington, Texas, November 1, 2004

Peter Westen, telephone interview, Berkeley, California, December 18, 2004
Russ White, telephone interview, Lake Mary, Florida, October 30, 2004
George Will, telephone interview, Washington, D.C., February 17, 2004
Barbara Williams, Los Angeles, California, January 23, 2005
Ralph Wimbish Jr., telephone interview, New York, New York, February 3, 2005
Phil Wood, telephone interview, Columbia, Maryland, November 1, 2004
Woody Woodward, telephone interview, Palm Coast, Florida, February 17, 2005
Carl Yastrzemski, telephone interview, Boca Raton, Florida, February 25, 2005
Bill Zeigler, telephone interview, Fort Worth, Texas, November 1, 2004
Allan Zerman, Palm Desert, California, March 13, 2004, and January 24, 2005, and Clayton, Missouri, August 23, 2004, and e-mail, May 24, 2005

BOOKS

Aaron, Hank, with Lonnie Wheeler. *I Had a Hammer: The Hank Aaron Story*. New York: HarperCollins, 1991.
Aaron, Henry, with Furman Bisher. *Aaron*. New York: Crowell, 1974.
Adelson, Bruce. *Brushing Back Jim Crow: The Integration of Minor-League Baseball in the American South*. Charlottesville: University Press of Virginia, 1999.
Allen, Maury. *Jackie Robinson: A Life Remembered*. New York: Franklin Watts, 1987.
Baker, Liva. *The Justice from Beacon Hill: The Life and Times of Oliver Wendell Holmes*. New York: HarperCollins, 1991.
Baldwin, James. *Collected Essays*. New York: Library of America, 1998.
Barkley, Charles, edited by Michael Wilbon. *I May Be Wrong but I Doubt It*. New York: Random House, 2002.
The Baseball Blue Book. Fort Wayne, Ind.: 1956 and 1957.
Berkow, Ira. *Red: A Biography of Red Smith*. New York: Times Books, 1986.
Bingham, Howard L., and Max Wallace. *Muhammad Ali's Greatest Fight: Cassius Clay vs. the United States of America*. New York: M. Evans and Company, 2000.
Bouton, Jim. *Ball Four: The Final Pitch*. North Egremont, Mass.: Bulldog Publishing, 2000.
Branch, Taylor. *Parting the Waters: America in the King Years 1954–63*. New York: Simon & Schuster, 1988.
———. *Pillar of Fire: America in the King Years 1963–65*. New York: Simon & Schuster, 1998.
Brock, Lou, and Franz Schulze. *Stealing Is My Game*. Englewood Cliffs, N.J.: Prentice-Hall, 1976.
Broeg, Bob. *Bob Broeg's Redbirds: A Century of Cardinals' Baseball*. St. Louis: River City Publishers, 1981.
———. *Memories of a Hall of Fame Sportswriter*. Champaign, Ill.: Sagamore Publishing, 1995.
Brosnan, Jim. *The Long Season*. New York: Harper & Brothers, 1960.

Burk, Robert F. *Never Just a Game: Players, Owners, and American Baseball to 1920.* Chapel Hill: University of North Carolina Press, 1994.

———. *Much More Than a Game: Players, Owners, and American Baseball Since 1921.* Chapel Hill: University of North Carolina Press, 2001.

Burke, Michael. *Outrageous Good Fortune: A Memoir*. Boston: Little, Brown, 1984.

Campanella, Roy. *It's Good to Be Alive*. 1959. Lincoln: University of Nebraska Press, 1995.

Cosell, Howard. *Cosell*. Chicago: Playboy Press, 1973.

Cosell, Howard, with Peter Bonventre. *I Never Played the Game*. New York: William Morrow, 1985.

Craft, David, and Tom Owens. *Redbirds Revisited: Great Memories and Stories from the St. Louis Cardinals*. Chicago: Bonus Books, 1990.

Cramer, Richard Ben. *Joe DiMaggio: The Hero's Life*. New York: Simon & Schuster, 2001.

———. *What Do You Think of Ted Williams Now?* New York: Simon & Schuster, 2002.

Dawidoff, Nicholas. *The Catcher Was a Spy: The Mysterious Life of Moe Berg*. New York: Random House, 1994.

Dean, John W. *The Rehnquist Choice: The Untold Story of the Nixon Appointment That Redefined the Supreme Court*. New York: Free Press, 2001.

D'Emilio, John. *Lost Prophet: The Life and Times of Bayard Rustin*. New York: Free Press, 2003.

Devine, Bing, with Tom Wheatley. *The Memoirs of Bing Devine: Stealing Lou Brock and Other Winning Moves by a Master GM*. Sports Publishing, 2004.

Diamond, Norman. *A Practice Almost Perfect: The Early Days at Arnold, Fortas & Porter.* Lanham, Md.: University Press of America, 1997.

Di Salvatore, Bryan. *A Clever Base-Ballist: The Life and Times of John Montgomery Ward.* New York: Pantheon, 1999.

Dolson, Frank. *Jim Bunning: Baseball and Beyond*. Philadelphia: Temple University Press, 1998.

Dorinson, Joseph, and Joram Warmund, eds. *Jackie Robinson: Race, Sports, and the American Dream*. Armonk, N.Y.: M. E. Sharpe, 1998.

Douglas, William O. *Go East, Young Man: The Early Year. The Autobiography of William O. Douglas*. New York: Random House, 1974.

Duberman, Martin Bauml. *Paul Robeson: A Biography*. New York: Ballantine Books, 1989.

Edwards, Harry. *The Revolt of the Black Athlete*. New York: Free Press, 1970.

Einstein, Charles. *Willie's Time: Baseball's Golden Age*. 1979. Carbondale: Southern Illinois University Press, 2004.

Erardi, John, and Greg Rhodes. *Opening Day: Celebrating Cincinnati's Baseball Holiday.* Cincinnati: Road West Publishing, 2004.

Eskenazi, Gerald. *Bill Veeck: A Baseball Legend*. New York: McGraw-Hill, 1988.

Falkner, David. *Great Time Coming: The Life of Jackie Robinson from Baseball to Birmingham*. New York: Simon & Schuster, 1995.

Flood, Curt, with Richard Carter. *The Way It Is*. New York: Trident Press, 1971.

Galbraith, John Kenneth. *A Life in Our Times: Memoirs*. Boston: Houghton Mifflin, 1981.

Garagiola, Joe. *It's Anybody's Ballgame*. Chicago: Contemporary Books, 1988.

Garrow, David J. *Bearing the Cross: Martin Luther King, Jr., and the Southern Christian Leadership Conference*. New York: William Morrow, 1986.

———. *Liberty and Sexuality: The Right to Privacy and the Making of* Roe v. Wade. New York: Macmillan, 1994.

Gibson, Bob, and Lonnie Wheeler. *Stranger to the Game: The Autobiography of Bob Gibson*. New York: Viking, 1994.

Gibson, Bob, with Phil Pepe. *From Ghetto to Glory: The Story of Bob Gibson*. Englewood Cliffs, N.J.: Prentice-Hall, 1968.

Goldberg, Arthur J. *Equal Justice: The Warren Era of the Supreme Court*. New York: Farrar, Straus & Giroux, 1971.

Goldberg, Dorothy Kurgans. *A Private View of a Public Life*. New York: Charterhouse, 1975.

Golenbock, Peter. *Bums: An Oral History of the Brooklyn Dodgers*. 1984 2d ed. New York: Pocket Books, 1986.

———. *The Forever Boys: The Bittersweet World of Major League Baseball As Seen Through the Eyes of the Men Who Played One More Time*. New York: Birch Lane Press, 1991.

———. *The Spirit of St. Louis: A History of the St. Louis Cardinals and Browns*. New York: Avon Books, 2000.

Goulden, Joseph C. *The Benchwarmers: The Private World of the Powerful Federal Judges*. New York: Weybright & Talley, 1974.

Greenberg, Hank, with Ira Berkow. *The Story of My Life*. New York: Times Books, 1989.

Greenhouse, Linda. *Becoming Justice Blackmun: Harry Blackmun's Supreme Court Journey*. New York: Times Books, 2005.

Grunwald, Lisa, and Stephen J. Adler, eds. *Letters of the Century: America, 1900–99*. New York: Dial Press, 1999.

Gunther, Gerald. *Learned Hand: The Man and the Judge*. Cambridge, Mass.: Harvard University Press, 1994.

Guthman, Edwin O., and Jeffrey Shulman, eds. *Robert Kennedy in His Own Words: The Unpublished Recollections of the Kennedy Years*. New York: Bantam, 1988.

Halberstam, David. *The Best and the Brightest*. New York: Random House, 1969.

———. *October 1964*. New York: Villard, 1994.

Hall, Kermit L., ed. *The Oxford Companion to the Supreme Court of the United States*. New York: Oxford University Press, 1992.

Harrelson, Ken, with Al Hirshberg. *Hawk*. New York: Viking, 1969.

Helyar, John. *Lords of the Realm: The Real History of Baseball*. New York: Ballantine Books, 1995.

Hemingway, Ernest. *Across the River and into the Trees*. 1950. New York: Scribner's, 1978.

Hernon, Peter, and Terry Ganey. *Under the Influence: The Unauthorized Story of the Anheuser-Busch Dynasty*. New York: Simon & Schuster, 1991.

Holaday, J. Chris, ed. *Baseball in the Carolinas: 25 Essays on the States' Hardball Heritage*. Durham, N.C.: Baseball America, 2001.

———. *Professional Baseball in North Carolina: An Illustrated City-by-City History, 1901–1996.* Jefferson, N.C.: McFarland, 1998.

Holtzman, Jerome. *The Commissioners: Baseball's Midlife Crisis.* New York: Total Sports, 1998.

Horwitz, Morton J. *The Warren Court and the Pursuit of Justice.* New York: Hill & Wang, 1998.

Howard, Arlene, with Ralph Wimbish. *Elston and Me: The Story of the First Black Yankee.* Columbia: University of Missouri Press, 2001.

Howe, Mark DeWolfe, ed. *Holmes-Laski Letters: The Correspondence of Mr. Justice Holmes and Harold J. Laski 1916–1935.* Cambridge, Mass.: Harvard University Press, 1953.

Hutchinson, Dennis J. *The Man Who Once Was Whizzer White: A Portrait of Byron R. White.* New York: Free Press, 1998.

Irvin, Monte, with James A. Riley. *Nice Guys Finish First: The Autobiography of Monte Irvin.* New York: Carroll & Graf, 1996.

James, Bill. *The Bill James Historical Baseball Abstract.* New York: Villard Books, 1986.

———. *The New Bill James Historical Baseball Abstract.* New York: Free Press, 2001.

———. *The Politics of Glory: How Baseball's Hall of Fame Really Works.* New York: Macmillan, 1994.

Jeffries, John C., Jr. *Justice Lewis F. Powell, Jr.: A Biography.* New York: Scribner's, 1994.

Johnson, Lyndon Baines. *The Vantage Point: Perspectives of the Presidency 1963–1969.* New York: Holt, Rinehart & Winston, 1971.

Johnson, Marilynn S. *The Second Gold Rush: Oakland and the East Bay in World War II.* Berkeley: University of California Press, 1996.

Kahn, Roger. *The Boys of Summer.* New York: Harper & Row, 1972.

———. *The Era 1947–1957: When the Yankees, the Giants, and the Dodgers Ruled the World.* New York: Ticknor & Fields, 1993.

Kalman, Laura. *Abe Fortas: A Biography.* New Haven: Yale University Press, 1990.

Kluger, Richard. *Simple Justice: The History of* Brown v. Board of Education *and Black America's Struggle for Equality.* New York: Alfred A. Knopf, 1976.

Korr, Charles P. *The End of Baseball As We Knew It: The Players Union, 1960–81.* Urbana and Chicago: University of Illinois Press, 2002.

Kuhn, Bowie. *Hardball: The Education of a Baseball Commissioner.* New York: Times Books, 1987.

Lamb, Chris. *Blackout: The Untold Story of Jackie Robinson's First Spring Training.* Lincoln: University of Nebraska Press, 2005.

Lanctot, Neil. *Negro League Baseball: The Rise and Ruin of a Black Institution.* Philadelphia: University of Pennsylvania Press, 2004.

Lazarus, Edward. *Closed Chambers: The First Eyewitness Account of the Epic Struggles Inside the Supreme Court.* New York: Times Books, 1998.

Leavy, Jane. *Sandy Koufax: A Lefty's Legacy.* New York: HarperCollins, 2002.

Lewis, Anthony. *Gideon's Trumpet.* New York: Vintage Books, 1964.

Lipman, David, and Ed Wilks. *Bob Gibson: Pitching Ace.* New York: G. P. Putnam's Sons, 1975.

Lisanti, Tom. *Fantasy Femmes of Sixties Cinema: Interviews with Twenty Actresses from Biker, Beach, and Elvis Movies*. Jefferson, N.C.: McFarland, 2001.

Lowenfish, Lee. *The Imperfect Diamond: A History of Baseball's Labor Wars*. 1980. New York: Da Capo Press, 1991.

MacPhail, Lee. *My 9 Innings: An Autobiography of 50 Years in Baseball*. Westport, Conn.: Meckler Books, 1989.

Marshall, William. *Baseball's Pivotal Era: 1945–1951*. Lexington: University Press of Kentucky, 1999.

Mays, Willie, with Lou Sahadi. *Say Hey: The Autobiography of Willie Mays*. New York: Simon & Schuster, 1988.

McCarver, Tim, with Phil Pepe. *Few and Chosen: Defining Cardinal Greatness Across the Eras*. Chicago: Triumph Books, 2003.

McCarver, Tim, with Ray Robinson. *Oh, Baby, I Love It!* New York: Villard Books, 1987.

Meggyesy, Dave. *Out of Their League*. Berkeley, Calif.: Ramparts Press, 1970.

Mikan, George, as told to Bill Carlson. *Mr. Basketball: George Mikan's Own Story*. New York: Greenberg, 1951.

Mikan, George, and Joseph Oberle. *Unstoppable: The Story of George Mikan, the First NBA Superstar*. Indianapolis: Masters Press, 1997.

Miller, Marvin. *A Whole Different Ball Game: The Sport and Business of Baseball*. New York: Birch Lane Press, 1991.

Moffi, Larry, and Jonathan Kronstadt. *Crossing the Line: Black Major Leaguers, 1947–1959*. Iowa City: University of Iowa Press, 1994.

Montville, Leigh. *Ted Williams: The Biography of an American Hero*. New York: Doubleday, 2004.

Moody, Anne. *Coming of Age in Mississippi*. New York: Dell, 1968.

Murphy, Bruce Allen. *Fortas: The Rise and Ruin of a Supreme Court Justice*. New York: William Morrow, 1988.

———. *Wild Bill: The Legend and Life of William O. Douglas*. New York: Random House, 2003.

Newman, Roger K. *Hugo Black: A Biography*. New York: Pantheon, 1994.

Nixon, Richard. *RN: The Memoirs of Richard Nixon*. New York: Grosset & Dunlap, 1978.

Novick, Sheldon M. *Honorable Justice: The Life of Oliver Wendell Holmes*. Boston: Little, Brown, 1989.

O'Brien, David M. *Storm Center: The Supreme Court in American Politics*. 1986. 3d ed. New York: W. W. Norton, 1993.

Pappas, Milt, with Wayne Mausser and Larry Names. *Out at Home: Triumph and Tragedy in the Life of a Major Leaguer*. Oshkosh, Wisc.: Angel Press, 2000.

Parker, Richard. *John Kenneth Galbraith: His Life, His Politics, His Economics*. New York: Farrar, Straus & Giroux, 2005.

Parrott, Harold. *The Lords of Baseball: A Wry Look at the Game the Fan Seldom Sees—the Front Office*. Atlanta: Longstreet Press, 2001.

Patterson, James T. *Grand Expectations: The United States, 1945–1974.* New York: Oxford University Press, 1996.

Perry, H. W., Jr. *Deciding to Decide: Agenda Setting in the United States Supreme Court.* Cambridge, Mass.: Harvard University Press, 1991.

Peterson, Robert W. *Cages to Jump Shots: Pro Basketball's Early Years.* New York: Oxford University Press, 1990.

Pietrusza, David. *Judge and Jury: The Life and Times of Judge Kenesaw Mountain Landis.* South Bend, Ind.: Diamond Communications, 1998.

Polner, Murray. *Branch Rickey: A Biography.* New York: New American Library, 1982.

Rains, Rob. *The St. Louis Cardinals: The 100th Anniversary History.* New York: St. Martin's, 1992.

Rampersad, Arnold. *Jackie Robinson: A Biography.* New York: Alfred A. Knopf, 1997.

Rehnquist, William H. *The Supreme Court.* Rev. ed. New York: Alfred A. Knopf, 2002.

Reichler, Joseph L., ed. *The Baseball Encyclopedia: The Complete and Official Record of Major League Baseball.* 7th ed. New York: Macmillan, 1988.

Remnick, David. *King of the World: Muhammad Ali and the Rise of an American Hero.* 1998. New York: Vintage Books, 1999.

Ritter, Lawrence S. *The Glory of Their Times: The Story of the Early Days of Baseball Told by the Men Who Played It.* 1966. New York: Colliers Books, 1971.

Robinson, Frank, with Dave Anderson. *Frank: The First Year.* New York: Holt, Rinehart & Winston, 1976.

Robinson, Frank, with Al Silverman. *My Life Is Baseball.* New York: Doubleday, 1968.

Robinson, Frank, and Berry Stainback. *Extra Innings.* Chicago: McGraw-Hill, 1988.

Robinson, Jackie, and Charles Dexter. *Baseball Has Done It.* Philadelphia: J. B. Lippincott, 1964.

Robinson, Jackie, with Alfred Duckett. *I Never Had It Made.* New York: G. P. Putnam's Sons, 1972.

Robinson, Jackie, with Wendell Smith. *Jackie Robinson: My Own Story.* New York: Greenberg, 1948.

Robinson, Rachel, with Lee Daniels. *Jackie Robinson: An Intimate Portrait.* New York: Harry N. Abrams, 1996.

Robinson, Sharon. *Stealing Home: An Intimate Family Portrait by the Daughter of Jackie Robinson.* New York: HarperCollins, 1996.

Roeder, Bill. *Jackie Robinson.* New York: A. S. Barnes, 1950.

Roth, Philip. *Our Gang: (Starring Tricky and His Friends).* New York: Random House, 1971.

Rowan, Carl, with Jackie Robinson. *Wait Till Next Year: The Story of Jackie Robinson.* New York: Random House, 1960.

Russell, Bill, and Taylor Branch. *Second Wind: The Memoirs of an Opinionated Man.* New York: Random House, 1979.

Russell, Bill, as told to William McSweeney. *Go Up for Glory.* New York: Coward-McCann, 1966.

Sammons, Jeffrey T. *Beyond the Ring: The Role of Boxing in American Society*. Urbana and Chicago: University of Illinois Press, 1988.

Schlesinger, Arthur M., Jr. *Robert Kennedy and His Times*. New York: Ballantine Books, 1978.

Schneider, Russell J. *Frank Robinson: The Making of a Manager*. New York: Coward, McCann & Geoghegan, 1976.

Schwartz, Bernard J. *The Ascent of Pragmatism: The Burger Court in Action*. Reading, Mass.: Addison-Wesley, 1990.

———. *Super Chief: Earl Warren and His Supreme Court—a Judicial Biography*. New York: New York University Press, 1983.

Shogan, Robert. *A Question of Judgment: The Fortas Case and the Struggle for the Supreme Court*. Indianapolis: Bobbs-Merrill, 1972.

Sickels, John. *Bob Feller: Ace of the Greatest Generation*. Dulles, Va.: Brassey's, 2004.

Simon, James F. *The Center Holds: The Power Struggle Inside the Rehnquist Court*. New York: Simon & Schuster, 1995.

Smalling, Jack. *The Baseball Autograph Collector's Handbook, Number 12*. Durham, N.C.: Baseball America, 2003.

Smith, Red. *The Red Smith Reader*. Edited by Dave Anderson. New York: Vintage Books, 1982, 1983.

Smith, Sam. *Second Coming: The Strange Odyssey of Michael Jordan—from Courtside to Home Plate and Back Again*. New York: HarperCollins, 1995.

Snyder, Brad. *Beyond the Shadow of the Senators: The Untold Story of the Homestead Grays and the Integration of Baseball*. Chicago: McGraw-Hill, 2003.

Stebenne, David L. *Arthur J. Goldberg: New Deal Liberal*. New York: Oxford University Press, 1996.

Sumner, Jim L. *Separating the Men from the Boys: The First Half-Century of the Carolina League*. Winston-Salem, N.C.: John F. Blair, 1994.

Thorn, John, ed. *The Armchair Book of Baseball*. New York: Scribner's, 1985.

Thorn, John, et al., eds. *Total Baseball: The Official Encyclopedia of Major League Baseball*. 6th ed. New York: Total Sports, 1999.

Tushnet, Mark. *The NAACP's Legal Strategy Against Segregated Education, 1925–1950*. Chapel Hill: University of North Carolina Press, 1987.

Tygiel, Jules. *Baseball's Great Experiment: Jackie Robinson and His Legacy*. New York: Oxford University Press, 1983; Vintage Books, 1984.

———, ed. *The Jackie Robinson Reader: Perspectives on an American Hero*. New York: Dutton, 1997.

———. *Past Time: Baseball as History*. New York: Oxford University Press, 2000.

Veeck, Bill, with Ed Linn. *The Hustler's Handbook*. New York: G. P. Putnam's Sons, 1965.

———. *Veeck As in Wreck*. New York: G. P. Putnam's Sons, 1962.

Waller, Spencer Weber, et al. eds. *Baseball and the American Legal Mind*. New York: Garland, 1995.

White, G. Edward. *Creating the National Pastime: Baseball Transforms Itself 1903–1953.* Princeton, N.J.: Princeton University Press, 1996.

———. *Justice Oliver Wendell Holmes: Law and the Inner Self.* New York: Oxford University Press, 1993.

Whitfield, Shelby. *Kiss It Goodbye.* New York: Abelard-Schuman, 1973.

Whitford, David. *Extra Innings: A Season in the Senior League.* New York: HarperCollins, 1991.

Williams, Juan. *Thurgood Marshall: American Revolutionary.* New York: Times Books, 1998.

Woodward, Bob, and Scott Armstrong. *The Brethren: Inside the Supreme Court.* New York: Simon & Schuster, 1979.

Yarbrough, Tinsley E. *John Marshall Harlan: Great Dissenter of the Warren Court.* New York: Oxford University Press, 1992.

———. *The Rehnquist Court and the Constitution.* New York: Oxford University Press, 2000.

Zimbalist, Andrew. *May the Best Team Win: Baseball Economics and Public Policy.* Washington, D.C.: Brookings Institution Press, 2003.

ARTICLES

Ali, Muhammad. "'I'm sorry, but I'm through fighting now.'" *Esquire*, May 1970, 120–22, 226–27.

"A Loss for Curt Flood." *Newsweek*, July 3, 1972, 67.

"Arthur J. Goldberg's Legacies to American Labor Relations." 32 *J. Marshall L. Rev.* 667 (1999).

"At Last, Professional Bargaining in Baseball." *Sport*, October 1967, 98.

Axthelm, Pete. "Let's Make a Deal." *Newsweek*, November 15, 1982, 96.

———. "Slap on the Wrist." *Newsweek*, April 13, 1970, 48.

"Baseball's Forgotten Man." *Newsweek*, April 2, 1979, 18.

Bingham, Walter. "Frolic in the Spring." *Sports Illustrated*, March 9, 1959, 58–59.

"The Black Scholar Interviews: Muhammad Ali." *The Black Scholar*, June 1970, 32–39.

Blount, Roy, Jr. "Birds of a Feather Flock to Bob." *Sports Illustrated*, November 2, 1970, 26–28, 31.

Bourginon, Henry J. "Second Mr. Justice Harlan: His Principles of Judicial Decision Making." 1979 *Sup. Ct. Rev.* 251.

Boyle, Robert H. "This Miller Admits He's a Grind." *Sports Illustrated*, March 11, 1974, 22–26.

———. "The Private World of the Negro Ballplayer." *Sports Illustrated*, March 21, 1960, 16–19, 74–80, 82, 84.

Breyer, Stephen. "Clerking for Justice Goldberg." *Supreme Court Historical Society 1990 Yearbook*, 4.

Bright, Myron H. "The Power of the Spoken Word: In Defense of Oral Argument." 72 *Iowa L. Rev.* 35 (1986).

Briley, Ron. "Baseball and America in 1969: A Traditional Institution Responds to

Changing Times." *Nine: A Journal of Baseball History & Social Policy Perspectives* 4, no. 2 (Spring 1996): 265–81.

Brill, Steven. "Benching of Bad Judges." *Esquire*, April 10, 1979, 20–21.

———. "How Could Anyone Have Believed Then?" *American Lawyer*, November 1989, 5, 35–41.

Carroll, Brian. "Wendell Smith's Last Crusade: The Desegregation of Spring Training." In *The Cooperstown Symposium on Baseball and American Culture 2001*. William M. Simons, ed. Jefferson, N.C.: McFarland, 2002.

Craft, David. "Curt Flood: Just Around the Corner to the Light of Day." *Baseball Cards*, September 1988: 72–74.

Curran, Ron. "Curt Flood and the Baseball Revolution." *LA Weekly*, April 1–7, 1994, 1, 16–17, 24–25, 27.

"Curt Flood's Troubles." *Newsweek*, May 10, 1971, 67.

"Curt Flood, Featured in *Ebony*'s 50th Anniversary Issue, Battles Cancer." *Jet*, November 13, 1995, 51.

Davis, Jack E. "Baseball's Reluctant Challenge." *Journal of Sports History* 19, no. 2 (Summer 1992): 144–62.

"Day in Court." *Time*, March 30, 1962, 16.

Deford, Frank. "Heirs of Judge Landis." *Sports Illustrated*, September 30, 1974, 82–96.

Dickey, Glenn. "Curt Flood." *Inside Sports*, August 1985, 76–77.

"Ebbing Flood." *Sports Illustrated*, August 11, 1975, 6, 8.

Eskridge, William N., Jr. "Overruling Statutory Precedent." 76 *Geo L.J.* 1361 (1988).

Fimrite, Ron. "Marvin Miller: Yankee Stadium, Opening Day, 1980?" *Sports Illustrated*, March 3, 1980, 58–70.

Flood, Curt. "A New Idea: The United Baseball League." *Sport*, April 1995, 43.

———, with Stu Black. "The Legacy of Curt Flood." *Sport*, November 1977, 34–40.

———, as told to John Devaney. "Why I Am Challenging Baseball." *Sport*, March 1970, 10. In *The Armchair Book of Baseball*, John Thorn, ed. New York: Scribner's, 1985: 125–34.

"Flooding the Market." *Sport*, January 1994, 12.

"Found—An 'Abe Lincoln' of Baseball." *Ebony*, March 1970, 110.

Garrow, David. "The Brains Behind Blackmun." *Legal Affairs*, May–June 2005.

———. "Mental Decrepitude on the U.S. Supreme Court: The Historical Case for a 28th Amendment." 67 *U. Chi. L. Rev.* 995 (2000).

———. "The Supreme Court and *The Brethren*." 18 *Const. Comment.* 303 (2001).

Goldberg, Arthur J., and Alan M. Dershowitz. "Declaring the Death Penalty Unconstitutional." 83 *Harv. L. Rev.* 1773 (1970).

———. "Memorandum Conference Re: Capital Punishment—October 1963 Term." 27 *South Tex. L. Rev.* 493 (1986).

Gross, Milton. "The Ballplayers' Drive for Independence." *Sport*, August 1969, 14–15, 82–83.

Gross, Nell. "Curt Flood—Ballplayer and Artist." *St. Louis Globe-Democrat Sunday*

Magazine, March 31, 1968, 1, 4–7. Reprinted in *Sporting News*, April 20, 1968, 9; *Ebony*, July 1968, 70–76.

Hertoff, Nat. "The Constitutionalist." *New Yorker*, March 12, 1990, 60.

Holtzman, Jerome. "Attendance and Litigation Were Up in 1970." In *Official Baseball Guide for 1971*. St. Louis: Sporting News, 1971, 272–303.

———. "Two Divisions, Rules, Player Demands, Etc." In *Official Baseball Guide for 1970*. St. Louis: Sporting News, 1970, 271–275.

———. "Expansion, Canadian Club, Feature 1968." In *Official Baseball Guide for 1969*. St. Louis: Sporting News, 1969, 185–89.

———. " '71 Saw Gate Up, Short Move, Alex Angry." In *Official Baseball Guide for 1972*. St. Louis: Sporting News, 1972, 277–311.

Jacobs, Michael S., and Ralph K. Winter Jr. "Antitrust Principles and Collective Bargaining by Athletes: Of Superstars in Peonage." 81 *Yale L. J.*, 1 (1971–72).

Jordan, David, Larry Gerlach, and John Rossi. "A Baseball Myth Exploded." In *The National Pastime: A Review of Baseball History*, no. 18 (Cleveland, Ohio: SABR, 1998), 3–13.

"The Judge Takes the Stand." *Time*, August 17, 1962, 16–17.

Kahn, Roger. " 'I'm not discouraged either. Got it?' " *Saturday Evening Post*, January 29, 1966, 85–89.

Katz, Fred. "Life with the Cardinals." *Sport*, July 1968, 54–61.

Keith, Larry. "Someone Old, Someone New." *Sports Illustrated*, April 26, 1980, 46, 49.

King, Coretta Scott. "Martin's Legacy." *Ebony*, January 1986, 105–6, 108.

Kraft, Joseph. "Putting It All Together for Goldberg." *New York*, April 13, 1970, 7–8.

Leggett, William. "The Big Leagues Select a Fan." *Sports Illustrated*, February 17, 1969, 16–17.

———. "Futile Surge amid the Shuffle." *Sports Illustrated*, September 21, 1964, 98–101.

———. "Not Just a Flood, but a Deluge." *Sports Illustrated*, August 19, 1968, 1, 18–21.

Lewis, Anthony. "Supreme Court Confidential." *New York Review of Books*, February 7, 1980, 3–8.

Linn, Ed. "The Man Who Begs, Buys and Borrows Trouble." *Sport*, May 1971, 66–67, 91–93.

Lukas, J. Anthony. "Playboy Interview: Bob Woodward." *Playboy*, February 1989, 62–63.

McCarver, Tim, with Cal Fussman. "Curt Flood." *ESPN the Magazine*, January 8, 2001, 12.

McDonald, Kevin D. "Antitrust and Baseball: Stealing Justice Holmes." *J. of Sct. Hist.* 2 (1998): 89–138.

McKenna, Dave. "The Forgotten Flood of 1971." *Washington City Paper*, April 30, 2004.

Mann, Jack. "Ted Williams and Bob Short: Baseball's Odd Couple Meets the Wild Bunch." *Look*, May 4, 1971, 71–75.

Mikva, Abner. "In Memoriam—Arthur J. Goldberg, The Practitioner." *Supreme Court Historical Society 1990 Yearbook*, 1.

"Mr. Goldberg Runs for Office." *New Yorker*, June 13, 1970, 27–29.

Navasky, Victor. "In Washington, You Just Don't Not Return a Call from Abe Fortas." *New York Times Magazine*, August 1, 1971, 7–24, 32–33, 67–68.

"Needed—Abe Lincoln of Baseball." *Ebony*, April 1964, 110–11.

Noble, John Wesley. "The Coach Nobody Wanted." *Saturday Evening Post*, May 10, 1958, 31.

O'Brien, David M. "Join-3 Votes, the Rule of Four, the Cert. Pool, and the Supreme Court's Shrinking Plenary Docket." 13 *J. L. & Pol.* 779 (1997).

"Oil in the Outfield." *Sport*, March 1968, 8.

Okrent, Daniel. "The 10 Most Influential Athletes of the Century." *Time*, June 14, 1999, 93.

Olsen, Jack. "In the Back of the Bus: Part 2, the Black Athlete." *Sports Illustrated*, July 22, 1968, 28–41.

Pepe, Phil. "How Flood Finally Made It." *Sport*, November 1962, 44–45.

Raskin, A. H. "A Conciliator Goes to the U.N." *New York Times Magazine*, August 8, 1965, 10, 62–64.

Reeves, Richard. "'Goldilocks may not be the most exciting fellow in town but he's the only one who can win this year.'" *New York Times Magazine*, June 14, 1970, 7, 60, 64, 68.

———. "The Last Angry Men." *Esquire*, March 1, 1978, 41–48.

———. "This Is the Battle of the Titans?" *New York Times Magazine*, November 1, 1970, 224.

Remnick, David. "How Muhammad Ali Changed the Press." *SportsJones Magazine*, October 29, 1999, at http://www.sportsjones.com/ali4b.htm.

"The Return of Curt Flood." *Sport*, July 1992, 8.

Roberts, Robin. "The Game Deserves the Best." *Sports Illustrated*, February 24, 1969, 46–47.

Robinson, Jackie. "A Kentucky Colonel kept me in baseball." *Look*, February 8, 1955, 82–90.

———. "Now I know why they boo me!" *Look*, January 25, 1955, 22–28.

———. " 'Your temper can ruin us!' " *Look*, February 22, 1955, 78–87.

Rodell, Fred. "The 'Warren Court' Stands Its Ground." *New York Times Magazine*, September 27, 1964, 23, 120–21.

Ross, Stephen F. "Reconsidering *Flood v. Kuhn*." 12 *U. Miami Ent. & Sports L. Rev.* 169 (1995).

Rovell, Darren. "The Early Days of Free Agency." ESPN.com, November 21, 2000, at http://espn.go.com/mlb/s/2000/1121/893718.html.

Rumill, Ed. "With Glove, Bat and Brush." *Baseball Digest*, August 1967, 63–64.

Shapiro, Fred. "Arthur Goldberg You Owe Me $587.50." *Esquire*, September 1970, 146, 187–99.

Shaplen, Robert. "Peacemaker-I." *New Yorker*, April 7, 1962, 49–112.

———. "Peacemaker-II." *New Yorker*, April 14, 1962, 49–105.

Shills, Edward B. "Arthur Goldberg: Proof of the American Dream." *U.S. Department of Labor Monthly Labor Review*, January 1997, 56–71.

Skefos, Catherine Hetos. "The Supreme Court Gets a Home." *Supreme Court Historical Society 1976 Yearbook.*

Smith, Claire. "Baseball's Angry Man." *New York Times Magazine*, October 13, 1991, 28–31, 53, 56.

Smith, Red. "Gardella Hales Baseball into Court." *Sports Illustrated*, vol. 1, no. 2 (Dell Publishing), March 1949, 10–11, 71–72.

Snyder, Brad. "How the Conservatives Canonized *Brown v. Board of Education.*" 52 *Rutgers L. Rev.* 383 (2001).

Speers, William J. "Why Curt Flood Won't Play for the Phillies." *Philadelphia Inquirer Magazine*, May 17, 1970, 6–14.

Stark, Jayson. "The Decision That Changed the Game." ESPN.com, November 22, 2000, at http://espn.go.com/mlb/columns/stark_jayson/891711.html.

———. "Part II: Free Agency Increased Competitive Balance." ESPN.com, November 22, 2000, at http://espn.go.com/mlb/columns/stark_jayson/ 893655.html.

———. "Part III: Player Movement Part of Life." ESPN.com, November 23, 2000, at http://espn.go.com/mlb/columns/stark_jayson/896430.html.

Stump, Al. "Curt Flood in the Midnight League." *Sport*, March 1965, 32–33, 78–79.

"Supreme Court Memo from Rehnquist." *Newsweek*, December 13, 1971, 32–37.

"Thanks, Curt." *Sports Illustrated*, March 12, 1979, 13.

Thompson, Cordell S. "Man Who Fights Power Structure of Baseball." *Jet*, February 12, 1970, 1, 50–54.

Topkis, Jay H. "Monopoly in Professional Sports." 58 *Yale L.J.* 691 (1949).

Tygiel, Jules. "The Court-Martial of Jackie Robinson." *American Heritage*, August–September, 1985, 34–39.

Underwood, John. "They're Ho-Hummers No More." *Sports Illustrated*, March 15, 1971, 26–28, 33.

Van Tassel, Emily Field. "Justice Arthur J. Goldberg." In *The Jewish Justices of the Supreme Court Revisited: Brandeis to Fortas*, ed. Jennifer M. Lowe. Washington, D.C.: Supreme Court Historical Society, 1994.

Vecsey, George. "How Curt Flood Inspires the Cardinals." *Sport*, October 1968, 64–68.

Ward, John Montgomery. "Is the Base-Ball Player a Chattel?" *Lippincott's Monthly Magazine*, August 1887, 310–19.

"Whatever happened to . . . Curt Flood." *Ebony*, March 1981, 55–56.

"Where the Negro Goes from Here in Sports." *Sport*, September 1966, 56–59, 87–88.

White, Russ. "Baseball's Roaming Son Back at 'Kid's Game' and Liking It." *Washington Star Sportsweek*, November 22, 1970, S-4, S-6, S-14.

Whitford, David. "Curt Flood." *Sport*, December 1986, 102–7.

Wilks, Ed. "Curt Flood and the Handwriting on the Wall." *Super Sports*, November 1969, 15–17, 60.

Winkelman, Nancy. "Just a Brief Writer." *Litigation*, Summer 2003, 50–53.

THESES AND DISSERTATIONS

Jacobson, Josh. "The Danny Gardella Story." Senior honor's thesis, University of Minnesota, 1987.

Smith, Maureen M. "Identity and Citizenship: African American Athletes, Sport, and the Freedom Struggles of the 1960s." Ph.D. diss., Ohio State University, 1999.

TELEVISION SOURCES

Burns, Ken. *Baseball.* Innings 6, 8, and 9. 1994.

ESPN. "Curt Flood," *SportsCentury.*

Firestone, Roy. *Sports Look,* June 10, 1986.

Lee, Spike. "The Curt Flood Story." *Real Sports* with Bryant Gumbel, March 10, 1997.

Moyers, Bill. "Mr. Justice Blackmun: In Search of the Constitution with Bill Moyers," Public Affairs Television, 1987.

Vanderbilt University, Television News Archive.

UNPUBLISHED SOURCES

Karen Brecher, mailgram to Toastmaster, California Coaches' Association, January 30, 1981.

Ken Burns interview with Curt Flood for *Baseball* documentary, transcript.

Early, Gerald. "Curt Flood, Gratitude, and the Image of Baseball." Unpublished paper, delivered at Harvard University, October 30, 2003.

Curt Flood, letter to Lawrence Williams, January 9, 1978.

Curt Flood, letter to Lawrence Williams, March 2, 1978.

Curt Flood Christmas Letters, 1994 and 1996.

Curt Flood file, Cincinnati Reds Museum, Cincinnati, Ohio.

Curt Flood file, FBI, San Francisco, California, and Washington, D.C.

Curt Flood file, National Baseball Hall of Fame Library, Cooperstown, New York.

Curt Flood file, Sporting News Archives, St. Louis, Missouri.

Curt Flood file, State Department, Washington, D.C.

"Curt's Ninth Inning," Funeral Program.

Bob Gibson, letter to Curt Flood, January 12, 1981.

Buddy Gilbert Scrapbook, 1956 and 1957.

Major League Baseball Players Association Meeting Minutes and Notes, December 13–14, 1969.

Frank Robinson Hall of Fame Induction Speech, transcript, August 1, 1982, National Baseball Hall of Fame Library, Cooperstown, New York.

Gabriel Schechter interview with Marvin Miller, transcript, March 24, 1992.

"A Tribute to Curt." Oakland Board of Education, March 24–29, 1980.

Lawrence Williams, telegram to Curt Flood, January 10, 1978.

George Will's Eulogy.

INDEX